Why You Need This New Edition

This new edition has been thoroughly updated and revised to take into account many new and significant studies by sociologists and other behavioral scientists. Here is a sampling of some of the new information you will find:

- New research that finds a difference in brain structures between gay people and straight people.

- A new review of 30 studies in various countries indicating that drug users are much more likely than nonusers to commit a crime.

- A recent study suggesting that the perpetrators of murder-suicide kill their victims as a way of demonstrating their dominance or control over them.

- New statistics showing many more billions of dollars being spent on drug law enforcement than on prevention and treatment.

Here are just a few of the current, high-interest topics examined in this new edition:

- The search for the causes of the shootings at Virginia Tech University.

- The essence of mass murder, which is often committed by extraordinarily ordinary rather than emotionally disturbed people, illustrated by a discussion about a young suicide bomber killing and wounding many students before he is shot dead.

- The controversy over the death penalty as a possible deterrent for murder.

- The increasing numbers of teenagers today who turn to oral sex because they don't consider it real sex, although they engage in it with only one partner rather than many.

TENTH EDITION

Deviant Behavior

Alex Thio

Ohio University

Allyn & Bacon

Boston   New York   San Francisco
Mexico City   Montreal   Toronto   London   Madrid   Munich   Paris
Hong Kong   Singapore   Tokyo   Cape Town   Sydney

Editor-in-Chief: *Karen Hanson*
Editorial Assistant: *Courtney Shea*
Senior Marketing Manager: *Kelly May*
Production Supervisor: *Patty Bergin*
Manufacturing Buyer: *Debbie Rossi*
Editorial Production Service: *TexTech International*
Photo Researcher: *Martha Shethar*
Cover Designer: *Joel Gendron*

Photo credits: Page 3, Peter Hvizdak/The Image Works; **p. 16,** Mike Theiler/epa/Corbis; **p. 33,** Micah Walter/Reuters/Corbis; **p. 55,** AP Wide World Photos; **p. 83,** Deborah Davis/Photo Edit. All rights reserved; **p. 112,** Viviane Moos/CORBIS; **p. 137,** Royalty-Free/Corbis; **p. 167,** Dennis MacDonald/Alamy; **p. 203,** Photofusion Picture Library/Alamy; **p. 234,** Marilyn Humphries Photography; **p. 269,** David Hoffman Photo Library/Alamy; **p. 300,** Elke Van de Velde/Getty Images; **p. 333,** AP Wide World Photos; **p. 363,** David Young-Wolff/Photo Edit; **p. 387,** vario images GmbH & Co.KG/Alamy

Library of Congress Cataloging-in-Publication Data

Thio, Alex.
   Deviant behavior / Alex Thio. —10th ed.
     p. cm.
   ISBN 0-205-69323-7 (alk. paper)
  1. Deviant behavior. I. Title.
   HM811.T46 2010
   302.5'42—dc22
                        2008048381

Printed in the United States of America

10 9 8 7 6 5 4   HAM 13 12 11

Allyn & Bacon
is an imprint of

www.pearsonhighered.com

ISBN-10: 0-205-69323-7
ISBN-13: 978-0-205-69323-8

BRIEF CONTENTS

CONTENTS

PREFACE

This new edition of *Deviant Behavior* is designed to make teaching and learning as interesting and rewarding as possible. Deviant behavior is already by itself an exciting subject, but I have tried to make it more exciting with a simple style of writing. No matter how complex and dry the theories and data about deviance may appear in scholarly journals and books, they are here presented simply, yet accurately. In addition, stimulating, ironic, and thought-provoking remarks are often thrown in to make the book come alive. I have enjoyed working on this edition, and I hope that students will have fun reading it while learning about deviance.

Features

The current edition retains all the features that have made the book a success. These features include comprehensive coverage, lively writing, real-life vignettes, student-oriented illustrations, and critical analyses of theories and data. Also unique to this text are the sections on social profile and global perspective in all the chapters on specific forms of deviant behavior. The social profile sections spotlight certain groups of deviants, such as serial killers, suicide bombers, depressed teens, swinging couples, college binge drinkers, and corporate crooks. The sections on global perspective—a critically important approach in the globalization of our lives and society today—compare specific deviances in the United States with those in other parts of the world. Examples of these deviances are family violence, mental disorder, prostitution, homophobia, smoking, and official corruption. Another unique feature of this text is a list of myths and realities at the opening of each of the behavior chapters. Perhaps the most important feature is the blend of style and substance that runs through all the chapters.

A wide spectrum of theories and specific deviant behaviors are analyzed here. In addition to covering all the standard subjects, I have dealt with many important and current topics, including feminism, postmodernism, shaming theory, and ethnography as well as such newly recognized deviances as Internet deviance, suicide bombing, female genital mutilation, risky teen sex, prescription drug abuse, and the stigma of obesity. I have also provided an abundance of research data, including a substantial amount that demolishes common assumptions about deviant behavior.

Students will be exposed to the full range of theories and data about deviance. More important, they will be challenged to think about and evaluate the preconceptions and biases they may have picked up from conventional society. In the chapter on gays and other victims of stigma, for example, students will learn that homosexuals, transsexuals, intersexuals, transvestites, the obese, and the tattooed are definitely not weird and grotesque at all and that people with physical disabilities are far from helpless and pitiful.

New to This Edition

This updated and revised text takes into account many significant and interesting new studies by sociologists and other behavioral scientists as well as suggestions and criticisms from the reviewers and adopters of this book. The most significant updates and revisions include the following:

- Chapter 2 (*Positivist Theories*) opens with a new vignette about the shootings at Virginia Tech University, showing how the search for the causes of this tragedy exemplifies the pursuit of positivist theories. A new study indicates how certain factors such as gender and ADHD can strengthen the impact of strain on deviance.
- Chapter 3 (*Constructionist Theories*) opens with a new vignette about the increased difficulty of getting an abortion, which reflects the increased support for the idea that abortion is a deviant act. But pro-life forces do not see abortion as deviant. These conflicting views on whether a certain act is deviant or not suggest that deviance is a matter of perception rather than actual behavior, which is the essential point of constructionist theories.
- Chapter 4 (*Physical Violence*) opens with a new vignette about a young suicide bomber killing and wounding many students before he was shot dead. The bomber fits the typical profile of a suicide terrorist. Also, more recent data are given on the perpetrators of murder-suicide. School violence is extensively revised and updated. More information on stalking and genocide is offered. And the issue of whether the death penalty deters murder is substantially revised.
- Chapter 5 (*Rape and Child Molestation*) begins with a new vignette about three high school students charged with sexually assaulting a 16-year-old girl in their school, which illustrates one of the major forms of sexual violence relatively common in the United States. New data further clarify (1) the myth that victims of rape contribute to their victimization and (2) the nature of male rape that takes place outside the prison.
- In Chapter 6 (*Family Violence*) new data show how elders are abused by their family members.
- Chapter 7 (*Suicide*) opens with a new vignette about how a college student committed suicide, a cause of death that ranks second among young people, after motor-vehicle accidents. New information further shows (1) higher suicide rates among professionals such as physicians, (2) controversy over whether antidepressant drugs increase the risk of teen suicide, (3) why smaller living-and-learning environments in college protect students against suicide, and (4) the cause of the soaring suicide rate among young men in Norway.
- Chapter 8 (*Mental Disorder*) begins with a new vignette about a lawyer who has struggled with depression for nearly a decade, an example of mental disorder besetting millions of Americans. Other new materials include the popular belief about the epidemic of autism among children, the continuing dominance of the biological view in the psychiatric profession, and the gender factor in the development of internally oriented mental disorder.
- In Chapter 9 (*Heterosexual Deviance*), new data show that many female teenagers engage in oral sex with just one partner and most men in Denmark find hardcore pornography beneficial to their lives. There is also more information about nude dancing, sexual harassment, call girls, and pimps.

- Chapter 10 (*Gays and Other Victims of Stigma*) includes new research in Sweden that finds a difference in brain structures between gays and straights and a recent study suggesting why heterosexual women with an AIDS-afflicted relative tend to engage in homoerotic activities.
- Chapter 11 (*Drug Use*) offers a new review of 30 studies in various countries indicating that drug users are much more likely than nonusers to commit a crime, new statistics showing many more billions of dollars being spent on drug law enforcement than on prevention and treatment, and a new survey indicating a relatively high rate of cigarette smoking among the very young—from age 12 to 17.
- Chapter 12 (*Drinking and Alcoholism*) opens with an updated vignette that dramatizes binge drinking on campus. This chapter also presents new conflicting studies on whether teenagers are more, or less, likely to binge drink when drinking with parents.
- Chapter 13 (*Privileged Deviance*) begins with an updated vignette about a corporate executive caught stealing regularly from his company. Included here is a new example of deviance against the government perpetrated by a giant German technology corporation.
- Chapter 14 (*Underprivileged Deviance*) opens with a new vignette about street gangs engaging in various underprivileged deviances. Also included is the new observation that robbers today are more likely to use a gun than before and why.
- Chapter 15 (*Internet Deviance*) begins with an updated vignette suggesting why online deviance is a very common problem.

Pedagogy

Each chapter opens with a meaningful photo, a list of myths and realities, and a real-life vignette, not only to stimulate student interest but also to portray an important theme of the chapter. The summary of each chapter is laid out in a question-and-answer format to promote thinking as well as retention. The list of books for further reading is annotated to help students decide which publications will suit their need for more information. Finally, at the end of each chapter is a set of two questions designed to encourage students to think critically about the subject they have just studied.

Supplements

Instructor's Manual and Test Bank

Kenneth Culton of Niagara University and Adrian Tan of Southern Methodist University have prepared a detailed, comprehensive Instructor's Manual and Test Bank to accompany this text. The Instructor's Manual includes chapter summaries; key concepts; suggestions for lectures, demonstrations, student activities, and research projects; annotated lists of films and videos; and additional resources pertinent to each chapter. The Test Bank portion of the manual offers multiple-choice, true/false, fill-in-the-blank, and essay questions. The Instructor's Manual and Test Bank are available for download at www.pearsonhighered.com.

Computerized Test Bank

The Test Bank is also available through Pearson's new online test-generating program, *MyTest*. The user-friendly interface allows you to view, edit, and add questions; transfer questions to tests; and print tests. Search and sort features allow you to locate questions quickly and arrange them in whatever order you prefer.

PowerPoint Lectures

The PowerPoint lecture slides have been created by Jim Taylor of Ohio University. The slides feature lecture outlines for each chapter, and include many of the figures and tables from the text. The PowerPoints are available for download at www.pearsonhighered.com.

Readings in Deviant Behavior, Sixth Edition, compiled by Alex Thio, Thomas Calhoun, and Addrain Conyers, is available to supplement the text. This collection of readings represents the full range of deviance sociology, dealing with many different theories and data collected via different research methodologies.

Readings in Deviant Behavior includes selections with high student appeal. All of the readings have been carefully edited for clarity and conciseness to ensure that students will find them easy and enjoyable to read while learning what deviance is all about. The sixth edition features many new articles that reflect current trends, especially those dealing with noncriminal deviance as well as those that emphasize the constructionist perspective. A special package is available with *Deviant Behavior,* Tenth Edition, and *Readings in Deviant Behavior,* Sixth Edition, offering students a discount off each book. Contact your publisher's representative for more information.

Acknowledgments

I would like to express my profound gratitude to the numerous professors who have adopted the past nine editions of this book for their classes. My thanks also go to those sociologists who have enhanced the quality of the earlier editions as well as the current one with their criticisms and suggestions:

Roy Austin, Pennsylvania State University
Dodd Bogart, University of New Mexico
Julie V. Brown, University of North Carolina, Greensboro
James T. Carey, University of Illinois, Chicago
Brenda Chaney, Ohio State University
Steven R. Cureton, University of North Carolina, Greensboro
Phillip W. Davis, Georgia State University
Estelle Disch, Boston State College
Jackie Eller, Middle Tennessee State University
Raymond A. Eve, University of Texas at Arlington

Charles E. Frazier, University of Florida
John R. Hepburn, Arizona State University
Arthur C. Hill, Minneapolis Community College
Richard C. Hollinger, University of Florida
Gary Jensen, Vanderbilt University
Margaret S. Kelley, University of Oklahoma
Michael Kimmel, SUNY–Stony Brook
Gang Lee, University of Texas–El Paso
Hong Liu, University of Pittsburgh
Ruth X. Liu, San Diego State University
Scott Magnuson-Martinson, Normandale Community College

Charles H. McCaghy, Bowling Green State
  University
Karen E. B. McCue, University of New Mexico
James Messerschmidt, University of Southern
  Maine
Joyce D. Meyer, Parkland College
Eleanor M. Miller, University of Wisconsin,
  Milwaukee
James J. Nolan III, West Virginia University
Michael Olson, Frostburg State University
Michael P. Perez, California State University
David Prok, Baldwin Wallace College
Marion Sherman-Goldman, University
  of Oregon

Deanna Shields, Fairmont State College
Steven Stack, Wayne State University
Larry Stokes, University of Tennessee,
  Chattanooga
Kenrick S. Thompson, Northern Michigan
  University
Gunnar Valgeirsson, California State University,
  Fresno
Jerry Van Hoy, Purdue University
Timothy N. Veiders, Niagara County Community
  College
J. D. Wemhaner, Tulsa Junior College
Arthur L. Wood, University of Connecticut
Anthony Zumpetta, West Chester University.

Alex Thio

ABOUT THE AUTHOR

Alex Thio (pronounced TEE-oh) has long been a sociology professor at Ohio University. Born of Chinese parentage in Penang, Malaysia, he grew up in a multicultural environment. He acquired fluency in Mandarin Chinese, Malay, and Indonesian. He also picked up a smattering of English and Dutch. He took French and German in high school and college.

Professor Thio attended primary school in Malaysia and high school in Indonesia. He then came to the United States and worked his way through Central Methodist University in Missouri, where he majored in social sciences. Later, he studied sociology as a graduate student at the State University of New York at Buffalo, and he completed his doctorate while working as a research and teaching assistant.

Professor Thio has regularly taught courses in deviance, introductory sociology, social problems, and criminology. In addition to teaching, he enjoys writing. Aside from this book, he is the author of the popular text *Sociology: A Brief Introduction,* Seventh Edition (2009), and has written many articles. The author is grateful for the feedback he often receives from faculty and students, which he believes improves the quality of his books. If you have any comments, suggestions, or questions, please write to him at the Department of Sociology, Ohio University, Athens, OH 45701, or via e-mail at thio@ohio.edu.

He lives in Athens, Ohio. His hobbies include traveling, reading, and walking.

PART ONE

Perspectives and Theories

1

What Is
Deviant Behavior?

Bonnie Pitzer, a middle schooler, was taking a vocabulary test. When she drew a blank on the word *desolated,* she did not panic but instead quietly searched the Internet for the definition. Was she cheating? If she was, her behavior may be regarded as deviant. In the Internet age today, however, a growing number of educators, including Bonnie's teacher, do not consider her behavior cheating or deviant. To them, intelligent online surfing and analysis are more important than rote memorization. To her teacher, Bonnie aced the test not only because she knew how to surf the Internet for the meaning of a word but also because she was able to use the word in a sentence. As her teacher explains, "I want the kids to be able to apply the meaning, not to be able to memorize it." Many other teachers, though, would regard Bonnie as deviant for cheating on her test (Gamerman, 2006).

There is, in fact, a great deal of disagreement among people as to what they consider deviant. In a classic study, J. L. Simmons (1965) asked a sample of the general public who they thought was deviant. They mentioned 252 different kinds of people as deviants, including prostitutes, alcoholics, drug users, murderers, the mentally ill, the physically challenged, communists, atheists, liars, Democrats, Republicans, reckless drivers, self-pitiers, the retired, divorcees, Christians, suburbanites, movie stars, perpetual bridge players, pacifists, psychiatrists, priests, liberals, conservatives, junior executives, smart-aleck students, and know-it-all professors. If you are surprised that some of these people are considered deviant, your surprise simply adds to the fact that there is a good deal of disagreement among the public as to the conception of deviant behavior.

A similar lack of consensus exists among sociologists. We could say that the study of deviant behavior is probably the most "deviant" of all the subjects in sociology. Sociologists disagree more over the definition of deviant behavior than they do on any other subject.

Conflicting Definitions

Some sociologists simply say that deviance is a violation of any social rule, while others argue that deviance involves more than rule violation—that it also has the quality of provoking disapproval, anger, or indignation. Some advocate a broader definition, arguing that a person can be a deviant *without* violating any rule or doing something that rubs others the wrong way, such as individuals with physical or mental disabilities. These people are considered deviant in this view because they are disvalued by society. By contrast, some sociologists contend that deviance does not have to be conceived as only negative but instead can also be positive, such as being a genius, saint, creative artist, or glamorous celebrity. Other sociologists disagree, considering "positive deviance" to be an oxymoron, a contradiction in terms (Heckert and Heckert, 2002; Goode, 1991; Dodge, 1985; Harman, 1985).

All these sociologists apparently assume that, whether it is positive or negative, disturbing behavior or disvalued condition, deviance is real in and of itself, that is, endowed with a certain quality that distinguishes it from nondeviance. The logic behind this assumption is that if it is not real in the first place, it cannot be considered positive, negative, disturbing, or devalued. But other sociologists disagree, arguing that deviance does not have to be real in order for behaviors and conditions to be labeled deviant. People can be falsely accused of being criminal, erroneously diagnosed as mentally ill, unfairly stereotyped as dangerous because of their skin color, and so on. Conversely, committing a deviant act does not necessarily make the person a deviant, especially when the act is kept secret, unlabeled by others as deviant. It is, therefore, the label "deviant"—not the act itself—that makes the individual deviant.

Some sociologists go beyond the notion of labeling to define deviance by stressing the importance of power. They observe that relatively powerful people are capable of avoiding the fate suffered by the powerless—being falsely, erroneously, or unjustly labeled deviant. The key reason is that the powerful, either by themselves or through influencing public opinion or both, hold more power for labeling others' behavior as deviant. Understandably, sociologists who hold this view define deviance as any act considered by the powerful at a given time and place to be a violation of some social rule (Ermann and Lundman, 2002; Simon, 2006).

From this welter of conflicting definitions we can discern the influence of two opposing perspectives: positivism and social constructionism. The positivist perspective is associated with the sciences, such as physics, chemistry, or biology. The constructionist perspective is fundamental in the humanities, such as art, language, or philosophy. Each perspective influences how scientists and scholars see, study, and make sense of their subject. The two perspectives have long been transported into sociology, so that some sociologists are more influenced by the positivist perspective while others are more influenced by the constructionist one.

In the sociology of deviance the positivist generally defines deviance as positively real, while the constructionist more often defines deviance as a social construction—an idea imputed by society to some behavior. Each perspective suggests other ideas about deviance, so that it has been referred to in various terms. Thus the positivist perspective has also been called objectivist, absolutist, normative, determinist, and essentialist (Goode, 2005b; Wittig, 1990). The constructionist perspective has also been referred to by such terms as humanist, subjectivist, relativist, reactivist, definitionist, and postmodernist (Heckert and Heckert, 2002; Lyman, 1995). Each perspective suggests how to *define* deviance, but reveals through the definitions what *subject* to study, what *method* to use for the study, and what kind of *theory* to use to make sense of the subject.

The Positivist Perspective

The positivist perspective consists of three assumptions about what deviance is. These assumptions are known to positivists as absolutism, objectivism, and determinism.

Absolutism: Deviance as Absolutely Real

The positivist perspective holds deviance to be absolutely or intrinsically real, in that *it possesses some qualities that distinguish it from conventionality*. Similarly, deviant persons are assumed to have certain characteristics that make them different from conventional others. Thus, sociologists who are influenced by such a perspective tend to view deviant behavior as an attribute that inheres in the individual.

This view was first strongly held by the early criminologists who were the progenitors of today's sociology of deviance. Around the turn of the last century, criminologists believed that criminals possessed certain biological traits that were absent in law-abiding people. The biological traits were believed to include defective genes, bumps on the head, a long lower jaw, a scanty beard, and a tough body build. Since all these traits are inherited, criminals were believed to be born as such. Thus, if they were born criminals, they would always be criminals. As the saying goes, "If you've had it, you've had it." So, no matter where they might go—they could go anywhere in the world—they would still be criminals.

Criminologists then shifted their attention from biological to psychological traits. Criminals were thought to have certain mental characteristics that noncriminals did not. More specifically, criminals were thought to be feebleminded, psychotic, neurotic, psychopathic, or otherwise mentally disturbed. Like biological traits, these mental characteristics were believed to reside within individual criminals. And like biological traits, mental characteristics were believed to stay with the criminals, no matter what society or culture they might go to. Again, wherever they went, criminals would always remain criminals.

Today's positivist sociologists, however, have largely abandoned the use of biological and psychological traits to differentiate criminals from noncriminals. They recognize the important role of social factors in determining a person's status as a criminal. Such status does not remain the same across time and space; instead, it changes in different periods and with different societies. A polygamist may be a criminal in our society but a law-abiding citizen in Islamic countries. A person who sees things invisible to others may be a psychotic in our society but may become a spiritual leader among some South Pacific peoples. Nevertheless, positivist sociologists still regard deviance as absolutely or intrinsically real. Countering the relativist notion of deviance as basically a *label* imposed on an act, positivist Travis Hirschi (1973), for example, argues: "The person may not have committed a 'deviant' act, but he did (in many cases) do *something*. And it is just possible that what he did was a result of things that had happened to him in the past; it is also possible that the past in some inscrutable way remains with him and that if he were left alone he would *do it again*." Moreover, countering the relativist notion of mental illness as a label imputed to some people's behavior, Gwynn Nettler (1974) explicitly voices his absolutist stance: "Some people are more crazy than others; we can tell the difference; and calling lunacy a name does not *cause* it." These positivist sociologists seem to say that just as a rose by any other name would smell as sweet, so deviance by any other label is just as real.

Because they consider deviance real, positivist sociologists tend to focus their study on deviant behavior and deviant persons, rather than on nondeviants who label others deviants, such as lawmakers and law enforcers, which constructionist sociologists are more likely to study, as will be explained later.

Objectivism: Deviance as an Observable Object

To positivist sociologists deviant behavior is an observable object in that a deviant person is like an object, a real something that can be studied objectively. Positivist sociologists, therefore, assume that they can be as objective in studying deviance as natural scientists can be in studying physical phenomena. The trick is to treat deviants as if they were objects, like those studied by natural scientists. Nonetheless, positivist sociologists cannot help being aware of the basic difference between their subject, human beings, and that of natural scientists, inanimate objects. As human beings themselves, positivist sociologists must have certain feelings about their subject. However, they try to control their personal biases by forcing themselves not to pass moral judgment on deviant behavior or share the deviant person's feelings. Instead, they try to concentrate on the subject matter as it outwardly appears. Further, these sociologists have tried to follow the scientific rule that all their ideas about deviant behavior should be subject to public test. This means that other sociologists should be able to analyze these ideas to see whether they are supported by facts.

Such a drive to achieve scientific objectivity has made today's positivist sociologists more objective than their predecessors. They have, therefore, produced works that can tell us much more about the nature of deviant behavior. No longer in vogue today are such value-loaded and subjective notions as evil, immorality, moral failing, debauchery, and demoralization, which were routinely used in the past to describe the essence of deviance. Replacing those outmoded notions are such value-free and objective concepts as norm violation, retreatism, ritualism, rebellion, and conflict.

To demonstrate the objective reality of these concepts, positivist sociologists have used official reports and statistics, clinical reports, surveys of self-reported behavior, and surveys of victimization. Positivists recognize the unfortunate fact that the deviants who are selected by these objective methods do not accurately represent the entire population of deviants. The criminals and delinquents reported in the official statistics, for example, are a special group of deviants, because most crimes and delinquent acts are not discovered and, therefore, not included in the official statistics. Nevertheless, positivists believe that the quality of information obtained by these methods can be improved and refined. In the meantime, they consider the information, though inadequate, useful for revealing at least some aspect of the totality of deviant behavior. A major reason for using the information is to seek out the causes of deviant behavior. This brings us to the next, third assumption of the positivist perspective.

Determinism: Deviance as Determined Behavior

According to the positivist perspective, deviance is determined or caused by forces beyond the individual's control. Natural scientists hold the same deterministic view about physical phenomena. When positivist sociologists follow natural scientists, they adopt the deterministic view and apply it to human behavior.

Overly enthusiastic about the prospect of turning their discipline into a science, early sociologists argued that, like animals, plants, and material objects that natural scientists study, humans do not have any free will. The reason is that acknowledgment of free will would contradict the scientific principle of determinism. If a murderer is thought to will or determine a murderous act, then it does not make sense to say that the murderous act is caused by forces (such as mental condition or family background) beyond the person's control. Therefore, in defending their scientific principle of determinism, early sociologists maintained their denial of free will.

However, today's positivist sociologists assume that humans do possess free will. Still, this assumption, they argue, does not undermine the scientific principle of determinism. No matter how much a person exercises free will by making choices and decisions, the choices and decisions do not just happen but are determined by some causes. If a woman chooses to kill her husband rather than continue to live with him, she certainly has free will or freedom of choice as long as no one forces her to do what she does. Yet some factor may *determine* or *cause* the woman's choice of one alternative over another, that is, determine the way she exercises her free will. One such causal factor may be a long history of abuse at the hands of her husband. Thus, according to today's positivist sociologists, there is no inconsistency between freedom and causality.

Although they allow for human freedom or choice, positivist sociologists do not use it to explain why people behave in a certain way. They will not, for example, explain why the woman kills by saying "because she chooses to kill." This is no explanation at all, since the idea of choice can also be used to explain why another woman does not kill her husband—by saying "because she chooses not to." According to positivists, killing and not killing, or more generally, deviant and conventional behavior, being contrary phenomena, cannot be explained by the same factor, such as choice. Further, the idea of choice simply cannot explain the difference between deviance and conventionality; it cannot explain why one person chooses to kill while the other chooses not to. Therefore, although positivists do believe in human choice, they will not attribute deviance to human choice. Instead, they explain deviance by using such concepts as wife abuse, broken homes, unhappy homes, lower-class background, economic deprivation, social disorganization, rapid social change, differential association, differential reinforcement, and lack of social control. Any one of these causes of deviance can be used to illustrate what positivists consider to be a real explanation of deviance because, for example, wife abuse is more likely to cause a woman to kill her husband than not. Positivist theories essentially point to factors such as these as the causes of deviance.

In sum, the positivist perspective on deviant behavior consists of three assumptions. First, deviance is *absolutely real* in that it has certain qualities that distinguish it from conventionality. Second, deviance is an *observable object* in that a deviant person is like an object and thus can be studied objectively. Third, deviance is *determined* by forces beyond the individual's control.

The Constructionist Perspective

Since the 1960s the constructionist perspective has emerged to challenge the positivist perspective, which had earlier been predominant in the sociology of deviance. Let's examine the assumptions of the constructionist perspective that run counter to those of the positivist perspective.

Relativism: Deviance as a Label

The constructionist perspective holds the relativist view that deviant behavior by itself does not have any intrinsic characteristics unless it is thought to have these characteristics. The so-called intrinsically deviant characteristics do not come from the behavior itself; they come instead from some people's minds. To put it simply, an act appears deviant only because some people think it so. As Howard Becker (1963) says, "Deviant behavior is behavior that people so label." So, no deviant label, no deviant behavior. The existence of deviance depends on the label. Deviance, then, is a mental construct (an idea, thought, or image) expressed in the form of a label. Deviance, in other words, is socially constructed, defined as such by society.

Since, effectively, they consider deviance unreal, constructionists understandably stay away from studying it. They are more interested in the questions of whether and why a given act is defined by society as deviant. This leads to the study of people who label others as deviants—such as the police and other law-enforcing agents. If constructionists study so-called deviants, they do so by focusing on the nature of labeling and its consequences.

In studying law-enforcing agents, constructionists have found a huge lack of consensus on whether a certain person should be treated as a criminal. The police often disagree among themselves as to whether a suspect should be arrested, and judges often disagree among themselves as to whether those arrested should be convicted or acquitted. In addition, since laws vary from one state to another, the same type of behavior may be defined as criminal in one state but not so in another. Young adult males who father babies born to unwed teenage females, for example, can be prosecuted for statutory rape in California but not in most other states (Gleick, 1996). There is, then, a *relativity* principle in deviant behavior: Behavior gets defined as deviant relative to a given norm or standard of behavior, which is to say, to the way people react to it. If it is not related to the reaction of other people, a given behavior is in itself meaningless—it is impossible to say whether it is deviant or conforming. Constructionists strongly emphasize this relativistic view, according to which, deviance, like beauty, is in the eye of the beholder.

Subjectivism: Deviance as a Subjective Experience

To constructionists, the supposedly deviant behavior is a subjective, personal experience and the supposedly deviant person is a conscious, feeling, thinking, and reflective subject. Constructionists insist that there is a world of difference between humans (as active subjects) and nonhuman beings and things (as passive objects). Humans feel and reflect, and are thus distinguishable from animals, plants, things, and forces in nature, which cannot. Humans also have sacred worth and dignity, but things and forces do not. It is proper and useful for natural scientists to assume nature as an object and then study it, because this study can produce objective knowledge for controlling the natural world. It can also be useful for social scientists to assume and then study humans as objects because it may produce objective knowledge for controlling humans, but this violates the constructionist's humanist values and sensibilities.

As humanists, constructionists are opposed to the control of humans; instead, they advocate the protection and expansion of human worth, dignity, and freedom. One result of this humanist ideology is the observation that so-called objective knowledge about human behavior is inevitably superficial whenever it is used for controlling people. To control its black citizens, for example, the former white racist regime in South Africa needed only the superficial knowledge that they were identifiable and separable from whites. To achieve the humanist goal of protecting and expanding a certain people's human worth, dignity, and freedom, a deeper understanding is needed. This understanding requires appreciating and empathizing with each individual or group, experiencing what they experience, and seeing their lives and the world around them from their perspective. We must look at their experience from the inside as a participant rather than from the outside as a spectator. In other words, we must adopt the internal, subjective view rather than the external, objective one.

The same principle, according to constructionists, should hold for understanding deviants and their deviant behavior. Constructionists contrast this subjective approach with positivists' objective one. To constructionists, positivists treat deviance as if it were an immoral, unpleasant, or repulsive phenomenon that should be controlled, corrected, or eliminated. In consequence, positivists have used the objective approach by staying aloof from deviants, by studying the external aspects of their deviant behavior, and by relying on a set of preconceived ideas for guiding their study. The result is a collection of *surface facts* about deviants, such as their poverty, lack of schooling, poor self-image, and low aspirations. All this may be used for controlling and eliminating deviance, but it does not tell us what deviant people think about themselves, society, and their daily activities.

In order to understand the life of a deviant, constructionists believe, we need to use the relatively subjective approach, which requires our appreciation for and empathy with the deviant. The aim of this subjective approach is to understand the deviants' personal views, seeing the world as it appears to them. Thus, constructionists tend to study deviants with such methods as ethnography, participant observation, or open-ended, in-depth interviews.

As a result of their subjective and empathetic approach, constructionists often present an image of deviants as basically the same as conventional people. The deaf, for example, are the same as the nondeaf in being able to communicate and live a normal life. They should therefore be respected rather than pitied. This implies that so-called deviant behavior, because it is like so-called conventional behavior, should not be controlled, cured, or eradicated by society.

Voluntarism: Deviance as a Voluntary Act

The constructionist perspective holds that supposedly deviant behavior is a voluntary act, an expression of human volition, will, or choice. Constructionists take this stand because they are disturbed by what they claim to be the dehumanizing implication of the positivist view of deviant behavior. The positivist view is said to imply that the human being is like a robot, a senseless and purposeless machine reacting to everything in its environment. But constructionists emphasize that human beings, because they possess free will and choice-making ability, determine their own behavior.

To support this voluntarist assumption, constructionists tend to analyze how social control agencies define some people as deviant and carry out the sanctions against them. Such analyses often reveal the arbitrariness of official action, the bias in the administration of law, and the unjustness of controlling deviants. All these convey the strong impression that control agents, being in positions of power, exercise their free will by actively, intentionally, and purposefully controlling the "deviants."

Constructionists also analyze people who have been labeled deviant. The "deviants" are not presented as if they were robots, passively and senselessly developing a poor self-image as conventional society expects of them. Rather, they are described as actively seeking positive meanings in their deviant activities. In constructionist Jack Katz's (1988) analysis, for example, murderers see themselves as morally superior to their victims. The killing is said to give the murderers the self-righteous feeling of defending their dignity and respectability because their victims have unjustly humiliated them by taunting or insulting them. Katz also portrays robbers as feeling themselves morally superior to their victims—regarding their victims as fools or "suckers" who deserve to be robbed. Such insight into the subjective, experiential world of deviance constitutes a noncausal, descriptive, or analytical theory.

In brief, the constructionist perspective consists of three assumptions. First, deviant behavior is not real in and of itself; it is, basically, a *label*. Second, supposedly deviant behavior is a *subjective* experience and therefore should be studied with subjectivity and empathy. And, third, putatively deviant behavior is a *voluntary, self-willed* act rather than one caused by forces in the internal and external environments.

An Integrated View

To know what deviant behavior is, then, we need both positivist and constructionist perspectives. (See Table 1.1 for a quick review of these two perspectives.)

The combination of the two can give us a better picture than either one can by itself. The two perspectives may appear to be in sharp contradiction, but their differences are largely in emphasis. By giving consideration to one side, we do not necessarily deny the reality of the other. Both positivist and constructionist sociologists, in emphasizing their own views, assume in a way their opponents to be correct. Each group merely thinks of the other's argument as less important than its own. Thus, while they accept constructionists' view of deviance as a label, positivists simply take it for granted, considering it less important than their own assumption of deviance as real behavior. On the other hand, while constructionists accept positivists' view of deviance as an act that has really occurred, they consider it more worthwhile to focus on society's definition of the act as deviant.

Now that we know the two opposing perspectives, we can bring them together. As Chinese people are fond of saying, "Things that oppose each other also complement each other" (Mao, 1967). Thus we may see deviant behavior as being both a real act and a label. One cannot exist without the other. If there is no real act, there is no deviant *behavior*; if there is no label, there is no *deviant* behavior. In order for us to use the label "deviant," the *behavior* must occur. Similarly, for us to understand that behavior, the *label* "deviant" must be used. Deviance, then, is both behavior and label.

But in complementing each other, the two conflicting perspectives are not necessarily equally applicable to all types of deviant behavior. On the contrary, one perspective seems more relevant than the other in studying the types of deviance that more easily fit its assumptions and the temperaments of the sociologists embracing that perspective.

TABLE 1.1 A Summary of Two Perspectives

Positivist Perspective	Constructionist Perspective
Absolutism: Deviance is absolutely, intrinsically real; hence, deviance or deviants can be subject of study.	*Relativism:* Deviance is a label, defined as such at a given time and place; hence, labelers, labeling, and impact of labeling can be subject of study.
Objectivism: Deviance is an observable object; hence, objective research methods can be used.	*Subjectivism:* Deviance is a subjective experience; hence, subjective research methods can be used.
Determinism: Deviance is determined behavior, a product of causation; hence, causal, explanatory theory can be developed.	*Voluntarism:* Deviance is a voluntary act, an expression of free will; hence, noncausal, descriptive theory can be developed.

Specifically, the positivist perspective is more relevant to the study of what society considers relatively *serious* types of deviant behavior, such as murder, rape, armed robbery, and the like. The study of these types of deviance responds well to the positivist perspective for three reasons. First, these forms of deviant behavior, which characteristically enter into the official statistics analyzed by positivists, can be defined as really deviant. Such deviant acts are intrinsically more harmful than conforming behavior, are likely to elicit wide consensus from the public as to their deviant characteristics, and, therefore, are easily distinguishable from conforming behavior. Second, people who commit serious crimes, such as murder and robbery, generally come from the lower classes, quite unlike the positivists who study them. These are crimes that positivists themselves—as researchers, scholars, or professors—generally would not commit or could not conceive themselves capable of committing. It is easy, therefore, for positivists to stay aloof from these criminals, analyzing their behavior objectively, without empathizing with them or romanticizing their behavior. Third, since positivists can easily separate themselves from the people who commit serious deviant acts, it is natural for them to study these deviants as if they were passive objects "out there" rather than active subjects "in here" (like positivists themselves). It is thus natural for positivists to investigate these "passive" individuals with an eye to seeking out the causes of their deviance rather than understanding the operation of their free will.

In the same way, the constructionist perspective is more pertinent to the *less serious* kinds of deviance, particularly those that do not gravely harm other people. Thus this perspective finds itself at home in the world of adulterers, prostitutes, drug users, strippers, sex tourists, tax evaders, and the like. Again, three reasons explain the convenient fit between perspective and subject matter. First, there is a relative lack of consensus in society as to whether the less serious forms of deviant behavior are indeed deviant. Some members of society may label them deviant, while others may not. It is, therefore, logical for constructionists to emphasize that deviant behavior is basically a matter of labeling. Second, those so-called deviants are considered by society as less dangerous than the criminals typically studied by positivists. They also engage in the so-called deviant activities that constructionists themselves could enjoy, participate in, or at least feel themselves capable of engaging in—quite unlike the more dangerous acts committed by "common" criminals. Therefore, constructionists can more easily empathize with these supposed deviants and consider the latter's subjective experience useful for understanding deviance. Third, since they can empathize with these relatively harmless deviants, it is natural for constructionists to consider them active subjects like themselves rather than passive objects. This may be why they emphasize the voluntary, self-willed nature of the putative deviants' experience.

At bottom, the types of deviant behavior—seen through the positivist and constructionist perspectives—differ in the *amount of public consensus* regarding their deviant nature. On the one side, a given deviant act is, from the positivist standpoint, "intrinsically real," largely because there is a relatively great public consensus that it is really deviant. On the other side, a given deviant act is, from the constructionist perspective, "not real in itself but basically a label," largely because there is a relative lack of public consensus supporting it as really deviant. We may integrate the two views by defining deviant behavior with public consensus in mind.

Deviant behavior, we may say, is *any behavior considered deviant by public consensus, which may range from the maximum to the minimum.* Defined this way, deviant behavior should not be regarded as a discrete entity that is clearly and absolutely distinguishable from conforming behavior. Instead, deviance should be viewed as an act located somewhere on a continuum from total conformity at one extreme to total deviance at the other. Given the pluralistic nature of U.S. society, with many different groups having conflicting views of whether a given act is deviant, most of the so-called deviant behaviors can be assumed to fall in the large gray areas between the two poles of the continuum. Hence, deviant behavior actually means being more or less, rather than completely, deviant. It is a matter of degree rather than kind. Keeping this in the back of our minds, we may classify deviant behavior into two types, one more deviant than the other: higher- and lower-consensus deviance. *Higher-consensus deviance* is the type that has often been studied by positivist sociologists. *Lower-consensus deviance* is the type that has more frequently been studied by constructionist sociologists. Today, however, both positivists and constructionists are more interested than before in investigating both types of deviance, as we will see in many of the following chapters. This is probably because positivists are nowadays more likely to regard traditionally lower-consensus deviances (e.g., corporate fraud and governmental abuses) as harmful and dangerous as higher-consensus deviances such as homicide and robbery (Liddick, 2004; Rosoff et al., 2002). And, to be politically correct, constructionists tend more to "define deviancy down," showing greater sensitivity and empathy toward murderers, robbers, and other higher-consensus deviants (Hochstetler, 2004; Skrapec, 2001).

We have seen in this chapter how positivists and constructionists define what deviant behavior is. In Chapter 2 we will see how positivists explain what causes deviance. Then in Chapter 3 we will see how constructionists show what deviance means to certain people and how this meaning affects them or others.

A Word about Deviance and Crime

Students tend to think that deviance is basically the same as crime. Thus, the sociology of deviance is sometimes confused with criminology. But the two fields do differ. Although the sociology of deviance includes crime, it deals much more with deviance that is not crime. Criminology, on the other hand, covers only crime, although it has been profoundly influenced by the sociology of deviance.

How, then, does deviance differ from crime? First, crime *always* involves violating a law, but deviance does not. Deviance may involve breaking the law, so that some deviances such as murder, robbery, and rape are also crimes. So, in that sense, the sociology of deviance overlaps with criminology. But these two fields are mostly different, because most deviances are not crimes—they merely depart from some societal norm, rule, or standard, such as nude dancing, binge drinking, joining a cult, and being emotionally disturbed. Such subjects clearly distinguish the sociology of deviance from criminology.

Second, crime is a violation of a *formal* norm, which the law is, but deviance is more a violation of an *informal* norm that derives from a popular belief. Thus, crime as a violation of a formal norm is subject to imprisonment, fines, and other punishments by formal control agents such as the police, judges, prison guards, and other law-enforcement agents. On the other hand, deviance as a violation of an informal norm is subject to criticism, ridicule, condemnation, rejection, and other negative reactions by informal control agents such as relatives, friends, neighbors, peer groups, and even strangers.

Third, the number and variety of deviances are infinitely greater than those of crimes. Crimes can *only* be *behavioral* in nature, because there are only laws against some unacceptable behaviors, not some strange beliefs and attitudes. But deviances include more than behaviors and even more than beliefs and attitudes. Many deviances involve having certain physical or psychological conditions, characteristics, or traits, such as obesity, mental illness, and being grossly unattractive, for which the individual can in no way be prosecuted.

Fourth, as has been suggested, not all deviances are crimes, but are all crimes deviances? Most crimes, such as murder, rape, and robbery, are deviant because they violate informal norms in addition to breaking the law as a formal norm. But a few crimes are *not* deviant because they are relatively acceptable throughout society. They are, in other words, normative behavior, such as gambling and cohabitation. Such practices hardly raise an eyebrow because they are very common. They are nonetheless criminal because in some places the *old* laws against them are still on the books. Other popular practices such as drinking among young people under age 21, smoking inside public buildings, and driving without buckling up have become criminal in many states because of the passing of *new* laws to prohibit them.

The subject of crime was the preoccupation of the positivists in the sociology of deviance before the 1960s. The emergence of the constructionist perspective in the 1960s transformed the sociology of deviance into a lively field. The sociology of deviance continues to be vibrant today. Its positivist approach to deviance has revitalized criminology (see, for example, Messner and Rosenfeld, 2001; Tittle, 1995; Hirschi and Gottfredson, 1994), while its constructionist approach has renewed the sociology of deviance. On the one hand, for example, an increasing number of studies delve into the subjective world of deviance, revealing how deviants see themselves and others. On the other hand, the constructionist approach has caused the sociology of deviance to focus less on crime and more on deviance, bringing in many new subjects on deviance for study, such as binge drinking, prescription drug abuse, transgenderism, exotic dancing, physical disabilities, obesity, tattooing, and cyberdeviance, as presented in this text.

Summary

1. How do sociologists define deviant behavior? In sociology there are many different definitions of deviant behavior. They can be divided into two major types, one influenced by the positivist perspective and the other by the constructionist perspective. The positivist perspective holds the absolutist view that deviant behavior is absolutely real, the objectivist view that deviance is an observable object, and the determinist view that deviance is determined behavior, a product of causation. The constructionist perspective consists of the relativist view that the so-called deviance is largely a label applied to an act at a given time and place, the subjectivist view that deviance is itself a subjective experience, and the voluntarist view that deviance is a voluntary, self-willed act.

2. Can we integrate those two perspectives? Yes. We can integrate them into a larger perspective that sees deviant behavior as an act located at some point on a continuum from maximal to minimal public consensus regarding the deviant nature of the act. With this integrated view, we can divide deviant behavior into two major types. One, *higher-consensus deviance,* is generally serious enough to earn a great amount of public consensus that it is really deviant. This type has often been the subject of research by positivist sociologists. The other, *lower-consensus deviance,* is generally less serious and thus receives a lesser degree of public consensus on its deviant reality. This type has more often attracted the interest of constructionist sociologists. The sociology of deviance has been a lively field since the 1960s and continues to be today.

FURTHER READING

Adler, Patricia A. 2006. "The deviance society." *Deviant Behavior,* 27, 129–148. Arguing that the sociology of deviance continues to be a vibrant subfield of sociology.

Bendle, Mervyn F. 1999. "The death of the sociology of deviance?" *Journal of Sociology,* 35, 42–59. A critical analysis of the problems besetting the sociology of deviance and the emergence of a new paradigm for the field.

Best, Joel. 2004. *Deviance: Career of a Concept.* Belmont, Calif.: Wadsworth. An attempt to argue that deviance is no longer a thriving field of study in sociology.

Conrad, Peter, and Joseph W. Schneider. 1992. *Deviance and Medicalization: From Badness to Sickness.* Philadelphia: Temple University Press. An analysis of the changing definitions of deviance, from religious to criminal to medical definitions.

Cullen, Francis T. 1984. *Rethinking Crime and Deviance Theory: The Emergence of a Structuring Tradition.* Totowa, N.J.: Rowman & Allanheld. Arguing the importance of the "structuring perspective" for understanding deviance, which shows how certain social and social-psychological conditions can determine the transformation of a general deviant tendency into a specific form of deviant behavior.

Dodge, David L. 1985. "The over-negativized conceptualization of deviance: A programmatic exploration." *Deviant Behavior,* 6, 17–37. Argues that sociologists would do well to start studying positive deviance.

Goode, Erich, and Nachman Ben-Yehuda. 1994. *Moral Panics: The Social Construction of Deviance.* Cambridge, Mass.: Blackwell. A constructionist analysis of how societies periodically overreact with excessive fear or outrage to such social events as witchcraft, drug abuse, and satanism.

Henslin, James M. 1988. "Structuralism and individualism in deviance theory." *Deviant Behavior,* 9, 211–223. Illustrating an example of the difference between the positivist and constructionist perspectives in the sociology of deviance.

Konty, Mark. 2007. "'When in doubt, tell the truth': Pragmatism and the sociology of deviance." *Deviant Behavior,* 28, 153–170. Arguing that the study of deviance is about the rules that govern people's lives as well as the effects of rule breaking on them and others.

Lauderdale, Pat (ed.). 2003. *A Political Analysis of Deviance.* Toronto, Canada: de Sitter Publications. A collection of articles dealing with the political nature of deviance and the various aspects of political deviance.

Lyman, Stanford M. 1995. "Without morals or mores: Deviance in postmodernist social theory." *International Journal of Politics, Culture and Society,* 9, 197–235. A critical analysis of the constructionist view that the concept of deviance reflects an unjustifiable attempt to distinguish one group from another.

Pfohl, Stephen J. 1994. *Images of Deviance and Social Control: A Sociological History,* 2d ed. New York: McGraw-Hill. Presents nine perspectives of deviance, ranging from the earliest view of deviance as a demonic act to the latest conception of deviance as a way of "asserting lost power."

Thio, Alex, Thomas C. Calhoun, and Addrain Conyers (eds.). 2010. *Readings in Deviant Behavior,* 6th ed. Boston: Allyn and Bacon. An anthology that includes articles on definitions, images, notions, characteristics, and explanations of deviance.

CRITICAL THINKING QUESTIONS

1. Are liberals more likely than conservatives to hold the positivist or constructionist view of deviance? Why? Which view makes more sense to you and why?

2. Conduct a survey by asking a sample of your fellow students "What is deviant behavior?" and then "Why do you think it is deviant?" How do their responses fit either of the two perspectives of deviance?

2 Positivist Theories

Soon after 7 A.M. on April 16, 2007, campus police at Virginia Tech University found two students in a dormitory shot to death. About two hours later, the killer, Cho Seung-Hui, a Virginia Tech senior, arrived at the school's engineering building. First, he chained all the outside doors shut, preventing anyone from entering or leaving the building. He then headed to a German class and peered in as if he was looking for somebody. He left but soon returned. Quiet and purposeful, Cho first shot the German teacher in the head, then methodically went around the room and took out the students one by one, pumping at least three bullets into each victim. He then moved on to three other classrooms to carry out the massacre in about the same way. After killing 32 people, Cho committed suicide by shooting himself in the temple (Gibbs, 2007).

What caused Cho Seung-Hui to perpetrate those horrendous acts? Various theories were reported in the media but the most commonly mentioned were his mental illness and the easy availability of guns in the United States. Such a focus on the causes of deviant behavior like Cho's killing spree and suicide characterizes positivist theories of deviance. There are many positivist, causal theories of deviance. Here we will discuss only the most important ones, namely, anomie-strain theory, social learning theory, and control theory.

Anomie-Strain Theory

In 1938 Robert Merton developed what later became known as anomie theory, attributing deviance to *anomie,* the breakdown of social norms that results from society's urging people to be ambitious but failing to provide them with the opportunities to succeed. Albert Cohen (1955) extended Merton's theory to explain the emergence of delinquent boys. Then, two other sociologists, Richard Cloward and Lloyd Ohlin (1960), tried to improve on Merton's theory by adding the concept of differential illegitimate opportunity. Finally, since the early 1990s, other attempts have been made to extend the theory by emphasizing how the *strain* generated in people by anomie or other social conditions causes them to commit deviant acts (Messner and Rosenfeld, 2001; Agnew, 1992). The theory may thus be called anomie-strain theory.

Merton: The Goal–Means Gap

Merton found something wrong with Freud's psychoanalytic theory of deviant behavior. The psychoanalytic theory says that criminal, pathological, or socially dangerous behavior represents the free expression of the libido, biological impulses, or animal desires the individual is born with. The defect of this theory, according to Merton, lies in its assumption that "the structure of society primarily restrains the free expression of man's fixed native impulses." That is, society *discourages* the individual from engaging in deviant activities. Merton called this assumption a "fallacious premise," because he believed just the opposite: Society *encourages* the individual to engage in deviant activities. With such a premise, Merton developed his anomie theory.

Many sociologists have long believed that Merton's theory was inspired by Émile Durkheim, who was the first to use the term *anomie* as a sociological concept. Thus they have called it *anomie theory.* But the implication of Durkheim's concept of anomie is contrary to the premise of Merton's theory. By *anomie* Durkheim referred to the absence of social norms, which he equated with the failure of a society to rein in its members' limitless pursuit of material success. Durkheim assumed that the lack of this normative control causes deviance. This is similar to Freud's assumption that deviance will break out if society fails to discourage it by restraining individuals' impulses. But Merton's theory assumes just the opposite: Deviance will occur if society encourages it by pressuring individuals to commit it. Precisely how does society do this?

In Merton's view U.S. society heavily emphasizes the cultural value of success. From kindergarten to college your teachers motivate you to achieve a high scholastic record and to have great ambition for your future. The books, magazines, and newspapers you read often carry success stories that encourage you to become successful yourself. The games, sports, and athletic events that you watch in the stadium or on television impress you with the supreme importance of winning. If you participate in an athletic event, the coach will prod you to win. If you simply want to enjoy the pleasure of playing the game and sarcastically argue that "winning is not everything," the coach may argue back even more sarcastically: "Right, winning is not everything—winning is the *only* thing!" This cultural value of success is so pervasive in this society that people of *all* classes are expected to be ambitious, to entertain high aspirations; everyone is expected to have the desire to be a winner, to be somebody. Even poor people are told that their children have the chance of becoming president of the United States if they have as much ambition as the young, poverty-stricken Abraham Lincoln did. In this sense, the cultural *goal* of success is freely available to all people, regardless of their social-class backgrounds.

In contrast, the institutionalized, legitimate *means* of achieving the high success goal, such as getting a good job, are not freely available to all classes of people. The society is structured in such a way that people of the lower social classes, when compared with those of the higher, have less opportunity to realize their success aspirations. Lower-class people thus find themselves trapped in a very difficult situation. They have been encouraged by the society to hold high success aspirations, but they are not given the opportunity to realize those aspirations. To get themselves out of that predicament, many lower-class people resort to the *illegitimate* means of achieving their success aspirations, such as stealing, robbing, and other similar forms of deviant activities. So, lower-class people are more likely to engage in deviant activities.

We have just seen that the *cause* of those lower-class deviant activities is the societal condition marked by the inconsistency between society's overemphasis on the success goal and its *under*emphasis on the use of legitimate means for achieving that goal. Merton (1938) describes this goal–means disjunction in this way: "Contemporary American culture continues to be characterized by a heavy emphasis on wealth as a basic symbol of success, without a corresponding emphasis upon the legitimate avenues on which to march toward this goal." With this encouragement of high aspirations and denial of success opportunities, U.S. society produces a great deal of strain that pressures us to commit deviance.

However, given this societal pressure toward deviance, not all of us would respond to it in the same way. Many lower-class people, as the previous discussion has implied, may respond to it by accepting the success goal while rejecting the use of legitimate means for realizing that goal. Merton refers to this deviant behavior as *innovation*. It is also the case that many other individuals of various social classes may respond differently to that same social condition. Therefore, along with innovation, Merton presents other types of response (see Table 2.1).

1. *Conformity* is the most popular form of response. It involves accepting both the cultural goal of success and the use of legitimate means of working toward that goal. Presumably most of us choose this response.

2. *Innovation* is largely found among lower-class people, who reject the use of legal means in favor of illegal ones in their attempts to achieve the high success goal that they have learned to accept. This form of deviant response is the central subject of strain theory, and Merton discusses it much more than any other.

TABLE 2.1   A Typology of Responses to Goal–Means Gap

In U.S. society, according to Merton, there is too much emphasis on success but too little emphasis on the legitimate means for achieving success. Such inconsistency may cause deviant behavior, yet various people respond to it differently.

Response	Success Goal	Legitimate Means
1. Conformity	+	+
2. Innovation	+	−
3. Ritualism	−	+
4. Retreatism	−	−
5. Rebellion	− +	− +

Note: + indicates accepting; − signifies rejecting; and − + means rejecting the old and introducing the new.
Source: Adapted from Robert K. Merton, *Social Theory and Social Structure.* New York: Free Press, 1957.

3. *Ritualism* is common among lower-middle-class people who lower their aspirations or abandon high success goals so that they can more easily realize their aspirations. But in their attempts to realize these modest aspirations, they compulsively—hence, ritualistically—abide by the institutional norm of toiling as conscientious, loyal workers. They tend to be proud of their hard, honest work while shrugging off their modest incomes.

4. *Retreatism* is a withdrawal from society into the shell of one's self. The retreatist does not care about success, nor does he or she care to work. Examples of such people are psychotics, outcasts, vagrants, vagabonds, tramps, alcoholics, and drug addicts.

5. *Rebellion* involves rejecting the prevailing social expectation that we work hard in the so-called rat race to reach the goal of great success. The rebel also attempts to over-throw the existing system and put in its place a new one with new goals and new means of reaching those goals. Thus, the rebel may abandon both the pursuit of fame and riches and the cutthroat competition needed to achieve this worldly goal. At the same time, the rebel may encourage people to seek goodwill toward others and to cooperate in attaining this heavenly goal.

Cohen: Status Frustration

The version of anomie-strain theory proposed by Cohen (1955) is fundamentally the same as Merton's. Like Merton, Cohen suggests that U.S. society encourages all classes of people to achieve status while at the same time making it difficult for lower-class people to really achieve it. As a consequence, lower-class people are compelled to achieve status in their own way—that is, to engage in deviant acts. Although the theme is the same as in Merton's theory, Cohen tells the story differently, replacing Merton's word *success* with *status*.

According to Cohen, lower-class boys, like their middle-class peers, want to have status. An important place to achieve status is the school, which they are forced to attend. But the school turns out to be a most unlikely place for lower-class boys, because it ensures their failure. How so? The school is run by middle-class teachers, promotes middle-class values and behavior, and judges the student's achievement by middle-class standards of behavior and performance. The school, then, is a middle-class status system. To achieve the status of a successful, competent, or good student in the middle-class setting, youngsters must possess middle-class values, virtues, and traits, such as verbal fluency, academic intelligence, the ability to delay gratification, courtesy, opposition to fistfights, and respect for property. In this status system, middle-class boys obviously have a good chance of becoming successful. Yet lower-class boys, who have not been socialized in the same way as middle-class boys, are thrown into a status system where they are expected to compete with middle-class boys. The result is not surprising: Lower-class boys fail disastrously. In Cohen's words, "they are caught up in a game in which others are typically the winners and they are the losers and the also-rans."

Being a loser or also-ran is obviously very frustrating. Driven by this frustration, which Cohen calls *status frustration,* lower-class boys go back to their own lower-class neighborhood and set up their own competitive system, which Cohen refers to as a *delinquent subculture.* In that subculture they can compete more fairly among themselves for high status in accordance with their own criteria of achievement. Their criteria of achievement are in direct opposition to the "respectable" middle-class, conventional criteria. They judge as wrong whatever values and behaviors are considered right by conventional standards, and they judge as right whatever values and behaviors are considered wrong by conventional standards. Given this, it is obvious that the lower-class boys' very attempt to achieve status among their peers is—according to conventional standards—delinquent. The so-called delinquent activities include stealing "for the hell of it," fighting, terrorizing "good" children, destroying property, and defying various conventional taboos.

In short, Cohen extends Merton's theory by adding the concept of status frustration. As you may remember, Merton suggests that the goal–means gap (discrepancy between success aspiration and opportunity) *by itself* creates a lot of strain that pressures lower-class people into deviance: Goal–means gap → deviance. But Cohen's theory suggests that the goal–means gap can lead lower-class boys toward deviant activities only if the boys encounter *status frustration.* In other words, status frustration serves as the third, intervening variable that enables the goal–means gap to produce delinquent subculture: Goal–means gap → *status frustration* → deviance.

Nevertheless, Cohen's theory is basically the same as Merton's. Both assume that lower-class people are more likely than others to engage in deviant activities because society fails to help them fulfill the aspirations (for success or status) that it has induced in these people.

Cloward and Ohlin: Differential Illegitimate Opportunity

You may recall the way Merton formulates his theory: The lower classes tend to engage in deviance because they, like the middle and upper classes, have been encouraged to hold high success goals but, unlike the higher classes, are denied the *legitimate* means or opportunity of achieving the success goals. Cloward and Ohlin (1960) accept this general idea. At the same time, however, they want to extend it by introducing the concept of differential *illegitimate* opportunity.

First, Cloward and Ohlin point out that Merton correctly directs our attention to the problem of differential legitimate opportunity—that the lower classes have less opportunity than other classes for achieving success in a legitimate, conforming manner. But Merton wrongly assumes that the lower classes, when confronted with the lack of opportunity, would automatically and successfully engage in deviant activities. In other words, Merton fails to recognize the fact that the lower classes, after being confronted with the problem of differential *legitimate* opportunity, are further confronted with the additional problem of differential *illegitimate* opportunity. The fact is that some members of the lower classes have less opportunity than others of the same classes for achieving success in an *illegitimate, deviant* manner. What Cloward and Ohlin want to emphasize is that while all lower-class people suffer from the same lack of opportunity for engaging in legitimate and conforming activities, they do not have the same opportunity for participating in illegitimate and deviant activities. Thus, when some lower-class persons are pressured toward committing a deviant act such as theft or robbery, there is no guarantee that they will actually do it. Whether or not they will actually do it depends on whether they have access to illegitimate opportunity in the lower-class neighborhood.

There are three types of illegitimate opportunity, each provided by a deviant subculture. The *criminal* subculture offers illegitimate opportunities for achieving success goals. If lower-class youngsters are integrated into this subculture, they are able to achieve success by stealing, robbing, and fencing. This is the kind of deviant activity to which Merton assumes all lower-class youngsters will turn when they are denied conventional opportunities in the larger society. But, according to Cloward and Ohlin, many of these lower-class youths are not part of the criminal subculture and therefore do not enjoy criminal opportunities.

Yet some of those youths may find themselves in another neighborhood where the *conflict* subculture flourishes. In this subculture, a youngster has the opportunity to achieve "rep" or status within a violent delinquent gang. But that opportunity is available only to those youngsters who can meet such requirements as possessing great fighting skill and demonstrating enthusiasm for risking injury or death in gang warfare. Some lower-class adolescents fail to meet these requirements and are therefore denied the opportunity for achieving status within the conflict subculture.

There is, finally, a third, *retreatist* subculture, in which the only requirement for membership is the willingness to enjoy the use of drugs. Persons who are recruited into the retreatist subculture are likely to be those who have failed to achieve success in the criminal subculture or to attain status in the conflict subculture. Because of their failure to achieve success or status in *both* the delinquent underworld and the conventional upperworld, the retreatists have been called "double failures."

In brief, Cloward and Ohlin extend Merton's anomie-strain theory by introducing differential illegitimate opportunity as the third, intervening variable through which the goal–means gap leads to three different kinds of deviant activities: goal–means gap → *differential illegitimate opportunity* → different deviant activities. (Table 2.2 shows how this version of anomie-strain theory compares with the other two.) Nevertheless, Cloward and Ohlin basically agree with Merton that lower-class people are more inclined than others toward deviance because they are more likely to experience the discrepancy between success aspirations and the opportunity for realizing those aspirations.

TABLE 2.2   Three Versions of Anomie-Strain Theory

Merton: Goal–means gap → deviance

Cohen: Goal–means gap → status frustration → deviance

Cloward and Ohlin: Goal–means gap → differential illegitimate opportunity → different deviant activities

Note: The sign "→" indicates "antecedes or causes," as in "*A* antecedes or causes *B*."

Recent Developments

Over the last decade a number of sociologists have moved anomie-strain theory in new directions. Steven Messner and Richard Rosenfeld (2001), for example, argue that Merton focused too much on the "inequality in access to the legitimate means for success" as the source of the strain that leads to deviance. It is not so much the relative lack of opportunity that causes people to resort to the illegal means of achieving success, Messner and Rosenfeld contend, rather it is the overwhelming culture of the American Dream that causes deviance by encouraging people to adopt an "anything goes" mentality in the pursuit of success. According to Mark Konty (2005), the pursuit of the American Dream or economic success can cause deviance because it reflects a strong *self* interest with little or no *social* interest. Self interests focus on personal success or dominance over others, while social interests emphasize concern for the welfare of others. Research has suggested that people tend to engage in deviance if they have strong self interests while lacking social interests.

Robert Agnew (1992) has also found Merton inadequate for focusing only on failure to achieve economic success goals as the strain that directly causes deviance. There are two other kinds of strain that are noneconomic in nature, Agnew theorizes. One is what he calls the "removal of positively valued stimuli," such as "the loss of a boyfriend/girlfriend, the death or serious illness of a friend, moving to a new school district, the divorce/separation of one's parents, and suspension from school." The other form of strain involves the "presentation of negative stimuli," which includes such unpleasant experiences as child abuse and neglect, criminal victimization, physical punishment, and problems with parents or peers. These strains are said to cause frustration, fear, and anger, which in turn lead to deviant actions such as theft, aggression, and drug use. Certain factors, however, may strengthen the influence of strain on deviance. When experiencing strain, for example, men tend to commit a greater amount of violent crime than do women, and college students with attention deficit hyperactivity disorder (ADHD) are more likely than other students to get involved in crime (Baron, 2007; Johnson and Kercher, 2007).

Evaluating Anomie-Strain Theory

This theory has at least two problems. First, there is no reliable evidence to support its claim that people of the lower classes are more likely than those of other classes to engage in deviant activities. It is true that the official statistics on crime and delinquency, which anomie-strain theorists rely on, do support the theory. But the official statistics are largely unreliable and invalid. They are unreliable because law enforcers are much more likely to catch lower-class criminals and delinquents than higher-class ones. They are invalid because they do not reflect the total picture of deviance—they measure instead a very small portion of the totality of deviance, namely, the relatively serious types. If we modify the theory and say that lower-class people are more likely to commit what society considers *serious* types of deviance, then the theory does have adequate empirical support from both the official and unofficial reports on criminality and delinquency.

Second, there is no evidence to support the assumption of anomie-strain theory that lower-class people tend to hold the same level of success aspirations as do upper- and middle-class people. On the contrary, both theoretical analysis and empirical data show that lower-class people hold a significantly lower level of success aspirations. It is true, as anomie-strain theorists claim, that U.S. society *encourages* lower-class people to embrace high-success goals. But it is *not* necessarily true, as anomie-strain theorists assume, that lower-class people will end up embracing high-success goals. Merton and other anomie-strain theorists appear to have ignored the fact that while the manifest, intended function of U.S. success ideology is to get all social classes to entertain high aspirations, its latent, unintended, and real consequence turns out to be the higher social classes holding far higher aspirations than the lower classes.

Whatever its shortcomings, anomie-strain theory does have important redeeming value, aside from its being considered by many sociologists as highly interesting. Foremost to consider is that the theory has contributed greatly to the sociological idea that the society, not the individual, causes deviant behavior. Before the theory was first published in 1938, many sociologists tended to seek the causes of deviance within the individual rather than without. The fact that today many sociologists take for granted the notion of deviance as caused by society is a testament to the contribution of anomie-strain theory.

Further, the theory seems to have a valid premise: The discrepancy between aspirations and the opportunity to realize these aspirations produces pressures toward deviation. This premise suggests that anybody, regardless of their social class backgrounds, tends to engage in deviance if they experience a significant gap between aspiration and opportunity. Indeed, much research has shown that wherever the aspiration–opportunity gap strikes, it tends to generate deviation (Parnaby and Sacco, 2004; Passas and Agnew, 1997; Menard, 1995).

Social Learning Theory

According to social learning theory, the brainchild of Edwin Sutherland (1939), deviant behavior is learned through one's interaction with others. More specifically, Sutherland developed the theory of differential association to explain how the learning of deviance comes about. Later, other sociologists presented different versions of the same theory.

Sutherland: Differential Association

More than 60 years ago—at about the same time that Merton proposed strain theory—Sutherland (1939) introduced the theory of differential association. The heart of the theory is this: If an individual associates with people who hold deviant (or criminal) ideas more than with people who embrace conventional ideas, the individual is likely to become deviant.

We should note two things about the meaning of this statement. First, although deviants typically hold deviant ideas, the people who hold deviant ideas do not have to be deviants—they can be anybody, even those who have not committed any deviance. What counts is the *idea* of committing deviance. If a father tells his children that it's all right to steal when you are poor, he is giving them an idea of committing a deviant act. On the other hand, if the father tells his children that it's wrong to steal, he is giving them an antideviant idea. The emphasis here is on whether the father gives his children deviant or antideviant ideas, not whether the father himself is a deviant or nondeviant. Therefore, if people are given more ideas of committing deviant acts than ideas of performing conventional acts, they are likely to engage in deviance.

Second, the theory does *not* refer to only one type of association, that is, deviant association or exposure to deviant ideas. The theory does not suggest that, if individuals have a lot of contacts with deviant ideas, they will become deviant. Lawyers, for example, may have a lot of contacts with their criminal clients, but they will not necessarily become criminals themselves. The theory instead refers to both deviant and conventional contacts or, more precisely, to the *excess* of deviant over conventional contacts. This means that it is all right to have both kinds of contacts; only if we have a *greater* number of deviant contacts than conventional ones are we likely to become deviant. This is suggested by the term *differential association,* which refers to the fact that deviants' *association* with deviant individuals and ideas *differs* from (or, more precisely, occurs more often than) their association with conventional ones. Defined in this way, differential association is theorized to be the cause of deviance: Differential association → deviant behavior.

Glaser: Differential Identification

According to Daniel Glaser (1956), Sutherland's theory actually conveys a "mechanistic image" of deviance. Such an image shows the individual as being mechanically pushed into deviant involvement by an association with deviants. It ignores the individual's role-taking and choice-making ability. Glaser, then, tries to correct this mechanistic image by suggesting that the experience of associating with deviants is harmless unless the individual *identifies* with them.

Glaser's theory may be taken to suggest that it is all right for us to associate with deviants in real life or get to know them in books and movies, as long as we do not take them so seriously that we identify with them, treating them as our heroes. But if we do identify with them, or more precisely, if we identify with them more than with nondeviants, we are likely to become deviants ourselves. In effect, Glaser suggests that deviance is likely to occur if differential identification intervenes between it and differential association: Differential association → *differential identification* → deviant behavior.

Burgess and Akers: Differential Reinforcement

According to Robert Burgess and Ronald Akers (1966), Sutherland merely suggested, in very broad terms, that people with differential association must go through a learning process before they become deviant. Sutherland failed, they contend, to specify what that learning process entails. In trying to correct this failure, Burgess and Akers offer the idea of *differential reinforcement* as the substance of that learning process.

Burgess and Akers derive their idea from a well-known theory in psychology, which has been variously referred to as *social learning theory, behaviorist theory, operant behavior theory, operant conditioning theory,* and *reinforcement theory.* Generally, the theory says that we are motivated to continue behaving in a certain way if we have been rewarded for doing so, or to discontinue the behavior if we have been punished for it. You are, for example, likely to continue studying hard if you have been rewarded by good grades for studying hard in the past. When applied to deviant behavior, reinforcement theory says that people will continue to engage in deviant activities if they have been rewarded for doing so. Robbers, for example, will continue to rob if they have made much money from their robberies or if they have not been caught for their crimes.

One aspect of reinforcement theory that is most relevant to the Burgess-Akers reformulation of Sutherland's differential association theory is the Law of Differential Reinforcement. This law can be expressed in simple terms as follows: If you are given several options, such as studying hard, going to the movies, drinking in a tavern, and attending a wild party the night before an exam, you will most likely choose the option that has been most satisfying to you in the past. When applied to deviant behavior, the law of differential reinforcement would explain that individuals will choose deviance over conventionality if they find deviance more satisfying than conventionality. However, this is likely to occur if they have been exposed to deviant ideas more than to conventional ideas. In short, Burgess and Akers's theory can be expressed as follows: Differential association → *differential reinforcement* → deviant behavior. Table 2.3 summarizes how this version of differential theory differs from the other two discussed earlier.

Evaluating Social Learning Theory

First, it is difficult to determine precisely what "differential association" in Sutherland's theory is in real-life situations. As Sutherland and Donald Cressey (1978) admit, people often cannot identify the persons from whom they have learned deviant and antideviant ideas. Although it is difficult to determine the exact, empirical meaning of differential association, many sociologists have claimed that their research data appear to support Sutherland's theory. But this need not be surprising. Actually, those sociologists have not found any empirical support for Sutherland's theory, but only for their *own* interpretations

TABLE 2.3   Three Versions of Social Learning Theory

Sutherland: Differential association → criminal behavior

Glaser: Differential association → differential identification → criminal behavior

Burgess and Akers: Differential association → differential reinforcement → criminal behavior

Note: The sign "→" indicates "antecedes or causes," as in "*A* antecedes or causes *B*."

of the theory. As James Short (1960), who has done considerable research to test the theory, observed: "Much support has been found for the principle of differential association *if* the liberties taken in the process of its operationalization [translation into empirical or testable terms] are granted." One study, for example, treats the concept of "differential association" as if it had to do with "association" only—and nothing to do with "differential." The concept is thus operationalized as a perception of friends' deviant attitudes and behaviors alone, not the friends' *excess of deviant over conventional* attitudes and behaviors (Hochstetler, Copes, and DeLisi, 2002).

Second, Glaser's differential identification theory appears to have received some support from empirical data. It has been found, for example, that high school boys who identified with delinquent friends were likely to become delinquent themselves. But there is no conclusive evidence that identification with delinquent friends is the cause of delinquency or occurs before a person becomes delinquent. It is quite possible that youngsters may identify with delinquent friends only after—not before—having become delinquent themselves.

Third, the Burgess-Akers differential reinforcement theory cannot explain why a person *initially* commits a deviant act. The theory is useful, however, for explaining repeated deviance, namely, why some people *continue* to get involved in deviance after committing a deviant act for the first time. The reason, according to differential reinforcement theory, is that they have in the past been rewarded more than punished for their deviance, whereas others do not repeat a deviant act because they have been punished more than rewarded for the act. This formulation has indeed been borne out by many studies (see, for example, Sellers, Cochran, and Branch, 2005; Chappell and Piquero, 2004; Akers and Lee, 1999).

Control Theory

Control theory differs in at least two ways from the other major theories discussed above. First, both anomie-strain and learning theorists approach the problem of explaining deviant behavior head-on and ask: What causes deviance? Control theorists approach the problem in a roundabout way: What, they ask, causes conformity? They assume, in other words, that if they find out what causes conformity, they will know what causes deviance, for what causes deviance is simply the *absence* of what causes conformity. Second, both anomie-strain and learning theorists reject the Freudian idea that deviance can naturally, or by itself, burst forth from our inborn animal impulses. Instead, anomie-strain and learning theories maintain that deviance originates from certain social conditions, namely, the discrepancy between goals and means in society and the experience of learning from others. In contrast, control theorists seem to accept the Freudian idea because they assume that people are naturally inclined to commit deviant acts and will do so *unless* they are properly controlled.

In the eyes of control theorists, then, what causes conformity is social control over the individual, and therefore the *absence of social control causes deviance*. There are, however, many different theories about the specific nature of social control. We will focus on only three of the more important ones.

Hirschi, Gottfredson, and Tittle: Social Bond, Self-Control, and Control Balance

Travis Hirschi (1969) assumes that all of us are endowed like animals with the ability to commit deviant acts. But most of us do not take advantage of this ability, Hirschi suggests, because of our *strong bond* to society. In other words, our strong bond to society ensures our conformity. Conversely, if our social bond is weak, we will commit deviant acts.

According to Hirschi, there are four ways for individuals to bond themselves to society. The first is by *attachment* to conventional people and institutions. In the case of juveniles, they may show this attachment by loving and respecting their parents, making friends with conventional peers, liking school, and working hard to develop intellectual skills. A *commitment* to conformity is the second way. Individuals invest their time and energy in conventional types of action, such as getting an education, holding a job, developing an occupational skill, improving a professional status, building up a business, or acquiring a reputation for virtue. At the same time, people show a commitment to achievement through these activities. The third way is *involvement* in conventional activities. People simply keep themselves so busy doing conventional things that they do not have time for partaking in deviant activities or even thinking about deviant acts. A *belief* in the moral validity of social rules is the fourth way in which people bond themselves to society. Individuals have a strong moral belief that they should obey the rules of conventional society. A young person may show such moral belief through a respect for the police or through a positive attitude toward the law.

If these four elements of the individual's bond to conventional society are strong, the individual is likely to get stuck in conformity. If these elements are weak, the individual is likely to slide into deviance. In more recent publications, Hirschi, along with Michael Gottfredson, argues that *weak self-control* is more useful for explaining deviance. People with weak self-control are said to be highly impulsive, reckless, and insensitive. They are a product of inadequate socialization. Their parents have often failed, for example, to discipline them in childhood for wrongful behavior. Such people then are likely to commit deviant acts (Langton, Piquero, and Hollinger, 2006; Love, 2006; Hirschi and Gottfredson, 1994).

According to Charles Tittle (2004, 1995), however, it is the *lack of control balance* that causes deviance. Individuals with a lack of control balance are said to have either a "control surplus" (such as the control we have over others being greater than the control others have over us) or a "control deficit" (the control others have over us being greater than the control we have over them). They are likely to engage in any kind of deviance, which may include such widely different deviances as exploitation of others, theft, vandalism, child molestation, and sexual harassment.

Braithwaite: Reintegrative Shaming

While Hirschi sees how society controls us through bonding, John Braithwaite (2000, 1989) looks at how society controls us through shaming. Shaming involves an expression of social disapproval designed to invoke remorse in the wrongdoer. There are two types of shaming: disintegrative and reintegrative. In *disintegrative shaming,* the wrongdoer is punished in such a way as to be stigmatized, rejected, or ostracized—in effect, banished from conventional society. It is the same as stigmatization. *Reintegrative shaming* is more positive; it involves making wrongdoers feel guilty while showing them understanding, forgiveness, or even respect. It is the kind of shaming that affectionate parents administer to their misbehaving child, or "hating the sin but loving the sinner." Thus, reintegrative shaming serves to reintegrate—or welcome back—the wrongdoer into conventional society.

According to Braithwaite, reintegrative shaming is more common in communitarian societies (marked by strong social relationships but weak individualism), such as Japan, whereas disintegrative shaming is more prevalent in less communitarian societies (characterized by weaker social relationships but stronger individualism), such as the United States. At the same time, reintegrative shaming usually discourages further deviance, whereas disintegrative shaming or stigmatization encourages it. This is taken to explain why crime rates are higher in the United States than in Japan.

Braithwaite concludes by arguing that the United States can significantly reduce its crime rates if it emphasizes reintegrative shaming rather than stigmatization in dealing with criminals, as Japanese society does. Since the early 1990s reintegrative shaming has appeared in the United States as "shaming penalties," which include drunk drivers being ordered by judges to display "DUI" bumper stickers, people convicted of public urination being ordered to sweep city streets, or men who solicit prostitutes being identified on newspapers, billboards, and radio shows. Dan Kahan (1997), a law professor at the University of Chicago, argues that the shaming is an effective deterrent to deviance.

The Deterrence Doctrine

While Braithwaite's theory deals largely with shaming as an *informal* social control (carried out by relatives, friends, neighbors, and the like), the deterrence doctrine focuses on formal social control (executed by judges and other law-enforcement agents). This version of control theory assumes that humans are basically rational, given to calculating the benefit and cost of committing a crime. If they find the cost greater than the benefit, they will refrain from committing the crime. The cost of crime, according to deterrence doctrine, is legal punishment, such as arrest, prosecution, imprisonment, or execution. Thus, the doctrine assumes that punishment (a form of social control) deters crime—and lack of punishment encourages it.

There are three ways in which punishment can be carried out, each being assumed to affect the likelihood of committing crime. First, punishment can be made more or less *severe*. According to deterrence doctrine, the more severe the punishment, the less likely the crime. Murder rates, for example, are expected to be lower in societies where convicted murderers are executed than in societies where the murderers are given a 20-year sentence. Second, punishment can be made more or less *certain*. Deterrence doctrine assumes that the more certain the commission of a crime will result in punishment, the less likely people will be to commit the crime. Shoplifting, for example, is expected to become less common if the chances of getting arrested for it go up from 50–50 to 100. Third, punishment can be made more or less *swift*. The more swiftly punishment is carried out, the less likely the crime is to occur. If it takes only several days for robbers to be arrested in a given city, the robbery rate in this city is likely to be lower than in another city where it takes longer to arrest robbers.

Whatever the mode of punishment, whether it be severe, certain, or swift, it is assumed to achieve two kinds of deterrence: general and specific. In *general deterrence* the punishment of a criminal deters the general public from committing crimes; in *specific deterrence* the punishment of a criminal deters the criminal alone from committing more crimes.

In sum, the three control theories suggest that some form of control prevents people from committing deviant acts, and the lack of controls prompts the commission of such acts. The theories differ largely in regard to what type of control can prevent deviance. Thus, they present various types of control, which include bond to society, self-control, reintegrative shaming, and legal punishment.

Evaluating Control Theory

First, many studies have supported Hirschi's social bond and self-control theory. Deviants such as juvenile delinquents, drug users, and drunk drivers have been found to have a weaker social bond or self-control than nondeviants (see, for example, Drapela, 2005; Pratt and Cullen, 2000). But most of these studies, being cross-sectional rather than longitudinal, could not have controlled for (canceled out) the reciprocal effect of deviance on social bond or self-control. Often, it is the deviant experience that causes people to have a weaker social bond and self-control rather than the other way around. Also, many studies that supposedly support the theory turn out to be tautological, using deviant acts (such as smoking, using drugs, speeding, and drunk driving) as the empirical indicators of weak self-control. These studies effectively suggest that deviance causes deviance (Li, 2004; Stylianou, 2002; Burton et al., 1998; Kempf, 1993).

Second, Braithwaite is only partly convincing in his argument that the United States can reduce crime with reintegrative shaming—by treating criminals in the same lenient, compassionate way as Japan does. This treatment may work if applied to first-time offenders who have committed relatively minor crimes and still retain a sense of shame for their crimes. But it can hardly have the same positive impact on hardened criminals who have lost their sense of shame for their crimes. Moreover, since reintegrative shaming is part and parcel of a communitarian society, it seems to be the pervasiveness of such society's strong social relationships rather than reintegrative shaming that largely keeps the crime rate low. This may explain why reintegrative shaming is less likely to deter deviance in Russia and other less communitarian societies marked by weak social relationships (Botchkovar and Tittle, 2005).

Third, the deterrence doctrine has received only conflicting support from research. Various studies show, for example, that arresting wife-beaters deters further violence more than less severe forms of punishment such as ordering the offender to leave the victim for eight hours. However, studies on released prisoners suggest just the opposite: The more severe their punishment (for example, the longer the sentence), the more likely former inmates will commit crimes again (Wright et al., 2004; Heckert and Gondolf, 2000; Berk and Newton, 1985).

Finally, various control theorists share a simplistic view of social control, regarding it as only a *preventer* of deviance. They fail to see control as a possible *cause* of deviance. The great ambition—along with excellent social and intellectual skills—that develops from social bond may prevent juvenile delinquency, as Hirschi's theory suggests, but the same ambition may cause corporate and political crimes. Similarly, contrary to Braithwaite's theory, reintegrative shaming may cause deviance, such as by encouraging judges to treat the accused as guilty, thereby violating their right to be presumed innocent. Also, contrary to the deterrence doctrine, the very process of law enforcement to deter crime may trigger lawbreaking acts. In taking action against a suspect, for example, a police officer may cause the suspect to commit such criminal acts as resisting arrest or assaulting an officer (Marx, 1981).

Table 2.4 presents the major points of all the theories discussed in this chapter.

TABLE 2.4   Positivist Theories of Deviance

Anomie-Strain Theory: Social strain causes deviance.

Merton's goal–means gap: Deviance is prevalent in society because the society encourages people to achieve success without providing equal opportunity for achieving it.

Cohen's status frustration: Deviance is prevalent among lower-class youths because they fail to achieve status in a middle-class school environment.

Cloward and Ohlin's differential illegitimate opportunity: Lower-class youths are likely to engage in delinquent activities if they have access to illegitimate opportunity.

Latest versions of the theory: The American Dream contributes to deviance by directly encouraging the use of illegal means to achieve success, while various social strains cause deviance by producing such emotions as frustration and anger.

Social Learning Theory: Deviance is learned through social interaction.

Sutherland's differential association: People are likely to become deviant if they associate with people holding deviant ideas rather than with people holding antideviant ideas.

Glaser's differential identification: People are likely to become deviant if they identify themselves more with deviants than with nondeviants.

Burgess and Akers's differential reinforcement: Deviants are likely to continue engaging in deviant activities if they have been rewarded rather than punished for their past deviance.

Control Theory: Lack of social control causes deviance.

Social bond, self-control, and control balance: People are likely to become deviant if their bond to society and their self-control are weak or if they have a control surplus or deficit.

Braithwaite's reintegrative shaming: People are likely to become deviant if they are not made to feel ashamed for their wrongdoing or to feel they are an integral part of society.

The deterrence doctrine: People are likely to become deviant if they know their deviant acts are not punished with severity, certainty, or swiftness.

Summary

1. How does anomie-strain theory explain the causation of deviant behavior? According to Merton's anomie-strain theory, lower-class people are more likely to get involved in deviant activities because the society has encouraged them to pursue a high-success goal without providing them with the means of achieving it. Cohen extends this theory by proposing that when their aspirations for status are frustrated in the middle-class milieu, lower-class youths are driven to achieve status among themselves by engaging in delinquency. Cloward and Ohlin extend Merton's theory by suggesting that whether potentially delinquent lower-class youth will actually become delinquent depends on whether they have access to illegitimate opportunity. Other sociologists extend Merton's theory by attributing deviance to the American Dream and forms of strain ignored by Merton. **How good is anomie-strain theory?** There is no reliable evidence for its assumption that, compared with middle and upper classes, the lower classes are more prone to deviance while holding the same level of success aspirations. Nevertheless, the theory has been valuable for replacing the psychological with the sociological explanation of deviance and for offering the valid premise that the aspiration–opportunity gap causes deviance.

2. According to various versions of social learning theory, why do some people become deviant? Sutherland's differential association theory states that people will likely become deviant if they associate more with individuals who hold deviant ideas than with those who embrace antide-viant ideas. Glaser extends this theory by suggesting that the determining factor for turning the differential association into criminal action is differential identification, while Burgess and Akers designate differential reinforcement the determining factor. **Are Sutherland's theory and its extended versions any good?** Sutherland's theory has been criticized for lacking a precise, empirical meaning of "differential association," but many researchers claim to have found data supporting the theory. As for Glaser's theory, it has received some, though not conclusive, empirical support. The Burgess-Akers theory cannot explain initial acts of deviance but is useful for explaining repeated deviance.

3. How does control theory explain deviance? According to the theory, what causes conformity is control, and, therefore, the lack of control causes deviance. Hirschi refers to this causal factor of conformity as our *bond to society,* or *self-control.* Braithwaite calls it *reintegrative shaming,* and, proponents of deterrence doctrine refer to it as *legal punishment.* **What are the strengths and weaknesses of various control theories?** Hirschi's theory has received a lot of support from research data, but weak social bond or self-control may be the effect rather than the cause of deviance. Braithwaite's theory about reintegrative shaming being able to reduce crime in the United States may work for first-time offenders but not hardened criminals. The deterrence doctrine has received support from some studies but has been refuted by others.

FURTHER READING

Adler, Freda, and William S. Laufer (eds.). 1995. *The Legacy of Anomie Theory.* New Brunswick, N.J.: Transaction. A series of essays that discuss the contribution of Merton's theory to the sociological research on and understanding of deviance.

Agnew, Robert. 1992. "Foundation for a general strain theory of crime and delinquency." *Criminology,* 30, 47–87. A revision of Merton's anomie-strain theory that takes into account many forms of strain that lead to deviance.

Akers, Ronald L. 1998. *Social Learning and Social Structure: A General Theory of Crime and Deviance.* Boston: Northeastern University Press. A clear presentation of his social learning theory as well as research data supporting the theory.

Braithwaite, John. 1989. *Crime, Shame and Reintegration.* New York: Cambridge University Press. A theory about how society deters crime through the imposition of a social control called "reintegrative shaming."

Cullen, Francis T. 1988. "Were Cloward and Ohlin strain theorists? Delinquency and opportunity revisited." *Journal of Research in Crime and Delinquency,* 25, 214–241. Shows why Cloward and Ohlin are more opportunity theorists than strain theorists.

Higgins, George E., and Rebecca J. Boyd. 2008. "Low self-control and deviance: Examining the moderation of social support from parents." *Deviant Behavior,* 29, 388–410. Shows the finding that parental support can reduce the influence of weak self-control on deviant behavior.

Hirschi, Travis, and Michael R. Gottfredson (eds.). 1994. *The Generality of Deviance.* New Brunswick, N.J.: Transaction. A collection of articles about the editors' theory of self-control, which essentially shows how a lack of self-control can result from ineffective child rearing and then cause deviance.

Johnson, Matthew C., and Glen A. Kercher. 2007. "ADHD, strain, and criminal behavior: A test of general strain theory." *Deviant Behavior,* 28, 131–152. An empirical study of how college students with self-reported ADHD symptoms are more likely than other students to participate in criminal behavior when experiencing strain.

Langton, Lynn, Nicole Leeper Piquero, and Richard C. Hollinger. 2006. "An empirical test of the relationship between employee theft and low self-control." *Deviant Behavior,* 27, 537–565. An exploratory study of how college students with low self-control are more likely than others to lie on their job applications and commit employee theft.

Love, Sharon RedHawk. 2006. "Illicit sexual behavior: A test of self-control theory." *Deviant Behavior,* 27, 505–536. Offers data to show how low self-control seems to contribute to sexual deviance such as masturbation, using pornography, and cross-dressing.

Messner, Steven F., and Richard Rosenfeld. 2001. *Crime and the American Dream.* Belmont, Calif.: Wadsworth. Shows how the culture of the American Dream causes deviance by encouraging people to pursue success in any way possible.

Passas, Nikos, and Robert Agnew (eds.). 1997. *The Future of Anomie Theory.* Boston: Northeastern University Press. A collection of articles analyzing, modifying, and expanding Merton's strain theory.

Stylianou, Stelios. 2002. "The relationship between elements and manifestations of low self-control in a general theory of crime: Two comments and a test." *Deviant Behavior,* 23, 531–557. Discusses the tautological problem with low self-control theory and shows the proper way of testing the theory.

Tittle, Charles R. 1995. *Control Balance: Toward a General Theory of Deviance.* Boulder, Colo.: Westview. Presents a complicated theory of how the interaction among deviant motivation, opportunity, and constraint determines the probability of deviance.

CRITICAL THINKING QUESTIONS

1. Which of the positivist theories makes the most sense to you and why?

2. What would you have the government do to fight crime, based on one or more of the positivist theories discussed in this chapter?

3 Constructionist Theories

Abortion has been legal since 1973 but today it is increasingly hard to get one. Consider Lisa, a 22-year-old unmarried woman who works in a restaurant. Several months ago she was pregnant and decided to have an abortion. But the only abortion provider in her area, 15 minutes from her home in Missouri, had just closed down. There were now merely four abortion doctors left in the entire state. The closest one to Lisa's town was at the Planned Parenthood clinic in St. Louis, an eight-hour round-trip away. Having no car, Lisa not only had to ask a friend to drive her but also had to miss two days of work. She had to take the long trip again two weeks later, for a follow-up exam that lasted five minutes. The whole expenditure for the clinic's bill, the abortion drug, gasoline, food, and incidentals added up to more than $600. "It was all very frustrating," she said a month after her abortion. "I only recently paid back everyone I borrowed money from" (Tumulty, 2006).

Besides Missouri, many other states have also made it more difficult to get an abortion nowadays. They not only have created a hostile environment that has led to the closing of many abortion clinics, but also have imposed legal restrictions on abortion, such as requiring pre-abortion counseling, a waiting period, and, for minors, parental consent or notification. They, in effect, treat abortion as a deviant act. So do positivist sociologists. To constructionist sociologists, however, abortion is not really deviant as an act but only appears deviant as a mental construction, a figment of human imagination. Thus constructionists have developed theories about how people impute the notion of "deviance" to behaviors such as abortion and what consequences this has for themselves and for others. This chapter discusses the more important of these theories.

Labeling Theory

In the early 1960s, a group of sociologists developed what soon became widely known as labeling theory. It is actually a version of symbolic interactionism, a well-known sociological theory about social behavior in general (Prus and Grills, 2003; Becker, 1974, 1963; Erikson, 1962; Kitsuse, 1962).

A Version of Symbolic Interactionism

In defining what deviance is, labeling theorists call on two central ideas in symbolic interactionism. These two ideas are suggested by the very two words that make up the name of the theory. First, as suggested by the word *interaction,* deviance—like any other kind of human activity—is a collective action, involving more than one person's act. According to labeling theory, we should not focus on the deviant person alone as positivist sociologists do but rather on the *interaction* between the supposed deviant and other, conventional people. As Becker (1974) says:

> The positivist style of studying deviance has focused on the deviant himself and has asked its questions mainly about him. Who is he? Is he likely to keep being that way? The new [labeling] approach sees it as always and everywhere a process of interaction between at least two kinds of people: those who commit (or are said to have committed) a deviant act and the rest of society, perhaps divided into several groups itself. The two groups are seen in complementary relationship. One cannot exist without the other.

Second, as suggested by the word *symbolic,* the interaction between the supposed deviant and the conformists is governed by the meanings that they impute to each other's actions and reactions. The meaning (variously referred to by symbolic interactionists as a symbol, significant gesture, interpretation, definition, or label) that people attach to an act is much more important than the act itself. The meaning, according to labeling theorists, comes through in how people respond to an act: A negative response means deviance; a positive response means nondeviance. As Kitsuse (1962) explains, "Forms of the behavior per se do not differentiate deviants from nondeviants; it is the responses of the conventional and conforming members of the society who identify and interpret behavior as deviant which sociologically transform persons into deviants."

In short, labeling theorists interpret deviance not as a static entity whose causes are to be sought out, but rather as *a dynamic process of symbolic interaction between both deviants and nondeviants*. Consequently, labeling theorists do not ask as positivists do: What causes deviant behavior? Instead, they ask at least two questions: (1) Who applies the *deviant* label to whom? and (2) What consequences does the application of this label have for the person labeled and for the people who apply the label? (These questions can be expressed in terms of symbolic interactionism: Who interprets whose behavior as deviant? And how does this interpretation affect the behavior of both parties involved in the interaction?)

Who Labels Whom?

According to labeling theorists, people who represent the forces of law and order as well as conventional morality typically apply the deviant label to those who have allegedly violated that law and morality. Examples of the *labelers* include the police, judges, prison guards, psychiatrists, mental hospital attendants, and other social control agents. On the other hand, examples of the *labeled* include criminals, juvenile delinquents, drug addicts, mental patients, and prostitutes.

Generally, the rich, white, or powerful and their representatives such as law-enforcing agents are more able to label others as deviant. As Becker (1974) says, "A major element in every aspect of the drama of deviance is the imposition of definitions—of situations, acts, and people—by *those powerful enough or legitimated to be able to do so*." On the other side of the same coin, the poor, black, or powerless are more likely to be labeled deviant. Thus a poor or black person is more likely than a rich or white person to be arrested, prosecuted, or convicted as a criminal, even if both have committed similar crimes; to be declared insane or committed to a mental institution, even if both suffer from similar psychiatric conditions; and so on. This idea of the powerful labeling the weak as deviant runs through other constructionist theories, especially the various versions of conflict theory, which will be discussed later.

Consequences of Labeling

Labeling a person deviant may have some consequences for the person so labeled and also for the labeler.

Consequences for the Labeled.   According to labeling theorists, being labeled deviant produces negative consequences for the individual so labeled. One major consequence is that once people are labeled deviant, they tend to see themselves as deviant, which in turn leads them to continue the so-called deviant behavior. The issue here is not whether they have actually committed deviant acts; rather—whatever the nature of their acts—whenever they are defined as deviant by others, they also tend to define themselves as deviant, then continue to engage in the acts, and, finally, become confirmed deviants. This process of becoming deviant was long ago discussed by Frank Tannenbaum (1938). In his view, a child may engage in many forms of activities—such as breaking windows, annoying people, climbing over the roof, stealing apples, and playing hooky—and innocently consider all these enjoyable. But the parents, teachers, and police may, and often do, define these activities as a type of nuisance, delinquency, or evil. So they may "dramatize the evil" of these activities by admonishing, scolding, spanking, hauling into court, or jailing the child. Thus, dramatically labeled a delinquent, the child will likely become one, and, later, a criminal.

In discussing the process of becoming a criminal, Tannenbaum implied that there are two types of deviant acts. One is the *first* act, which the child considers innocent but which adults define as delinquent, and the second is the *final* behavior, which both the child and adults define as delinquent. Later, Edwin Lemert (1951) made explicit the distinction between these two forms of behavior. He called the first *primary deviation,* and the second, *secondary deviation.*

Like Tannenbaum, Lemert sees the difference between primary and secondary deviance as more than temporal—more than the fact that one occurs earlier than the other, more than that primary deviance is committed only once while secondary deviance is continued or repeated deviance. Lemert sees primary deviance as a matter of value conflict, as a behavior that the society defines as deviant but that the performer of that behavior does not so define. This behavior becomes secondary deviance only when the person comes to agree with the society's definition of the behavior as deviant, seeing himself or herself as a deviant.

Labeling theorists are mostly interested in analyzing the process of becoming a secondary deviant—that is, in how a person goes from primary to secondary deviation. They refer to this analysis as a sequential, career, or identity-stabilizing model of deviance. This model suggests that when people are forced by society to see themselves as deviants, they become secondary deviants by repeatedly engaging in deviation as a way of life. Consider a man who has just been released from prison after serving a sentence for robbery. He is likely to be stigmatized as an "ex-con." As a stigmatized ex-con, he will find it difficult to get a good job. For that reason, he will see himself as an ex-con, feel compelled to commit another robbery, and thus launch his career as a robber.

In short, once labeled a deviant, the individual tends to suffer a negative consequence by continuing to engage in deviant activities as a secondary, confirmed, or career deviant. The individual also suffers other negative consequences, such as being ridiculed, humiliated, degraded, harassed, beaten, imprisoned, or otherwise dehumanized—treated as an object, animal, or nonperson. All this suggests that the deviant is "more sinned against than sinning" (Becker, 1963).

Consequences for the Labeler.   According to labeling theorists, labeling a person deviant tends to create positive consequences for the community that applies the label. One consequence is enhanced social order. As Erikson (1962) explains:

> As a trespasser against the group norms, he [the deviant] represents those factors which lie outside the group's boundaries: he informs us, as it were, what evil looks like, what shapes the devil can assume. And in doing so, he shows us the difference between the inside of the group and the outside. It may well be that without this ongoing drama at the outer edges of group space, the community would have no inner sense of identity and cohesion. . . . Thus deviance . . . may itself be, in controlled quantities, an important condition for preserving stability.

If some individuals are periodically singled out to be convicted and punished as criminals, conventional members of the community will know better the distinction between good and evil so that they will ally themselves with good and against evil. The deviant, in effect, does us a great service by teaching us what evil is like, presenting himself or herself as an object lesson for what we shall suffer if we do evil, and thus encouraging us to avoid punishment and do good. Therefore, when some individuals or groups are labeled deviant, there will follow some positive consequences for the community as the labeler, the most important consequence being the preservation and strengthening of social cohesion and social order.

Evaluating Labeling Theory

Labeling theory has enjoyed tremendous popularity among sociologists. They can easily see the significance of labeling in human interaction, and can find considerable research evidence to support the theory (see, for example, Adams, 2003; Davies and Tanner, 2003; Lauderdale et al., 1984). Nevertheless, the theory has also drawn a lot of criticisms, of which only the most important are addressed here.

First, many sociologists have criticized labeling theory for not being able to answer the question of what causes deviance in the first place. This criticism misses the mark, though, because the theory is not meant to explain what causes primary deviance. The theory is intended to be nonetiological; it is not concerned with causal questions about primary deviance, except as they might relate to how labeling causes secondary deviance.

Second, research has failed to produce consistent support to labeling theorists' assumption that the deviant label leads the individual into further deviant involvement. Some studies show that labeling encourages further deviance, but many others do not. According to one researcher, for example, teenagers who are publicly labeled as juvenile delinquents for having been convicted in court for an offense, more than their nonlabeled peers tend to get involved in delinquent activities again. Another researcher, however, finds that although they are often ridiculed in school as "sluts," "druggies," or "white trash," poor teenage girls with a relatively strong bond to their mothers or grandmothers do not engage in promiscuous, unprotected sex or use alcohol and other drugs (Victor, 2004; Farrington, 1977).

Finally, labeling theory cannot logically deal with hidden deviance and powerful deviants (Thio, 1973). By insisting that no behavior can be deviant unless labeled as such, labeling theory inevitably implies that hidden deviance, particularly the kind committed often in secrecy by powerful people, cannot be deviant because it is by definition unknown to others and, therefore, cannot be labeled by others as deviant. In addition, by stating that it is the more powerful people who typically impose the deviant label on the less powerful, labeling theorists in effect suggest that the powerful cannot be deviants because they can only be labelers.

Phenomenological Theory

Many sociologists have been influenced by labeling theory since the early 1960s. But toward the end of that decade, some sociologists took a step beyond labeling theory and developed another, new version of symbolic interactionism called *phenomenological theory*. (It has also been referred to as ethnomethodology, existential sociology, creative sociology, or sociology of everyday life.) As we have noted, labeling theory deals with societal reaction to deviance and the consequences of this reaction for the deviants and their labelers. But the theory does not get into the minds of these people. This is what phenomenological theory does. It delves into people's subjectivity (called a *phenomenon*), including their consciousness, perception, attitudes, feelings, and opinions about deviance. It assumes that all kinds of people, whether deviants or their labelers, are highly subjective in "constructing," defining, or interpreting deviance, although they may claim to be very objective (Roubach, 2004; Handel, 1982; Morris, 1977).

Critique of Positivism

Phenomenologists first launch a philosophical attack on sociologists who adopt the positivist view of deviance. As we saw in Chapter 1, positivists take an objective and deterministic approach to deviance. They view a deviant person as an object whose behavior is determined or caused by various forces in the environment. Consequently, positivists ignore how deviants think and feel about their own deviant experience. By contrast, phenomenologists consider the deviant's subjective experience the heart of deviant reality. At the same time, they regard positivists' supposedly objective notion of deviant behavior as unreal, because it reflects their own preconception of the deviant as an object rather than the reality of the deviant as a thinking and feeling human.

In other words, positivists do not study a phenomenon as it really is but rather study *their own conception* of the phenomenon. They are, in effect, highly subjective—or certainly not as objective as they claim to be. Positivists have long assumed that the real phenomenon and the positivist conception of it are identical. But to phenomenologists, the real phenomenon is different from the positivist conception of it. The real phenomenon, in phenomenologists' view, is the immediate experience and consciousness of the person under study. Consider, for example, how the positivist view of a psychiatrist might differ from the subjective view of quiet, withdrawn Hopi Indians. To the psychiatrist, the Hopi may be abnormal because their withdrawn behavior is defined by the psychiatric profession as a symptom of abnormality. The Hopi, to the contrary, see themselves as perfectly normal because their quiet demeanor is a virtue in Hopi culture.

Subjectivism as the Key to Deviant Reality

To phenomenologists, what deviance means is *fundamentally problematic*: People disagree over the meanings of deviance. Such disagreement frequently occurs among positivists when they try to observe and explain an individual's deviant behavior "objectively." In analyzing suicide, for example, constructionist sociologists find that doctors, coroners, and official statisticians—on whom positivist sociologists rely heavily for their definition of suicide—often disagree among themselves as to whether a given death is "suicide" (Pescosolido and Mendelsohn, 1986; Douglas, 1967). According to general agreement, a self-caused death should be interpreted as suicide if there is "intention to die." But since the *intention* to die is difficult to determine after the person is dead, disagreement is bound to exist over whether the deceased actually had this intention. Thus, those who believe there was intention to die would define the self-caused death as "suicide"; those who do not would interpret it as "accidental death." All this implies that since the meanings of deviance are fundamentally problematic for positivists, their conception of deviance cannot possibly get at the essence of a deviant phenomenon.

The meanings that positivists ascribe to deviance are *abstract* in nature, that is, *independent* of concrete situations in which the deviant person is involved. By contrast, the meanings that the deviant person imputes to his or her own behavior are *situated* in nature, that is, tied to the concrete situations in which the subject is involved. *Abstract meanings* are the positivist's so-called *objective,* scientific interpretation of the deviant subject's behavior, while *situated meanings* are the subject's *subjective* interpretation of the subject's own behavior. Alfred Schutz (1962), a founder of phenomenology, refers to the abstract, objective meanings as "constructs of the *second* degree," and the situated, subjective meanings as "constructs of the first degree." Phenomenologists insist that the positivists' supposedly objective idea about deviance is actually their own idea, far removed from, and at best a pale representation of, the deviant experience they study. Only the deviant person's subjective interpretation of the person's own experience is real. Thus, phenomenologists emphasize that to understand deviance, we should rely heavily on people's subjective interpretations of their own deviant experiences.

Ethnography: An Application of Phenomenology

Seeking to grasp the reality of deviance, phenomenologists analyze how their subjects feel and think about their deviance, themselves, and others. The method they use is called *ethnography*. Many sociologists who use ethnography to study deviance, however, call themselves ethnographers rather than phenomenologists. And they define ethnography as a style of research that seeks to understand the *meanings* the people under investigation ascribe to their experiences (Maso, 2001; Brewer, 2000; Ferrell and Hamm, 1998). But this is essentially the same thing sought by sociologists who call themselves phenomenologists (see, for example, Skrapec, 2001).

In his classic in-depth interview with 19-year-old Agnes, who had both male genitals and female secondary sex characteristics, Harold Garfinkel (1967) found that Agnes saw himself or herself not as a freak, as most people would, but as a normal person. Agnes was born as a male and raised as a boy until high school. During adolescence Agnes secretly took his mother's hormone medication and eventually developed large breasts, a slim waist, wide hips, and soft skin. At 17 she had an attractive female figure. By then she dropped out of school, left home, moved to another city, and tried to begin a new life as a woman. A year later, she went to the UCLA Medical Center to request a sex-change operation. Before such surgery was approved, Agnes had to be thoroughly investigated to ensure that she really felt like a woman. As a participant in this investigation, Garfinkel interviewed her extensively. He found that she saw herself as a normal woman, and did her best to convince others that she was. She told Garfinkel that she was merely a normal woman who happened to have a physical defect comparable to any other deformity, such as a harelip, clubfoot, or twisted spinal cord. Like any other normal person with a deformity, she felt that it was only natural for her to want to have hers—the penis—removed. Her self-concept as a normal woman further led her to claim that, as a sexual organ, her penis was "dead," that she had no sexual pleasure from it nor sexual attraction to women. She wanted to have it replaced by a surgically constructed vagina. Her self-concept as a normal woman also caused her to make sure that others would not suspect her of having a penis. Thus, on a beach she always wore a bathing suit with a skirt. In the apartment that she shared with a woman, she never undressed in her roommate's presence. On a date she always dodged necking and, in particular, petting below the waist.

Just as Agnes saw and presented herself as a normal person, Jack Katz (1988) found that criminals such as murderers and robbers also see themselves and their deviance in some positive way. More specifically, murderers perceive themselves as morally superior to their victims. This is because, in most cases of homicide, the *victims* have humiliated their killers by teasing, daring, defying, taunting, or insulting them. The resulting rage leads to killing but at the same moment gives the killers the self-righteous feeling of defending their identity, dignity, or respectability.

Katz also found that virtually all robbers feel themselves morally superior to their victims, regarding their victims as fools or suckers who deserve to be robbed. If robbers want to rob somebody on the street, they first ask the potential victim for the time, for directions, for a cigarette light, or for change. Each of these requests is intended to determine whether the person is a fool. The request for the time, for example, gives the robber the opportunity to know whether the prospective victim has an expensive watch. Complying with the request, then, is taken to establish the person as a fool and hence the right victim.

Most recently, many ethnographic studies that have delved into the subjective world of various kinds of deviants have come out with basically the same findings as those of Garfinkel and Katz. In his study of a family in which virtually all members were officially certified as "mentally retarded," Steven Taylor (2004) found that these people did not see themselves as mentally challenged. They carried on their daily lives as if they were like everybody else. In his analysis of tattoo collectors, Angus Vail (2004) found that they viewed their tattoos as normal as the car they drove and the hairstyle they wore on any given day. In his examination of the personal accounts of an 18-year-old girl who committed suicide, Thomas Cottle (2004) found that she had gone through many unpleasant experiences in her daily life, but she and other family members seemed not to notice their special significance—they were normal everyday events. Before killing herself, she had even made plans to attend a prestigious university that had admitted her. In her in-depth interviews with serial killers, Candice Skrapec (2001) was impressed by "their apparent ordinariness. They eat breakfast like the rest of us," which implies that they saw themselves as normal and acted accordingly.

Evaluating Phenomenological Theory

Phenomenologists have offered a convincing argument about the inadequacy of positivism: Positivists cannot get at the essence of deviant reality. But phenomenologists' assumption that they themselves can is less convincing. Phenomenologists only create a version of human reality. The phenomenologist version may be unique, but it is not necessarily superior to the positivist or other versions. Since sociologists, whether they are phenomenologists, positivists, or others, differ in their value systems, ideological inclinations, observational methods, and sensitivity to human experience, they are bound to create different, competing, or conflicting versions of human reality. In this regard, however, we may point out the contribution of phenomenological theory. Its view of deviant behavior as comprehensible through the individual's subjective experience does differ, compete, or conflict with the positivist emphasis on the objective side of deviant reality, thereby enabling us to look at the subject with a broader perspective and understanding.

Conflict Theory

More than 70 years ago, a number of sociologists began to point out the pluralistic, heterogeneous, and conflictive nature of modern society (Sellin, 1938; Waller, 1936). In a traditional or simple society, people share the same cultural values and, therefore, can have harmonious relationships with one another. Such value consensus and social harmony are absent in modern industrial societies, particularly in the United States. Instead, there is a great deal of social and cultural conflict. *Social conflict* has to do with the incompatible interests, needs, and desires of such diverse groups as business companies versus labor unions, conservative versus liberal political groups, whites versus blacks, and so on. *Cultural conflict* has to do with the discrepant norms and values that derive from definitions of right and wrong—that is, what is considered right in one culture is considered wrong in another. For example, in the 1930s a Sicilian father in New Jersey, after killing his daughter's 16-year-old seducer, felt proud of having defended his family honor in a traditional way, but was very surprised when the police came to arrest him (Sellin, 1938). Either social or cultural conflict has been said to bring about criminal behavior, not only among immigrants but also among African Americans and other poor or oppressed groups. Therefore, conflict as well as its resulting criminality is an inherent, normal, and integral part of modern society. Those sociologists who held this view 70 years ago may be regarded as *conflict theorists*.

But those conflict theorists failed to develop systematically the notion of conflict as the source of criminal *definition* rather than behavior. They were still very much tied to the traditional positivist concern with the causal explanation of criminal behavior. Only in the mid-1960s did a group of conflict theorists emerge to explore criminality systematically as a matter of definition. Since the mid-1970s, moreover, some of these new conflict theorists have begun to deal with the causation of deviance but in a different way from the early conflict theorists. Let's see how these new conflict theorists view deviance.

Legal Reality Theory

According to William Chambliss (1969), there are two kinds of law. One is the *law on the books,* the ideal of law, and the other is the *law in action,* the reality of law. According to the law on the books, legal authorities *ought* to be fair and just by treating all citizens equally. However, the law in action shows that legal authorities are *actually* unfair and unjust, favoring the rich and powerful over the poor and weak (Chambliss and Seidman, 1971).

Many people may blame the discrepancy between the two types of law on the evil character of lawmaking and law-enforcing individuals, but Chambliss rejects such an individualistic interpretation. He shows how those individuals are heavily influenced by the historical and organizational background of the law, as follows.

Modern Anglo-American law stems from the legal system of early England. The English legal system was established in the eleventh century. Its central feature is that personal wrongs are considered transgressions against the state and that only the state has the right to punish the transgressors. This legal principle replaced the earlier nonlegal norm that personal wrongs, being a highly personal matter, should be settled through reconciliation by the private parties concerned. To carry out the new legal principle, the government used force and coercion as the means for handling wrongs and disputes; created two separate bodies, the lawmakers (legislature) and the law enforcers (judiciary); appointed judges to settle disputes between the state and individual citizens or between individual citizens themselves; and relied on peers (juries) to ultimately decide disputes.

Such was the general structure of the legal system in early England, and it still prevails in contemporary U.S. society. But the specific content of the laws as well as the specific manner of enforcing them has often changed to reflect the interests of the ruling classes. The vagrancy laws in fourteenth-century feudal England, for example, reflected the powerful landowners' need for cheap labor because the law required poor able-bodied men to work at low wages, made it unlawful for them to move from one place to another to avoid the low-paying jobs or to seek higher wages, and prohibited giving alms to able-bodied beggars. Then, in the sixteenth century, the vagrancy laws were changed to protect the interests of prosperous merchants who had to transport their goods from one town to another, as the new vagrancy laws were applied to the rogues, vagabonds, and highwaymen who often preyed on the traveling merchants. Today, in both England and the United States, the vagrancy laws are meant to control down-and-outers, the undesirable, the criminal, and nuisances, thereby reflecting the desire of the influential middle and upper classes to make their streets safe and peaceful. Historically, criminal law has, in effect if not in intent, served the interests of the rich and powerful rather than the interests of the poor and powerless. Under this historical influence, the legislators of today understandably tend to make laws that favor the rich and powerful.

Law enforcers such as police, prosecutors, and judges also tend to become the tools of power and privilege. This tendency is mostly the consequence of *organizational imperative*. It is in the nature of any organization to compel its members to perform tasks that will maximize reward and minimize trouble for the organization. The reward to be sought by the law-enforcing agency is public support; the trouble to be avoided is the withdrawal of such support, or worse. Thus, it is rewarding for the law-enforcing officials to arrest, prosecute, and convict powerless people such as skid-row drunks, vagrants, gamblers, prostitutes, rapists, thieves, and robbers. But it will likely cause trouble for the agency if the law enforcers make the same effort to process respectable middle- and upper-class citizens for their white-collar offenses. In view of such an organizational imperative, the law-enforcing officials are very likely to make the law serve the interests of the rich and powerful (Chambliss, 1969).

Social Reality Theory

While Chambliss attributes the unjust practice of law to historical changes and organizational imperative, Richard Quinney (1974) blames the unjust law itself directly on the capitalist system. "Criminal law," he says, "is used by the state and the ruling class to secure the survival of the capitalist system, and, as capitalist society is further threatened by its own contradictions, criminal law will be increasingly used in the attempt to maintain domestic order."

Such a critical view of capitalism is based on Quinney's (1975) conflict theory of criminality, which he calls "the social reality of crime." According to this theory, four factors jointly produce the capitalist society's high crime rates but also help to consolidate its established legal order as well as its dominant class. First, the dominant class *defines* as criminal those behaviors that threaten its interests. This means that criminal laws are largely made by powerful members of society. Second, the dominant class *applies* those laws to ensure the protection of its interests. This involves having the police, judges, and other members of the criminal justice system enforce the laws. Third, members of the subordinate class are compelled by their unfavorable life conditions to engage in those *actions* that have been defined as criminal. The poor, for example, are likely to commit a crime because their poverty pressures them to do so. And, fourth, the dominant class uses these criminal acts as the basis for constructing and diffusing the *ideology* of crime. This is the belief that the subordinate class contains most of the society's dangerous criminal elements and therefore should most often be arrested, prosecuted, or imprisoned. These four factors are interrelated, supporting each other so as to produce and maintain a certain high level of crime in society. For example, such criminal acts as murder and robbery committed by the poor are likely to cause the dominant class to make and enforce the laws against the poor, which in turn would make life more difficult for the poor, thereby encouraging them to commit more crimes. Figure 3.1 summarizes Quinney's theory.

Quinney (1974) has also tried to turn his theory into a call for political action. As his theory implies, there is something terribly wrong with existing society. What is wrong is that members of the powerful class inevitably criminalize the actions of the powerless so as to exploit, oppress, and subjugate them, thereby preserving, consolidating, and perpetuating the status quo of social inequality. Thus, Quinney calls for the development of a revolutionary consciousness that should eventually lead to the creation of a democratic-socialist society that will end the oppression of the powerless by the powerful. More recently, a

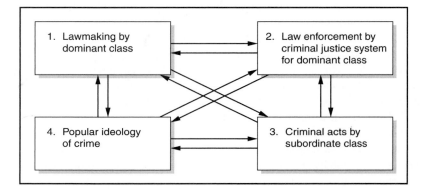

FIGURE 3.1 Quinney's Social Reality Theory. The interaction among these four factors helps produce and maintain a certain high level of crime in society.

"new sociology of social control" has emerged that goes far beyond Quinney's notion about the capitalist state controlling, by itself, the powerless, deviant population. According to this new control theory, many institutions, organizations, professions, and agencies are increasingly involved in controlling troublesome, deviant people on behalf of the state (Garland, 1993; Davis and Stasz, 1990; Scull, 1988).

Marxist Theory

In describing how the powerful define and control the powerless as deviants, most conflict theorists such as those discussed above have virtually ignored the causes of deviance. More recently, however, a number of conflict theorists have turned their attention to the question of causality. They draw their ideas mostly from Marxism; hence, they are often referred to as *Marxist theorists* (Greenberg, 1981).

According to these theorists, the cause of deviance can be traced to the exploitative nature of capitalism. To increase profit, capitalists must find ways to enhance productivity at low labor costs, including introducing automation and other labor-saving devices, forcing workers to work faster and work overtime, relocating industries to cheap labor locations, such as some nonunionized places in the southern United States or in labor-rich developing countries, and importing workers from poor nations. No matter what method is used, it inevitably throws some of the existing labor force out of work. These unemployed laborers become what Marxists call the *marginal surplus population,* relatively superfluous or useless to the economy. Their inability to maintain decent living conditions pressures them to commit crime.

Capitalism produces not only property crimes (such as robbery and theft) among the unemployed lower-class people; it also causes personal crimes (assault, rape, murder) and various other forms of deviance (alcoholism, suicide, and mental illness). As Sheila Balkan, Ronald Berger, and Janet Schmidt (1980) explained, economic "marginality leads to a lack of self-esteem and a sense of powerlessness and alienation, which create intense pressures on individuals. Many people turn to violence to vent their frustrations and strike out against symbols of authority, and others turn this frustration inward and experience severe emotional difficulties." This means that capitalism pressures people to commit crimes and become deviants by making them poor in the first place. Poverty, however, is not the only means by which capitalism generates deviance. According to Mark Colvin and John Pauly (1983), capitalist society can also produce crimes by exercising "coercive control" over the lower classes. Coercive control involves threatening to fire or actually firing poor workers in order to coerce them to work hard for their capitalist employers. It tends to create resentment. These workers are likely to feel alienated from society, showing an "alienative involvement" in it—a lack of attachment to it. Consequently, they are likely to engage in criminal activities.

However, the capitalistic pressure to commit crime and other forms of deviance is not confined to the lower classes, but reaches upward to affect the higher classes as well. By making possible the constant accumulation of profit, capitalism inevitably creates powerful empires of monopoly and oligopoly in the economy. These economic characteristics are an important cause of corporate crime. The reason is that "when only a few firms dominate a sector of the economy they can more easily collude to fix prices, divide up the market, and eliminate competitors" (Greenberg, 1981).

Feminist Theory

Virtually all theories about deviance are meant to apply to both sexes. The theories assume that what holds true for men also holds true for women. Feminist theorists, however, disagree. They argue that extant theories of deviance are actually about men only. Consequently, the theories may be valid for male behavior but not necessarily for female behavior. Consider, for example, Merton's anomie-strain theory. First, this theory assumes that people are inclined to strive for material success. This may be true for men but not necessarily true for women. In fact, under the influence of patriarchal society, women have been socialized differently than men. Thus, women are traditionally less interested in achieving material success, which often requires one-upmanship, and more interested in attaining emotional fulfillment through close, personal relations with others. Second, the theory assumes that if some women have a strong desire for economic success but no access to opportunities for achieving that goal, they would be as likely as men in the same situation to commit a crime. Today, given the greater availability of high positions for women in the economic world, the number of ambitious women in the "men's" world is on the rise. However, when these women are faced with the lack of opportunities for greater economic success, they are not as likely as men to engage in deviant activities. Finally, Merton's theory explicitly states that people in the United States are likely to commit a crime because their society overemphasizes the importance of entertaining high success goals while failing to provide the necessary opportunities for all its citizens to realize those goals. This may be relevant to men but less so to women. In fact, despite their greater lack of success opportunities, women still have lower crime rates than men (Heidensohn, 2002, 1995; Morris, 1987; Leonard, 1982).

The lack of relevancy to women in anomie and other conventional theories stems from a male-biased failure to take women into account. In redressing this problem, feminist theory understandably focuses on women. First, the theory deals with women as victims, mostly of rape and sexual harassment. These crimes against women are said to reflect the patriarchal society's attempt to put women in their place so as to perpetuate men's dominance (Heidensohn, 2002, 1995; Messerschmidt, 1986).

Feminist theory also zeroes in on women as offenders. It argues that although the rate of female crime has increased in recent years, the increase is not great enough to be significant. This is said to reflect the fact that gender equality is still far from being a social reality. Like employment opportunities, criminal opportunities are still much less available to women than men, hence women are still much less likely to engage in criminal activities. When women do commit crimes, they tend to commit the types of crime that reflect their continuing subordinate position in society. They are minor property crimes, such as shoplifting, passing bad checks, welfare fraud, and petty credit-card fraud. In fact, most of the recent increases in female crime involve these minor crimes. Largely, this reflects the increasing feminization of poverty—more women are falling below the poverty line today. Not surprisingly, most women criminals are unemployed, without a high school diploma, and single mothers with small children. They hardly fit the popular image of liberated women who benefit from whatever increase there has been in gender equality. There is no increase in female involvement in more profitable crimes, such as burglary, robbery, embezzlement, and business fraud, which are still primarily committed by men (Heidensohn, 2002; Chesney-Lind, 1997; Steffensmeier, 1996; Weisheit, 1992).

Power Theory

It seems obvious that power inequality affects the quality of people's lives: The rich and powerful live better than the poor and powerless. Similarly, power inequality affects the quality of *deviant* activities likely to be engaged in by people. Thus the powerful are more likely to engage in profitable deviant acts, such as corporate crime, while the powerless are more likely to commit less profitable deviant deeds, such as armed robbery. In other words, power—or the lack of it—determines to a large extent the *type* of deviance people are likely to carry out.

Power can also be an important *cause* of deviance. More precisely, the likelihood of powerful people perpetrating profitable deviance is greater than the likelihood of powerless persons committing less profitable deviance. It is, for example, more likely for bank executives to rob customers quietly than for jobless persons to rob banks violently. Analysis of the deviance literature suggests three reasons why the powerful are more likely to commit profitable deviance than the powerless to commit less profitable deviance.

First, the powerful have a *stronger deviant motivation*. Much of this motivation stems from *relative deprivation*—from feeling unable to achieve relatively high aspirations. Compared with the powerless, whose aspirations are typically low, the powerful are more likely to raise their aspirations so high that they cannot be realized. The more people experience relative deprivation, the more likely they are to commit deviant acts (Cookson and Persell, 1985; Harry and Sengstock, 1978; Merton, 1957).

Second, the powerful enjoy *greater deviant opportunity*. Obviously, a rich banker enjoys more legitimate opportunities than a poor worker to make money. But suppose they both want to acquire *illegitimately* a large sum of money. The banker will have access to more and better opportunities that make it easy to defraud customers. The banker, further, has a good chance of getting away with it because the kind of skill needed to pull off the crime is similar to the skills required for holding the bank position in the first place. In contrast, the poor worker would find his or her illegitimate opportunity limited to crudely robbing the bank, an illegitimate opportunity being further limited by a high risk of arrest (Ermann and Lundman, 2002; Vaughan, 1983).

Third, the powerful are subjected to *weaker social control*. Generally, the powerful have more influence in the making and enforcement of laws. The laws against mostly higher-status criminals are, therefore, relatively lenient and seldom enforced, but the laws against largely lower-status criminals are harsher and more often enforced. For example, many lower-class murderers have been executed for killing one person, but not a single corporate criminal has ever faced the same fate for marketing some untested drug that "cleanly" kills many people. Given the lesser control imposed on them, the powerful are likely to feel freer to use some deviant means to amass their fortune and power.

In sum, due to social inequality, the powerful are likely to have a stronger deviant motivation, enjoy greater deviant opportunity, and encounter weaker social control, as compared with the powerless. As a consequence, the powerful are more likely to get involved in profitable deviancy than the powerless in less profitable deviancy.

Postmodernist Theory

Postmodernist theory is probably the newest attempt in sociology to shed light on the nature of deviance. It first emerged in the early twentieth century as a philosophical movement in France that *questioned* the basic values of *modernism* such as innovation, rationality, objectivity, and other similar values represented by modern science and technology. These modernist values were criticized for encouraging, among other things, objectification, depersonalization, alienation, and other social problems that make it difficult for people to form genuine or close relationships. The French philosophers, then, called for greater attention to postmodernist values including subjectivity, feeling, and intuition, so that a richer, more meaningful life can be attained.

This philosophical thought started to influence the arts and social sciences in the United States in the 1960s, and since the late 1980s it has become a well-known, though poorly understood, theoretical perspective in American sociology.

Postmodernist theory contains both old and new ideas in the sociology of deviance. First is the theory's attack on modern science's emphasis on the search for objective truth. To postmodernists, the so-called objectivity in modern science is actually subjective because it involves the scientists imposing their own "privileged" professional view on the subject under their investigation. The subjective view of the subject, whether the subject is a deviant, victim, or anybody who reacts in some way to the deviant act, is therefore suppressed, discounted, disregarded, or ignored. But, to postmodernists, the subject's own views are important for understanding deviance. By thus attacking positivism (the scientist's so-called objectivity) and advocating subjectivity, postmodernist theory is similar to phenomenological theory.

Another old idea in postmodernist theory is what its developers call "deconstructionism." This term is defined as "tearing a text [which means any phenomenon or event, such as deviance] apart, revealing its contradictions and assumptions" (Rosenau, 1992). In other words, deconstruction is said to involve "the breaking up of something that has been built, as in 'demolition,' and exposing the way in which it is built" (Einstadter and Henry, 1995). This meaning of deconstruction is basically the same as the meaning of what is popularly called "analysis," which involves studying something by separating the whole into its component parts. "Deconstruction" is different, though, in that it serves to destroy, challenge, or question the conventional way of looking at things such as deviance. But, because of its emphasis on the importance of subjectivity, the postmodernist's concept of deconstructionism is similar to the phenomenologist's idea of "phenomenological bracketing," which requires eliminating preconceptions in order to maximize sensitivity to the subject's experiences.

Postmodernist theory does have some new ideas. At the heart of the theory is "linguistic domination," which assumes that a linguistic conflict exists in any social interaction, with the language of the strong dominating that of the weak (Arrigo and Bernard, 1997). To understand the significance of linguistic domination for deviants, consider, for example, the linguistic conflict between the government and rebellious citizens. The government often calls political dissidents "traitors," revolutionaries "criminals," and freedom fighters "terrorists." But the so-called deviants—dissidents, revolutionaries, and freedom fighters—refer to themselves as concerned citizens battling a corrupt government. The first set of words (traitors, criminals, and terrorists) is "privileged," respected, or taken seriously, while the second set (dissidents, revolutionaries, and freedom fighters) is "marginalized," ignored, or suppressed. Thus the government can receive considerable support from the masses and make life extremely difficult for the political deviants.

Evaluating Conflict Theory

In blaming the capitalist or inegalitarian society for the prevalence of deviant labeling and deviant activities, conflict theory seems to hold the *unconvincing* assumption that in the utopian, classless society, deviant labeling will stop and such nasty human acts as killing, robbing, raping, and otherwise hurting one another will disappear. It may be more realistic to assume as Durkheim did that deviance is inevitable, even in a society of saints, but that the type of deviance committed by saints can be expected to be mostly unserious or even trivial. More precisely, if full social equality were achieved, the serious forms of human nastiness would greatly decrease rather than completely disappear. This is because, with the abolition of poverty in a fully egalitarian society, there would not be any poor people left to produce, as they do now, a large volume of serious deviance and thus this volume would greatly shrink. But the formerly poor people would join the formerly rich to engage in less serious—or saintly—forms of deviant activities.

All the same, conflict theory greatly contributes to our understanding of how social inequality—such as in the form of capitalism and patriarchy—influences the making and enforcing of norms, rules, or laws or the definition, production, and treatment of deviance in society (Heidensohn, 2002; Akers, 1985; Williams and Drake, 1980). Moreover, conflict theory is useful for explaining the motivations behind the formulation of laws, even, for example, why the powerful bother to pass laws against such nonpolitical acts as illicit sex, gambling, drinking, and loitering—the kind of deviance that does not seem to threaten their dominant position in society. The reason, according to conflict theory, is that those seemingly trivial deviances do threaten powerful people's vested interests by challenging the underlying values of capitalism, such as sobriety, individual responsibility, deferred gratification, industriousness, and the belief that the true pleasures in life can only be found in honest, productive labor. Laws against those "trivial" deviant acts serve to preserve these capitalist values, the capitalist system, and hence the dominant position of the powerful (Hepburn, 1977).

Table 3.1 shows the main points of all the theories discussed in this chapter. These constructionist theories as well as the positivist theories in the preceding chapter are relatively high-level theories. They are, in effect, general analyses of deviance, dealing with deviance in general rather than a specific form of deviant behavior. They assume that all forms of deviant behavior are in some respect similar to one another, and they, as a general theory, are supposed to capture that similarity. This assumption inevitably ignores or misses many unique aspects of each specific form of deviant behavior. Thus, in the following chapters, we will discuss the concrete characteristics of various deviances. Logically, the high-level, general theories can be applied to specific deviances, but to get a closer, sharper view and deeper understanding of the specific deviant behaviors in the following chapters, we will mostly turn to lower-level, more concrete versions of positivist and constructionist theories.

TABLE 3.1 Constructionist Theories of Deviance

Labeling Theory: Relatively powerful persons are more likely to label the less powerful as deviant than vice versa, and being labeled deviant by society leads people to see themselves as deviant and live up to this self-image by engaging in more deviancy.

Phenomenological Theory: Looking into people's subjective interpretation of their own experiences is key to understanding their deviant behavior.

Conflict Theory:

Legal Reality: Law enforcement favors the rich and powerful over the poor and weak.

Social Reality: The dominant class produces crime by making laws, enforcing laws, oppressing subordinate classes, and spreading crime ideology.

Marxist: Deviance and crime stem from the exploitative nature of capitalism.

Feminist: Conventional theories of deviance are largely inapplicable to women, and the status of women as victims and offenders reflects the continuing subordination of women in patriarchal society.

Power: Because of strong deviant motivation, greater deviant opportunity, and weaker social control, the powerful are more likely to engage in profitable deviancy than are the powerless to engage in unprofitable deviancy.

Postmodernist: "Privileged" language of the powerful dominates the "marginalized" language and thus the lives of the weak as deviants.

Summary

1. What does labeling theory have to say about deviance? According to labeling theory, superordinate parties apply the deviant label to subordinate parties; being labeled deviant produces unfavorable consequences for the individual so labeled; and labeling some individuals as deviant generates favorable consequences for the community. The theory is generally convincing, and there are considerable data to support it. But it has been criticized for being unable to explain what causes deviance in the first place. It has also failed to receive consistent support from studies on the presumed negative consequences of labeling.

2. What is phenomenological theory all about? It claims that positivist sociologists cannot capture the essence of deviance, while phenomenological sociologists can cut into the heart of deviant experience with the scalpel of subjective interpretation, which they try to demonstrate with analyses of specific deviances. Phenomenologists are convincing in arguing that positivists cannot get into the essence of deviant reality. But their claim that they themselves can is excessive and unjustifiable. What they themselves can capture is only their own version of deviant reality, not necessarily the essence of that reality itself.

3. How do various versions of conflict theory deal with deviance? According to legal reality theory, the enforcement of law is unjust, favoring the rich over the poor, as a result of historical changes and organizational imperatives. Social reality theory attributes the capitalist society's high crime rates to the convergence of four forces: lawmaking by the elite, law enforcement for the elite, law violation by the masses, and popular beliefs about the poor as the criminal class. Marxist theory traces the source of lower-class deviance to the exploitative nature of capitalism, and the origin of corporate crime to capitalism-generated monopoly. Feminist theorists criticize all other theories for being mostly relevant to men and, therefore, ignoring women and ascribe the experience of women as offenders and victims to the patriarchal system of gender inequality. Power theory explains that the powerful are more likely to engage in profitable deviance than the powerless in less profitable deviance because the powerful experience stronger deviant motivation, greater deviant opportunity, and weaker social control. Postmodernist theory shows how "privileged" language (like that of the powerful government) influences the lives of deviants (such as political dissidents).

4. What are the weaknesses and strengths of conflict theory? Conflict theory can be faulted for assuming that only capitalism or inequality can produce deviance but the utopian, classless society cannot. Nonetheless, conflict theory contributes greatly to our understanding of the making and enforcement of norms and laws, of the power-influenced definition and production of deviance, and of the motivation behind the formulation of laws against seemingly trivial deviance.

FURTHER READING

Brewer, John D. 2000. *Ethnography*. Buckingham, Eng.: Open University Press. Explaining what ethnography is and how it is used for theory building and applied research.

Davies, Scott, and Julian Tanner. 2003. "The long arm of the law: Effects of labeling on employment." *Sociological Quarterly*, 44, 385–404. Shows how teenagers who were suspended from school or served time in prison grew up to suffer as adults such negative consequences as low occupational success, small income, and checkered employment.

Green, Gill, Nigel South, and Rose Smith. 2006. "'They say that you are a danger but you are not': Representations and construction of the moral self in narratives of 'dangerous individuals'." *Deviant Behavior*, 27, 299–328. A constructionist analysis of how mentally disordered offenders attribute their so-called deviant behavior to the failings of others and how they see themselves as normal people.

Hagan, John. 1992. "The poverty of a classless criminology —The American Society of Criminology 1991 presidential address." *Criminology*, 30, 1–19. An effort to convince criminologists that it is important to use the class-related concept of power to understand the nature of crime.

Jensen, Gary F., and Kevin Thompson. 1990. "What's class got to do with it? A further examination of power-control theory." *American Journal of Sociology*, 95, 1009–1023. Reflects the continuing refusal of many sociologists to see the connection between class or power and deviance.

Katz, Jack. 1988. *Seductions of Crime: Moral and Sensual Attractions in Doing Evil*. New York: Basic Books. A phenomenological analysis of how various deviants, such as murderers and robbers, feel about their deviant acts.

Maso, Ilja. 2001. "Phenomenology and Ethnography." In Paul Atkinson et al. (eds.), *Handbook of Ethnography*. London: Sage Publications. An analysis of how phenomenology and ethnography are so closely related that they appear nearly identical.

Patterson, E. Britt. 1991. "Poverty, income inequality, and community crime rates." *Criminology*, 29, 755–776. Offers data showing that absolute poverty is significantly associated with higher rates of violent crime.

Prus, Robert C., and Scott Grills. 2003. *The Deviant Mystique: Involvement, Realities, and Regulation*. Westport, Conn.: Praeger. Presents a symbolic interactionist approach to the study of deviance and social control.

Regoli, Robert M., Eric D. Poole, and Finn Esbensen. 1985. "Labeling deviance: Another look." *Sociological Focus*, 18, 19–28. Calling for a revision of labeling theory that focuses on the process of labeling before the occurrence of a reaction to certain behavior.

Simpson, Sally S., and Christopher S. Koper. 1992. "Deterring corporate crime." *Criminology,* 30, 347–375. Analyzing the evidence concerning the deterrent impact of legal sanction on criminal corporate behavior.

Sorokin, Pitirim, and Walter Lunden. 1959. *Power and Morality: Who Shall Guard the Guardians?* Boston: Porter Sargent. A classic sociological statement on how power corrupts so that the ruling groups tend to become more criminal than the ruled.

Ward, David A., and Charles R. Tittle. 1993. "Deterrence or labeling: The effects of informal sanctions." *Deviant Behavior,* 14, 43–64. Offers data showing how primary deviance leads to secondary deviance as suggested by labeling theory.

Winter, Michael F. 1996. "Social reaction, labeling, and social control: The contribution of Edwin M. Lemert." *History of the Human Sciences,* May, 53–77. Presents the main ideas of a major contributor to labeling theory.

CRITICAL THINKING QUESTIONS

1. In various versions of conflict theory it is always the poor and powerless who suffer as deviants. Is there a way for them to turn their fate around? If so, how? If not, why not?

2. Ask a sample of your fellow students to give a list of behaviors that they believe most people would consider to be deviant but they themselves do not. Then ask them to explain the difference. What would their answers tell you about labeling and phenomenological theories?

PART TWO

Interpersonal Violence

4 Physical Violence

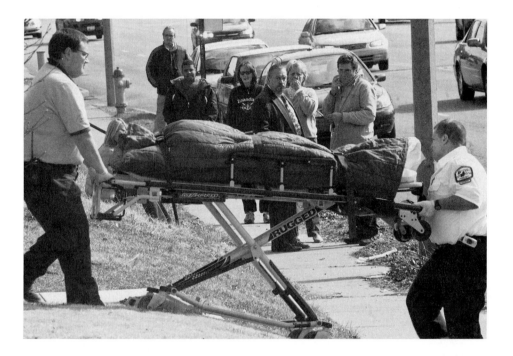

Myths and Realities

Myth: Given the long history of discrimination and prejudice by whites, African Americans are understandably more likely to kill whites than other blacks.

Reality: Most killings are intraracial, with blacks more likely to kill other blacks than whites, just like whites are more likely to do away with other whites than blacks (p. 58).

Myth: Because of their larger population, small cities, which have as many as 50,000 residents, generally have higher rates of homicide than do rural areas.

Reality: Rural areas have more homicides than small cities because they have less community integration brought about by the population dispersion in the country (p. 59).

Myth: When women kill their husbands, it is mostly because their victims have cheated on them.

Reality: Women rarely kill in response to their husbands' infidelity. They usually send their husbands to the hereafter as a desperate attempt to get out of an abusive relationship (p. 60).

Myth: Teenagers in poor inner cities often carry guns in order to seek status among their peers or make an impression on others as being tough.

Reality: The primary reason they carry guns is to protect themselves in their dangerous, high-crime neighborhoods (p. 60).

Myth: As everyone knows "guns don't kill; people do." So it is futile to outlaw the possession of guns.

Reality: Of course, guns by themselves cannot kill, nor can their absence reduce the motivation to kill. But were guns less available, potential killers would use less lethal weapons, which would result in fewer deaths (p. 62)

Myth: Strangers don't care about us as much as our family, friends, and acquaintances do; so it is not surprising that most murder victims are killed by strangers.

Reality: The majority of murder victims are related to or know their killers (p. 63).

Myth: Given the shocking nature of their crimes, most mass murderers, who kill many people at about the same time and place, must be and are somehow emotionally disturbed.

Reality: The majority of mass murderers are far from mentally ill. They appear to be extraordinarily ordinary, indistinguishable from everybody else (p. 67).

Myth: Genocide perpetrators, who kill hundreds or thousands of people, are mostly abnormal because they get a great deal of pleasure from making many others suffer.

Reality: They are mostly normal, like you and me, except that they have the job of killing others under the order of their superiors (p. 73).

Myth: The U.S. war against al Qaeda as well as the war in Iraq has been a total failure.

Reality: There have been both successes and failures. Over half of al Qaeda's key leaders have been killed or captured but the terrorists continue to threaten the United States. Iraq seems to be on the way to democracy, but many U.S. soldiers have died and still nobody knows when the Iraqi government will be able to take care of its country's security without American military assistance (p. 75).

Myth: If people know that if they kill somebody they will be executed, they will think twice or more and decide against committing murder. It can thus be concluded that the death penalty deters murder.

Reality: The death penalty does not seem to deter murder, as suggested by, for example, the fact that many states that still practice the death penalty have higher murder rates than do other states that have abolished the death penalty (p. 77).

In 2008, Abu Dhaim, a 25-year-old Palestinian, filled a cardboard television box with a semiautomatic rifle, two pistols, and plenty of ammunition. He then called his girlfriend, 17, and discussed their plan to go shopping the next day in Jerusalem. They were going to get married soon and hoped to honeymoon in Turkey. After he hanged up the phone, Abu Dhaim drove to a Jewish seminary in Jerusalem. He went into a library, where he killed eight students and wounded ten before he himself was shot dead. His girlfriend was totally surprised. She could not have imagined him as a suicide terrorist. After all, she had known him to be cheerful and gentle. Furthermore, he came from a relatively wealthy and well-educated family (McGirk, 2008).

Actually, contrary to his girlfriend's preconceptions, Abu Dhaim fits the typical profile of a suicide terrorist. Instead of being poor and uneducated, most suicide terrorists come from families with money and education, as we will see in this chapter. We will also examine other types of violence including assault, homicide, mass and serial murder, school violence, hate-motivated killing, and genocide, along with stalking as a threat of violence.

Assault and Aggravated Assault

Considerably less serious than homicide, assault is understandably far more prevalent. Assault involves the unlawful use of physical force against another person. It can be legally divided into two types: aggravated and simple. Aggravated assault involves an atrocious attack with the intent to kill or the use of a deadly weapon. It is considered a felony carrying a relatively severe penalty. All other forms of assault are simple, hence considered a misdemeanor, for which the punishment is less severe. As an act, aggravated assault is basically similar to homicide. Aggravated assault differs mostly in consequence: The victim survives rather than dies.

Since assault is behaviorally similar in some ways to homicide, most of the research findings about homicide that we will discuss also hold true for assault. Thus, like murderers, assaulters are more likely to be poor than nonpoor, to be black than white, to victimize people of the same race than of a different race, to live in the South than other regions, to reside in large cities than small towns, to be men than women, to have a violent past than not, to commit the crime during the weekend than during the weekday, and so on. At the same time, research has suggested at least two ways in which assault differs from homicide.

First, for obvious reasons, assaulters are less likely than murderers to use firearms in committing the crime. Second, in the summer, the number of homicides increases only slightly, but assault rises significantly. In the hot season, people tend to go out more, especially the poor whose homes are not comfortably air-conditioned. Going out increases social interaction, especially among strangers, who are likely to get involved in assault. Heat stress and increased consumption of alcoholic beverages further heighten aggression. A combination of all these factors enhances the likelihood of assault (Livingston, 2008; Parker with Rebhun, 1995; Harries, 1990).

Who Is More Likely to Kill?

The most striking thing about killers is that they are mostly poor. Not surprisingly, blacks, being generally poorer than whites, are more likely than whites to commit homicide. Poor countries have higher rates of homicide than rich nations. Similarly, societies and individuals with violent pasts have relatively high rates of homicides. The South has more homicides than any other region in the United States. Here and abroad large cities have more killings than smaller cities. Men are far more likely than women to kill, and young men (aged 18 to 24) are more likely than other age groups to commit murder. Let us take a closer look at each of these facts.

Class and Race

Various studies have clearly indicated that homicides are concentrated heavily in the lower class. Over 90 percent of the murderers in the United States are semiskilled workers, unskilled laborers, and welfare recipients. Poverty is definitely a factor in homicide. As such, poverty crosses racial lines: Poor whites have higher murder rates than better-off whites, and poor blacks have higher rates than richer blacks. There are several reasons for the strong link between poverty and murder. Compared with people of the higher classes, the poor are more likely to have financial, marital, and other stressful problems, which in turn tend to cause interpersonal conflict. The poor also tend more to resort to physical violence as a way of dealing with interpersonal conflict. Violence is, in effect, a mechanism for getting respect, because the poor generally consider violence a badge of toughness and masculinity (Pridemore, 2008; Hannon, 2005; Parker with Rebhun, 1995; Parker, 1989).

Blacks generally have a much higher rate of homicide than whites. This fact makes it appear as if race plays an important role in homicide. Actually, though, being black has nothing to do with such violence. Instead, African Americans' higher rate of homicide simply reflects their higher rate of poverty, which, along with racial discrimination, generates greater frustration and alienation. In expressing their frustration, however, blacks tend more to kill their fellow blacks than to kill whites. In fact, most killings are *intra*racial, for whites also do away with whites more than blacks. *Inter*racial murders—in which blacks kill whites and vice versa—are rare because racial discrimination discourages interaction between blacks and whites (Strom and MacDonald, 2007; Shihadeh and Flynn, 1996; Greenberg and Schneider, 1994; Rose and McClain, 1990).

Regions, Large Cities, and Rural Areas

Generally, the southern region has the highest murder rate, the western region has the next highest rate, and the northeastern and midwestern states have the lowest rate (FBI, 2008). There is nothing new about these regional differences; they have been around for a long time. What accounts for the southern leadership in homicide rates? Some sociologists have attributed it to the "culture of violence" in the South, where violent behavior seems more acceptable than in other regions. For example, gun ownership and execution of murderers, along with the history of lynching, which are assumed to reflect a violent culture, are the most common in the South (Lee, Hayes, and Thomas, 2008; Messner, Baller, and Zevenbergen, 2005). Another reason could be the greater prevalence of rurality in the South. A study by Kenneth Wilkinson (1984) shows that the average murder rate in rural areas exceeds the rate in most cities. According to Wilkinson, the dispersion of people in rural areas (as contrasted with the congestion of people in most cities) reduces community

TABLE 4.1   How Urban and Rural Murder Rates Differ

Where People Live	Murder Rate in 2006 (per 100,000 population)
Large cities with population of	
250,000 or more	13.1
100,000 to 249,999	7.7
50,000 to 99,999	4.8
Rural areas	4.1
Small cities with population of	
25,000 to 49,999	3.6
10,000 to 24,999	2.8
Fewer than 10,000	2.5

Source: FBI, *Crime in the United States,* 2007.

integration, thereby forcing family members, friends, and acquaintances to spend too much time with each other. This enhances the opportunity for violent disruption in primary relationships (among relatives and acquaintances), and it is in such relationships that most homicides take place, a strange fact that we will discuss in another section.

The rurality–homicide connection, however, seems to run counter to the popular belief that there are more killings in *large* cities. Actually, it does not; large cities do have more killings. Rurality is related to homicide only if we compare the homicide rates of rural areas with those of *most* cities, which are relatively *small,* having populations of fewer than 50,000 people. Rural areas do have higher homicide rates than these small cities. However, larger cities, with populations exceeding 100,000, have significantly higher murder rates than those for small cities and rural areas (see Table 4.1).

Paradoxically, like rurality, large city size encourages homicides by reducing community integration. But unlike rurality, which reduces community integration through *population dispersion,* large city size diminishes community integration via *population heterogeneity.* However it comes about, the lack of community integration drives individuals—anonymous urbanites as much as isolated ruralites—into the same matrix of interactions among relatives and acquaintances that is likely to lead to homicides. Although there are many more relatives and acquaintances than strangers killed in both urban and rural areas, anonymous urbanites are more likely than isolated ruralites to kill strangers while isolated ruralites tend more to kill family members or intimate partners (Gallup-Black, 2005).

Gender and Age

Those homicidal interactions are far more likely to cause men than women to kill because men are far more concerned about defending their manhood. Most of the killings involve a man doing away with another man. If a man and a woman are caught up in a homicidal interaction, he is more likely to be the offender and she the victim. Men who kill their wives or girlfriends do so mostly because they have persistently tried to *keep their victims in an abusive relationship*. Such killing, then, is the culmination of a long series of physically violent acts perpetrated by the men against their female victims. Moreover, men tend to kill in response to their wives' infidelity. Men would also kill their wives as part of a murder-suicide or a family massacre (Wilson and Daly, 1992).

In the fewer cases in which women kill, they differ from their male counterparts in the choice of victims. Unlike male offenders, who are more likely to kill others of the *same sex,* female offenders are more likely to kill members of the *opposite sex.* In these opposite-sex killings, the female and male murderers usually commit the crime for different reasons. The women rarely kill in response to their husbands' infidelity even if their husbands are extremely adulterous. They usually send their husbands to the hereafter as a desperate attempt to *get out of an abusive relationship*. The women basically kill for self-preservation or in self-defense. Violence by women, then, is primarily defensive, in contrast to violence by men, which is distinctly offensive. Such defensive killing serves as "self-help social control" against abusive husbands. Not surprisingly, it often takes place in states where there are no laws requiring mandatory arrests for domestic violence (Gauthier and Bankston, 2004; Peterson, 1999; Mann, 1996; Wilson and Daly, 1992; Goetting, 1989).

Males also kill at a younger age than females. When killing, people are more likely to target others of the same age group than older or younger victims. This is largely because people of about the same age spend more time interacting with one another than with others of a different age. In the few cases in which older persons quarrel with younger ones, the older persons are more likely to end up dead, because the younger persons are more impulsive and hence quicker to shoot. While most homicides involve relatives and acquaintances, the younger killers are more likely than their older peers to target strangers and commit murder and robbery together (U.S. Census Bureau, 2008; Eigen, 1981; Mulvihill and Tumin with Curtis, 1969).

The homicide rate in the United States is lower today than ten years ago. But, from the mid-1980s to the early 1990s, there was a stunning upsurge in murders committed by *teenagers*. Most of these killings took place in large cities' poor neighborhoods, where gang violence, drive-by shootings, and crack cocaine were relatively common. More important, many teenagers in poor inner cities carried guns, a new phenomenon in those years. Contrary to popular belief, the primary reason for carrying guns was not seeking status among one's peers or trying to make an impression on others. Teenagers carried guns to protect themselves in their dangerous, high-crime neighborhoods (Fox, 1996; Blumstein, 1995; Wright, Sheley, and Smith, 1992). All the same, the increased possession of guns contributed to the surge in teen murders. Other contributing factors included the larger number of dysfunctional families, the greater prevalence of drugs among the urban poor, the lower quality of public schools, and the increased glorification of violence on television, in the movies, and in video games. Since 1994, however, the teen murder rate has declined, largely as a result of the falloff in the crack market and increased confiscation of handguns from juveniles by police departments (FBI, 2005; Steinberg, 1999; Kleck and Hogan, 1999; Grossman, 1995).

Patterns of Killing

Various studies have found certain patterns in the majority of murder cases. However, these patterns mainly involve murders committed by lower-class people, not by middle- and upper-class persons. Traditionally, researchers have concentrated on lower-class homicides simply because they make up the overwhelming majority of murders. Thus, in this section, we will focus on the patterns of lower-class homicides, but will also note the characteristics of higher-class murders in cases in which they differ.

Time of Killing

Most murders are committed in the heat of passion, and there does seem to be some, though relatively weak, connection between season of the year and murder. The number of homicides increases slightly during the hot late spring and summer, peaking in July and August, during which potential killers and victims, who are relatives, friends, and acquaintances rather than strangers, tend most to get together and drink cold beer in public places such as restaurants and taverns. Homicide decreases during the cool autumn and early spring, and drops even more during the winter months of January and February (U.S. Census Bureau, 2008; Wolfgang, 1958). But the number of homicides peaks again during the cold month of December, primarily due to its being a holiday season, which, like July and August, brings together the kinds of people who are more likely to get involved in homicide (Anderson, 1989).

Far stronger than the association between homicide and season is the link between homicide and days of the week as well as hours of the day. Homicide occurs most frequently during the weekend evenings, particularly on Saturday night. This may explain why the handgun most often used in homicide is popularly called a Saturday night special. These weekend killings are more likely to involve family members than the homicides occurring during the weekdays—the weekday homicides tend more to involve strangers. The reason is that people usually spend more time at home on weekends (Messner and Tardiff, 1985).

All this does not, however, hold true for the minority of cases involving middle-class and upper-class offenders. These relatively affluent offenders are likely to kill on any day of the week while poor offenders tend more to kill during the weekend. Why this class difference? Because murders in the middle and upper classes are more likely to be *calculative* or *premeditated,* while lower-class killings are more often carried out in a burst of rage, usually after some heavy drinking during the weekend (Parker with Rebhun, 1995; Green and Wakefield, 1979).

What about the evening when the moon is full? Does the popularly believed lunar effect on homicide exist? Is it true, as "every policeman, bartender, and emergency-room attendant knows, that people tend to act crazy and become more violent when the moon is full"? One psychiatrist claimed to have found a higher incidence of homicides in Cleveland and Miami at the times of new and full moons. However, in analyzing the same data and other relevant studies, an astronomer found no correlation between lunar phases and homicide rates (*Sky and Telescope,* 1985).

Place of Killing

Men are more likely to kill at public places, but women are far more likely to kill in the home (Miethe and Regoeczi, 2004). In the past women most often did the killing in the kitchen, apparently because it is the place where women traditionally were accustomed to handling a knife—which can turn into a dangerous weapon when a quarrel flares up (Wolfgang, 1958). But nowadays, less likely to be confined to the kitchen as a result of greater gender equality, women tend more to kill in the living room (Mann, 1996). However, the bedroom is a more dangerous place for women than for men, as women are more frequently killed there by their husbands, boyfriends, or exes (Totman, 1978). Perhaps men have been socially conditioned to use the bedroom as a place for demonstrating their "manliness" by sexually conquering women and end up using it as a place for physically subjugating them to death.

While women are more likely to kill at home, they are also more likely to be killed at home. A major reason is simply that they spend more time at home. Other types of people who spend more time at home are also more likely to have the same fate. These include the very young, the very old, minority groups, the married, and the unemployed (Messner and Tardiff, 1985).

Method of Killing

Killing a human may appear extraordinary when compared with, say, killing a rabbit. This consequently fires the imagination of many mystery writers, who help spread the popular notion that murderers often use mysterious, exotic, ingenious, or superclever methods to get rid of their victims. Yet research often shows that there is nothing special about the methods of killing. Most objects can be readily turned into murder weapons, as long as they are conveniently accessible when the murderous anger erupts. In our society firearms are easily available, and so they are most often used as murder weapons (Miller et al., 2007; Kristof, 1996b). Perhaps, seeing a gun while embroiled in a heated argument may incite a violent person to murderous action. As Shakespeare has it, "How oft the sight of means to do ill deeds, makes ill deeds done."

Of course, firearms in themselves cannot cause homicide, nor can their absence reduce the motivation to kill. It is true that "guns don't kill people, people do." Still, were guns less available, many heated arguments would have resulted in aggravated assaults rather than murders, thereby reducing the number of fatalities. An analysis of over 20,000 homicides and aggravated assaults in Chicago suggests that attacks with knives are five times *less* likely to result in death than attacks with guns (Wright, Rossi, and Daly, 1983). An enormous number of guns are in private hands: Half of all U.S. households own firearms of some kind, and a quarter of all families have handguns. It is, therefore, not surprising that many deaths in the United States result from gun homicides. Every year, our country has over 15,000 handgun homicides compared with less than 100 in other industrialized nations such as Canada, England, and Japan, where guns are much harder to get (Cook and Moore, 1999; Wright, 1995).

The easy availability of guns in the United States appears to be a great equalizer for the poor. It gives power to the powerless. This may explain why lower-class people are more likely to use firearms than any other weapon when they kill. Shooting is also the most popular mode of murder among people of the higher classes. However, higher-class killers are much more likely than their lower-class peers to use more refined techniques of killing, such as poisoning, staging a hit-and-run car death, and hiring somebody else to do the killing (Green and Wakefield, 1979).

Characteristics of Homicide

Most killings are carried out against family members, friends, or acquaintances rather than strangers. Some killings happen as if the victim asks to be put to death. Some involve an attempt to win a seemingly trivial argument. Some serve as an adjunct to suicide. Let us take a closer look at each characteristic of killing.

Warm-Blooded Murder

Many people are apparently afraid of getting attacked and killed by strangers, particularly in big cities. Such fear came through clearly in the mid-1980s when Bernhard Goetz, the so-called Subway Vigilante, shot four young African Americans on a subway car in New York, though they allegedly had merely approached and asked him for money. It was also the same fear that drove many people to hail him as a hero. The fear that strangers will kill us unless we kill them first does not reflect reality. Compared with other major crimes, such as robbery, rape, and assault, homicide is the least likely to involve strangers. Of all the murders that occur every year, only a small percentage are committed by strangers (Baker, 2007). In fact, the majority of the murders involve relatives, friends, or acquaintances, as Figure 4.1 indicates. This situation is not unique to our society. It exists in many other countries as well.

It seems incredible that the people we know or even love are more likely to kill us than are total strangers. But, as three sociologists have explained, "This should really not be very surprising. Everyone is within easy striking distance of intimates for a large part of time. Although friends, lovers, spouses, and the like are a main source of pleasure in one's life, they are equally a main source of frustration and hurt. Few others can anger one so much" (Mulvihill and Tumin with Curtis, 1969). Ordinarily, killing requires a great deal of emotion. Therefore, it may be more difficult to kill a stranger about whom we don't have much feeling—unless we are professional killers, who typically dispatch their victims in a cold-blooded, unemotional manner. In sum, we are far less likely to become victims of cold-blooded murders carried out by strangers but more likely to die from warm-blooded, emotional murders at the hands of our relatives, friends, or acquaintances.

Doing the Victim a Favor

The general public often sympathizes with the murder victim but not with the offender at all. The public assumes that the murder victim is weak and meek, helplessly slain by the strong and aggressive offender. This assumption is not always correct. In at least one out of four homicides, the victim has first attacked the subsequent slayer, and such murder has

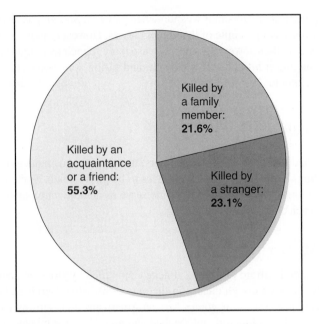

FIGURE 4.1   Most Victims Know Their Killers

Source: FBI, *Crime in the United States,* 2007.

been called *victim-precipitated homicide* (Wilbanks, 1984; Felson and Steadman, 1983). The following are typical cases of victim precipitation (Klinger, 2001):

- A drunken husband, beating his wife in the kitchen, gave her a butcher knife and dared her to use it on him. She warned him that she would use it if he should strike her again. At the very instant he heard this warning, he slapped her in the face—and he was fatally stabbed.
- A drunken man, with knife in hand, approached a person during a quarrel. When this person showed a gun, the drunk dared him to shoot. He did.
- A man who had just robbed a jewelry store was fleeing. Outside, he saw three police officers, but he ran toward them. At gunpoint, they ordered him to stop. Instead, he pulled out a gun, whereupon he was shot dead. Later, his gun was found to be unloaded.

Because they provoke another person to kill them, Marvin Wolfgang (1967) assumes that these self-precipitated murder victims may have secretly wanted to kill *themselves.* This assumption may well be correct. But if they have suicide wishes, why do they not take it on themselves to end their own lives? Perhaps they have been influenced by what may be considered a culture of *showy masculinity,* characteristic of a sexist society. This culture encourages males to show off their toughness and hide their tenderness, to act like a "man" and avoid acting like a "woman," or to engage in "manly" braggadocio and shun "feminine" quietism. Under the pressure of this culture, suicidally inclined men may *avoid* revealing their "sissy cowardice" or pleading for condescending sympathy from others in quietly ending their own lives. Instead, they are inclined to display masculine bravado and earn from others some "respect" as the worst person imaginable, by making an ostentatious assault on another person that is secretly designed for their own annihilation—the result being a victim-precipitated murder.

Winning a Trivial Argument

Murder is an extremely serious human act, yet the motive for committing it often appears downright trivial. Ordinary quarrels, which often seem to be over nothing, are the most common reason for poor people to kill. As a retired homicide detective in New York reports, "When you get a guy to 'fess up as to why he did it, you get very shoddy answers: 'He took my coat,' 'He stepped on my girlfriend's foot'" (Wilentz, 1985). Similar examples follow (Mulvihill et al., 1969):

- A man was fatally shot in front of a tavern because he had refused to lend his assailant $1.
- Two men were arguing over a $5 bet and became involved in a scuffle. One then took out a gun and pulled the trigger on the other.
- Two fellow workers were drinking beer; they argued over a $1 pool bet. One wound up in a morgue.
- A man was drunk when he came home. He told his uncle to move over in bed. Seeing that his uncle would not, he stabbed him to death.
- "Hey, you're lookin' at me."
  "No, I ain't."
  "Yes, you are. Why you lookin' at me?"
  Minutes later one of them lay still in a puddle of blood.

Murder, then, is apparently a quick and effective way for the poor to win an argument—over trifles. Middle-class people usually use a much less drastic means, such as verbal or intellectual ability, to settle an argument. But the poor tend more to suffer from lack of such ability, and thus they are more often compelled to use their physical strength to end an argument with—and sometimes the life of—another person.

We may also note that arguments such as those illustrated above may appear trivial to us. Yet the same arguments are apparently taken by poor males as reasons for defending their dignity or honor as men. A dirty look, a little insult, a jostle would not usually get middle-class people into an argument, let alone impel them to spill another person's blood. The same triviality may be perceived differently by the poor. Why would the poor make such a mountain out of a molehill, and with such deadly consequences for themselves?

The explanation can be found in the economic and social oppression of the poor. The poor man's dignity as a man—or, for that matter, as simply a human being—has been substantially diminished by the frustrating and humiliating forces in his life. Some of these forces are impersonal, such as the general condition of poverty, so that the poor man cannot fight back against them. Other humiliating forces can be found in people, such as the police, bureaucrats in a welfare or unemployment office, and employers—who usually treat him with far less respect than they do the more successful, higher-status persons. But since these people are more powerful, the poor man cannot fight back at them either.

As a consequence, he has extremely little dignity left in him, and so, in order to live with at least more worth than an animal, he dearly hangs on to it. Although he cannot maintain this fragile dignity in the larger society or in the presence of those more powerful than himself, he certainly can at his own home and in his neighborhood, among his equally dignity-deprived family members, friends, and acquaintances. Because his dignity as a man is already extremely fragile, the pressure of daily frustration and tension can easily crush it. Thus even a small insult from his relatives, friends, or acquaintances (who are, after all, his last strand of hope for keeping his dignity) can mean, to him, the threat that all his dignity will be taken away. With such a perception, he will very likely fight like mad to defend his dignity, even to the extent of killing the person who has "dissed" him. In fact, as many researchers have found, most homicides result from what they call character contests, in which the offender and victim try to defend their honor after it has been threatened by the other (Mullins, 2006; Athens, 1985; Felson and Steadman, 1983).

An Adjunct to Suicide

We have speculated that the so-called victims of victim-precipitated homicide may have wanted to die and contributed greatly to their own deaths. There is yet a different group of offenders with the same suicidal tendency. They are homicide-suicide offenders, who first kill another person and then finish themselves off. The difference between these two types of offenders is obvious. While the "victim" of victim-precipitated homicide conceals his or her suicidal wishes, the homicide-suicide offender reveals them.

Homicide-suicide is relatively rare, no more than 3 or 4 percent of all murders in the United States and approximately 10 percent in Canada. Virtually all homicide-suicides are male and their victims female. The perpetrators are extremely frustrated, depressed, and violent, killing their wives and, often, their children as a way of expressing their dominance or control over them (Harper and Voigt, 2007; Gillespie, Hearn, and Silverman, 1998).

Two conflicting views can be found on the nature of homicide-suicide: one sociological, seeing homicide-suicide as a form of *normality*; the other, psychiatric, viewing it as a symptom of *abnormality*. According to the sociological view, the murderer-suicide is a normal person because, after killing the loved one, he is able to feel remorse, just as we would expect normal people to feel after they had done such a horrible thing. By contrast, the psychiatrist sees the murderer-suicide as a psychotic, believing that, instead of feeling remorse, the offender anticipates a reunion with the victim in another world, and, therefore, kills himself in order to achieve that goal.

These two conflicting views can be reconciled. It is true that some murderer-suicides are "normal." It is also true that other murderer-suicides are "psychotic." But these two types of murderer-suicides may have one thing in common—both are unaffected by the culture of showy masculinity discussed before. Instead of acting like "tough guys," as required by that culture, both behave like "weaklings." In effect, the normal one begs the mortally wronged victim (who is usually his wife or girlfriend) for pardon, and the psychotic one dreams for some happy reconciliation in another world. Both behave like—when seen from the standpoint of the "tough guy" culture—mushy characters in a tear-jerking love story.

Sociologist David Phillips (1981, 1980a) has discovered homicide-suicides of a third kind. They resemble the so-called victims of victim-precipitated murder in that they conceal their suicidal wishes, but they carry out these wishes with more ingenuity. They "disguise their homicide-suicides as accidents to protect their survivors from insurance problems and from social stigma." One example of these disguised homicide-suicides is a pilot who deliberately crashes his airplane with passengers onboard, but who makes the crash appear convincingly like an accident. Phillips argues that many plane crashes actually involve the pilots committing murder-suicides. This argument is based on his finding that after a murder-suicide is publicized in the mass media there is an increase in both noncommercial and commercial plane crashes, a trend that persists for approximately nine days. Phillips assumed that the mass media, with their spate of murder-suicide stories, encourage those suicidal pilots to commit murder-suicides. He later reinforced this assumption by showing in another study the impact of mass media on homicides in general. That study indicated that between 1973 and 1978, homicides increased by more than 12 percent on the third day following highly publicized heavyweight championship prizefights (Phillips, 1983; see also Baron and Reiss, 1985; Phillips and Bollen, 1985).

Mass and Serial Murder

In 1997 Andrew Cunanan killed the famous fashion designer Gianni Versace in Miami Beach after having murdered four other men in other cities. In 1992 Jeffrey Dahmer of Milwaukee, Wisconsin, pleaded guilty to killing 15 young men, one after another. He reportedly had sex with some of the corpses, dismembered some of the bodies, and kept in his refrigerator a severed head as well as a heart that he planned to eat later. Earlier, in 1985, another serial killer struck terror in the Los Angeles area. Called the Night Stalker, he sneaked into the homes of 19 people at night and killed them as they slept. Just a year before, a mass murderer walked into a McDonald's restaurant in San Diego carrying a rifle, a shotgun, and a pistol with hundreds of rounds of ammunition. He opened fire on everybody, killing 21 people—mostly children—and wounding 19 others. These types of killing—mass and serial murders—attract considerable attention from the media and public. Just the same, they are extremely rare.

Mass murder involves killing a number of people at about the same time and place. It usually ends with the murderer dying at the scene of the carnage. The murderer's death results from either committing suicide or forcing the police to take lethal action. Despite the shocking nature of their crime, most mass murderers are not mentally ill. As sociologists Jack Levin and James Fox (1985) conclude after studying mass murderers, "The mass killer appears to be *extraordinarily ordinary*. He is indistinguishable from everyone else. Indeed, he may be the neighbor next door, a coworker at the next desk, or a member of the family."

Some mass murderers are *disgruntled employees* who want to get even with their boss who has wronged them in some way, by firing them, for example. But in the process of killing their boss, they end up murdering their coworkers as well. Other mass murderers are *heads of family* who kill their wives and children after having long felt alone, alienated, helpless, and depressed, aggravated by heavy drinking. Some mass murderers are *pseudocommandos,* who turn their home into an arsenal and then lash out at what they consider to be an unjust or evil world. Finally, some mass murderers *work as a team under the direction of a charismatic leader,* such as the September 11 suicide bombers who attacked the United States under the direction of their leader, Osama bin Laden (Meloy et al., 2004; Holmes and Holmes, 1992).

Slightly more common than mass murder is serial murder, which involves killing a number of people one at a time. But the media has wildly exaggerated the incidence of serial murder by calling it an "epidemic." This exaggeration originated from the claim by a Justice Department official that serial murder accounts for about 20 percent of all homicides. Actually, the most credible figure, based on careful analysis by sociologists, is only 2 or 3 percent. Another myth about serial murder is that its perpetrators roam from one city to another to carry out their killing. The fact is that most (70 to 75 percent) serial murderers commit their crime in one city alone (Kappeler, Blumberg, and Potter, 1993).

While mass murderers are nearly always caught, serial killers are far more elusive because they are practiced and accomplished at what they do. First, they stalk their victims from a distance, studying the victims' routine activities and habits. They then win the victims' confidence by befriending them, or gain entry into the victims' house that they have staked out for days. Next, they lure the victims into a trap or simply hold them captive by closing off all possibility of escape. Finally, they kill the victims. In the process of killing, they "often torture their victims, taking delight in the victims' agonies, expressions of terror, cries of despair, and reactions to pain" (Norris, 1989). This should not be surprising, because most serial killers have in their childhood tortured dogs and cats for the thrill of watching them suffer. They have also been subjected to a lot of physical and emotional abuse by their parents. Such experiences have apparently taught the serial killer to become a sociopath, incapable of feeling remorse or guilt for hurting others. Nonetheless, the vast majority of serial killers are not mentally ill. They appear as normal people who go to school or work, come home, and blend into their immediate neighborhood (Knight, 2006; Fox, Levin, and Quinet, 2005). For more on serial killers, see the following Social Profile.

A Social Profile of Serial Killers

According to one popular myth, serial killers are monsters. You would think so too if you had seen many movies like *Friday the 13th,* which portray serial killers as glassy-eyed lunatics bent on getting their kicks from inflicting human destruction. Another myth is just the opposite, regarding serial killers as unusually handsome and charming. This myth may stem from a few well-known cases, such as those involving the debonair "lady-killer," Theodore Bundy, who murdered dozens of women, and the "Los Angeles Night Stalker," Richard Rameriz, who attracted many women even after he was in prison and married there. A third myth presents serial killers as extremely brilliant, like Hannibal Lecter, the character in the novel and movie, *The Silence of the Lambs.* Contrary to these myths, most serial killers are unusually ordinary.

In one study of 107 serial killers, only 16 percent attended college and only 4 percent graduated with a bachelor's degree; the majority had blue-collar jobs. Despite their relatively low level of education and employment, most serial killers do possess a certain amount of cunning and are especially skillful in presenting themselves as friendly and trustworthy (Fox, Levin, and Quinet, 2005).

Most serial killers are white men in their late twenties or early thirties. In one study of nearly 400 serial killers, 84 percent were found to be male and 80 percent white, with an average age of 28 when their first murder was committed. All this distinguishes serial killings from single-victim homicides, which are more likely to be carried out by non-whites. Also, while murderers with a single victim tend to target people whom they know, serial killers are more likely to kill strangers—especially vulnerable ones such as children, prostitutes, and the elderly (Fox, Levin, and Quinet, 2005).

The motive behind most serial murders is an intense desire for power and sadism. Serial murderers typically kill for the fun of it, not for love, money, or revenge. It makes them feel good to kill while also being able to torture the victim in the process.

A Global Perspective on Homicide

The influence of poverty on homicide shows up in comparison between rich and poor countries. In general, developing countries such as those in Latin America, Asia, and Africa have higher homicide rates than do developed countries such as those in North America and Western Europe.

Among the developed countries, however, the United States has by far the highest rate. This is largely due to the greater amount of poverty—and economic inequality—in our society compared to the other developed areas, namely, Western Europe and Japan. If Russia is considered a developed country, it has an even higher homicide rate than the United States, because it has much more poverty. The prevalence of guns can also explain why the homicide rate in the United States is much higher than in Western Europe and Japan. Within Western Europe, countries such as Finland, where many private citizens own guns, have higher homicide rates than those such as England, where guns are scarcer (Chamlin and Cochran, 2005; Moniruzzaman and Andersson, 2005; LaFree, 1999).

But among the poor, developing countries, those in Latin America have unusually high homicide rates, apparently the highest in the world. Some sociologists have attributed these high rates to a "culture of violence," which encourages the use of violence to deal with unbearable interpersonal conflict. This culture seems to have a powerful element of machismo, the belief that men should be concerned about their manhood. In such a culture, men are encouraged to respond aggressively to an insult about their manhood. If they do not respond aggressively, they are made to feel like cowards. In any country, however, killers seem to have developed a similarly tough, macho attitude from a violent past. A killer's violence usually begins with minor assaults against others, gradually escalates to more and more serious assaults, and finally culminates in homicide. Also in every country in the world, men are much more likely than women to kill, which apparently reflects the influence of machismo, though to a lesser degree than in Latin America. In highly patriarchal societies in the Middle East, women are likely to fall victim to "honor killings" by their male relatives, like their father or brother, if they engage in premarital or extramarital sex even as rape victims. The woman is considered to have shamed the family and the killing is meant to bring back the family honor (Baron, 2006; Moniruzzaman and Andersson, 2005; LaFree, 1999).

School Violence

In the late 1990s, boys as young as 11 gunned down classmates or teachers in the public schools of such little-known places as Littleton, Colorado; Edinboro, Pennsylvania; Jonesboro, Arkansas; Pearl, Mississippi; West Paducah, Kentucky; and Stamps, Arkansas. It appears that school violence, long known as a phenomenon of large and noisy cities, has now spread to small and tranquil towns, suburbs, and rural areas. More recently, similar violence has also taken place at Virginia Tech University and Northern Illinois University.

Following the massacre of 32 students and professors at Virginia Tech in 2007, many people wondered what had brought about such a violent act. The media tried to explain the carnage largely by focusing on the killer's mental problems. Through interviews with students who knew the killer, he was said to be a loner, never talking to anybody. One teacher called him a bully, declaring that "there was something mean about this boy." He was once caught using his cell phone to take pictures of female classmates under the desks. Another teacher found him so angry and sad that she conveyed her concerns to campus police and counselors. An acquaintance also found him to be suicidal. When police requested a temporary detention order after he stalked two female students, he was evaluated at a psychiatric facility, and a judge wrote on a court document that he "is mentally ill and in need of hospitalization, and presents an imminent danger to self or others as a result of mental illness" (Gibbs, 2007).

It is true that mental illness plays a role in school shootings, as more than half of the shooters have experienced severe depression. But only an extremely small number of even the most depressed persons turn into mass murderers. Depression, then, cannot by itself cause the killing. Other factors are also likely to be implicated, such as having been abused by parents and rejected, taunted, or ostracized by peers. All these personal experiences are especially likely to lead to violence if they occur under the influence of some larger social forces. One is the easy availability of *guns,* without which depressed and angry young men would have difficulty acting out a lethally violent tendency. Another social force is the glamorization of violence in such *media* as movies, television, and video games. Media violence cannot cause actual violence among the overwhelming majority of young men, but it is likely to turn a few susceptible, violence-prone young men to violence. A third social force is the *culture* of violence, which favors the possession of firearms and accepts the use of force for settling interpersonal conflict (Newman, 2004).

Despite its horror, school killing is extremely rare. According to the Centers for Disease Control and Prevention (CDC), less than one percent of all youthful homicides take place in or around the school. Besides, school shooting has, along with weapon carrying and physical fighting, gone down in recent years (CDC, 2008; Fox, Levin, and Quinet, 2005; Brener et al., 2004; Stolberg, 1999).

Stalking

Stalking is pursuing someone in a way that creates the fear of being assaulted or killed. The offenders may follow or spy on the victims; send them unsolicited letters; make unsolicited phone calls; stand outside their homes, schools, or workplaces; show up at places where they are present; give them unwanted items; vandalize their property; or kill their pets. Stalkers, if not stopped, may end up assaulting and killing the victim; even if they do not, the stalking may be nearly as bad as being attacked and killed. The ordeal of assault or murder usually lasts only a few minutes, but victims of stalking endure their tormentors' cruelty for nearly two years, the average duration of stalking. Stalking is also more prevalent than nearly all other forms of physical violence discussed in this chapter. According to a survey by the National Institute of Justice, 8 percent of women and 2 percent of men in the United States encounter stalking at some time in their lives (Moffatt, 2000; Mullen et al., 2000).

The majority of stalkers know their victims as ex-intimates, fellow employees, and acquaintances. The following are typical cases (Albrecht, 2001):

- A woman with two young children left her abusive husband to start a new life, but he stalked her and later killed her, saying, "If I can't have her; nobody will."
- A high school girl broke up with her boyfriend. He then stalked her and eventually set fire to a room in her house, killing an infant her mother babysat.
- A wife had a one-night stand with a man she met in a bar. Later, he stalked, kidnapped, and raped her for getting back together with her husband.
- A man repeatedly asked a female coworker to go out with him but without success. He then stalked her for many months. After he was dismissed from his job, he killed seven former coworkers and injured four others, including the victim of his stalking.

A few stalkers victimize strangers, especially celebrities. The most well known is probably John Hinckley. Infatuated with movie actress Jodie Foster, he repeatedly sent her letters with poems and messages to get her interested in him. Finally, in 1981, in order to attract her attention, he tried to assassinate President Ronald Reagan, wounding the president and two other people. In 1989, Robert Bardo was obsessed with TV actress Rebecca Schaeffer, videotaping every episode of her show *My Sister Sam*. He repeatedly wrote to her, and after seeing her in bed with another actor in one episode, he flew into a rage. He went to her apartment and shot her to death. He later told a court-appointed psychiatrist, "She was a whore, and God appointed me to punish her." Most recently, in 2008, Jack Jordan was convicted of stalking movie star Uma Thurman on and off for two and a half years, sending her love letters and on one occasion ringing her doorbell from early in the morning to late at night (Steel, 2008; Moffatt, 2000).

Most of the stalkers are male, and most of the victims are female. There is no racial difference in stalking—stalkers are as likely to be white as black. Stalkers are generally older than their victims. The majority of stalkers are loners, mentally unhealthy, and socially incompetent. They are most likely to inflict violence on persons with whom they have had an intimate relationship (Wondrak and Hoffmann, 2007; Moffatt, 2000; Mullen et al., 2000).

Hate Killing

According to the FBI, every year more than 9,000 Americans fall victim to hate or bias crimes, offenses committed because of the victim's race, religion, national origin, or sexual orientation. Slightly more than half of these victims were only intimidated. Nearly half are assaulted and less than 1 percent murdered. Hate-motivated homicides are comparatively rare, but they have received great attention from the media, which presumably reflects the profound concern of many Americans on this issue (Fox, Levin, and Quinet, 2005).

African Americans and gay Americans are more likely than any other group to be victims of hate homicide. Such killing is targeted not only at the particular person but also at all the other members of that person's group. In June 1998, when three white men in Jasper, Texas, dragged James Byrd, an African American, behind their pickup truck to his death, they were in effect telling every black person in town to get out or suffer the same fate as Byrd. Similarly, in October 1998, when two young men in Laramie, Wyoming, beat gay college student Matthew Shepard into a coma and left him to die tied to a fence in the desert, they were effectively warning all gay people that they too could suffer the same fate.

Hate-motivated killers are also more likely than perpetrators of other, less serious hate crimes to have joined an organized hate group. James Byrd's three killers, for example, had met each other in prison and joined the Aryan Brotherhood, a white supremacist group. For someone filled with hate, membership in such a group assures them that they are not alone in their bigotry. They are also likely to feel bolder and more willing to take risks when encouraged by the group to attack the victim of their hate.

In their research on hate killers, James Fox, Jack Levin, and Kenna Quinet (2005) found that the killers can be divided into three types. First are the *thrill* hate killers, who, being young, bored, and idle, are seized with the idea of going out together to look for someone to attack. As marginalized and alienated youngsters, these offenders often feel important and powerful from the thrill attacks. Then, there are the *defensive* hate killers, who feel the need to defend what they consider to be their birthright. A black family moving into a white neighborhood or a gay man attending a predominantly heterosexual party, for example, is seen as encroaching on the hatemonger's birthright of being white or straight. Finally, there are the *mission* hate killers. These are the rarest but the most dangerous of the three types. While the thrill and defensive killers usually target a single victim, the mission killers seek to destroy all members of a hated group. Thus, they may kill members of a group indiscriminately, target many people simultaneously, and carry on a killing spree in various places. Their mission is to eliminate or weaken an entire group of people so that they themselves can attain the most powerful position in society.

Genocide

If the mission hate killers turn out to be the political leaders of a state, they are able to carry out their mission by committing *genocide,* the wholesale killing of members of a racial or ethnic group. There have been numerous cases of genocide around the world. During the nineteenth century, Dutch settlers in South Africa exterminated the native Hottentots, and British settlers on the island of Tasmania, near Australia, wiped out the entire native population, hunting them like wild animals. During the pioneer days of the United States, white settlers from Europe slaughtered many Native American tribes. In the early part of the twentieth century, the Turks massacred more than one million Armenians. Between 1933 and 1945, the Nazi Germans systematically murdered six million Jews. More recently, in the early 1990s, the Serbs in Bosnia killed and tortured numerous Muslims and Croats as part of an "ethnic cleansing" campaign. From 1993 to 1996, over half a million Tutsis were eliminated by Hutus in Rwanda, Africa. In 2004 and 2005 the Arab government in Sudan killed more than 200,000 of its non-Arab citizens in the Darfur region of western Sudan. In the twentieth century as a whole, the victims of genocide were four times more numerous than the victims of all the wars and revolutions. Since 1968, the number of genocide victims throughout the world has *tripled* (Morrison, 2006; Leaning, 2004; Alvarez, 2001).

One way to grasp the nature of genocide is to take a look at the people who are involved in it as victims, perpetrators, and bystanders. The victims are killed, "not for what they have done, but for who they are." They are, however, seen not as individuals, but as members of a stigmatized category of people. Thus, even if friends and neighbors happen to belong to a despised group, they are perceived as deserving to be killed. This is why, for example, many Muslims in Bosnia were killed by their Serbian friends (Weitz, 2003; Alvarez, 2001).

As for the perpetrators of genocide, common sense would suggest that they are monsters, sadists, and psychopaths, who derive great pleasure from making others suffer. But in reality they are mostly normal, like you and me, except that they have the job of killing others under the order of their superiors. The people who participated in the Holocaust, for example, came from a cross section of German society, representing a variety of careers, religious backgrounds, and socioeconomic classes. They lived normal, law-abiding, family-centered lives before and after the Holocaust. During the Holocaust, many suffered from stress, insomnia, nervous breakdown, or even committed suicide, because they were not psychopathic killers but ordinary people unaccustomed to killing human beings.

Finally, average citizens play the role of bystanders by doing nothing. In virtually all cases of genocide, the majority of citizens stay quiet and let their genocidal government carry out its campaign of exterminating the victims. A typical example is a high official of a university in Rwanda: He closed his eyes to the killing of tens of thousands and turned a deaf ear to the screams of dying people around him. Similarly, many nations play the role of bystanders by ignoring the genocide in the African countries of Rwanda and Sudan (Cose, 2008; Snyder, 2008; Alvarez, 2001).

Scholars from various disciplines have offered a number of theories to explain genocide. One theory says that the cause of genocide is the *physical and psychological separation* between perpetrators and victims, which makes it easy for the former to kill the latter. A second theory attributes genocide to the *dehumanization* of the victims, who are treated as objects rather than persons. A third theory argues that the syndrome of "*obedience to authority,*" which is widespread in society, causes people to participate in genocide when ordered or asked to do so by the government. A fourth theory traces genocide to the perpetrators' *psychological ability to dissociate* their normal selves from the insanity of mass killing as if the killing is done by somebody else. And a fifth theory blames genocide on *power,* in that the more power the government has, the more able and willing it is to kill on a massive scale, which may explain why genocide occurs far more frequently in authoritarian and totalitarian states than in democratic nations (Valentino, 2004; Alvarez, 2001).

Terrorism: The September 11 Attacks

Terrorism is violence aimed at a government, though the victims are usually innocent citizens. Terrorists are basically powerless individuals futilely fighting a powerful government. Some fight their own governments. An example here is Timothy McVeigh, who was convicted of and executed for bombing the Alfred P. Murrah federal office building in Oklahoma City in 1995. Others are international terrorists, who leave their country to attack a foreign government. The Islamic radicals from the Middle East who used hijacked planes to destroy the World Trade Center and damage the Pentagon on September 11, 2001, are a more recent example.

On that day Muslim terrorists from the Middle East hijacked passenger planes and crashed them into the World Trade Center in New York City and the Pentagon in Washington, D.C., killing about 3,000 innocent people. It was far and away the worst terrorist attack on U.S. soil, the most devastating terrorism in human history. Why did the terrorists commit this heinous crime with the certain knowledge that they would die, too? Were they insane?

The suicide attacks happened because the terrorists believed they were waging a holy war against the infidels, calling the United States "the Great Satan." But they were far from mentally ill. Like the Palestinian suicide bombers who blow themselves up along with innocent Israeli citizens, the September 11 attackers were members of a terrorist organization. But unlike the Palestinians, who belong to local groups, the September 11 terrorists belonged to an international organization called al Qaeda ("the base"), with members spread out all over the world. The September 11 attacks were part of al Qaeda's mission to destroy the United States and its interests abroad. Those terrorists were following the orders of their organization's leader, Osama bin Laden.

According to bin Laden, the U.S. culture of secularism, materialism, and free immorality threatens the traditional Islamic way of life. Moreover, U.S. foreign policy—including support for Israel, the stationing of American troops in Saudi Arabia, and the war and blockade against Iraq—purportedly destroys Muslim lives and wounds Muslim dignity as proud inheritors of a great religion. To redress these wrongs, bin Laden told his followers to engage in a holy war against the United States. He further mesmerized them with the seductive message that should they die as martyrs, they would go to heaven, where they each would be rewarded with 72 virgins (MacFarquhar, 2001). All this apparently resonated well with the young and unattached suicide terrorists who were already intensely religious and patriotic. It should not be surprising, then, that they carried out the horrendous crime on September 11, 2001.

Since that day, the U.S. government has tried to fight the war against the terrorists with some success. The Taliban rulers of Afghanistan, who used to provide sanctuary to Islamic fundamentalist terrorists, have been eliminated. With cooperation from other governments, the United States has "hacked" into foreign banks' computer systems to find people who finance terrorist activities. The Americans also have obtained assistance from friendly Muslim countries such as Saudi Arabia and Pakistan in tracking down terrorists. Most Muslim publics express less support for terrorism than in the past, fewer Muslims believe that suicide bombings are justified in the defense of Islam, and confidence in Osama bin Laden has dropped sharply in some Arab countries. Over half of al Qaeda's key operational leaders have been killed or captured, along with some 3,000 of their associates. But al Qaeda has changed from an organization to a movement, made up of a loosely affiliated network joined together by local terrorists in many different countries, the Internet, and a shared hatred of Western governments. Similarly, a combination of achievements and problems has emerged from the war in Iraq. The country seems to be on the way to democracy, having put in place a legitimate constitution and electoral process. But more than 4,000 U.S. soldiers have died, the insurgency continues to threaten the U.S. and Iraqi forces along with innocent Iraqi civilians, and nobody knows for sure when the Iraqi government will be able to take care of its country's security so that the American soldiers can come home (Falkenrath, 2006; Kaplan and Whitelaw, 2004; Al-Arian, 2004).

Why Do People Kill?

Some sociologists have used positivist theories of deviance such as anomie-strain, control, and social learning to explain why people commit homicide (see, for example, Fox, Levin, and Quinet, 2005). The assumption is that whatever causes deviance in general also cause homicide in particular. But here we will discuss two positivist theories that are specifically designed to explain the causes of homicide, theories that are derived from studies on homicide as opposed to other forms of deviance.

External Restraint Theory

Developed by Andrew Henry and James Short (1954), the external restraint theory is intended to explain why some people who are extremely frustrated commit suicide and others who are just as frustrated turn to homicide instead. Henry and Short consider suicide and homicide to be basically the same—both are acts of aggression fueled by frustration. Yet, these sociologists point out, the two acts differ in that suicide is aggression directed inward against oneself, while homicide is aggression directed outward against another person. This theory attempts to explain why intensely frustrated people are likely to choose one type of aggression rather than the other. The explanation is that intensely frustrated people would choose *self*-directed aggression (suicide) if they experience *weak* external restraint, but would choose *other*-directed aggression (homicide) if they suffer *strong* external restraint.

Henry and Short define the *strength of external restraint* as "the degree to which behavior is required to conform to the demands and expectations of other persons." In other words, the strength of external restraint is the amount of social control imposed on people so as to limit their freedom and range of behaviors. According to the theory, people who suffer a great amount of that kind of social control are more inclined toward homicide than suicide because they can legitimately blame others for their frustration.

Martin Gold (1958) has extended the theory of external restraint to include a factor that mediates between strong external restraint and murder. The mediating factor is the *socialization in aggression by physical punishment*. Gold believes that there are two types of socialization—that is, techniques of bringing up a child. One involves the parents using *physical* punishment (e.g., spanking, slapping, hitting, or punching) to deter their misbehaving child from further misbehavior. The other involves the parents employing *psychological* punishment (e.g., threatening withdrawal of love, or lecturing to induce guilt) to correct their child's misconduct. Gold theorizes that physical punishment leads to outward aggression against another person, while children psychologically punished turn their aggression against themselves. When they become frustrated adults ready for aggressive action, those who have been physically punished will likely choose murder over suicide, while those who have undergone psychological punishment would choose suicide.

There is some evidence to suggest that strong external restraint is associated with homicide. As we have observed, the lower classes and blacks have significantly higher homicide rates than do the middle classes and whites. Such a finding can be said to support the theory because the lower classes and blacks suffer stronger external restraint. There is also evidence to support Gold's theory that physical punishment received in childhood increases the likelihood of homicide in adulthood (Straus, 1991). Still, all this does not mean, as the theories imply, that external restraint or physical punishment has a direct, causal impact on homicide. Instead, as more recent studies suggest, external restraint can lead to homicide only through a third variable called "external attribution of blame"—blaming others rather than oneself for one's own frustration (Unnithan, Huff-Corzine, Corzine, and Whitt, 1994). In other words, excessive external restraint or physical punishment encourages people to blame others rather than themselves for their own problems in life, which in turn causes them to engage in physical violence against others.

Subculture of Violence Theory

After analyzing his abundant data on homicide, Marvin Wolfgang (1958) concludes:

> There may be a subculture of violence which does not define personal assaults as wrong or antisocial; in which quick resort to physical aggression is a socially approved and expected concomitant of certain stimuli; and in which violence has become a familiar but often deadly partner in life's struggles.

Wolfgang then theorizes that the subculture of violence is the basic cause of high homicide rates in poor neighborhoods.

According to Wolfgang, the violent subculture has such a grip on the poor that they engage in a wider range of violent behavior than the nonpoor. This is because they associate and identify with the model of violence as provided by their parents, peers, and others in the poor neighborhood. At the same time they are discouraged from following the countermodel of nonviolence from the larger society. Consequently, violence becomes a part of their lifestyles and their way of solving interpersonal problems. Not surprisingly, they consider the use of violence not only normal but necessary for survival. They do not feel guilty about their aggression at all (Wolfgang and Ferracuti, 1967).

Critics, however, have questioned the implication that a violent act necessarily reflects the actor's placing a high value on violence. In fact, studies have shown that people who engage in violence do not value violence any more than those who refrain from violence, and that prisoners convicted of murder and other violent crimes do not value violence any more than other inmates convicted of burglary and other nonviolent crimes

(Erlanger, 1974; Ball-Rokeach, 1973). Other studies have suggested that the cause of high homicide rates among the poor and African Americans is not the subculture of violence but rather poverty, relative deprivation, or social inequality (Williams, 1984; Messner, 1982). Nevertheless, as it propagates the belief in using violence to solve interpersonal problems, the subculture of violence does encourage—though not cause—homicide, especially among those frustrated by the structural problems of poverty and inequality (Corzine, Huff-Corzine, and Whitt, 1999; Messner, 1983).

Does the Death Penalty Deter Murder?

Nowadays, most people believe that the death penalty is an effective deterrent to murder. Not surprisingly, to win an election, most politicians vow that convicted killers shall be put to death. Many sociologists, however, have observed that the death penalty does not have its hoped-for effect. The evidence supporting this observation has come in several forms.

The first indication is the homicide rates in *states that have retained* the death penalty law are generally much higher than in *states that have abolished* it. (See examples in Figure 4.2.) This clearly suggests that the death penalty does not deter homicide. It might even suggest to some observers that the death penalty causes more homicides. It could be the other way around: That is, the higher homicide rates cause the states to bring back the death penalty. Moreover, the South, where all the states practice the death penalty, has a very large black population and a culture of violence, as reflected by its traditionally high rate of criminal violence and high level of gun ownership. Thus the distinctive population and cultural characteristics of the South, rather than its death penalty, may be responsible for its higher homicide rate.

In view of this, some sociologists have excluded the southern states from analysis of the relationship between capital punishment and murder. Instead, they focused on northern and western states that have about the same population composition and cultural tradition. The result has consistently shown that the death penalty states still have higher homicide rates than their neighboring states without the death penalty. Although this finding does not prove that capital punishment encourages murder, it does show that the death penalty does not deter murder.

A second type of evidence comes from comparing the homicide rates that occurred *before and after abolition* of the death penalty within the same states. Such comparisons have shown no significant difference in homicide rates before and after the states abolished capital punishment. Furthermore, the *restoration* of the death penalty in states that had earlier abolished it had *not* led to any significant decrease in homicides. This further suggests that the death penalty does not deter people from committing murder.

A final piece of evidence comes from comparing the numbers of homicides *shortly before and shortly after executions* of convicted murderers that have been widely publicized. If the death penalty has a deterrent effect, the execution should so scare potential killers that they would refrain from killing, and the number of homicides in the area should decrease. Apparently, this is not the case. In Philadelphia during the 1930s, for example, the number of homicides remained about the same in the period from 60 days before to 60 days after a widely publicized execution of five murderers. This finding, among others,

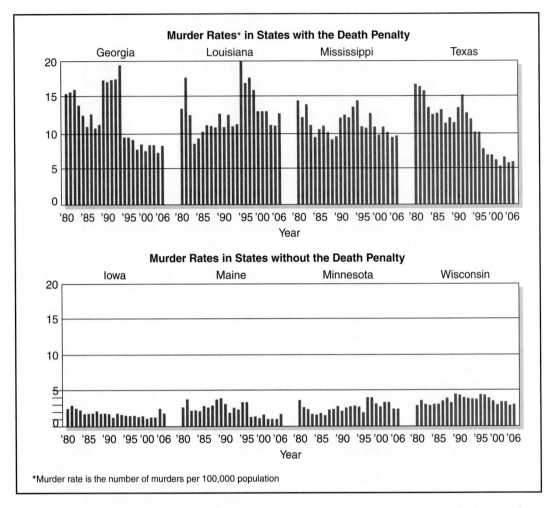

FIGURE 4.2   The Death Penalty and Murder. Murder rates are generally much higher in the 38 states that still retain the death penalty than in the 12 states that have abolished it, as exemplified above.

Source: FBI, *Crime in the United States,* 2007.

suggests that the death penalty, even when the state shows people that it means business with it, apparently does not frighten potential killers from killing.

In fact, publicized executions may have the opposite, *brutalizing effect* on potential murderers, indirectly encouraging them to kill, possibly by diminishing respect for human life or by stimulating imitative violence. In California between 1946 and 1955, the state always chose Friday mornings to carry out executions, and there were more murders during the weekends following executions than during the weekends without the Friday-morning executions. Also, in New York between 1907 and 1963, there was an average increase of two homicides in the month after each execution (Bailey, 1998; Bowers and Pierce, 1980). In a few other cases, the brutalizing effect did not exist, but there was no indication of the deterrent effect either, because the number of homicides remained about the same whether there was a publicized execution or not (King, 1978).

What we have discussed can be summed up by the conclusion from a 14-nation analysis of the death penalty: "If capital punishment is a more effective deterrent than the alternative punishment of long imprisonment, its abolition ought to be followed by homicide rate increases. The evidence examined here fails to support and, indeed, repeatedly contradicts this proposition. In this cross-national sample, abolition was followed more often than not by absolute *decreases* in homicide rates, not by the increases predicted by deterrence theory" (Archer and Gartner, 1984; also see Simon and Blaskovich, 2002).

Nevertheless, a few studies appear every now and then to challenge that conclusion. The most well known is economist Isaac Ehrlich's (1975) conclusion from his statistical analysis that one execution can prevent about eight murders. This particular analysis has been criticized for its methodological problems, such as the use of unreliable data on homicides. More devastating to Ehrlich's conclusion is another economist's analysis that uses the same statistical method as Ehrlich's but produces essentially contrary results (Avio, 1979). Like Ehrlich, a number of other economists also claim to have found the deterrent effect of the death penalty, but again they have been criticized for using flawed methodologies or insufficient data (Liptak, 2007).

We may conclude that the death penalty does not deter murder. But why not? One reason is that murder is mostly a crime of passion, carried out under the overwhelming pressure of a volcanic emotion, which makes it difficult for the individual involved to stop and think that he or she will end up being executed for killing the victim. Another reason is that the causal forces of homicide, such as the experiences of abuse, brutality, and poverty, are so powerful that the threat of capital punishment could not stop the homicide-prone person from committing the crime.

Summary

1. How do assaults differ from homicide? In assaults the victim survives, and compared to killers, the assaulters are less likely to use firearms and more likely to commit the offense in the summer.

2. What kinds of people are more likely than others to commit homicide? They include the poor, African Americans, men, and young adults. They are also more likely to live in the southern region of the United States, and in large cities and in rural areas rather than in small towns.

3. Are there any patterns to the occurrence of homicide? Yes. Homicides are somewhat more likely to occur during the hot summer months than the cold month of February. They are most likely to occur on Saturday night. They are likely to take place outside the home if the killers are male, but tend more to occur at home if the offenders are female. Firearms are more often used than any other weapon.

4. What are the characteristics of homicide? First, homicide is generally warm-blooded killing, involving a relative, a friend, or an acquaintance. Second, it may involve the victim helping to bring about the killing. Third, it often involves killing for trivial reasons. And fourth, it sometimes involves the killer first doing away with the victim and then finishing himself off.

5. What is the nature of mass and serial murder? In mass murder a number of people are killed at the same time, while in serial murder the victims are killed at different times and places. Mass murderers are mostly ordinary people who are disgruntled employees, heads of family, pseudocommandos, and followers of a charismatic leader. Serial murderers are more clever in eluding the police and more likely to torture their victims before killing them. **What is the social profile of serial killers?** Most serial killers have not attended college but are cunning and able to present themselves as friendly and trustworthy. They are mostly white men, generally kill strangers, and are motivated to kill by sadism and a desire for power. **What does homicide look like from the global perspective?** Homicide appears associated with poverty, as shown by its greater prevalence in developing countries than in developed countries. It also has to do with a culture of violence, which characterizes Latin America more than other poor regions in the world.

6. What causes school violence? Contributing factors include the easy availability of guns, the media glamorization of violence, and the culture of violence, which favor the use of force to settle interpersonal problems. Given this environment, youngsters who are emotionally troubled or have been abused by parents or rejected by peers may engage in school violence.

7. What are stalkers like? Most stalkers target ex-intimates, fellow employees, and acquaintances, although a few go after celebrities. Stalkers are more likely to be male than female,

and their victims are mostly female. A majority of stalkers are loners, mentally unhealthy, and socially incompetent.

8. How do hate-motivated killers act? They are more likely to target gays and African Americans than any other group. They use their killing to intimidate the entire group of which the victim is a member, and they usually belong to a hate group. They may kill for thrill, for defense of their birthright, or for the mission of eliminating the groups they hate.

9. What kinds of people are involved in genocide? The victims of genocide are members of a stigmatized group, the perpetrators are normal people following orders to kill, and the bystanders are average citizens who do nothing to stop the killing. **What causes genocide?** According to various theories, the causes include the physical and psychological separation between offenders and victims, dehumanization of the victims, widespread obedience to authority, psychological dissociation between the normal self and the insane act of genocidal killing, and the immense power of the state.

10. What is the nature of terrorism? Terrorism is violence aimed at a government and usually involves victimizing innocent citizens. Terrorists can go after foreign or domestic targets. **What caused the September 11 terrorist attacks?** The attacks were directed by Osama bin Laden, the leader of the terrorist organization al Qaeda, who exhorted or ordered its extremely religious and patriotic young members to attack the United States as "the Great Satan."

11. Why do some people kill? One sociological theory points to strong external restraint as the cause of homicide, while another indicates the subculture of violence as a breeding ground of homicides. **Is the death penalty an effective deterrent to murder?** Sociologists usually say "no," though economists tend to say "yes."

FURTHER READING

Alvarez, Alex. 2001. *Government, Citizens, and Genocide: A Comparative and Interdisciplinary Approach.* Bloomington: Indiana University Press. Discusses the history of genocide, the political nature of genocide, the institutional and organizational supports of genocide, and the contribution of ordinary men and women to genocide.

Baker, Jean A. 1998. "Are we missing the forest for the trees? Considering the social context of school violence." *Journal of School Psychology,* 36 (Spring), 29–44. Showing how school violence derives from a breakdown of community in schools where students do not feel a sense of belonging.

Beeghley, Leonard. 2003. *Homicide: A Sociological Explanation.* Lanham, Md.: Rowman and Littlefield. Discusses the connection of homicide to gun availability, illegal drugs, violence history, racial discrimination, and economic inequality.

Combs, Cindy C. 2000. *Terrorism in the Twentieth-First Century.* Upper Saddle River, N.J.: Prentice Hall. A systematic discussion of many aspects of terrorism, ranging from terrorist ideology and terrorist organizations to counterterrorist measures.

Dunn, Jennifer L. 2002. *Courting Disaster: Intimate Stalking, Culture, and Criminal Justice.* New York: Aldine de Gruyter. Provides an intimate look at the nature of stalking through the victims' experiences.

Fox, James Alan, Jack Levin, and Kenna Quinet. 2005. *The Will to Kill: Making Sense of Senseless Murder.* Boston: Allyn and Bacon. Analyzes the nature of various forms of murder, including serial murder, school shootings, mass murder, and cult killings.

Holmes, Ronald M., and Stephen T. Holmes. 1998. *Serial Murder,* 2d ed. Thousand Oaks, Calif.: Sage Publications. Presents various types of serial killers, their behavioral patterns, and the motivations behind their killings.

Levin, Jack, and James Alan Fox. 2002. *Dead Lines: Essays in Murder and Mayhem.* Boston: Allyn and Bacon. A series of essays about homicide, school shootings, workplace violence, hate crimes, serial murder, the culture of killing, guns, official responses to murder, capital punishment, and crime victims.

Levin, Jack, and Gordana Rabrenovic. 2004. *Why We Hate.* Amherst, N.Y.: Prometheus Books. Discusses the various sources of hate crime and ways of combating it.

Mann, Coramae Richey. 1996. *When Women Kill.* Albany: State University of New York Press. An analysis of both qualitative and quantitative data on nearly 300 women arrested for homicide in six large U.S. cities.

Martinez, J. Michael, William D. Richardson, and D. Brandon Hornsby (eds.). 2002. *The Leviathan's Choice: Capital Punishment in the Twentieth Century.* Lanham, Md.: Rowman and Littlefield. A collection of articles presenting various perspectives on the death penalty, including the philosophical, theological, social science, and legal perspectives.

Miethe, Terance D., and Wendy C. Regoeczi, with Kriss A. Drass. 2004. *Rethinking Homicide: Exploring the Structure and Process Underlying Deadly Situations.* Cambridge, U.K.: Cambridge University Press. An empirical analysis of homicide as a nexus of offender and victim characteristics and social situations, showing homicide, for example, as an expressive act of violence that men carry out with guns in large cities against acquaintances of a similar race, gender, and age during a heated argument.

Mullen, Paul E., Michele Pathe, and Rosemary Purcell. 2000. *Stalkers and Their Victims.* Cambridge, U.K.: Cambridge University Press. Discusses numerous aspects of stalking, from the epidemiology of stalking to various types of stalkers and stalking situations.

Mullins, Christopher W. 2006. *Holding Your Square: Masculinities, Streetlife, and Violence.* Portland, Ore.: Willan. An analysis of how threat to masculinity often triggers street violence.

Newman, Katherine S., with Cybelle Fox, David Harding, Jal Mehta, and Wendy Roth. 2004. *Rampage: The Social Roots of School Shootings.* New York: Basic Books. Research report on how school shootings usually erupt from a combination of five factors: social marginality, emotional problems, cultural scripts, failed surveillance, and gun availability.

Reuter, Christoph. 2004. *My Life as a Weapon: A Modern History of Suicide Bombing.* Princeton, N.J.: Princeton University Press. An analysis of suicide bombings in different parts of the world.

Sageman, Marc. 2004. *Understanding Terror Networks.* Philadelphia: University of Pennsylvania Press. Based on the biographies of Osama bin Laden and 171 other terrorists, this analysis shows how alienated young men turned into fanatics eager to kill and to become martyrs and then got together to form a global network of terrorism.

Simon, Rita J., and Dagny A. Blaskovich. 2002. *A Comparative Analysis of Capital Punishment: Statutes, Policies, Frequencies, and Public Attitudes the World Over.* Lanham, Md.: Lexington Books. A brief historical survey of the views and practices of the death penalty in various countries.

Smith, M. Dwayne, and Margaret A. Zahn (eds.). 1999. *Homicide: A Sourcebook of Social Research.* Thousand Oaks, Calif.: Sage Publications. A collection of detailed analyses of the theories, methodologies, substantive studies, and prevention of homicide.

Vanden Heuvel, Katrina. 2002. *A Just Response: The Nation on Terrorism, Democracy, and September 11, 2001.* New York: Thunder's Mouth Press/ Nation Books. A collection of essays on the meanings and implications of the September 11 terrorist attacks.

Waters, Tony. 2007. *When Killing Is a Crime.* Boulder, Colo.: Lynne Rienner. Illustrates how killing is socially constructed so that it is not always and everywhere viewed as a crime.

Weitz, Eric D. 2003. *A Century of Genocide: Utopias of Race and Nation.* Princeton, N.J.: Princeton University Press. Shows how the zealous attempt to create a homogeneous utopia led the leaders of nations as well as the masses of ordinary people to genocide.

CRITICAL THINKING QUESTIONS

1. Analyze the various forms of homicide discussed in this chapter. What are the similarities and differences among them?

2. Genocide is the most horrendous kind of killing. How can it be prevented?

5 Rape and Child Molestation

Myths and Realities

Myth: Because rape is a serious, horrible crime, the offender tends more to victimize a stranger than someone he knows.

Reality: Most of the victims know their rapists (p. 85).

———

Myth: As a result of increased racial integration, men are today more likely to rape women of a different race than women of the same race.

Reality: Although there are now more interracial rapes than before, most rapes still involve members of the same race (p. 85).

———

Myth: Rapes tend to occur during the hot summer months because the season of summer increases the heat of passion and hence the likelihood of rape.

Reality: Summer doesn't fuel passion; it merely increases the social interaction between potential offender and victim that makes rape more likely to happen. Similarly, there are many more rapes during the weekend than on any other day because the potential offender and victim are more likely to meet during the weekend (p. 86).

Myth: As some psychiatrists suggest, gang rape can be interpreted as an expression of latent homosexuality in that the fellow rapists have an unconscious wish to have sex with each other.

Reality: Such an interpretation makes as much sense as the suggestion that several men who rob a store together unconsciously want to rob each other or that a bunch of guys who go hunting together have a latent wish to kill each other (p. 88).

Myth: When raping their dates, most young men regard the date rape as a criminal offense just like most of their victims do.

Reality: Most young rapists do not regard date rape as real rape. Many victims of date rape do not identify their experience as rape, either, because they find it hard to believe that someone they know well could have raped them (p. 89).

Myth: Regardless of how they react, whether combatively or passively, when they are raped, the victims tend to suffer the same way afterward, having great difficulty readjusting to their lives.

Reality: Rape survivors who have resisted their attackers by screaming and kicking readjust more easily to life than passive survivors who have yielded to crying and pleading (p. 93).

Myth: After a woman is raped, her husband tends to show her more love, affection, or understanding because, after being raped, she needs emotional support as a human being the most.

Reality: After a woman is raped, she is often said to have been "ravaged," "ravished," "despoiled," or "ruined," as if she were a piece of property that has been damaged. Not surprisingly, a man whose wife has been raped tends to show her less love than before, consequently increasing the likelihood of their marriage ending in divorce (p. 95).

Myth: Whether submissive or assertive, virtually all women have about the same potential of getting raped.

Reality: Submissive women are more likely than their assertive peers to be chosen as potential victims of rape, and when they are approached by a potential rapist, they are more likely to be raped (p. 99).

Myth: Some men are likely to rape other men in prison in order to relieve their sexual deprivation.

Reality: The primary motive for the rape in prison is not the need for sexual release but instead the need to subjugate and humiliate the victim, as evidenced by the use of such language by the rapist as "Fight or fuck" or "I'm gonna make a girl out of you" (p. 104).

Myth: Most of the same-sex rapes involve homosexual men as offenders or victims or both.

Reality: The majority (more than half) of the same-sex rape victims are heterosexual, as are the majority of the offenders (p. 104).

In 2008, three students from a high school in New Jersey were charged with sexually assaulting a 16-year-old special education student at one of their homes. One suspect was 18 years old and the other two were 16. The older youngster, Romal Roberts, invited the girl to come into his house. For the next four hours or so, Roberts and his two friends forced her to perform sex acts on them and abused her with a broomstick. According to an acquaintance, Roberts was a "stand-up kid who played video games and wanted to go to college." A neighbor described him as "a polite teenager who would shovel snow for them" (Fahim and Schweber, 2008).

Sexual violence against women is relatively common in the United States. According to a nationwide survey, 22 percent of women ages 18 to 90 reported having been sexually assaulted (Elliott et al., 2004). In other studies, rape victims were found to make up between 13 and 16 percent (Kilpatrick et al., 2007). In any case, the most conservative estimate has put the average woman's chance of being raped at "an appalling 1 in 10" (Russell and Bolen, 2000; Koss, 1995). Also significantly, the overwhelming majority of these women know their rapists (Campbell and Wasco, 2005).

In this chapter we will first explore the patterns of rape, seeking answers to such questions as: Who is likely to rape? How are rapes generally planned and executed? What is involved in different forms of rape? Why can't the victim be blamed for the rape? We will in turn examine the reactions of both victims and law enforcers to rapes, analyze the pervasive culture that encourages men to assault women sexually, discuss the major explanations for rape, and look at the issue about men being victims of rape. Finally, we will analyze the problem of child molestation.

Patterns of Rape

Certain patterns can be detected in rape. Let us first see what kind of men are likely to rape and how they plan and carry out such a crime. We then will take a close look at the nature of gang rape, acquaintance or date rape, and rape on the college campus along with the controversial issue of victim-precipitated rape.

Racial, Age, and Situational Factors

In his classic analysis of 646 rape cases from the Philadelphia police files for the years 1958 and 1960, sociologist Menachem Amir (1971) found that most of the rapists were poor. He also found that blacks were more likely than whites to be both rapists and victims. Amir further discovered that, contrary to the then widespread white fear of black men being more likely to rape white women than black, rape was mostly *intraracial*—black men raping black women and white men raping white women. In about 95 percent of the rapes in Philadelphia, both offenders and victims were of the same race; in only 3 percent were the rapists black and their victims white. In other words, rape was as intraracial as murder. The intraracial nature of rape can be attributed to at least two factors. One is the unusually severe legal penalty against blacks who raped white women. Another reason is racial segregation, which made black women more accessible than white women to those black men who were inclined to express their aggression in rape.

Today, rape continues to be mostly intraracial but has become considerably less so— or more interracial. Already by the early 1980s black-against-white rapes had soared to 19 percent (from 3 percent in the late 1950s and early 1960s) of all rapes committed by both blacks and whites (Wilbanks, 1985). This may have resulted from increased racial integration and hence more contact between potential offenders and victims of different races. It should be pointed out, though, that most rapes still involve members of the same race.

Age is another factor in the relationship between rapists and their victims. Females from the age of one year all the way up to above the age of 80 are subject to rape. The age group most vulnerable to rape, however, is 16 to 20 years of age. In intraracial rapes, offenders are generally somewhat older than their victims. But in *inter*racial rapes, black offenders tend to be *younger* than their white victims. This does not mean that the black offenders prefer older white women. Instead, it is largely a matter of availability, because many of these black–white rape episodes involve the commission of burglary or robbery in addition to rape (Russell, 1984). While this may reflect black hostility toward white society, as suggested, it may also reflect the influence of a sexist society. Burglars and robbers usually feel that "if you rob a woman, you might as well rape her too—the rape is free" (Lear, 1972). Such criminals simply consider rape "an added bonus" to their property crime (Scully, 1990).

There is also a situational factor in rape. The number of rapes, especially gang rapes, tends to increase during the hot summer months. Most significant is the finding that most rapes occur on weekends (Michael and Zumpe, 1983). Does summer increase the heat of passion and hence the likelihood of rape? No, summer merely increases the social interaction between potential offender and victim that makes rape more likely to happen. Most rapes also involve drinking on the part of offenders, just like most homicides. The use of alcohol serves as an excuse for sexual aggression ("It wasn't my fault; I was drunk"). Because this excuse is to a significant degree socially acceptable, it helps reduce the inhibition against raping as it does against killing. But compared with murderers, rapists are generally less violent, less likely to have previous arrest records for aggravated assault. Since rapists are not as violent as murderers, most rapes do not happen as explosively or impulsively as murders do; they do not spring from a sudden, uncontrolled sexual desire. Instead, rapes are mostly planned.

Planning and Execution

Since most rapes involve acquaintances, friends, or lovers, the planning largely entails the offender using sweet talk, romantic moves, alcoholic beverages, or some other means to induce the woman to have sex, and then single-mindedly striving to achieve his aim without paying any attention to her wishes.

But rapists operate differently if they do not know the victim well or at all. In such cases, offenders tend to choose women who, they believe, are vulnerable to attack. Such targets are in a disadvantaged situation so that they cannot react appropriately or swiftly to the threat of rape. Examples include a mentally challenged girl, a sleeping female, an old woman, or a young woman under the influence of alcohol or drugs. Other women are also more vulnerable to rape if they appear passive or submissive, lacking in assertiveness or confidence. A woman is said to suggest submissiveness to a potential rapist if she "walks slowly and tentatively, stares at the ground and moves her arms and legs in short, jerky motions." Yet some rapists prefer the opposite type of women—those who appear too aggressive or domineering. As many convicted rapists in one study indicated, "they wanted to put a particular uppity woman in her place" (Bart and O'Brien, 1985). Apparently, women who project confidence without appearing too aggressive are less subject to rape.

If they cannot easily determine the vulnerability of a woman, rapists will likely work out a strategy to test her. They might first try to determine whether or not their selected target is a friendly and helpful person. A rapist might approach a woman on the street and ask her for a light or a street direction. If she provides it, he may proceed to ask her an intimate question, make some sexually suggestive remarks, put his arm around her, or touch her in a sexually provocative place to see how she reacts. If she reacts submissively or fearfully, he knows that she can be intimidated into submitting to his sexual demands. Another rapist might ask a woman to let him into her house to make an emergency phone call or for any other bogus reason. If the woman falls for such a ploy, the rapist may establish her as a prospective victim. An example follows:

> The rapist would walk into an apartment house and ring several doorbells asking for "Sally." When he found a woman who was helpful, attractive and presumably alone, he would explain how hot and tired he was and ask for a drink of water. Then he asked to use the bathroom so he could look around and make sure the victim was alone. Finally he would ask for a second drink of water and then approach the victim as she stood at the kitchen sink. With a knife at her throat and cut off from help, the victim usually capitulated. (Selkin, 1975)

After they have successfully identified a target for rape, the offenders initially do not resort to intimidation with such violent means as brandishing a weapon or administering a brutal beating. The majority of rapes involve only verbal coercion and nonphysical aggression, such as "Don't scream or I'll cut you to pieces," and "If you don't take your clothes off, I'll kill you!" Rapists ordinarily become more violent only when they are ready to carry out the crime. According to Pauline Bart and Patricia O'Brien (1985), the majority of the rapists in their study were rough—pushing, shoving, slapping, or choking their victims. Some rapists would not merely subject their victims to forced intercourse; they would also force them to submit to oral or anal sodomy and repeated vaginal assault. Sometimes rapists make jokes at their victims' expense. After he was through, one rapist proclaimed to his victim: "I'll marry you if you get pregnant" (Macdonald, 1995, 1971).

Gang Rape

Of all the rapes studied by Amir (1971), 43 percent were gang rapes. The most significant fact about these rapes is that the perpetrators are largely adolescents aged 14 to 19. Most of these young rapists come from lower-class families, and are members of street gangs. They find their victims in several ways. First, they may cruise an area looking for a female hitchhiker to pick up and drive the unsuspecting victim to a deserted area to rape her. Second, they may use a knife or gun to kidnap a woman from the street at night. Third, a member of the gang may make a date with a woman and then drive her, without her knowledge or consent, to a predetermined location where he and other members will rape her (Zezima, 2004; Scully, 1990).

Occurring less frequently are gang rapes on college campuses, committed by middle- and upper-class youths. Gang rape takes place at various kinds of schools: large state universities, well-known liberal arts colleges, religious schools, and Ivy League institutions, where gang rape is often referred to as "running a train" on the victim. There is a pattern to the way campus gang rapes occur: At a party, the men encourage a woman to drink or take drugs and rape her when she gets drunk or high on drugs (Sanday, 1990).

Why do those lower-class adolescents and college men participate in gang rapes? Psychiatrists generally interpret gang rape as an expression of latent homosexuality, arguing that the fellow rapists have an unconscious wish to have sex with each other (Sanday, 1990). Such an interpretation, however, makes as much sense as the suggestion that several men who rob a store together unconsciously want to rob each other or that a bunch of guys who go hunting together have a latent wish to kill each other. It seems more convincing to theorize that participation in a gang rape fulfills a social need more than a sexual desire, particularly for young boys who feel peer pressure to prove that they are not "chicken" (Groth and Birnbaum, 1979).

Similarly, college men who share a close relationship may find it hard to resist the pressure to participate in a gang rape because they are afraid of having their masculinity questioned. Moreover, through their camaraderie, they can playfully urge each other to participate in a gang rape without seeing it as a serious crime. This may explain why fraternity brothers and college athletes on some campuses are more likely than other students to engage in gang rape (Schwartz and DeKeseredy, 1997; O'Sullivan, 1991). In fact, the likelihood of committing gang rape is relatively great in other similarly cohesive or tightly knit groups. Examples are Serbian soldiers gang-raping Muslim women in Bosnia in the early 1990s, Japanese soldiers gang-raping women in China and other Asian countries during World War II, and U.S. soldiers gang-raping women in Vietnam during the Vietnam War.

Acquaintance Rape

Compared with their counterparts in stranger rape, the offenders in acquaintance or date rape are more likely to use verbal or psychological coercion and less likely to resort to guns or knives. Verbal coercion may involve pressuring the victim by saying "C'mon, I know you really want it;" psychological coercion may involve making the victim feel inadequate as an object by ignoring her wishes when she says "Stop it!" Also, while stranger rapists typically premeditate the rape, acquaintance rapists tend more to premeditate only a sexual relation, which leads to rape when the victim refuses and the offender brushes her refusal aside, often assuming that she means yes when saying no (Jasper, 1992). Most victims of acquaintance rape see themselves as victims, but they are more likely than victims of stranger rape to blame the rape partly on themselves, such as for being careless or trusting the man too much (Bechhofer and Parrot, 1991). As one victim of acquaintance rape said,

> One summer while I was in college, I worked at a hamburger stand. There was a regular there. He seemed like a nice guy, and we'd gotten to know each other pretty well. He asked if I wanted to come over to his apartment that afternoon when I got off work and listen to a record he'd been telling me about. Once we were up there, he grabbed me, and when I pulled away, he turned up the music really loud and said I'd better not fight unless I wanted to lose some teeth. The music was blasting away—no one could have heard me if I yelled— and I knew he wasn't kidding, so I just let him do it. Afterward I told him what a jerk he was and tried to make him feel bad, but *I was the one who felt awful—how could I have been so stupid to let something like that happen, how could I have been so dumb?* (Mithers, 1980)

Acquaintance rape has always been a common offense. In the 1950s, Clifford Kirkpatrick and Eugene Kanin (1957) asked a representative sample of 291 college women whether they had been sexually assaulted during the academic year. More than half (55.7 percent) replied that they had—at least once. Their experiences ranged from forced necking to forced petting to forced vaginal penetration. In the late 1970s, Kanin and Stanley Parcell (1981) did a follow-up study and found about the same result. In the mid-1980s *Ms.* magazine also found a similarly high incidence of sexual offenses in its nationwide survey of more than 7,000 college students on 35 campuses: 52 percent of all the women surveyed had encountered some form of sexual assault. The *Ms.* survey further showed that 15 percent were actually raped—forced to have sexual intercourse. Similar studies today can be expected to show about the same result. In short, of all college women, *more than half* are sexually assaulted in one way or another and about *15 percent* are forcibly raped by their dates (Fisher, Cullen, and Daigle, 2005; Jackson, 1996; Koss et al., 1987; Sweet, 1985).

Acquaintance rape is this common because it appears to be an extension of, rather than a departure from, the conventional pattern of male sexual behavior. In our culture, where men are expected to be aggressive rather than shy in dealing with women, young men can easily go too far and use too much force to execute a sexual conquest. Not surprisingly, as suggested by one study, the more sexually active they are, the more likely they are to commit date rape (Kanin, 1985). Moreover, most of the rapists and even many of their victims do not regard date rape as real rape. In the *Ms.* survey, about 8 percent of the college men admitted to committing the sexual offenses that can be legally defined as rapes or attempted rapes, but virtually none of these men identified themselves as rapists. In the same survey, of the women who had been raped, nearly 75 percent did not identify their experiences as rape. They simply found it hard to believe that someone they knew could have raped them. But such victims are likely to regard their experiences as rape if they talk to supportive others. As one victim said, "I felt it was my fault, for drinking and flirting and leaving the party, but a close male friend of mine convinced me that it was sexual assault" (Harned, 2005; Koss, 1995; Sweet, 1985).

Campus Rape

As we have observed, rape is particularly prevalent on college campuses, with about 15 percent of college women having been sexually assaulted. But most of the campus rapists, and even the majority of their victims, do not see the offense as forcible rape. Why not? The reason, as has been suggested, lies in the culture of the larger society that defines aggressiveness with women—rather than gentleness—as a highly desirable quality for young men to have. Campus rape, in other words, represents an extension of this culturally idealized male behavior. Thus the more sexually active men, who can be said to have acquired the highly desirable masculine trait as proved by their great success with women, are more likely than other men to commit date rape (Mohler-Kuo et al., 2004; Gilbert, 1995; Koss, 1995; Kanin, 1985).

While the larger society exerts its cultural influence on the college campus, is there something unique about the campus itself that also encourages sexual aggression? The answer from researchers on campus rape is yes. In her analysis of small tribal societies, Peggy Sanday (1981) found that many are "rape-free" and a few "rape-prone." Rape-free societies have a culture that discourages sexual aggression while rape-prone societies have a culture that encourages it. More recently, Sanday (1996b) observed that there are also rape-free campuses and rape-prone campuses. On a rape-free campus, sexual assault is treated as a serious offense punishable by expulsion, fraternities discourage heavy drinking, women are respected as friends rather than used as sex objects, and gays and lesbians are accepted in the same way as straights. But on a rape-prone campus, sexual assault is not seriously dealt with, heavy drinking is encouraged, taking advantage of an intoxicated woman is accepted, bragging about sexual conquests is prevalent, homophobia is rampant, and pornography is a popular guide to female sexuality. Thus we can expect a higher incidence of sexual offense on rape-prone campuses.

Other researchers have made similar observations about what causes the high incidence of campus rape. Patricia Martin and Robert Hummer (1995) conclude from their study of fraternities that such student groups contribute heavily to campus rape in a number of ways through their unique norms and practices. First, the brotherhood norm requires "sticking together," which discourages anyone's stopping rapes when they occur or reporting them to outsiders. This form of "participation" effectively condones and encourages sexual violence. Second, fraternity norms emphasize the value of maleness and masculinity over femaleness and femininity, causing members to devalue women by using them as mere sex objects, which can lead to rapes when women resist. Third, certain fraternity practices that often lead to coercive sex include excessive use of alcohol and pressure from fellow members to prove one's masculinity through sexual conquests. Studies on male athletes have also found them to be more rape-prone than other students. The athletes subscribe to the same norms and practices as the fraternity brothers (Adams-Curtis and Forbes, 2004; Benedict, 1998; Crosset et al., 1996).

The Myth of Victim Precipitation

In his classic study of the rapes in Philadelphia, Amir (1971) found that 19 percent were precipitated by the victims themselves. He refers to this kind of offense as "victim-precipitated rape," explaining that "the victim actually—or so it was interpreted by the offender—agreed to sexual relations but retracted before the actual act or did not resist strongly enough when the suggestion was made by the offender." A common victim behavior that Amir interprets as an invitation to sexual intercourse occurs when a woman agrees to have a drink or ride with a stranger. The implication here is that the victim is as much to blame as her offender. The following case has been given as an example of victim-precipitated rape:

> An 18-year-old girl was standing in the parking lot of a hamburger drive-in when some men in a car called to her to come over to the car. When she reached the car, she thought she recognized one of the men so she sat in the front seat and started talking to them. Suddenly the driver started the car and drove off. They explained that they were looking for a friend. As they were driving, one of the men asked, "Do you want to fuck?" She laughed and said no. After stopping briefly at another drive-in, the man sitting alongside her put a gun to her head and said, "Are you scared?" She replied, "I don't like having a gun to my head and I am scared shitless, but I don't feel like crying and begging you because I don't feel like hassling you. You won't get any enjoyment out of being sadistic to me." The man turned to the men in the back of the car and said, "Well, what about it, do you want to or not?" They agreed to go ahead and rape her. (Macdonald, 1971)

The concept of victim-precipitated rape reflects a *biased,* male-centered view rather than an accurate description of the crime, and it has drawn criticisms for being a sexist myth. In the example quoted above, the young woman can be said to have "asked for it" only from a biased perspective. As attorney Camille LeGrand (1973) says, "Hitchhiking and walking alone at night in a rough neighborhood may be considered behavior encouraging a sexual attack. This view of what a *man* can assume to be a sexual invitation is unreasonable, because when the female hitchhiker first sets out to get a ride, she normally is not expecting—or hoping for—a sexual encounter."

Sociologist Eugene Kanin (1984) also argues that the concept of victim precipitation, which has been applied to some homicides as discussed in the preceding chapter, is not applicable to rapes. But Kanin contends that some victims do "contribute" in some way to being raped, in the same way as a man contributes to the burglary of his house by failing to stop newspaper delivery while away on vacation. Thus Kanin suggests using the term *victim contribution* to describe those cases of rape in which the victims have willingly engaged in deep kissing or some other form of advanced intimacy prior to the occurrence of the assault.

There could also be problems, however, with the concept of victim contribution. Most important, it amounts to suggesting that virtually all dating women contribute to rape because they usually engage in uncoerced intimacy with their dates. We should note that rape victims only contribute to the *pre*rape intimacy, comparable to the way the man whose house is burglarized contributes to the burglary by failing to stop newspaper delivery while away on vacation. The rape victims cannot be said to contribute to the rape itself because they try to stop it at the moment of the crime, just as the burglary victim cannot be said to contribute to the burglary if he had come home and tried to stop it. In brief, a fundamental difference exists between prerape intimacy, which does not involve the use of force and hence is not a crime, and rape itself, which involves the use of force and therefore is a crime.

Many men, however, do not seem to recognize this difference between consensual prerape intimacy and forced sex. According to one study, 50 percent of the young men interviewed consider it "acceptable for a man to force a girl to have sexual intercourse when she initially consents but then changes her mind, or when she has sexually excited him" (Shotland and Goodstein, 1983). A more recent study found that 76 percent of high school male students regard forced sex as acceptable under similar circumstances (White and Humphrey, 1991). These young men, in effect, blame the victim. It reflects the popular myth that it is her fault if she is flirting, if she is attractively dressed, if she is in the man's perception "a tease," if she joins him for a drink, if she invites him to her apartment for coffee after having gone to a movie with him, or, sometimes, even if she only says "hello" to him at the office (Morris and Cubbins, 1992; Burt, 1991).

Consequences of Rape

Rape is in a way unique, different from murder, robbery, and most other crimes. While each of these other crimes is largely a finished act after it has occurred, rape is more likely to be a continuing process, in which the survivor keeps on suffering after the rape is over. Let us examine the survivor's experiences in the aftermath of the sexual assault.

The Rape Survivor's Response

The response to rape varies from one survivor to another. At one extreme are the survivors who show a lack of concern. One such survivor, when asked what happened between the two attacks of rape by her assailant, replied, "We went out for hamburgers." Some fall asleep after the rape; others are more upset over the theft of a purse, a ring, a cell phone, or similar property than over the rape; some survivors may voluntarily engage in sexual relations with their assailant when they meet him again after the rape; other survivors may later marry their rapists, whom they may or may not have met prior to the rape (Macdonald, 1995, 1971). At the opposite extreme are the survivors who are so traumatized that they sink into deep depression, attempt to commit suicide, or actually kill themselves. In between these two extremes are the great majority who initially experience shock, disbelief, anger, anxiety, or depression, but eventually pull themselves out of it.

This diversity of reactions to rape is apparently related to such factors as the degree of violence, the age of the survivor, her social class or cultural background, and prior sexual experience. If she has been violently raped, is relatively young, comes from a middle- or upper-class family, or has had no or little previous sexual experience, she is likely to suffer relatively severe consequences. Other factors also have a significant impact on how rape survivors feel. The trauma will be much greater, for example, if the survivor has experienced a major life change (divorce, separation, or unemployment) within a year prior to the rape (Ruch, Chandler, and Harter, 1980). Similarly, survivors of stranger rape are far more likely than survivors of acquaintance rape to have the most persistent depression, fear, and interpersonal problems because stranger rapes are generally more violent. But survivors of acquaintance rape suffer more from self-blame, primarily because society holds them responsible in some way. They also distrust men more and longer, because their earlier trust in men has been betrayed through rape (Gidycz and Koss, 1991; Katz, 1991; Mandoki and Burkhart, 1991).

Most rape survivors go through two phases of disorganization before they gradually and finally regain their ability to live normally. From the time immediately following the rape to a few days or weeks thereafter is the *acute phase* of disorganization. During this phase most survivors succumb to *extreme* fear, shock, humiliation, embarrassment, self-blame, or anxiety. After this initial, acute phase is over, survivors generally go through a *longer, lingering phase* of disorganization, which often lasts for a few months, but may persist for several years. In this phase survivors experience a variety of phobic reactions, including the fear of being alone and fear of sex. Understandably, survivors suffer from an increased risk of divorce, reduced income, and unemployment (Byrne et al., 1999; Burgess, 1995).

You may notice the nature of the survivors' feelings: Fear, depression, anxiety, and self-blame are inward-directed. Other possible feelings are outward-directed, such as anger, revenge, and the courage to have the rapist kept behind bars. While most rape survivors are gnawed by the passive, inward-directed feelings, a few others express the outward-directed feelings. One rape survivor with these feelings said, "I have fantasies about cutting off his dick and balls," and another said, "Never in my life had I felt such hate for another human being. I wish I had jammed my fingers into his eyes" (Madigan and Gamble, 1991). Interestingly, such active, angry survivors tend to feel better about themselves and swing back faster to their normal lives. As Pauline Bart and Patricia O'Brien (1984) have found, rape survivors who have resisted their attacker by screaming and kicking readjust more easily to life than passive survivors who have yielded to crying and pleading. Survivors of acquaintance rape can also recover faster if they learn to see the rape as totally their attacker's fault (Gidycz and Koss, 1991).

The Feeling of Being Raped Again

In the 1960s and 1970s both popular writers and social scientists published many horror stories about how police officers were grossly insensitive in dealing with rape survivors. For example, when a survivor gave a calm, rational account of the rape, she was asked, "What are you, some kind of sociologist?" If the woman was not physically attractive, her report of rape was dismissed as just another fantasy of a sex-starved woman. A middle-aged mother who reported having been raped might be asked by a young policeman: "Did he come?" (Geis and Geis, 1979).

When those blatant insults from the police were added to the physical and psychological injury from the rapist, survivors of sexual assault could not help feeling that they were being raped again. Although the "second rape" by the police described above is only psychological, the impact can be just as painful or traumatic as that of the first rape by the criminal (Nagel et al., 2005; Madigan and Gamble, 1991). Today, police officers are generally much more polite and respectful, but many survivors continue to suffer the second rape because the police tend to make them feel responsible for the first rape by questioning their moral character. In many cases police officers ask a woman who comes to report being raped whether, for example, "she agreed to have drinks with the man, accepted or offered him a ride, or left with him after a party," whether she "has ever been arrested for soliciting or is a known prostitute," or whether she has resisted by squirming, struggling, and screaming even if the rape was carried out with a gun or knife (Madigan and Gamble, 1991). The presumption behind these questions is that the rape survivor might have "asked for it." The police in effect blame the victim rather than the criminal.

If the police find their "blame the victim" presumption proven wrong, they will proceed to file a complaint against the alleged rapist. In the court, however, the woman is likely to suffer another psychological rape. This is largely because defense attorneys focus on the victim's sexual history or reputation in order to discredit her. In effect, they put her on trial, accusing her of having "asked for it." Since the mid-1970s there have been some legal reforms. At least eight states have renamed rape "criminal sexual assault" or some other term designed to focus the law on what the alleged criminal rather than the victim did. Nearly all states have tried to make the rape survivor's day in court less horrendous by enacting "rape shield" laws, which ostensibly prohibit the admissibility of evidence regarding the victim's previous sexual experience. Nevertheless, defense lawyers can still get around the rape shield laws by subtly revealing the rape survivor's sexual history.

In one typical case, for example, the defense called the jury's attention to the fact that the rape survivor's address was the same as that of her boyfriend, whom she had known for just one week. This was obviously meant to suggest that she was sexually immoral. The tactic worked, as one juror later admitted, "We weren't supposed to judge her as to her past relations, but it came out that she was living with her boyfriend of one week. It was hard not to judge her" (LaFree, Reskin, and Visher, 1985). Many defense lawyers continue to use similar tactics to put the victim on trial. They will dig out testimony about the victim's drinking, drug use, extramarital sex, birth of an illegitimate child, prior acquaintance or sex between her and the alleged rapist, or some other aspect of her lifestyle that can be used to make jurors question her character and credibility (Sanday, 1996a; Vachss, 1994).

Many judges allow such evidence to be presented to the jury because they believe that without it the defendant cannot get a fair trial. This is what a judge did in 1993 at the trial of four young men in Glen Ridge, New Jersey, who were charged with raping a 17-year-old woman. The judge allowed in evidence of the woman's past experiences of sexual promiscuity on the ground that the defendants could only get a fair trial if they were allowed to use the evidence. In presenting the evidence, the defense argued that the woman had willingly performed the sex acts with the young men (Lewin, 1993). Similarly, in 2004, the judge at the trial of basketball player Kobe Bryant let the defense present evidence about the accuser's previous sexual activities with somebody else. The ensuing public scorn and ridicule forced her to withdraw from the trial.

The Culture of Rape

Obviously many societies openly condemn rape as a serious crime. Less obviously, however, those same societies have a hidden culture of rape—a culture that encourages men to sexually assault women. The rape culture does not affect all men in the same way; otherwise, all men would rape. Some men are more inclined than others to rape, though they all live under the influence of the same culture. Research has suggested that those who are immature, irresponsible, and lacking in social conscience are more influenced by the rape culture (Sapp et al., 1999; Rapaport and Burkhart, 1984). But what is the nature of this rape culture? We can see it through the prevailing attitudes toward women as well as through the popular concept of male and female sex roles.

Treating Women Like Men's Property

On the face of it the law against rape appears to protect the interests of the female. Actually it protects to a larger degree the interests of the male. This is because the female is treated like a piece of property that before marriage belongs to her father and after marriage belongs to her husband. If a man rapes an unmarried girl, he is, in effect, considered to be committing the crime of vandalism against her father. If a man rapes a married woman, he is considered to be committing the crime against her husband. Thus statutory rape laws "help preserve the 'market value' of virginal young women as potential brides, rather than [protect] the naive girls from sexual exploitation" (LeGrand, 1973). As for forcible rape laws, Susan Griffin (1971) explains:

> The laws against rape exist to protect rights of the male as possessor of the female body, and not the right of the female over her own body. Even . . . the laws themselves are clear: [In some states a man cannot be] accused of raping his wife. How can any man steal what already belongs to him? It is in the sense of rape as theft of another man's property that Kate

Millett writes, "Traditionally rape has been viewed as an offense one male commits against another—a matter of abusing his woman." In raping another man's woman, a man may aggrandize his own manhood and concurrently reduce that of another man. Thus a man's honor is not subject directly to rape, but only indirectly, through "his" woman.

In marriage men traditionally feel entitled to use their wives as a sexual commodity in any way they want. As one senator opposed to making marital rape a crime said, "When you get married, you kind of expect you're going to get a little sex" (Blakely, 1983).

The absence of marital-rape laws in some countries or the rarity of husbands being imprisoned for raping their wives in most countries reflects the treatment of women as men's property. This component of the rape culture also comes across in other ways: For example, when a woman has been raped, it is often said that she has been "ravaged," "ravished," "despoiled," or "ruined." These words connote the idea that a raped woman is like a piece of property that has been damaged. Further, when a man's wife has been raped, he tends to feel as if she is less "lovable" than before—in about the same way as he would feel about a piece of damaged property. If he regards her as a human being who has feelings rather than an object that does not have feelings, logically the husband should show her more love, affection, or understanding—particularly because, after being raped, she needs emotional support as a human being the most. Instead, her husband tends to show her less love than before, as if she had turned into a piece of damaged property with no feeling and very little value. This is why many men say something like "I can't see how I can face my wife again if she has been raped." It is not surprising that rape has the tendency to wreck or strain the victim's relationship with her husband, fiancé, or boyfriend. In fact, 75 to 85 percent of the marriages in which the wife has been raped end in divorce within two years following the sexual assault (Gordon and Riger, 1989).

Continuing to uncover these parallel assumptions, it is accepted that the more often an object has been used, the less valuable it is considered. Similarly, in a society where women are treated as sex objects, the more often a woman has engaged in sex with various men, the less valuable a property she is judged to be. A woman with very little value is referred to as a "cheap woman," "loose woman," "easy lay," "slut," or "whore." Thus, just as a man who steals or damages another's relatively worthless property can easily get away with it, so a man who ravages a relatively "cheap" woman—"common" property—can get away with it. This may be why it is difficult for a rapist to be convicted if his victim is known to have engaged in sexual relations with more than two men—and it is virtually impossible for the rapist to be convicted if his victim is a known prostitute. Also, since black or poor women are considered as less valuable sex objects than white or rich women, raping the former carries a lesser risk of conviction than raping the latter. Raping a woman who is simultaneously African American, poor, and sexually experienced is especially unlikely to result in conviction. This is why, in a case involving the rape of a young, poor, black woman, a juror argued for acquittal by saying that "a girl her age from 'that kind of neighborhood' probably wasn't a virgin anyway" (LaFree, Reskin, and Visher, 1985). In fact, many convicted rapists themselves do not feel guilty for having raped known prostitutes, "loose" women, "promiscuous" women, or women with an "illegitimate" child. The rapists apparently see these women as cheap ("available") sexual commodities that men are entitled to use (Scully and Marolla, 1984).

Lastly, the widespread availability of pornography, especially the type that shows violence against women, reinforces the popular image of women as men's sex objects. By degrading women in this way, pornography increases men's callousness toward women. As several studies have shown, extended exposure to pornography tends to cause men to trivialize rape. After viewing pornography for some time, the men in these studies advocated less severe punishment for rapists and expressed less sympathy for the victims (Segal, 1993; Linz, Donnerstein, and Penrod, 1984; Zillman and Bryant, 1982). Pornography apparently encourages rape by producing sexual callousness toward women. This does not mean that pornography by itself causes rape, as it does not have the same impact on all men. But it does make certain men dangerous to women. As research has demonstrated, pornography tends to incite violent, angry men to rape (Gray, 1982).

Since women are culturally defined as men's property, men may find it difficult to respect women as human beings. It is through a lack of respect for women that men are encouraged to rape women, as rape expresses the very essence of this lack of respect for women. Not surprisingly, as sociologists Diana Scully and Joseph Marolla (1985) found in their interviews with 114 convicted rapists, "the overwhelming majority of these rapists indicated they never thought they would go to prison for what they did. These men regard women as sexual objects that they are entitled to use for pleasure, or as one young rapist confided to Scully, "Rape is a man's right. If a woman doesn't want to give it, the man should take it. Women have no right to say no. Women are made to have sex. It's all they are good for. Some women would rather take a beating, but they always give in; it's what they are for" (Scully and Marolla, 1985).

Using Women in Men's Masculinity Contests

In a society that places a high premium on competition, men are pressured to engage in what may be called a masculinity contest to prove their male prowess and to earn a macho reputation among peers (Fields, 1993). To come out a winner, a man has to make out with the largest number of women possible.

> And that means sex under whatever conditions the particular man can stand. Whether in a whorehouse or the backseat of a Toyota, the object is to score. However, your score counts more if you don't pay for it in cold hard cash. The most respected player in the game is the one who best outwits the most females by coaxing, lying, maneuvering; the one who, with the least actual cost to himself, gets the most females to give him the most sex. (Medea and Thompson, 1974)

This masculinity contest is comparable to such competitive sports as football, baseball, soccer, and tennis. In any one of these sports, the players need an object—say, a ball—to grab, hit, kick, or smash. Their goal is to score, and they couldn't care less whether they hurt the ball. Similarly, in the masculinity contest, the male participants need an object—namely, a woman—to play with. They don't care whether they may end up humiliating, degrading, hurting, or terrifying her as a human being. Their goal is to score, as was well illustrated in 1993 by the Spur Posse, a gang of high school boys in the Los Angeles suburb of Lakewood. Members of this group competed with one another to score points for sexual conquests, one point for each sexual encounter, whether the girl consented or not. In such a masculinity contest, men see the woman as merely an object, often referring to her as a "piece of meat," a "piece of ass," a "box," or a "whore." A victim of a gang rape reported that she was indeed treated that way; after they had finished with her, one of the rapists said, "Let's dump this one and find another piece of meat" (Medea and Thompson, 1974).

Such a dehumanizing attitude toward women can further be found in the language that men use to refer to sexual intercourse as if it were a manly game of violence and conquest. American soldiers in Vietnam used to speak of dragging women into the woods for a little "boom boom," as if the penis—the rape weapon—sounded like a gun. To "bang" a woman—to have sex with her—also has the violent sound of a gun. Words, such as *whacking off, screwing, fucking, scoring, shooting off,* and *knocking up,* also give off the tough sound of conquest (Blakely, 1983). This dehumanizing language and attitude toward women may encourage men to play the masculinity game. Whether they will actually do so depends on at least two things: (1) the social pressure to play the game and (2) learning some basic pointers for playing it.

The social pressure often comes from friends who ask something like "Did you score?" "Had any lately?" "Does she put out?" If you answer no, they may say, "What's the matter? You ain't got no balls?" Such social pressure tends to make men, especially teenage males, afraid of showing any sign of "femininity"—being soft, gentle, and considerate. It also tends to make them want to show off their "masculine" qualities—being aggressive, forceful, and violent. A likely consequence is that these men will engage in sexual violence, of one degree or another, against women at some point. As research has shown, the most important factor that distinguishes sexually aggressive males from others is the peer pressure, which comes from sexually aggressive friends (Alder, 1985).

As to the pointers for playing the masculinity game, they come with the masculine role that men have been taught to play. This role requires that the man take the active part in achieving the social and then the sexual relations with a woman. He should be as aggressive as possible to carry out his sexual conquest. He need not concern himself with how much force he is allowed to use. Our culture puts that burden on the woman, who is held responsible for determining the limit of the force he is allowed. But even when the woman bluntly tells him to stop or puts up a fight to ward off his sexual advances, he may still ignore her resistance (Sanday, 1996a; Fillion, 1991). Men often get this lesson in sexual conquest from the stereotype of the television or movie hero who forcefully, persistently embraces and kisses the heroine despite her strong resistance and is finally rewarded by her melting in his arms. In real life such sexual aggression may lead to forcible rape.

The Myth That Women Ask for It

There is a popular myth that women have a secret wish to be raped. As shown by various studies, many people believe that women have an unconscious rape wish. This myth is expressed in various ways and often: "She asked for it," "She actually wanted it," "She lied about it," "She earlier consented to sex but later decided to 'cry rape'," "She was not really hurt," and "It was only a form of sex, though without her consent." Even sex researchers claim that between 31 and 57 percent of women have rape fantasies (Critelli and Bivona, 2008; Lonsway and Fitzgerald, 1994; Brinson, 1992). As a result, many people—particularly men with low income and little education—hold the victim responsible for the rape. They assume that the victim did something that provoked the man to rape her. That "something" involves being in the "wrong" place (going to a bar or walking alone at night), wearing the "wrong" clothes (short shorts, miniskirts, or some other sexy dress), or turning the man on (letting him kiss or pet her) (Nagel et al., 2005; Vachss, 1994; Brinson, 1992).

These blame-the-victim rationalizations reflect society's sexist attempt to "put women in their place," denying them the freedom that men enjoy. The rationalizations also stem from the popular assumption that rape is only sexually motivated. This explains why men tend to blame physically unattractive women more than attractive ones for rape. They find it difficult to believe that a man would try very hard to have sex with an unattractive woman if she keeps on resisting. They assume that, since it is less easy for unattractive women to attract men, they would be more inclined to encourage rapes by flirting, dressing sexily, or in some other way presenting a sexually provocative appearance. In short, men tend to consider unattractive women more likely to fantasize about rape and ask for it when a rapist appears (Vachss, 1994; Deitz et al., 1984; Thornton and Ryckman, 1983).

The myth about women wanting to be raped is understandably popular with rapists, which may help explain why they committed the crime in the first place. According to various studies, most convicted rapists, even those serving long prison terms, deny their culpability. Stubbornly, they insist that their victims have encouraged and enjoyed the experience, or that their victims have seduced them, meant yes while saying no to the sexual assault, and eventually relaxed and enjoyed the rape (Vachss, 1994; Scully and Marolla, 1985; Selkin, 1975). The willing-victim myth also prevails in the courtroom. While a man charged with rape is presumed innocent until proven guilty, the rape victim is often presumed guilty until proven innocent of provoking the rape. In the past, defense lawyers often argued to the court how impossible it is to rape a woman if she resists with statements such as "You can't thread a moving needle" or "You can't put a pencil through a moving doughnut." Today, most defense lawyers have abandoned such crude tactics to suggest that the victim "has asked for it." But they manage to convey the same message by emphasizing that she has willingly danced with him at a bar, accepted his invitation to go to his apartment, or asked him to wear a condom before the intercourse. These less blatant tactics often result in the acquittal of the accused rapist because many jurors are influenced by the same popular myth (Vachss, 1994; LaFree, Reskin, and Visher, 1985).

Because of the willing-victim myth, when a woman declines a man's sexual invitation, he is likely to keep on pressuring her: "What's the matter, are you frigid? Oh, come on, you know you really want to." If he eventually rapes her, he will assume that she has consented, even though she has strongly resisted all along (Sanday, 1996a; Vachss, 1994).

Socializing Girls to Be Victims

To make it easier for men to rape women, the rape culture teaches girls to play the stereotypically feminine role. In contrast to boys, who are taught to be "snips and snails and puppy dogs' tails," girls are taught to be "sugar and spice and everything nice." In other words, while boys learn to be tough and active, girls learn to be sweet and passive. Girls also learn from the movies and other mass media that women like macho men and expect such men to be rough with them. Slasher films and rock videos, in particular, teach young women to associate sex with violence. In learning all this as part of the feminine role, the girl acquires two tendencies that make her a potential victim of rape. One is to be "feminine"—passive, gentle, weak, childlike, and dependent on men. The other is to be submissive to aggressive or violent men.

To be feminine means that she is physically unaggressive and psychologically unprepared to defend herself in hand-to-hand combat. Thus, when she encounters her would-be rapist, especially one who is her acquaintance or date, she is unlikely to gouge his eyes, kick him in the groin or genitals, or otherwise blind, maim, or kill him. Being ladylike also involves being submissive to men. A "lady" does not shout, scream, scratch, hit, or otherwise make a scene when she is offended by a man. In public places such as buses, subways, elevators, and theaters, she is not supposed to react aggressively to sexual harassment. She is expected to find it too embarrassing to make a public scene in response to such "sex grabs" as the touching of her legs or behind by a molesting male (Weis and Borges, 1973). It is, therefore, not surprising that, as studies have suggested, traditionally passive or submissive women are the ideal victims for rapists. They are more likely than assertive women to be chosen as potential victims, and when they are approached by a potential rapist, they are also more likely to end up raped (Bart and O'Brien, 1985; Myers, Templer, and Brown, 1984).

A Global Perspective on Wartime Rape

Throughout history, when a conquering army destroyed or confiscated the conquered population's property, it also raped the women as if they were part of that property. During World War II, German soldiers raped massive numbers of Jewish and Russian women after occupying many villages and cities in Europe, and the Japanese army systematically raped women and girls as it invaded Korea, China, and various Southeast Asian countries. In 1971, when the Pakistani army marched into Bangladesh, soldiers were first shown pornographic movies and then let loose to rape at least 200,000 women. In 1992 Serbian soldiers in Bosnia raped thousands of Muslim women as part of an "ethnic cleansing" campaign. In 1994 the Hutus in Rwanda, who at that time dominated the country, raped immense numbers of minority Tutsi women. In 1999 when the Serbian forces took over Kosovo, they raped ethnic Albanian women. In 2004 pro-government Arab militias in Sudan used rape as a weapon of war to humiliate black African women in the region where rebels were fighting the government. All these rapes reflect the universally shared attitude that women are men's property, the same attitude in the U.S. culture that we have discussed (Lacey, 2004; Farwell, 2004).

Given that attitude it is not surprising that wartime rapes are especially dehumanizing and brutal. In Bosnia, for example, the victims were corralled like cattle in concentration camps where they were repeatedly raped, often in front of family members, neighbors, and other prisoners. The women were not only subjected to extreme humiliation; they were sexually tortured as well. As one victim says, "They would ask women if they had male relatives; I saw them ask this of one woman and they brought her 14-year-old son and forced him to rape her. If a man couldn't rape, he would use a bottle or a gun or he would urinate on me." Worse, many women were killed after being raped. Those who did survive became extremely traumatized from being raped by many men for many months. This is particularly true of traditional and conservative Muslim women who had never even been seen naked by their husbands (Carlson, 2006; Diken and Laustsen, 2005; McGirk, 2002).

After having been raped by foreign soldiers, women tend to be regarded as irreparably damaged property and therefore valueless. In some traditional countries, their husbands or other male relatives would throw them out of their homes as they would a piece of junk. Sometimes they would even kill the victims. In the minds of those men, though, their raped relatives have brought their family unbearable dishonor and shame.

While most victims of wartime rape are women, some are men. As investigations of the prisons in former Yugoslavia and the Abu Ghraib prison in Iraq indicate, the sexual assaults against male detainees included forced masturbation, anal rape, and beating or kicking of the genitals. They were carried out to humiliate the hated enemy or to serve as a "college fraternity prank" (Carlson, 2006).

Why Men Rape Women

Various researchers have tried to explain why some men are more likely than others to rape women or why some groups or societies have a higher incidence of forcible rape. Psychologists generally attribute rape to some psychological problem in the offender. Sociologists, on the other hand, see rapists as basically normal, psychologically no different from the average population. Various sociologists, however, explain rape differently: Some use a social-psychological theory to attribute rape to sexual permissiveness in society and others rely on a feminist theory to view rape as an expression of gender inequality. These three theories are positivist in nature, focusing on the causation of rape.

Psychological Theory: Sexual Inadequacy

Generally, psychologists, psychiatrists, and psychoanalysts agree that rapists suffer from some personality defects or emotional disturbance. "The majority of such offenders are not insane," write two psychologists, "nor are they simply healthy and aggressive young men 'sowing some wild oats.' The rapist is, in fact, a person who has serious psychological difficulties which handicap him in his relationships to other people and which he discharges, when he is under stress, through sexual [violence]" (Groth, 1983; Groth and Birnbaum, 1979). And a group of psychiatrists state, "It is true that classic neurotic symptoms are a rarity, but all types of neuroses, character disorders, and more severe borderline and psychotic states are represented in rapists. It is equally clear that there are some specific characteristics present in rapists which differentiate them from other criminals and from other sexual offenders" (Cohen et al., 1971). One psychologist sums up all this by saying, "What's wrong with a sex offender is what's between his ears, not his legs" (Gelman et al., 1994).

Disagreement abounds over what the specific psychological problem is. The problem that has been theorized to reside in rapists ranges from feelings of sexual inadequacy to fear of homosexual tendency to sexual addiction (Herman, 1995; Goldner, 1972). According to a typical psychological theory, the rapist is a man who, as the result of his unpleasant childhood experiences, has developed such a personality defect that he cannot relate successfully to women—a defect called "sexual inadequacy." This inadequacy drives the rapist to indulge in fantasy and then act out this fantasy by raping a woman. Here is how a rapist describes his fantasy:

> I had a complete fantasy life that involved my being stronger than all men, irresistible to all women, a doer of great things. . . . I had fantasies about the woman I was raping, how she felt physically, where she had been in life, some resentment that she's done things in life without me. I had a longing to do things in general with people. Sometimes I'd verbalize these fantasies if the woman was quite submissive, otherwise I'd just take the trip within myself. (Selkin, 1975)

But psychological theories such as this can explain only a few cases of rape. True, there are some rapists who, because of their psychological problems, cannot relate to women well. However, they make up only a small minority of rapists. In prisons, for example, the majority of rapists appear quite normal, no different from other convicts who have committed robbery, theft, or some other nonsexual crime. In an experimental study in which the subjects were asked to chat with a woman for as long as they wanted, the convicted rapists were just as skilled and relaxed as the nonrapists (Lussier, Proulx, and LeBlanc, 2005; Scully, 1990; Alder, 1984).

The psychological theory of sexual inadequacy is even less applicable to the countless rapists, especially acquaintance rapists, outside of prisons. Far from sexually inadequate, most of these rapists are highly skillful in dealing with women. In fact, as indicated by Eugene Kanin's (1985) study, the date rapists in college are far more heterosexually successful than other male students—they have had more dates and more consensual sexual experiences (see also Lalumiere et al., 2005; Rapaport and Posey, 1991).

Social Psychological Theory: Sexual Permissiveness

Sociologist Duncan Chappell and his colleagues (1971) ask why the rate of rape is higher in some societies than in others. The reason, they theorized, is that the society with a higher rape rate is, ironically, more sexually permissive—full of opportunities for men to have consensual nonmarital sex with women. Why would more men resort to force to get sex in a society where it is relatively easy to get sex without the use of force? The answer, according to the theorists, lies in the concept of relative frustration: When encountering the *same* experience of being rejected by a woman, the men in a sexually permissive society feel *more frustrated* than the men in a sexually restrictive society in which premarital and other nonmarital sex is prohibited. But why?

In a sexually restrictive society, a man is more able to take a woman's rejection in stride. This is because he can protect his ego by rationalizing that she has rejected him not because he is in some way undesirable but because the restrictive society prevents her from accepting his sexual invitation. He may take comfort from the fact that women are too sexually conservative, too afraid to engage in nonmarital sex, that their religion condemns such sex, or that laws against nonmarital sex are too stringent. In a sexually permissive society the rejected man cannot use this kind of rationalization. Instead, he is more likely to take the woman's rebuff personally, seeing that it is he himself who is responsible for his own failure to win the woman's favors. As a consequence, he is likely to feel hurt, thereby experiencing sexual frustration. This sexual frustration is said to drive many men in a permissive society such as the United States or Sweden to rape women (Geis and Geis, 1979; Chappell et al., 1971).

In short, the social atmosphere of sexual permissiveness produces a great number of rapes because it generates a great deal of relative frustration by causing men to take a woman's rejection personally. This theory may explain why modern societies such as the United States and Sweden have higher rates of rape today than a century ago or why modern societies have higher rates than traditional societies. It seems obvious that modern societies are more sexually permissive than traditional ones. Feminists, however, question the theory's assumption that rape is mostly sexually motivated. To feminists, rape is primarily motivated by the man's desire to dominate the woman because of gender inequality.

Feminist Theory: Gender Inequality

The social-psychological theory of sexual permissiveness seems to suggest that gender equality produces more rapes than does sexual inequality. This is because relative gender equality is more prevalent in the more sexually permissive societies such as Sweden and other industrialized Western societies than in the more sexually restrictive, traditional societies in the developing world. But feminist theorists blame rape on sexual inequality. To feminists, rape is primarily an expression of men's dominance over women, which in turn is a reflection of society's sexual inequality. Rape, then, serves to intimidate women, keeping them in their place to maintain sexual inequality (Edwards, 1993; Peterson, 1992; Schwendinger and Schwendinger, 1983; Brownmiller, 1975).

The evidence on rape as an expression of male dominance exists everywhere. All over the world, no matter which society we go to, we are bound to find that the overwhelming majority of rapes involve men raping women rather than women raping men. At the same time, men generally have greater physical, political, or economic power than women. We may therefore conclude that rape is largely an expression of male power over women. An abundance of more specific evidence also exists to support the feminist theory. In her study of tribal societies, for example, Peggy Sanday (1981) found that some of these societies are relatively free of rapes while others are full of rapes. She discovered that male dominance is a key feature of rape-prone societies, defined as societies in which rape is treated as a ceremonial expression of masculinity or in which men are allowed to use rape to punish or threaten women. Other researchers have further found that the incidence of rape is high in colleges where masculinity and male dominance are highly valued (Schwartz and DeKeseredy, 1997; Martin and Hummer, 1995).

Nevertheless, the feminist theory of gender inequality has drawn fire for exaggerating the influence of male dominance on rape. As the major inspiration of the theory, Susan Brownmiller (1975) has often been faulted for arguing that "from prehistoric times to the present, I believe, rape has played a critical function. It is nothing more or less than a conscious process of intimidation by which *all men* keep *all women* in a state of fear." But critics have observed that not all men would use rape to intimidate all women, and that it is easy to think of numerous men who do not want to dominate women by raping them, especially if the women are their mothers and daughters. Through her forceful statement, however, Brownmiller probably means to say that rape is a primary expression—rather than the sole expression—of male dominance.

Males as Victims

According to popular belief, men are simply "too big," "too strong," or "too much in control" to be sexually assaulted. But men can and do become victims of rape in prison as well as outside the prison.

Inside the Prison

The experience of a man being raped by another in the prison is relatively common. It is more prevalent than man-on-woman rape is outside the prison. About one in five inmates in U.S. prisons have been raped, compared with one in ten females in the larger society. Moreover, while the female rape victims typically get raped only once, the male victims are raped multiple times. Why so many more rapes in prison? The reasons include: (1) The general public has little or no sympathy for convicts. (2) The rapists go unpunished. (3) The "wolves" (rapists) are not segregated from the "punks" (the victims). And (4) rape is used as a prison-management tool to pacify violent inmates so that they will not turn against the staff (Hensley and Tewksbury, 2005; Lehrer, 2001; Cahill, 1985; Lockwood, 1985).

In an average state prison system, virtually every slightly built young man is approached for sex within one or two days after arrival. Many of these young men are repeatedly raped by gangs of inmates. Some of these victims commit suicide; others manage to escape gang rape by seeking protection from a more powerful inmate. However, they have to pay for that protection by serving as the protector's slaves, providing sexual services as well as keeping house for their "masters." Sometimes punks are forced into prostitution so that they can earn such goods as cigarettes for their keepers. Some new inmates are lured into a trap for forced sex. They are offered goodies such as cigarettes, drugs, or extra food stolen from the kitchen, and after a day or so the gift giver will demand sexual repayment. Sometimes the new inmate is lured into gambling, rolling up large debts, and then being told to "pay or fuck" (Lehrer, 2001; Knowles, 1999; Davis, 1982). This stratagem for forced sex is basically the same as that often used by male rapists on their prospective female victims in the larger society: offering a drink at a bar, a dose of sweet talk, an invitation into his apartment, and then forcibly demanding sex.

Male rapists and their male victims in prison are comparable to male rapists and their female victims in the larger society in several ways. The rapists within the prison, like the rapists without, are heterosexual. Moreover, the prison rapists are like the men who rape women outside the prison (and the male victims in prison are like the female victims outside) in that both types of rapists are generally older, heavier, taller, and more violent than their victims. However, compared with heterosexual rapes outside the prison, same-sex rapes in prison are much more likely to be interracial—blacks raping whites. Still, the two types of rape are similar in the sense that both involve members of the *dominant* group (the males outside the prison and the blacks inside) raping members of the *subordinate* group (the females outside and the whites inside).

Common sense may suggest that the rape in prison is intended to relieve one's sexual deprivation. But that is not the primary motive for prison rape. If an inmate simply wants to relieve his sexual deprivation, masturbation would be a much more convenient and normal method of relief than same-sex rape. Instead, the primary motive for same-sex rape is the need to subjugate and humiliate the victim, as evidenced by the fact that the prison rapists often use such language as "Fight or fuck," "We're going to take away your manhood," "You'll have to give up some face," and "We're gonna make a girl out of you." Of course, this does not mean that the rape serves only to express the need for dominance—if it did, the offenders should be content *only* to bully or beat up others. The rape, then, is also sexually motivated. But the drive for power appears to be a stronger motivation for the rape in prison (Lehrer, 2001; Knowles, 1999; Davis, 1982). The same is true of the majority of the men who rape other men in the larger society. As one such rapist says:

> I had the guy so frightened I could have made him do anything I wanted. I didn't have an erection. I wasn't interested in sex. I felt powerful, and hurting him excited me. Making him suck me was more to degrade him than for my physical satisfaction. (McMullen, 1990)

Outside the Prison

In the larger society, the risk of a man being raped by another man or by a woman is still far less than the risk of a woman being sexually assaulted by a man. According to a national survey, only 3.8 percent of men have ever suffered sexual assault compared to 22 percent of women (Elliott et al., 2004). Surveys on U.S. campuses reveal considerably more male victims: 12 to 48 percent of male college students are forced or pressured to have sex, more commonly known as nonconsensual sex. But virtually all of these sexual coercions are not legally and popularly considered rapes because they involve women using verbal pressure such as pleading, demands, or blackmail rather than physical force. In the fewer cases in which men rape men, however, most offenders do use physical force, with sodomy being the most common mode of assault (Gillespie, 1996; Struckman-Johnson, 1991). Male offenders are more likely than their female counterparts to use physical force, apparently because the men are generally stronger than the women. But another reason is that the men's victims are much more likely than the women's victims to be strangers, who tend to put up relatively strong resistance. On the other hand, female offenders are more likely to use verbal pressure because their victims are more likely to be their acquaintances.

Although male offenders are more likely than their female peers to be strangers to the victim, nearly half the male offenders know their victim as their peer, coworker, subordinate, or date. These acquaintance rapes include attacks by men meeting their victims at parties or bars, gang rapes in the Navy and other military settings, and seduction with pressure by trusted men, such as doctors, psychotherapists, priests, and teachers. Most victims are in their late teens or early twenties. More than half of the victims are heterosexual, so are more than half of the offenders. The rapist assaults his victim mostly with an intent to punish or dominate, rather than for sexual pleasure (Scarce, 1997; Struckman-Johnson, 1991).

Same-sex rape can be illustrated with a few actual cases of a man sexually assaulting another: (1) A heterosexual man became intoxicated at an office party. He let his boss drive him home. He passed out in the car, but he soon woke up to find himself in the backseat, with his pants down, being anally entered by the boss. (2) A college male student, who was gay, met an older man at a bar. He went to the older man's apartment, where he was sodomized despite his protests. (3) Three Navy men overpowered, beat, and dragged a shipmate to a secluded area of the ship to rape him, but the victim escaped. Three weeks later the same attackers overpowered the victim and then two of the assailants held him down while the third raped him anally. Victims of male rape such as in these examples are highly unlikely to report their victimization, however, largely because of the myths that "male rape is a gay crime" and "male rape doesn't happen" (Rumney, 2008; Tewksbury, 2007; Struckman-Johnson, 1991).

The male victim reacts in about the same way to same-sex rape as the female victim does to heterosexual rape. The reactions include shock, self-blame, shame, anger, and depression. These reactions are more distressing to men than women because men are expected to be strong, aggressive, and avoidant of sexual contact with other men. Given this male-role expectation, the male victim is also more likely to control his emotion by denying or minimizing the trauma of rape. Still, unlike the female victim, the male victim tends to feel a loss of masculinity. As one victim said, "Hell, I've got no manhood left. He's made me into a woman" (Walker, Archer, and Davies, 2005; Elliott et al., 2004; Pelka, 1995; Struckman-Johnson, 1991).

Can Women Rape Men?

Women can rape men because rape, as feminists emphasize, is basically an expression of power. As we have seen, male prison rapists are more powerful than their male victims. Similarly, the rapists in the larger society are more powerful than their female victims. Since men are typically in a position of power in relation to women, rapes characteristically involve men as the aggressors and women as the victims. But men are not always in the power position; neither are women always vulnerable. Therefore, to the extent that a woman can overpower a man in a sexual encounter, she is able to rape him.

If it is sociologically possible for a woman to rape a man, is it physiologically possible? To the general public, the answer may appear to be "no," because it is assumed that men cannot perform sexually if frightened or anxious. But medical doctors have observed that "all anxieties are not the same. Neither are all men the same. Some men can and do have erections while they are anxious" (Sarrel and Masters, 1982; Sarrel and Sarrel, 1981). Further, even if some men cannot engage in sexual intercourse under stress or duress, they still are vulnerable to rape because they can be forced to perform oral sex or other sex acts that are meant to humiliate them but fulfill their attackers' need for asserting power and dominance.

Therefore, it should not be surprising that there are actual cases of women using physical force to rape men, but such rapes are extremely rare. Presumably, if there is a trend for women to become increasingly powerful, there may well be more women raping men. The cases that have occurred so far usually involve a single victim and two or more offenders—an apparent attempt on the part of the women to compensate for their traditional lack of power. As John Macdonald (1995) reports:

A 37-year-old man was accosted late one evening by two women who forced him at gunpoint inside an abandoned building. They made him undress, tied his hands, manipulated him to erection and had intercourse with him a number of times. When he could no longer maintain an erection, they abused his genitals and rectum. When he fainted, they untied his hands and left him.

However, instead of using physical force as illustrated here, most female offenders resort to verbal persuasion and other nonviolent methods. Examples include an older woman seducing a teenage boy or younger man, a female babysitter sitting on a younger boy and forcing his penis into her vagina, and a female college student persistently "getting fresh" with her date until he gives in to intercourse (Gavey, 2005; Struckman-Johnson, 1991). We may argue, though, that the use of verbal persuasion alone does not legally constitute rape if the victim is no longer under the age of consent.

The use of physical force is a different matter. It is rape and may traumatize the male victim as much as it does the female victim. He is likely to feel a loss of masculinity and consequently suffer such sexual dysfunction as impotence, premature ejaculation, or loss of sexual desire. But since most female offenders do not resort to physical force, most male victims are far from being traumatized. Therefore, the most common effect is avoidance of aggressive women and pressured sex (Struckman-Johnson, 1991). As things stand now, even those male victims who are badly shaken by the more violent assault may not get much sympathy. "A former police officer in San Diego," report Philip Sarrel and Lorna Sarrel (1981), "told us that a few years ago a sailor came into his precinct house to report that he had been raped by a woman. The police in the station house thought he must be drunk, out of his mind, or simply weaving a good tale. They laughed him out the door."

Child Molestation

Child molestation can be considered a form of rape because the victims are too young and hence not legally capable of giving their consent.

Some Basic Facts

There are all kinds of studies giving vastly different estimates of how common child molestation is. It is impossible, therefore, to know with any certainty the true incidence of this sex offense. But we can have more confidence about the accuracy of these basic facts: (1) Girls are far more likely than boys to be molested. (2) The overwhelming majority of child molesters are men rather than women. (3) Molesters are more likely to be acquainted with, than to be strangers to, their victims. (4) The molester is usually unmarried; never or rarely dates; and lives alone or with his parents. (5) While only a few molesters have serious mental problems, most have a personality disorder characterized by "a relative lack of human attachments and social relations," as shown by their social incompetence or deficiency in social skills (Bolen, 2001; Macdonald, 1995; Lanning, 1992).

Another basic fact concerns the effects of child molestation on the victim. A review of 45 such studies has clearly demonstrated that molested children are more likely than other children to suffer from various problems. The problems include posttraumatic stress disorders (such as nightmares or nervousness), behavior problems (hyperactivity, immaturity, delinquency, or running away), sexualized behaviors (putting objects in vaginas or anuses, or excessive masturbation), and poor self-esteem (Bruni, 1997; Kendall-Tackett, Williams, and Finkelhor, 1993).

A Social Profile of Child Molesters

Compared with men who rape adult women, men who molest young girls have the following characteristics: (1) Molesters are much older; most are over 35 years of age, while most rapists are under 20. (2) Molesters are more likely than rapists to have been abused as children. (3) Molesters are more gentle and passive, while rapists are tougher and rougher. (4) Molesters are less likely to resort to physical force or vaginal penetration and more likely to restrict themselves to fondling the victim. (5) Molesters are much less capable than rapists of getting along with adult members of the opposite sex—less skilled, more nervous, and less assertive in interacting with women. (6) Most molesters commit the offense against the same child for a certain length of time, while rapists attack different victims. (7) Most molesters admit their guilt, while most rapists refuse to do so (Bolen, 2001; Lanning, 1992).

All this suggests that child molesters fail to meet the sexist cultural standard of "masculinity"—being dominant over women. This may explain why they are scorned and often raped by their tougher fellow inmates in prison. Their lack of masculinity may also explain why, unlike rapists who resort to rape to dominate women, child molesters feel inadequate with adult women but dominant over children. Moreover, while the culture of rape—which is related to the ideal of masculinity and male domination over females in society—encourages rapists to blame their victims, this same culture fails to have the same impact on molesters. This is why, unlike rapists, most molesters fully and frankly admit their guilt. Nonetheless, child molesters are at bottom similar to rapists: Both victimize a person who is less powerful than they are (Bolen, 2001; McCaghy, 1968).

Molesting Boys

Child molestation does not only involve men victimizing young girls. Men also molest young boys. There is some evidence that most of these molesters are not gay. Although they molest children of their own gender, they are usually married, have no sexual interest in other men, and do not identify themselves as gays. There are, of course, gay molesters, such as the pedophile priests who recently scandalized their church. But they are a minority. Whether gay or straight, however, the men who molest boys are not much different from those who victimize girls. They are by and large emotionally troubled. More specifically, they are lacking in human attachments, obsessed with their own fantasies, unable to feel empathy for others, and inclined to control and dominate less-powerful others. As for their victims, they are more likely than other boys to grow up to become child abusers themselves (Bolen, 2001; Finkelhor, 1984).

What about women who molest young boys? This type of molester is extremely rare. Perhaps because of their extreme rarity, they have not become a popular subject of scholarly investigation. It is also quite possible that, like the general public, researchers feel that if a woman molests a young boy she could hardly do any harm without a penis or, related to this attitude, that he should consider himself "lucky" (Mathis, 1972). In fact, this kind of sex can anger the boy so much that he may later as an adult take it out on other women by raping them. In an investigation of 83 rapists in a California prison, two researchers found that 59 percent of them had been molested as children by older women (Petrovich and Templer, 1984).

There is, however, a gender difference in the way victims deal with the anger caused by their victimization. Men who have been molested as boys by older women or men are likely to *act out* their smoldering anger from the sexual traumas by becoming rapists or child molesters themselves. In contrast, women who have been molested as children appear more likely to *internalize* their anger by becoming victims of additional abuse, such as rape victims, wife-abuse victims, drug addicts, or prostitutes (Finkelhor, 1984; Russell, 1984). This gender difference can be attributed to traditional sex-role socialization, which encourages boys to be aggressive and girls to be passive.

The Scandal of Pedophile Priests

Early in 2002, the media started reporting that a few Roman Catholic priests in the United States were found to have sexually molested children in their care. This trickle of cases turned into a flood several months later, with child-molesting priests reported in virtually every region of the country. For many years the church hierarchy had protected the child molesters by silencing the victims and their parents while transferring the molesters to other posts—and new potential victims. In one case, for example, Boston's Cardinal Bernard Law allegedly moved the Rev. John Geoghan in 1984 from one parish to another even after he was told that Geoghan had molested children. Geoghan was finally sentenced to nine to ten years in prison in 2002 for fondling a 10-year-old boy, but he had been accused of molesting more than 130 children over a period of thirty years. In 2005 another child-molesting priest, Paul Shanley, was given 12 to 15 years in prison (*USA Today,* 2005; Cannon and Sheler, 2002).

As a result, many people now wrongly conclude that the majority of priests are child molesters. The fact is that only a few priests are. Probably only about 4 or 5 percent of Catholic priests are pedophiles, most being emotionally troubled, socially incompetent, or sexually immature. The great majority of priests are normal and mature. The general public also believes the myth that the celibate, sexless life imposed by the Catholic Church on its priests frustrates them so much as to drive them into perversion and molestation. If this were true, the majority of priests would have become child molesters. Instead, the majority, both straight and gay, keep their vows of celibacy and lead happy, healthy, and productive lives serving their church and community (Greeley, 2004). What, then, could have caused the church to have child-molesting priests?

One reason, say some observers, is the absence of women and married men serving as priests. As has been observed, women rarely commit sexual abuse against children. It is also obvious that most women are more emotionally and sexually mature than the priests who molest children. So are most married men, when compared to child-molesting priests. Therefore, if numerous women and married men became priests, the scandal of child molestation might not have blown up in the church.

Another reason for the presence of deviant priests in the church, critics argue, is the declining number of priests and candidates for priesthood. The number of U.S. priests has dropped from 60,000 to 40,000 over the last four decades and an average of 1,200 priests have left the priesthood annually during the last three decades, mostly to marry (Berry, 2000). And because of the church's continuing refusal to ordain women and married men as well as its rejection of many increasingly popular American practices such as birth control, divorce, and remarriage, considerably fewer men are interested in joining the priesthood. Thus, the argument goes, the church hierarchy has become so desperate that it has lowered its recruitment standards. As a result, emotionally and sexually immature men who would later molest children were allowed into the priesthood.

And the third reason offered for the child-molestation scandal is the church leaders' failure to dismiss offending priests from their jobs. Such priests were often placed in new positions where they would have continued access to vulnerable children. The church leaders in effect aided and abetted child molestation (Broder, 2005). A major cause of such behavior is the culture of secrecy in which the church hierarchy operates. Specifically, church leaders are required to "keep in confidence anything that, if revealed, would cause a scandal or harm to the church" (McGeary, 2002). Church leaders were thus under pressure to refrain from firing a priest for child molestation; to do so, according to their calculation, would invite publicity for the scandalous act and thus hurt their church. In addition, there is the church's culture of forgiveness, which encourages protection of the offender as a sinner to be pardoned, rather than punishment of the offender as a criminal to be turned over to the police.

Summary

1. What are the major patterns of rape? Blacks are more likely than whites to commit rape. Rapes are mostly intraracial, though interracial rapes are more common today than before. Females between ages 16 and 20 are most vulnerable to rape. Most rapists plan their assault rather than act it out impulsively. Gang rape involves mostly young men pressuring each other to prove their masculinity by raping the same woman. More common than stranger rape, acquaintance rape is an extension of men's socially accepted aggressive sexual behavior. Campus rape is relatively prevalent because of the influence of the rape-prone culture. The myth of victim precipitation in effect blames the rape survivor for having asked to be raped.

2. What consequences does rape have for its survivors? Most survivors are beset with anxiety and guilt. A few, but increasingly more, survivors feel outraged and revengeful, and they have also stimulated the growth of organizations for helping rape survivors and other women fight sexual attack. There have been legal reforms to treat rape survivors better, but they are still made to feel that they have "asked for it."

3. What is the culture of rape? It is made up of the prevailing male attitudes toward women as well as the traditional ideas of appropriate sex roles. In such a culture, women are treated as if they were men's property; women are used as objects to enable men to prove their masculinity; women are believed to have a secret desire to be raped; and girls are taught to play the feminine, submissive role. All these jointly encourage men to rape. **What does the global perspective reveal about wartime rape?** The army that invades a country tends to rape its women, treating them as if they are the conquered country's property.

4. Why do men rape women? Psychological theory attributes rape to a psychological problem, such as the offender's feelings of sexual inadequacy. Social psychological theory traces the source of rape to a sexually permissive culture that intensifies the male's feeling of rejection by women and thus increases his sexual frustration. Feminist theory explains that since rape serves to preserve male dominance in a sexually unequal society, men are likely to assault women.

5. What is the nature of same-sex rape in prison? In many respects, male-against-male rape in prison is comparable to male-against-female rape in the larger society. It is basically a phenomenon of a more powerful person raping a smaller, weaker person; it is an expression of dominance more than sexual desire. **How can men be raped in the larger society?** Men can be raped by other men as well as pressured by women to engage in nonconsensual sex. Male offenders are more likely to be strangers to their victims while female offenders tend to be acquaintances. More than half of the male victims are heterosexual, so are half of the offenders. **Can women rape men?** Yes. To the extent that some men are weak and submissive and some

women are powerful and aggressive, women can rape men. But most such rapes involve verbal pressure rather than physical force.

6. What are some of the common characteristics of child molestation? Most victims are likely to be girls; most child molesters are men; molesters are more likely to be acquainted with, not strangers to, their victims; and molesters tend to lack social skills. **What is the social profile of child molesters?** Compared to rapists of women, child molesters are older, more likely to have been abused themselves, more gentle and passive, less likely to resort to physical force, less skilled in interacting with women, more likely to victimize the same child repeatedly, and more likely to admit their guilt. **What could have caused the scandal of child molestation in the U.S. Catholic Church?** Some suggested causes are: (1) the lack of women and married men as priests, (2) the declining numbers of priests and candidates for priesthood, which has lowered the recruitment standard and allowed child molesters to become priests, and (3) keeping rather than dismissing child-molesting priests.

FURTHER READING

Barstow, Anne Llewellyn (ed.). 2000. *War's Dirty Secret: Rape, Prostitution, and Other Crimes Against Women*. Cleveland, Ohio: Pilgrim Press. A collection of articles about how rape is used as a weapon of war.

Benedict, Jeffrey R. 1998. *Athletes and Acquaintance Rape*. Thousand Oaks, Calif.: Sage Publications. A detailed analysis of three court cases involving athletes charged with committing acquaintance rape, showing why such rape is relatively common in sports.

Bolen, Rebecca M. 2001. *Child Sexual Abuse: Its Scope and Our Failure*. New York: Kluwer Academic/Plenum Publishers. Discusses the history of child sexual abuse, the scope of the abuse, and professional responses to the problem.

Brownmiller, Susan. 1975. *Against Our Will: Men, Women, and Rape*. New York: Simon & Schuster. A hard-hitting classic on how men use rape to intimidate and keep women in their place.

Cahill, Ann J. 2001. *Rethinking Rape*. Ithaca, N.Y.: Cornell University Press. Analyzing the nature of rape from the feminist perspective.

Fairstein, Linda. 1993. *Sexual Violence: Our War Against Rape*. New York: William Morrow. An analysis of rape from the author's vantage point as chief of New York's Sex Crime Prosecution Unit for nearly 20 years.

Gavey, Nicola. 2005. *Just Sex? The Cultural Scaffolding of Rape*. London: Routledge. A feminist analysis of rape showing the interrelationships among gender, power, and sexuality.

Henry, Nicola, Tony Ward, and Matt Hirschberg. 2004. "A Multifactorial Model of Wartime Rape." *Aggression and Violent Behavior*, 9, 535–562. An analysis of how wartime rape has its roots in peacetime culture.

Jackson, Thomas L. (ed.). 1996. *Acquaintance Rape: Assessment, Treatment, and Prevention*. Sarasota, Fla.: Professional Resource Press. A collection of articles on various aspects of acquaintance rape, including its impact on victims, treatment of victims, and prevention of the sexual assault.

Madigan, Lee, and Nancy C. Gamble. 1991. *The Second Rape: Society's Continued Betrayal of the Victim.* New York: Lexington Books. A critical analysis of the various ways society makes the rape survivor's life worse.

Meloy, Michelle. 2006. *Sex Offenses and the Men Who Commit Them: An Assessment of Sex Offenders on Probation.* Boston: Northeastern University Press. A thoroughgoing analysis of both quantitative and qualitative data on sex offenders.

Reddington, Frances P., and Betsy Wright Kreisel (eds.). 2005. *Sexual Assault: The Victims, the Perpetrators, and the Criminal Justice System.* Durham, N.C.: Carolina Academic Press.

Russell, Diana E. H., and Rebecca M. Bolen. 2000. *The Epidemic of Rape and Child Sexual Abuse in the United States.* Thousand Oaks, Calif.: Sage Publications. An evaluation of the prevalence of rape and child molestation that concludes that the problem is very widespread.

Sanday, Peggy Reeves. 1996. *A Woman* Scorned*: Acquaintance Rape on Trial.* New York: Doubleday. Illustrates how the U.S. culture and legal system help make victims of acquaintance rape responsible for their own victimization.

Scarce, Michael. 1997. *Male on Male Rape: The Hidden Toll of Stigma and Shame.* New York: Insight Books. The first-ever book-length analysis of male rape outside of prison settings.

Schwartz, Martin D., and Walter S. DeKeseredy. 1997. *Sexual Assault on the College Campus: The Role of Male Peer Support.* Thousand Oaks, Calif.: Sage Publications. Provides a critical review of various theories and studies on campus rape, and shows how male peer groups encourage college men to engage in sexual aggression.

Scully, Diana. 1990. *Understanding Sexual Violence: A Study of Convicted Rapists.* Boston: Unwin Hyman. An insightful analysis of how rapists see themselves and their crime.

CRITICAL THINKING QUESTIONS

1. The culture of rape is all around us. What can you do to resist it?

2. Can the Catholic Church prevent more scandal about child molestation by its priests? If yes, why? If not, why not?

6   Family Violence

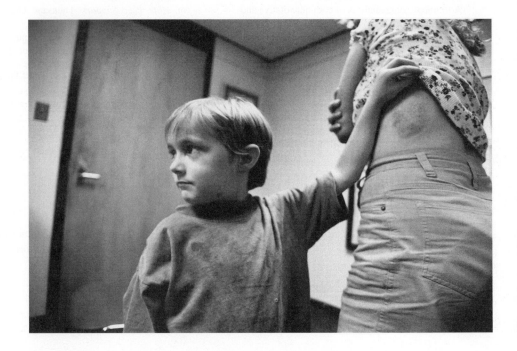

Myths and Realities

Myth: Violence can be found within the majority of blue-collar or poor families in the United States.

Reality: Violence is more likely to occur in blue-collar families than white-collar families, but this only means that the percentage of violent blue-collar families is higher than the percentage of violent white-collar families. As for the percentage of violent blue-collar families, it is far less than 50 percent, which means that only a minority of such families are violent (p. 114).

———

Myth: Violence and love are so completely opposite that they cannot exist together in marriage and family.

Reality: Parents often resort to violence as a way of punishing their misbehaving children, whom they love dearly. Violent spouses often express love for their victim, along with apology or remorse for their bad behavior (p. 114).

Myth: The abuse of alcohol is the cause of family violence.

Reality: Heavy drinking does play a role in family violence as suggested by the fact that husbands who drink heavily are nearly three times more likely than their nondrinking peers to beat their wives. But heavy drinking is not the real cause of wife abuse. The real cause is personal or financial problems (p. 115).

Myth: Thanks to the function of marriage as a haven for love, marital rape—the raping of a woman by her husband—is relatively rare, at least less common than the raping of a woman by a stranger or acquaintance.

Reality: Marital rape is the most prevalent form of forced sex, more common than stranger or acquaintance rape (p. 116).

Myth: Like the rapes against strangers, acquaintances, and others, most of the rapes perpetrated by men against their wives involve vaginal penetration.

Reality: The majority of marital rapes do not involve vaginal penetration. They involve instead forced anal intercourse and other extremely degrading sexual coercions (p. 117).

Myth: Most women who have been abused by their husbands continue to put up with the abuse and continue to live with their husbands. Apparently, the women love their husbands too much and so can forgive them.

Reality: The overwhelming majority of abused wives do leave their husbands. They do so to seek help or refuge from police, social workers, mental health agencies, shelters, parents, or friends (p. 119).

Myth: Most of the children who have been abused by their parents grow up to become abusive parents themselves.

Reality: The majority (about 70 percent) of child-abuse victims do not grow up to abuse their own children (p. 122).

Myth: There is no need to worry about spanking and slapping a misbehaving child because it is relatively harmless; besides, you don't want to spare the rod and spoil the child.

Reality: There is a tendency for physical punishment to escalate into child abuse. Research has shown that parents who approve of physical punishment are four times more likely to abuse their children than are parents who disapprove of this physical discipline (p. 122).

Myth: Adult children are more likely than anybody else to abuse their elderly parents.

Reality: Elderly people themselves are more likely to abuse their spouses than to be abused by their adult children (p. 125).

Myth: Since most of the states in the United States have passed laws against marital rape, men are now more likely than not to be arrested for raping their wives.

Reality: The laws against marital rape are rarely enforced, and too many people still refuse to treat marital rape as real rape, often saying something about the victim, such as "She has had sex with him a thousand times before. What is one more time?" (p. 129).

Marlon Gill, age 23, was driving with his girlfriend Melinda Abell, 24, on a highway in Missouri. In a jealous rage, he yelled at her, demanding to see the call history of her cell phone. When she resisted, he drove to a parking lot. There he used his hands to force open her mouth and jammed her cell phone down her throat. Doctors later had to perform a tracheotomy to save her life. Gill was charged with first-degree assault, for which he could be sent to prison for at least 10 years. This was not the first time he was accused of battering his girlfriend. He had earlier been convicted of misdemeanor battery against her. This time, though, the bizarre case has triggered some gallows humor, causing the prosecutor to say, "I'm disturbed by some of the levity I've heard surrounding this case. What we're talking about here is a severe case of domestic violence, and it's time we started taking this issue more seriously" (Johnson, 2006).

Indeed, family violence is no laughing matter. It is serious and also relatively common. Every day thousands of women, like Melinda Abell, in the United States, along with many children and older persons (mostly over age 75), are targets of family violence. In fact, Americans are so much more likely to be attacked by family members than strangers that two researchers on the subject have called the family the "most violent institution, with the two exceptions of the police and the military" (Gelles and Straus, 1988). In this chapter we will examine some popular myths about family violence, then analyze various forms of family violence and the effects of the violence on the victims, construct a social profile of family abusers, see how family violence differs in poor and affluent societies, understand the theories of family violence, and look at social responses to the problem.

Myths about Family Violence

Because family violence involves the most cherished and intimate social institution in our lives, we may find it difficult to see the discomforting subject with neutrality or objectivity. We may think, for example, that violence happens only in poor, disorganized, and dysfunctional families, not in middle-class or richer homes. Let's take a closer look at this myth and others that have been discussed in a text on family violence (Barnett, Miller-Perrin, and Perrin, 2005).

Myth 1: Family Violence Hits the Poor Only

A great deal of evidence does indicate higher rates of family violence among lower-income people. According to one survey, for example, there is five times as much marital violence in families at or below the poverty level as in families above the poverty level. This means merely that poor people are *more likely* to experience family violence; it does *not* necessarily mean that *most, let alone all,* poor families are violent. In fact, most studies suggest that only a minority of poor families are violent. Take a careful look at this typical finding: 13.4 percent of blue-collar husbands were violent in the past year, compared with 10.4 percent of white-collar husbands (Kantor and Straus, 1990). Findings such as this are often reported to mean that blue-collar husbands are more likely than their white-collar counterparts to be violent, but only a *minority* (13.4 percent) of blue-collar husbands are violent.

Myth 2: Violence and Love Cannot Happen Together

Many people assume that violence and love are so totally opposite they cannot exist together in marriage and the family. But parents do often resort to violence as a way of disciplining their children, whom they love dearly. While married persons may not inflict violence on their spouses in the name of love, couples with one partner battering another do stay together for about the same length of time (six years) as the average marriage lasts (Walker, 1990; Browne, 1987). This is because violent spouses often express love for their victim, along with apologies or remorse for their bad behavior, and most victims do not leave immediately every time their violent spouses become abusive. All this, of course, does not imply that violence is good for marriage, as most battered wives do eventually leave their husbands. It only means that violence does occur in many love relationships.

Myth 3: Most Abused Children Grow Up to Be Abusive Parents

Having been abused as a child is associated with being a child abuser. As research has consistently shown, parents who abuse their child are more likely than nonabusive parents to have been victims of child abuse themselves, but this does not mean that abused children will necessarily become abusive parents. In fact, as will be discussed later, the majority of child-abuse victims do *not* grow up to abuse their children (Kaufman and Zigler, 1993; Widom, 1989; Gelles, 1985).

Myth 4: Alcohol and Drugs Are Involved in Most Family Violence

It is true that users of alcohol and drugs are more likely than nonusers to get involved in family violence. As one study (Kantor and Straus, 1990) shows, for example, the proportion of male binge drinkers who abuse their wives (19.2 percent) is nearly three times higher than that of nondrinkers (6.8 percent). This finding can be taken to mean that heavy drinking plays a role in, but is not the real cause of, family violence. After all, only a minority (19.2 percent) of men who engage in binge drinking beat their wives—the large majority do not. Moreover, even among many of those who drink or use drugs and then hit their spouses, the real reason for spouse abuse is not the psychoactive substance but some personal or financial problems. For men with such problems, alcohol and drugs are often used as an excuse for abusing wives, because, as suggested in Chapter 12, the substance by itself cannot diminish the user's moral competence.

The Extent of Family Violence

There are many different forms of family violence, ranging from fights among siblings to killings of parents by children. Here we will focus on the types that have so far interested sociologists the most: marital rape, wife beating, child abuse, and elder abuse.

The extent of family violence varies from one research report to another. Researchers who define the problem broadly would report a very high incidence of family violence, while those who define it more narrowly would find a lower incidence. For example, if child abuse is broadly defined to include spanking, slapping, cursing, or threatening to send a child away as a traditional way of disciplining a misbehaving child, at least 85 percent of all U.S. parents are found to be child abusers. But if the abuse is defined more narrowly to comprise only such physical violence as punching, hitting, kicking, or throwing the child down, then the proportion of child abusers drops sharply to 5 percent (Lewin, 1995).

If we settle for the more narrow definition of family violence as relatively severe physical or sexual violence—severe enough to cause injury—we will find from various surveys the following percentages of Americans who fall victim to family violence (Martin et al., 2007; Matthews, 2004; Lewin, 1995; Russell, 1990; Pillemer and Finkelhor, 1988).

- Marital rape: 8 to 14 percent of wives since marriage
- Wife beating: 3 percent of wives every year
- Child abuse: 6 percent of children every year
- Elder abuse: 2 percent of older people every year

It should be noted that these figures are only the minimum, most conservative estimates of the prevalence of family violence.

The real extent of serious family violence may well be *much higher* than suggested by these percentages because people are generally reluctant to reveal their family problems to researchers. Moreover, even though these percentages appear relatively small, the numbers of women, children, and older people suffering from severe family violence run to millions. Six percent of child-abuse victims, for example, means that more than 4.5 *million* children are sexually or physically abused every year. We should also remember that family violence is considerably more common if many forms of abuse short of severe physical violence are taken into account, such as slapping, verbal abuse, or child neglect. In addition, if financial exploitation is included in the definition of elder abuse, a much greater percentage of older people are victims. Considering all this, we may say that family violence is a common, serious social problem.

Marital Rape

In early 1994 the well-publicized case of Lorena Bobbitt, who cut off her husband's penis after he raped her and then went to sleep, made many people aware of marital violence. But still unknown to the general public, marital rape—the raping of a woman by her husband—is probably the most prevalent form of forced sex, more common than stranger or acquaintance rape. Of the representative sample of women in San Francisco studied by Diana Russell (1990), 8 percent have been raped by their husbands, as opposed to 3 percent by strangers and 5 percent by acquaintances. By focusing on married women rather than all women, Russell and other researchers have found that 10 to 14 percent of wives have suffered marital rape.

The Nature of Marital Rape

Most of the rapes in marriage involve physical violence or the threat of it. A typical example is reported by a victim as follows: "He wanted to make love with me, and I didn't want to. He got mad and tried to force me to take off my panties. He actually did it himself, so I fought back. I pushed him away, but he was stronger than me, so he forced me down, spread my legs, and forced penetration." Some of these rapes result in serious injury to the victim; as one woman said, "He'd hold me so hard I'd have black and blue marks on my throat. And he gave me black eyes too. . . . One time I was so full of blood, the neighbor called the police." Marital rapes also include those accomplished with threats of physical harm ("He said if I didn't do what he wanted he'd choke me."), with coercive, nonphysical threats ("He said, 'You have sex now or I'll get sex elsewhere. I'll leave you.'"), and by forcing sex on the victim when she is asleep, extremely drunk, or helpless from drugs (Russell, 1990).

Contrary to what you may assume, the majority of marital rapes do not involve vaginal penetration. Vaginal rapes account for less than half of marital rapes, while forced anal intercourse occurs slightly more often. Other forms of extremely degrading rapes in marriage include inserting objects into the wife's private parts, coercing her to have sex in front of children, or forcing sex on her right after she is discharged from a hospital—usually after giving birth (Barnett, Miller-Perrin, and Perrin, 2005).

Most offenders assume that they are entitled to have sex with their wives whether the spouses want to or not. But marital rape is as traumatic to the victim as stranger rape, striking tremendous fear into the raped wife. As one victim said, "It was as though he wanted to annihilate me. More than the slapping, or the kicks . . . as though he wanted to tear me apart from the inside out and simply leave nothing there" (Browne, 1987). After the assault, victims who are employed or able to be economically independent tend to get a divorce, while those who are not employed tend to stay married. Those who stay married, however, usually avoid sex or develop a negative attitude toward sex (Barnett, Miller-Perrin, and Perrin, 2005; Bergen, 1996).

Causes of Marital Rape

Marital rape can be attributed to at least three causes (Bergen, 1996). One is the sexist belief that husbands are *entitled* to have sex in any way they want with their wives. This belief is part of the popular patriarchal myth that wives cannot be raped because they are considered as "belonging" to their husbands—that is, as their husbands' property (Ferro et al., 2008). Not surprisingly, although all the states have finally made marital rape a crime, it is still rare for a man to be charged with raping his wife.

A second cause of marital rape could be the husband's attempt to *punish* the wife for what he considers her unfaithfulness or some other "sin." Here is how a victim describes why her husband raped her:

> A lot of times it [rape] happened because he was so jealous. He always thought that I was looking at other men. Like the time my brother and his friend—who I grew up with—were over, and he thought I was looking at his friend, and he was really mad. He started hitting me and then forced me to have sex. (Bergen, 1996)

A third cause of marital rape is the husband's attempt to use rape as a form of *control* over the wife. As one victim reports on what happened to her:

> The more control he thought he was losing, the worse it got. If I got a job or I was doing good, he would take it away. He would beat me up and force me [to have sex] just to get that control back. (Bergen, 1996)

These three causes of rape are an integral part of the patriarchal society that encourages men to dominate women, with marital rape the essence of male dominance over women. Presumably, the more strongly a husband believes in patriarchy, the more likely he is to rape his wife as an entitlement to sex, a punishment for her "sin," or a control over her. Due to the paucity of research on the subject, though, it is difficult to explain adequately why, under the same patriarchal, rape-inducing culture, some men are more likely than others to accept patriarchy in the first place.

The same culture that justifies marital rape also tends to lead the victim to blame herself. Here is an example of self-blame as expressed by one victim: "I'm not the most sexual person in the world and there was some unwanted sex. When I tried to say no, he would make me say yes. I'm really a very tight person. I don't send out signals about sex. I was not sexually communicative" (Russell, 1990).

Wife Beating

It has been estimated that about one-third of all U.S. married persons assault their spouses every year, and that two-thirds do so at least once during their marriage. The researchers who came up with these estimates have found that wives are as likely as, if not more likely than, husbands to be the offenders (Straus, Gelles, and Steinmetz, 1980). The problem is that these researchers lumped together violent and nonviolent acts as if they were the same. They defined all acts of slapping, for example, as violence, ignoring the fact that some slaps, particularly those often carried out by women, are not violent at all, while other kinds of slaps, especially those more likely to be perpetrated by men, are violent. Consequently, a wife playfully slapping her husband on the hand to chastise him for trying to steal her dessert was regarded as a violent act, no different from a husband angrily slapping his wife on the face and knocking out several teeth (Loseke and Kurz, 2005; Holtzworth-Munroe, 2005; Dobash et al., 1992). To avoid trivializing the problem, we will focus here on really violent acts, namely, acts serious enough to cause injury, which are much more likely to happen to wives at the hands of their husbands. Some women do seriously hurt their husbands, but they make up only a small minority of all spouse batterers (Durose et al., 2005; Busch and Rosenberg, 2004; Gelles and Straus, 1987).

The Nature of Wife Beating

Of the people who are involved in spouse abuse, husbands are overwhelmingly more likely to severely assault their wives than the other way around. As Martin Schwartz (1987) has found in an analysis of several national surveys on crime victimization, 1,641 women said they had been assaulted by their husbands, while only 102 men claimed to have been assaulted by their wives. The latest survey has also shown that the overwhelming majority of spouse abuse involve women being victimized by their husbands (Durose et al., 2005). While the percentage of wives being beaten by husbands every year is very small (3 percent), the number reaches more than 2 million, a figure large enough for wife beating to be considered a serious social problem (Browne, 1993; Gelles and Straus, 1987).

In committing the offense, abusive husbands usually act as if they had the license to batter their wives. This is why, after they commit the violence, they usually do not show genuine remorse by fully admitting guilt. Instead, they often attempt to neutralize or rationalize their violent act in one of three ways (Barnett, Miller-Perrin, and Perrin, 2005; Dutton, 1986):

- Blaming the victim for provoking the offense ("She kept yelling at me; she didn't want to shut up after I told her to.")
- Minimizing the harm done to the victim ("I didn't really hurt her; I just gave her a little slap.")
- Attributing the violence to some problem beyond their control ("I drank a little too much; I had a bad day in the office.")

The effects of wife beating on the victim go beyond physical injury. Generally, the victim tends to develop what psychiatrists call "posttraumatic stress disorders," similar to the disorder that some U.S. soldiers have developed from their combat experiences in Vietnam or Iraq. The syndrome consists of feelings of depression, anxiety, and helplessness. Here is an illustration of posttraumatic syndrome suffered by a typical wife-beating victim named Ginger:

> Ginger closed herself off from friends and family. She lost interest in her life and avoided any situation that could "put her in jeopardy." In fact, Ginger appeared more depressed and anxious than many of the patients in the psychiatric unit of the hospital. (LaViolette and Barnett, 2000)

Some victims with this disorder develop *battered woman syndrome,* a specific deadly pattern of losing self-esteem, feeling trapped, expecting constantly the terror of violence, but eventually striking back by killing their abusive husbands (LaViolette and Barnett, 2000).

Why Don't Some Battered Wives Leave?

It has been widely assumed that most victims of wife beating continue to put up with the abuse and continue to live with their husbands. On the contrary, however, the overwhelming majority of abused women *do* leave the abusive relationship (DeKeseredy and Schwartz, 1996). They leave their homes to seek help or refuge from police, social workers, mental health agencies, shelters, parents, or friends. The victims, though, continue to show some symptoms of the posttraumatic syndrome while finding themselves at some risk of being stalked and killed by the abusive husbands (Gelles, 1995; Gibbs, 1993b; Wilson and Daly, 1992).

Nevertheless, why do some women continue to live with their abusive husbands? One reason is that they are for the most part *the most socially and economically isolated* of all women as a result of having too little education and not being gainfully employed. The lack of education and employment, coupled with the isolation, forces them to be economically dependent on their abusive husbands as well as discourages them from seeking help from others outside their home. Another reason for remaining in an abusive relationship is the victims' *fear that their husbands will retaliate* if they leave. By staying, however, these women are also more likely to end up getting killed by their husbands or being forced into a corner where they struggle desperately to survive by killing their husbands (Matthews, 2004; Mann, 1996; Goetting, 1995; Wilson and Daly, 1992).

Causes of Wife Beating

According to feminist theorists, a major cause of wife beating is *the sexist, patriarchal nature of society,* which treats women as if they were their husbands' property. This kind of patriarchy can be seen, for example, in the fact that in many states an aggravated assault against a stranger is a felony but assaulting one's own wife is a misdemeanor, for which the husband is rarely arrested, much less jailed (Gibbs, 1993b). There is evidence to suggest the impact of patriarchy on wife beating. For example, husbands who hold patriarchal beliefs are more likely to assault their wives than those who do not, and wife beating is generally more prevalent in patriarchal societies than in those with greater gender equality (Boy and Kulczycki, 2008; Brown, 1992; Smith, 1990; Levinson, 1988).

Obviously, however, patriarchy is not the only cause of wife beating. If it were, every husband would become a wife beater. In fact, only about 30 percent of U.S. husbands have ever physically abused their spouse in the entire course of their marriage (Dutton, 1994). In other words, patriarchy influences some husbands more than others, encouraging some more than others to abuse their spouses. But what kinds of husbands are more vulnerable to the influence of patriarchy? Possibly, it is those who have *lost control of their lives* to poverty, unemployment, drug abuse, and alcoholism. Deprived of the sense of power over their lives, those men are understandably more receptive to the patriarchal idea that men may dominate and control their wives. And since they do not have money and other precious resources that rich men can use to control their wives, poor men are compelled to resort to violence as a way of controlling their wives. This may explain why research has often shown poor or unemployed men to be more likely than other men to beat their wives, especially the employed ones, whose work represents a threat to their husbands' power and control (Brush, 2003; Cazenave and Straus, 1990).

Child Abuse

Of the different forms of family violence, child abuse seems to be the most serious or shocks people the most. Yet it is not confined to "sick" families; it is quite prevalent, victimizing millions of children every year. Not surprisingly, child abuse has been called a national emergency (Barnett, Miller-Perrin, and Perrin, 2005). There are two broad types of child abuse, one sexual and the other physical.

The Nature of Child Abuse

Some children suffer sexual abuse at the hands of family members, mostly their fathers and stepfathers. Such abuse is popularly called incest. According to one study, anywhere from 10 to 20 percent of women have been victimized this way during their childhood and adolescence, while 1 to 3 percent of men have had the same experience. These figures appear quite large in part because they include what has happened both in childhood and in adolescence, a long span of 17 years. According to another survey, which focuses on what has happened within the past 12 months only, about 2 percent of all children are sexually abused every year (Meiselman, 1990).

Researchers have found a few significant facts about this kind of deviance: Most cases of incest involve fathers as offenders and daughters as victims. Stepfathers are much more likely than biological fathers to commit incest. Incestuous fathers are more likely than average fathers to be isolated from others outside their home. There is, however, no significant difference in incest rates among social classes and racial or ethnic groups—various classes and groups have about the same rate. Incest usually gives rise to a strong sense of shame and guilt as well as anxiety, depression, and isolation among the young victims. When they become adults, the victims are more likely than other people to be dissatisfied with sexual relationships and to encounter marital problems (Johnson, 2004; May, 1991; Finkelhor et al., 1989).

Nevertheless, the majority of child abuses in the family involve the parents *physically* abusing their children. The entire gamut of this kind of child abuse exists, ranging from assaults on the child that cause minor bruises to severe battering that results in death. About three million children, or 4 percent of all children age 17 or younger, are severely assaulted every year (Lewin, 1995). An enormous increase in child abuse has often been reported in various media over the last 20 years. Much of the reported increase, however, is a result of the 1974 federal law, the Child Abuse Prevention and Treatment Act. Until that year, it was seldom that anyone came to the aid of child-abuse victims because the crime was rarely reported and routinely covered up.

The 1974 law requires professionals, such as health-care providers, law-enforcement officials, teachers, and school administrators, to report suspected child abuse to the appropriate child protection agency. Failure to report may subject such professionals to fines, or even prison sentences. To avoid violating the law, many have tended to report child abuse as more common than it is. The same federal law has encouraged child protection agencies to overreport because the more people they report as child abusers, the more money they receive from the government. Thus they have developed a foolproof technique for "proving" child abuse: It involves routinely defining suspects as "noncredible" witnesses, accepting their testimony as true only when they agree with the allegations, and routinely seeing victims as "credible" witnesses, rejecting their testimony only when they say suspects are innocent (Margolin, 1992). In reality, according to one survey, very severe violence toward children has declined, thanks to increased publicity about child abuse and prevention programs for child abuse (Gelles, 1995).

Nonetheless, the number of children being severely physically abused (three million a year) remains disturbingly large. More disturbing is the real 48 percent *increase* of children killed by parents since the mid-1980s, with at least 1,200 such deaths occurring in 1994, the year when a young mother in South Carolina, Susan Smith, shocked the nation by drowning her two children, one 3 years old and the other 14 months old (Barnett, Miller-Perrin, and Perrin, 2005).

Sociologists have discovered a few significant facts about child abuse: Very young children, under age 5, are at higher risk than older ones for being physically abused, principally because they are more dependent and powerless. Child abuse occurs more frequently in lower-income families than in higher-income ones. Child abusers are more likely than nonabusers to have some emotional, behavioral, familial, or interpersonal difficulties. Examples of these difficulties include depression and low self-esteem, being quick to anger and to lose self-control, and marital problems and isolation from relatives and friends (Barnett, Miller-Perrin, and Perrin, 2005).

In addition to suffering physical injury, children who have been abused are more likely than their nonabused peers to experience many social and psychological problems. These problems include emotional and social difficulties, learning disabilities and poor academic performance, and running away from home, as well as delinquency, criminality, and violent behavior. When they become adults, they are more likely than others to abuse drugs and alcohol, engage in criminal activities, suffer from psychiatric disturbances, and become child abusers themselves (Goode, 1999; Gelles, 1995).

Causes of Child Abuse

Sociologists have discovered a number of causal factors in child abuse. One is the *intergenerational transmission of violence*: Parents are likely to abuse their children if they have learned in childhood that it is all right to use violence in dealing with child-rearing problems. This learning may come from *the experience of being abused as children*. Indeed, research has shown that child-abusing parents are more likely than nonabusing parents to have been abused themselves as children. More specifically, about 30 percent of child abusers have been abused themselves, while only 3 or 4 percent of nonabusers had the same experience in the past. But this should not be taken to mean that receiving early abuse inevitably leads to later abuse-giving because, contrary to popular belief, the *majority* (about 70 percent) of child-abuse victims do *not* grow up to become abusers (Rein, 2001; Peterson, 2000; Kaufman and Zigler, 1993). A history of the abuser being abused is only one of the causal influences on child abuse, and not its only cause. The other learned influence—the legitimacy of using violence to deal with problems—also comes from *having observed as children how parents and other significant adults use violence* to express anger, to react to stress, or to deal with marital problems. This explains why researchers often find that child abusers are more likely than nonabusers to have been raised in homes with a great deal of marital conflict and violence (Barnett, Miller-Perrin, and Perrin, 2005).

Another contributing factor to child abuse is the *acceptance of the popular view that physical punishment is a proper way of disciplining children*. Nearly half of all U.S. parents resort to physical punishment in an attempt to correct a child's misbehavior. But there is a tendency for physical punishment (say, spanking or slapping) to spill over into child abuse (punching or kicking). As a researcher has found, parents who approve of physical punishment are four times more likely to abuse their children than are parents who disapprove of such physical discipline. Because of the social acceptance of physical punishment, child abusers tend to see their abusive behavior as good and proper. This can be illustrated by the case of a father who had severely beaten his two boys, one 5 years old and the other only 18 months old. In the hospital where the boys were brought in for treatment of multiple bruises, lacerations, and fractures, the father said to the examining physicians, "Children have to be taught respect for authority and be taught obedience. I would rather have my children grow up afraid of me and respecting me than loving me and spoiled" (Berger, 2004; Lewin, 1995; Straus, 1991).

Other social factors that have been found to contribute to child abuse include *poverty, unemployment, family problems, and lack of education*. Poverty, unemployment, and family problems are likely to cause considerable stress for parents, and stress, as research has shown, is a major factor in child abuse. Moreover, the parents, given their lack of education, will find themselves less able to cope with the enormous stress that weighs on them, and as a result, they are likely to explode by assaulting people in their immediate environment, including their children. The stress that triggers violence against children can be defused if social and emotional support is available from friends and relatives. But child abusers are more likely than nonabusers to be socially isolated and without a telephone in the house (Barnett, Miller-Perrin, and Perrin, 2005; Berger, 2004).

Finally, *problematic interaction between parent and child* has been found to increase the risk for child abuse. Interaction becomes problematic if parent, child, or both have problems that make child care demanding, difficult, or stressful. Parent problems include lack of parenting skills, lack of knowledge about normal childhood behavior, unrealistic expectations for the child, or punitive parenting. Child problems comprise antisocial behavior, aggressive behavior, or mental and physical disabilities. Parents with problems when interacting with children with problems can feel so frustrated and angry that they become violent and abusive toward the helpless youngsters (Barnett, Miller-Perrin, and Perrin, 2005; Denham, Renwick, and Holt, 1991; Anderson, Lytton, and Romney, 1986).

Female Genital Mutilation

Euphemistically called "female circumcision," female genital mutilation involves cutting off some of the female genitalia such as the clitoris, its foreskin, or the labia. It takes place mostly in Africa, where it has been practiced as part of some African cultures for hundreds of years. The genital mutilation is usually performed on girls aged 4 to 14. Most of the performers are "ritual leaders," well-respected elderly women in the community who are specially designated for the task (Hassanin et al., 2008; Gruenbaum, 2001; Toubia and Izett, 1998).

The mutilation has recently generated a firestorm of outrage in the West. It has been called the worst human rights violation against the female gender. The Western media has portrayed it as extremely cruel as it is carried out without anesthetics. Most Western social scientists have observed how the victims suffer from numerous health problems. Some are physical, such as death, hemorrhage, infection, and severe pain. Some are psychological, such as anxiety, depression, low self-esteem, and recurring memories of the mutilation. Some problems are sexual, with the women unable to experience sexual pleasure and orgasm, or their husbands choosing to have sex with other, "uncircumcised" women. A few social scientists, however, contend that only a small minority suffer any of those problems (*Nation's Health,* 2008; Barstow, 2004; Gruenbaum, 2001).

Female genital mutilation has been blamed on *patriarchy* with the argument that in societies where the mutilation is a common practice, men dominate women in virtually all aspects of social life. The mutilation is seen as men's attempt to discourage women from having extramarital sex so as to turn them into obedient and subservient wives. But numerous patriarchal societies do not practice female genital mutilation. Patriarchy may be a cause of the practice, but not the only cause. There are other, more specific reasons why the practice takes place only in some patriarchal societies in Africa (Ahmadu, 2000).

First is the *cultural belief* that genital mutilation makes women more desirable. In the societies that practice the mutilation, the clitoris and the labia are seen as masculine and unsightly on a woman. They should, therefore, be removed, so that the genitalia will look highly feminine and aesthetically pleasing. Female genital mutilation is thus similar to the use of cosmetic surgery to reshape noses, enlarge breasts, or shrink bellies to make women look more desirable in Western societies.

A second reason for the mutilation is the high social value of *virginity* and *marriageability*. If a woman is not circumcised, men would suspect that she is not a virgin and would not think of marrying her. This is because female circumcision is taken as proof of virginity, which in turn makes the woman marriageable.

A third reason is the reward of *social and psychological benefits*. The ritual of female circumcision helps the woman become respected among her peers as well as the entire community of women. Further, the experience of bravely going under the knife in the presence of other women enables the participant to feel strong and powerful. Making all this possible is the social support from the community. Once the circumcision is over, a party is given in honor of the participant, and many friends, neighbors, and others will come to offer congratulations.

Elder Abuse

The majority of older people are capable of taking care of themselves, but a significant minority have difficulty doing so. Today, about 25 percent of elders require long-term care. A few live in nursing homes, but the vast majority live at home, often cared for by their spouses or other relatives (Dobrzynski, 1996; Kart, 1990). Some of these older dependents suffer abuse at the hands of their caretakers.

The Nature of Elder Abuse

Elder abuse often appears in the form of neglect, emotional abuse, financial exploitation, or physical abuse. The perpetrators are frequently adult children. Elder people are thus more likely to be abused if they live with adult children than if they live alone. This is probably because the full-time care administered to live-in elders is more stressful to the caregiver than the part-time care rendered to live-alone elders. Since older men are more likely than older women to live with relatives, older men are more vulnerable to abuse. Older persons are also more likely to suffer abuses if they are socially isolated, with relatively few contacts with friends and relatives other than the caregiver. Without the support of friends and relatives, elders are more liable to become sitting ducks for abuse by the overstressed caregiver. Research has so far found no class difference in rates of elder abuse: Middle-class elders are just as likely as their lower-class peers to be abused (Matthews, 2004; Paveza et al., 1992; Bachman and Pillemer, 1991).

In physically abusing elders, caregivers often feel stressed out from doing what they consider an unpleasant job. But when it comes to financial exploitation as a form of elder abuse, it has little to do with stress and more to do with greed. Yet it is not the unscrupulous financial adviser, scam artist, or morally bankrupt professional caregiver who is most likely to cheat the elderly. It is instead the victim's own family. Examples include a daughter using her power of attorney over her mother's bank accounts to withdraw her life savings; a son caring for his father paying for substandard care to preserve assets he expects to inherit; and a nephew coercing his elderly aunt to designate him as the beneficiary of her life insurance policy. Most well known is the case of the wealthy philanthropist Brooke Astor, whose son, who was supposed to be her legal caretaker, not only neglected his mother's care but also enriched himself with millions from her $45 million fortune (Black, 2008).

Abused elders generally suffer from a variety of psychological problems, especially depression and sleep disorders. They are also likely to be withdrawn, shrinking from contact with younger adults like those who have abused them (Wallace, 1996). But not enough research has been done to provide more detailed data on the consequences of elder abuse.

Causes of Elder Abuse

Helping elders is for the most part a highly stressful job. It is particularly hard on the female members of the *sandwiched generation,* the middle-aged group squeezed between raising children of their own and taking care of their parents. For many of these women, the trap between child care and elder care prevents them from working outside the home. Having been on the "mommy track" with the expectation of eventually returning to their careers, they now find themselves on an even longer "daughter track," taking care of older parents with chronic and disabling conditions.

Given the enormous stress from elder care, we may expect, as research has shown, that caregiving daughters are more likely than their noncaregiving peers to abuse parents (Hinrichsen, Hernandez, and Pollack, 1992). We should emphasize, though, that the majority of stressed caregivers do not abuse their elders. Elder abusers are distinguishable for having *severe personal problems,* including alcoholism, drug addiction, unemployment, antisocial behavior, arrest records, or emotional instability. In addition, abusers are generally *beset with money problems or financially dependent* on their victims, which may explain why elder abuse differs from child abuse in that elder abuse often involves financial exploitation and rarely takes the form of physical abuse.

In general, we may conclude that stress from the burden of caregiving tends to trigger elder abuse, and this is usually related to the fact that the abuser has personal and financial problems (Barnett, Miller-Perrin, and Perrin, 2005; J. Shapiro, 1996). Some studies show that elder abusers are more likely to be sons or other male relatives than daughters or other female relatives, but other studies suggest the reverse. Regardless of whether the abusers are male or female relatives, they usually have personal and financial problems (Barnett, Miller-Perrin, and Perrin, 2005; J. Shapiro, 1996).

Ironically, though, a famous study of a random sample of people in the Boston area indicates that older persons themselves are more likely to abuse their spouses than to be abused by their children (Pillemer and Finkelhor, 1988). In other words, most elder abuses turn out to be *spouse* abuses. Again, most of these older abusers are financially dependent on the victim or suffer from some physical or emotional disabilities that prevent them from properly caring for their spouses. But older people are much less likely than younger people to abuse their spouses (Desmarais and Reeves, 2007; Krummel, 2001; Suitor, Pillemer, and Straus, 1990).

As for most of the caregiving daughters, who are free of personal and financial problems but overburdened with the stress of taking care of their parents, why are they not likely to abuse their elders? A major reason may be that women have been socialized to feel close to their parents and to take family responsibilities more seriously than men. As caregivers they may "see their efforts as a chance to repay the time and care their parents gave them—a chance to say, again, *I love you,* before it's too late" (Beck, 1990). More generally, women are more likely than men "to respond to the interdependencies of lives by altering their own situations to fit the needs of others" (Moen, Robison, and Dempster-McClain, 1995).

In short, elder abuse arises from problems that plague caregivers: stress, severe personal problems, and financial difficulty and dependence. An additional explanation suggested by social exchange theory, which has empirical support, is that the cost of caregiving exceeds the benefit the caregiver expects to receive. As Ola Barnett and her colleagues (2005) observe:

> Taking care of an elder can be very time consuming and unpleasant and offers few benefits to the caregiver. Imagine the frustration of a wife who spends several hours cooking a birthday meal for her husband who is suffering from a severe memory impairment and decides that it is not his birthday, so he will not eat any dinner at all.

But the frustration of this caregiver should not be exaggerated, because she does receive some benefits from her caregiving role that make the frustration bearable. To understand this, we should know that the social exchange between the giver and the recipient of elder care differs from an economic exchange. The benefits in economic exchange are material in nature—only money, as we say—but the benefits that providers of elder care often receive are emotional or even spiritual in nature, such as the feeling of satisfaction from being able to repay the material and emotional support received in the past. Another benefit is the caregivers' expectation of receiving aid in the future when they become old and dependent themselves. Such benefits are made possible by societal norms of reciprocity in families (Horwitz, Reinhard, and Howell-White, 1996).

A Social Profile of Family Abusers

Research has produced enough data to suggest what the average abusers in the U.S. family are like. They are more likely than nonabusers to have the following characteristics (Rein, 2001; Peterson, 2000; Suitor, Pillemer, and Straus, 1990).

Age.   Young husbands and parents, particularly those under age 30, are more likely than older ones to assault wives and abuse children. This may reflect the greater tendency among young men to commit violence in general.

Class. Family violence cuts across all income levels, but it occurs more often among lower-income people. It also takes place more frequently among individuals without a college education. This may be because, compared to those in higher social classes, lower-class people have less ability, resources, or opportunities to demonstrate personal power outside the home. But in their own homes, they find themselves in a position of dominance as husbands over their wives or as mothers over their children. Thus lower-class men are more likely to abuse their wives and lower-class women their children.

Gender. At home, men are more likely than women to inflict serious injury on their victim, but women are as likely as, or more likely than, men to abuse their spouse without seriously harming the victim. As for the physical abuse of children, women are more likely than men to be the offenders. An obvious reason is that mothers have greater responsibility for child care and spend more time with children and thus have more opportunity to be abusive. Understandably, in families where men have more responsibility for child care, they are more likely to be abusive.

Stressful Life. People with a more stressful home life are more likely to commit family violence. A stressful life includes having financial problems, being pregnant, being a teenage mother, being a single parent, and having sexual difficulties.

Social Isolation. To reduce stress and thus the likelihood of family violence, most people are able to call for help from relatives other than those at home or from neighbors, friends, and other members of the community. But those who are likely to get involved in family violence tend to be socially isolated.

A Global Perspective on Family Violence

Family violence is a worldwide phenomenon, taking place in every society. The nature of the violence is basically the same in all countries. It involves physical, emotional, or sexual abuse. The most common acts of physical abuse include pushing, shaking, slapping, hitting with a thrown object, and twisting the arm. In most cases of emotional abuse, the victim is publicly humiliated, constantly scolded, or being put down in one way or another. Sexual abuse typically involves forcing the spouse or some other family member to have sex. While such acts of family violence are universal, they seem to occur more frequently in developing countries than in the United States and other developed countries. In many poor countries most victims still cannot get help from the police, shelters, and other public agencies or facilities. But such help is much more accessible to victims in the United States and other affluent societies, thanks largely to the feminist movement that has, over the last 30 years, striven to end violence against women. Not surprisingly, the rate of family violence in affluent societies is now much lower than before (Durose et al., 2005; Kishor and Johnson, 2004; Summers and Hoffman, 2002).

Since the 1990s many poor countries, including formerly communist regimes, have started to protect women against violence by men, but the tradition of patriarchy—male dominance—continues to exert its powerful influence. In Romania, for example, many victims of family violence dare not report the violence to authorities because they believe that they as women deserve to be beaten every now and then. In Russia, when a battered woman called the police for help, she was told, "You're still alive. When we get a corpse, then we'll investigate." In countries such as South Africa and Uganda, the custom of paying a dowry to the bride further reinforces the traditional belief that the husband owns his wife as a piece of property. With such patriarchal attitudes toward women, it shouldn't be surprising that family violence is very prevalent in those countries (Stickley et al., 2008; Gosselin, 2005).

Patriarchy is still alive in affluent societies such as the United States, but it is much less influential than in poorer countries, due in large part to the feminists' three-decades-long push for gender equality. This has apparently made family violence less common in the United States. The demand for gender equality, however, may have brought about an unintended consequence: American women seem more likely than their counterparts in third world countries to abuse their husbands. But much of this so-called husband abuse is carried out in self-defense or retaliation against an abusive husband in a male-dominated family. Husband abuse represents, in effect, a resistance to patriarchy. It is therefore more likely to occur in a society such as the United States, where women expect greater gender equality than women in the third world. Third world women are more submissive to patriarchy so they are less likely to fight back against their abusive husbands (Straus, 2005; Loseke and Kurz, 2005; Saunders, 2002).

Theories of Family Violence

We have discussed the causes of each of the five specific types of family violence individually, as if they totally differ from each other. But, with the exception of female genital mutilation, the four different forms of family violence in the United States do have something in common. The experience of stress, for example, can be found in the perpetrator of family violence whether the violence is marital rape, wife beating, child abuse, or elder abuse. It is this commonality among various types of family violence that has led some sociologists and other social scientists to develop positivist theories that can simultaneously explain different forms of family violence. Here we will discuss only a few theories (Kurst-Swanger and Petcosky, 2003; Gosselin, 2000; Gelles, 1998; Kemp, 1998).

Social Learning Theory

According to this theory, people are likely to engage in family violence if they have been exposed to violence. They may have experienced violence as offenders or victims or known about others committing violence in their social environment. From these experiences, the individual learns that violence is the appropriate way to deal with interpersonal problems. Given this kind of learning, when a man is arguing with his wife, when a woman is having difficulty stopping her child from misbehaving, or when a financially strapped person is having a hard time caring for an elderly relative, they all tend to commit violence against the other person in the family.

Stress Theory

All of us experience stress every now and then unless we are pushing up daisies. But some people suffer greater stress than others, and they are more likely to turn violent. Still, given the same stress, some people are more likely than others to commit violence. Whether stress leads to violence in the family partly depends on whether the individual has adequate personal resources (such as money, intelligence, and fortitude) or social support from relatives, friends, and others. Those who lack the resources and social support are more likely than others to buckle under stress and turn violent against a family member.

Exchange Theory

This theory is based on the principle of benefit and cost, akin to the law of reward and punishment. According to this theory, if the benefit or reward for committing family violence is greater than the cost or punishment for it, people will likely commit the violence. Thus, violence occurs in many families because the reward for it, such as the enjoyment of power and control over the victim, outweighs the risk of getting arrested. Law enforcers are generally not particularly enthusiastic about making arrests because of the private nature of the family.

Social Responses to Family Violence

U.S. society is caught in a bind in its battle against family violence. On the one hand, violence by strangers against women, children, and elders is widely condemned as a serious crime for which the offender is often severely punished. On the other hand, the same violence by a family member is more likely to be treated leniently or even ignored because of the traditional belief in the sacredness and privacy of the family. It is thus very difficult to protect vulnerable women, children, and elders against family violence with fully satisfying results (Gelles, 1995).

Protecting Women

Today all the states have passed laws against marital rape, but these laws are rarely enforced. Too many people still refuse to treat marital rape as "real" rape. It is often said of the victim: "She has had sex with him a thousand times before. What is one more time?" Some apparently find it hard to tell the difference between consensual sex and forced sex in marriage (Barnett, Miller-Perrin, and Perrin, 2005). As a result, very few victims succeed in having their offending husbands convicted and sent to prison. Victims can, nonetheless, get help from advocacy groups such as the National Clearinghouse on Marital and Date Rape. Since victims of marital rape are also often beaten by their husbands, some victims can find protection as battered women.

A battering victim can call the police and have the husband or boyfriend taken away. Since the late 1980s, most states have required or encouraged the arrest of husbands for wife assault. Thus many offenders today are arrested. Another solution to the problem is for the battered woman to obtain a civil order of protection, which empowers the police to evict the offender from the house—and to arrest him only if he returns. This kind of police intervention effectively deters most abusive husbands, but it can backfire in cases in which the offender is unemployed, alcoholic, or has other deep-seated problems. These offenders usually become more violent toward their victims (Gelles, 1995; Zorza and Woods, 1994).

Another way for battered women to seek protection is to go to a shelter or safe house. There they can receive not only physical protection and social support but many important services such as counseling, legal aid, or even occupational counseling. Occupational counseling is ultimately the most useful assistance because it helps the victim obtain employment. Holding down a job, she can free herself from her abusive husband by ending her social isolation and her economic dependence on him (Barnett, Miller-Perrin, and Perrin, 2005; Gelles, 1995).

Finally, the criminal justice system helps to protect women by requiring their abusers to participate in some counseling programs. Generally, as confirmed by research, abusive husbands who have completed a counseling program are significantly more likely to stop beating their wives when compared with those who have not received any counseling. Unfortunately, only a minority of wife beaters are court-mandated to complete the program. Most who are arrested are not prosecuted or convicted, and thus they are not required to seek counseling. Some batterers voluntarily seek counseling, but most drop out before completing the program (Barnett, Miller-Perrin, and Perrin, 2005; Mills, 2003; Gelles, 1995).

Protecting Children

Since the mid-1970s every state has passed laws requiring teachers, health-care providers, and other professionals to report child abuse to a government agency called Child Protective Services. When the protective service agents determine after investigating the report that a child has indeed been abused, they are empowered to do one of two things: (1) to provide the family with social support, such as counseling, day care services, and food stamps, or (2), if the parents are dangerous, to remove the child from the parents and place the child in a foster home, in the care of relatives, or in a residential treatment center. The majority (about 75 percent) of identified children are placed in foster care (Gelles, 1995; George, Wulczyn, and Funshel, 1994).

Neither solution is ideal. There is risk in providing the family with social support while leaving the child with the abusive parent. The child may continue to be abused, even to the point of being killed. In fact, some children are killed *after* abuse of the child has been reported to Child Protective Services. This is because the agency is usually so understaffed and overworked that some reports of child abuse are left uninvestigated or open pending further action. There are also risks in removing the child from the abusive parents. For one, children may not fully comprehend why they are taken away from their parents; they may think that they are being punished for having done something wrong. A second problem is that since mistreated children require special care because of the physical and emotional damage done to them, it may be too heavy a burden for foster parents to care properly for them, so that their condition may become worse. Child advocacy groups have often criticized protective service agencies for failing to adequately protect abused children either in the home or out of it. Still, most analyses conclude that the children would have been in even worse shape without Child Protective Services (Barnett, Miller-Perrin, and Perrin, 2005; Gelles, 1995).

Sometimes, though, protective service agents can become so zealous in their mission that innocent parents are hauled into court or jailed. The most notorious case involved the Child Protective Services in East Wenatchee, Washington. This agency used "intense recovered-memory therapy" to encourage suspected child victims to confirm having been sexually abused by their parents or other adults. In 1994 and 1995 more than 80 adults in the small town were charged with child sexual abuse. Of the 80 accused, more than 20 were convicted and sent to prison. Of those in prison, most are poor and functionally illiterate. No one who could afford to hire a lawyer and fight the charges has gone to jail (Carlson, 1995; Nathan, 1995). But such a blatant abuse of recovered-memory therapy to accuse innocent parents of child abuse seems relatively rare.

Protecting Elders

There are no formal government protective services agencies for vulnerable elders as there are for children, but all states have some type of elder protection program. In addition, most states have mandatory elder reporting laws similar to the reporting laws for children. According to critics, however, such laws demean elders by treating them like children. This criticism has some validity, as many older individuals (at least one-fourth) refuse intervention or services from outsiders after they have been abused by their relatives (Mixson, 1995; Fredriksen, 1989). Nonetheless, the laws require most health and mental health professionals and law-enforcement officers to report elder abuse to social service departments.

Social service departments provide a wide spectrum of services to abused elders, including homemaker assistance, legal services, medical care, counseling, meals and income assistance, housing or relocation assistance, and guardianship among many other forms of assistance. Two types of service seem most useful to abused elders (Barnett, Miller-Perrin, and Perrin, 2005):

- Medical services: providing doctors, nurses, physical therapists, and community health nurses (who visit patients' homes).
- Legal services: obtaining restraining orders to remove abusers, providing guardianship of elders and their estates, safeguarding elders' Social Security and other incomes, and protecting elders against involuntary commitment.

Summary

1. What myths are there about family violence? There are myths that family violence hits the poor only, that violence and love cannot happen together, that most abused children grow up to be abusive parents, and that alcohol and drugs are involved in most family violence.

2. How common is family violence in U.S. society? The extent of family violence depends partly on the definition of the problem. If family violence is defined as severe enough to cause injury, the percentages of Americans victimized are as follows: 8 to 14 percent of wives raped by husbands since marriage, 3 percent of wives beaten by husbands annually, 6 percent of children sexually or physically abused every year, and 2 percent of elders abused every year.

3. What is the nature of marital rape? Most of the rapes in marriage involve physical violence or the threat of it and include, aside from anal and vaginal rapes, extremely degrading sex acts. Most offenders feel entitled to have sex with their wives regardless of the latter's wishes. But, like stranger rapes, rapes by husbands have a traumatic effect on the victims. **What causes marital rape?** Such rape can be attributed to: (1) the belief in entitlement to sex, (2) the use of rape as punishment, and (3) the use of rape as control.

4. What is the nature of wife beating? Husbands are more likely to severely assault their wives than vice versa. Abusive husbands act as if they had the license to batter their wives, hence are unlikely to show genuine remorse afterward. Wife beating causes not just physical injury but posttraumatic stress disorders or, more specifically, battered woman syndrome. **Do most battered wives leave their husbands?** Yes, most do leave. But some remain because of social and economic dependence on the husband as well as fear of retaliation from the husband for leaving. **What causes wife beating?** Causes of wife beating can be traced to the sexist, patriarchal nature of society and to the abusers losing control of their lives to poverty, drug abuse, and the like.

5. What is the nature of child sexual abuse in the family? Child sexual abuse in the family, also called incest, mostly involves fathers as offenders and daughters as victims. Stepfathers are more likely than natural fathers to commit incest. Offenders are more likely than nonoffenders to be socially isolated outside the family. Incest usually causes victims to suffer many problems, especially a strong sense of shame and guilt, anxiety and depression, and social isolation. **What is the nature of child physical abuse?** In the family, physical abuse of children is far more common than sexual abuse. A wide gamut of child physical abuse exists, ranging from abuse that causes minor injury to abuse that causes death. Very young children are more likely than older ones to be abused; child abuse occurs more often in lower-income families; abusers have more problems than nonabusers; and victims suffer, in addition to physical injury, many social and psychological problems.

6. What causes child abuse? Factors that have been found associated with child abuse include intergenerational transmission of violence; acceptance of the popular view of physical punishment as proper for disciplining children; poverty and other problems that cause considerable stress for parents; and problematic interaction between parent and child.

7. Why do some African societies practice female genital mutilation? The reasons include the general condition of patriarchy combined with specific factors including (1) the perception of the clitoris as masculine and hence unsightly on a woman, (2) female circumcision being regarded as proof of highly valued virginity and marriageability, and (3) the ritual of circumcision providing the participant with social and psychological benefits such as social respectability and feeling strong.

8. What is the nature of elder abuse? Elder abuse is more likely to happen to older persons who live with relatives, are male, and are socially isolated outside the family. Elder abuse tends to cause psychological and social problems for the victim. **What causes elder abuse?** Causes of elder abuse include such caregiver problems as stress, severe personal problems, financial difficulty and dependence, as well as the cost of caregiving being greater than the benefit.

9. What is the social profile of family abusers? Compared with nonabusers, abusers are more likely to be under age 30, to be lower-class, to be men in the case of spouse abuse and women in the case of child physical abuse, to have a stressful home life, and to be socially isolated.

10. What can a global perspective tell us about family violence? The nature of violence is basically the same; it involves inflicting some physical, emotional, or sexual abuse on a family member. But the problem seems more prevalent in poor than in affluent societies, because the traditional influence of patriarchy is stronger in poor countries. The greater demand for gender equality in affluent societies, however, may have produced more husband abuses than in poor countries, where women are more submissive to their abusive husbands and thus less likely to retaliate against them.

11. What are the theories of family violence? One is social learning theory, which attributes family violence to learning violence from personal experience or the social environment. Another is stress theory, which blames family violence on the lack of personal resources and social support in dealing with a stressful life. There is exchange theory, which explains family violence as a result of the offender getting more reward than punishment for abusing a family member.

12. How are vulnerable women protected against sexual and physical abuse? All states have laws against marital rape, but the laws are rarely enforced. Victims of marital rape, however, can find protection as physically abused wives do in several ways: calling the police to have the husband taken away, going to a shelter or safe house, and expecting the court to require the abusive husband to get counseling. **How are children protected?** Mandatory reporting laws require professionals to report child abuse to government agencies, which can either provide the family with social support or remove the abused child from the dangerous home and place the child in foster care. **How are elders protected?** Most states have mandatory reporting laws for elders like those for children. Government departments of social services provide victims with a wide range of services, such as medical and legal services.

FURTHER READING

Arriaga, Ximena B., and Stuart Oskamp (eds.). 1999. *Violence in Intimate Relationships*. Thousand Oaks, Calif.: Sage Publications. A collection of articles about the characteristics, correlates, and consequences of family violence.

Barnett, Ola W., Cindy L. Miller-Perrin, and Robin D. Perrin. 2005. *Family Violence Across the Lifespan: An Introduction,* 2d ed. Thousand Oaks, Calif.: Sage Publications. A wide-ranging review of numerous studies on abuses against children, spouses, and elders.

Bergen, Raquel Kennedy. 1996. *Wife Rape: Understanding the Response of Survivors and Service Providers*. Thousand Oaks, Calif.: Sage Publications. Covers all aspects of wife rape, including the nature of the offense, the survivor's reactions, and services for survivors.

Berry, Dawn Bradley. 1998. *The Domestic Violence Sourcebook*. Los Angeles, Calif.: Lowell House. Discusses family violence from the historical, psychological, sociological, and legal perspectives, and concludes with ideas on how to reduce and prevent the problem.

Buzawa, Eve S., and Carl G. Buzawa. 2003. *Domestic Violence: The Criminal Justice Response,* 3d ed. Thousand Oaks, Calif.: Sage Publications. A review of various law-enforcement approaches, such as mandatory arrest and protective orders, for dealing with the problem of family violence.

Doak, Melissa J. 2007. *Child Abuse and Domestic Violence*. Detroit, Mich.: Thomson Gale. A condensed book presenting various aspects of family violence such as the causes and effects of child abuse and domestic violence.

Hammer, Rhonda. 2002. *Antifeminism and Family Terrorism: A Critical Feminist Perspective*. Lanham, Md.: Rowman & Littlefield. A feminist scholar's view of family violence and critique of conventional ideas about the problem.

Jackson, Nicky Ali, and Giselé Casanova Oates (eds.). 1998. *Violence in Intimate Relationships: Examining Sociological and Psychological Issues*. Boston: Butterworth-Heinemann. A collection of articles about various forms of family violence including child abuse, wife abuse, husband battering, homosexual domestic violence, and elder abuse.

Kirkwood, Catherine. 1993. *Leaving Abusive Partners: From the Scars of Survival to the Wisdom for Change*. Newbury Park, Calif.: Sage Publications. An analysis of how victims of marital abuse learn to overcome their dependence on their abusive partners.

Kurst-Swanger, Karel, and Jacqueline L. Petcosky. 2003. *Violence in the Home: Multidisciplinary Perspectives*. New York: Oxford University Press. Discusses various forms of family violence including child maltreatment, spouse abuse, and elder mistreatment as well as strategies for solving and preventing the problems.

LaViolette, Alyce D., and Ola W. Barnet. 2000. *It Could Happen to Anyone: Why Battered Women Stay,* 2d ed. Thousand Oaks, Calif.: Sage Publications. A critical analysis of various theoretical, empirical, and policy issues on why some battered wives do not leave their abusive husbands.

Loseke, Donileen R., Richard J. Gelles, and Mary M. Cavanaugh (eds.). 2005. *Current Controversies on Family Violence,* 2d ed. Thousand Oaks, Calif.: Sage Publications. A collection of conflicting views on some aspects of family violence such as whether women's violence toward men is a serious social problem, whether spanking is necessary and effective, or whether alcohol and drugs cause violence.

Malley-Morrison, Kathleen, and Denise A. Hines. 2004. *Family Violence in a Cultural Perspective: Defining, Understanding, and Combating Abuse*. Thousand Oaks, Calif.: Sage Publications. An analysis of family violence in four ethnic communities in the United States: Native American, African American, Hispanic/Latino American, and Asian American.

Mignon, Sylvia I., Calvin J. Larson, and William M. Holmes. 2002. *Family Abuse: Consequences, Theories, and Responses*. Boston: Allyn and Bacon. A wide-ranging analysis of family abuse, including various forms of physical, sexual, and psychological abuses that take place within the family.

Mills, Linda G. 2008. *Violent Partners: A Breakthrough Plan for Ending the Cycle of Abuse*. New York: Basic Books. Instead of using the legal system or focusing on the abuser alone, the author finds it more useful to treat the couple and even the whole family in order to end the abuse.

Nguyen, Tuyen D. (ed.). 2005. *Domestic Violence in Asian American Communities*. Lanham, Md.: Lexington Books. Offers insights into the nature of family violence from the cultural perspectives of Cambodian, Chinese, Korean, Japanese, and other Asian communities in the United States.

Pryor, Douglas W. 1996. *Unspeakable Acts: Why Men Sexually Abuse Children*. New York: New York University Press. Analyzing the views of men who sexually abuse their sons, daughters, stepdaughters, nieces, and nephews in order to find the reasons for the abuse.

Summers, Randal W., and Allan M. Hoffman (eds.). 2002. *Domestic Violence: A Global View*. Westport, Conn.: Greenwood Press. A collection of 13 articles with each discussing the problem of family violence in a given country ranging from South Africa, Australia, Germany, Russia, and Canada to Jamaica, Japan, Thailand, and the United States.

Wallace, Harvey. 1996. *Family Violence: Legal, Medical, and Social Perspectives*. Boston: Allyn and Bacon. Discusses many forms of family violence, including sibling abuse and gay/lesbian abuse, along with related issues such as stalking and victims' rights.

Websdale, Neil. 1999. *Understanding Domestic Homicide*. Boston: Northeastern University Press. A study of how and why husbands kill wives and vice versa, and why they kill children, with special attention to the ways cultural influences and everyday interactions are involved in the killings.

Winton, Mark A., and Barbara A. Mara. 2001. *Child Abuse and Neglect: Multidisciplinary Approaches*. Boston: Allyn and Bacon. Offers a comprehensive coverage of child abuse, including the sexual, physical, and emotional abuse of children and the treatment and prevention of the abuse.

CRITICAL THINKING QUESTIONS

1. Family violence may sound as oxymoronic and unreal as cruel love. Yet that is what it is: cruel love. The family is supposed to be a place to practice love, but it often turns into a place to practice cruelty. If you are thinking of marrying, what would you do to prevent the love between you and your spouse from degenerating into cruelty?

2. Female genital mutilation has been practiced as part of the culture of many African societies. Thus, to ban this practice would risk being charged with ethnocentrism and racism. But to allow the practice to continue would risk being charged with cruelty and inhumanity. What would you do? Would you seek a middle ground by ensuring that the practice is as safe as cosmetic surgery in the United States? If yes, why? If not, why not?

Self-Destructive Deviance

PART THREE

Self-Destructive Deviance

Myths and Realities

Myth: Since they like themselves more than others as a result of living in a highly individualistic society, Americans are less likely to kill themselves than others.

Reality: Every year Americans are far more likely to kill themselves than others as indicated by the much higher rate of suicide than homicide in the United States (p. 139).

Myth: Depression is the cause of suicide.

Reality: Depression is a risk factor for suicide as it is often found in people who kill themselves. But this does not mean that depression is the cause of suicide. There are other risk factors and depression is not the most important one, let alone the cause of suicide. After all, teenagers, who have a higher incidence of depression than the

137

elderly, are *less* likely to kill themselves than are the elderly (p. 139).

_____

Myth: Most people who commit suicide are successful on their first try.

Reality: The majority (about two-thirds) of those who commit suicide are known to have made at least one prior attempt to kill themselves (p. 141).

_____

Myth: Life must be more stressful in densely populated states, such as New York and New Jersey, than in wide-open areas, such as Montana and Wyoming. Not surprisingly, people in densely populated states are more likely to commit suicide.

Reality: People in densely populated states have lower suicide rates (p. 144).

_____

Myth: More likely to be victims of racism and poverty, African Americans tend to commit suicide more often when compared with whites.

Reality: The rate of suicide is much higher among whites than blacks in the United States (p. 145).

_____

Myth: Because of gender prejudice and discrimination, women are more likely than men to find their lives oppressive and consequently commit suicide.

Reality: Men are much more likely than women to kill themselves (p. 146).

_____

Myth: Footloose and fancy-free, the unmarried are generally more likely than the married to have the time of their lives and thus are less likely to kill themselves.

Reality: The unmarried are more likely than the married to kill themselves (p. 147).

_____

Myth: Suicide bombers are generally psychotic, or at least irrational, and poor and uneducated.

Reality: Suicide bombers generally come from *relatively* well-off, middle-class families, are better educated than most of their countrymen, and are apparently rational enough to know that they can seriously threaten an enormously powerful nation (p. 149).

_____

Myth: Among the affluent, industrial societies, those that enjoy greater income equality, such as Finland, Denmark, and Switzerland, generally have lower suicide rates than do those with less equality, such as the United States, Britain, and Australia.

Reality: The opposite is true: the greater the equality, the higher the suicide rate (p. 155).

_____

Myth: There are more suicides in the winter than in the spring because it is easier to feel depressed in the cold, dark season and cheerful in the warm, sunny season.

Reality: There are far fewer suicides in the winter or many more suicides in the spring. In the winter, people tend more to stay home and relax with family and friends and are thus more able to console the distressed and forestall their suicides. By contrast, in the spring, most people are so active and busy that they pay little attention to the distressed, suicide-prone individuals (p. 155).

_____

Adam looked like a normal college student. He gave no hint of any emotional problem. He was 6 feet, 4 inches tall and had the body of an athlete. In high school he had competed in cross-country and track. Now in college, he was smart, about to graduate with a major in physics. He did not seem to have any dark moods, did not use drugs or alcohol, and did not have a girlfriend who might have jilted him. One day he went out to buy a gun. He shot himself in the bedroom of his student apartment, ending whatever suffering he had endured without being able to share it with family and friends. When this happened, his roommates were away, and he left no suicide note, so nobody knows exactly when he died (Dalmas, 2007).

Like Adam, about 31,000 Americans die by their own hand every year. As a cause of death, suicide ranks eighth among adults, but second among adolescents or college students, after motor-vehicle accidents. There is something ironic about suicide. In a highly individualistic society, we are supposed to be more concerned with ourselves than others, to like ourselves more than others. Yet every year we are far more likely to kill ourselves than others as indicated by the fact that the U.S. suicide rate is nearly twice as high as the homicide rate (U.S. Census Bureau, 2008).

Since suicide is a horrible, tragic loss of life, most people feel sympathy for the victim and the surviving relatives and friends. But probably because religion and other cultural forces have long frowned on suicide, many people may see suicide as an easy way out of a terrible life and therefore a cowardly act. This view does not reflect reality, however. Many studies have suggested that suicide is not easy to do because it requires overcoming the fear of death. The fear of death is a powerful biological and sociological force, which stems from the self-preservation instinct instilled in us by eons of evolution and from the anti-death culture and socialization we have absorbed since birth from our society and parents. To surmount this powerful fear of death is no easy task. It requires *practice,* going through such experiences as attempting suicide multiple times, hurting oneself, learning how to work a gun, searching for an overdose drug, and learning how to tie a noose. Such experiences often appear in researchers' analyses of what suicide victims did before killing themselves (Joiner, 2005).

Since suicide also looks like an unnatural act, many people assume that those who kill themselves must be abnormal, mentally ill, that they suffer from severe depression, and therefore that depression is the cause of suicide (Williams, 2006). It is true that depression is a risk factor for suicide as it is often found in people who kill themselves. But this does not mean that depression is the cause of suicide because there are other risk factors and depression is not the most important one, let alone the cause of suicide. After all, teenagers, who have a *higher* incidence of depression than the elderly, are less likely to kill themselves than are the elderly (Joiner, 2005).

If depression is not the cause of suicide, what is? It seems to be the inability to cope effectively with depression, and this inability has to do with certain social forces in U.S. society. In other words, the overwhelming majority of depressed Americans do not kill themselves. Those extremely few who do commit suicide do so usually because they have been under the influence of certain social forces in their lives. One of these forces is lack of social support, as shown by the inability to talk about one's problems with family and friends. Other social factors such as race, gender, and age also play a role in suicide. In this chapter we will take a closer look at these social factors associated with the act of suicide. We will also discuss various forms of suicidal experience, social responses to suicide, and theories that explain why and how some people commit suicide.

Varieties of Suicidal Experiences

On the tragic road to suicide can be found different types of sad travelers with a distinctive kind of experience. Some *threaten* to kill themselves but do not make good on their threats. Others *attempt* to take their own lives but do not succeed. And still others actually *commit* suicide. Although they all share the same feeling that their lives are unbearable, these three types of individuals differ in their approaches to suicide.

Threatening Suicide

Those who threaten suicide do so explicitly, directly, or clearly. They clearly want to live rather than die, since their suicide threats are intended as a means of achieving some objective in life. This does not necessarily mean that they will never carry out their threats. They may do so if the threats fail to achieve their objectives. Given the lack of knowledge about them, it is not possible to determine the percentage of suicide threateners who successfully carry out their threats (Stephens, 1995; Lester, 1988). Obviously, those whose threats are heeded will more likely refrain from killing themselves than those whose threats are ignored. One classic study has indicated various ways in which suicide threats have traditionally been used to produce positive results for individuals:

> The threat of suicide forces persons to marry, prevents marriage dissolution, coerces companionship between persons despite their mutual infidelity, prevents marriages, forces parents to acquiesce in their offspring's vicious habits, precludes institutionalization, is rewarded by escape from further military duty, is used to obtain favored treatment over siblings, is employed as a device to avoid military induction. (Siegal and Friedman, 1955)

Attempting Suicide

Unlike the threateners, who clearly want more to live than to die, suicide attempters are ambiguous in their intent. They are often seized with the mood of "I don't care whether I live or die." Thus, compared with those who issue threats in unmistakable terms, the attempters are less explicit in communicating their suicidal feelings. They may simply show others how depressed they are, or tell others that they cannot sleep, but generally avoid using the word *suicide*. As a result, most of them do not succeed in conveying their distress signals to others. Only somewhere between 14 and 53 percent of suicide attempters are known to have forewarned others of even an ambiguous intention to die (Bettridge and Favreau, 1995; Wilkins, 1967). When they succeed in communicating their message, others tend not to take it seriously because of its vagueness. This is why suicide attempters eventually resort to dramatic and dangerous methods to express—still implicitly—their appeal for help.

The methods include wrist cutting, swallowing large amounts of sleeping pills, and gas poisoning in the house or car. Although these methods can be lethal, they are less foolproof than those generally used by real suicides, such as shooting and hanging (Peck, 1985–86, 1984). In addition, most suicide attempts are carried out in a setting or in a manner that makes rescue possible, probable, or even inevitable. Some may remain near others during the attempt, or call up a friend immediately afterward. This reflects their lack of determination to die, and most suicide attempts have been therefore described as "a road to life, not death" (*Psychology Today,* 1976).

Suicide attempters are more likely to be women than men, to be young (ages 24 to 44) than old (ages 55 to 66), and to come from lower classes than upper classes. By contrast, those who actually commit suicide are more likely to be men than women, to be old than young, and to come from upper than lower classes. Suicide attempters are also more likely to abuse drugs (O'Boyle and Brandon, 1998; Hendin, 1995; Harry, 1983). Since the 1960s, however, the gender difference in suicide attempts has narrowed significantly, thanks to the increased independence among women (Kushner, 1995; Kessler and McRae, 1983). Many women are more able today than before, for example, to cope with the emotional impact of divorce because they have worked outside the home prior to the marital breakup. But traditional women, such as stay-at-home parents or homemakers, are still more likely to attempt suicide. They are more likely to have been socialized to rely heavily on others for emotional support and to feel helpless when having to deal with crises alone. Aside from this "trained dependency and helplessness," suicide attempters in general are also more likely to be rigid in thinking and to see events with a narrow perspective, when compared with nonsuicidal persons (Clifton and Lee, 1995).

Committing Suicide

About two-thirds of those who commit suicide are known to have made at least one prior attempt to kill themselves. Also, most have openly or subtly communicated their suicidal ideas to others (Hendin, 1995, 1979). Completed suicides comprise a mixed category, which includes suicide threateners who have failed to get what they desperately wanted, suicide attempters who have not been rescued in time, and individuals who were simply more determined to die. From notes left by suicides and from reports given by suicide attempters, we can discern at least five types of suicidal feeling.

First, most suicides may feel so *depressed* that they withdraw themselves from their daily activities. A deeply depressed college student, for example, cut classes, slept too much, and ate too little. Just before killing himself, he wrote (Wartik, 1995):

> I sit alone, sad and quiet, contemplating death. My hopes and dreams have turned to dust; inside my soul, emptiness. I look back on the bright, bubbly, always contented child that I was, every day and everything was just so great, nothing could really go wrong. Even as I sit and contemplate the end of my life by my own hand, I'm so empty I can't even cry.

Second, many suicides feel *apologetic* toward their survivors. In the following suicide note, for example, a young man apologizes to his parents (Folse and Peck, 1995):

> Mom and Dad,
> I was supposed to be the model son, doing the best of everything I did. I let you down all those times. I've really screwed up now. I can never be your model son again. I know I can't say anything to let you know how bad I feel about all this, but please try to accept this humble apology and realize this is what I thought best. See you in heaven.
> Gary

Third, some suicides feel *vindictive* toward their survivors or themselves. Blaming others for their misery and death, they seek revenge by punishing those they leave behind. This can be illustrated by the following suicide note from a 38-year-old divorced woman (Shneidman, 1975):

> Bill,
>   You have killed me. I hope you are happy in your heart, if you have one which I doubt. Please leave Rover with Mike. Also leave my baby alone. If you don't, I'll haunt you the rest of your life and I mean it and I'll do it. You have been mean and also cruel. God doesn't forget those things and don't forget that. And please no flowers; it won't mean anything. Also keep your money. I want to be buried in Potters Field in the same casket with Betty. . . . You know what you have done to me. That's why I did this. It's yours and Ella's fault, try and forget if you can. But you can't . . .
>
> > Your wife.

Some suicides may feel genuinely angry with *themselves* for having done a wrongful act and for that reason use self-killing to punish themselves. A common example of this suicidal experience is the man who kills himself after murdering another person. This has been referred to as *atonement suicide*. Here is how anthropologist Raymond Firth (1961) describes a case of atonement suicide involving a man on a South Pacific island:

> About the oddest [form of suicide] was that chosen by Pu Sao, who, having broken wind in a public gathering, in his shame climbed a coconut palm and sat down on the sharp-pointed, hard flower-spathe, which pierced his rectum and killed him—a bizarre case of making the punishment fit the crime.

Fourth, suicides may become *magnanimous* toward the world they choose to leave behind. In their suicide notes, some request that their bodies be donated to medical schools, others bequeath their property and money to charitable organizations, and still others forgive whoever has wronged them, as the following indicates (Shneidman, 1975):

> Mary:
>   We could have been so happy if you had continued to love me. I have your picture in front of me. I will look at it the last thing. I do love you so much. To think you are now in the arms of another man is more than I can stand . . . I am giving my life for your indiscretion. Please don't let me pay too high a price for your happiness. All your faults are completely forgotten and your sweetness remembered. You knew I would do this when you left me—so this is no surprise. Good-bye darling—I love you with all of my broken heart.
>
> > W. Smith

Fifth, suicides usually become suffused with *surrealistic* feelings during the very act of ending their lives. The stormy tension that has initially driven them to suicide dies down, and an overwhelming calm takes over just before they consciously breathe their last breath. In this state of calmness, they experience surrealistic feelings. A number of suicide attempters who have cut their wrists report that wrist slashing was not painful. They felt that the sight and smell of their blood was enlightening, leading them to "return to reality and life from the state of dead unreality" of this world. Some wrist cutters even likened the experience to orgasm, followed by a soothing feeling of relaxation and then deeply comfortable sleep (*Psychology Today,* 1976). This type of suicidal experience, however, is becoming less common today because an increasing number of suicides choose the immediately lethal method—firearms—to end their lives. In fact, the proportion of suicides by firearms has grown so much that guns have replaced asphyxia (which includes drowning, suffocation, and hanging) as the most popular means of suicide today.

Groups with Higher Suicide Rates

In general, sociologists, psychiatrists, and researchers in other fields have ignored suicide threateners and attempters and focused instead on suicides. In their efforts to assess the social characteristics of suicides, sociologists have relied heavily on suicide statistics compiled by coroners and other government officials. Usually these statistics are expressed in the form of a *suicide rate,* which refers to the number of suicides for every 100,000 people of a given population. At the same time, sociologists have recognized, to one degree or another, that the official statistics are not highly reliable. At least two reasons have long been suggested for the relative unreliability of official suicide statistics (Labovitz, 1968; Douglas, 1967).

The first is that officials in different countries, states, and local areas use different procedures to determine what constitutes suicide. Consequently, what is judged suicide in one place is considered a natural, accidental, or homicidal death in another. Even within the same country, state, or local area, coroners sometimes disagree whether a given death is caused by suicide—or by homicide or accident. Thus, when officials report a death as suicide, it may not be a suicide. On the other hand, when officials fail to report a death as suicide, it may actually be a suicide. When a corpse is found floating in a river, for example, it may be reported as a case of suicide when it is actually an accident, or vice versa. Also, deaths from victim-precipitated homicide (as discussed in Chapter 4, "Physical Violence") may be considered suicides but are routinely not reported as such but as homicides. In short, official statistics on suicide are far from reliable, not only because different officials define suicide differently, but also because it is sometimes difficult to distinguish a suicide from a homicide, an accident, or a natural death.

Second, the official data on suicide are relatively unreliable because suicide victims or their relatives may conceal the evidence that the deaths were self-inflicted. They would report the suicide as an accidental death. This is particularly the case if suicide is considered a disgrace for the self-killer and his or her family. Furthermore, many automobile fatalities (about 15 percent) are actually suicides but are routinely reported as accidents (Madge and Harvey, 1999; Lester, 1985). Thus, official statistics tend to consistently underestimate the suicide rate.

Although sociologists recognize the relative unreliability of official suicide statistics, there are no data showing the *amount* of the unreliability. Consequently, sociologists differ in their estimations of how unreliable official statistics are. Those who want to search for the social meanings rather than causes of suicide are extremely critical of official statistics, arguing that they are grossly unreliable. In contrast, those who want to seek out the causes of suicide assume that official statistics are fairly reliable or at least the best available for studying suicide. Some sociologists have found that systematic misreporting—consistently underreporting suicides—does exist but that it does not significantly distort the analysis aimed at finding out which social groups are more likely than others to commit suicide (Phillips, 1993; Pescosolido and Mendelsohn, 1986). Let's turn to such an analysis.

Residents in Rural, Wide-Open Areas

In the past, most researchers found a positive correlation between urbanization and suicide. Their studies suggest that during the nineteenth century and well into the twentieth century in practically all countries, urban dwellers were more likely than rural residents to kill themselves. The higher urban suicide rate has been attributed to certain characteristics of city life. The heterogeneous population, conflicting social norms, and fast-changing lifestyles in the city were assumed to weaken the individual's ties to others, thereby increasing the potential for suicide. But today much of those differences between urban and rural life have greatly diminished because the mass media and other institutions have spread the urban culture to the rural areas. This social change may have weakened the traditional social support in the rural areas in most countries. Consequently, today, in most countries, the rural areas have higher suicide rates (Hill et al., 2005; Levin and Leyland, 2005; Goldsmith, 2002).

The rurality–suicide connection can also be found in the United States. As shown by Table 7.1, the five states with the highest suicide rates are considerably more rural and more sparsely populated than the five states with the lowest suicide rates. Moreover, in every state in the United States, predominantly rural counties generally have higher suicide rates than do urban counties. Why is suicide the most prevalent in such mostly rural states as

TABLE 7.1   States with Highest and Lowest Suicide Rates

State	Suicides per 100,000 Residents	Percent Rural	Population per Square Mile
Alaska	23.6	34.4	1.1
Montana	18.9	45.9	6.2
Nevada	18.8	8.5	18.2
New Mexico	18.7	25.0	15.0
Wyoming	17.4	34.9	5.1
Average	**19.5**	**29.7**	**9.1**
Rhode Island	7.9	9.1	1,003.2
New Jersey	6.9	5.6	1,134.4
Massachusetts	6.6	8.6	809.8
New York	6.2	12.5	401.9
D.C	6.0	0	9,316.4
Average	**6.7**	**7.2**	**2,533.1**

Source: U.S. National Center for Health Statistics, 2008; Statistical Abstract of the United States, 2008.

Montana and Wyoming, where people can enjoy a quiet and wide-open space as opposed to the traffic- and people-congested life in New York and New Jersey? And why are people who live in the rural counties more likely than those in urban counties to commit suicide? One reason is that people who live in those wide-open or rural areas tend to be more socially isolated, more individualistic, more dependent on themselves or less willing to seek help from others when facing a personal crisis, the type of social characteristics significantly associated with suicide. Another reason is that the share of whites is higher in those areas, and whites have higher suicide rates than blacks.

Whites

Indeed, the rate of suicide is much higher among whites than blacks in the United States. Among males, whites have a rate of about 21 suicides for every 100,000 whites, compared with only 13 for blacks. And among females, whites have a suicide rate of five, compared with two for blacks. Whites also have higher suicide rates than Asian and Hispanic Americans. Why do whites have higher suicide rates than minorities? The reason is that whites experience less social regulation or more individual freedom, which is associated with a higher suicide rate. But in the last two decades the suicide rate among *black youths* has risen sharply, though still not approaching the rate for their white peers. The sharp rise in black suicide reflects a significant move to middle-class life, which weakens social regulation as shown by a splintering of community and family support networks and a decline in bonds to religion (Belluck, 1998).

But whites of various younger age groups (ages 15–24, 25–34, and 35–44) have consistently *lower* suicide rates than Native Americans of the same age groups. Only among older age groups (beginning age 45) are whites more likely to kill themselves than Native Americans. Put another way, Native Americans of the younger age groups have the highest suicide rate of all racial groups. The basic reason is that the dominant, white society has largely destroyed their traditionally proud culture, creating an identity crisis, self-doubt, and self-criticism, which is particularly likely to lead young people to suicide. Suicide rates are lower, though, among many of the Southwestern Pueblos and the Navajo because these peoples have managed to retain their traditional cultural values and practices (U.S. Census Bureau, 2008; Young, 1991; U.S. Congress, 1990).

The Less Religious

On the whole, Protestants have higher suicide rates than Catholics, who in turn have higher rates than Jews. Sometimes, though rarely, research reveals no real difference in suicide between Catholics and Protestants (van Poppel and Day, 1996; Breault, 1986). But the type of religion people subscribe to is not as important as the strength of their religious identity or the degree of their religious conservatism. Thus, regardless of what religion people have, the weaker their religious identity or the less religiously conservative they are, the higher their risk of suicide. During the period 1900 to 1910 in the Netherlands, for example, the Jewish suicide rate far exceeded both the Catholic and Protestant rates, apparently because the Jews, unlike those in other countries, did not have a strong Jewish identity. Also, in New Zealand, among the Protestants, Congregational church members have the highest suicide rate, Baptists the next highest, and Church of Christ members the lowest (Goldsmith et al., 2002; Stack, 1983). This is apparently because the Congregational church is the most liberal and the Church of Christ the most conservative. However, if religious identity or conservatism is held constant, religious type does play a significant role in suicide. Thus in the United States those who adhere to Confucianism, Buddhism, or Hinduism, which have no strong prohibition against suicide, are more likely to kill themselves than those who believe in Christianity or Islam, which prohibit suicide (Ibrahim, 1995).

Most sociologists explain the religious differences in suicide rates by using Durkheim's concept of social integration. Thus, the higher Protestant rates are seen as having to do with Protestants' lesser degree of integration into their church, when compared with Catholics or Jews. In essence, weak religious identity, religious liberalism, and lack of religious integration seem to reflect the same thing—inadequate social involvement. Regardless of whether they are Protestant, Catholic, or Jewish, people are apparently more likely to commit suicide if they do not go to church or do not participate in some other religious activities. In fact, as research suggests, nominal Christians are more likely than practicing Christians to kill themselves (Kay and Francis, 2006; Van Tubergen et al., 2005; Goldsmith et al., 2002).

Males

In most societies, men are much more likely to kill themselves than are women. This probably has to do with the social inequality between the sexes. Given their greater freedom and opportunities for success, men may find it harder to blame others when having serious problems in life. Instead, they tend more to blame themselves for their own problems and therefore become more likely to commit suicide as an aggression against themselves. Thus, the greater the sexual inequality, the greater the gender difference in suicide. But many studies have suggested that as sexual inequality has decreased since the 1960s, so has the gender difference in suicide (Steffensmeier, 1984; Stack, 1982). Still, the male suicide rate remains much higher, as we have observed. In contrast, though, the attempted suicide rate is considerably higher among women than among men (Hawton and Harriss, 2008; Canetto and Lester, 1995; Kushner, 1985).

There is also a gender difference in methods of committing suicide. As Table 7.2 indicates, men are more likely than women to use firearms, while women are more likely to

TABLE 7.2   Gender and Suicide Methods

Suicide Method	Male	Female
Firearms	66%	39%
Poisoning*	14	35
Hanging	15	13
Other	5	13

*Includes drug overdoses and gassings.

Source: National Strategy for Suicide Prevention, 2005.

use poisoning, including gas and sleeping pill overdose. This gender difference reflects the overrepresentation of men in completed suicides and the preponderance of women in attempted suicides. Most of the completed suicides involve using the immediately lethal method, which firearms are. But most attempted suicides involve the use of less immediately lethal methods, such as gas poisoning and drug overdose (Miller and Hemenway, 1999; Gunnell, Wehner, and Frankel, 1999).

It is true that in most societies, particularly in the West, more women than men attempt suicide but fewer women succeed because they tend more to use those less lethal methods. But evidence is mounting that in rural China and India women who attempt suicide are far more likely to employ more deadly methods such as hanging, drowning, swallowing pesticides, and setting oneself on fire. Consequently, in Asian countries more women die from suicide than men, contrary to the higher rates of suicide among men in the West (NewsRx.com, 2004; Pearson and Liu, 2002). Most of the suicides by Western men are *anomic,* resulting from having much less social regulation or greater individual freedom than women. But most of the suicides by Asian women are *fatalistic,* brought on by greater regulation or less freedom, which makes the women feel trapped in an unjust social situation such as being forced by their parents to marry.

The Divorced or Single

There are large differences in suicide rates by marital status. In general, divorced persons have the highest rate, married persons the lowest rate, and those who are single or widowed have intermediate rates. Married couples are most immune to suicide. Those with children are even more immune to suicide than those without children (Goldsmith et al., 2002; Lester, 1991; McIntosh, 1991). All this has been taken to suggest that the more and stronger ties we have to other people, the less likely we are to escape our problems through suicide.

Older People

In the United States the suicide rate tends to rise with increasing age, with the young having the lowest rates and the old the highest. Most notably, the suicide rate starts to increase sharply with age 64 and peaks in the oldest age group. But this relationship between age and suicide holds only for white males. For black males, black females, and white females, suicide rates remain low in old age. More significantly, while suicide rises with age for white men, it drops with age for African American men (see Figure 7.1).

Why does the suicide rate increase so much among white older men? According to a sociological explanation, the social ties that have been formed through marriage, children, work, friendships, community participation, and other social commitments and activities start to diminish with the commencement of old age. The social ties inevitably weaken when "adult children leave home, loved ones die, careers end, and health declines" (Girard, 1993). Without the support of the significant others, older men, when faced with serious life problems, tend more to commit suicide.

Still, as Chris Girard (1993) points out, more women are widowed and living alone in old age but their suicide rate does not go up. Apparently, there is something more than the mere lack of social ties that causes high suicide rates. That something more, according to

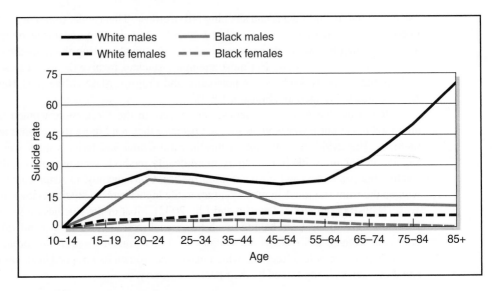

FIGURE 7.1   Age and Suicide

Source: National Strategy for Suicide Prevention, 2005.

Girard, is the distressing decline in physical and mental capacities. This is conducive to suicide because it threatens men's self-identity as a capable, worthy person. Male self-identity is likely to be threatened in old age because it is oriented to performance—that is, based on demonstration of talent, competence, and accomplishment—in the business or professional world. In contrast, female self-identity is less performance-oriented and more intrinsically oriented—that is, based more on "me as I am, just because I am this way." Thus older women tend to see themselves as a senior citizen, a caring person, a religious person, a person with a hobby, or some other kind of person who is less likely to be threatened by old age. But as more women enter the business world, their self-identity will increasingly be oriented to performance and their suicide rate can be expected to rise in old age (Girard, 1993).

What about older African American men and women? Why don't their suicide rates increase as sharply as those of older white men? Apparently, their self-identity is less performance-oriented, because racism has long denied them entry into business or professional careers. But, again, like white women, their growing participation in the business world can be expected to push their suicide rates upward. This upward push cannot go too far, though, because African American culture strongly condemns suicide (Early and Akers, 1995; Early, 1992).

The Relatively Well-Off

Inconsistencies abound in the observations and findings on the relationship between social class and suicide. Sociologists have long observed that the rich are more likely to kill themselves than the poor because, given their higher status and aspirations, they have farther to fall in times of economic crisis (Henry and Short, 1954; Durkheim, 1897). Supporting evidence can be found in the finding that the richer, more industrialized countries generally have higher suicide rates than the poorer, developing countries. Within a rich country such as the United States, occupations with low unemployment rates and high incomes have been found to have higher suicide rates than those with higher unemployment and lower incomes. This is particularly true of doctors, who have the highest rate of suicide of any profession (Noonan, 2008; Lester, 2000). Moreover, in developing countries such as Mexico, the more affluent middle class has a higher suicide rate than the lower class (Stack, 1982). Such a positive relationship between class and suicide, however, does not always appear in sociological research. Some studies have shown just the opposite—a negative relationship—with the poor having higher suicide rates than the rich (Stack, 1982). This is consistent with the common finding that unemployment, which is more likely to happen to the poor, is associated with suicide (Platt, 1984). According to the researchers, poverty and unemployment may cause suicide by generating stress or exacerbating a preexisting depression. There is yet a third type of study, which has found no relationship at all between class and suicide (Marks, 1980).

The contradiction in those findings stems largely from the different ways researchers define social class or test the relationship between class and suicide. Some use income and others employ occupation to define social class. Some control for the impact of intervening variables such as race, age, or divorce in analyzing the class–suicide relationship; others do not. Given the conflicting data, we obviously do not know with total certainty whether the rich are more suicidal than the poor or vice versa. But we can be *reasonably* certain that the rich are more suicidal because of the consistent evidence that suicide rates are higher in affluent societies than in poor ones and also higher among whites (a relatively well-off group) than among blacks (whose poverty rate is higher).

A Social Profile of Suicide Bombers

Since the September 11 attacks, some Westerners have assumed that suicide bombers must be psychotic, or at least irrational, and poor and uneducated since they come from third world countries. But evidence suggests just the opposite. According to a study on the 149 Palestinian suicide bombers who tried to attack Israel between 1993 and 2002, the majority shared the same social profile as the September 11 terrorists. The suicide bombers in Iraq who have frequently targeted U.S. soldiers also have the same social background as the September 11 terrorists. They came from relatively well-off, middle-class families. They are also better educated than most of their countrymen. Thus, they are apparently rational enough to know, for example, that they can resort to suicide bombings as their ultimate, powerful weapon in an asymmetrical war with Israel. They know, like the September 11 terrorists, that they can't fight a conventional war because they have no tanks, no artillery, and no air force, while their enemy has one of the world's most powerful and modern militaries (Nordland et al., 2007; Pape, 2005).

Evidence further shows that suicide bombers are mostly young, male, and single. Like the September 11 terrorists, the Palestinian and Iraqi suicide bombers consider themselves martyrs, rather than terrorists. They are also seen that way by many people in the

Middle East. Their parents are proud of them, as well. After the Palestinian suicide bomber Saeed Hotari blew himself up, his father said, "I am very happy and proud of what my son did. He has become a hero! What more could a father ask? My prayer is that Saeed's brothers and friends will sacrifice their lives too. There is no better way to show God you love him." The bombers further receive other, more concrete social support. After they die carrying out a suicide mission, their family is rewarded with a permanent pension from the terrorist organization that sponsors the bombing. Finally, the bombers are assured that they will earn a special place in heaven (Begley, 2004; Dickey, 2002; Ripley, 2002).

Suicide attacks are not new, nor have they originated only from the Middle East. In 1911 in China, 72 pro-democracy revolutionaries, mostly students, sacrificed their lives by charging an overwhelming garrison of the Ching Dynasty in order to prod the apathetic Chinese masses to overthrow the tyrannical government. In 1945 toward the end of World War II, Japanese kamikaze pilots crashed their fighter planes into U.S. warships in the Pacific. Today in Sri Lanka, the separatist rebels known as the Tamil Tigers, who are fighting their government for an independent Tamil state, have launched about 200 suicide attacks. All these terrorists had about the same social characteristics as the Iraqi, Palestinian, and September 11 suicide bombers (Gambetta, 2005).

Situational Factors in Suicide

We have just observed that individuals with certain social characteristics are more inclined to commit suicide. We also know that they are even more likely to kill themselves if they find themselves in certain social situations or undergoing certain social experiences. These situations or experiences may include going through adolescence, going to college, being in prison, being infected with the AIDS virus, and being exposed to media influences.

Going through Adolescence

Every year about 2,800 young people between ages 10 and 21 kill themselves and many more high school students (about three million, or 20 percent) have seriously considered suicide in the previous year. Among adolescents, suicide ranks as a leading cause of death. It is the third most frequent cause of death after accident and homicide, but many accidents, especially car crashes, that take the lives of teenagers, are actually suicidal, though reported as accidental (U.S. Census Bureau, 2008; Hosansky, 2004; Phillips, 1979). More significant, while their suicide rate is still lower than that of older adults, teenagers today are much more likely than their peers of the past to kill themselves. Of all U.S. age groups, adolescents have experienced the largest increase in suicide rates over the last 30 years. As shown in Table 7.3, the greatest increase involves ages 15 to 19. By contrast, suicide rates have declined among the older age groups—from age 35 to above 65.

The huge rise in youthful suicide may stem from the fact that adolescence as a life crisis has gotten worse over the last 30 years. It is well known that adolescents are often caught in the transition between childhood and adulthood. Treated simultaneously like children (e.g., being considered too young to drink, to stay out late, or to have sex) and like adults (being old enough to drive, work, or vote), adolescents tend to feel "conflicted" and

TABLE 7.3   Changes in Suicide Rates by Age Groups

Age	Suicide Rate		% Change
	1970	**2004**	
15–19	5.9	8.2	+39
20–24	12.2	12.5	+2
25–34	14.1	12.7	−10
35–44	16.9	15.0	−11
45–54	20.0	16.6	−17
55–64	21.4	13.8	−36
65+	20.8	14.0	−33

Source: Statistical Abstract of the United States, 2008.

confused—resentful of being treated like children and fearful of being unable to discharge adult responsibilities adequately. This feeling is often expressed in the form of defiant and rebellious behavior toward parents, delinquency, drug use, reckless driving, or some other action designed to attract attention from others (Hendin, 1995). Such problems are part of the transition from childhood to adulthood, which youths of every generation, with social support from adults, have gone through and come out of without too much difficulty.

However, over the last 30 years, significant changes have occurred in the family as well as in the economic and religious lives of adolescents that make it more difficult to deal with the transition problems. Today there are proportionately more parental divorces, more single-parent families, more two-career families, and more latch-key kids who come home to empty houses after school. Teenagers are also less likely to work part-time during the school year and full-time during the summer than were their peers of 30 years ago. The rate of church attendance and participation in other religious activities is also lower among teenagers today. In other words, contemporary youngsters have effectively suffered a decline in social integration and regulation (traditionally provided by the family, job market, and religion), hence the increase in suicide rates (Hawton and Harriss, 2008; Stockard and O'Brien, 2002; Mulrine, 2001; Stack, 1986). (Lack of social integration and regulation being associated with suicide will be discussed later.)

A controversy has emerged, though, over whether antidepressant drugs such as Prozac, Paxil, and Zoloft increase the risk of teen suicide (Carey, 2008). Parents have testified before the U.S. Food and Drug Administration that their children committed suicide after taking antidepressants, and some psychiatrists agree that antidepressants can cause teen suicide (Fritz et al., 2007). But many other psychiatrists blame the suicide on depression rather than the antidepressant drug itself, pointing out that teens who are most likely to commit suicide tend to have suffered from the most severe depression. Those psychiatrists further argue that without antidepressants the teen suicide rate would have increased. There is some evidence to support this argument: When prescriptions for youths with depression dropped more than 50 percent between 2003 and 2005, the number of teen suicides went up 18 percent between 2003 and 2004 (Rosack, 2007; Dokoupil, 2007).

Going to College

More than one thousand students at U.S. colleges and universities commit suicide every year. Many more students (about 1.5 million, or 10 percent) on campus have seriously considered suicide in the last 12 months. These problems have also become more common today, leading many colleges to step up efforts to prevent suicide on their campuses (Kisch et al., 2005; Hosansky, 2004; Arenson, 2004). Among college students, those who attend more prestigious universities are more likely to kill themselves because of greater pressure to achieve in an intensely competitive atmosphere. At any given institution, suicide-prone students generally do better than others in their studies, but their grades typically drop to Ds and Fs when they begin to think about killing themselves. Most give some warning of their intentions to parents and friends by appearing troubled or depressed (Sontag, 2002; Lester, 2000; Hendin, 1995; Peck and Schrut, 1971).

Since college life is relatively stressful, the greater stress experienced by students may be an important factor in their higher risk of suicide. But something else also contributes to their suicides, something that makes it difficult to cope with the stress, namely, their lack of social ties or social support, a common problem among suicidal students. As one such student says about his university, "This place is just so damned big! Nobody here really cares what happens. So, nobody here will notice when I'm gone" (Rickgarn, 1994). Another suicidal student says, "Nobody wants to associate with me. I've never felt so alone. I eat alone and no one comes to see me in my room" (Rickgarn, 1994). The significance of the lack of social ties or support as a factor in suicide can also be discerned from the fact that college students are mostly single. Without a spouse and children, college students lack the social ties that typically help married couples relieve their stress as well as restrain them from killing themselves. This is why, to protect their students against suicide, many universities have created smaller living-and-learning environments, which reduce student isolation and encourage feelings of belonging (Silverman, 2008).

Being in Prison

Suicide in prison is relatively common. It is, in fact, the leading cause of death among prison inmates. In a number of countries, suicide rates are considerably higher inside prison than outside. Prisoners are five to eight times more likely to kill themselves than free citizens. Moreover, the rate of prison suicides has, over the last 20 years, increased considerably more than the rate of suicides among the general population (Fazel et al., 2005; Hayes, 1995; Liebling, 1992).

Those who kill themselves in prison are predominantly whites, in their early twenties, and are single, divorced, or lacking stable and supportive relationships. The majority die by hanging, which is the most easily available method. Ironically, proportionately more inmates commit suicide in local jails while awaiting trial or sentencing than in state prisons after conviction or sentencing. Even more ironically, most of the suicides have been charged with relatively minor crimes. Does this mean that they are probably mentally ill or emotionally disturbed? No, because they are far less likely than the suicides in the larger society to have a history of mental depression or psychiatric treatment. The immediate cause seems to be fear of other inmates or imprisonment itself, which arises from the *radical transformation* of a free person in a familiar, safe environment into a confined person in an unaccustomed, dangerous milieu, further compounded by the *uncertainty* of judicial outcome (Hayes, 1995; Lester and Danto, 1993; Liebling, 1992).

During the initial phase of imprisonment the level of stress is the highest; it diminishes only with adjustment to prison life. Not surprisingly, inmates are most likely to kill themselves during the first few days of their imprisonment. However, death-row inmates, who are imprisoned for life or awaiting execution, also have a higher suicide rate than the general prison population. But the *immediate* cause of such suicides is an overwhelming sense of despair or hopelessness (Hayes, 1995; Lester and Danto, 1993; Liebling, 1992).

Being Stricken with AIDS

Research has found higher rates of suicide among people who are stricken with fatal diseases such as terminal cancer. Since AIDS (acquired immune deficiency syndrome) is a fatal disease, it shouldn't be surprising that AIDS patients are more likely than healthy people to kill themselves. As a study shows, the yearly suicide rate of male AIDS patients in New York City is nearly 700 suicides for every 100,000 patients, compared with only 20 for men free of AIDS (Mancoske et al., 1995). The standard explanation is that dying from AIDS produces an enormous sense of hopelessness while the social stigma attached to the disease brings the additional burden of social rejection and isolation (Beckerman, 1995).

But less sick patients, those who are only infected with HIV (human immunodeficiency virus, the virus that causes AIDS) and have a chance of surviving, are even more likely to kill themselves. It takes them only one to four weeks after their HIV diagnosis to attempt suicide (Cooperman and Simoni, 2005). Why are these less sick HIV-infected patients more suicidal than the dying AIDS patients? One reason has to do with the tremendous tension resulting from the *uncertainty* about the outcome of HIV infection—which may or may not lead to death. By contrast, the certainty of death facing the AIDS patient tends to induce an attitude of resignation or acceptance, which reduces stress and hence the risk of suicide. Another reason is the sudden, *radical transformation* from being a totally healthy person to being a seriously—possibly deathly—ill patient. Being struck with this transformation is bound to be extremely stressful. Such stress tends to diminish when the HIV infection becomes, after some passage of time, full-blown AIDS because the patient will have learned to master the fear of death. In fact, some terminally ill AIDS patients may have the same low risk of suicide as healthy people (McKegney and O'Dowd, 1992). In other words, the stress that triggers suicide among HIV-infected patients is basically the same as the stress that provokes suicide among newly jailed inmates. In both cases, the stress comes from uncertainty about a new, frightening situation and from failure to cope with the radical transformation of status.

Under Media Influence

Research has demonstrated the mass media's influence on suicide. When the suicide of a famous person, such as the novelist Ernest Hemingway, the movie star Marilyn Monroe, or the grunge-rock star Kurt Cobain, is widely publicized, the nation's suicide rate tends to go up (Stack, 1987; Wasserman, 1984). This does not mean that celebrity suicide causes imitative suicide among all kinds of ordinary people. Rather, imitative suicide is more likely to occur among the suicidally inclined persons with the social characteristics (such as being male and white) that we have seen associated with high suicide rates. Why, then, does celebrity suicide encourage imitative suicide among those individuals? Apparently it is because celebrities are regarded as role models, and, by killing themselves, celebrities demonstrate the act of suicide as well as legitimize it as a way of solving a terrible life problem. Note too that the news about an ordinary person's suicide can also raise the country's suicide rate *if* the news is so widely disseminated that it reaches a truly national audience. Such publicity has the same impact on imitative suicide as TV commercials featuring an ordinary person have on consumer purchases (Stack, 1991). The mass media can further influence what method to use to kill oneself. The choice of a certain suicide method such as firearms, hanging, or drugs may depend on seeing that method used by suicide victims in movies or TV shows (Crabb, 2005).

Country music can also exercise a significant influence on suicide. As research has shown, the greater the radio airtime given to country music, the higher the white suicide rate is. Country music tends to promote suicide by reinforcing preexisting suicidal moods in suicidally inclined listeners. This is because country music conveys many suicide-related themes, such as marital strife and dissolution, alcohol abuse, financial strain, and exploitation at work. A content analysis of 1,400 hit country songs reveals that nearly three-fourths deal with the travails of love. Hopelessness further pervades most country songs. While country music cannot by itself drive people to suicide, it can increase suicide risk among those with suicidal tendencies (Stack and Gundlach, 1992).

A Global Perspective on Suicide

Generally, the more industrialized a society, the higher its suicide rate. Thus people in the United States and other Western societies are usually more suicidal than people in the developing world. Western societies have higher suicide rates because they, being more modern and individualistic, place greater importance on self-reliance so that distressed individuals are more likely to be left alone to fend for themselves. But developing countries, more traditional and group-oriented, put a higher premium on interdependence so that distressed individuals are more likely to receive support from others.

In the developing world, however, the fast-industrializing countries of China, Hong Kong, South Korea, and Singapore now have higher suicide rates than do Western societies. In addition to rapid industrialization, other dramatic social changes may also lead to higher suicide rates by disrupting the traditional pattern of social life (Pritchard and Baldwin, 2002). In Russia, for example, the collapse of the Soviet Union in the early 1990s brought about huge increases in suicide, primarily because the collapse also brought about huge increases in such social problems as unemployment, poverty, divorce, and alcohol consumption (Pridemore and Spivak, 2003). Also in South Africa, the collapse of the white-dominated government in the early 1990s greatly increased the suicide rates among the blacks. Now enjoying greater freedom and opportunity, South African blacks feel more stress from the increased social pressure to achieve, while the traditional social ties have buckled under the pressure to be self-reliant. As the stepmother of a man who killed himself said, "We're different now . . . [there] used to be people who would be interested in you and help you. But now, where were his friends when he needed them? No one trusts each other anymore, and everyone just does his thing" (Laubscher, 2003).

Among the affluent, industrialized societies, those that enjoy greater income equality, such as Finland, Denmark, and Switzerland, generally have higher suicide rates than do those with less equality, such as the United States, Britain, and Australia. Greater equality may cause more suicides by bringing more individual freedom. Given the freedom, individuals tend to rely on themselves more than on others in trying to solve personal crises. Some people, being far too subjective or emotional when faced with a crisis, will find it difficult to solve the problem and, therefore, increase their risk of suicide.

Also in the Western industrialized societies there has, for the last 100 years, been a certain pattern of temporal variation in suicide rates. The rates peak in the spring and bottom in the winter, and rise substantially at the beginning of the week and decline sharply during the weekend. The cause can be found in the ebb and flow of social life. In the spring and the beginning of the week, most people tend to be so active and busy that they pay little attention to the few distressed, suicidally prone individuals among them, which makes suicide more likely. But in the winter and on the weekends, people tend more to stay home and relax with relatives and friends, and are, therefore, more able to render social support to the distressed and forestall their suicides (Painter, 2008; Bjorksten, 2005; Lester, 2000).

Social Responses to Suicide

Whether suicide is common or rare depends to some degree on how society responds to it. As two sociologists observed more than 70 years ago, "Where custom and tradition accept or condone it, many persons will take their own lives; where it is sternly condemned by the rules of the Church and State, suicide will be an unusual occurrence" (Dubin and Bunzel, 1933). There is much evidence to support this observation. Islamic nations, which condemn suicide more strongly than other societies, usually have lower suicide rates. Similarly, African Americans have a relatively low suicide rate in the United States because their culture strongly condemns self-destruction (Early and Akers, 1995). Also, in Western societies, suicide has become more common in the present century than in previous ones largely because of the increasingly permissive attitude toward suicide. In the past, those who committed suicide were treated as criminals to be punished; today, suicides are considered victims to be sympathized with. In medieval England and Europe, for example, suicides were punished by denial of Christian burial, confiscation of property, or burial at a crossroads with a stake driven through the heart—presumably to keep the condemned spirit from wandering. Such harsh treatments of suicides are unheard of today. Instead, an upsurge of posthumous love, or at least tender feeling, toward the self-killer typically fills the hearts of the surviving relatives, friends, and others.

Survivors' Reactions

When a loved one, such as a friend or family member, commits suicide, those who are left behind tend to feel guilty. Parental suicide is particularly traumatic to young children, who may be so overwhelmed with guilt feelings that they become seriously disturbed. The children typically think that they were in some way responsible for their parent's death (Carter and Brooks, 1991). Mature adults also can hardly avoid the assault of guilt feelings. They often blame themselves for having failed to perceive the self-killer's suicidal intent, for having been unable to prevent the suicide, or for having done something that might have caused the suicide (Shellenbarger, 2001). Society further intensifies their self-blame by holding them responsible in some way for the death. However, unlike young children, mature adults are capable of neutralizing their guilt. As shown in one study, adults can rationalize their guilt in several ways: (1) They can regard themselves as having been good to the person who committed suicide. (2) They can view the suicide as inevitable, believing that even if they had been extraordinarily nice to the deceased, they still could not have stopped the suicide. (3) They can consider the suicide as a good thing for the person involved because the deceased is no longer suffering in this world (Henslin, 1970).

Most people also suffer from some symptoms of physical illness and emotional disturbance (such as migraine headache, hypertension, crying spells, and depression) subsequent to a close relative's suicide. These symptoms are comparable to, but more prolonged and devastating than, bereavement effects from natural or accidental death. They continue to plague the survivors even six months after the suicide. Within the same period, however, the relationships among the surviving family members are frequently strengthened, largely because the suicide prompts them to feel closer to each other in their common plight. The survivors also receive considerable support from other relatives and friends, who tend to be sympathetic, to listen, and to avoid the topic of death in order to focus on living (Shellenbarger, 2001; Farberow, 1991). Not surprisingly, health problems tend to remain in those who continue to think about their loved one's suicide and avoid discussing it with friends, keeping it as a "psychological skeleton in their emotional closet" (Pennebaker and O'Heeron, 1984).

While a parent's suicide has the greatest impact on the surviving child, a child's suicide has the most severe effect on the surviving parents. In addition to having the inevitable sense of shock and devastation in the wake of a child's suicide, the parents tend to feel totally responsible for the death because they are acutely aware of the tremendous stigma society attaches to parents whose child commits suicide. Research has shown that most people blame the parents of a child suicide more than they blame survivors of other suicides. Typically, the general public asks how this tragic event could possibly have happened (Calhoun, Selby, and Faulstich, 1980).

Advocating Suicide

Since the U.S. Supreme Court ruled in 1990 that Nancy Cruzan's parents had the right to remove the feeding tube that kept their comatose daughter alive, a growing number of Americans have come to believe that there is no virtue in heroically prolonging life against the patient's wishes. In fact, most Americans believe that terminally ill patients should be allowed to die with dignity rather than live in a deathlike, vegetative state. In response to this development, Congress has passed the Patient Self-Determination Act, which requires hospitals to inform patients of their right to control their treatment through living wills—advance instructions about what they want their doctors to do in the event of a terminal illness. This, in effect, allows patients to kill themselves by refusing life-sustaining treatments. More than half of U.S. doctors support this option. Further, increasing determination on the part of the government and general public to cut medical costs can be expected to encourage or pressure more doctors to withhold extremely expensive life-prolonging treatments from terminally ill or permanently unconscious patients (Gibbs, 1995; Davis, 1990).

Suicide involving the withholding of treatment, however, is different from physician-assisted suicide, in which the doctor helps the patient die by prescribing a lethal drug. According to a national survey, most Americans (72 percent) believe that terminally ill people have a right to die. But it is still illegal in virtually all the states in the United States. And only a small number (less than 5 percent) of American physicians have helped patients end their lives (*Contexts,* 2004).

Even in Oregon, the only state where assisted suicide is legal, doctors had helped only 71 patients (or 5 per 100,000 population) die between 1998 and 2005. By contrast, in the Netherlands, where assisted suicide is also legal, doctors help roughly 4,000 patients (or 25 per 100,000 population) commit suicide every year. A major reason for the difference is that it is easier to get assisted suicide in the Netherlands. There, children as young as 12 may qualify with parental consent, but in Oregon only those who are at least 18 are eligible. Also, Dutch patients may qualify if they are merely chronically ill and cannot bear their suffering, but their peers in Oregon must be terminally ill and have only six months or less to live. Apparently, then, the Dutch are more liberal than the Americans in Oregon (Yen, 2005; Nelson, 2004; Liptak, 2002; Cloud, 2001).

Still, the assisted suicide law in Oregon has been gaining support throughout the United States. In 2006 the U.S. Supreme Court upheld the Oregon law, fueling other states' efforts to pass similar legislation. An apparent reason is recognition of the patient's unbearable pain. Some critics argue that the medical profession is to blame for this problem because the vast majority of doctors do not know how to treat pain, so that up to 90 percent of patients die in too much pain (Guthrie, 2006; Gibbs, 1993a). The critics assume that if the medical profession could eliminate the pain, terminally ill patients would stop requesting suicide. But unrelievable pain is not the only reason for suicide. In the eye of right-to-die advocates, the quality of life (such as loss of dignity, loss of autonomy, or loss of meaning of life) is more important than merely being alive. It is argued, therefore, that people should be allowed to die if they find their lives worthless or unbearable. There is also the legal argument that the right to die is the same as the constitutionally guaranteed right to privacy, the right to be left alone (Ganzini et al., 2008; Rosenfeld, 2004; Gianelli, 1999).

Preventing Suicide

All this has alarmed right-to-life groups. They are more concerned with the sanctity of life. Considering every life sacred, they argue that it is morally wrong to take one's own life just as it is to take another's and that it is the state's duty to help preserve rather than destroy life. They fear that doctor-assisted suicide would lead down the "slippery slope" to widespread euthanasia. They believe that, although they would not necessarily want to die, the physically or mentally different, the poor, and others devalued by society, along with many terminally ill patients, would be eliminated in the same way as their counterparts were in

Nazi Germany. Their lives would be regarded from the quality-of-life perspective as worthless, and it would be considered justifiable and even merciful to terminate them. If these "worthless" people are not legally required to die, they would still be under great social pressure to commit suicide as an act of love and patriotism because their death would remove a costly burden on family and society (Hendin, 1997; Mauro, 1996). As an author who opposes mercy killing of the terminally ill sums it up, "From there, it's a hop, skip and a jump to killing people who don't have a good 'quality' of life, perhaps with the prospect of organ harvesting thrown in as a plum to society" (Smith, 1993).

While the right-to-life forces try to stop doctor-assisted suicide, another group is more interested in discouraging large masses of distressed, suicidal people from killing themselves. Since the 1950s, many suicide-prevention centers have appeared in various countries. At least 150 such organizations now exist in Great Britain and over 200 in the United States. Their primary function is to encourage troubled individuals to telephone them for help. They have friendly, compassionate, and dedicated volunteers working around the clock (Hendin, 1995).

There is some evidence that these organizations, using the psychological method of counseling, can effectively deal with a few individual cases of potential suicide. But they cannot substantially reduce suicide rates. Thus, despite the tremendous increase in the number of suicide prevention centers in the United States over the last 40 years, the suicide rate has not declined significantly. One study even shows that there is little overall difference in suicide rates between counties that have suicide prevention centers and those that do not (Miller et al., 1984). The reason is that suicide is basically a sociological problem (caused by larger social factors) rather than a psychological problem (caused by factors within the individual).

It is worth noting that people who are characteristically prone to suicide, such as older men, tend to stay away from suicide prevention centers, and, in the few cases when they do call the centers for help, tend to go ahead and kill themselves anyway. On the other hand, people who are less inclined to commit suicide, such as young white women, constitute the majority of those who call up the centers and are likely to refrain from taking their lives (Hendin, 1995; Greer and Weinstein, 1979). In other words, suicide prevention centers are more useful to people who are *less* likely to commit suicide, but less useful to people who are *more* likely to end their own lives. Apparently the organizations cannot deal with the social forces that cause some older men and other seriously suicide-prone individuals to kill themselves. What exactly is the nature of these social forces? Some of the theories discussed below may give us the answer.

Sociological Theories of Suicide

Efforts to explain suicide can be divided into two broad categories: psychiatric and sociological theories. Psychiatric theories generally assume that there is *something wrong* with the person who commits suicide, whereas sociological theories assume that there is *nothing wrong* with that person. More specifically, to psychiatrists, suicidal people are in one way or another mentally ill—hence, mental illness is considered the cause of suicide. A few other psychiatrists hold the classical Freudian view that the death instinct, thanks to the breakdown of ego defenses, drives individuals to kill themselves. Most psychiatrists, however, theorize that the cause of suicide is mental depression, morbid anxiety, intense hopelessness, deep frustration, or a traumatic experience during early childhood. An exception is psychiatrist Thomas Joiner's (2005) theory that puts forth a confluence of three social-psychological factors as the cause of suicide. To kill themselves, people must first *overcome the fear of death*—the self-preservation instinct that has long evolved in humans. They can overcome the fear of death by repeatedly experiencing violence, pain, or injury so that they can ultimately acquire the ability to fatally injure themselves. Then they must *feel being a burden* on their loved ones and others. And finally they must *feel socially isolated,* disconnected, and alienated from others.

To most sociologists, the psychiatric theories that attribute suicide to some mental problem are useless because they're not able to explain why some individuals (who are, say, men, whites, or older persons) are more likely to commit suicide than other individuals (who are women, blacks, or younger persons). If we used the psychiatric theories for an explanation, we would have to insist that men, whites, and older persons are somehow psychologically abnormal, which is, of course, far from the truth. Also, to sociologists, the causes of suicide do not reside within the individual, but within the group to which the individual belongs. But not all sociologists are positivists, looking for the social causes of suicide. Some sociologists are constructionists, more interested in seeking out the meanings of suicide. In the following sections we will discuss two positivist theories of suicide and then two constructionist theories of suicide.

Classical Durkheimian Theory

Although French sociologist Émile Durkheim (1897) presented his positivist theory of suicide many years ago, it remains the most influential theory in the field. If we examine it very closely, as we would the trees of a forest, we can get confused by its many ambiguities and inconsistencies. But if we look at it as a whole, as we would the forest, we may see with clarity a very useful theory for explaining various types of group influences on suicide rates. Let's look at the theory as a whole.

According to Durkheim, there are two major causes of suicide: One has to do with *social integration,* the other, with *social regulation.* Social integration involves individuals voluntarily attaching themselves to a group or society of which they are members. Social regulation involves individuals being restrained, constrained, or controlled by a group or society of which they are members. Social integration or regulation varies from one individual to another. Compared with unmarried individuals, for example, married persons experience more social integration by virtue of their being a spouse and parent, an important part of a group called the family. Similarly, compared with males, females are subjected to greater social regulation by a society with gender inequality, as exemplified by girls experiencing greater parental control than their brothers.

According to Durkheim, people who experience *too little* social integration as well as people who experience *too much* integration are more likely to commit suicide, when compared with those who experience *moderate* integration. In like manner, those who are subjected to *too little* social regulation as well as people who are subjected to *too much* regulation are more likely to kill themselves, when compared with those who are subjected to *moderate* regulation. There are, then, four types of suicide, as shown in

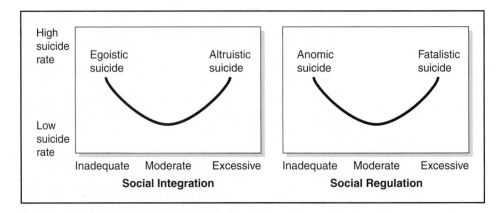

FIGURE 7.2   Schematic Presentation of Durkheim's Theory

Figure 7.2: (1) *egoistic suicide,* which is caused by too little social integration; (2) *altruistic suicide,* brought about by too much integration; (3) *anomic suicide,* generated by too little social regulation; and (4) *fatalistic suicide,* produced by too much regulation.

A few examples can be used to explain how the theory works. Compared with married persons, unmarried ones are more likely to commit *egoistic* suicide, because they are *less socially integrated,* and are unable to receive love, affection, or moral support from a spouse and children when deeply frustrated with their lives. Compared with the average citizens of a country, members of a close-knit terrorist group are more likely to commit *altruistic* suicide by becoming suicide bombers, because they are *more integrated* into their organization. Rich countries have higher rates of *anomic* suicide than poor countries. This is because the citizens of rich countries, being *less socially regulated,* are more encouraged to expect too much from life, and thus more liable to greater frustration when their expectations fail to materialize. In ancient societies slaves were more likely than free persons to commit *fatalistic* suicide, for, as Durkheim reasoned, the slaves were *more regulated* in that their "futures were pitilessly blocked and passions violently choked by oppressive discipline" (Durkheim, 1897). Fatalistic suicide is also relatively common today among rural women in China, where the women are often made to feel worthless and helpless because of their gender (Pearson and Liu, 2006; Rosenthal, 1999).

Many studies have supported Durkheim's theory. Here are a few examples:

- Anders Barstad (2008) found that young Norwegian men's soaring suicide rate since 1970 seems to have resulted from their decreasing likelihood to marry, which signals a decline in social integration.
- Nick Danigelis and Whitney Pope (1979) found that the married have lower suicide rates than the single, divorced, or widowed, because, as Durkheim's theory suggests, married people are more socially integrated than others.
- Steven Stack (1979) discovered that a sharp increase in political regulation—indicated by such events as declarations of martial law and banning of a political party—is associated with an increase in suicide.

■ Walter Gove and Michael Hughes (1980) found that living alone, which reveals a lack of social integration, is a powerful predictor of suicide.

A Modern Durkheimian Theory

A number of modern positivist theories of suicide derive their core concepts from Durkheim's classical theory. The most persuasive and interesting is the theory developed by Andrew Henry and James Short (1954).

Henry and Short first define *suicide* as an act of aggression directed against oneself, the aggression having been induced by one's frustration with life. They then theorize that this self-directed aggression results from three different factors, which are (1) sociological, (2) psychological, and (3) economic in nature.

The sociological factor consists of two parts: *a weak relational system* and *weak external restraint*. The first term refers to a lack of involvement with other people, so the term *weak relational system* means about the same thing as Durkheim's *inadequate social integration*. As Durkheim would have anticipated, Henry and Short point out that individuals who are inadequately involved with others are prone to suicide. These suicide-prone people include those who are unmarried rather than married and those who are older (over age 65) rather than younger.

The second term, *weak external restraint,* has the same meaning as Durkheim's *inadequate social regulation*. Like Durkheim, Henry and Short argue that higher-status persons are more likely than lower-status ones to commit suicide, because higher-status individuals have less external restraint so that they tend to blame themselves rather than others for their own problems. By higher-status persons, Henry and Short refer to whites, males, individuals with high income, and army officers. By low-status persons, Henry and Short have in mind blacks, females, individuals with low income, and army recruits.

With respect to the psychological factor of suicide, Henry and Short suggest that a strong superego, which is thought to result from "internalization of harsh parental demands and discipline," produces a high psychological propensity to suicide. This means that if people have been conditioned by their parents to develop a strong conscience, they are likely to blame themselves rather than other people for their problems and frustrations. Since they blame themselves (instead of others), they will likely kill themselves (instead of others).

As for the economic factor of suicide, Henry and Short show that suicide rates rise in times of economic depression and fall in times of prosperity. Economic depression, then, is a major cause of high suicide rates. Henry and Short also observe that, although people of both higher and lower statuses find economic depression frustrating, the frustration is greater for higher-status individuals and, therefore, more likely to cause them to kill themselves. This is because, during an economic depression, higher-status individuals, who by definition occupy a higher social position than lower-status people, fall harder and hurt more.

These three factors in suicide are interrelated through the concept of social status. In terms of the sociological factor, the higher-status person is more likely to be part of a weak relational system and to experience weak external restraint and therefore to commit suicide. In terms of the psychological factor, the higher-status person is likely to have a stronger superego and consequently a greater tendency toward suicide. Finally, in terms of the economic factor, the higher-status person is likely to experience greater frustration during an economic depression and is thus more prone to suicide. By integrating the sociological, psychological, and economic concepts into one theory, Henry and Short have contributed a great deal to our knowledge about the causes of suicide. Research has also largely supported their theory (Unnithan, Huff-Corzine, Corzine, and Whitt, 1994; Lester, 1990).

Phenomenological Theories

Ultimately the validity of the Durkheimian theories, both classical and modern, depends on the reliability of the official suicide statistics that have been used as the source of empirical support for the theories. Durkheimian theorists assume that these statistics are reasonably reliable; consequently, they consider their theories reasonably valid. Phenomenological sociologists, however, believe that the official statistics are seriously unreliable; therefore, they develop a different perspective on suicide.

Two basic differences exist between Durkheimian and phenomenological theories: (1) Durkheimian theories are positivist and thus etiological, primarily concerned with seeking out the *causes* of group differences in suicide rates. In contrast, phenomenological theories are constructionist and thus nonetiological, dealing with the popular *meanings* of suicide or with how the suicidal person acts on these meanings. In a way, though, the meanings may cause the individual to commit suicide. (2) Durkheimian theories look at suicide *from a distance*—through abstract official statistics. On the other hand, phenomenological theories look at suicide *up close*—through actual suicide notes, interviews with the suicide victim's surviving relatives and friends, and interviews with suicide attempters.

Theory of Suicidal Meanings.   According to Jack Douglas (1967), before committing suicide, individuals impute certain meanings to their own prospective suicidal acts. These personal meanings, however, differ from the widely shared meanings that the society attaches to suicide.

Douglas believes that our society attaches to suicide three types of meaning: (1) "*Suicidal actions are meaningful.*" This means that many people typically ascribe some motive to suicide, such as depression, hopelessness, or drug abuse. (2) "*Something is fundamentally wrong with the suicidal person's social situation.*" The general public often blames a suicide on the victim's parents, spouse, lover, or employer. (3) "*Something is fundamentally wrong with the suicidal person himself.*" Most people are jolted with shock, bewilderment, or disbelief on hearing that someone they know has committed suicide. The reason is that the society has conditioned them to view suicide as a very unnatural act. Individuals who kill themselves are consequently thought of as psychologically abnormal.

Unlike these three popular meanings of suicide, the meanings that suicidal people construct to make sense of their prospective self-destruction make it easier for them to end their own lives. Douglas divides these personal meanings into four types: (1) "*Suicide is a way of transporting the soul from this world to the other world.*" By killing themselves, people believe that they will leave behind their tumultuous lives for a tranquil, peaceful world. (2) "*Suicide is a way of changing the view of oneself held by others in this world.*" Feeling that their family and others have taken them for granted while alive, people expect their suicide to attract a great deal of attention, believing that they will be greatly missed and their fine qualities appreciated after they die. (3) "*Suicide is a way of achieving fellow-feeling."* In a surrealistic, dreamlike way, people expect their suicide to generate a great deal of sympathy, thereby bringing their family and friends closer to them. (4) *"Suicide is a way of getting revenge."* Some people want to use their suicide to get even with others by making them feel guilty for having made their lives miserable.

To suicidal people, these personal meanings of suicide are *positive* in nature, and, therefore, make it easier for them to commit suicide. While Douglas focuses on the positive types of suicidal meanings that facilitate suicides, the theorist we will turn to now views suicidal meanings as *negative* in that they discourage suicides. Individuals must, therefore, go through a process of rejecting the negative meanings before they can commit suicide.

Theory of Suicidal Process.   Jerry Jacobs (1967) views the meanings of suicide as social prohibitions against the act because suicide is defined by society as "a violation of the sacred, God-given trust of life." Thus, according to Jacobs, suicidal people must overcome the social prohibitions before taking their own lives. This entails going through a series of experiences, conceptualizations, or rationalizations.

1. Individuals find themselves faced with unexpected, intolerable, and unsolvable problems.
2. They view these problems not as isolated incidents, but as part of a long-standing history of problems. At the same time, they expect more problems in the future.
3. They believe that death is the only way to solve these problems.
4. Their belief in the efficacy of death intensifies through increasing social isolation, because they cannot share their problems with others.
5. They now diligently look for ways to overcome the social prohibition against suicide, which they have so internalized that they view suicide as immoral.
6. They succeed in overcoming the prohibition because they already feel isolated from others and, therefore, feel freer to act on their own.
7. They succeed in overcoming the prohibition by rationalizing their intended suicide in such ways as, "Killing myself doesn't necessarily mean I don't hold life sacred. In fact, I still hold life sacred despite my suicide."
8. They convince themselves that the problem they experience is not of their own making and cannot be solved except through suicide.
9. Defining suicide as the necessary solution, they feel that they do not have the choice not to kill themselves, thereby freeing themselves from a sense of guilt and responsibility for their impending suicide.
10. Finally, just to make sure that they will not be punished in the afterlife, they pray to God for forgiveness or leave a suicide note requesting the survivors to pray for their souls. Then they decisively kill themselves.

Summary

1. How do suicidal people approach suicide? There are three types of suicidal people, each with a different way of dealing with suicide.

(1) Suicide threateners are explicit in communicating their suicidal intention to others. (2) Suicide attempters are less explicit with their suicidal

messages but more likely to actually try to end their lives. (3) Suicide committers may have threatened or attempted suicide or neither in the past. Suicide committers may feel depressed, apologetic, vindictive toward others, angry with themselves, magnanimous, or surrealistic just before they die.

2. Who are more likely than others to commit suicide? Suicide rates are higher among residents in sparsely than in densely populated areas or in rural than in urban areas, among whites than blacks, among the less than the more religious, among men than women, among the divorced than the married, among older than younger people, and among the affluent than the less well-off.

3. What is the social profile of suicide bombers? They are relatively rational, well-off, and well-educated and mostly young, male, and single. They do not work alone but instead receive significant support from terrorist organizations.

4. How are some social situations or experiences conducive to suicide? The rate of youthful suicide has increased sharply over the last three decades because of declining social integration and control in the teenager's life. College students are also more likely than before to commit suicide not only because of the greater stress in college life but also because of the diminishing support to cope with the stress. Prison inmates are more likely than free citizens to kill themselves because of tension and stress resulting from the new, unaccustomed experience of confinement and the uncertainty of what will happen to them. HIV-infected patients are more suicidal than those with full-blown AIDS because of extreme stress from having suddenly become seriously ill as well as from uncertainty about the outcome of their sickness. Ordinary suicidal people tend to kill themselves after a celebrity suicide is widely publicized because the celebrity serves as a role model and lends legitimacy to

suicide. The frequent radio broadcast of country music also promotes suicide by reinforcing the suicidal moods of suicidally inclined listeners.

5. How does society respond to suicide? While societal response to suicide was punitive in the past, it is sympathetic today. Consequently, suicide tends to generate guilt feelings and even symptoms of physical and mental illness in the survivors. Further, sympathy toward suicides has generated two different social responses. One involves advocating the right to die with dignity, especially when suffering a terminal illness or unrelievable pain. The other involves preventing suicide either by generally supporting the right to preserve the sanctity of life or by specifically helping suicide-prone individuals to avoid killing themselves.

6. What is the global pattern of suicide? Industrialized societies have higher suicide rates than less industrialized ones, but fast-industrializing counties in Asia now have high rates. In the West, high suicide rates are associated with greater equality and freedom, and suicide tends to occur more in the spring and the beginning of the week.

7. How do sociologists explain suicide? While psychiatrists generally attribute suicide to mental disturbance of one type or another, sociologists view the suicidal person as normal. There are two categories of sociological theories: (1) Durkheimian theories are etiological, designed to explain the causes of group differences in suicide rates. Durkheim's original theory suggests that high suicide rates result from either excessive or inadequate social integration and regulation. Henry and Short's theory includes sociological, psychological, and economic factors as causes of high suicide rates. (2) Phenomenological theories are nonetiological, focusing on the meanings of suicide and on how individual suicides behave in accordance with the meanings. One such theory, developed by Douglas, deals with how society and the suicidal person differ in defining suicide and how the personal meanings imputed to suicide facilitate the process of suicide. Another meaning-based theory by Jacobs shows how individuals have to overcome the moral prohibition against suicide through certain experiences, conceptualizations, or rationalizations before they can take their own lives.

FURTHER READING

Balkin, Karen F. (ed.). 2005. *Assisted Suicide*. Detroit, Mich.: Greenhaven Press. A series of essays presenting conflicting views on various aspects of assisted suicide.

Dorais, Michel, and Simon Lajeunesse. 2004. *Dead Boys Can't Dance: Sexual Orientation, Masculinity, and Suicide*. Montreal, Canada: McGill-Queen's University Press. A sociological analysis of suicides among young gay men.

Early, Kevin E. 1992. *Religion and Suicide in the African-American Community*. Westport, Conn.: Greenwood. An empirical analysis of how the African American community and culture keeps the black suicide rate low.

Friedman, Lauri S. (ed.). 2005. *What Motivates Suicide Bombers?* Detroit, Mich.: Greenhaven Press. A presentation of various and conflicting views on what motivates suicide bombing, with some, for example, pointing at nationalism and American imperialism as the motives and others blaming Islam and the promise of an afterlife.

Gambetta, Diego (ed.). 2005. *Making Sense of Suicide Missions*. New York: Oxford University Press. A collection of articles about suicide missions in various countries involving the Japanese kamikaze pilots, Tamil Tigers, Palestinians, al Qaeda suicide bombers, and others.

Girard, Chris. 1993. "Age, gender, and suicide: A cross-national analysis." *American Sociological Review,* 58, 553–574. An empirical analysis of how role identities, economic development, and kinship institutions affect the age and gender patterns of suicide—such as highest suicide risks for men in old age and for women in middle age in economically developed countries.

Hendin, Herbert. 1997. *Seduced by Death: Doctors, Patients, and the Dutch Cure*. New York: Norton. A critical analysis of the practice of euthanasia and suicide in the Netherlands.

Holmes, Ronald M., and Stephen T. Holmes. 2005. *Suicide: Theory, Practice, and Investigation*. Thousand Oaks, Calif.: Sage. A brief book about how and why various kinds of people such as the youth and the elderly commit suicide.

Joiner, Thomas. 2005. *Why People Die by Suicide*. Cambridge, Mass.: Harvard University Press. An empirically based analysis of three related causes of suicide: the acquired ability to enact lethal self-injury, the feeling of being a burden on others, and the feeling of disconnection from others.

King, Robert A., and Alan Apter (eds.). 2003. *Suicide in Children and Adolescents*. New York: Cambridge University Press. A collection of articles on youthful suicide analyzed from sociological, psychological, and biological perspectives.

Lester, David. 2000. *Why People Kill Themselves,* 4th ed. Springfield, Ill: Charles C. Thomas Publishers. Summarizing the main findings of numerous research studies on suicide conducted in the 1990s.

Macdonald, Charles J. H. 2007. *Uncultural Behavior: An Anthropological Investigation of Suicide in the Southern Philippines*. Honolulu: University of Hawaii Press. Offers the theory that suicide can be explained by a combination of three interrelated factors: a biologically inherited predisposition, a catastrophic event, and being influenced by suicidal relatives, friends, and acquaintances.

Pickering, W. S. F., and Geoffrey Walford. 2000. *Durkheim's Suicide: A Century of Research and Debate*. London: Routledge. A collection of articles that review and evaluate critical analyses and empirical studies of Durkheim's theoretical ideas about suicide.

Rickgarn, Ralph L. V. 1994. *Perspectives on College Student Suicide*. Amityville, N.Y.: Baywood. An analysis of various aspects of campus suicide, including how suicidal students view college and suicide and how to prevent student suicides.

Stack, Steven, and Jim Gundlach. 1992. "The effect of country music on suicide." *Social Forces,* 71, 211–218. An empirical study of the influence of radio-broadcast country music on white suicide rates in large cities.

Unnithan, N. Prabha, Lin Huff-Corzine, Jay Corzine, and Hugh P. Whitt. 1994. *The Current Lethal Violence: An Integrated Model of Suicide and Homicide*. Albany: State University of New York Press.

Reformulating Henry and Short's classic theory to explain how attribution of blame leads to suicide rather than homicide or vice versa.

CRITICAL THINKING QUESTIONS

1. Sociologists have long discovered that the lack of social integration is related to suicide. Given this social fact, could you prevent a depressed friend who is highly independent from taking his or her life? If you could, what would you do? If you couldn't, why not?

2. Would you support or oppose the doctor-assisted suicide law for people who suffer a terminal illness or unrelievable pain? Why or why not?

8 Mental Disorder

Myths and Realities

Myth: In general, the mentally ill are extremely "weird" or greatly disturbed.

Reality: Most mental patients are far from greatly disturbed. Even among schizophrenics—the most severely mentally ill—the flamboyant symptoms of hallucinations and delusions are not the most important characteristics of their disorder (p. 169).

Myth: Mental illness is essentially incurable; most mental patients will never recover.

Reality: The majority of mental patients can recover and live relatively normal lives. Even schizophrenics can eventually recover. According to research in the United States and Europe, about half of all schizophrenics *spontaneously* get better over the course of

20 years. Professional treatment further makes the recovery easier and faster (p. 170).

Myth: The mentally ill can be easily and clearly distinguished from the mentally healthy.

Reality: Most of the time even psychiatrists cannot clearly differentiate the vast majority of the mentally ill from the mentally healthy (p. 170).

Myth: The mentally ill are mostly crazed, violent, and therefore dangerous.

Reality: The great majority (about 90 percent) of mental patients are not prone to violence and criminality. They are more likely to hurt themselves than others (p. 170).

Myth: We are likely to become depressed in the middle of winter because of its coldness and lack of sunshine.

Reality: Depression is more likely to strike us in the summer than in winter, presumably because we spend less time with our loved ones during the warm season than the cold season (p. 170).

Myth: Compared to men, women are more likely to become mentally ill because their lives as victims of gender inequality are more restrictive and oppressive.

Reality: Some studies show women to have a higher rate of mental illness but other studies show men to have a higher rate. There are no conflicting findings, however, in regard to *specific* disorders: Women are more likely to suffer from depression and anxiety attacks while men are more likely to have antisocial personality and paranoia (p. 177).

Myth: Nowadays, older people are more likely than young people to suffer from depression.

Reality: Over the last several decades the problem of depression has increased so much among young people that today they are more likely than older people to suffer from depression (p. 178).

Myth: Urban residents are more likely than rural and small-town dwellers to suffer from severe depression because it is more stressful to live in the city.

Reality: While they exhibit higher levels of neurotic and personality disorders, urban dwellers are *less* likely to experience severe depression (p. 180).

Myth: Today the mentally ill are no longer stigmatized as moral lepers. Most people treat them with respect and understanding. Only a few uneducated people still regard them as second-class citizens.

Reality: Most people, whether old or young, well educated or with little schooling, feel that the mentally ill are somehow dangerous, violent, unpredictable, or worthless (p. 184).

Myth: In the United States today, mentally ill criminals are more likely to be sent to a mental institution than to a prison.

Reality: They are more likely to be sent to a prison (p. 187).

Bob Antonioni, a 48-year-old attorney, has struggled with depression for nearly a decade. In public he appeared normal, appearing in court on behalf of his clients. But in private he was irritable and short-tempered, and became easily frustrated by small things, such as deciding which television show to watch with his girlfriend. Working at his office, he often would get so exhausted by noon that he would go home and collapse on the couch, where he would stay for the rest of the day. When he decided to seek help, he kept it a secret from his friends and family. He saw a therapist in secret, and he had his prescriptions for antidepressants filled at a pharmacy 20 miles away (Scelfo, 2007).

Like Antonioni, millions of Americans suffer from depression. If other, less serious psychiatric problems are also taken into account, mental disorder is indeed very common. According to the latest national survey, about half of all adult Americans have experienced at least one episode of psychiatric disorder during their lifetime, and a quarter within the past year alone (Sergo, 2008; Kessler et al., 2005a, 2005b).

In fact, *all* of us have been mentally ill at one time or another in the same way as all of us have been physically ill. Of course, most of our mental disorders are not serious at all, just as most of our physical illnesses are not. But, just as we all have occasionally come down with a minor physical ailment such as the flu, we all have occasionally come down with a relatively minor mental disorder such as mild depression. Indeed, mild depression is so prevalent that it has been called "the common cold of mental illness" (Cherry and Cherry, 1973).

Yet, because of the stigma attached to mental illness, most people associate it with only severe forms of illness such as major depression and schizophrenia. Therefore, if we come down with the flu and call in sick we would say to our boss, "I'm ill today," but if we are too depressed to go to work, our family would be too afraid to tell our boss that we are mentally ill. If we say we are *physically* ill, most people would *not* automatically assume we are suffering from a serious illness such as heart disease, cancer, or AIDS. But if we say we are *mentally* ill, most people would jump to the conclusion that we need to be sent to a mental institution right away.

While the general public equates "mental illness" only with the relatively severe and uncommon forms of mental disorder, most of the mental illnesses that occur every day are far from severe and are extremely common. They are basically problems of everyday life, ranging from being sad, anxious, irritable, or antisocial to being dependent on drugs, alcohol, or coffee to doing poorly in reading, writing, or math as a youngster. Psychiatrists define all such problems as mental disorders (Ratey and Johnson, 1997; APA, 1994), but we would not if we associate mental illness only with its relatively serious forms, such as being too depressed to function adequately in one's daily life (Horwitz and Wakefield, 2006; Kutchins and Kirk, 1997). In this chapter we will deal mostly with serious forms of mental disorder. First, though, we will discuss a number of popular beliefs about mental disorder. Then, we will take a look at various types of mental disorder, examine a number of social forces behind mental disorder, analyze a series of societal responses to the problem, and see how different psychiatrists and sociologists view or explain mental disorder.

Popular Beliefs

The mentally ill are popularly believed to be extremely weird. In fact, most are far from greatly disturbed. This is the first of several common misconceptions. Only a few inmates of mental institutions spend their time cutting out paper dolls, screaming and yelling, talking to the air, or posing as kings or queens. Even among the most severely mentally ill—schizophrenics—the flamboyant symptoms of hallucinations and delusions are not the most important characteristics of their disorder. Instead, the less demonstrative symptoms of apathy and inertia constitute the core of schizophrenia. In fact, most patients are like ourselves, "much more simply human than otherwise" (Zimmerman, 2003; Boffey, 1986).

Mental illness is—to take up a second popular belief—hopeless, essentially incurable. Even after people are discharged from a mental hospital as recovered, they are likely to be viewed with suspicion. In reality, the majority (some 70 to 80 percent) of hospitalized mental patients can recover and live relatively normal lives if their treatment has been adequate and received in time. Even many schizophrenics, whose illness is probably the most debilitating and devastating, can eventually recover. According to studies in the United States and Europe, about half of all schizophrenics *spontaneously* get better over the course of 20 years, and professional treatment with support from family and friends further makes the recovery easier and faster (Kopelowicz and Bidder, 1992; Boffey, 1986).

A third popular belief is that there is a sharp, clear distinction between "mentally ill" and "mentally healthy." This is widely taken for granted, but it is true only if we compare the extremely few mentally ill persons who are extraordinarily disturbed with average "normal" people. Most of the time even a psychiatrist cannot clearly differentiate the vast majority of the mentally ill from the mentally healthy. Thus the dividing line between mental health and illness is mostly arbitrary (Brody, 1997; APA, 1994). This is not only because the behavior of different individuals ranges by imperceptible degrees from normal to abnormal, but also because an individual may shift at different times to different positions along that range, appearing normal at one time and abnormal at another.

The fourth popular belief is that the mentally ill are mostly crazed or violent, as often portrayed in news media, movies, and television programs. In fact, the great majority (about 90 percent) of mental patients are not prone to violence and criminality. They are more likely to engage in behavior harmful to themselves rather than to others. Most significant, they are six or seven times more likely than other citizens to become *victims* of homicide (Harris and Lurigio, 2007; Cuvelier, 2002; Monahan, 1992).

The fifth popular belief is about midwinter depression, which psychiatrists call SAD (seasonal affective disorder). Many people assume that we are likely to become depressed in the middle of winter because of its coldness and lack of sunshine. Research has shown otherwise: Depression is more likely to strike people in the summer than winter (Smyth and Thompson, 1990; Christensen and Dowrick, 1983). Presumably, the summer is more likely to give us the blues because we spend less time with our loved ones than we do in the winter.

Most recently, a new popular belief has emerged that there is an epidemic of autism—characterized by serious problems with language and social bonding—among American children. According to the U.S. Department of Education, the nationwide rate of autism had jumped 657 percent over the last decade, leading a congressman to declare, "We have an epidemic on our hands." But many behavioral scientists disagree. They point out that much of the startling rise in autism results from, among other things, a broader definition that includes many more children with mild symptoms who would not be considered autistic in the past and a school policy that causes many children with mental retardation or learning disabilities to be labeled autistic (*Current Science,* 2008; Lilienfeld and Arkowitz, 2007; Monastersky, 2007).

Types of Mental Disorder

Psychiatry has two opposing views on what constitutes mental disorder. One is the medical view, which defines mental disorder chiefly as a *biologically* caused disorder, similar to a physical disease. This view dominates psychiatry today, and its influence can be found in the current edition of a manual published by the American Psychiatric Association for helping psychiatrists diagnose patients. This diagnostic manual contains a long list of mental disorders with numerous symptoms the same way as a medical manual does for physical diseases. The other view of mental disorder is psychoanalytic, which defines mental disorder primarily as an emotional problem that is *psychological* in origin. This view dominated psychiatry in the 1950s and 1960s and is less popular with psychiatrists today. But its traditional classification of mental disorders into fewer and broader types still provides insight into what it is like to be mentally ill (Wilson, 1993).

Traditional Classification

In the traditional classification system, mental illness is divided into two broad types: *organic* and *functional* disorders. Both types may show the same symptoms, such as hallucination, delusion, impaired judgment, and other behavioral disturbances, but they can be differentiated on the basis of their underlying causes. Organic disorder is caused by damage to the brain, which in turn may have originated from a tumor, head injury, viral meningitis, brain syphilis, lead poisoning, deterioration from old age, drug abuse, or other acute physical damage. Functional disorder, on the other hand, is believed to result from psychological and social factors, such as unpleasant childhood experiences, interpersonal conflict, or social stress. Functional disorder constitutes a much larger category of mental disorders than organic disorder. Psychiatrists, psychologists, and sociologists are primarily interested in the study of functional disorder.

Functional disorder can be further divided into three major categories: *psychosis, neurosis,* and *personality disorder* (see Figure 8.1). In general, psychosis is typified by losing touch with reality, and neurosis by an inability to face reality. As Freud put it, "Psychosis denies reality and tries to substitute something else for it; neurosis does not deny reality, it merely tries to ignore it" (quoted in Kolb and Brodie, 1982). Since psychotics have lost contact with reality, they do not recognize that they are mentally ill and, therefore, have no desire to seek treatment. Neurotics, conversely, still know what reality is, keenly feel their suffering, and consciously want to get well. Their problem is an inability to accept reality for what it is, causing them to be unreasonably worried about it, terrified by it, or obsessed with it. A psychotic can be likened to a person who thinks that two plus two is equal to 10 and strongly believes it, whereas a neurotic can be compared to a person who thinks that two plus two is equal to four but constantly worries about it. What about the third type of disordered person, who has the personality disorder? This individual is basically too self-absorbed, unsociable, or antisocial, and may say, "The hell with two plus two; what a silly game to play." Let's get a closer view of these three categories of functional disorder.

Psychosis. Psychosis is more serious than neurosis and personality, or character, disorder. More important, because psychosis involves the loss of touch with reality, the patient

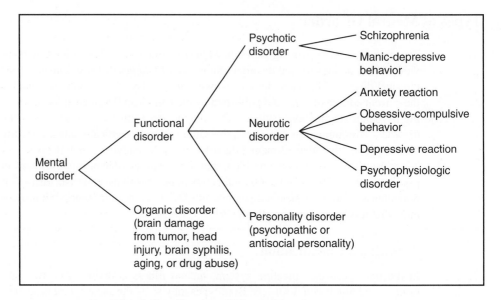

FIGURE 8.1   Traditional Classification of Mental Disorders

cannot attend school or work or do other things that normal people do. There are many different types of psychosis, but we will discuss only two major ones here for purposes of illustration.

Schizophrenia is the most common type of psychosis. Schizophrenics think and talk in unconventional, illogical, or ambiguous ways; they may say things such as "My body is a bottle." They express emotions inappropriately, for example, by laughing in response to sad news and crying in response to happy news. They withdraw from others into their inner selves, often becoming totally unresponsive to their surroundings. They may simply sit, mute, motionless, and emotionless, sunk in deep apathy. Sometimes they engage in such infantile acts as thumb sucking. They have delusions of grandeur (e.g., thinking themselves to be presidents) and delusions of persecution (e.g., believing the whole world is plotting to assassinate them). They have hallucinations, hearing voices where there is only silence and seeing things that do not exist. They will talk to themselves or scream loudly to voices only they can hear. Actually, these experiences of distorted reality are not rare; all of us may have encountered them once in awhile. But psychiatrists would not consider us schizophrenic unless these experiences occur so frequently that our school, job, or family functions are severely disrupted. Because of the severe nature of their mental disorder, schizophrenics are thought to require hospitalization.

Another major type of psychosis is *manic-depressive disorder,* also called bipolar disorder. This involves fluctuating between two opposite extremes of mood. One extreme, called *mania,* is characterized by great elation, exuberance, confidence, or excitement. Individuals in this mood are constantly joking, laughing, and making speeches, although they are far from happy or content. They are continually on the move, not because they enjoy it but because they are driven to it by powerful tension within them. In this hyperactivity, they are enveloped by grandiose delusions, thinking that they are superior or godlike, capable of achieving anything. After going through this manic phase, they suddenly find themselves in the opposite extreme, called *depression*. When brought down to a depressive state, the victims feel an overwhelming despair, experience the delusion of worthlessness, and think of committing suicide. Consequently, they lose the desire to talk, move, eat, and sleep, and spend a lot of time crying.

Neurosis.   Neurosis is less severe than psychosis. There is little distortion of reality, and most neurotics are still able to appear normal and do most of the things that normal people do, such as staying in school, keeping jobs, and maintaining family relations. The only problem is that their neurotic symptoms prevent them from being as happy as they want to be. There are various types of neurosis, each characterized by a certain syndrome.

One is *anxiety reaction,* which is a generalized, vague, freely floating apprehension. The object of apprehension cannot be identified. Normal people occasionally experience such anxiety, such as the nervousness we feel before taking an exam, giving a speech, or being interviewed for a job. But the anxiety that attacks the neurotic is far more serious. Consider the case of a 25-year-old secretary: When she was about to leave her office one evening, she suddenly had an intense panicky sensation that something dreadful was going to happen. She had difficulty breathing, feeling as though she was choking. She also felt dizzy. Waves of fear ran through her. Her heart was pounding strongly and loudly, making her think she might be dying. Her legs became rubbery, but she managed to make it outside to get some fresh air. Gradually, the panic subsided. Relieved but still shaky, she made her way home. Later, she described the terror of her anxiety attack: "It could not be worse if I were hanging by my fingertips from the wing of a plane in flight. The feeling of impending doom was just as real and frightening" (Fishman and Sheehan, 1985).

If neurotics can identify a specific object of their anxiety, they are said to suffer from *phobia.* Phobic neurotics may have an extreme, unreasonable fear of animals (*zoophobia*), fear of heights (*acrophobia*), fear of closed spaces (*claustrophobia*), fear of open spaces (*agoraphobia*), or any of a variety of other specific fears. These are simple, monosymptomatic phobias, triggered by specific animals or situations, such as cats or open spaces. Another type of fear is *social phobia,* brought on by the presence of other people. The neurotic with social phobia cannot speak before an audience, eat in restaurants, or write his or her name when someone else is around.

The second type of neurosis is a combination of *obsession* and *compulsion.* Obsession involves some bothersome idea that keeps interrupting the individual's train of thought. One college student describes his earlier obsession this way: "When I was about eight years of age . . . I thought I was going to cut my throat from ear to ear with a certain large butcher knife in my grandmother's kitchen. I couldn't throw off the idea. . . . I was afraid to go near the knife" (Cashdan, 1972). A compulsion involves some ritualistic action that neurotics feel they must perform. An example of this can be found in people whose extreme fear of germs and contamination by others drives them to wash their hands repeatedly. Yet the more they wash to get rid of their anxiety about germs, the more anxious they become.

The third type of neurosis is *depressive reaction.* Neurotic depression is distinguishable from psychotic depression, which is much more severe both in degree and in duration. The milder neurotic depression is characterized by the feeling of sadness, dejection, and self-deprecation. Although this depressive reaction may last for weeks or even months, it usually clears up eventually. If it does not, it may become psychotic depression.

The fourth type of neurosis is *psychophysiologic disorder,* also known as *psychosomatic illness.* Its symptoms range from the relatively minor to the very severe, including headaches, ulcer, amnesia, and paralysis. These symptoms have no basis in physical injury or nerve damage; they represent the neurotic's way of solving a psychological problem. This can be illustrated with the case of a young army draftee who had been a dancer and circus acrobat. He found his life in the army too restrictive and monotonous and longed for the travel and excitement he had previously enjoyed. But he could not leave the army for fear of being treated as a deserter. The situation became so intolerable that he developed a psychophysiologic disorder. He could neither walk nor stand, and his legs could not even respond to vigorous prickings by a pin. A few months later, he was discharged from the army on a physician's certificate of disability. Soon his legs began to recover, and in another three months he left the hospital practically well (Kolb and Brodie, 1982).

Personality Disorder.   This is a general category for all sorts of deviant behavior the psychiatrist can describe but cannot diagnose as either psychotic or neurotic. This mental disorder has also been called *character disorder* or *sociopathic (psychopathic) disorder.* Its most prominent feature is blatant disregard for society's rules. Its cause is thought to be a lack of moral development—failure to develop conscience, acquire true compassion, or learn how to form meaningful relationships. People with personality disorder include con men, dope pushers, pimps, criminals, unprincipled businesspeople, shyster lawyers, quack doctors, and crooked politicians. Such people come across as merely self-centered nonconformists rather than seriously disturbed patients.

This traditional classification system provides insight into the characteristics of various types of mental disorder by explaining in some detail how they differ. It also encourages psychiatrists to analyze their patient's life in order to find and eliminate the causes of his or her mental disorder. But, to medically oriented psychiatrists, the types of mental disorders presented in the traditional system are too broadly and ambiguously defined, so that they cannot be precisely identified in terms of specific symptoms. Related to this problem, the system presents only a small number of disorders, thereby missing a large number of more specific ones, which are discussed in the following section.

The DSM-IV Classification

A much greater number of mental disorders, totaling over 300, can be found in the DSM-IV, an acronym for The Diagnostic and Statistical Manual of Mental Disorders, Fourth Edition, published in 1994 by the American Psychiatric Association (see Table 8.1). Each of the mental disorders is defined as having a list of symptoms. Panic disorder, for example, is defined as having symptoms such as the following:

1. Shortness of breath or smothering sensations
2. Dizziness, unsteady feelings, or faintness

3. Palpitations or accelerated heart rate
4. Trembling or shaking
5. Sweating
6. Choking
7. Nausea or abdominal distress
8. Chest pain or discomfort
9. Fear of dying

Checking a patient against lists of symptoms such as this, psychiatrists can determine what mental disorder their patient is suffering from. By using this mechanical, routinized

TABLE 8.1   The DSM-IV Classification of Mental Disorders

DSM-IV provides a list of over 300 specific disorders. The following are the major types:

1. DISORDERS USUALLY FIRST EVIDENT IN INFANCY, CHILDHOOD, OR ADOLESCENCE. *Examples:* separation anxiety, stuttering, defiance, doing poorly in reading, math, or writing
2. DELIRIUM DEMENTIA, AMNESIC AND OTHER COGNITIVE DISORDERS. *Examples:* delirium from intoxication, substance-induced loss of sanity, amnesia, caused by a medical condition
3. SUBSTANCE-RELATED DISORDERS. *Examples:* excessive use of alcohol, cigarettes, coffee, cocaine, and other psychoactive drugs
4. SCHIZOPHRENIA AND OTHER PSYCHOTIC DISORDERS. *Examples:* being paranoid, disorganized, catatonic, delusional
5. MOOD DISORDERS. *Examples:* major depression, substance-induced mood swings
6. ANXIETY DISORDERS. *Examples:* panic attack, social phobia, acute stress
7. SOMATOFORM DISORDERS. *Example*s: psychosomatic illness, hypochondria
8. FACTITIOUS DISORDERS. *Examples:* intentional feigning of pains or distress of some physical illness
9. DISSOCIATIVE DISORDERS. *Examples*: multiple personality, amnesia without any medical condition
10. SEXUAL AND GENDER IDENTITY DISORDERS. *Examples:* premature ejaculation, voyeurism, sexual masochism or sadism, transsexualism
11. EATING DISORDERS. *Examples:* anorexia, bulimia
12. SLEEP DISORDERS. *Example:* insomnia, sleepwalking, having nightmares
13. IMPULSE CONTROL DISCORDERS. *Examples:* compulsive gambling, kleptomania (stealing repeatedly), pyromania (being excited about setting fires)
14. ADJUSTMENT DISORDERS. *Examples:* responding to stressful life changes with anxiety or depression
15. MENTAL RETARDATION. *Examples:* mild, moderate, or severe mental retardation
16. PERSONALITY DISORDERS. *Examples:* antisocial, paranoid, schizoid, dependent personalities
17. OTHER CONDITIONS THAT MAY BE A FOCUS OF CLINICAL ATTENTION. *Examples:* academic problem, marital problem, child abuse

method of diagnosing mental disorders in the same way as physicians diagnose physical diseases, psychiatrists can dispense with the time-consuming psychoanalysis required by the traditional classification system. Psychiatrists can also use the DSM-IV to collect payments for their services from insurance companies or government agencies, which insist that the manual be used (Kutchins and Kirk, 1997). Many patients, though, do get significant relief from the distressing symptoms of their mental disorders because their doctors can use the DSM-IV to prescribe appropriate medications.

But the scientific value of DSM-IV falls short. One problem is that the diagnostic manual is merely *descriptive,* describing mental disorders with lists of symptoms without explaining how the disorders differ from one another in terms of their causes. DSM-IV also arbitrarily defines disorders in terms of a specific number of symptoms: To be diagnosed as suffering from mania, for example, a patient must have three symptoms from a list of seven, but the manual does not explain why three, not five or six, is required for defining mania (Davison and Neale, 1996). Moreover, the focus on symptoms tends to lead to a misdiagnosis of some normal behaviors as mental disorders. Symptoms such as being depressed, losing appetite, having difficulty sleeping, and being unable to concentrate may naturally occur and therefore be normal in response to such stressful events as the loss of a job, the breakdown of a marriage, and the death of a loved one (Horwitz and Wakefield, 2006). Finally, the focus on symptoms inevitably encourages psychiatrists to eliminate the symptoms rather than the cause of the problem. Influenced by the medical view of mental disorder as a biologically caused disease, the elimination of symptoms often involves prescribing medication, just as physicians do for physical illness. But the mental disorder usually persists because its nonbiological cause remains.

Since its first edition, published in 1952, the DSM has been criticized for promoting the medical view of mental disorder as a biologically caused disease. But in its more recent editions, especially DSM-IV, psychiatrists are encouraged to see social factors as possibly additional causes of mental disorder. Thus, after identifying the symptoms of a patient's disorder, users of DSM-IV are instructed to find out whether the patient has experienced any "environmental" problems, such as those involving education, occupation, money, or housing. Nevertheless, the medical, biological view continues to dominate the psychiatric profession, so that the mentally disordered are routinely treated with drugs (Garber, 2008; Sorboro, 2007).

Social Factors in Mental Disorder

Sociologists have long discovered the influence of social factors on mental disorder. We will discuss the more important factors here.

Social Class

Of all the social factors assumed to be related to mental disorder, social class has been most consistently and most clearly demonstrated in various studies to be associated with the disorder. More specifically, people from the lower classes are more likely than those from other classes to become mentally ill. Although the mental illness among the lower classes is more likely to be *reported* to the authorities, surveys on random samples of Americans have consistently found a greater percentage of lower-class people suffering from psychiatric symptoms (Skapinakis, 2007; Littlejohn, 2004; Dohrenwend, 1975).

This finding, however, has prompted two conflicting explanations. One, called *social causation,* suggests that lower-class people are more prone to mental disorder because they are more likely to experience social stress (such as unemployment and divorce); to suffer from psychic frailty, infectious diseases, and neurological impairments; and to lack quality medical treatment, coping ability, and social support. This means that low social status is, through those problems, a *cause* of mental illness. The other explanation, called *social selection* or *drift,* suggests that mentally ill people from higher social classes often drift downward into the lower-class neighborhood, helping to increase the rate of mental illness in that neighborhood. This means that the lower-class position is a *consequence* of mental illness among formerly higher-status people. Both explanations have been found to have some basis in fact: Some lower-class people do become mentally ill because of their stressful lives and some middle-class people with emotional problems do drift into the lower-class neighborhood (Jones et al., 1993; Link, Lennon, and Dohrenwend, 1993; Rodgers and Mann, 1993).

Gender

There are conflicting findings as to which gender is more likely to become mentally ill. In most studies, women are found to have higher rates of mental disorder. But in some studies, men are the ones with the higher rates. Still other studies fail to find any difference between the sexes (Schwartz, 1991; Dohrenwend and Dohrenwend, 1976).

These conflicting findings, however, concern mental illness *in general*. Studies on *specific types* of disorder do indicate a gender difference. They usually show that women are more likely to suffer from depression, anxiety attacks, and posttraumatic-stress disorder, while men tend more to have antisocial personality, paranoia, and drug and alcohol abuse disorders (Norris et al., 2002; Yonkers and Gurguis, 1995). How can we account for this gender difference?

Most sociologists attribute it to the difference in gender roles. The female role is relatively restrictive and oppressive, likely to confine the woman to her inner self, so that she tends to internalize her problems (e.g., keeping her frustration and anger to herself) rather than externalize them (e.g., aggressively taking them out on others). Hence women are more likely than men to fall victim to depression and anxiety attacks, which essentially involve the victims hurting themselves. In contrast, the male role is more liberating, more likely to encourage men to be assertive, bold, and aggressive in social relations. If frustrated and angry, they tend more to take it out on others, behaving like antisocial and paranoid individuals. All this can be summarized in Durkheimian terms: Women are more likely to respond to social stress by developing depressive disorders because they are *more* socially integrated and regulated, whereas men are more likely to respond to social stress by developing antisocial personality disorders because they are *less* socially integrated and regulated (Rescorla et al., 2007; Schwartz, 1991).

Research has further suggested that the female role has taught women to value emotional attachment to others, to be sociable, while the male role has trained men to be emotionally detached from others, to be aggressive. Women, then, become more vulnerable to "social loss" such as death of a loved one, while men are more vulnerable to "material loss" such as unemployment (Lewis, 1985; Gove, 1984). However, as more and more women enter the man's competitive world of economic struggle, they would suffer less depression and anxiety. As research has suggested, the increase in women's employment over the last 30 years has caused a decline in their psychiatric distress. During the same period, though, there has been a decline in men's employment, triggering a rise in antisocial personality disorders among men. As a consequence, the gender difference in psychological distress has narrowed in the last several decades (McLanahan and Glass, 1985).

Young Age

Many studies before the mid-1980s suggested that in our society older persons are more likely to suffer from mental disorder than younger persons. This was typically attributed to societal neglect of older persons: Older individuals are not given meaningful and satisfying roles to play in society, since these roles are largely allocated to the young, on whom industrial production depends heavily. Deprived of respect by others, older individuals become isolated. As they begin to develop psychopathological symptoms, their families and other close relatives do not bother taking them to a hospital or psychiatrist. By the time their psychopathology becomes hopelessly severe, they are brought to a mental institution where they will be kept out of their families' sight for a long time (Gallagher, 2002; Kaplan, 1972).

However, more recent studies in the 1980s and 1990s show that the elderly are the least likely among all age groups to become mentally ill. According to a national survey published in 1994, for example, relatively young people, aged 25 to 34, have the highest rate of mental illness (Kessler et al., 1994). Another study by a research team called the Cross-National Collaborative Group (1992) also found a significant increase in major depression among the younger generations, especially over the last several decades. In countries as diverse as the United States, Taiwan, Lebanon, and New Zealand, each successive generation has been growing more vulnerable to depressive disorders. In those countries, people born after 1955 are more than three times as likely as their grandparents to have a major depression. Among Americans, about 6 percent of those born after 1955 have become severely depressed by age 24, while only 1 percent of those born before 1905 have suffered similar depression by age 75.

The increasingly greater prevalence of depression among young people can be attributed to changes in modern society—more specifically, to an increase in social stresses and a decrease in social resources for coping with the stress. Most of the stresses come from family problems, such as divorce, child abuse, or parental indifference to children's needs for love and support. And the difficulty in coping with these stresses comes largely from the loss of the extended family and close-knit, village-like community in modern society.

A Social Profile of Depressed Teens

There are three types of depression. If you experience *mild* depression, you may feel slightly sad over some ordinary disappointment, such as getting a *B* instead of an *A* on a test. In *situational* depression, you would be sadder because of a more unpleasant experience, such as having a loved one die, breaking up with a boyfriend or girlfriend, or losing a job. But you would get over it soon. The most serious is *major* depression, which is a mental disorder involving the kind of sadness that is extreme, out of proportion to the event that has triggered it, as if it is the end of the world. As many as 8 percent of U.S. teens suffer from this type of depression at some time during any one year. The problem is worse for American college students, of whom more than 40 percent said in a 2003 survey that they felt "so depressed, it was difficult to function" at least once during the year (Krislov, 2007; McGinn and Depasquale, 2004; Furr, 2001).

If asked which feelings in the following list they have, they are likely to check off at least four that last longer than two weeks:

- I feel extremely sad and very irritable.
- I feel guilty, and have no confidence.
- I feel I'm a failure or let my family down.
- I lose interest in hobbies like music or sports, and I'd rather be alone.
- I often feel restless or tired.
- I have trouble concentrating on things like homework or TV watching.
- I have trouble sleeping or I sleep too much.
- My appetite increases or decreases a lot.
- I often think about death, and sometimes about suicide.
- I use drugs or alcohol regularly.

In addition to having symptoms of depression like the above, depressed teenagers are more likely than their healthy peers to be overwhelmed with certain *stressful events,* as we suggested earlier. The stresses may originate from family problems, such as parental divorce and childhood sexual abuse, the pressure to do well in school, the diffi-culty of fitting in and forming relationships, problems with the boyfriend or girlfriend, and loneliness. Given these stresses, depressed teens are more likely to lack *social resources* to deal with their problems. Their parents and friends may respond by simply telling them to "cheer up and get on with it," which won't do much good. What the teens need are responses that come from tremendous patience and thoughtful listening, which is hard to come by in a modern, highly individualistic society (Empfield and Bakalar, 2001; Martin, 2001).

Race and Ethnicity

Like gender, race and ethnicity have not been consistently found to be related to mental illness in general. Many studies have shown higher rates of psychiatric distress among American blacks, Hispanics, and Asians than whites. The standard explanation for this finding is that minorities experience more social stresses stemming from discrimination, poverty, and cultural conflict (Kessler and Neighbors, 1986; Yamamoto et al., 1983). On the other hand, there are studies showing no significant difference in psychiatric problems between minorities and whites. An equally plausible reason has been given for this finding: The minorities' group identification, group solidarity, or social network protects them against those social stresses (Kuo and Tsai, 1986; Kessler et al., 1985). The same explanation has been used to account for the lower level of mental illness among Great Britain's minorities, for example, among Pakistanis and Indians. These minorities are the most isolated from Britain's mainstream society because of the whites' prejudice and the minorities' desire to maintain their separate traditions. Yet they are the least vulnerable to psychological disorders because they are said to have strong "community integration," resulting from the very same factors that have brought about their isolation (Shrout et al., 1992; Cochrane, 1983).

More consistent data are available on the relationship between race or ethnicity and specific forms of mental disorder. Among the lower classes, Puerto Ricans and African Americans are more likely than Irish and Jewish Americans to have sociopathic inclinations ("I can easily make people afraid of me and sometimes do just that for the fun of it"), as well as paranoid tendencies ("Behind my back people say all kinds of things about me"). While African Americans are more likely to show paranoid disorders (viewed by researchers as anger expressed outwardly—against others), Jewish Americans tend more to manifest depressive disorders (anger turned inward—against oneself) (Ruiz, 1982; Kaplan, 1972). Asian Americans, particularly those of Korean ancestry, also have more depressive symptoms than whites (Kuo, 1984).

Urban Environment

Many studies have suggested that the urban environment is a major producer of mental disorders. Surveys in the United States and the Netherlands, for example, indicate higher rates of mental disorders in urban areas, particularly the inner city, than in rural areas, including the suburbs and small towns (Peen et al., 2007; Robins et al., 1984). According to many sociologists and psychiatrists, the urban environment produces a lot of mental problems because it generates an abundance of physical and social stresses—in the forms of traffic congestion, excessive noise, population density, tenuous social relations, loneliness, and lack of social support.

Some community studies also reveal a link between urban living and specific psychiatric problems. Generally, urban residents exhibit higher levels of neurotic and personality disorders while the more serious psychotic conditions, especially severe depression, are more prevalent among rural and small-town dwellers (Dohrenwend and Dohrenwend, 1974). Why? Perhaps rural and small-town residents are more likely to find their lives in the nonurban areas too restrictive. They cannot freely express frustration and anger in the presence of relatives, friends, acquaintances, and even strangers—who can easily find out who the troublemakers are. By suppressing their frustration, the ruralites and small-towners may get deeper and deeper into themselves until they become psychotic, totally withdrawing into themselves, breaking the ties between themselves and others, or losing touch with conventional reality. In contrast, urban dwellers can more easily get away from family and friends and are freer to express frustration in the midst of strangers, who tend to tolerate unconventional behavior or antisocial outbursts. If they persist in doing so, the urbanites may become neurotics, who, unlike psychotics, still retain their grip on conventional reality. Otherwise, they may develop an antisocial psychopathic personality, which essentially is an "acting-out" disorder.

September 11

Virtually all Americans were shocked when terrorists hijacked commercial planes and crashed them into the twin towers of the World Trade Center in New York and the Pentagon in Washington, D.C., on September 11, 2001. Since then, researchers have tried to find the extent and severity of the damage to the American psyche.

According to a national survey of 560 randomly selected U.S. adults conducted *three to five days* after September 11, the terrorist attacks dealt a psychological blow to all Americans, not just those in New York and Washington. Many suffered a high level of stress, with about 44 percent of Americans experiencing serious symptoms of posttraumatic stress disorder (PTSD), such as difficulty sleeping, being irritable, inability to concentrate, being overly vigilant, and exaggerated startle (Schuster et al., 2001). Another survey was taken of 1,008 adults living in Manhattan *five to nine weeks* after the attacks on the towers. This study showed that about 8 percent of the New Yorkers experienced symptoms of PTSD and 10 percent came down with symptoms of major depression. And those residing closest to the attack site were nearly three times as likely to suffer from PTSD as those living farther away (Galea et al., 2002).

The most comprehensive survey is the National Study of Americans' Reactions to September 11, which sought information from a representative sample of 2,273 adults throughout the United States *one to two months* after the terrorist attacks. First, it found that geographic proximity to the World Trade Center was related to the prevalence of posttraumatic stress. More specifically, a significantly higher percentage of New Yorkers reported symptoms of PTSD than did the percentage of people in other parts of the nation. (The prevalence of PTSD was 11.2 percent in New York City, compared with 3.6 percent in other major U.S. cities, 2.7 percent in Washington, D.C., and 4.0 percent in the rest of the country.) Second was the surprising finding that the rate of PTSD in Washington, D.C., was about the same as that in other parts of the United States. This was probably because the target was military, thereby reducing the civilian population's identification with the victims and perception of personal vulnerability. A third finding was that the more hours people spent watching TV coverage of the attacks, the more they experienced posttraumatic stress (Schlenger et al., 2002).

To provide some perspective on these findings, the seriousness of the stress suffered by those 2.7 percent to 11.2 percent of Americans was comparable to that found among survivors of motor vehicle crashes and survivors of sexual assault. Thus, the stress caused by the September 11 terror could be considered a significant public health problem (Schlenger et al., 2002).

A Global Perspective on Mental Disorder

The incidence of mental disorder is generally higher in modern industrial societies such as the United States and France than in traditional agricultural societies such as China and Nigeria. A major reason is the culture of individualism and competitiveness in modern societies, where individuals with personal problems often have to fend for themselves, doing without the relatives and friends who are more readily available to offer support in group-oriented, traditional societies. The United States, being presumably the world's most individualistic and competitive society, has the world's highest incidence of mental disorder. According to the latest survey, over 26 percent of Americans suffer from mental disorders, compared with 18 percent of French, 15 percent of Dutch, 9 percent of Chinese, and 5 percent of Nigerians (Kessler et al., 2004; Demyttenaere et al., 2004).

Some types of mental disorder appear in certain societies but never or rarely in others. In Latin America, some people are tormented by *susto,* the pathological fear that their souls have left their bodies. In Malaysia, some people suffer from *latah,* known in the West as hyperstartle syndrome, which makes the victim scream, swear, or gesture for a prolonged period when startled by something like a loud noise or a snake. These mental disorders are unheard of in the United States. In the United States, though, some women are afflicted with anorexia nervosa, the extreme fear of weight gain, which is rarely or never found in third world societies. These abnormal behaviors seem to reflect in an exaggerated and distorted way the cultures in which they occur. Susto, for example, apparently reflects the widespread and profound belief in religion in Latin America, while anorexia nervosa reflects the popular belief in thinness in the United States (Lemelson, 2001).

The symptoms of a given mental disorder may also mirror the culture in which they take place. Depression is more likely to show itself as a physical illness in developing countries than in the United States and other Western societies. This is because in the culture of developing countries it is shameful to admit to emotional distress. In the United States, however, people suffering from obsessive-compulsive disorder (the compulsion to perform a task repeatedly) usually wash their hands over and over, because concern with cleanliness and health is widely considered important in U.S. culture. By contrast, in Bali, Indonesia, one common symptom of the compulsive disorder is the uncontrollable urge to collect information about people. A Balinese man with the disorder would find out the name of every person who passes by his house, so that he could treat even strangers like friends. This is of great importance in Balinese society, famous for its extreme friendliness to everybody (Osborne, 2001).

In short, there are some *differences* between societies in the incidence, types, and symptoms of mental disorder. But there are also *similarities*. Virtually everywhere, women are more likely than men to suffer from anxiety and depression, men are more likely to have alcohol disorders, and young people are more likely than older people to have mental disorders (Wolpert, 2000).

Societal Responses to Mental Disorder

To understand mental disorder, it is not enough to focus on the problem itself, as we have so far done. It is also important to turn our attention to how various parts of society respond to mental illness because these responses can have an enormous impact on the sufferer's life or illness. Let us begin by taking a look at how people in the past dealt with the mentally ill (Cashdan, 1972).

Historical Background

For hundreds of years in ancient Greece, mental illness was viewed with awe. Even the famous philosopher Socrates believed that mental illness was a greatest blessing, for which both states and individuals in Greece should be thankful. Epilepsy, which was then equated with mental illness, was considered sacred—a sign of divine favor. Later, in the Middle Ages, the mental patient was sometimes portrayed by artists and writers as the only one in touch with ultimate reality.

However, for most of human existence, the mentally ill have been badly treated. During the Stone Age, mental illness was attributed to some evil spirit that had somehow entered the body. Archaeological evidence suggests that Stone Age people were the first to perform what is today called *lobotomy* on their mental patients. Their psychosurgical technique, called *trephining,* involved boring a hole in the skull to allow the evil spirit to escape.

With the beginning of the Hebrew and early Greek civilizations, the evil spirit was still considered the cause of mental illness. The fear surrounding the mentally ill is reflected in the Bible: "A man also or woman that hath a familiar spirit, or that is a wizard, shall surely be put to death" (Leviticus 20:27). This pronouncement later provided the rationale for witch burning in medieval Europe, when the church defined the mentally ill as witches who had invited the devil to reside in their bodies. Witch burning took several forms: Some witches were burned alive; others were strangled or beheaded before being burned; and still others were mutilated before being thrown into the fire. In 1636 a man in Konigsberg, Germany, claimed that he was God, and the authorities treated his "demon possession" by cutting out his tongue, chopping off his head, and burning his body.

By the middle 1700s, demonology and witch burning began to disappear, but the mentally ill were still harshly treated. Those who were believed to be dangerous were kept in jails and poorhouses, while those considered less violent were allowed to beg for food on the streets. There were also a few institutions for treating the mentally ill. One such institution, Bethlehem Hospital in London, became widely known as "Bedlam." It handcuffed and chained patients to the walls. It even put patients on display for the amusement of the public. Tickets were sold for a sideshow featuring the wilder, more agitated patients. Similarly, in France not only were the mentally ill treated like animals, but their asylums were much worse than zoos. One French physician of the period reported:

> I have seen them naked, or covered with rags, and protected only by straw from the cold, damp pavement. I have seen them in squalid stinking little hovels, without air or light, chained in caves where wild beasts would not have been confined. There they remain to waste away in their own filth under the weight of chains which lacerate their bodies. Whips, chains, and dungeons are the only means of persuasion employed by keepers who are as barbarous as they are ignorant. (Cashdan, 1972)

In 1793 a revolutionary change in attitude toward the mentally ill occurred when the doctor Phillippe Pinel was placed in charge of a large asylum in Paris. Pinel removed the chains from the inmates. Then he administered to them what has become known as *moral treatment*—treating them like human beings and encouraging them to have hope and confidence in themselves. As a result, instead of acting wild and destructive as they were popularly believed to be, the patients became thankful and docile, and some who had been chained for more than 20 years were able to leave the hospital a few months later. Soon Pinel's moral treatment was adopted in England and the United States. Many mentally ill inmates in jails and poorhouses were moved to new asylums to receive the new humane treatment. But gradually the asylums became overcrowded and served largely as warehouses for the mentally disordered. The conditions in many mental institutions became almost as dismal as before (Gamwell and Tomes, 1995). By 1955, however, new alternatives to mental institutions began to emerge. They included general hospitals that opened outpatient clinics, private psychiatrists, private clinics, and community mental health centers, all of which attempted to be more therapeutic than asylums had been in the past. But even today this therapeutic objective is still far from fulfillment for many mental patients.

The Public

One major difficulty in trying to help the mentally ill lies in the public's negative attitude toward them. Although the public today does not believe in burning the mentally ill as devils, basically the attitude of the past still remains: The mentally ill are stigmatized as moral lepers. Most people, whether they are old or young, highly educated or with little schooling, feel that the mentally ill are somehow dangerous, violent, unpredictable, or worthless (Markowitz, 2005; Link and Phelan, 1999; Trad, 1991). But unlike the barbaric ancients, who openly showed their intolerance, today's apparently civilized people try to conceal theirs by presenting a front of tolerance, publicly expressing sympathy for the mentally ill. Nonetheless, the intolerance often comes through, as can be illustrated by the experience of a female lawyer who is mentally ill in addition to being a recovering alcoholic. Here is how she describes her experience:

> Several years ago, a nurse told me that she dropped out of a therapy group because there were too many "crazies"—some of them *even took lithium*! (Unknown to her, I take lithium.) Some of my recovering alcoholic brothers and sisters maintain that a person on psychiatric drugs is not "clean and sober." This perverse philosophy is reinforced by social agencies caring for the less fortunate; in my city, most halfway houses willingly accept recovering alcoholics and addicts, but not those taking psychiatric medications. When I told one of my lawyer coworkers about my "problem," he was markedly uncomfortable. (Collier, 1993)

The public's negative attitude about the mentally ill can also be discerned from popular, stereotypical jokes about them. For example, a character in the popular TV show *Roseanne* says that "only murderers, psychos, and schizos can beat a lie-detector test." Even presidential candidate Ross Perot told a cheering crowd during the 1992 campaign: "We're all crazy again now! We got buses lined up outside to take you back to the insane asylum." An award-winning TV commercial for Daffy's, a chain of discount clothing stores, shows a straitjacket with the caption, "If you're paying over $100 for a dress shirt, may we suggest a jacket to go with it?" And an analysis of Disney animated movies shows that 85 percent of them stereotype the mentally ill as "crazy," "mad," and "nuts" (Lawson and Fouts, 2004; Socall and Holtgraves, 1992).

The negative public attitude toward the mentally ill is so pervasive that it even gets into, of all people, psychiatrists, who are supposed to be compassionate to do their job well. As one psychiatrist observes,

> The curious thing to note about psychiatrists as doctors is in the realm of what they do. They never touch their patients. . . . The exceptions to this are rare and are frowned upon by the

profession. I can clearly remember one of my supervisors confiding to me during my training that he sometimes patted his patients on the back on their way out of the office. Horrors!
If discovered, he may be branded as an infidel. (Torrey, 1974)

It is indeed difficult for psychiatrists to approach the mentally ill as equals. According to
R. D. Laing (1985), most psychiatrists believe that "an unbridgeable gulf," "an abyss of difference," or "a total difference" exists between psychotics and the rest of us. Of course,
some psychiatrists do befriend mental patients by spending much time in their company.
But their conventional colleagues often call them "the lunatic fringe of the psychiatric
profession" (Laing, 1985).

The Court

Since the public does not appreciate having the mentally ill around, the court can oblige by
putting them away in mental institutions or prisons. This can be done by using (1) involuntary commitment proceedings, (2) denying the right to trial, and (3) allowing the defense of
insanity.

Involuntary Commitment.   The court can hospitalize the mentally ill against their will.
This involuntary hospitalization is for an indefinite period; it may be just for a few days or
for a lifetime. Individuals can be released only if they can convince the hospital authorities
of their recovery from mental illness. In order for individuals to receive involuntary commitment, they need not commit a crime, or be convicted of a crime, or even be charged with
a crime. They only have to be judged by a court-appointed psychiatrist as mentally ill or,
more commonly, as dangerous to themselves or others.

　　Since involuntary hospitalization is a serious matter, elaborate safeguards have
been set up to protect the rights of the mentally ill. But these safeguards were often side-
stepped or ignored in the 1960s. The judge, the psychiatrist, and the attorney were relatively careless in handling commitment proceedings. Usually they took only two or three
minutes to decide whether to commit the individual to a mental institution for an indetermi-
nate period. In addition, court psychiatrists were typically incompetent. As a result, many
persons who were not really mentally ill or dangerous were coercively committed (Scheff,
1966, 1964).

　　Since the early 1970s, many higher courts have clamped down on the abuse. Most
laws today are much more concerned with protecting the civil liberty of the mentally ill
than with committing them to psychiatric hospitals for treatment. And many lower-court
judges would not commit patients to a mental hospital even if the patients are severely
mentally ill. While this judicial approach has greatly enhanced the rights of the mentally ill,
it has ironically created a new problem. Many of the patients whom the courts have
released into the community suffer from serious mental illness and do not receive any treatment. These released patients tend to end up homeless or in jails and prisons for disorderly
conduct, disturbing the peace, or vagrancy. But now most states (42 in 2006) try to combat
this problem with a law that requires the mentally ill to receive psychiatric treatment. Consequently, for example, Jeff Demann, diagnosed as schizophrenic, is forced to drive to a
clinic every other week where he drops his pants and gets a shot of some antipsychotic

drug, even though he says the drug makes him sick. If he doesn't show up at the clinic, he will be committed to a mental institution (Fritz, 2006).

Denying Rights.   The court can confine in the mental institution presumably mentally ill people by denying them the right to be tried. It is our fundamental right to stand trial if we are charged with a crime. But this right can be taken away from the mentally ill. When individuals are accused of a crime, the court will decide whether to try them or not. If they are found to be mentally ill, the court can rule that they are not competent to stand trial. Thus, without the benefit of a trial and without having been found guilty, the mentally ill defendants can be committed to a mental institution for an indefinite period. In fact, these unconvicted defendants can end up being confined in the institution longer than convicted criminals are in the prison. At one time, over half of nonconvicted defendants—considerably more than convicted criminals—spent the rest of their lives in mental institutions (Hess and Thomas, 1963). Today, however, because of the closing of many state-run mental health facilities, most of these patients are confined in prisons. Their number is now estimated to be 300,000, compared with only 70,000 in state psychiatric facilities (Fields, 2006).

In some states, ex-convicts with a history of violent sex crimes can be judged in court as having a "mental abnormality" that causes them to lose control of their sexual impulses and become sexual predators. They can, therefore, be sent back to prison to be indefinitely locked up for treatment at its psychiatric facilities. One ex-convict who is thus reincarcerated protests:

> There's a wrong being done here. I served my time and stayed clean during the five months I was out. I'm not a sexual predator. They even talked to girls I dated after I got out and couldn't find anything wrong. (Richards, 1992)

Insanity Defense.   The court can put away a mentally ill person for a crime by allowing a defense of insanity. If judged "insane," the defendant is sent to a mental institution; if judged "sane," the defendant is sent to prison. But the legal concept of insanity is not necessarily the same as the popular or psychiatric notion of mental illness. Consider the 1992 case of Jeffrey Dahmer, who was convicted of murdering 15 young men. Dahmer drugged some of his victims and crudely operated on their brains in an attempt to turn them into zombie-like companions. He had sex with some corpses. And he dismembered bodies, cooking some hands in a kettle and storing a severed head in the refrigerator, where he also saved a heart to be eaten later (Toufexis, 1992b). Given these facts, we will most likely agree with psychiatrists that Dahmer was mentally ill. But the court pronounced him sane, found him guilty, and sent him to prison.

There have been two major rules for establishing an insanity defense. The first is the M'Naghten Rule, according to which the accused are insane and, therefore, not guilty if at the time of committing the crime they did not know what they did was wrong. Another way of saying this is that they did not know the difference between right and wrong; hence the M'Naghten Rule is also known as the *right-or-wrong test*. This test has been in existence for over 100 years and has been used in about two-thirds of the states in this country. Then in 1954 the U.S. Court of Appeals broadened the definition of the M'Naghten Rule by handing down the Durham Rule. This new rule states that the accused are not guilty if they are mentally ill, because their crime is considered the "product" of their mental illness. Hence this rule is also called the *product test*.

For about 30 years until the mid-1980s, many defense lawyers successfully used the product test to win acquittal for their clients. One reason is that acquittal can be easily won if the defendant is clearly mentally ill—the defendant's behavior is so bizarre that everybody readily agrees that the individual is insane. Another reason is that, in cases in which the accused is *not* clearly mentally ill, acquittal by reason of insanity can also be easily won. This is primarily because the burden of proof lies with the *prosecution* rather than the defense. To win conviction, the prosecution must prove "*beyond a reasonable doubt*" that the defendant is sane. This is extremely difficult to accomplish because defense psychiatrists, by presenting evidence on the defendant's illness, can easily convince the jury that there is at least some possibility of the defendant's being insane, which in effect will create *some doubt* in the jury's mind that the defendant is sane.

A good example is the case of John Hinckley, who tried to assassinate President Ronald Reagan in 1981. Hinckley was acquitted by reason of insanity because the prosecution failed to prove that he was sane at the time of his crime. Commenting on how difficult it was for the prosecution to prove Hinckley sane, President Reagan said, "If you start thinking about even a lot of your friends, you would have to say, 'Gee, if I had to prove they were sane, I would have a hard job'" (Carrithers, 1985).

Well-known cases such as Hinckley's caused many legislators to believe that the insanity defense had helped too many guilty people to get away with murder. Consequently, in 1984, Congress passed a law that shifts the burden of proof from the prosecution to the defense. Now it is *the defense* that must prove the defendant's insanity, which can be easily refuted by the prosecution psychiatrists' testimony about the defendant not being insane all the time. More important, the defense must prove that the defendant, if proved insane, did not know right from wrong at the time of the alleged crime. But this, too, can be easily refuted by prosecution psychiatrists' testimony that it is possible for even the most severely mentally ill people to know what they did was wrong when committing the alleged crime. Thus, since the mid-1980s, it has been extremely difficult for defendants to win acquittal by reason of insanity. Consequently, most of the mentally ill criminals today are sent to prisons rather than mental institutions. Mental patients now constitute about 16 percent of the prison population (Toufexis, 2002; Butterfield, 1999; Schmitt, 1996).

The Mental Hospital

The mental hospital is a "total institution," a place of residence and work where a large number of individuals are cut off from the greater society and lead an enclosed, regimented life. The patients' needs and desires are subordinated to the smooth operation of the hospital, and consequently the hospital staff tends to treat the patients as if they were objects rather than humans. Psychiatrist D. L. Rosenhan (1973) and his fellow researchers saw various aspects of this dehumanizing treatment after they had gotten themselves admitted to

12 different mental hospitals by pretending to be psychotic. Rosenhan gives these revealing and telling examples of the dehumanizing attitude toward the patients:

> A nurse unbuttoned her uniform to adjust her brassiere in the presence of an entire ward of viewing men. One did not have the sense that she was being seductive. Rather, she didn't notice us. A group of staff persons might point to a patient in the dayroom and discuss him animatedly, as if he were not there.

Considering patients (who are also called inmates, as prisoners are) as objects that can neither see nor feel, staff people tend to show them no respect. Staff members may enter patients' rooms and examine their possessions at any time. Hospital personnel sometimes even monitor their patients' personal hygiene and waste evacuation in the toilet. The situation is particularly bad in state institutions. The air inside these institutions is often thick with the odor of cigarette smoke and urine. Patients are often lined up like cattle to be showered in succession, or sometimes gang-showered without curtains. Deliberate and systematic physical abuse of patients, including tying patients to beds in isolation rooms, can be found in some institutions. Sexual abuse of female patients, overuse of drugs, and medical neglect are also common. These are part of the "dangerous routine" of state institutions that has been reported in testimony before the U.S. Senate (Weicker, 1985). Moreover, institutional psychiatrists are on the whole incompetent. Ironically, their charges are the most severely disturbed. These patients obviously need the most competent psychiatrists, but such psychiatrists prefer the far easier and more lucrative private practice of treating the "worried well"—mildly neurotic rich people. As a former APA president admits, psychiatry is "one of the few specialties where the most skilled practitioners take care of the least impaired patients" (Boffey, 1986).

The combination of staff incompetence and patient dehumanization tends to produce certain unexpected consequences. First, patients often exhibit symptoms that the staff consider to be indicative of their mental illness, but actually the symptoms result from the staff's action. When staff members strip recalcitrant patients and put them in isolation, for example, the patients may tear up mattresses or write with feces on the wall. The staff will then interpret such behavior as befitting very sick people, but the behavior actually expresses patients' attempt to stand apart from the dehumanizing place forced on them (Goffman, 1961). Second, some patients develop what has been called "hospitalitis" or "institutionalism," a hospital-caused problem characterized by a deep sense of hopelessness, pervasive loss of initiative, deterioration of social skills, and inability to function in the larger society. Third, the professional staff becomes less capable than many mental patients in diagnosing mental illness. As Rosenhan (1973) discovered, when he and his normal associates had themselves committed to mental hospitals, many of the mental patients quickly found out that Rosenhan and his associates were normal—but the hospital staff did not. Actually, this need not be surprising. The psychiatric staff, aloof from the patients, cannot see the latter as whole, multidimensional persons. In contrast, the patients, living intimately with one another day in and day out, can develop deeper insight into one another's behavior and thus into mental illness in general (Kaysen, 1993).

But this negative view of the mental hospital has not emerged from every study on the subject. According to Raymond Weinstein (1983, 1981), there are two kinds of data about the goings-on in the mental hospital. One is *qualitative* data, which the researcher collects from participant observation, in the same way as Rosenhan and his associates did, observing closely the mental-hospital patients while living or interacting with them. The other is *quantitative* data, which the researcher gathers by taking a representative sample of patients, questioning them about the hospital, using objective tests or scales, and presenting the findings in a statistical format. The qualitative data are overwhelmingly critical of the mental hospital, as we have seen. But Weinstein claims that most (about three-quarters) of the quantitative studies reviewed by him show the mental institution as a nice place for the patients. The basis for this claim is that a majority of the patients in these studies told the interviewers that "hospital personnel understood their problems, helped them to get well, treated them with kindness and respect, took a personal interest in them, and were attentive to their needs" (Weinstein, 1981).

Weinstein's analysis, however, has drawn fire. Critics have argued, among other things, that in most of the quantitative studies where the researchers are detached and aloof from their subjects, as they are professionally required to be, the patients may not reveal their true feelings. As one critic says, the patients' "expressions of a positive attitude [toward the hospital and its staff] may be designed to impress the staff with their 'progress' and thereby secure a quicker release from the hospital" (Essex et al., 1981).

But over the last 20 years, fiscal problems have forced many communities to significantly cut back on social services for people with disabilities. In the past, mental patients stayed in the hospital for years, if not decades. But today the median length of their hospitalization is only about two weeks. By thus being "deinstitutionalized" (discharged) so much sooner than before, many mental patients are now homeless on the streets, in jails, or in prisons (Gove, 2004; Lewis, 2003; Torrey, 1997). But the majority of deinstitutionalized individuals live in state-financed group homes, apartments, or single-family homes, receiving treatment in general hospitals, Veteran's Administration hospitals, or outpatient clinics. Some of this treatment is community-based, provided by community mental health centers throughout the country (Winerip, 2002; Sharpe, 1997; Foderaro, 1995).

The Community Mental Health Center

The notion of community mental health care was initiated in the 1950s, and then, in 1963, Congress passed a law to provide funds for helping states and communities to build and staff community mental health centers. Today such centers exist all over the country. Their objective is to offer professional and paraprofessional help to the emotionally disturbed. Resources such as hospitals, courts, police departments, welfare agencies, schools, churches, employers, coworkers, neighbors, and other concerned citizens are integrated in order to provide support to anyone in time of stress. Patients can receive inpatient or outpatient care in their communities. This is a very important option, for individuals already under stress do not have to suffer either the inconvenience of leaving their usual surroundings or the disturbance of being "put away" in some distant, isolated, large, and dehumanizing institution. Patients are free from the stigma usually attached to incarceration in a mental institution, and have a better chance of recovery because of the active participation of family members and others who are genuinely concerned and treat them with respect.

Interestingly, the *nonprofessional* method of treatment provided by a network of family and friends—hence the name *network therapy*—has proved highly effective in bringing deinstitutionalized patients back to normal life. It involves offering a support system to former hospital patients who otherwise would feel lonely and isolated. Relatives, friends, neighbors, and whoever knows the patient get together to discuss what each can do for him or her. Some will promise to call the patient more often, others will volunteer to bring him to church, still others will help him find a job, and so on. In addition, a crisis team is available 24 hours a day, ready to make house calls at any time to resolve crises. Through network therapy even schizophrenics, who are severely mentally ill, are rarely readmitted to mental hospitals. They have lower rates of relapse, show far fewer symptoms of schizophrenia, and are more satisfied with their lives, when compared with those who are hospitalized or under drug treatment alone (Prior, 2007; Goleman, 1986).

Why do laypersons who provide network therapy seem to do a better job in treating mental disorders than professional psychiatrists? The reason is probably that many psychiatrists, especially the medically oriented ones, are so professional that they cannot relate to their patients on their social level, let alone spend a lot of time with their patients as their friends. To these psychiatrists, being professional often means treating a mental illness as a medical doctor would a heart disease. But treating a mental disorder is radically different. A heart ailment may require only objective professionalism to effect a treatment, but curing a mental illness requires more than that—it demands a great deal of genuine compassion and empathy, as does network therapy (Breggin, 1997). However, psychiatrists usually treat mental disorder in the same way as physical illness, that is, with medications alone. Not surprisingly, their rate of success in treating mental patients is quite low, with less than half of their patients getting effective care. Their success rate will go up significantly if they supplement the drug therapy with a large dose of compassion by ensuring that the patient develops a relationship with a compassionate other who may be a social worker, a nurse, a doctor, or a family member (Neugeboren, 2006; Elias, 2005; Wang et al., 2005).

Perspectives on Mental Disorder

There are three different ways of looking at mental disorder, represented by the *medical, psychosocial,* and *labeling models.* The first two derive from the positivist perspective and the third from the constructionist perspective. More specifically, the medical model defines mental disorder as a disease with a biological origin, so that the psychiatrist who embraces this model treats the illness by using physical means such as drugs, electric shock, and surgery. The psychosocial model can be found in many psychological and sociological theories, such as behaviorist, social-learning, cognitive, psychoanalytic, and social-stress theories. Here we will discuss only the two most important ones: psychoanalytic and stress theories. The psychoanalytic theory attributes mental disorder to emotional conflict (developing largely from child–parent interaction) and consequently treats the illness by using talk therapy to resolve the conflict. The stress theory is principally aimed at explaining mental disorder as a result of stressful social experiences rather than suggesting how to treat the disorder. Finally, the labeling model is neither explanatory nor treatment-oriented.

It has often been called antipsychiatric because it is a radical critique of what psychiatrists think and do about mental disorder. Let's take a closer look at each model.

The Medical Model

According to this model, mental illness is similar to a physical disease in that its causes are biological; it should be treated, then, in the same way as a physical disease (Gottesman, 1995). This model has been dominating psychiatry since the 1970s when drug treatment emerged as a promising alternative to talk therapy. Advocates of this model, who are known as medical or biological psychiatrists, often point to one of two kinds of evidence to support their belief in the biological causes of mental disorder.

One type of evidence comes from studies on genetically related individuals. According to one of these studies, if one *identical* twin suffers a major depression, the other has a 78 percent chance of suffering the same condition, but the figure is only about 20 percent among *fraternal* twins (Goleman, 1992). Since identical twins are more genetically alike than fraternal twins, it is assumed that mental depression runs in the family. A similar study shows that schizophrenia is three-and-a-half times more common among schizophrenic adopted children's biological relatives than among their nonbiological relatives (Kety, 1974). As a review of such studies concludes, "Genetic factors are at least as important in the etiology of schizophrenia as they are in the etiology of diabetes, hypertension, coronary artery disease, and ulcers" (Kendler, 1983).

Another type of evidence that seems to support the biomedical model comes from numerous cases of successful treatment of mental patients with antipsychotic and antidepressant drugs. In the 1950s hospitalized schizophrenics were first treated successfully with a drug called Thorazine. For the next 20 years, Thorazine and other antipsychotic drugs enabled as many as 500,000 schizophrenics to leave hospitals. Since the 1970s more new psychiatric drugs—including lithium, Clozaril, and Prozac, the most popular antidepressant drug of the 1990s—have been proven relatively effective in treating schizophrenia, depression, and other mental disorders. ("Relatively effective" means that the drugs work in two-thirds to three-quarters of the cases.) Aside from their relative effectiveness, the drugs are so convenient to use that most psychiatrists today routinely prescribe them for their patients (Harris Interactive, 2004; Kluger, 2003; Goode, 2002). The success of these psychopharmacological treatments is taken to suggest that mental illness originates from a chemical imbalance in the brain.

Actually, however, these drugs treat only the symptoms, not the causes, of mental disorders. Since the causes remain, the drug treatment must continue in order to avoid relapse, that is, to prevent the symptoms from returning. Logically, then, the chemical imbalance in the brain cannot be the cause of mental disorder. If it were, the drug treatment alone would have eliminated it. As for the twin and other genetic studies, they do not necessarily mean that mental disorder is genetically determined. If some defective genes were the cause of mental illness, the chance of one identical twin being mentally ill in the event of the other having the same illness would be 100 percent. We cannot ignore, though, the fact that the concordance rate of mental illness is significantly higher among identical twins than fraternal twins. This does suggest that some people may be more genetically vulnerable than others to mental disorder (Van Mourik, 2007; Begley, 1996; Crossen, 1996). But genetic vulnerability cannot by itself lead to mental disorder. It has to be triggered by some psychosocial forces, such as emotional conflict or social stress.

The Psychosocial Model

One version of the psychosocial model is psychoanalytic theory. The other version is social stress theory, which has in recent years attracted a great deal of attention from sociologists and psychologists.

Psychoanalytic Theory.   Presented by Sigmund Freud a century ago, psychoanalytic theory traces mental disorder to some unresolved psychic or emotional conflict in the patient. To Freud, conflict is inevitable within the personality of every human being. This is because personality is made up of three conflicting parts: the id, the ego, and the superego. The id consists of the animal desires for sex and aggression, which all humans are born with. The id is governed by the "pleasure principle." It seeks self-gratification however it can get it, with no regard for reason, logic, or morality. The ego, on the other hand, operates in accordance with the "reality principle." Developed from ages one to three through interacting with the environment, especially the parents, the ego is rational and logical, able to deal with the environment realistically. It, therefore, conflicts with the id by setting limits on how far the id can go in gratifying its impulses. The superego also seeks to restrain the id, but for moral reasons. It emerges in ages three to six when the child internalizes the parent's, or society's, morals in the form of ideals and restrictions. The superego is roughly the same as what is traditionally called "conscience."

But, in Freud's view, the superego is just as completely unreasonable as the id. While the id wants to have, among other things, sex with *anybody* (e.g., one's own parent), the superego prohibits *any* form of sexual pleasure, including sex between husband and wife. Being the only reasonable one, the ego has to mediate between the id and the superego, trying to resolve the conflict between them. The ego may try to persuade the id to stop being completely animal-like while pointing out that the id can still enjoy pleasure in a civilized way, say, having sex with one's spouse. Simultaneously, the ego may try to persuade the superego to give up its total opposition to any form of pleasure seeking and let the id enjoy marital sex, while pointing out that such sex does not destroy the morality upheld by the superego. There are, of course, many other issues for the id and superego to fight over, and each time the fight occurs, the ego will try to settle it. Most of these conflicts take place during childhood. If the ego succeeds in resolving the conflicts, the child will grow up to be normal. But if the ego fails to resolve a conflict, the unresolved conflict will develop into a neurosis or psychosis.

The conflict is usually such a painful experience that the patient "represses" it, pushing it into the unconscious area of the mind. The conflict manifests itself, however, in the form of psychiatric symptoms such as anxiety, depression, or compulsion. To help cure the patient, the psychoanalyst must bring the conflict out into the open, so that the patient can understand and solve the problem (Edmundson, 1999).

Suppose the patient is a male university president suffering from the compulsion of making phone calls to women who advertise child-care services and asking them whether they enjoy having sex with children. After each call, he feels extremely guilty but does not know why he has made the call. To treat this patient, a psychoanalyst would meet with him several times a week for four to six years, with each meeting lasting about one hour. At each session, the psychoanalyst may encourage the patient to say anything that comes into his mind. Meanwhile, the psychoanalyst analyzes everything the patient says, in order to dig out the unresolved conflict that has long been buried in the unconscious.

Finally, the patient may say something that the psychoanalyst is looking for: When he was eight years old, his mother first asked him to have sex with her, and then when he was 11, she forced him to have sex again and again for many months. This experience, according to psychoanalytic theory, must have been so traumatic that it became repressed, or buried, in the unconscious. But why must the experience be traumatic? Because it involves a conflict between the id's sexual gratification with the mother and the superego's total disapproval of it. The ego obviously has failed to resolve the conflict; otherwise it would not have been repressed. The unresolved conflict later appeared in the form of a neurotic compulsion, which caused the patient to make obscene phone calls to child-care workers. This compulsion involved the patient's "projecting" (unconsciously attributing) his sexual feelings for his mother to those child-care workers. In other words, in the patient's unconscious mind, making the obscene phone calls to the child-care workers was effectively the same as having sex with his mother. With all this out in the open, the patient can resolve the conflict, with the psychoanalyst's help (Berendzen and Palmer, 1993).

Psychoanalytic theory, however, is not empirically testable. It is difficult, if not impossible, to operationally define and measure the key concepts of the theory, namely the id, ego, and superego. One has to rely on faith to accept them as real in the same way as accepting ghosts as real. Once the concepts are accepted as real, though, the theory sounds convincing because there is enough logical reasoning and "talking cure" to support it.

Social Stress Theory.   Since the 1980s there has been an avalanche of studies on social stress as a significant contributor to the development of mental illness (Monroe and Hadjiyannakis, 2002; Coyne and Downey, 1991). Various studies on the impact of life crises on the victims, for example, show that a large minority—from 20 to 40 percent—fail to recover fully from depression or other psychiatric problems despite a long passage of time (Kessler et al., 1985). These sufferers usually have gone through life crises such as divorce, unemployment, and death of a loved one. Even less serious experiences can be stressful enough to develop mental problems. Research has shown, for example, that an increasing number of Americans, from school principals to shoe salespersons, are suffering emotional breakdown from their jobs. Blue-collar jobs are particularly stressful because of their unpleasant work conditions—characterized by hazard, noise, heat, humidity, fumes, and cold. These have been found to play an important etiologic role in the prevalence of schizophrenia among lower-class people (Link, Dohrenwend, and Skodol, 1986).

While stress can lead to mental disorder, most people exposed to stressful situations do not develop any psychiatric symptoms. The reason is that they have the coping resources for dealing with stress. Several types of coping resources have been found effective in offsetting stress. One is *social support,* otherwise called strong social ties, intimate personal relationships, or social network. Another is *personal skill* in actively solving problems, seeking information, using distraction or humor, or reducing tension. A third type of coping resource is *high self-esteem* (Kessler et al., 1985).

In short, social stress can cause mental illness if the coping resources are inadequate. Since some individuals encounter more stress and have less coping resources than others, they are more likely to develop psychiatric symptoms. Society can be seen as promoting (through, for example, its structure of social inequality) mental illness in two ways: first, by putting some people in more stressful situations and, second, by depriving them of the social and psychological resources required for dealing with the stress. Critics, though, have observed that most of the studies on stress and psychopathology have not clearly demonstrated stress as the *cause* of mental disorder. This is because stress is also often the *effect* of the problem—that is, troubled individuals are more likely to experience stresses such as joblessness and divorce (Coyne and Downey, 1991; Mitchell and Moos, 1984).

The Labeling Model

Advocates of the medical or psychosocial model assume that mental illness is real; otherwise they would not bother to look for the causes and cures of the illness. But a few psychiatrists and many sociologists question that assumption. They use the constructionist perspective to see mental disorder not as a sickness but as a label imposed on some disturbing behavior. Such an argument has appeared in three versions.

Mental Illness as a Myth.   Psychiatrist Thomas Szasz (1994, 1974b) has sharply criticized the medical model for assuming that mental illness is just as real and objective as a bodily disease. Psychiatrists who embrace the medical model, according to Szasz, are actually spreading a kind of psychiatric propaganda: "Mental illness is a myth, whose function it is to disguise and thus render more palatable the bitter pill of moral conflicts in human relations." In saying that mental illness is a myth, Szasz does not imply that the behavior labeled "mental illness" does not exist. Szasz simply objects to the use of the label because it masks as well as distorts the true nature of the behavior by implying that it is similar to physical disease.

   "Mental illness," in Szasz's view, can be more accurately referred to as "a problem in living," "a moral conflict in human relations," or "a communication expressing some socially unacceptable idea." All these terms imply that so-called mental illness is not a medical problem, but a social and moral one. It does not originate from within the individual—as physical illness does—but from without. More precisely, it is a conflict between the "mental patients" and those around them, such as family, neighbors, friends, or the whole society. But, in labeling them mentally ill as if they had a disease *within* them, psychiatrists use such means as drug therapy, electroshock treatment, or psychiatric incarceration to control *them alone,* exempting their family or others involved in the moral conflict with them. As a woman who was committed as a teenager to a mental hospital for being "uncertain about life issues" says, "Often an entire family is crazy, but since an entire family can't go into the hospital, one person is designated as crazy and goes inside" (Kaysen, 1993). To Szasz, those psychiatric treatments violate the sufferers' civil rights—the rights to freedom and privacy. The treatments are, in effect, less for the good of the "patients" than for the good of the others, who end up enjoying the double benefit of freedom from being "treated" and freedom from being disturbed by the "patients."

   If mental illness is merely a label imposed on an interpersonal conflict, it should not be surprising that today many normal people are treated as mental patients simply because they have problems with others. When DSM-I (the first edition of the APA's diagnostic manual of mental disorders) came out in 1952, only about 100 types of behavior were listed as mental disorders. That number has jumped to more than 300 with the publication of DSM-IV in 1994. This means that many problems, such as reacting angrily to criticism or losing one's temper, which have never been treated as mental disorders, are now included in DSM-IV and are, therefore, expected to be controlled. Moreover, psychiatrists are recruited by various social and government agencies to treat or control youngsters who behave in some ways like Tom Sawyer or Huckleberry Finn—whose behaviors offend or disturb others, behaviors such as being defiant, using drugs, fighting, hating school, or being disrespectful (Diller, 1998). Actually, many of these youngsters are victims of poverty, child abuse, or family misery, and their behaviors reflect a normal response to their abnormal environment. But, instead of dealing with the abnormal environment that causes those troublesome behaviors, psychiatrists label those normal children "emotionally disturbed," then give them drug treatments or isolate or incarcerate them. In short, kids who stand out as different are labeled mentally ill and controlled accordingly. As one of the victims says, "The Bart Simpsons of this world do not wind up in the cartoons. They wind up in the hatch" (Armstrong, 1993).

The Impact of Labeling. Sociologist Thomas Scheff (1966) also views mental illness as a myth. More precisely, he sees it as an ambiguous label. He calls mental illness "residual rule-breaking" because it is such a residue of diverse kinds of rule violations that society does not clearly define it as rule-breaking. Society does clearly define as rule-breaking other forms of deviant behavior, such as crime, perversion, immoral acts, and bad manners. As rule violations, these behaviors are punishable in one way or another. But the mentally ill may only appear to violate social norms, but do not exactly or actually do so—not in the same way as criminals and other rule breakers. In other words, most people do not clearly regard the mentally ill as rule breakers who should be punished. Therefore, the mentally ill can be said to belong in the residual, leftover category of deviance, which is ambiguously defined as a sort of rule violation after all the other rule-breaking acts have been clearly defined as such. The ambiguity of mental illness makes it easy for people to label a person as mentally ill. Such labeling, Scheff emphasizes, can lead the person to develop stabilized, chronic mental disorder.

Scheff assumes that psychiatric symptoms arise from diverse sources. These sources may include genetic, biochemical, physiological, and psychological factors, or whatever you can think of—fear of combat, overwork, continuous lack of sleep, ingestion of psychoactive drugs, and so on. Many people, after being influenced by one of these factors, show such psychiatric symptoms as hearing voices, seeing visions, or imagining fantastic events. Yet their families, friends, and others who know them do not label them mentally ill. This is because most symptoms appear in apparently normal people and last only for a short while. However, a small minority of these people do get labeled mentally ill, which will eventually cause them to become chronically mentally disturbed.

According to Scheff, after people are labeled mentally ill, they are encouraged to acknowledge their mental illness. If they refuse to see themselves as mentally ill, they will be forced to enter a mental hospital, where staff and patients will pressure them to admit their illness. If they ask to be admitted to mental hospitals, they will be complimented for "doing the right thing." After release, they may try to resume their normal lives, but, as former mental patients, they are likely to be rejected by others. Consequently, they may become extremely confused, anxious, or ashamed. In such an emotional crisis, they tend to accept their families', psychiatrists', and community's judgment that they are mentally ill. All this leads Scheff to conclude that labeling a person mentally ill is the single most important factor in making that person become a chronic mental patient. Indeed, research evidence can be found to demonstrate the power of such labeling in aggravating the mental patient's condition (Link, Mirotznik, and Cullen, 1991).

Insanity as Supersanity.   The British psychiatrist R. D. Laing (1967) also considers mental illness a myth, but his way of attacking the myth differs from Szasz's. Laing criticizes his fellow psychiatrists for believing in the myth that their mental patients' experiences are somehow unreal, invalid, false, perverse, or otherwise inferior to their own and other normal people's experience. He asks rhetorically: "How can the so-called insane's experiences be inferior, when it is the normal people who have killed over 100 million of their fellow human beings since the outbreak of the First World War in 1914?" He further writes: "The statesmen of the world who boast and threaten that they have Doomsday weapons are far more dangerous, and far more estranged from 'reality' than many of the people on whom the label 'psychotic' is affixed" (Laing, 1965). This is why Laing sees psychotics as more sane than normals—and their psychosis as a sane response to an insane world. He invites us to imagine a single bird that drops away from its flock in midflight. The flock is heading toward disaster while that deviating bird will land safely on the ground. But most psychiatrists see the psychotic unfavorably, assuming that the sufferers are disoriented as to space and time.

Laing, however, criticizes the psychiatrists for failing to understand the nature of space and time. There are, in Laing's view, two types of space and time, one being outer and the other inner. When a psychiatrist prejudicially considers a mental patient disoriented, the patient actually is oriented to *inner* space and time, while the psychiatrist is oriented to *outer* space and time. By inner orientation, Laing refers to the experience of seeing those realities that have no external or objective presence, as in imagination, dreams, fantasies, contemplation, or meditation. If we simply experience God's presence, for example, we are having an inner experience; but if we try to prove rationally or objectively that God exists, we are demonstrating our orientation to the outer world. Mentally ill people are *inner-oriented,* attuned to themselves, not concerned with what others think of them. By contrast, normal people are *outer-oriented,* attuned to others and sensitive to what they think of them. To Laing, inner orientation is superior to outer orientation. As a form of inner orientation, insanity involves entering a state of more rather than less reality, of supersanity rather than subsanity, of mental breakthrough rather than breakdown.

If insanity is supersanity, why do many mental patients appear so unhappy with their experience? Their unhappiness, Laing suggests, can be traced to society's extremely negative attitude toward madness. Due to our society's greater appreciation for outer orientation than for inner, we are conditioned to *respect* individuals who climb Mount Everest, fly a balloon across the Atlantic, rocket to the moon, or embark on other similar adventures. But we do *not* respect the other kind of travelers, who journey into inner space and time. This is why when astronauts return from outer space, they are welcomed back as heroes, but when schizophrenics return from inner space, they are stigmatized as ex-mental patients. Given our far more positive attitude toward outer exploration, highly competent persons from favorable home environments would willingly embark on a voyage into outer space and with such advantages as moral support from others, prevoyage training and preparation, and all the information and apparatus necessary for making the voyage a successful one. By contrast, most mental patients have been forced into inner space and time by being placed in an untenable, unlivable position in the "normal" world. Therefore, unknowledgeable about and unprepared for the voyage into inner consciousness, they do not know how to deal with the terrors, voices, or images to be encountered on the voyage. As a result, they get lost in the inner world, which is why they appear so spaced-out and unhappy.

However, since he regarded insanity as supersanity, Laing did not use drugs to dull his psychotic patients' sensitivity to their inner world. Instead, he let them live freely in his group home, with only minimum psychiatric supervision. In effect, he gave his patients the opportunity to engage in deep thinking, so that they could more effectively explore their inner world, come to terms with the demons, and eventually return to the outer, "normal" world. This unique program reportedly cured most of the patients who stayed at Laing's unconventional hospital (Mishara, 1983).

Criticisms of the Labeling Model.   A number of sociologists have criticized the labeling model, arguing that mental illness is not a myth but real behavior that exists all over the world. For example, John Clausen and Carol Huffine (1975) argue that "If mental illness is a myth, as Szasz and Scheff and others propose, it is remarkable that the manifestation of the myth should be found in antiquity and in preliterate societies as in modern industrial societies, in the People's Republic of China as in fascist states." Apparently Clausen and Huffine misunderstand what Szasz means by calling mental illness a myth. By "myth," Szasz refers to the use of the *label* "mental illness," not to the *behavior* so labeled. Further, Clausen and Huffine's criticism serves to divert attention from Szasz's reason for calling mental illness a myth, which is to show how the label "mentally ill" unjustly victimizes individuals so labeled.

Scheff also assumes that the label unjustly victimizes the individual. To Scheff, the victimization involves committing individuals to mental institutions, and thereby causing them to become chronic mental patients, even though they may have only mild, harmless psychiatric symptoms. This labeling argument has also been attacked by critics. One of them, Walter Gove (1970), argues that many research studies have refuted Scheff's labeling argument:

> The evidence shows that a substantial majority of the persons who are hospitalized have a serious psychiatric disturbance. . . . Once prospective patients come into contact with public officials, a substantial screening still occurs, presumably sorting out persons who are being railroaded or who are less disturbed. [In addition], the studies reviewed, while in no way denying the existence of the processes outlined by [Scheff], suggest that mental hospitalization does not necessarily or even typically lead to [chronic mental illness].

Therefore, Gove concludes that the evidence supports his own medical model more than Scheff's labeling model. In response, Scheff (1974) claims that the studies that he analyzes give stronger support to his own labeling model. But Gove (1982) argues that many of the studies employed to support labeling theory are methodologically flawed.

Summary

1. What are some popular myths about mental disorder? The myths are: (1) The mentally ill are extremely weird; (2) mental disorder is hopeless, mostly incurable; (3) a sharp difference exists between "mentally ill" and "mentally healthy"; (4) the mentally ill are mostly crazed and violent; (5) people are likely to be depressed in the coldness of winter; and (6) autism has become an epidemic.

2. What is the traditional classification of mental disorders? There are two broad types of disorders: organic and functional. Organic disorders are physically caused, while functional disorders are psychologically and socially caused. Functional disorders are further divided into three types: psychosis, neurosis, and personality disorder. Psychosis is the most debilitating, neurosis is less so, and personality disorder is the least. Psychosis is characterized mostly by being out of touch with reality, neurosis by being constantly fearful or worried about apparently unimportant things, and personality disorder by being self-absorbed, antisocial, or a nonconformist. Each of these three types of functional disorder is further divided into various subtypes. **What is the DSM-IV classification of mental disorders?** Over 300 disorders are listed, each defined as having a set of symptoms. In using DSM-IV, psychiatrists can determine what mental disorder their patient is supposedly suffering.

3. What social factors are involved in mental disorders? The lower classes have higher rates of mental disorder than other classes. Women are more likely to suffer from depression and anxiety, and men from antisocial personality, paranoia, and drug and alcohol abuse disorders. Young people today are more likely than older persons to have psychological problems, particularly depression. They suffer from major depression, with such symptoms as extreme sadness and difficulty sleeping. They are overwhelmed with stressful events but lack social resources to deal with them. Puerto Ricans and African Americans are more likely to have sociopathic and paranoid tendencies, and Jewish and Asian Americans tend more to suffer from depressive disorders. Urban areas have higher rates of mental illness in general than do rural areas. And urbanites also tend more to suffer from neurotic and personality disorders, but ruralites tend more to suffer severe depression. Finally, the September 11 terrorist attacks have caused some posttraumatic stress among Americans all over the country.

4. How does mental disorder vary among societies? There is generally more mental disorder in modern industrial societies than in traditional agricultural societies. Some types of disorder, such as hyperstartle syndrome and anorexia nervosa, appear in some societies but rarely, if ever, in other societies. And symptoms of mental disorder may reflect the culture in which they take place; for example, depression often appears as a physical illness in traditional societies where it is shameful to reveal emotional distress.

5. How does society respond to mental disorders? In the past, the mentally ill were believed to be possessed with the devil and so were sometimes burned alive. By the mid-seventeenth century, they were chained or otherwise treated like animals. Today, the treatment of the mentally ill is no longer barbaric but remains unpleasant. The public as well as many psychiatrists treat the mentally ill like moral lepers; the courts put them away through involuntary commitment, denial of rights, and granting of the insanity defense; and the mental hospitals dehumanize them. The number of hospitalized mental patients has declined significantly, while increasing numbers receive treatment from community mental health centers.

6. What are the current perspectives on mental disorder? The medical model views mental disorder as similar to a physical disease, attributes its causes to some biological factors, and, therefore, treats it with drugs and other physical means. The psychosocial model, including psychoanalytic and social-stress theories, attributes mental disorder to nonbiological factors such as emotional conflict and stressful social experiences. While both the medical and psychosocial models assume that mental illness is real, the labeling model sees mental illness as only a label that has undesirable consequences for individuals to whom the label is applied. Critics of labeling theory insist that mental illness does involve real behavior. Yet the labeling model does not question the reality of the behavior, but opposes the unjust imposition of the label "mental illness" on the behavior.

FURTHER READING

Beam, Alex. 2002. *Gracefully Insane: The Rise and Fall of America's Premier Mental Hospital*. New York: Public Affairs. An entertaining narrative of the history of a mental hospital that catered to rich patients, coupled with an account of the changing conceptions and treatments of mental illness within the context of the larger culture.

Chesler, Phyllis. 2005. *Women and Madness*. New York: Palgrave Macmillan. A critical analysis of the sexist bias in the knowledge and practice of psychiatry.

Corrigan, Patrick W. (ed.). 2005. *On the Stigma of Mental Illness*. Washington, D.C.: American Psychological Association. An anthology of articles presenting sociological and other perspectives on mental illness stigma and ways to change it.

Cross-National Collaborative Group. 1992. "The changing rate of major depression: Cross-national comparisons." *JAMA (Journal of the American Medical Association)*, 268 (December 2), 3098–3105. An empirical study showing an overall increase in major depression in widely different countries as well as increasing depression among successively younger generations.

Glenmullen, Joseph. 2000. *Prozac Backlash: Overcoming the Dangers of Prozac, Zoloft, Paxil, and Other Antidepressants With Safe, Effective Alternatives*. New York: Simon & Schuster. Showing how old-fashioned psychotherapy may be more effective than the currently popular psychopharmacology.

Grinker, Roy Richard. 2007. *Unstrange Minds: Remapping the World of Autism*. New York: Basic Books. Shows how social and cultural conditions cause autism to look like an epidemic.

Hobson, J. Allan, and Jonathan A. Leonard. 2001. *Out of Its Mind: Psychiatry in Crisis: A Call for Reform*. Cambridge, Mass.: Perseus Publishing. A critique of the split in modern psychiatry into drug therapy and talk therapy, and a proposal to bring together these conflicting approaches to mental disorder.

Karp, David A. 1996. *Speaking of Sadness: Depression, Disconnection, and the Meanings of Illness*. New York: Oxford University Press. A phenomenological analysis of a common type of mental disorder, as experienced by 50 people and the author himself.

Kaysen, Susanna. 1993. *Girl, Interrupted*. New York: Turtle Bay Books/Random House. An interesting account of the author's two-year stay at an expensive private mental hospital, revealing, among other things, that often the psychiatric staff seems less rational or more insane than the patients.

Kutchins, Herb, and Stuart A. Kirk. 1997. *Making Us Crazy*. New York: Free Press. Shows how the DSM (Diagnostic and Statistical Manual of Mental Illness) contains "a strange mix of social values, political compromise, scientific evidence, and material for insurance claim forms."

Lane, Christopher. 2007. *Shyness: How Normal Behavior Became a Sickness*. New Haven, Conn.: Yale University Press. Argues that the psychiatric definition of social anxiety disorder is so broad that it includes many people who are shy but normal.

Luhrmann, T. M. 2000. *Of Two Minds: The Growing Disorder in American Psychiatry*. New York: Alfred A. Knopf. A critical analysis of how the dominance of drug therapy over talk therapy has caused more harm than good to patients.

Rosenberg, Morris. 1992. *The Unread Mind: Unraveling the Mystery of Madness*. New York: Lexington Books. An interesting sociological analysis of mental illness as a breakdown in human relations in which the patients and nonpatients each cannot see the world through the other's eyes.

Schaler, Jeffrey A. (ed.). 2004. *Szasz Under Fire: The Psychiatric Abolistionist Faces His Critics*. Chicago: Open Court. Twelve critical essays about Thomas Szasz's views on mental illness and his response to each of them.

Slater, Lauren. 1996. *Welcome to My Country: A Therapist's Memoir of Madness*. New York: Random House. Offers an intimate look into the world of mental illness with the insight of the author as a former sufferer.

Szasz, Thomas. 1994. "Mental illness is still a myth." *Society,* 31, 35–39. An updated version of the author's provocative view that mental illness is a myth.

Vaughan, Susan C. 1997. *The Talking Cure: The Science Behind Psychotherapy*. New York: Grosset/Putnam Books. Presents the new view that psychotherapy, like medication, can cure patients by altering their brains.

Wolpert, Lewis. 2000. *Malignant Sadness: The Anatomy of Depression*. New York: Free Press. A review of the theories and studies of depression, with some accounts of the author's personal experiences.

CRITICAL THINKING QUESTIONS

1. Suppose you find a good friend extremely depressed for too long over the death of a pet, which strikes you as downright irrational. Would you try to reason with your friend and say, "It doesn't make sense to feel that way for so long"? If yes, why? If not, what else would you do?

2. Consider the case of the Texas mother, Andrea Yates, who was convicted of killing her five children in 2002. She was clearly psychotic, suffering from schizophrenia and depression. Would you find her guilty and send her to prison? Or would you find her not guilty by reason of insanity and commit her to a mental hospital? Provide an argument and rationale for your answer.

PART FOUR

Diverse Lifestyles

CHAPTER

9

Heterosexual Deviance

Myths and Realities

Myth: A growing number of teenagers today engage in oral sex with many partners because they do not see it as real sex like intercourse.

Reality: There are now more teenagers having oral sex but mostly with only one partner rather than many (p. 205).

Myth: When it comes to sex education for their children, most parents want schools to teach abstinence as either the preferred option or the only option.

Reality: The majority (at least 75 percent) of parents want schools to teach both contraception and abstinence without emphasizing which option is better (p. 206).

――――――

Myth: Extramarital sex is far more exciting or satisfying than marital sex.

Reality: Most (about two-thirds of) married men find their marital sex "very pleasurable," but fewer than half of the unfaithful husbands gave the same rating to their extramarital intercourse (p. 206).

――――――

Myth: Some married men and women have affairs because they are oversexed.

Reality: Those who engage in adultery are far from oversexed. They generally have considerably less sex than monogamous couples (p. 207).

――――――

Myth: Swinging helps improve marriage, confirming the swingers' belief that "the couple that swings together stays together."

Reality: Swinging may improve marriage if the couple is able to divorce sex from emotion, enjoying sex with other couples as pure entertainment without getting emotionally involved with them. But swinging tends to have a negative impact on those who are more conventional, unable to totally separate sex from emotion (p. 210).

――――――

Myth: Pornography is always harmful.

Reality: Violent pornography is harmful as shown by laboratory studies, but erotic, nonviolent pornography is harmless as suggested by "real world" studies outside the lab (p. 212).

――――――

Myth: The dancers at nude bars can make an enormous amount of money because most of their customers are wealthy.

Reality: Most of the nude dancers' customers are working-class men, far from wealthy (p. 214).

――――――

Myth: Most prostitutes are sexually frigid, unable to enjoy sex.

Reality: When having sex with their boyfriends or husbands, prostitutes as a group are more responsive than other women, more able to achieve orgasm. Many call girls even have orgasms with their clients (p. 216).

――――――

Myth: Prostitutes are mostly heavy drug users, victims of low self-esteem, socially immature, emotionally disturbed, or pitifully abnormal in some other way.

Reality: Most prostitutes, largely like conventional women, do not have those social and psychological problems. Only a small minority, mostly streetwalkers, have such problems (p. 220).

――――――

Myth: Largely liberal, broad-minded, and freedom-loving, most Americans support the idea of legalizing prostitution.

Reality: Most Americans not only oppose the legalization of prostitution but also want the existing antiprostitution laws strictly enforced (p. 227).

――――――

When she was 13, Kristie ran away from home in the Southwest. Friends introduced her to a tall and good-looking man who made her feel good by saying she was very smart and sexy. Soon he had persuaded her to prostitute herself on the streets of Las Vegas—and then other cities such as Los Angeles, Atlanta, and Phoenix. The pimp had other girls working for him, and he would bring them along with Kristie to a city, make them sell sex through-out the night, and then move on. Kristie stopped only when she was arrested at age 15, two years after she started prostituting herself. During the preceding six months, she estimates, she had had at least 100 customers, but she had stopped counting long before her arrest (Fang, 2005).

This kind of prostitution, which involves women selling sex to men, is an example of heterosexual deviance. In this chapter, we will take a look at various aspects of prostitution. But first we will examine other forms of heterosexual deviance: teen sex, extramarital sex, pornography, phone sex, nude dancing, and sexual harassment.

Teen Sex

Most Americans today no longer consider premarital sex deviant as they did 20 or 30 years ago. More precisely, though, they find premarital sex acceptable for adults, but not for teenagers (Risman and Schwartz, 2002). It is okay for people aged 20 or older to engage in premarital sex, but it is still a no-no for those under age 20. Teenage sex, then, continues to be deviant in the eyes of U.S. society. The acceptability of premarital sex for adults apparently reflects the influence of the sexual revolution that has been going on since the 1960s. But why not for teenagers as well? Probably because teens are still *not* considered mature and responsible enough to have sex. Most adults seem to be afraid that if teens were allowed to have sex, they would end up having "illegitimate" babies. In fact, this seems to be a major reason for today's sex education programs that emphasize the importance of sexual abstinence.

Still, teenagers nowadays are much more likely than their peers of two or three decades ago to be sexually active. Teens now have sex younger, have more sexual partners, and are more likely to have "hookups" or one-night stands. More than half of teens (aged 15 to 19) are now sexually active. Further, teens are more likely to get a sexually transmitted disease (STD) such as herpes, gonorrhea, or HIV, and have the highest rate of premarital pregnancy in the industrial world. The sex education that urges teens to abstain from sex until marriage has worked in some ways, but with some unintended consequences. In some schools, for example, teens who have pledged abstinence tend to delay having sex for 18 months, but once they start having sex, they are less likely to use contraception. Also, partly because of the "just say no" emphasis in sex education, growing numbers of teens have been trying to maintain "technical virginity" by having oral sex, which they do not view as real sex, presumably because it cannot cause pregnancy. But most of these "virgins" have oral sex with just one partner, not a lot of partners as popularly believed (Sharon, 2008; Mosher, 2005; Bearman, Moody, and Stovel, 2004).

There is, however, a gender factor in teens having sex or abstaining from it. As shown by a study of youngsters aged 12 to 14, boys with high self-esteem are more likely to engage in sex, but girls with high self-esteem are more likely to abstain (Spencer et al., 2002). Apparently, the traditional double standard still holds sway over the teen world: Sexually active boys are looked up to as studs, while sexually active girls are looked down on as sluts. Girls are further caught in a double bind: If they continue to maintain their virginity, they risk being stigmatized as a tease. To get around both the "slut" and "tease" stigmas, many teenage girls become sexually active within a relationship—by having sex with their boyfriend or somebody they know well rather than a stranger or mere acquaintance (Dunn, 2004).

In the meantime two groups of adults continue to battle over what to do about teen sex. Conservative Christians want schools only to teach teenagers to abstain from sex, while liberals support a comprehensive sex-education program that teaches both abstinence and contraception. To the conservatives, the teaching of contraception contradicts the teaching of abstinence because the former will lead to sex. But to the liberals, teaching abstinence without contraception will leave teens defenseless against pregnancy and STDs when they have sex, as some are bound to because the abstinence-only program cannot be expected to be 100 percent successful.

Thus, the nature of sex education varies from school to school. Among schools that teach sex education, about 51 percent discuss contraception but teach abstinence as the preferred option. Approximately 35 percent teach abstinence as the only option. The remaining 14 percent teach both options without emphasizing which is better. But, ironically, the majority (at least 75 percent) of *parents* want schools to take this third, comprehensive approach. Also, ironically, research has shown the comprehensive program to be the most effective in reducing teen pregnancy and STDs (Kelly, 2005; Irvine, 2002). However, since 2002, a new sex education has emerged that may help boost the effectiveness of the abstinence-only program. It teaches only the health benefits of abstinence, totally ignoring the moral issues. Students are taught, for example, that the cervix of teenage girls is more vulnerable than that of adult women to certain STDs, particularly viral diseases such as human papillomavirus (HPV), so that a sexually active girl can still get the diseases even though her partner uses condoms (Parker-Pope, 2002).

Extramarital Sex

Extramarital sex, popularly known as adultery, infidelity, or an affair, is sex that a married person has with "the other" woman or man. An overwhelming majority of Americans frown on extramarital sex: Nearly 90 percent of men and 94 percent of women said in a national survey that they considered adultery "always wrong" or "almost always wrong." Not surprisingly, only a relatively small minority engage in extramarital sex: 25 percent of married men and 17 percent of married women reported having at least one affair. These data, however, can also be taken to suggest that adultery is very common because the ratios (25 and 17 percent) mean that at least 19 million American men and 12 million American women have committed adultery. "That's a helluva lot of people being unfaithful," said a sex researcher in Florida (Norman, 1998; Michael et al., 1994).

Seductive Myths

Although faithful to their spouses, most married Americans, especially men, wish at one time or another to have an extramarital affair. According to the classic Kinsey Report, over 70 percent of married men had such a wish in the late 1940s. While women tend to associate an affair with love more than sex, men are more likely to think of it as a sexual escapade (Glass and Wright, 1992). As a result, many men seem to believe in the myth that extramarital intercourse is far more exciting or satisfying than marital sex. But data show otherwise. Perhaps because extramarital copulation is mostly carried out in secrecy, and frequently charged with tension and guilt, the experience is far from gratifying. According to one study, two-thirds of married men rated their marital sex "very pleasurable," but fewer than half of the unfaithful husbands gave the same rating to their extramarital coitus. And

53 percent of married women regularly reached orgasm with their husbands, but only 39 percent of the straying wives did so in extramarital intercourse (Katchadourian, 1985).

Another myth about extramarital sex may be equally popular with both men and women: "People have affairs because they are oversexed." Research suggests, however, that those who engage in adultery are far from oversexed. They generally are much less sexually active—having a lot less sex—than monogamous couples (Adler, 1996; Pittman, 1993). If being oversexed is not the cause of infidelity, what is? The cause can be found in a set of social and cultural factors, as suggested by the fact that the incidence of extramarital sex varies from one group to another in the United States as well as from one culture to another in the world.

Cultural Variations

There are legitimate and illegitimate adulteries, and each appears in different forms in different cultures. First, consider the different forms of illegitimate adulteries. Among the Lozi of eastern Africa, adultery does not involve sexual intercourse. If a man walks with a married woman he is not related to, or if he gives her a beer, he has committed adultery. By contrast, in most other societies, illegitimate adulteries always involve copulation. To conservative Christians who interpret the Bible literally, even divorce and remarriage, which involves copulation, is condemned as adultery. As Jesus says in Mark 10:11, "Whoever divorces his wife and marries another commits adultery against her; and if she divorces her husband and marries another, she commits adultery." In various societies, however, women have historically been punished for adultery more harshly than men. In Muslim societies, for example, unfaithful wives could be stoned to death. Generally, because illegitimate adulteries are socially condemned, they do not occur frequently (Fisher, 1992; Lawson, 1988).

Legitimate adulteries, however, take place more often in societies where they are by definition socially approved. Among the Kofyar of Nigeria, a woman who is unhappy with her husband but does not want to divorce may, without seeking his consent, take an extra lover, who lives openly with her in her husband's house. A Kofyar man may do the same for the same reason. In many Italian towns on the Adriatic coast, virtually every married man has a lover whom he visits regularly. Most of these affairs are between men and women who are married to others. Sometimes younger male servants visit rich men's wives, while rich men occasionally copulate with their maids or cooks. But it is taboo for any married person to ever speak of his or her affair. This is because boasting, gossiping, or even whispering to others about one's dalliance can expose the extensive network of extramarital relationships, seriously threatening their highly cherished community cohesion and family life (Fisher, 1992). However, legitimate adulteries such as these do not exist in American society.

All this points to the significant influence of culture on extramarital sex. Whatever form of adultery a culture considers acceptable is likely to be prevalent. Research that focuses on U.S. society alone further suggests the influence of certain social factors on extramarital sex.

Social Factors

Under the influence of the same culture that basically discourages infidelity, some groups of Americans are nonetheless more likely than others to cheat on their spouses. As shown by various studies, extramarital sex is more common among those who have experienced premarital coitus than among those who have not; men are more likely than women to have an affair; the less religious generally have a higher incidence of extramarital sex than the more religious; and lower-income people are more likely than higher-income Americans to be unfaithful to their spouses (Duncombe et al., 2004; Janus and Janus, 1993).

Sociobiologists regard the gender difference in adultery as the most significant finding because it exists in virtually all societies. Sociobiologists trace it to humankind's long evolutionary past when men had to impregnate more women to produce more young so as to ensure the survival of their genes (Norman, 1998; Fisher, 1992). But the last thing that today's philandering men want is to produce babies. After all, most people, both male and female, now regard the primary purpose of sex as recreation rather than procreation. Far from scientific and valid, the evolutionary theory merely reflects the patriarchal belief that men should prove their masculinity by screwing around. It is this widely shared belief that causes men to philander more than women do. Most male philanderers also differ from their affair partners. The men tend to attach too little significance to the affair, being far from deeply in love with the women. But women tend to attach too much significance to the affair, believing that they no longer love their husband and that their affair partner is the true love of their life (Allan, 2004; Pittman, 1993).

Many affairs begin accidentally. The straying spouse may have drunk too much, got caught up in the moment, or just had a bad day. Here is how a typical accidental infidelity "just happens" to a 47-year-old college professor:

> I had my first affair with a young faculty member who was divorced. We had known each other for several years, and there was no great passion, but she was a woman and I a man. It was strange how it came about. We were both out of town at a professional conference. . . . The very first night, after some drinks, I found myself in bed with her. The sex was fine, but the guilt was awful. She kept telling me, "Grow up, we're both adults, and if we can give each other some pleasure, what's the sin in that?" It wasn't easy; I could see my poor sad-sack wife, and the dread of my kids ever finding out. The conference lasted a week but I carefully avoided my colleague for the rest of it. (Pittman, 1993)

Infidelity is likely to lead to divorce (Previti and Amato, 2004). But more often the betrayed wife or cuckolded husband strives to do whatever they can to save their marriage, although they initially feel deeply hurt and outraged. The marriage usually survives if the affair is stopped, brought into the open, and dealt with (Pittman, 1993).

A Social Profile of Swingers

The extramarital sex that we have just discussed involves having an affair behind the spouse's back. Another form of extramarital sex is an open sexual activity in which both husband and wife agree to participate. It is popularly known as *swinging,* also called "comarital sex" or "mate swapping" in sociological research. It involves married couples exchanging spouses for sex only. In the eye of the general public, swinging is much more deviant than infidelity, the traditional form of extramarital sex. This could explain why swinging is considerably less common than infidelity. While about 20 percent of married couples have cheated on their spouses, only about 1 or 2 percent have engaged in swinging. Still, thanks to the Internet, it is now much easier than before to find swinging couples at any locale. In addition, swinging couples are available in sex clubs in large cities (Gould, 2000; Levy, 1999; Jenks, 1998).

Most swingers are middle-class, suburban whites. The majority are between 25 and 45 years of age. Politically they are somewhat conservative, particularly if they live in Middle America. They are also mildly prejudiced against racial and ethnic minorities. Most are Protestant. Although they themselves do not attend church regularly, they often send their children to Sunday school or give them religious instruction. Both the men and women lack outside interests, hobbies, and activities. In general, swingers appear bored, frustrated, and incapable of living a joyful and stimulating life—much like ordinary Americans living lives of "quiet desperation." Such is the profile of the swingers that emerged from Gilbert Bartell's (1971) classic research.

Brian Gilmartin (1975) took another look at swingers by comparing them with a control group of nonswingers. The two groups appear closely similar in age, occupation, income, number of children, and involvement in local clubs and organizations. The swingers are no more unhappy, bored, or neurotic than the nonswingers. These findings largely support Bartell's observation. "Other than their sexual deviance," Gilmartin concludes, "the most remarkable thing about the swingers is how unremarkable they are." But Gilmartin also discovered significant differences between the two groups: (1) swingers have a much lower rate of church attendance; (2) swingers tend more to have had unhappy childhoods; (3) swinging husbands are more likely than nonswinging husbands to have unhappily married or divorced parents, though there is not much difference for the wives; (4) swingers began dating earlier, dated more frequently, had their first sexual intercourse at a younger age, were more sexually active before marriage, and married earlier; (5) swingers are more likely to have been divorced before; and (6) swingers are less politically active and less involved in community activities.

In sum, compared to nonswingers, swingers have looser ties to the three traditional institutions of social control, namely, religion, family, and community. This does not mean, though, that swingers are alienated from society, living on the fringes of conventional social life. Swinging takes up only a small portion of their lives. They still spend more time with conventional people and on traditional, marital sex.

More recent research has largely confirmed the findings of those earlier studies. Richard Jenks (1998, 1985), for example, has found swingers less subjected to social control but no more alienated from society than conventional people. The swingers in Jenks's study have moved more often, have been living in their communities for fewer years, and are less likely to have a religious identification. Given these experiences, they presumably feel less restricted or controlled by social institutions. Yet there is no significant difference between them and nonswingers in responses to questions designed to measure alienation. They are no more likely than nonswingers, for example, to feel that their votes do not make much difference in political elections or that they have little influence over their own lives. In short, swingers are basically ordinary people who happen to resist social control by swinging.

Since they resort to swinging as a way of expressing their liberation from social control, many swingers seem to think that they are the vanguard of sexual revolution, replacing male–female inequality with equality. It is obviously true that the swinging husband and wife have an equal share of sexual promiscuity, but this does not necessarily mean that they have abolished sexual inequality. In fact, swinging seems to be basically a male institution. In almost all cases of mate swapping, it is the husband who initiates the idea of swinging, which is often objected to by his wife. Then the husband strong-arms, subtly coerces, or persuades his wife into swinging (Henshel, 1973; Palson and Palson, 1972). This may be less likely to occur today, though, given the increased social power of women.

Finally, swingers regard their comarital sex as a marital enhancement, believing that "the couple that swings together stays together." Indeed, swinging has been found to improve marital relations for some couples. One study shows that swinging couples consistently report a higher level of marital happiness than nonswinging couples. There is a greater amount of intimacy, affection, and communication, as well as a higher frequency of marital sex, between swinging spouses than between conventional spouses (Gilmartin, 1975). Another study finds swinging couples "more harmonious, more self-accepting, and more accepting of their mates" when compared with nonswinging couples. Swinging couples also report more pleasurable sexual experiences with their own spouse (Rubin and Adams, 1986; Wheeler and Kilmann, 1983).

Does this mean that swinging tends to improve marriage? The answer is yes, *if* the swinging couple is able to divorce sex from emotion, enjoying sex with other couples as pure entertainment without getting emotionally involved with them (de Visser and McDonald, 2007). But swinging tends to have a negative impact on those who are more sensitive or romantic, unable to totally separate sex from emotion. Having expected to be treated by their swinging partners as *persons,* they are likely to be disappointed when they are used as mere sex *objects*. They are, as research has suggested, likely to drop out of swinging, often in disgust (Denfeld, 1974). In short, swinging is like a two-edged sword: It may swing in the direction of positive consequences or in the opposite direction of negative consequences. The nature of the consequences depends on the individual who uses the sword rather than on the sword itself.

Pornography

It is against the law to distribute what is called pornography—sexually explicit materials— in the media, but the law is not strictly enforced because the meaning of pornography is subject to different interpretations. A large majority of Americans are also opposed to the distribution as well as the consumption of pornography (Maguire and Pastore, 1996). Yet sexually explicit materials can be found everywhere, and most people, especially men, have used it. The film about *Hustler* magazine's founder, *The People vs. Larry Flynt,* raises the interminable controversy over whether the constitutional right to free speech allows even the most vulgar form of expression. Some would endlessly debate this kind of issue, but here we will focus more on what the producers and distributors of pornography sell and what effects the merchandise has on the consumers.

The Porn Industry

Pornography has become an enormous industry today. A major reason is that the demand for sexually explicit materials has soared over the last decade. The number of hard-core video rentals, for example, skyrocketed from only 75 million in 1985 to 665 million in 1996. Today, the United States has become by far the world's leading producer of hard-core videos, churning them out at the astonishing rate of about 150 new titles a week. Also widely consumed, though to a lesser extent than hard-core videos, are sex magazines, adult cable programming, peep shows, live sex acts, phone sex, and computer porn. The amount of money spent on all the adult materials ($10 billion in 2000) is much larger than Hollywood's domestic box office receipts or the entire revenue from rock and country music recordings. Strip clubs alone bring in more money than all the opera, ballet, and jazz and classical music performances combined (Egan, 2000; Schlosser, 1997).

The porn industry's fantastic growth has stemmed mostly from the invasion of pornographic videos into mainstream society. In the past, most people were too embarrassed to go to seedy movie theaters and adult bookstores, but today they can watch porn videos in the privacy of their homes. Not surprisingly, the number of those traditional suppliers of porn has declined. Now, not only mom-and-pop video stores but also cable-TV companies profit greatly from pornographic videos. Even large hotel chains such as Hyatt, Holiday Inn, and Marriott reportedly earn millions each year by making their guests feel at home with adult films to watch in their rooms (Ackman, 2004; Egan, 2000).

There is a wide spectrum of hard-core videos to meet every conceivable consumer demand: videos that feature gay, lesbian, straight, transsexual, interracial, or older couples; "cat fighting" videos that show naked women wrestling each other or joining forces to beat up a naked man; videos for sadomasochists, aficionados of bondage or spanking, or people fond of verbal abuse; and other kinds of videos too numerous to list. Other forms of pornography, particularly phone sex and computer porn, have also emerged on the scene, generating significant revenues for Internet service providers such as Verizon, Sprint, and Time Warner Cable (Koch, 2008; Egan, 2000; Schlosser, 1997).

The Effects of Pornography

Research has produced seemingly conflicting findings on the effects of pornography. Some studies seem to support the antiporn feminist and conservative view that pornography is harmful. Other studies appear to confirm the anticensorship, liberal view that pornography is harmless. Let us take a closer look at each of these two views and the studies supporting them.

Pornography as Harmful.   Some feminists support the idea that a woman has the legal right to free expression via pornography even though they may personally find the material distasteful. But many other feminists are opposed to pornography and want it banned because they believe that pornography is harmful to women.

To support this view, antiporn feminists usually point out many laboratory studies showing that exposure to violent pornography encourages male aggression against women (Linz and Malamuth, 1993; Donnerstein et al., 1987). In one experiment, for example, male subjects were divided into two groups: One watched a film depicting sexual violence against women; the other watched a nonviolent film. After seeing the movies, the subjects who had watched the violent film were more likely to adminster electrical shocks to women than were those who had watched the nonviolent film (Donnerstein et al., 1987). But we cannot generalize, as some feminists do, from the laboratory finding to what goes on in the larger society by insisting that violent pornography contributes significantly to the prevalence of antiwomen sexual aggression *in the society at large*. The reason is simply that, as research has indicated, *most* of the pornographic materials in the United States are not violent at all, and nonviolent pornography, which merely shows nudity and consensual sex, generally does not cause male aggression against women (Donnerstein et al., 1987).

Conservatives also find pornography harmful. They believe that sexually explicit materials can destroy traditional family values and, thereby, the entire society. Often cited to support this belief is the research finding that long exposure to explicit depictions of common sex acts often leads men to seek portrayals of less common, more deviant practices, such as violent, sadomasochistic, or bestial sex. Such men are then more likely to engage in various deviant sexual activities, which they find exciting. At the same time, however, they become more likely to find conventional, monogamous, or marital sex boring. All this is considered to have "devastating consequences" for traditional monogamy, marriage, family, and society (Paul, 2004; Linz and Malamuth, 1993). There is, however, no clear-cut evidence that pornography wrecks many marriages, let alone threatens the survival of the society.

Pornography as Harmless.   Liberals may personally find pornography distasteful, but they are opposed to the censorship of sexually explicit material not only because it violates the freedom of expression but also because they view pornography as basically harmless.

To support their belief that pornography is harmless, liberals usually call on studies showing that, in the real world outside the laboratory, exposure to sexually explicit materials does not cause rape or other sex crimes. For example, the availability of pornography in the United States increased substantially between 1960 and 1969 but the incidence of rape did not go up as much during the same period. Similarly, the advent of the VCR has vastly increased the dissemination of hard-core videos, but the rate of rape has not increased to the same extent. U.S. cities with high circulation of sexually oriented magazines have basically the same rates of rape as cities with low circulation. In Denmark, in the late 1960s, after all legal prohibitions on the sale of pornography were removed, sex crimes did not rise but instead dropped sharply. Today most Danes even find hard-core pornography beneficial to their lives, which they credit with improving not only their sex lives but their general quality of life (Hutson, 2008; Linz and Malamuth, 1993). To liberals, all these data strongly suggest that pornography is harmless.

We may conclude that pornography may be harmless for the majority of men but harmful for a few men who are already inclined to be sexually violent. Porn is also more likely to be harmful if it portrays sexual violence, but more likely to be harmless if it merely shows nudity or nonviolent sex acts (Hutson, 2008; Kingston et al., 2008; Procida and Simon, 2003).

Phone Sex

In phone sex the operator, who is most likely a woman, essentially sells sexual fantasies to the caller, most likely a man. She is good at faking interest in the caller, talking about anything the caller wants, and playing along with whatever fantasies he has. The trick is to maximize profit by getting him to stay on the phone for as long as possible. If a caller says "I love you," the operator is likely to answer "I love you, too. Now what else do you want to do with me?" If the caller wants her to go down on him, she may pretend to do it by making the appropriate sound and saying the right things.

The operator is extremely unlikely to meet the caller for fear of getting beaten, raped, or even murdered. But she will do practically anything on the phone, regardless of what kind of man the caller is. As an operator says,

> There hasn't been a caller that I didn't really like. There have been callers that just basically ticked me off, but it's really not a like or dislike thing. I don't think of those callers as people that I like or dislike. It's just another John, you know? I mean, I'm a telephone whore, so this is just my trick. It's not that I like them or dislike them. (Flowers, 1998)

In other words, the operator has the typical business attitude toward her work. She needs the job primarily to make money, and she will sell her service to whoever the caller is.

There are five types of callers, says sociologist Amy Flowers, who spent four months working as an operator in a phone sex company while observing and interviewing 21 colleagues. Knowing what the five types are can help us understand the men's various reasons for engaging in this kind of sexual deviance.

First, *quick-sex callers,* the majority of customers, do not stay on the phone long enough to accumulate a hefty charge. They offer little or no conversation, usually asking the operator to perform a fast sex act. Second, *psychos* are violent and angry callers, who like to talk about beating or raping women. Third, *lonely, lovelorn callers* keep calling the same operator, proposing marriage, and making plans for the future with her, but refraining from discussion of sexual matters. Fourth, *sexually possessive callers* resemble the lovelorn for being infatuated with a particular operator, but they are jealous of her sexual involvement with other men and demand that she give sex only to him. And fifth, *likable callers* sound attractive, and are able to arouse the operator's personal or sexual interest. They are well spoken and educated with high-status professions, for example, physicians, celebrities, and government officials. They often insist that they called the phone sex line "only out of curiosity" (Flowers, 1998).

Nude Dancing

Like phone sex, nude dancing enables the male customer to fulfill his fantasy of sexual intimacy with an attractive woman, except that in nude dancing he can see the woman's partially clad or totally naked body. At topless bars and lingerie shows, the dancers are partly clothed but often do not wear panties so they can flash their customers. At nude clubs, however, the dancers remove all their clothing. Since they make most or all of their money from tips, dancers do their best to please the customers. Not surprisingly, then, dancers pay only scant attention, if any, to the art and aesthetics of dancing, which they know is not the audience's interest. Instead, maximum effort is made to catch and hold the customers' attention on what they have come to the club to see. Thus, as customers seated near the edge of the stage are prepared with cash in hand to tip her, the dancer may move from one man to another exposing her vagina for his close-up view. She may later lie on her back, spread her legs, separate her labia, and repeatedly stroke her clitoris. If her vagina becomes profusely wet, she may snatch the baseball cap off the head of a client and wipe it between her legs and give it back to him (Schiff, 1999).

Most customers are working-class men. They are not only far from wealthy, they are also not good-looking, young, and assertive. In a patriarchal society where successful or wealthy older men often get trophy wives, it may be difficult or impossible for those working-class men to get a young and attractive woman to be romantically interested in them. In their everyday lives, such a woman might not even look at them or talk to them, let alone expose herself to them. But they can fantasize having such a woman treat them like a million bucks, and this fantasy is what the nude dancer seeks to fulfill (Schiff, 1999).

What about the dancer? What can she get out of this work? In 1999 she could expect to make $25,000 to $75,000 a year. This could be considered an excellent wage, given the fact that most nude dancers have only a high school education and few job skills. Unsurprisingly, money is by far the number one reason for becoming a nude dancer. Despite the high pay, though, nude dancing is still widely regarded as highly disreputable. But this does not seem to disturb most dancers, because they do not identify themselves with their stigmatized career. They identify themselves instead as wives, single mothers, or some other conventional role, and may not even tell family, friends, and others what they do. They feel that their dancing job does not reflect their true self, their true values and characteristics, who they really are. More positively, most dancers find their work empowering because it enables them to command so much attention and interest from an audience that it is willing to pay them handsomely. They even are able to stop rowdy customer behavior. When a customer touches her private parts, for example, the dancer may use her hips to bump his head and face, knocking him backward (Spivey, 2005; Wood, 2001; Schiff, 1999; Reid, Epstein, and Benson, 1995).

Sexual Harassment

Sexual harassment can be defined as an unwelcome act of a sexual nature. The U.S. Supreme Court has provided a more precise, legal definition: Sexual harassment is any sexual conduct that makes the workplace environment so hostile or abusive to the victims that they find it hard to perform their job.

The Supreme Court's definition came with its ruling on the suit that Teresa Harris filed against her former boss, Charles Hardy. In 1987 Harris quit her job in despair because she felt she had been sexually harassed by Hardy. According to Harris, Hardy often asked her—and other female employees—to retrieve coins from the front pockets of his pants. He once asked Harris to go with him to a hotel room to negotiate her raise. And he routinely made such remarks to her as, "You're a woman; what do you know?" She spent six years trying to convince judges that she was sexually harassed in violation of federal law, but to no avail. The judges found Hardy's conduct not severe enough to "seriously affect her psychological well-being." But Harris persisted, and finally the Supreme Court ruled that sexual harassment does not have to inflict "severe psychological injury" on the victim. As the Court said, federal law "comes into play before the harassing conduct leads to a nervous breakdown" (Sachs, 1993). More recently, in 1998, the Supreme Court further broadened the definition of harassment: A female employee can sue her employer even if she gets a salary raise or promotion after resisting unwanted sexual advances from her supervisor (Lavelle, 1998).

Since the early 1990s, the number of harassment charges has increased substantially. To avoid being sued, many companies, as well as universities and colleges, have instituted antiharassment policies, guidelines, or educational programs, especially since 1998 when the Supreme Court ruled that companies can protect themselves against lawsuits only if they have a strong and effective program to prevent and discipline harassment (Lavelle, 1998). Even primary and high schools have started to prevent harassment after the Court ruled in 1999 that schools can be sued if they fail to stop a student from "severely" harassing another (Greenhouse, 1999).

The problem, however, is too prevalent to soon go away. According to various studies, about half of all working women have been sexually harassed at some point in their careers, and about 40 percent of college women have been harassed. Examples of harassment range from unwanted sexual remarks to actual rape. Also, among high school and junior high students, close to 70 percent of girls have been touched, groped, or pinched on school grounds. And as many as 1 in 10 students from kindergarten to twelfth grade may be subjected to some form of sexual harassment by teachers and other school employees (Gregory, 2004; Hendrie, 2004; Crouch, 2001; Reed, 2000).

Generally, sexual harassment reflects men's attempt to preserve their traditional dominance over women. Men are, therefore, more likely to harass a woman if they feel threatened by her "invasion" into their male-dominated world. This may explain why sexual harassment seems to occur most frequently in traditionally and heavily male-dominated occupations, such as the U.S. military. For the same reason, in poor countries where men have long been better educated than women, women with more education are more likely to be sexually harassed than those with less education (Merkin, 2008; Walters, 2005). At bottom, however, sexual harassment is an expression of power, involving a more powerful person victimizing the less powerful, such as school employees taking advantage of their young charges. It is also possible for a female boss to sexually harass a male employee. But, given the predominance of men in positions of power, they are the offenders in most cases.

The World of Prostitution

Prostitution, the exchange of sex for money, is legal in many countries in Europe and elsewhere. By contrast, it is not legal in the United States, except in some counties of Nevada. Nonetheless, prostitution has long been big business here. Every year billions of dollars are spent on the sexual favors of prostitutes, whose profit amounts to at least 10 times the annual budget of the U.S. Department of Justice. The number of prostitutes has been estimated to range from 84,000 to 336,000 (Potterat et al., 1990). But such estimates grossly underrepresent the real number of prostitutes because the figures are almost entirely derived from sex workers who are known to the police and fail to take into account those who are not. According to one survey that asked a nationwide sample of American women ages 18 to 64 whether they had ever had sex for money, nearly 6 percent said yes. This seemingly small percentage translates into a huge number—at least 4.2 million women (Janus and Janus, 1993). Although there are so many prostitutes, we know very little about them. Here we will take a look at various aspects of prostitution.

Myths about Prostitution

We often hear that prostitution is the oldest profession in the world. This is a myth, however, because priesthood is the oldest profession. We frequently encounter other myths about prostitutes such as those that follow (Weitzer, 2005a; Perkins, 1991).

First, it is often mentioned in both folklore and sometimes even in scientific literature that prostitutes typically are nymphomaniacs, having an insatiable desire for sexual intercourse with many men. This is male fantasy, not substantiated by facts. Before going into the sex business, most prostitutes did not have many more sex partners than other, average women. What is true is that prostitutes have started having sex at a younger age than other women (Perkins, 1991).

Second, some clinical psychologists assume just the opposite of the first myth: Prostitutes are sexually frigid. Actually, when they have sex with their husbands or boyfriends, prostitutes as a group are more responsive than other women—more able to achieve orgasm. The majority of call girls even frequently have orgasms with their clients, primarily because those men tend to treat them like girlfriends. Only streetwalkers are unlikely to experience orgasms with their customers, who are much less friendly than call girls' clients.

Third, there are two contradictory beliefs about how prostitutes treat their clients: On the one hand, they are believed to be nasty and hard-hearted—as suggested by the popular saying "as cold as a whore's heart"—and on the other, they are romanticized as sweet and warmhearted—"a woman with a heart of gold." In reality, however, the average prostitute's attitude toward her clients is quite similar to that of anyone who provides services to a diverse clientele. Some clients she likes, a few others she dislikes, and toward most of them she simply feels neutral. However, being paid more and treated better, call girls, escorts, and brothel prostitutes are more likely than streetwalkers to like their clients.

Fourth, according to popular belief, most prostitutes are drug addicts or have turned to prostitution to support their drug habits. They are also assumed to have emotional problems. It is true that streetwalkers are more likely than conventional women to be addicted to drugs, but streetwalkers make up only a minority (10 to 30 percent) of prostitutes. Most prostitutes, including call girls, escorts, house prostitutes, and others who work indoors rather than on the street, are not drug addicts. They are also relatively free of emotional problems, while streetwalkers are more prone to have psychological problems resulting from the stress and danger of working the streets.

Types of Prostitutes

There is a great variety of prostitutes. Some researchers have found as many as 18 different types (Benjamin and Masters, 1964). Most of these kinds are relatively rare, however, so we need to know only the more common types, namely, streetwalkers, child and adolescent prostitutes, house prostitutes, and call girls. These sex workers are employed in a highly stratified occupation, so that they vary from one another in their status in prostitution, the price they charge, or the quality of their social and work life. The status, price, or life quality rises as one goes from streetwalkers, who occupy the lowest status, to call girls, who have the highest status.

Streetwalkers.   In prostitution, soliciting customers on the street is probably the most ancient method. Generally, compared with most other types of prostitutes, streetwalkers are less educated, more likely to shoot drugs and get AIDS, and more often arrested by the police.

Streetwalkers normally use a standard method of soliciting. When a streetwalker sees a potential customer strolling on a sidewalk, she is likely to smile at him. She may then say to him such things as: "Hi. How are you today?" or "Which direction are you heading?" If the man responds, she may ask, "Do you want company?" or "Want a date?" or "Wanna do something?" Then she tells him her price, although very often, the man himself takes the initiative and simply asks, "How much?" Once a deal is struck, she typically takes him to a hotel room.

Sometimes, streetwalkers solicit business from cruising motorists. For most of these transactions, the service is rendered in the car. Because many customers find their cars too cramped for intercourse, a large number of "car jobs" involve oral sex only. By contrast, virtually all the sexual services in hotel rooms involve vaginal intercourse. Wherever and however the sexual act is carried out, most streetwalkers, not being well paid, strive to minimize its duration. Thus, most of the sexual services in the room last 15 to 30 minutes, while most of the car jobs last only 4 to 15 minutes (van Gelder and Kaplan, 1992; Freund et al., 1991). Many car customers may whine about the shortness of the service, but most streetwalkers consider their job finished when the customer ejaculates. And it does not take long for this to occur, as a streetwalker says, "The men who are driving around here are so excited and horny. When you touch that thing, well, it almost happens right away" (van Gelder and Kaplan, 1992). That's why, despite the complaint, most customers repeatedly return for the same kind of service.

Traditionally, streetwalkers tend to ply their trade in lower-class areas, where they can afford to solicit blatantly and openly, without much fear of getting arrested by the police. But in many suburban areas today streetwalkers are more careful to avoid arrest. This presents a problem, though. How can customers know the identity of a streetwalker if she camouflages it to avoid being too obtrusive to the general public? To solve this problem, streetwalkers resort to a unique strategy: alternating between actively soliciting when spotting a potential customer and discreetly blending into the street scene when seeing a police officer. Thus, most streetwalkers tend to stand near a bus or taxi stop, a public telephone booth, street corner, or hotel entrance. This enables a customer to distinguish a streetwalker from other pedestrians, and when she sees him approaching her she will know him to be a customer. At the same time, such public places enable a streetwalker to loiter like any other pedestrian when a police officer appears (Riccio, 1992).

The prospect of being arrested is not the only problem facing streetwalkers. More than other types of prostitutes, streetwalkers are often abused by customers, pimps, and even police. Customers frequently force them to engage in kinky sex, rape them, refuse to pay them, rob them, or beat them. Pimps regularly beat them, too. Policemen sometimes beat them or demand free sex. Serial killers often murder them one after another, knowing prostitutes' families would not miss them and the police would not look too hard for them. Young streetwalkers, particularly those under age 16, are most likely to suffer these forms of victimization. Older streetwalkers are more able to protect themselves. They know how to "manipulate anonymity" before soliciting, concealing their true identity while trying to determine which customers are trustworthy or dangerous (Skipp and Campo-Flores, 2006; Weitzer, 2005b; Silbert and Pines, 1981; Merry, 1980).

Child and Adolescent Prostitutes.   Some prostitutes are only 8 to 12 years old. These child prostitutes are often called "baby pros." Most have been brought up in poor and chaotic families, where they are accustomed to seeing their mothers or older sisters engaged in sex with different men, in pornography, or in prostitution. Many have suffered physical or sexual abuse at the hands of their parents or other adults. Consequently, when first approached by a man with an offer to pay them for sex, they were "ready" to accept. Still too young, though, they continue to live with their parents and attend school, working as prostitutes only on a part-time basis.

Somewhat older than these children are adolescent prostitutes, aged 13 to 17. Most have also been brought up in disorganized families. They, too, have suffered physical or sexual abuse in childhood. But, unlike their younger counterparts, many adolescent prostitutes have run away from home and most have become heavy drug users. The need to support themselves, further intensified by the craving for drugs, is the most common motivation among the adolescents to sell sex for money (Weisberg, 1985). But often the pimp plays a significant role in their entry into prostitution. Alone in a large city, many young runaways from small towns or rural areas are fair game for pimps, who frequently look for new prey to entice or force into prostitution (Fang, 2005).

Adolescent prostitutes comprise only a small minority of prostitutes in the United States and other Western societies. The situation is different in poor countries, where far greater numbers of youngsters are forced or tricked into prostitution by pimps, parents, or poverty. In many poor villages in Thailand, many young girls are sold by penniless parents to brothel operators, are tricked into coming to big cities where they are forced to work in whorehouses, or are enticed to marry German tourists and then brought to Germany to serve as house prostitutes. In Nepal's poor Himalayan villages, some 7,000 adolescents are sold every year to the brothels in the Indian city of Bombay. In Brazil, about 25,000 girls from poor families have been forced into prostitution in remote Amazon mining camps. In Eastern Europe, many poor parents have forced their young daughters to sell sex, and those who work in brothels are often beaten to make them submit. As one official in a European aid group observes, "Many of the girls have broken teeth. They say they fell downstairs. But there are so many of them that either this business has the worst-maintained stairs in the world or these girls have been punched" (Perry and Sai, 2002; Kristof, 1996a; Hornblower, 1993).

Poverty is not the only driving force behind the prevalence of adolescent and child prostitution in those countries. A great demand for this kind of prostitution is another important factor. In recent years, the widespread belief among customers that very young sex partners are less likely to have AIDS has fueled a surging demand for youthful prostitution. In addition, many more tourists from rich, Western countries and Japan today flock to those poor countries for sex with children. These tourists know that they can exploit the children without any fear of being arrested for child abuse, as they would be in their home countries (Kristof, 1996a; Serrill, 1993; Simons, 1993).

House Prostitutes.   A brothel is a place where prostitutes meet their customers and share their earnings with its operator. It has been variously referred to as a cathouse, whorehouse, parlor house, and bordello. Very often it is simply called a "joint" or "house." In the 1920s and 1930s many brothels existed in this country. Since 1945, most of them have been forced to shut down. Some houses today still operate openly in Nevada and clandestinely in other parts of the country.

In Nevada, where prostitution is legal, brothel prostitutes are fingerprinted and carry prostitute identification cards issued by the police or district attorneys. The women are generally required to have a weekly medical checkup. When a customer enters the house, the madam (proprietor) will direct a young woman to him. Before the sex act, most prostitutes in Nevada always make sure their clients wear condoms, though their counterparts in other states are less likely to do so (Hilts, 1987).

In many states where the brothel is covertly operated, the madam usually ensures that the potential client is not from the "pussy posse," which is what the vice squad is called in the sex industry. The madam will, of course, readily admit a regular customer. In cases in which she does not know him, she will first meet him at a nearby bar or send a cooperating cab driver to size him up. Only when convinced he is a genuine customer will the madam admit him into the brothel. Some prostitutes wait in the brothel, while others wait in their own apartments for phone calls from the madam, to whom she typically gives half her earnings. Since the clients often look for variety, the house prostitute usually does not work in a brothel for an extended period—the longest she will stay in one brothel is four or five years and the more enterprising ones will jet around the country to work in each city for only a few weeks. To minimize the risk of arrest, many houses simply operate as escort agencies (Campo-Flores, 2002; Potterat et al., 1990).

Most house prostitutes find that they have a distinct advantage over streetwalkers: Working in the house is safer and more secure. For lonely women, the brothel can offer opportunities for regular contact with other women, which may further blossom into friendship. Similar opportunities are rare for streetwalkers, because they have to work alone. But there are also disadvantages to working in a brothel. House prostitutes are not free to set their own working hours and must give half of their earnings to the house. These are restrictions that streetwalkers do not have. House prostitutes who work as escorts seem to have the best deal. Although they have to split the take 50/50 with the house, there are better opportunities for receiving a fat tip from a satisfied customer after a good night out. There is a downside to escort work, though, as one prostitute explains: "You are very vulnerable in the client's room and have no control over the situation, which can be pretty frightening if things get nasty . . . you could be dead" (Perkins, 1991).

Call Girls.   Occupying the highest status in the sex business, call girls have been referred to as "the aristocrats of prostitution" (Greenwald, 1970). As befitting this title, they usually charge from several hundred dollars for each sexual intercourse to, occasionally, even more. Every year they can earn as much as or more than a successful lawyer or doctor. They are generally better educated or more sophisticated than other types of prostitutes. They dress expensively, and they live in affluent neighborhoods. Call girls are acutely aware of their high status and will feel insulted if they are treated like an ordinary streetwalker or brothel prostitute. In fact, many call girls will not apply the term *prostitute* to themselves.

It has been typical for call girls to find their customers by placing ads in newspapers and magazines, but in recent years many have turned to the Internet. They post their own websites, including their pictures, biographical sketches, and contact information. With the Internet, they can now more easily reach clientele, particularly high-paying ones, who are expected to respond with a phone call or email (Richtel, 2008; Castle and Lee, 2008).

Compared to lower-paid prostitutes, the call girl tends more to dress in good taste rather than poorly or garishly. She is skilled in making her commercial transaction appear noncommercial by, for example, acting like her clients' girlfriend in public. She may adhere to a professional code of ethics. For example, if a client is a prominent person, she would not even mention his name in her conversation with other call girls. She would not steal from her customers or let them overpay her when they are drunk and thus temptingly exploitable. She would do her best to satisfy her clients, even in cases when a client has difficulty getting an erection.

Most call girls claim that they fare much better than housewives and women with legitimate employment. They crow that they can afford to live in style because of the huge sums of money they are making. They also contend that they have found fulfillment of their desire for independence in their profession: "The difference between being a prostitute and being a wife is the security a wife's got. But it's also the difference in having a lot of men versus having just one. If you have a lot of men—like if you have 10 a day—then you're not dependent on any one of them. They can always be replaced . . . that's the thing I wanted— never to be dependent" (Rosenblum, 1975). While it is easy to accept their claim to the big bucks and high living, it may be harder to agree with their claim to independence. This is because call girls are heavily dependent on their customers for the high income they get, which requires taking orders from customers. Even in the case of a masochistic client, who likes to follow orders himself, the call girl still has to follow *his* order to give him orders (Rosenblum, 1975). Nonetheless, call girls generally see themselves as the ones who call the shots. As one call girl says:

> I think that they [clients] think, a lot of times, that they've rented me for an hour so I should have to do anything that they want to. I think, maybe, it takes them by surprise that I walk in and take charge of the situation, and I'm like, "OK, let's do this," and they can make suggestions but if I don't want to do something I'm not gonna do it. (Lucas, 2005)

Social and Sexual Backgrounds

According to sociologist Roberta Perkins (1991), many studies give a distorted picture of prostitutes as heavy drug users, victims of low self-esteem, or as being socially immature, emotionally disturbed, or pitifully abnormal in some other way. These studies are biased, Perkins contends, because they have focused mostly on adolescent streetwalkers or prostitutes who have been arrested by police or helped by social agencies. Such prostitutes indeed have more problems in their lives than other sex workers. But they are a minority, representing only about 10 to 30 percent of all prostitutes, and they differ significantly from most other prostitutes (Perkins, 1991).

The prostitutes in Perkins' study, however, are a reasonably representative sample of the women in the sex business. Although these prostitutes are Australians, they are comparable to their counterparts in the United States and other Western societies (Weitzer, 2005a). Perkins found that most prostitutes do not differ significantly from conventional women in their social and sexual backgrounds. For example:

- They have the same desire as conventional women to be married and have a traditional family life. Among those who already have young children, there is a plan to quit turning tricks when the children are old enough to begin catching on to their mothers' stigmatized occupation. As one prostitute says, "My oldest son will be 13 this year, and I don't want to be at work much after that."
- Prostitutes have about the same level of education as the general population of women. The percentages of prostitutes having been brought up in white-collar and blue-collar families are similar to those of conventional women.
- Most prostitutes are not friendless, loveless, or particularly "promiscuous" in their private lives. Like most women, they live with their husbands, lovers, or children, or share apartments with friends. But since their occupation is highly stigmatized, they are significantly more likely than other women to be raped.

Reasons for Becoming Prostitutes

According to public opinion, the common reasons for entering prostitution are drug addiction, severe poverty, low self-esteem, and emotional problems. Most of these reasons have to do with personal, social-psychological deficiencies. Such problems have indeed driven most teenage streetwalkers into prostitution, but these young hustlers differ from the large majority of prostitutes. Thus, when prostitutes in a representative sample were asked why they become prostitutes, a different set of reasons emerged. The most common reasons are economic, such as wanting to make more money, being unemployed, supporting a family, or paying for an education, an overseas trip, a car, or some other specific thing. Money, then, is the most important reason for going into the sex business. This is no different from the reasons that most other people have for working in conventional businesses.

Those economic reasons, however, merely serve as a predisposing factor in entering prostitution. They are not enough for a woman to become a prostitute—she needs to know something about the business before entering it. Necessary knowledge usually comes from an acquaintance, as illustrated by the following accounts from two prostitutes (Perkins, 1991):

- I needed some money because I was having legal hassles and my present job wasn't bringing in enough to pay for this. A girlfriend of mine had an escort agency, and this seemed the quickest way to get the amount of money I needed.
- I met an old school friend, and we had lunch together. She told me she was a prostitute, and how much money she made. She asked me if I would [go out with] her one night. But the fellows kept asking for me, not her. So, I thought, I must be sitting on a gold mine. And that's how I started.

The Subculture of Prostitution

Like any other profession, prostitutes hold certain beliefs about themselves and their work. One belief is that prostitutes are morally superior to conventional people. This is because prostitutes see themselves as honest and others as dishonest. To prostitutes, conventional women who marry so they can depend on their husbands for lifelong financial support— especially the young women who marry wealthy older men—are, in effect, prostitutes, except that they are not honest enough to regard themselves as such. Prostitutes also see their so-called respectable customers as hypocrites. As one prostitute says, "We come into continual contact with upright, respected citizens whose voices are loudly raised against us in public, and yet who visit us in private" (Hirschi, 1962). If most customers do not publicly condemn prostitutes, they in essence cheat on their wives by patronizing prostitutes. Many prostitutes, therefore, despise their customers, and try to exploit them by maximizing the fee and minimizing the service. Such an attitude and behavior is common among streetwalkers and other low-paid prostitutes who immerse themselves in the prostitution subculture by associating only with one another. Other prostitutes are less contemptuous and exploitative toward their customers. They include call girls and other higher-priced prostitutes who are less alienated from conventional society because their circle of friends includes straight people. These prostitutes are more likely to accept another, more positive aspect of the prostitution subculture to be true.

The more positive aspect of the subculture is the belief that prostitution is good for society because it performs many important services. One service is believed to involve preventing sex crimes; as one prostitute puts it, "I believe that there should be more prostitution houses and what have you, and then we wouldn't have so many of these perverted idiots, sex maniacs, all sorts of weird people running around." Another service is believed to involve contributing to marital success: "I could say that a prostitute has held more marriages together as part of her profession than any divorce counselor . . . the release of talking about an unhappy home situation may well have saved many a marriage, and possibly even lives, when nerves have been strained to a breaking point." Prostitutes liken themselves not only to marriage counselors but also to humanitarians, social workers, psychologists, or psychiatrists. One prostitute explains, "I don't regret doing it because I feel I help people. A lot of men that come over to see me don't come over for sex. They come over for companionship, someone to talk to. . . . They talk about sex. . . . A lot of them have problems" (Bryan, 1966; Hirschi, 1962).

This professional self-image has fueled civil rights movements among prostitutes in Western societies. In Great Britain, for example, prostitutes have long campaigned against the laws that prohibit public solicitation, as in streets, hotels, and bars, arguing that peaceful soliciting should be as lawful as peaceful picketing (*The Economist,* 1979). In the United States, prostitutes have formed unions in various cities with the aim of decriminalizing prostitution so that their working conditions can be improved and their sex work can be respected like any other legitimate profession. The most famous prostitutes' rights organization is COYOTE (Call Off Your Tired Ethics). It fights for full decriminalization and the elimination of all legal restrictions on prostitution. COYOTE argues that prostitutes have the right to sell sex because selling sex is no different from other kinds of work women do:

A woman has the right to sell sexual services just as much as she has the right to sell her brains to a law firm where she works as a lawyer, or to sell her creative work to a museum when she works as an artist, or to sell her image to a photographer when she works as a model, or to sell her body when she works as a ballerina. (Jenness, 1990)

COYOTE asserts that arresting or jailing prostitutes violates their civil rights, and that their sex work should be respected and protected like other legitimate professions. However, most feminists have rejected COYOTE's crusade to turn prostitution into a legitimate, respectable profession, because they consider prostitution a form of sexual slavery—which they want prostitutes to get out of, not into. COYOTE has also failed to get support from most of the general public, legislators, and law enforcers (Weitzer, 1991).

Other Participants in Prostitution

Aside from prostitutes, three other kinds of people are involved in the so-called skin trade. They are the madam, the pimp, and the customer.

The Madam.   The general public uses the term *madam* to refer to the owner or manager of a brothel; brothel owners themselves call one another "landlady." Most are former prostitutes with a great deal of experience "in the life" behind them. They run their establishments in about the same way as legitimate businesspeople run theirs, except that they must deal with problems arising from the illegal nature of their trade. There are three major forms of activities that the madam characteristically engages in. The first has to do with the employees, the second the customers, and the third the police.

The madam recruits her prostitutes largely through her current employees, but also from pimps and other madams. She trains the new employee to be clean, develop social skills, and observe such old customs of prostitution as asking for payment before giving the sexual service and refraining from getting emotionally involved or spending too much time with a customer. After the employees become professional, the madam supervises their work, keeps them happy, prevents quarrels and jealousy among them, and makes and enforces rules governing their behavior. The nature of her work is such that she usually functions as if she were the employees' mother. Some madams even insist that they are in effect running a charm school—where they teach social graces (*Time,* 1980).

The madam is responsible for finding customers. She keeps a "john book," which contains the customers' names and telephone numbers; she uses it when there is not much business in the house. Usually, customers call her. The madam's main concern is to make the client happy so that he will become a regular visitor. This means, among other things, that she has to find and hire new women constantly, because it is the variety of women that many customers look for in prostitution.

To avoid arrest, the madam must know how to deal with the police. She is usually skilled in recognizing a police officer disguised as a customer. As one madam says, albeit boastfully, "I could spot a copper a mile away—if I don't see him I can smell him" (Winick and Kinsie, 1971). Nonetheless, madams often have to work out some stable arrangements with the law officers. One arrangement involves bribing them. But more often the madam develops an understanding with the police that they will go through the motion of arresting her every now and then—thereby keeping up the appearance of performing their duty to appease the public's moral outrage against prostitution—while allowing her to continue her business. If all this cannot be done, a madam would ask her employees to wait for her calls at their own residences. Such a madam essentially runs a "call house"—euphemistically referred to in the sex business as an "escort agency"—by maintaining a list of prostitutes on call. She simply sits by a telephone, gets calls from customers, and then sends prostitutes to customers, or sends customers to prostitutes, or arranges for both to meet in some other place.

The Pimp.   Many of the prostitutes who do not work for a madam work for a pimp. While the madam gets a large portion—usually about half—of her employees' earnings, the pimp typically gets all of them. Also, unlike the madam, who has to find customers for her prostitutes, the pimp generally just tells his prostitutes to go out in the street and hustle. He does not want to be bothered with the details of their working life. The pimp, then, is *not* what many dictionaries say he is—"a pander, a procurer, or a man who solicits customers for a prostitute in return for a share of the proceeds." Rather, he is simply a man who lives off the entire proceeds of one or more prostitutes. For this reason, most people in conventional society would consider him "the lowest of the low."

A pimp may have anywhere from one to twenty women, his "stable," but most pimps have only one or two women. Pimps and their stables live in a subculture that is in many ways the opposite of conventional culture. In the pimping subculture, men are extremely dominant, women are extremely submissive, and the ideal union is between a black man and several white women. Also, the men are obsessed with their own appearance, spending many hours a day on their hair, clothes, and jewelry in order to make themselves look beautiful. The women, who consider themselves "wives-in-law," or "wifies," are the real economic providers, working hard to support the household. Since the women routinely have sex with other men—their customers—paternity of their children often comes from outside the subcultural group. In this subculture, then, men are expected to demonstrate great style and creativity in the way they dress and groom themselves; women generally sleep during the day and work at night; money is worshiped as a god; conspicuous consumption is indulged in every day; and there is little concern for future security (Hodgson, 1997; Milner and Milner, 1972).

The pimp often resorts to violence to control his women. As a former prostitute says, "I saw a girl walk into a bar and hand the pimp a $100 bill. He took it and burned it in her face and turned around and knocked her down on the floor and kicked her and said, 'I told you, bitch, $200. I want $200, not $100.' Now she's gotta go out again and make not another hundred, but two hundred" (Millett, 1973). The pimp's violent method of controlling his women is apparently effective. According to one study, over 50 percent of the prostitutes who had been beaten by their pimps "accepted it as a way of life, felt they deserved it, or were flattered by it as a sign of caring" (Caplan, 1984; Silbert and Pines, 1981). According to another study, a pimp's women generally worship him as if he were a god. They invest in him all their hopes, dreams, and goals for the future. They wear his beatings proudly as symbols of his love. Everything that he does to them is considered right, proper, or admirable. When a prostitute was asked what her pimp did to deserve all her earnings, she replied, "He doesn't do *nothing*. But the way he does nothing is *beautiful*" (Sheehy, 1971). In short, the prostitutes are so emotionally entangled with their pimp that they cannot see themselves being controlled and abused by him (Kristof, 2008; Barry, 1995).

The John.   In the argot of the sex trade, the prostitute's customer is called "john" or "trick." Research has shown that men who have slept with different women are more likely than monogamous men to become a john (Pitts et al., 2004; Michael et al., 1994). If sexually active men can get sex with conventional women for free, why would they want to buy sex from prostitutes? One reason, according to radical feminists, is that prostitution gives the customer the benefit of being a sexual master and the prostitute his sexual servant. As one prostitute says, "What they're buying, in a way, is power. You're supposed to please them. They can tell you what to do, and you're supposed to please them, follow their orders" (Overall, 1992). In this structure of power inequality between the sexes, the johns are, in effect, the prostitute's oppressors or victimizers.

But there are other reasons for buying sex (Pitts et al., 2004; Winick and Kinsie, 1971; Benjamin and Masters, 1964). First is the desire to get *quick, easy sex*. Finding a willing woman for sex requires time, effort, or ability. There are men who do not have the time to find such a woman, particularly if they are too busy pursuing a career or if they are strangers in a city far away from their wives or girlfriends. There are also men who simply want to have sex—not conversation, not companionship, not cultivation of friendship or love. For these individuals, the ritual of dating—taking a woman to a restaurant, a movie, a bar, and possibly a bedroom—demands too much effort. They prefer a prostitute from whom they can effortlessly get what they want. There are yet other men who are too shy or are otherwise lacking the ability to attract and persuade a woman to go to bed with them. For such men, a prostitute can be easily gotten without risking rejection.

A second reason for going to a prostitute is the desire to get *untangled sex*. There are men who do not want to get seriously involved with women. They want to dodge emotional entanglements, obligations, or interpersonal conflict. More specifically, they want to avoid getting entangled with a woman in courtship or marriage; avoid being obligated to her if she becomes pregnant; or avoid the risk of breaking up a marriage—their own or the woman's if she is married. What these men want is impersonal, untangled sex, which can free them from the conventional strictures regarding the responsibility of sex. Sex of this kind is characteristically available from the prostitute. Here's how a john describes the straightforward, no-strings-attached sex: "I like the basic rawness of it . . . the basic honesty of it. There's a lot of honesty in that. You girl, me have sexual desire, you have the object of my sexual desire, me give you money, you give me what I want, no bullshit, no play, no games. . . . It's raw, honest, and it's good" (Holzman and Pines, 1982).

A third reason for patronizing prostitutes is the desire to get a *variety of sexual experiences*. There are men who want to have sex with a variety of women rather than with the same one only. Some men may want to engage in certain types of sex, such as oral sex, anal sex, or sadomasochistic sex, that turn off their wives or girlfriends. All these needs can be easily met with a visit to prostitutes.

The majority of the men who buy sex are *occasional johns,* while a few are *habitual* and *compulsive johns* (Greenwald, 1970). Occasional johns, who buy sex only occasionally, are psychologically normal. They are hardly different from most men who do not visit prostitutes (Pitts et al., 2004). But habitual and compulsive johns are less normal. Habitual johns want to get emotionally attached to one special prostitute. They are fond of asking the prostitute many questions, telling her about their lives, offering to help her in whatever way they can, or trying to make her enjoy having sex with them. Compulsive johns also seem a little abnormal: They cannot keep away from prostitutes. Generally, compulsive johns feel that sex is dirty and would not want to defile a "good" woman, so that they will copulate only with "bad" ones—namely, prostitutes. Some compulsive johns can be sexually potent only with prostitutes; they cannot have an erection with their wives or other conventional women.

Societal Reaction to Prostitution

In ancient civilizations, prostitution was not condemned as evil. It was even considered sacred by some religious sects, so that only priestesses had the privilege to practice it. Nowadays, it is regarded as an evil in virtually all societies; but in most societies, it is recognized as an evil that cannot be eradicated. Consequently, one of two situations usually prevails: (1) prostitution is legal but public solicitation for it is not, as is the case in many European and Asian countries (Davis, 1993), or (2) prostitution is illegal but the law is not strictly enforced, as is the case in the United States.

Before 1900, prostitution was illegal but practiced openly in the United States, particularly in the Wild West, where prostitutes were as much a part of the new frontier as miners, cowboys, town preachers, and small merchants. In the early part of the twentieth century, various organizations, such as the YMCA and the American Purity Alliance, mounted an increasingly powerful campaign against prostitution. These vice crusaders eventually won; most brothels that had openly operated were closed down by the mid-1940s. Today, the few houses that continue to do business openly exist in several sparsely populated counties of Nevada, where prostitution is legal. In other parts of the country, where prostitution is not legal, the majority of prostitutes find their customers outside the house. The streetwalkers, who bear the brunt of law enforcement against prostitution, are periodically arrested. Soon after they pay a fine in court or are released from jail, however, they go right back to hustling on the street.

If prostitution is so tough to wipe out, why bother trying to enforce the antiprostitution laws? Conservatives have over the years developed the following rationales for the continued attempt at enforcement: (1) Prostitution often brings about mugging, robbery, or assault. (2) Prostitution provides a breeding ground for organized crime activities. (3) Prostitution helps spread the AIDS virus and other sexually transmitted diseases. (4) Prostitution often subjects innocent citizens to offensive public solicitation. (5) Prostitution is destructive to public morals, which enforcement of the laws helps to preserve (Bryant, 1977). Many feminists also condemn prostitution as degrading to women, robbing them of their dignity and worth as human beings. One feminist regards prostitution as "female sexual slavery" because she believes that most prostitutes, being controlled by pimps, cannot get out of it (Barry, 1995; Farley, 1994).

On the other hand, liberals have argued for the legalization of prostitution. They contend that most problems associated with prostitution stem largely from antiprostitution laws themselves. Treated as criminals, prostitutes are bound to operate secretly and stay as far away from the watchful eye of the law as possible. As a result, they and their customers are likely to commit crime against each other or transmit venereal diseases (VD) or AIDS to each other. If prostitution is legalized, liberals argue, those problems will disappear as they have in Europe because specific statutes can be enacted to control prostitutes' activities (Bilefsky, 2005). Prostitutes will be required to undergo regular medical checkups, be made to confine their business activities within a specified area, or be prohibited from soliciting on the street. Some liberals also argue that antiprostitution laws do not necessarily uphold national moral standards but instead encourage corruption among the police as well as moral hypocrisy and disrespect for the law among the general public. It is further argued that it costs too much to prosecute prostitutes and that precious law-enforcement efforts would be better employed against more serious crimes (*The Economist,* 2004; Quindlen, 1994).

The general public favors the conservative position over the liberal one. According to a survey, when Americans were asked whether they support or oppose the legalization of prostitution, 72 percent said "oppose" and only 23 percent said "support." Another survey also found significantly more people who want the current antiprostitution laws strictly enforced (Weitzer, 2000, 1991). However, no matter how strictly enforced the laws are, prostitution cannot be eradicated because of the substantial demand for it on the part of large numbers of ordinary men.

A Global Perspective on Prostitution

Due to the poor economic condition after the collapse of the Soviet Union, many unemployed women in Russia and Eastern Europe have drifted into Western Europe and other prosperous countries to sell sex. In Germany, today, at least a quarter of the prostitutes originate from the former Communist world. In Israel, many newspaper ads offering "entertainment services" brag about "hot new Russians." In Japan, blond and blue-eyed Russian women have become the latest addition to fancy "hostess" bars. Even in deeply religious Saudi Arabia, many Russian women have arrived to work as prostitutes. Some of these women have chosen to enter the skin trade. But most have been forced into it after arriving in those foreign countries with phony promises of singing, dancing, modeling, or waitressing jobs—the promises having been given earlier by pimps or mafia-style criminals posing as businessmen in their home countries (Gearan, 2006; Pristina and Chisinau, 2001).

Many prostitutes in those prosperous countries have also come from Latin America. Most of these women also have been tricked and coerced into prostitution. They are offered legitimate-sounding jobs overseas, such as working in a nightclub. They are then given money for visas and airline tickets as well as cash to pass as tourists to immigration authorities. Once abroad, they are forced to work as prostitutes to pay a huge fee. Smuggling women this way has become attractive to organized criminals, who find it easier and cheaper than trafficking drugs and arms (Pratt, 2001).

Many more poor women in Asia have also been lured into Western Europe, the United States, and Japan with promises of legitimate jobs only to be sold to brothels. Most of the Asian prostitutes, however, ply their trade in their home countries. Some of these women have come from poor villages to work in large cities and then are forced into prostitution. Others choose to sell their bodies. They all cater to not only local men but also hordes of Japanese and Western male tourists who come to the poor Asian countries primarily or solely for sex. In fact, prostitution has become a major component of those Asian countries' tourist industry, which represents a significant sector of their national economy (Pristina and Chisinau, 2001; Kuo, 2001).

One key factor behind the prevalence of prostitution in Asia is *abject poverty* in its rural areas. As Manju, a Nepalese prostitute in India, said, "Even if you work 24 hours a day in Nepal, you do not get enough to eat. One can endure anything except hunger. If I were a man, maybe I would have committed murder to fill my stomach. But as a woman, I became a prostitute." The rural poverty may have partly resulted from globalization. For example, large U.S. agribusinesses such as Dole and Del Monte have used up a massive expanse of farmland in the Philippines to plant pineapples and bananas for export, which drove many peasants out of their farms and caused widespread poverty. Another factor behind the prevalence of prostitution in Asia is *patriarchy,* the social and cultural system of men's domination over women. It forces poor women to sell their bodies as commodities while encouraging men to exploit them (Kuo, 2001; Hornblower, 1993).

Theories of Prostitution

There are at least three positivist theories about prostitution: functionalist, feminist, and social-psychological theories. Functionalist and feminist theories focus on prostitution, explaining why prostitution exists despite efforts to eradicate it. But social-psychological theory zeroes in on the individual prostitute, explaining why some women are more likely than others to become prostitutes.

Functionalist Theory

According to sociologist Kingsley Davis (1971), there are two reasons why prostitution exists. The first is the very system of *sexual morality* that ostensibly condemns prostitution but unintendedly or ironically causes prostitution to exist as a social institution. The moral system causes prostitution by creating advantages for it in at least two ways. First, the moral system divides sex into two types: Sex with one's spouse is part of a "meaningful" relationship and sex with a prostitute is "meaningless." This has the effect of encouraging men to go to a prostitute if they want to have "meaningless" sex. Second, by defining certain sex acts such as oral or anal sex as immoral and hence not to be indulged in with one's "moral" wife or girlfriend, the moral order encourages men to turn to "immoral" women—namely, prostitutes—for these sex acts. The moral system, in effect, creates a demand for prostitution.

Another reason for the existence of prostitution is also ironic: *prostitution's function of strengthening sexual morality.* More specifically, prostitution exists because it serves to strengthen sexual morality by "keeping the wives and daughters of the respectable citizenry pure" (Davis, 1971). In other words, the sex industry encourages men to go to prostitutes for premarital sex, extramarital sex, or other "immoral" sex so that they do not have to persuade or pressure "respectable" women to engage in the same "immoral" sex. By thus preserving the sexual morality of conventional women, who constitute nearly half of humankind, the level of a society's morality should be higher than if many women engage in the same sexual "immoralities" as prostitutes and men do.

In short, Davis's theory suggests that prostitution exists because the moral system paradoxically encourages it, and it in turn serves the important function of protecting "feminine virtue." This theory runs counter to the popular belief that "an evil such as prostitution cannot cause a good such as feminine virtue, or vice versa" (Davis, 1971).

There is some evidence to support the theory. In traditional Asian societies where prostitution is prevalent, "respectable" women are relatively unlikely to engage in "immoral" sex, while in modern Western societies where prostitution is less common, "respectable" women are more likely to get involved in "immoral" sex. Also, on many U.S. campuses, male students are more likely to think of having sex with college women than with prostitutes, so that they are more likely than their counterparts in Thailand to persuade or pressure college women to engage in premarital sex. There is, however, a basic problem with functionalist theory. It defines sexual morality and feminine virtue in sexist terms, implying that only women, particularly prostitutes, are immoral and virtueless when committing "meaningless" or "immoral" sex. That's why functionalist theory does *not* regard sexually "promiscuous" men, especially those who often patronize prostitutes, as a threat to the moral order.

Feminist Theory

To feminists, functionalist theory merely reflects a sexist society's view that "promiscuous" men are not a threat to the moral order, only "promiscuous" women such as prostitutes are. This explains why in a sexist society prostitutes are far more likely to be arrested than their male customers for committing the same sexual act. But why are "promiscuous" men not considered a threat to the moral order in the first place? Because the moral system reflects the larger patriarchal, gender-stratified system in which men dominate and exploit women.

According to feminist theory, the patriarchal system encourages prostitution by creating both demand and supply for it. On the demand side, boys are socialized under the influence of patriarchy to be dominant over girls, and when boys become adults, they are expected to desire sexual domination of women, which can be easily realized through sex with prostitutes. If a young man does not want to visit a prostitute, his peers will pressure him to do so. On the supply side, girls are socialized to be submissive to boys and, later as adults, to men in work, play, or sex. At the same time, women are relegated to predominantly low-status employment, including prostitution. All this explains why prostitution is usually more prevalent in traditional societies marked by great gender inequality, when compared with more modern societies with less gender inequality.

While the patriarchal system with its gender inequality encourages prostitution, prostitution in turn reinforces patriarchy. Some feminists have observed that prostitution "serves to perpetuate women's social subordination" (Overall, 1992) or "perpetuates socially hegemonic belief which oppresses all women in many domains of their lives" (Miller, 1991). In other words, by selling their bodies as a commodity, prostitutes convey the message that women can be bought or used as an object. This directly reinforces the prevailing patriarchal "notion that all women are whores at heart; all women have a price" (Overall, 1992). Consequently, many men, for example, find this sexist joke funny: A man asks a woman, "Would you sleep with me for a million dollars?" The woman answers, "I guess I would." Then the man asks, "Would you sleep with me for five dollars?" The woman turns angry, saying, "What do you take me for?" But the man responds, "We've already established that; now we're just negotiating your price" (Overall, 1992). Learning from prostitutes that women can be bought like an object, as implied in this joke, many men will continue to support the patriarchal structure of gender inequality, which in turn encourages prostitution.

The feminist theory is indeed convincing for suggesting that gender inequality significantly contributes to prostitution as the majority of prostitutes are women selling sex to men rather than men selling sex to women. But some feminists put forth the radical view that all prostitutes are basically the same for being victims of oppression, exploitation, or violence by their customers. There is no evidence, however, to support this view. It is true that some prostitutes, especially if they are streetwalkers, do experience those abuses. But those women represent a small minority of all prostitutes. Most of the prostitutes work indoors as call girls, escorts, brothel prostitutes, or massage-parlor prostitutes, and they are typically well protected from violence and other abuses (Weitzer, 2006, 2005a).

Social-Psychological Theory

According to this theory, a combination of social and psychological factors causes some women to become prostitutes. These factors include the following:

- *Predisposing* factors—exemplified by such unpleasant experiences as struggling with parental "promiscuity," parental neglect, child abuse, or other traumatic events that cause psychological problems.
- *Attracting* factors—exemplified by the expectation based on popular belief that a woman can have an easy life or lots of money as a prostitute.
- *Precipitating* factors—exemplified by such social situations as being unemployed, meeting a prostitute friend, or being pressured by a pimp to sell sex (Brown, 1979; Benjamin and Masters, 1964).

Most psychologists and psychiatrists stress the predisposing factors as the key to entering prostitution. According to Harold Greenwald (1970), for example, prostitutes sell their sexual service because they have suffered parental neglect, rejection, or abuse in childhood and consequently have developed such abnormal symptoms as feelings of loneliness and unworthiness, lack of self-control, and inability to establish stable relations with others. This implies that a woman must be psychologically abnormal to become a prostitute.

From the sociological perspective, however, we need not assume that prostitutes are abnormal even if they have been abused by their parents. It seems largely a matter of emotional socialization that teaches the victim to be a normal prostitute, one who is able to detach herself emotionally from her johns. This is because parental abuse teaches the victim to detach herself emotionally from her parent and, by extension, anyone who treats her like an object in the same way as her parent does. With this emotional detachment, the victim may later find it easier to enter into prostitution, detaching herself emotionally from her customers, who in a way treat her as her abusive father has done, that is, as an object. In short, some women are more likely than others to become prostitutes not because they are abnormal, but because they are *normal* for being able to withhold affection from their customers in the same way as a normal child-abuse victim withholds affection from her parent. But this capacity for emotional detachment may only *predispose* a woman toward entering prostitution; it is not enough to cause her to sell sex. She is more likely to do so if the attracting and precipitating factors also appear in her experience, as has been suggested by the theory and some research (Perkins, 1991).

Summary

1. How does U.S. society view teenage sex?
Most Americans consider teen sex unacceptable,
apparently because of the presumption that
teenagers are still not mature enough to handle sex
responsibly. **Do teenagers conform to the society's expectation that they refrain from sex?**
No. They are instead more sexually active than
before. They also engage in oral sex more, which
they do not see as real sex. But girls with high self-esteem are less likely to have sex, though boys
with high self-esteem are more likely.

**2. What are the myths about extramarital
sex?** One myth is that extramarital sex is more
exciting or satisfying than marital sex. Another
myth is that people have affairs because they are
oversexed. **How does adultery vary from one
culture to another?** Adultery is socially approved
in some societies but not so in others. Legitimate
adultery varies in form from one culture to
another and so does illegitimate adultery. **Which
groups of Americans are more likely than
others to engage in extramarital sex?** The
groups that are more likely to have an affair
include men, the less religious, and lower-income persons.

3. What is the profile of swingers? They are
largely middle-class, white, aged 25 to 45, and
somewhat conservative. They are not strongly
tied to traditional institutions of social control
such as religion, family, and community, but they
are basically no different from other middle-class
couples who do not swing. They claim that
swinging improves their marital relations, but
this may be true only if they are capable of having sex without any feeling.

**4. How big is the pornography industry
today?** It has grown to be an enormous industry
today, much more profitable than all the Hollywood movies distributed in the United States.
What are the effects of pornography? Some
argue that pornography is harmful, but others say
it is harmless. Evidence suggests that while the
erotic, nonviolent type of pornography is generally harmless, the violent type is harmful.

5. Why do some men call phone sex lines?
They want the phone sex operator to fulfill their
sexual fantasies for one of five reasons: They are
requesting quick sex, expressing anger, seeking
love, demanding sex for oneself only, and being
curious about the phone sex. **What is nude
dancing all about?** In nude dancing the performer takes off all her clothes and shows customers her genitalia to encourage them to tip her
generously. Most customers are working-class
men who expect nude dancers to fulfill their sexual fantasies. The dancers make a relatively large
amount of money and find their job disreputable
but empowering.

6. What is sexual harassment? It is an
unwelcome act of a sexual nature, but if it
involves workers it means, according to the U.S.
Supreme Court, any conduct that makes the
workplace environment so hostile that the victim
finds it harder to perform her or his job. **What
causes sexual harassment?** An apparent cause
is the threat posed by women to male dominance,
which may explain why sexual harassment often
occurs in traditionally and heavily male-dominated occupations.

7. What are the popular myths about prostitutes? The myths are that prostitutes are
nymphomaniacs, that they are sexually frigid,
that they are nasty and hard-hearted or sweet and
warmhearted, and that they are mostly drug
addicts, afflicted with emotional problems. **Are
all prostitutes largely the same?** No, there are
many different types of prostitutes. They
include—in ascending order of status, price, or
life quality—streetwalkers, child and adolescent
prostitutes, house prostitutes, and call girls.

8. What kinds of backgrounds do prostitutes come from? Most prostitutes have about the same social and sexual backgrounds as conventional women, desiring marriage and traditional family life, having the same level of education as other women, and not particularly "promiscuous" in their private lives. **What have been their reasons for becoming prostitutes?** The most common reasons are economic, such as wanting to make more money, being unemployed, or supporting a family. **What is the subculture of prostitution?** Prostitutes believe that they are morally superior to conventional people and that their so-called respectable customers are hypocrites. Prostitutes also regard their work as good for society because they compare it to the service rendered by a marriage counselor, social worker, or some other helping profession.

9. Who are the prostitute's coparticipants in prostitution? They include madams, pimps, and johns. The madam is a brothel owner or manager who employs prostitutes to serve her customers. The pimp is primarily the prostitute's nonworking lover or husband, who often uses violence to keep her under his thumb. The john visits prostitutes to enjoy being a sexual master or to seek quick and easy sex, untangled sex, and sexual variety. **How do conservatives and liberals want to deal with prostitution?** Conservatives want strong enforcement of antiprostitution laws, believing that prostitution causes many problems, such as crime and disease. Liberals want to legalize prostitution, arguing that legalized prostitution can be more effectively controlled and that the very problems currently associated with illegal prostitution will disappear.

10. How does prostitution vary from one society to another? Prostitution in Eastern Europe is more likely than in the West to have resulted from young women being tricked or forced into the skin trade. Asian and Latin American prostitutes are also more likely to have the same experience. In Asia, prostitution is a significant part of the tourist industry, and it thrives from abject poverty and patriarchy.

11. How do various theories explain prostitution? According to functionalist theory, prostitution exists because it is encouraged by society's system of sexual morality and prostitution in turn serves the function of strengthening sexual morality. According to feminist theory, the patriarchal system encourages prostitution by creating demand and supply for it, and prostitution in turn reinforces the patriarchal structure of gender inequality. Social-psychological theory offers three factors—predisposing, attracting, and precipitating factors—to explain why some women are more likely than others to become prostitutes.

FURTHER READING

Barry, Kathleen. 1995. *The Prostitution of Sexuality*. New York: New York University Press. An analysis of how prostitution represents the essence of sexual exploitation that serves to oppress womankind.

Bruckert, Chris. 2002. *Taking It Off, Putting It On: Women in the Strip Trade*. Toronto: Women's Press. A sociological analysis of nude dancing based on interviews with fifteen strippers, illustrating the feminist theory that emphasizes the agency, or power, rather than helplessness of women in this deviant career.

Christopher, F. Scott. 2001. *To Dance the Dance: A Symbolic Interactional Exploration of Premarital Sexuality*. Mahwah, N.J.: Lawrence Erlbaum Associates. Discusses the nature of premarital sex among various age groups.

Clift, Stephen, and Simon Carter (eds.). 2000. *Tourism and Sex: Culture, Commerce and Coercion*. London: Pinter. A collection of articles on various dimensions of sex tourism in different cities around the world.

Crouch, Margaret A. 2001. *Thinking about Sexual Harassment: A Guide for the Perplexed*. New York: Oxford University Press. A historical, theoretical, and empirical analysis of sexual harassment.

Duncombe, Jean, et al. (eds.). 2004. *The State of Affairs: Explorations in Infidelity and Commitment*.

Mahwah, N.J.: Lawrence Erlbaum Associates. A collection of articles covering the interpersonal, social, and cultural aspects of marital infidelity from different perspectives.

Fisher, Helen E. 1992. *Anatomy of Love: The Natural History of Monogamy, Adultery, and Divorce.* New York: Norton. A sociobiological attempt to explain the universality of adultery, though providing data on cultural differences in form and frequency of adultery.

Flowers, Amy. 1998. *The Fantasy Factory: An Insider's View of the Phone Sex Industry.* Philadelphia: University of Pennsylvania Press. Using participant observation, the author studies the operation of a phone sex company and interviews its employees.

Gibson, Pamela Church, and Roma Gibson (eds.). 1993. *Dirty Looks: Women, Pornography, Power.* London: British Film Institute. A volume of articles that deal mostly with nonviolent, erotic pornography, showing the harmlessness of pornography and the harmfulness of censorship.

Gould, Terry. 2000. *The Lifestyle: A Look at the Erotic Rites of Swingers.* Buffalo, N.Y.: Firefly Books. Provides an inside look at the past and current state of swinging.

Gregory, Raymond F. 2004. *Unwelcome and Unlawful: Sexual Harassment in the American Workplace.* Ithaca, N.Y.: Cornell University Press. A thorough analysis of sexual harassment of women by men, harassment of men by women, and same-sex harassment.

Hicks, George. 1995. *The Comfort Women: Japan's Brutal Regime of Enforced Prostitution in the Second World War.* New York: Norton. A documentation of how the Japanese army forced massive numbers of young women in Korea, China, and other Asian countries to become sex slaves for Japanese soldiers.

Irvine, Janice M. 2002. *Talk about Sex: The Battles over Sex Education in the United States.* Berkeley: University of California Press. An analysis of the clash between professional sex education advocates and the politicized Christian conservatives.

Linz, Daniel, and Neil Malamuth. 1993. *Pornography.* Newbury Park, Calif.: Sage Publications. Presenting the conservative, liberal, and feminist views of pornography as well as the data employed to support them.

Malarek, Victor. 2003. *The Natashas: Inside the New Global Sex Trade.* New York: Arcade Publishing. An investigation into the business of shipping women and girls from relatively poor countries in Eastern and Central Europe to Western and other prosperous countries for prostitution.

O'Donohue, William (ed.). 1997. *Sexual Harassment: Theory, Research, and Treatment.* Boston: Allyn and Bacon. A series of articles dealing with many different issues about sexual harassment, including the legal concepts, epidemiology, theories, effects, and prevention of such deviant behavior.

Procida, Richard, and Rita J. Simon. 2003. *Global Perspectives on Social Issues: Pornography.* Lanham, Md.: Lexington Books. Presents diverse societal reactions to pornography in North America, Australia, Western and Eastern Europe, Asia, and Africa.

Ryan, Chris, and C. Michael Hall. 2001. *Sex Tourism: Marginal People and Liminalities.* London: Routledge. Discusses the history of sex tourism, the interactions between sex workers and tourists, and the relationship between sexual slavery and sex tourism.

Smith, Diane Shader. 2005. *Undressing Infidelity: Why More Wives Are Unfaithful.* Avon, Mass.: Adams Media. Drawing from in-depth interviews with more than 150 women, this book presents intimate details of how unfaithful wives conducted their extramarital affairs.

Sheehan, Jack. 2006. *Skin City: Uncovering the Las Vegas Sex Industry.* New York: HarperCollins. A report on what strippers, swingers, porn stars, and prostitutes in Las Vegas do and a guide to sex-driven travelers on how to enjoy themselves with those entertainers.

Weitzer, Ronald (ed.). 2000. *Sex for Sale: Prostitution, Pornography, and the Sex Industry.* New York: Routledge. A collection of articles on various aspects of the sex industry, from the perspectives of sex workers and their customers to prostitutes as victims and the social control of sex work.

CRITICAL THINKING QUESTIONS

1. Do you approve of teen sex? Do you find adults' objection to teen sex justifiable? Defend the position you take on this issue.

2. Are phone sex and nude dancing harmful to young people? If yes, how and why are they harmful? If not, how can they be beneficial and why?

10 Gays and Other Victims of Stigma

Myths and Realities

Myth: Gay men are more likely to be "promiscuous"—sexually active—than straight men because they are homosexual rather than heterosexual.

Reality: The greater likelihood of promiscuity among gay men has nothing to do with being gay. It is instead a product of *heterosexual* society,

which socializes men, both gay and straight, to be more sexually active than women (p. 239).

Myth: Compared to their peers brought up by heterosexual parents, children raised by homosexual parents are more likely to experience depression, anxiety, and other psychological problems.

Reality: Children raised by homosexual parents are just as mentally healthy as those brought up by heterosexual parents. Apparently, the gay parents know how to protect their children from the homophobia around them. This may be due to the fact that, compared to heterosexual parents, homosexual parents are generally older and better educated and thereby have better parenting skills and spend more time taking care of their children (p. 243).

――――――

Myth: If children grow up in a home with homosexual parents, they are likely to become gay.

Reality: Children brought up by homosexual parents are no more likely than children raised by heterosexual parents to become gay and identify themselves as gay (p. 243).

――――――

Myth: Homosexuals are born as such, deriving their same-sex orientation from biology.

Reality: Homosexuals are both born and bred. They are born with a biological predisposition to same-sex orientation and bred through socialization and social approval to turn that predisposition into full-blown homosexuality (p. 246).

――――――

Myth: Homophobia reigns throughout U.S. society, with most Americans being opposed to gays and lesbians in every way.

Reality: Most Americans are homophobic in some ways but not in other ways. They are antigay on emotional issues, opposing, for example, the legalization of same-sex marriage. But they support gays in regard to less emotional issues such as granting gays the same civil rights and job opportunities as other Americans (p. 251).

――――――

Myth: Nowadays gay teenagers are so acutely aware of their homosexuality that they often call themselves gay or lesbian.

Reality: Today's gay teens usually avoid using the label "gay" or "lesbian" to refer to themselves in the same way as their straight peers avoid using the label "heterosexual" to refer to themselves. The gay teens see themselves as much more than being gay, in the same way as their straight peers see themselves as much more than being straight, for example, as a good student, a nice person, an athlete or sports fan, a music lover, and so on (p. 253).

――――――

Myth: Transvestites are mostly homosexuals who cross-dress in order to feel like members of the opposite sex.

Reality: Transvestites are mostly male heterosexuals, distinguishable from drag queens and drag kings, who are homosexuals wearing clothing associated with the opposite sex (p. 257).

――――――

Myth: The problems of helplessness, dependency, and low self-esteem in some people with physical disabilities usually originate from their impairment.

Reality: The problems that some people with disabilities experience often result from the stigmatization of the disabilities by normal people, which makes life more difficult for people with disabilities (p. 259).

――――――

Myth: Because the number of obese or overweight Americans has increased so much that they now represent a majority in U.S. society, being heavy has become more acceptable or less stigmatized than before.

Reality: The social stigma attached to fatness has increased, so that many more Americans, especially women, feel unhappy about their figures (p. 260).

――――――

Myth: Since they get tattoos in order to seek freedom from their conventional middle-class lives by being a little deviant, many tattooed young people tend to become more and more deviant until they reject most of the conventional values of society.

Reality: While their initial desire to get tattooed marks a search for *freedom* from conventional society, many tattooed young people end up using their tattoos to strengthen their *connection* to conventional society (p. 262).

――――――

Gary and Greg, a gay couple both in their thirties, are known to neighbors in a small, fairly conservative town in central Pennsylvania simply as "the guys." They call each other "honey" in the stores, and their straight friends call them "uncle" and "uncle." At their offices, their straight coworkers seem more familiar with gay issues than the gay couple themselves. As Gary says, "They realize we have the same worries they do. Now in tax season, they'll say, "That sucks, you can't put Greg on your return." All this friendliness shown by straights to Gary and Greg in a conservative town represents significant progress in U.S. attitudes toward gays. More recently, in 2006, large numbers of Americans across the country responded positively to *Brokeback Mountain,* a movie about the love affair between two gay cowboys, helping it to rake in millions as well as win multiple awards. Now, for the first time in U.S. history, only a minority (46 percent) of Americans consider homosexuality a sin. But at the same time, a majority (57 percent) are still opposed to gay marriage, while more than 32 states have passed new laws banning same-sex marriages (Corliss, 2006; Leland, 2000). In this new century, then, U.S. society still has a long way to go toward treating gays the same as straights.

The continuing rejection of gays suggests that homosexuality is still a *social stigma,* something a person has or does that others see as bad in some way. A stigma is practically the same as deviance, so that all the deviances discussed in this text can be considered stigmas. It is a stigma to be a prostitute, a mental patient, a suicide, a child abuser, a murderer, a rapist, and so on. Some of these stigmas are *justifiable.* Murderers, rapists, and other nasty criminals, for example, deserve to get what is coming to them. But most stigmas are *unjustifiable* because people such as gays and lesbians, suicides, mental patients, the obese, and the tattooed do not hurt others, and yet they are stigmatized—punished as victims of stigma. In this chapter we will focus on gays and lesbians as well as other victims of unjustifiable stigma, including bisexuals, transgenderists, people with physical disabilities, the obese, and the tattooed. By studying these people as victims of stigma, we may get a clearer understanding of how and why conventional society treats them as deviants and how they react.

Myths about Homosexuality

According to one popular myth, gay men are typically effeminate and lesbians masculine. Gays are believed to walk like women, talk like women, or look like women, and lesbians are believed to walk, talk, or look like men. In reality it is difficult to differentiate most gays and lesbians from straights. Most gays look and behave just like most heterosexual men, and most lesbians look and behave just like most heterosexual women (Marcus, 1993; Dunkle and Francis, 1990).

A second myth is that gay men like to molest or seduce young children. The fact is that the great majority of gay men have no more sexual interest in young boys than the great majority of straight men have in little girls. Actually, most child molesters are male *heterosexuals.* For one year, between 1991 and 1992, at the Children's Hospital in Denver, Colorado, there were 387 cases of suspected child molestation. Only one perpetrator was gay; all the rest were heterosexual men (Marcus, 1993).

A third myth is that gays and lesbians consistently play one specific role—either as an active or passive partner—in their sexual activities. The active partner is assumed to perform oral sex on the passive partner. The truth is that most gays and lesbians engage in a lot of alternation between those two roles. Same-sex couples are also popularly expected to behave like traditional couples, one mate playing the role of dominant husband, the other the submissive wife. Again the reality is quite different: Partners in a same-sex relationship often resemble best friends, who, being equal, "share and share alike" so that *both* may cook, make money, or disclose deep feelings (Peplau, 1981).

According to a fourth myth, same-sex orientation is a symptom of mental illness. Some gays and lesbians, particularly those who go to psychiatrists, are perhaps emotionally disturbed, but so are some straights, especially those who go to psychiatrists. Therefore, just as it is wrong to conclude that straights are mentally ill, it is wrong to conclude that lesbians and gays are. This is one reason why the American Psychiatric Association has, since 1973, removed "homosexuality" from its *Diagnostic and Statistical Manual* as a mental illness. There are still some psychiatrists, psychoanalysts, and psychologists, though, who continue to believe that same-sex orientation is a mental illness that can be cured (Socarides et al., 1997).

A fifth myth is that lesbians and gays cannot be expected to have a satisfactory sex life because it is abnormal or unnatural. Research, however, has shown no real difference between gays/lesbians and straights in their physical capacity to enjoy sex. The basic difference involves styles of making love. Same-sex couples tend to treat sex as play, spending much time on foreplay—focusing on kissing and caressing various parts of the body—before directing attention specifically to genitals for reaching orgasm. Heterosexual couples are more likely to treat sex as work, bent on a quick attainment of orgasm (Masters and Johnson, 1979).

According to a sixth myth, gays and lesbians are obsessed with sex, having sex all the time. In reality, gay men have about as much sex as their heterosexual peers—two or three times a week. As for lesbians, they seem less interested in sex when compared to heterosexual women: no more than once a week for lesbians but two or three times a week for married heterosexual women (Blumstein and Schwartz, 1990).

Finally, a seventh myth suggests that most people are either completely gay or completely straight. In reality, as biologist-turned-sexologist Alfred Kinsey (1948) wrote,

> [People] do not represent two discrete populations, heterosexual and homosexual. The world is not to be divided into sheep and goats. . . . It is a fundamental of taxonomy that nature rarely deals with discrete categories. Only the human mind invents categories and tries to force facts into separate pigeon holes. The living world is a continuum in each and every one of its aspects.

The difference between the sexes is mostly a matter of kind: People are either male or female. But the difference between sexual orientations is a matter of degree: Some people are more, or less, heterosexual (or homosexual) than others. Thus Kinsey assigned people varying positions on a scale from one extreme of being exclusively heterosexual to the other extreme of being exclusively homosexual (see Figure 10.1).

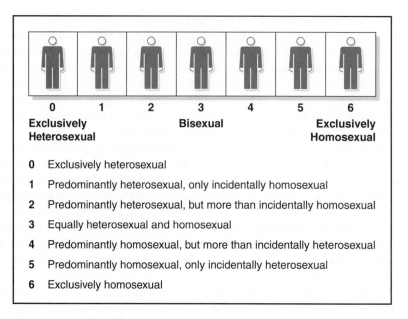

FIGURE 10.1   The Kinsey Heterosexual–Homosexual Continuum

Source: Adapted from Alfred C. Kinsey, Wardell B. Pomeroy, and Clyde E. Martin, *Sexual Behavior in the Human Male,* 1948, Philadelphia: W. B. Saunders, p. 638. Reproduced by permission of the Kinsey Institute for Sex Research, Inc.

Gays and Lesbians

Exclusively homosexual men and women are called gays and lesbians. In this section we will discuss how many they are, what they are like, how they "come out" (reveal to others their sexual orientation), their lifestyles, and various theories about why some people become homosexuals.

How Many Are There?

How many gays and lesbians are there in the United States? The answer depends first on the definition of what constitutes being a gay or lesbian. It appears from various studies that a lesbian or gay is a person with one or more of these characteristics: (1) *same-sex feeling*— being attracted to a person of the same gender, (2) *same-sex behavior*—having sex with a same-gender person, and (3) *identifying oneself as gay or lesbian* (Savin-Williams, 2005c).

Keeping in mind these different definitions of same-sex orientation, let us consider the following data from a study of a representative sample of the U.S. adult population (Laumann et al., 1994; Michael et al., 1994):

- Persons with same-sex feeling: 6 percent of men; 4 percent of women
- Persons who have ever engaged in same-sex behavior: 9 percent of men; 4 percent of women
- Persons with gay or lesbian self-identification: 2.8 percent of men; 1.4 percent of women

Most of these numbers fall significantly below the 10 percent that gay activists have long cited from Kinsey's classic studies as the proportion of gays and lesbians. In the late 1940s and early 1950s, Kinsey found that 10 percent of the U.S. adults were "predominantly" or "more or less exclusively homosexual." However, he discovered that only 2.5 percent were "exclusively homosexual," which is quite similar to the proportion of today's Americans identifying themselves as gay or lesbian, even though the people in Kinsey's survey were not a representative sample of the U.S. adult population (Voeller, 1990; Kinsey et al., 1953, 1948). Nonetheless, the real number of gays and lesbians must be higher than 2.5 percent because the homophobia in our society discourages identifying oneself as "homosexual," particularly among young people with same-sex orientations.

It should also be noted that while many studies have found more homosexuality among men than among women, the latest sex survey seems to find just the opposite: a higher percentage of women than men having "homosexual experiences." But this is not really true because the men and women in the survey were asked different questions. The men were specifically asked if they had had anal or oral sex with another man, and to that question 6.5 percent of the men said "yes." But the women were asked a general or vague question, whether they had had a "sexual experience of any kind" with another woman, and 11 percent of the women answered "yes." Many of these women may not have really committed a homoerotic act because their same-sex experience may only include hugging, kissing, or other practices that often occur among heterosexual women (Mosher, 2005).

What Are Gays Like?

Compared with male heterosexuals, gay men are more likely to be "promiscuous"—sexually active (Blumstein and Schwartz, 1990). Contrary to popular belief, though, the greater likelihood of promiscuity among gay men does not originate from gayness itself. It is in the main a product of *heterosexual* society, which socializes men to be more sexually active than women. Through its male-dominated culture, heterosexual society imposes a double standard of sexual behavior on men and women. If a woman is very sexually active, she is likely to be scorned as a "slut," but a man with the same experience is more likely to be praised as a "stud." Men, then, are encouraged to be more sexually active. Since they have been brought up in the same heterosexual culture as straight men, gay men equally have learned to be sexually active. Not surprisingly, just as heterosexual men are more sexually active than heterosexual women, gay men are more sexually active than lesbians. But why are *gay men* more sexually active than *heterosexual men*? Because the prospect of a heterosexual encounter involves only one person (a man) eager for casual sex—the other person (a woman) is less interested—but the prospect of a same-sex encounter involves two persons (both men) equally eager for casual sex.

Casual sex was extremely common among gay men during the heyday of the sexual revolution in the 1960s and 1970s. Since the AIDS crisis struck the gay community in the early 1980s, however, there has been a drastic shift from casual sex to monogamy. Afraid to play sexual "Russian roulette" by putting their lives on the line, gay men have greatly reduced the number of partners they have sex with. The streets and parks that used to bustle with men "cruising" for sex partners are nearly deserted. In gay newspapers and magazines, classified advertisements placed by men seeking "sex only" have declined significantly, while ads looking for "relationships" have increased. Ads for models or escorts have also decreased substantially, and gay men are more likely to seek out other men for baseball, soccer, choral groups, and other social activities as alternatives to bars, heavy drugs, and sex. Walking on the street, they are less likely to eye each other as potential sex partners and more likely to greet each other by saying hello and smiling (Feldman, 1985; Morin et al., 1984).

Today, while gay men are still more likely than straight men to be sexually active, the majority of gay men are involved in a steady, long-term relationship. In fact, most male couples are as satisfied with their relationships as most heterosexual couples are with theirs (Peplau and Cochran, 1990). Given the homophobic society's opposition to same-sex marriages, it seems remarkable for male couples to pull off the same level of love and happiness that heterosexual couples enjoy. What is the secret? Some researchers have analyzed gay couples' various personal and social characteristics, such as age, education, income, religion, ethnicity, or living arrangements. None of these was found to be associated with male couples' satisfaction. But researchers did find greater satisfaction among couples with one partner's income being about equal to another's. This finding is similar to the evidence from several other studies that male couples are happier when they perceive their relationships as egalitarian (Peplau and Cochran, 1990). In an egalitarian relationship, both partners make decisions together as equals, which is likely to occur if their incomes are roughly similar rather than widely different. In short, it is power equality that helps ensure "marital" happiness among male couples.

What Are Lesbians Like?

Brought up in the same heterosexual society, lesbians are in some ways *like other women,* which therefore makes them appear different from gay men. On the other hand, having the same sexual orientation, lesbians are in some ways just like gay men, which makes them *unlike other women.*

Like Other Women.   Like straight women, lesbians have been socialized to be less interested in casual sex and more interested in relationship and love. Thus they rarely look for one-night stands in gay bars, let alone go "cruising" in streets or parks. Lesbians are far more interested in making friends in the context of social gatherings, parties, mutual friends, and school. The relationship grows slowly, through a long process of knowing the other person, becoming good friends, dating, and cultivating deep affection. Usually, only after a fairly stable, prolonged, and affectionate bond has formed does sexual involvement take place (Nichols, 1990).

Also, like heterosexual women, a majority of lesbians carry on a comfortable relationship with straights by passing as one of them. The posture of heterosexuality is easy for lesbians to put on, because they—like other women—have been socialized to play the conventional female role. Some lesbians may look like men because of their severely tailored clothes, short hair, and masculine mannerisms, but the vast majority look like other women. Being a part of the straight community's social and occupational scene, lesbians can slip into its sexual scene as well. Thus, more than a third of lesbians exhibit a "partial bisexual style" by having sex with men, and about two-thirds are attracted to men (Rust, 1995; Nichols, 1990).

Finally, many lesbians have the same desire as heterosexual women to be mothers. They may decide to adopt a child or to bear one through artificial insemination. If they are already mothers by an earlier heterosexual marriage, they may fight for custody of their children. Stumbling blocks, however, are sometimes thrown in their way. In 1995, for example, the Virginia Supreme Court ruled in favor of a lower court that took away a child from his mother after declaring her "an unfit parent" simply because she is a lesbian. Nevertheless, today, lesbians are just as likely to be mothers as heterosexual women (Kantrowitz, 1996; Henry, 1993).

By sharing those characteristics with heterosexual women, lesbians appear different from gay men: less interested in casual sex, more involved socially and sexually with straights, and more interested in raising children—67 percent of lesbians are mothers, while only 27 percent of gay men are fathers (LeVay and Nonas, 1995).

Unlike Other Women. Lesbians are more likely than heterosexual women to reject the traditional female role. In a study of lesbians and a control group of heterosexual women, only one-third of the former said that they saw themselves as "appropriately feminine" (passive, dependent, or nonassertive) while most of the latter considered themselves "feminine" (Saghir and Robins, 1980).

While still teenagers, lesbians are far and away less likely than their straight peers to know their sexual identity. While virtually all heterosexual youths know they are heterosexual, most adolescent lesbians are not aware or certain of being lesbian. They, therefore, tend to see their same-sex attraction in a nonsexual way, as the following description by a lesbian of her adolescent experience suggests.

> We started out just being friends and then it became something special. She taught me a lot of things. I love music and she taught me how to listen to it and appreciate it. She liked things I liked, like walking. We read a lot together. We read the Bible, we read verses to each other. We shared things together. We caressed each other and kissed. *I think it was a need to have someone there. And I was there and she was there and we just held on to each other.* (Simon and Gagnon, 1974)

By being different from heterosexual women in these ways, lesbians appear similar to gay men. Just as lesbians are more likely to reject the traditional female role, gay men are more likely to reject the traditional masculine role—by being, for example, both tough and gentle rather than tough only. And like lesbians, gay men are less likely than heterosexuals during adolescence to be aware of their sexual orientation.

Coming Out

In the argot of the gay community, becoming openly gay is called "coming out," because it involves people *publicly* identifying themselves as gays or lesbians. It is difficult for most gays and lesbians to come out by revealing their sexual orientation to parents, friends, or coworkers, because the latter may react with shock, rejection, or worse.

Before coming out, many young gays and lesbians do not even *privately* identify themselves as being gay, even though they feel attracted to a person of the same sex. Sociologist Richard Troiden (1979) presents a detailed analysis of how most of the gay men he studied came to acquire their gay identity. The identity acquisition involved going through four stages of experience.

In the first stage, *sensitization,* the gays felt that they were different from their peers. As one recalled, "I never felt as if I fit in. I don't know why for sure. I felt different. I thought it was because I was more sensitive." Another expressed a similar feeling: "I felt different due to my interest in school, ineptness at sports, and the like." Most gays had these feelings when their puberty began, that is, at about age 13. A few, though, knew they were gay when they were as young as six or seven, but such men tend to have been "sissy boys" who always identified with women (Bawer, 1993).

In the second stage, *dissociation,* the gays, about 17 years of age, began to feel that they might be gay but refused to define themselves as such. One described how he was in this stage: "Before I was publicly labeled a faggot, I realized that I wasn't very interested in women. I had had enough experiences with girls to realize that while I was aroused by them, I was also aroused by males and wanted to have sex with them. However, I thought this was something I'd outgrow in time, something that would straighten itself out as I matured." In this stage of dissociation, they might deny their own gayness by being hostile to gays, calling them "faggots."

In the third stage, *coming out,* the gays, roughly at age 19, regarded their sexual feelings as definitely gay, got involved in the gay subculture, and redefined gayness as a positive and viable lifestyle. While the very act of coming out is usually very painful, frightening, or overwhelming, the resulting experience is often highly positive. It has been described as "an incredible sense of relief and renewal . . . like being born. The burden had been lifted from my shoulders. For the first time I felt like I had a life" (Marcus, 1993).

In the final stage, *commitment,* the gays, now mature adults, are committed to gayness as a way of life. They insist that they are happy being gay, that they would not change even if given the opportunity, and that they cannot see any benefit in choosing heterosexuality. Such a positive feeling even prevails among those who have lost their jobs or have been rejected by their families and children (Marcus, 1993).

Even after gays and lesbians have publicly revealed their sexual orientation, the process of coming out never ends. "Coming out is not something you do just once and then forget about," observes gay writer Eric Marcus (1993). "For gay and lesbian people who choose to live out of the closet, coming out is something you may do almost every day. There are all kinds of chance encounters and conversations that force gay people to decide whether to answer honestly or not." Every time somebody at a party or some other place asks questions such as "Are you married?" openly gay men and women are forced to come out again by saying something like, "No, because I am gay." This is likely to occur to gays and lesbians all the time simply because the society in which they live is predominantly heterosexual—so that most people routinely assume others to be heterosexual like themselves, and ask questions based on that assumption. Thus, even though they have come out, openly gay men and lesbians continue to face the same challenges from heterosexual society as those who remain in the closet.

Gay and Lesbian Lifestyles

Due to their same-sex orientation, gay and lesbian life differs in some ways from straight life. But most gays and lesbians live a normal, happy life, as most straights do.

Family and Children.   Lesbians and gays encounter the same prejudice and discrimination as other minority groups. But there is a basic difference. In nearly all cases, the parents of African Americans are African American, the parents of Hispanics are Hispanic, or the parents of Jews are Jewish. In contrast, the overwhelming majority of the parents of homosexuals are *heterosexual*. Unlike the other minorities, gays and lesbians cannot always count on their families for support in dealing with society's homophobia. In fact, practically all parents are upset when they find out their son or daughter is gay. Some react with tears but eventually manage to deal with it in a loving way; others react with anger, refusing to have anything to do with the gay child. Actually, these parents are not to blame for their negative reaction. Because of societal homophobia, parents with a gay child are typically afraid of what friends, neighbors, relatives, or even strangers will think if they find out. The parents are in effect victims of society's antigay culture. Therefore, ironically, while their gay child has come out of the closet, they themselves go into the closet, hiding from others the fact that their child is gay. All these problems are less common today, thanks largely to groups such as Parents and Friends of Lesbians and Gays (P-FLAG), which help parents accept their child's same-sex orientation without fear or embarrassment (Johnson and Piore, 2004; Marcus, 1993).

What if parents are gay? How do their heterosexual children react? In cases in which children have been raised since birth or early childhood in a household with two gay parents, there is no real news for them to react to. The child has learned to accept the fact that they have two daddies or two mommies at home. As they grow older, particularly in adolescence, they may face teasing or even ridicule. But research has shown that children raised by homosexual parents are just as mentally healthy as those brought up by heterosexual parents. Apparently, the gay parents know how to protect their children from the homophobia around them. This may be due to the fact that, compared to heterosexual parents, homosexual parents are generally older and better educated and thereby have better parenting skills and spend more time taking care of their children (Stacey and Biblarz, 2001). Multiple studies have further shown that children raised by homosexual parents are no more likely than children raised by heterosexual parents to become gay—that is, to identify themselves as gay. However, children raised by homosexual parents tend less to conform to the traditional, heterosexual gender norms that require, for example, males to be masculine and females to be feminine. Thus, the sons of lesbian mothers tend to behave in less traditionally masculine ways than the sons raised by heterosexual single mothers. Further, young adult children raised by lesbian mothers are more likely to experience same-sex feelings or behaviors without becoming a full-fledged gay or identifying themselves as gay (Stacey and Biblarz, 2001). This may have resulted from inheriting the *biological predisposition* to same-sex attraction from a homosexual parent and from *being socialized* by homosexual parents to be open to diverse lifestyles or sexualities.

Dating and Marriage.   It is easier for gays and lesbians to find a date in a relatively large city than in a small town simply because there are many more gays and lesbians in the city. The places where they hang out include bars, restaurants, clubs, and organizations that cater to lesbians and gays. But, like straights, gays and lesbians can also meet in any place imaginable, such as at work, at social events, at the grocery store, or at the mall. At such places, though, most people are straight rather than gay. It is usually quite a challenge for people with same-sex orientation to differentiate gays from straights, but occasionally they can spot each other by such clues as the style of clothing or haircut popular among gays and lesbians.

When having dates, lesbians and gays mostly do what straights do. They may go to a restaurant, a movie, or some other social place. They tend, though, to avoid holding their date's hand or some other intimate act in public unless they are in a predominantly gay neighborhood. Since they, like straights, have been socialized to the standard boy–girl roles, they may initially be uncertain as to who should, for example, make the first move in getting a date. But most gays and lesbians quickly learn to do what a specific situation calls for, rather than rigidly acting out the traditional gender roles. Thus, who asks for a date depends on who is more interested or bold, who pays for dinner depends on who asked for the date or who makes more money, and so on. When they fall in love, they will get married. But, in most states, since they cannot get a marriage license, same-sex couples do not have the same legal protections and financial benefits as heterosexual couples, such as the right to be on each other's insurance and pension plans or receive Social Security survivor's benefits (Michels, 2006; Cloud, 1998).

Politics, Education, and Religion.   Because the Democratic Party has often espoused policies sympathetic to the sexual minority, gays and lesbians are most likely to be Democrats. Straights have about the same party affiliations. But gays and lesbians are much more politically active than straights: While straight Democrats are somewhat less likely than straight Republicans to vote, gay/lesbian Democrats are much more likely than gay/lesbian Republicans to vote (LeVay and Nonas, 1995). Apparently, homophobia makes the sexual minority more eager than the sexual majority to vote for gay-friendly candidates.

Lesbians and gays are generally better educated than straights. Some scholars attribute this to higher IQ among gays and lesbians. According to others, the stress of belonging to a stigmatized group drives many gay and lesbian teenagers into an "overachiever" mode (LeVay and Nonas, 1995). Perhaps, with few or no friends to socialize with because of anti-gay ostracism, lesbian and gay youngsters spend more time reading and studying than their straight peers do. Homophobia has also made the suicide rate among gay youth much higher than among straight youth. In response to this problem, some high schools in a few cities have set up counseling programs for gay and lesbian students, as well as programs designed to reduce the fear, prejudice, or hostility that straight students have toward gay people (Marcus, 1993).

Although many churches and synagogues condemn same-sex practices, gays and lesbians belong to various major faiths and denominations in about the same proportions as heterosexuals. Moreover, lesbians and gays are no more unreligious than straights (LeVay and Nonas, 1995). But gays and lesbians usually attend churches and synagogues that they know will welcome them. These gay and lesbian worshipers, along with their pastors and rabbis, believe that God loves them as much as anybody else. They do not regard their own sexuality as sinful in the same way that straights do not consider their own sexuality as sinful. An increasing number of pastors and other religious officials agree to such an extent that they are willing to perform same-sex marriage ceremonies (Niebuhr, 1998; Marcus, 1993).

Theories of Homosexuality

Scholars and researchers in various disciplines are mostly positivists trying to explain why some individuals become gays or lesbians. Their explanations may be classified into three major types: biological, psychiatric, and sociological theories.

Biological Theories. Same-sex orientation has been linked to at least three kinds of biological factors: hormones, genes, and the brain.

According to the *hormone theory,* gay men have lower levels of male sex hormones than straight men, and lesbians have less female sex hormones than male sex hormones, while straight women have more female sex hormones. But critics observe that most studies have found no hormonal difference between gays and straights (Burr, 1996; Porter, 1996).

According to the *genetic theory,* people are born, rather than bred to be, gay. Studies have suggested that the probability of two siblings becoming gay together is significantly higher among *identical* twins than among *fraternal* twins. This is taken to mean that same-sex orientation is largely determined by genes because identical twins are more genetically alike than fraternal twins. But the findings, critics point out, do not necessarily mean that same-sex orientation can be traced to genes. According to critics, social environment may contribute to the development of same-sex orientation because, when compared with fraternal twins, identical twins are more likely to elicit similar reactions from others. If parents react to an identical twin boy by treating him as if he were a girl, they will most likely treat his twin brother in the same way. Given similar experiences, identical twins are likely to develop similar behavior patterns, including same-sex orientation (Santtila et al., 2008; Wickelgren, 1999; Alessio, 1996).

The *brain theory* comes from a study in which Simon LeVay (1996) examined brain tissues from deceased gay and straight men. The researcher found, among other things, a difference in the size of the hypothalamus, the cluster of neurons, or nervous tissues, in the brain's lower area, which controls sex drive and body temperature. The gays' hypothalamus was less than half the size of the straights'. LeVay concluded that a relatively small brain could make a person gay. Critics of this theory argue that it could be the other way around, that is, that AIDS (which killed all the gay subjects that LeVay studied) or same-sex activities may change brain size, as suggested by the evidence that the brain's neural networks can change in response to certain experiences. In people who read braille after becoming blind, for example, the area of the brain controlling the reading finger usually grows larger (Ridley, 1996). More recently, researchers in Sweden also found a difference in brain structures between homosexuals and heterosexuals. They first found that the two halves of the brains of gay men are the same size while the right half of straight men's brains is slightly larger than the left. The researchers then found that homosexual females' brains resemble straight men's while heterosexual women's brains are like those of gay men. But the controversy over whether the structure of the brain causes homosexuality continues (Park, 2008b).

Psychiatric Theories. For many years, most psychiatrists regarded same-sex orientation as a form of mental disorder. But, in 1973, the American Psychiatric Association (APA) decided to define *homosexuality* as normal. Still, today the APA continues to find some, though not most, gays and lesbians to be suffering from what it calls *sexual orientation disturbance*. Most psychiatrists would help these troubled gays to accept their same-sex orientation and feel comfortable with themselves. But some psychiatrists would try to "cure" the "patients" of their same-sex orientation. Such psychiatrists continue to hold the belief that same-sex orientation is characterized by "hidden but incapacitating fears of the opposite sex" (Socarides et al., 1997; Berger, 1994).

This pathological fear is often attributed to an abnormal parent–son relationship. A young boy is said to become gay later in life if he has a domineering, overprotective, or seductive mother and a weak, detached, or hostile father. Alienated from his father, the boy will not look to him as a model for learning the masculine role. Instead, being driven by his hostile father into the arms of his loving mother, the boy will cling excessively to her, identify himself with her, and fail to develop a strong masculine identity. As a consequence, the theory argues, the boy will likely grow up to become gay (Socarides et al., 1997; Herman and Duberman, 1995).

Many psychiatrists have found most of their gay patients to have had disturbed relationships with their parents, but these patients do not represent the majority of the gay population. Numerous studies on average, *non*patient gays have found them to be no different from heterosexuals in parent–child relationships (Ross and Arrindell, 1988).

Sociological Theories.   A basic problem with biological theories is their assumption that same-sex orientation is universally the same. Were this true, we should expect different societies to have about the same incidence of gayness or lesbianism. The reality is that same-sex orientation varies greatly in form and frequency from one society to another.

Though relatively rare in many Western societies today, same-sex practices have been and are common in other societies, from ancient Greece and ancient Japan to the present-day Azande of Africa and various New Guinea societies. In some of these societies, male teenagers have sex regularly with older men as a normal way of growing up but later in their adulthood marry women and have children (Herdt, 1990). This suggests that society has much to do with the development of same-sex orientation. To most sociologists, then, same-sex orientation is just like heterosexuality, both developing from past social experiences. Only the specific nature of their social experiences differs.

While they do not believe that certain hormones, genes, or brain size causes same-sex orientation, many sociologists assume that gays and lesbians may be born with a biological *predisposition* that makes them more likely than other children to be attracted to members of the same sex, which often shows up in cross-gender behavior. By itself, however, this biological predisposition does not automatically cause a person to become gay or lesbian. As suggested by societal variations in the incidence of same-sex orientation, society can check—or encourage—it through some social force such as *socialization* (Bem, 2008; Rieger, 2008; Dickermann, 1995; Bullough, 1993).

Socialization may involve children acquiring sexual orientation from physical contact with parents during the sensitive period between birth and age three. As research has suggested, if a mother kisses, touches, or caresses her little girl much more than her little boy, as expected by the predominantly heterosexual society, then both the girl and the boy are likely to become heterosexual. If, contrary to the expectation of heterosexual society, the mother has much more physical contact with the boy than the girl, the boy will likely grow up to be gay and the girl, lesbian. Thus, parents can socialize, though often unintentionally, their children to feel like members of the opposite sex by treating them as such. Parents can also *intentionally* socialize children toward becoming gay or, for that matter, straight. But since their society condemns homosexuality and supports heterosexuality, parents are pressured to socialize their youngsters to become straight much more than gay, which explains why heterosexual adults far outnumber their homosexual counterparts (Fleishman, 1983).

In short, the origin of homosexuality is both biological and sociological. Growing up to become gay is like growing up to become left-handed. To grow up left-handed, one is usually first born with the *tendency* to be left-handed but, in order to become a lefty *as an adult,* the child must be socialized or allowed to use the left hand. Thus in societies such as the United States where left-handedness is socially approved there are relatively many left-handed adults. But left-handedness among adults is much less common in societies such as China where left-handedness is frowned on and left-handed children are taught or pressured to stop using their left hand. About the same social force can cause children born with the homosexual *tendency* to grow up gay—or straight.

The sociologists who basically agree with what has just been discussed are *positivists,* who regard same-sex orientation as real and, therefore, seek to explain how it has come about. Other sociologists may be *constructionists,* who are *not* interested in seeking the cause of same-sex orientation because they see the phenomenon not as real in and of itself but only as a social construct—society's definition of same-sex orientation as undesirable. To constructionists, then, how gays and lesbians live their lives depends on how society treats them, not on their sexual orientation. Constructionists are, therefore, mostly interested in studying societal responses to same-sex orientation, such as various expressions of homophobia, and how those responses affect the lives of gays and lesbians, as we discuss later in this chapter.

Same-Sex Practices among Straights and Bisexuals

As Kinsey suggested, many straights are not exclusively heterosexual, so it should not be surprising that some straights and all bisexuals do engage in same-sex activities. Although they may not see themselves as gays or lesbians, homophobes generally regard this kind of straight as "homosexual."

Trades

The straights whose sexual feelings and experiences are predominantly heterosexual and only incidentally gay are called trades. All trades are males. They are, or have been, married, and seek same-sex experiences mostly as a means of releasing tension. Were cheap brothels easily accessible to them, they would frequent them. They want other men to go down on them but refuse to reciprocate. They will not fellate other men because they consider themselves straight and have a masculine self-image. Defining themselves as straight and masculine, they tend to treat their partner's mouth as if it were a woman's vagina. Many trades find their male sex-objects in public parks and rest rooms. In his classic study of same-sex activities in public rest rooms, Laud Humphreys (1970) found that most trades come from lower classes, are Roman Catholics, and do not get enough sex with their wives.

Street Hustlers

This type of straight resembles the trade in having predominantly heterosexual feelings, but engages in a greater volume of same-sex activities. Like trades, all street hustlers are males. They are usually lower-class teenage boys who consider themselves heterosexual and masculine. But they frequently make money from letting adults perform oral sex on them, although, like the trade, they often refuse to reciprocate. Many street hustlers have grown up in broken homes, could not get along with parents, or have run away from home. They are lonely and penniless at the time of their initial hustling experience. They generally do not take the initiative to start hustling; it is, instead, some older men who encourage them to do so. Here is how a young runaway, Eddie, got his first trick:

> After arriving in the city by bus, Eddie was standing in the bus terminal, "getting my bear-
> ings," when the customer approached. . . . The man inquired, "Where are you staying?"
> "No place. Actually, I'm looking for my uncle." He suggested that they go to his place so
> they could look in the telephone book for the uncle's address. Shortly after they arrived at
> the customer's home, the man asked, "Have you ever had your dick sucked?" Eddie replied,
> "What? No!" He was shocked by the query, for "that was something I never heard of down
> in Selma, Alabama." The man said, "Well, how would you like to make $100?" Eddie
> accepted the offer. (Luckenbill, 1985)

Once youngsters such as Eddie are introduced into prostitution, they search for customers by standing around particular streets, parks, bus stations, or bookstore entrances. Since they are basically heterosexual, they are likely to abandon homosexual prostitution when they reach adulthood. There are, of course, street hustlers who continue prostituting themselves by finding customers in the gay bars or through escort agencies, but they are likely to have seen themselves as gay in the first place (Luckenbill, 1986, 1985).

Situationals

Some straight men and women would engage in same-sex acts in situations in which the opportunity presents itself. These situational "gays" and "lesbians" can be found among prison inmates, priests, stripteasers, and others in one-sex situations (Blumenfeld and Raymond, 1993). They are predominantly heterosexual, see themselves as heterosexuals, and are able to abandon same-sex activities if circumstances permit. But they are com-pelled or tempted by their life in a unisexual institution to resort to sexual release with same-sex others. Among strippers, for example, the availability of opportunities for same-sex contacts is considered comparable to having a martini after a hard day's or night's work. As one stripper says, "I usually don't get kicks out of other women, not really, but there are times. Sometimes you come home and you are just too tired to work at it. Then it's nice to have a woman around. You can lay down on the floor, relax, watch TV, and let her do it" (McCaghy and Skipper, 1969).

However, opportunities for same-sex involvement are not only available in one-sex institutions. Straight women who find something lacking in their marriage may have a lesbian lover on the side, although they do not see themselves as lesbians. As one such woman says, "I don't consider myself gay. I simply can't relate to that for me. I need a romantic involvement in my life and it happens to be with Victoria, but I was with a man before this. I love my husband in a way. I need the kind of anchoring or stability he gives me. . . . But I also have a romantic side" (Ponse, 1984). In fact, situational lesbianism has become an "in thing" at some colleges. It involves a straight female student experimenting sexually with a member of the same sex. Such students are known as "LUGs" (lesbians until graduation) or "four-year lesbians" because they give up their same-sex activities when leaving college. As a 25-year-old woman who has been a LUG at Wellesley College explains, "It was a real lesbian experience. It was a unique, phenomenal experience. Now it's not an issue anymore. I'm going to marry Richard" (Rimer, 1993). According to a more recent study, heterosexual women who have a relative diagnosed with AIDS are likely to engage in homosexual activities because they are afraid of getting the disease from men (Francis, 2008).

Bisexuals

Bisexuals can be found among men as well as women. The bisexual is about equally straight and gay. Most bisexuals are married to members of the opposite sex, but also have sexual relations with others of the same sex. In some cases only one spouse, most likely the husband, is bisexual. In other cases both husband and wife are bisexual:

> Happily married for 10 years, Richard Sharrard, a dance instructor, and Tina Tessina, a psychotherapist and writer, blend in nicely enough with their neighbors in the middle-class community of Long Beach, California. But the couple's lifestyle is far from ordinary: Richard and Tina are openly and unapologetically bisexual. During their unusually flexible marriage, Richard has enjoyed liaisons with half a dozen men, while Tina has taken two female lovers (Toufexis, 1992a).

According to popular belief, bisexuals are basically straights with a taste for exotic adventure or essentially gay and unwilling to acknowledge their true sexual orientation. However, most of these individuals do not see themselves as either straight in some ways or gay in other ways but as totally unique persons with a third kind of sexual identity. Thus they do not consider their bisexuality "a walk on the wild side" or "a run from reality" but a legitimate and healthy identity (Leland, 1995; Rust, 1995). As lovers, bisexuals appear to be more sensitive and empathic than others because their bisexual orientation enables them to see things from more than one perspective. Nonetheless, many bisexuals still cannot transcend the societal expectation that they are either basically straight or gay. Not surprisingly, they are racked by discomfort and conflict. As a bisexual explains, "Your feet are in both camps, but your heart is in neither. You have the opportunity to experience a kind of richness, but you constantly feel you have to make a choice" (Toufexis, 1992a).

This problem is likely to continue because bisexuals usually have sex with either straights or gays rather than with other bisexuals. The problem will diminish, though, if bisexuals develop their own bisexual community to the same extent as gays and lesbians have formed their own. Like the gay community, the bisexual community will be able to strengthen its members' unique sexual identity so that they can enjoy sex with one another without being torn with guilt and other psychological problems. The bisexual community will also bring social harmony to our multicultural society because bisexuals are uniquely qualified to mediate between the lesbian and gay community and the larger heterosexual society (LeVay and Nonas, 1995).

Homophobia

The word *homophobia* originally meant only the fear of same-sex orientation, but now it refers more broadly to antigay prejudice and discrimination. Homophobia is also called "heterosexism" for being comparable to racism and sexism. This is because the sexual minority often encounters prejudice and discrimination for their same-sex orientation in about the same way as racial minorities and women do for their skin color and gender.

The Homophobic View of Homosexuality

In the United States and other Western societies, the view of same-sex orientation as deviant can be traced to the Judeo-Christian scripture, where same-sex practices are strongly condemned:

> You shall not lie with a male as with a woman; it is an abomination. (Leviticus 18:22)
> If a man lies with a male as with a woman, both of them have committed an abomination; they shall be put to death, their blood is upon them. (Leviticus 20:13)

It is from these biblical passages that many ultraconservative, fundamentalist Christians get their idea about same-sex orientation as an "abomination" that should be punished by death. But most homophobes today presumably would not go that far by interpreting the Bible so literally. If they do, they would have to condemn many heterosexuals to death for committing adultery, having sex with a menstruating woman, telling fortunes, or cursing one's parent. This is because in the same book of Leviticus, all these practices are also condemned as abominations punishable by death. Nonetheless, all homophobes still regard same-sex orientation as deviant in some way. Why? Usually, an act is considered deviant if it deviates from a norm. What, then, is the norm that most homophobes use to define same-sex orientation as deviant?

On the face of it, the norm may appear to be simply that sex should only involve persons of different genders. But the norm that is often used to condemn same-sex practices is more than simply gender-related, as can be discerned from standard arguments that oppose same-sex marriages. In 1996, for example, the Hawaiian legislators who opposed same-sex marriage argued that marriage is "intended for the *propagation* of the human race by man-woman units." And former Vice President Dan Quayle's speechwriter, Lisa Schiffren (1996), contends, "'Same-sex marriage' is inherently incompatible with our culture's understanding of the institution. Marriage is essentially a lifelong compact between a man and woman committed to sexual exclusivity and the *creation* and nurture of offspring."

Even if Schiffren is persuaded that gay couples can have "lifelong sexual exclusivity" and "nurture" children just as heterosexual couples can, she still will consider same-sex marriage deviant, because such marriage *cannot create* offspring. It is, therefore, clear that procreation or reproduction is often used as the norm for defining same-sex marriage—and, by extension, same-sex orientation—as deviant.

The reproductive norm is a holdover from the past when the purpose of marital sex was widely believed to be procreation. Logically, according to this anachronistic norm, any sex engaged in without any intention of producing a baby is deviant. This means that the vast majority of married heterosexual couples today are deviant because they routinely engage in sex for *pleasure* or *love* alone rather than for procreation. Among the married heterosexuals who violate the reproductive norm are not only average couples but also infertile or childless couples, couples who marry past childbearing age, couples who use birth-control methods, and couples who engage in oral or other nonreproductive sex. If premarital sex, extramarital sex, or masturbation committed by countless other heterosexuals are also taken into account, it seems clear that all of the straights violate the reproductive norm as lesbians and gays do. Nevertheless, homophobic society illogically uses the same norm to define the sexual minority as deviant but the sexual majority (heterosexuals) as normal.

The Nature and Extent of Homophobia

Homophobia is both a negative *attitude* (hence prejudice) toward gays and lesbians and an unjust *action* (discrimination) against them. As an antigay attitude, homophobia is, therefore, covert and invisible. It may be in the form of an unfavorable *belief* about same-sex orientation—as, for example, abominable, evil, or unnatural. It may also be in the form of a negative *feeling* (such as fear, disgust, or hatred) toward lesbians and gays. Antigay discrimination, however, is overt and observable, in the form of an unfair action against the sexual minority (such as denying them jobs, calling them names, or assaulting them).

It is difficult to assess the extent of homophobia in U.S. society, but if homophobia involves condemning same-sex orientation as *morally wrong,* then nearly half of Americans may be considered homophobic. Asked in a national poll whether same-sex relationships between consenting adults are morally wrong, 46 percent indicated yes (Leland, 2000). Most Americans are, however, antigay in regard to other highly emotional issues. According to other surveys, 57 percent do not want the sexual-minority members to be legally married, and 56 percent do not want them to raise children. In the 2004 presidential election, the voters in 11 states overwhelmingly approved the constitutional amendment to ban same-sex marriages (Leland, 2000; Berke, 1998).

However, if homophobia involves denying the sexual minority the same *civil rights* enjoyed by the sexual majority, then most Americans do not appear to be homophobic: Over 83 percent say that gays and lesbians should have equal rights in job opportunities. And 50 to 58 percent also say that gay and lesbian partners should be treated equally in regard to health insurance, inheritance, and Social Security benefits (Leland, 2000).

In short, U.S. society is deeply ambivalent about its sexual minority, torn between an uneasy feeling about their same-sex orientation and a democratic tolerance for them as citizens (Loftus, 2001; Wolfe, 1998).

A Social Profile of Homophobes

Not all straights are homophobic, but some are. The more homophobic have certain characteristics that distinguish them from other straight people. They are generally:

- Less educated and less well-off
- More conservative—socially, politically, religiously, and sexually
- More negative toward racial and ethnic minorities
- More supportive of traditional gender roles, in which men are supposed to be aggressive and women gentle
- Men who see themselves as "masculine" and women who see themselves as "feminine"
- More likely to stereotype as "homosexual" a man whom they consider to be "feminine" in some way and a woman whom they consider to be "manly"
- Older, except in cases of extreme violence against gays, known as gay bashing or hate crime, which are more commonly committed by young men
- Less likely to know personally someone who is gay or lesbian
- More likely to be influenced by peers
- More likely to be men than women

Why are heterosexual men more homophobic than women? According to one explanation, straight men, accustomed to playing the stereotypically masculine role, do not want other men to look at them the way they themselves look at women. They are afraid of becoming what women in a sexist society often are: an object of unwanted sexual attention (Wilkinson, 2004; Kite and Whitley, 1996; Berrill, 1992).

The Impact of Homophobia

Homophobia strongly affects virtually all aspects of gay and lesbian life. The problems that homophobia creates for its targets can be social or psychological in nature.

Social Problems. The social problems caused by antigay forces in the lives of gays and lesbians include the following: Gays and lesbians cannot get legally married; same-sex couples are denied health insurance and other benefits enjoyed by heterosexual couples; and people with the same-sex orientation are often rejected by straight family members and friends, shunned or ostracized by fellow employees, discharged from the military for revealing their sexual orientation, and prohibited from discussing same-sex orientation with students in public schools. Indeed, there are countless other problems suffered by gays and lesbians as victims of antigay prejudice and discrimination (Blumenfeld, 1992). Due to the prevalence of homophobia, then, lesbians and gays have to struggle harder than straights to succeed and live a happy life in the same society.

Nowadays, however, young heterosexuals are much less antigay than the older generation, and consequently the majority of gay teens now find it easier to live their lives in the same way as their straight peers do. Thus, just as their straight peers take their heterosexuality for granted rather than as something special or unusual, the gay teens take their homosexuality for granted rather than as something special or unusual. That's why they usually avoid using the label "gay" or "lesbian" to refer to themselves in the same way as their straight peers avoid using the label "heterosexual" to refer to themselves. In other words, most gay teens today do not see themselves as merely being gay, in the same way as their straight peers do not see themselves as merely being straight. Instead, the gay teens see themselves as much more than being gay, in the same way as their straight peers see themselves as much more than being straight, for example, as a good student, a nice person, an athlete or sports fan, a music lover, and so on (Savin-Williams, 2005a, 2005b).

Psychological Problems. Homosexuality does not cause mental health problems, just as heterosexuality does not. But the homophobic nature of society does make lesbians and gays more likely to develop some psychological problems, such as constant tension, self-hatred, and depression, which in turn lead to higher rates of suicide and alcohol and drug abuse among gays and lesbians than among straights. Running through these problems is the failure to achieve a harmonious integration of one's diverse identities (O'Hanlan, 1996; LeVay and Nonas, 1995).

Raised in a predominantly heterosexual and homophobic society, gays and lesbians, like straights, usually grow up identifying themselves as loving sons or daughters to their heterosexual parents, as fun-to-be-with persons to their heterosexual friends, and as productive or respected members to various heterosexual groups and organizations. But all these self-identities are based on conformity to the heterosexual way of life, and are, therefore, in conflict with their sexual self-identity as gays and lesbians. The conflict itself creates tension and restlessness. Some gays and lesbians try to resolve the conflict by assimilating into the straight world and outwardly carrying on like heterosexuals, but they tend to feel miserable for living a lie, for betraying their true self, or for deceiving their significant others. Other lesbians and gays try to resolve the identity conflict by leaving the straight world for the gay community, but many still feel the need to commute, physically or emotionally, between their new gay and old straight worlds (LeVay and Nonas, 1995). Thus the identity conflict that causes tension and other psychological problems is likely to remain as long as homophobia continues to hold sway in society. But through constant support from fellow gays and lesbians as well as from sympathetic straights, most members of the sexual minority manage to transcend those psychological problems and to live a relatively normal, happy life, like most heterosexuals do. This is particularly true of today's gay teenagers, as the vast majority of them feel quite good about themselves with levels of self-esteem no different from those of their straight peers (Savin-Williams, 2005b).

AIDS, Gays, and Straights

When AIDS first broke out in the early 1980s, virtually all the victims were gay men. Today, notably, gay men are much less likely to get AIDS, thanks to dramatic increases in safer sex practices such as monogamy and condom use (Francis, 2008; Altman, 1999; Gagnon, Levine, and Nardi, 1997). The majority of *new* AIDS cases do not appear among gay men but among intravenous drug users, who often share contaminated needles when shooting drugs and consequently pass the AIDS virus on to one another. But, having been exposed to the virus longer, gay men still make up the largest proportion of AIDS patients today.

In the 1980s, the homophobic society blamed the emergence of AIDS on "promiscuity" among gay men. AIDS was then associated with the same-sex orientation itself, and the disease was called the "gay plague." Discrimination against gays visibly soared. Suspected of being infected with the AIDS virus simply because they were known as gays, gays were often denied insurance coverage, fired from their jobs, and evicted from their apartments. Those who were actually infected with the virus or ill with AIDS also received shabby treatment from society. Even the U.S. Justice Department said it was legal for employers to discriminate against AIDS-infected employees if the discrimination was based on fear of contagion. Often, those who were ill with AIDS could not even see their gay lovers or have them attend their funerals because their families prohibited it. Physical attacks on gays also became more common.

Some well-known conservatives fanned the hostility toward gays further with inflammatory public statements. Patrick Buchanan, a conservative columnist, made the argument that AIDS is a fitting punishment for gays: "They have declared war upon Nature, and now Nature is exacting an awful retribution." Some conservatives even demanded that gays be incarcerated "until and unless they can be cleansed of their medical problems" (Bayer, 1985). Because they wanted to see gays punished with AIDS, many conservatives were opposed to any government attempt to develop a vaccine against the deadly disease. They declared that by showing compassion in developing the vaccine the government was in effect approving and supporting gayness as a normal, legitimate lifestyle (Marcus, 1993).

But today the general public has become less condemnatory toward gays and more sympathetic to those with AIDS. Most states have passed laws protecting AIDS victims against job dismissal and other discriminations. A number of factors have caused this turnaround in public sentiment: (1) A growing number of *heterosexuals,* including not only drug addicts but children and babies, have been afflicted with AIDS. (2) Many widely admired and loved celebrities, such as actor Rock Hudson and dancer Rudolf Nureyev, were brought to light as gay when they died of AIDS. (3) The media have often portrayed AIDS-infected gays and their gay companions and friends in a positive way, as courageous, compassionate, and hardworking people. (4) The AIDS crisis has galvanized thousands of otherwise apathetic gays and lesbians into joining the fight against the disease, thereby gaining respect from the general public—because the gays' anti-AIDS crusade helped slow the spread of the disease among *heterosexuals* (LeVay and Nonas, 1995; Marcus, 1993).

Fighting Homophobia

For more than 60 years now gays and lesbians in the United States have been fighting for equal rights in a homophobic society. The gay rights movement began in the late 1940s with the discovery among many individual gays and lesbians that they were not alone. This "gay awakening" resulted in large part from the widely publicized Kinsey report that millions of men and women had engaged in same-sex activities. At first the gay and lesbian organizations focused on educating the public about same-sex orientation, counseling gays and lesbians in trouble, and providing them with recreational services.

Then, in June 1969, the police raided the Stonewall Inn, a gay bar in New York, simply for serving a gay clientele. The patrons, who used to be cowed by such raids, reacted by throwing bottles and stones at the police. This violent reaction against police harassment soon led many young gays and lesbians to form militant organizations. They tried to confront the country with the fact that gays are an oppressed minority group, whose aspiration for respectability is no different from that of African Americans, Hispanics, women, migrant farm workers, and the like. They marched in great numbers, shouting such slogans as "Two-four-six-eight, gay is twice as good as straight!" "Three-five-seven-nine, Lesbians are mighty fine!" and "Gay Power!" They also resorted to dramatic confrontation tactics in dealing with antigay political figures. One such tactic was "zapping"—disrupting, for example, a Foran for Governor rally in Chicago in 1971 by marching, dancing, and chanting "Ho, ho, hey, hey, freaking fags are here to stay" as well as "Foran is a macho pig" (Humphreys, 1972). By the mid-1970s the militant fervor had cooled, and there was renewed concern with providing counseling and other social services to gays who needed them.

The cooling of the gay militancy apparently resulted from the many victories achieved by the gay power movement between the early and mid-1970s. A dozen states legalized consensual sex between same-sex adults. The school boards in some cities banned discrimination in the hiring of gay teachers, and a number of court decisions upheld the gay's right to teach. The Bank of America, IBM, NBC, AT&T, and other big corporations, as well as the Civil Service Commission, announced their willingness to hire gays and lesbians. The American Psychiatric Association stopped listing same-sex orientation as a psychiatric disorder. And more than 300 same-sex marriages were performed in a church in Los Angeles.

With the outbreak of AIDS in the early 1980s, the lesbian and gay rights movement began to shift into high gear again. At first, efforts were focused on fighting the disease. Gays and lesbians provided care for the sick and dying, presented AIDS education programs, lobbied for increased government funding for AIDS research, pressured medical researchers and drug companies to go all out searching for treatments and a cure, and fought discrimination against people with AIDS or HIV. Then, in the early 1990s, a few young people at the forefront of the AIDS battle began to reinvigorate the lesbian and gay rights movement with confrontational tactics. Giving themselves such militant names as "Queer Nation" and "Queer Action," they shouted their demands for equal rights in the streets, city halls, and suburban shopping malls. They staged gay-pride marches, with some appearing in drag, wearing nipple rings, kissing each other ostentatiously, or exhibiting some other anticonventional behavior. They even organized a massive march on Washington in 1993, shouting slogans like "We're here! We're queer! Get used to it!" (Marcus, 1992). But given the conservative climate, those gay militants may have hurt rather than helped the cause of equal rights for gays. As gay writer Bruce Bawer (1993) explains, the confrontational and exhibitionist derring-dos in gay-pride marches helped "perpetuate the widespread view of homosexuals as freaks, outlaws, sex addicts, and sexual exhibitionists."

However, the majority of gay-rights activists are far from militant today. Consider, for example, the Human Rights Campaign, the largest lesbian and gay organization. Its members are moderate, engaging in the same campaigning, fund-raising, and lobbying tactics as conventional interest groups. They also emphasize the importance of equal rights in the same way as other minority groups. They have, in a word, mainstreamed. Thus gays and lesbians have become an important, powerful political force. They can now count on an increasing number of leaders from both political parties to take their equal rights seriously. Many states and cities have passed laws to protect the sexual minority against discrimination. Massachusetts has become the first state to legalize same-sex marriages. But homophobia remains throughout the society, and antigay forces continue their efforts to oppose gay rights by arguing that gay-rights laws not only give the sexual minority special treatment but also encourage gay lifestyles and threaten traditional marriages (Rosenberg, 2004; Lacayo, 2004; Levay and Nonas, 1995). Actually, the sexual minority only wants the same rights as other Americans, not wanting to attempt the impossible task of turning straights into gays and destroying traditional marriages.

A Global Perspective on Homophobia

As we have seen earlier, the homophobia in the United States makes life difficult for gays and lesbians. They have a hard time getting legally married, are often rejected or ostracized by straights, experience tension or depression, and suffer other social and psychological problems. In Japan, too, homosexuals are often denied, though quietly or politely, opportunities for jobs and loans for housing. But the problems created by homophobia are even more serious in less affluent societies. The International Gay and Lesbian Human Rights Commission has documented many cases of abuse committed by the governments in less developed countries against the sexual minority. The cases include gays or lesbians being beaten, raped, imprisoned, and institutionalized. One gay man in Romania, for example, reported that he and his partner were arrested after the police were told about their gay love. While in jail, other inmates raped him, and when he disclosed the rapes in court, the warden beat him (Hawkins, 2000).

In Russia, since the law against sodomy was abolished in 1993, personal ads in newspapers under sections labeled "Man to Man" have become as frank and easy to find as they are in New York City. But homophobia among the general public remains stronger in Russia than in the United States. According to a poll, 47 percent of the Russians said that gays should be executed or isolated, while only 29 percent said they ought to be left alone. Understandably, most Russian gays and lesbians are fearful of being beaten up by straights and of losing their jobs if they are discovered to be gay. As a result, Russian homosexuals are much more likely than their U.S. peers to stay in the closet (Specter, 1995).

In the African nation of Zimbabwe, the president has publicly announced that homosexuals have no legal rights, calling them "sodomists and perverts" and "worse than dogs and pigs." When 70 U.S. Congress members signed a letter of protest, the Zimbabwean president said, "Let the Americans keep their sodomy, bestiality—stupid and foolish ways." The Zimbabwean citizens are also intolerant of the sexual minority, especially lesbians. The family of a lesbian, for example, is reported to have "locked her up and had a man rape her so she would get pregnant. After she ran off and had an abortion, they caught her and did it again. Now she has the baby and is forced to live with the man." Similar atrocities are inflicted on homosexuals in other parts of Africa. In Egypt, for example, the police often entrap men through gay-related advertisements on the Internet. Once arrested, the gays tend to be beaten and tortured in jail, which sometimes results in deaths (Allam, 2004; McNeil, 1998, 1995).

Other Victims of Social Stigma

Like gays and lesbians, many other groups are unjustly stigmatized—judged as undesirable and mistreated in some way. Here we turn our attention to some of those groups.

Transgenderists: Transsexuals, Intersexuals, and Transvestites

A new concept called *transgenderism* emerged in the 1990s to refer to those having the characteristics of both sexes. Most people, including straights, gays, lesbians, and bisexuals are either male or female, but transgenderists, also called transpeople, are both. Thus, trans-people include transsexuals, who belong to one sex but feel like members of the opposite sex; intersexuals (hermaphrodites), who are simultaneously male and female for being born with organs of both sexes; and transvestites (cross-dressers), who sporadically or permanently wear clothes associated with the opposite sex. They are all stigmatized, suffering as victims of social stigma.

There are many more male, or male-to-female, transsexuals than female transsexuals. The predominance of transsexuality among men has been attributed to women being the primary socializer of children in most families. If both a boy and a girl end up getting too attached to their mother and identifying themselves with her, only the boy is likely to become a transsexual because his mother is a member of the opposite sex. Both male and female transsexuals typically go through a "rite of passage," moving from one status to another. Male transsexuals first have partial and ambivalent feeling of being feminine, then gradually feel more and more certain about being women, and finally completely identify themselves as women. They may undergo hormone treatments or sex-change operations to become complete members of the desired opposite sex (Rosenberg, 2007; Nanda, 2000).

Intersexuals are born having both male and female characteristics, but are forced to become either male or female. This is because pediatric surgeons routinely change their ambiguous sex to either male or female when they are still infants. Most operations involve changing the intersexual infants into girls instead of boys, primarily because of surgical convenience. As a surgeon said, "You can make a hole, but you can't build a pole" (Goode, 2005b; Hendrix, 1993). However, transgenderism has emerged as a social movement that encourages the freedom to choose any form of gender identity beyond the conventional binary view that there are supposed to be only two, opposite sexes. As a result, the decision on sex-reassignment surgery is now more client-centered and less determined by the medical profession (Gorman and Cole, 2004; Nanda, 2000).

Transvestites are heterosexuals who cross-dress to obtain erotic gratification or satisfy an irresistible urge to look like a member of the opposite sex. Most are men. They are by definition distinguishable from individuals who cross-dress for show or fashion, such as men performing on stage as female impersonators or women projecting a masculine look wearing a pantsuit with a tie. Because transvestites are heterosexual, they are also distinguishable from drag queens and drag kings, who are gays and lesbians wearing clothing associated with the opposite sex. One final distinction is that gays and lesbians may flaunt their cross-dressing in public, while transvestites usually keep theirs private for fear of being ridiculed and harassed if they go public (Suthrell, 2004).

In fact, transvestites are not the only ones subject to verbal and physical harassment. So are other transgenderists, such as transsexuals and intersexuals, if the public knows they are different from the average men and women. That's why they often try to pass as "real" men and "real" women in order to conceal their true identity as transgenderists. Passing successfully, however, is no simple matter. Many transsexuals, for example, have to resort to electrolysis, hormone treatment, voice therapy, breast binding, mastectomy, and plastic surgery. Still, they suffer frequently from discrimination at the hand of "normal" people, even more than do gays and lesbians (Rudacille, 2005; Seligman, 2003; Namaste, 2000).

People with Physical Disabilities

Studies on the stigma of physical disabilities tend to distort reality by assuming that people with disabilities are *always* less desirable than "normal" people. This distortion seems to come from the influence of common sense that pervades the society. Thus, a common assumption is that compared to an average sighted person, an average blind person is less competent in walking from one place to another. But this is not necessarily true. It is true only because an unfair criterion is used, which allows the sighted to walk with their eyes open. But if we use the fairer criterion of who can best walk with eyes closed, then the blind person will definitely be more competent. That is often the essence of what stigma really is: not the disability itself but the judging of the disability by using criteria of competence that are *biased* in favor of so-called normal people.

The literature on disabilities also tends to give the impression that a person's disability is the *core* or even the *totality* of his or her self. This is unreal because the self of most people with disabilities consists of many different parts, such as being a son, daughter, parent, spouse, worker, rights activist, church member, or a quiet, kind, gentle, understanding, or wise person, and so on, many of which may be more important than being a disabled person. As a person with cerebral palsy says,

> My name is not cerebral palsy. There's a lot more to me than my disability and the problems surrounding it. That's what I call the disability trap. This country has a telethon mentality toward disability that thinks disabled people are not supposed to talk about anything but their disabilities. (Hebl and Kleck, 2000)

It is even more unreal to suggest that a disability can define the *totality* of a person's self as if he or she is already six feet under. Only dead people are totally disabled. In short, people with disabilities have many different roles to play so that they cannot be said to be mostly or totally defined by their disabilities.

Other reviewers of the literature on the stigma of disabilities have found similar, unsubstantiated assumptions (Link and Phelan, 2001; Fine and Asch, 1988):

- Disability resides solely in biology or the body.
- The disabled person's problems result from the disability-produced impairment.
- The disabled person is a victim of the disability.
- Disability is central to the disabled person's self-concept, self-definition, social comparisons, and reference groups.
- Having a disability is the same as needing help and social support.

These erroneous assumptions largely stem from the researcher's misleading definition of the stigma of disabilities, which focuses on the disability in the person rather than on the subjective, biased perception that normal people have of the disability. In reality, then, the stigma is not the disability in the disabled person; it is the perception held by normal people (Green et al., 2005; Link and Phelan, 2001). Only in one sense can the stigma be a disability, but it is not located in the disabled person. It resides instead in the perception of normal people, and it often makes the disabled person's life more difficult. As a disabled person says, "My disability is how people respond to my disability" (Gill, 2001). This is comparable to what a victim of racism may say, "My problem is how racists respond to my skin color." So, to understand the stigma of disabilities, we should focus on stigma as a negative and often disabling perception in normal people and its impact on the disabled.

Certain characteristics of stigma can be found in normal people. First, stigma is *powerful*. As Bruce Link and Jo Phelan (2001) say, "it takes power to stigmatize." It is the *powerful,* namely the nondisabled majority, who are able to stigmatize the powerless, the disabled. The powerless may engage in reverse stigmatization by viewing the powerful as insensitive, stupid, or arrogant, but it does not mean much because it cannot significantly affect the powerful. But the powerful stigmatizers can greatly impact the lives of the disabled because they control educational institutions, employment, housing, health care, and other major life domains.

A second characteristic of stigma is the *stereotype* of disabled people as helpless, weak, and dependent, as shown by "Jerry's kids" on the annual Jerry Lewis telethons for muscular dystrophy. This is why many nondisabled people like to help wheelchair users without first asking the disabled if they need help. The stereotype of the disabled as helpless and dependent tends to make it difficult for the normal person to show disabled people respect rather than pity because the stereotype makes it impossible to know and appreciate the disabled's heroic effort to live with their disabilities and their admirable ability to achieve many things, such as finding increased meaning and value in life. The stereotype also tends to make even a compassionate normal person help the disabled in order to feel superior (Gill, 2001).

A third characteristic of stigma is how normal people *express* it through their behaviors in the presence of a disabled person. They usually feel uncomfortable and distressed, which show up in forms of behavior that vary from one individual to another. These behaviors include fidgeting, staring, lack of eye contact, avoidance, physical distancing, expressions of sympathy, and acting as if the disability does not exist. They may also laugh at, joke about, or overcompensate their dislike with feigned hospitality toward the disabled. One behavior that the disabled find particularly disturbing is the tendency of the nondisabled to help them without being asked. The disabled often consider this helpful act an expression of pity and nervousness rather than genuine compassion and respect (Gill, 2001; Hebl and Kleck, 2000).

The stigma imputed to disabilities is bound to affect the lives of the disabled. Most people with disabilities have to struggle with employment discrimination, educational segregation, and environmental obstacles. They are also likely to have some difficulty being "welcomed as helpful neighbors, reliable friends, desired lovers, competent spouses and parents." Some disabled people become activists fighting discrimination in various spheres of social life, such as employment, public accommodation, and public services. Many other disabled people strive to get along with the nondisabled by helping them to feel good about interacting with the disabled. Thus, they may "use humor to put others at ease, tactfully ignore others' lack of tact, respond graciously to others' intrusive curiosity, and routinely sacrifice their interpersonal equality to accept unsolicited help from others who need to feel superior through helping" (Gill, 2001; Hebl and Kleck, 2000).

The Obese

Americans are getting heavier. Two out of every three U.S. adults are now overweight, and one-third are severely or dangerously overweight—obese. This rate of obesity among adults is twice the rate of 20 years ago. And, worse, over the same period, the rates of obesity among children and teenagers have tripled. Today, obesity brings us more chronic illness and higher health-care costs than does smoking. The major culprit is overeating, especially of high-fat and high-sugar foods. Appetites have grown so big that businesses over the last two decades have greatly increased the amount of food served in restaurants and the quantity of potato chips, soft drinks, and other junk foods sold in grocery stores and from vending machines. Another reason for being overweight is the lack of physical exercise (Tumulty, 2006; Brownell and Horgen, 2004; Lemonick, 2004; Spake, 2002).

Logically, because there are many more obese and overweight Americans, being heavy should become more acceptable or less stigmatized. But, ironically, the social stigma attached to fatness has increased, so that many more Americans, especially the women among them, feel unhappy about their figures. The reason is that over the last several decades the U.S. paragon of feminine beauty has gotten much thinner, with many fashion models now looking almost anorexic (Park, 2008a).

The stigma attached to heaviness, however, varies in strength from group to group. In the United States and other developed countries, obesity is more prevalent among the poor, but in poor countries the well-to-do are more likely to be fat. Thus, since the poor are generally less respectable than others, the stigma for being heavy is stronger in rich countries than in poor. But there is also a racial factor. Being heavy is more prominent among African Americans than whites, so being heavy is more acceptable and less likely to be stigmatized in the black community. Finally, the amount of stigmatization depends on what the general nonfat public thinks is the cause of fatness. If it thinks the cause is overeating and lack of exercise, which is taken to mean the person is self-indulgent and lazy, then the stigma for obesity is greater. If obesity is attributed to genetic inheritance, which is beyond the heavy person's control, then the stigma is less great (Hebl and Turchin, 2005; Goode, 2004b; Winslow and Landers, 2002).

The stigma of fatness has brought on three kinds of consequences. First, some female victims *internalize* the stigma, agreeing with the stigmatizing others that they are to blame for their obesity. Some of these women feel depressed and isolated while others turn to diet and exercise. Second, some heavy women *reject* the stigma, getting together to form a group expressing their pride in being heavy and to fight antifat discrimination. And third, the stigma for fatness has spawned a *huge industry* selling diet books, exercise programs and equipments, diet pills, liposuction, bariatric surgery, and mechanical devices for reducing weight without moving a muscle—some of which turn out to be downright fraudulent or incapable of achieving the hoped-for results (Wang et al., 2004; Goode, 2004b; Falk, 2001).

The Tattooed

Tattoos have long been popular with drunken sailors, criminals, gangsters, prostitutes, and other disreputable people. They are used to express the identity of the wearers—who they are, what they believe in, or how they feel about the world (Vail, 2004; Schildkrout, 2004). If you see a man sporting a tattoo on his arms that says "Kill the Pigs," you will know how he feels about the police—you can be sure he is not a worshiper of law and order (Vail, 2004; Dalrymple, 2002). Because tattoos have long been associated with disreputable characters, their wearers are usually stigmatized. But since the early 1990s, tattoos have been gaining popularity among college students, young professionals, and other middle-class, respectable people, including many women. Today these people make up the majority of the recently tattooed (Atkinson, 2003).

Why do these people want to be tattooed? One reason is that they intend to seek freedom from the constraints of their relatively conservative middle-class lives by becoming a little deviant. And they see that they can experience this freedom by getting tattooed just like the drunken sailors, gang members, and other deviants. For young people such as college students, for example, becoming tattooed means independence from parents and other authorities. Another reason for wanting to be tattooed is to be as "cool" as the people who sport nice-looking tattoos on TV and in other public places. There are an increasing number of individuals with tattoos in advertisements, professional athletes with tattoos, and even such famous U.S. icons as Barbie with tattoos (Irwin, 2001).

However attracted they are to the idea of getting tattooed, those people still would not hastily go out to get a tattoo because they have to contend with some aversions to deviancy. One major aversion stems from the fear of damaging relationships with parents, who usually disapprove of tattoos because they not only are associated with disreputable characters but also threaten both the family's social status and the tattoo wearer's future career. How, then, can this aversion be overcome to make tattooing possible? In other words, how can tattoos be de-stigmatized or legitimated so that the tattooed can maintain their middle-class status with all its advantages? This can be done in four ways, according to the findings of sociologist Katherine Irwin (2001), who interviewed 43 clients of a tattoo shop.

The first way involves *condemning the condemner* of tattoos. As one of Irwin's interviewees explains, "If someone wants to treat me differently because of the tattoo I would have on my ankle, that is a pretty shitty person. It would not be someone that I want to deal with anyway." This negative, antagonistic attitude toward the critic of tattoos may facilitate the decision to get a tattoo. But it may not be effective for achieving the desired goal of having one's status as a tattooed person accepted by others. The other strategies for attaining this goal are much more effective.

The second strategy involves *using conventional motivations* to justify the desire for tattoos. Such motivations exist in cases in which people get a tattoo to commemorate special events in their lives, such as graduation from college, finishing final exams, getting married, or having a baby.

The third strategy involves *committing oneself to a conventional life*. This can be seen in people who prove that while getting tattooed they remain active in various conventional pursuits such as school, family, and careers. As a young man in Irwin's study says,

"How could my dad really oppose? I'm everything he could want a kid to be. I'm a serious student. I get great grades. I am doing well in a career that I love and he loves. I'm married. Someday soon I will give him plenty of grandchildren. With all that, what difference is a tattoo going to make?"

And the fourth strategy involves *conforming to conventional aesthetics*. To achieve this, many middle-class tattooees avoid having the antisocial, violent, and other shocking, "in your face" images popular with bikers, skinheads, punk rockers, and other deviants emblazoned on their bodies. Instead, they go for small, discreet tattoos that show butterflies, flowers, and other images that would please rather than offend others.

With those strategies for de-stigmatizing tattoos, middle-class people have helped increase the acceptance and popularity of tattoos in conventional society. Ironically, though, while their initial desire to get tattooed was to seek *freedom* from conventional society, they have ended up using their tattoos to strengthen their *connection* to conventional society.

Summary

1. What are the popular myths about the sexual minority? One myth is that gay men are effeminate, while lesbians are manly. Other myths hold that gay men often molest young children, that gays and lesbians are restricted to either the active or passive role, are mentally ill, have an unsatisfactory sex life, and are obsessed with sex.

2. How many gays and lesbians are there in the United States? About 2.5 percent of U.S. adults see themselves as gay or lesbian. **What are some of the characteristics of gays and lesbians?** Gay men are more likely than straight men to be sexually active, but the majority of gay men are involved in long-term relationships characterized by power equality between partners. Lesbians resemble heterosexual women in having been socialized to desire long-term relationships, in having a comfortable relationship with straights, and in having the desire to be mothers. But compared with conventional women, lesbians are less likely to play the traditional female role and less aware of their same-sex orientation during adolescence.

3. What is "coming out"? It involves people revealing to others that they are gay or lesbian.

What does the process of coming out entail? It entails going through four stages of experience: sensitization, dissociation, coming out, and commitment. **What are the other aspects of the gay and lesbian life like?** Despite the homophobia around them, lesbians and gays manage to live relatively normal, happy lives. They get along well with their straight parents and children. They date and get married like straights, except that their marriages are not legally recognized. They are mostly Democrats, better educated than straights, and belong to religious organizations as straights do.

4. What are the theories of homosexuality? According to biological theories, same-sex orientation can be traced to hormones, genes, and the brain. According to some psychiatrists, homosexuality is a form of mental illness that stems from strained parent–son relationships. Sociologists who hold the essentialist view of deviant behavior attribute the development of same-sex orientation to cross-gender socialization in childhood, but sociologists who embrace the constructionist view are more interested in studying homophobic reactions to gays and lesbians.

5. Do people who do not identify themselves as gays or lesbians engage in same-sex practices? Some do. They are called trades, street hustlers, situationals, and bisexuals.

6. How does homophobic society "deviantize" gays and lesbians? By using the anachronistic norm that people may only engage in reproductive sex. **What is homophobia and how widespread is it in the United States?** Homophobia is antigay prejudice and discrimination. The general public is deeply ambivalent about gays and lesbians. While it opposes their lifestyle, it nonetheless supports most equal rights for the sexual minority. **What is the social profile of homophobes?** They are distinguishable from others for being less educated, less well-off, more conservative, and more negative toward racial/ethnic minorities. **What is the impact of homophobia on the sexual minority?** Homophobia creates some social and psychological problems for gays and lesbians.

7. How has the AIDS crisis affected gays and lesbians? The sexual minority is more likely to practice safer sex now than before. When AIDS first emerged in the 1980s, however, homophobia grew more intense and gross insensitivity toward AIDS victims became common. However, today the general public has become more sympathetic thanks to factors such as the growing number of heterosexuals afflicted with AIDS and the effort of gays and lesbians to fight the disease for everybody.

8. What is the nature of the gay and lesbian rights movement? Most gay organizations were initially service-oriented, counseling gays in trouble or providing them with recreational activities. But in the late 1960s and early 1970s, they became militant, aiming to end antigay discriminations in all aspects of life. This brought some victories for the sexual minority, which cooled the militancy. Because the outbreak of the AIDS crisis led to greater homophobia in the 1980s, some

gay activists have become militant again, but the majority have remained moderate, engaging in antihomophobic activities much like any conventional interest group.

9. What is the condition of homophobia in other countries? Homophobia is generally more serious in less affluent societies than in the United States. Gays and lesbians are known to have been beaten, raped, imprisoned, and institutionalized. In Russia nearly half of the population say that gays should be executed or isolated. In Zimbabwe and Egypt, gays tend to be beaten and tortured in jail.

10. Who are the transgenderists? Transgenderists have the characteristics of both genders rather than those of only one. Common examples are transsexuals, intersexuals, and transvestites. They usually pass as "normal" men or women to avoid harassment in conventional society. **What are disabled people like?** Contrary to what common sense suggests, they are not totally or mostly defined by their disabilities because they play many roles that have nothing to do with being disabled. **What is the stigma of disabilities like?** It has these characteristics: (1) It comes from powerful people; (2) it involves stereotyping the disabled as helpless; and (3) it is expressed through "normal" people's behavior.

11. Why are more American women today stigmatized for being fat? Because food consumption has increased and the standard of feminine beauty has gotten thinner. **What consequences does the stigma of fatness bring?** Some of its victims accept the stigma, others reject it, and a huge industry has emerged to help the victims get slim. **How do middle-class people overcome the stigma of tattoos?** By condemning the condemner, using conventional motivations to justify the desire for tattoos, committing themselves to conventional life, and conforming to conventional aesthetics.

FURTHER READING

Albrecht, Gary L., Katherine D. Seelman, and Michael Bury (eds.). 2001. *Handbook of Disability Studies.* A collection of articles reviewing the literature on many aspects of disability, including the experiences of being disabled and the social factors behind disability.

Atkinson, Michael. 2003. *Tattooed: The Sociogenesis of a Body Art.* Toronto: University of Toronto Press. An ethnographic study of how it feels and what it means to get a tattoo in Canada.

Becker, Ron. 2006. *Gay TV and Straight America.* New Brunswick, N.J.: Rutgers University Press. An analysis of how the recent gay-themed TV shows reflect the anxieties that straight Americans feel about gays and lesbians.

Beemyn, Brett, and Mickey Eliason (eds.). 1996. *Queer Studies: A Lesbian, Gay, Bisexual, and Transgender Anthology.* A collection of articles on various dimensions of same-sex attractions and practices.

Blumenfeld, Warren J. (ed.). 1992. *Homophobia: How We All Pay the Price.* Boston: Beacon. A collection of articles on various aspects of homophobia, ranging from sources and manifestations of the problem to ways of breaking free from it.

Blumenfeld, Warren J., and Diane Raymond. 1993. *Looking at Gay and Lesbian Life.* Boston: Beacon. Discusses many different issues about homosexuality, including gay sex, causes of homosexuality, homophobia, the gay rights movement, and AIDS.

Brownell, Kelly D., and Katherine Battle Horgen. 2004. *Food Fight: The Inside Story of the Food Industry, America's Obesity Crisis, and What We Can Do About It.* Chicago: Contemporary Books. An analysis of how the food industry contributes to the epidemic of obesity in the United States.

Falk, Gerhard. 2001. *Stigma: How We Treat Outsiders.* Amherst, N.Y.: Prometheus Books. A survey of various types of socially stigmatized groups, including the mentally ill, the obese, the mentally challenged, the homeless, and alcoholics.

Garber, Marjorie. 2000. *Bisexuality and the Eroticism of Everyday Life.* New York: Routledge. Analyzing various aspects of bisexuality, such as its culture, politics, and history, its normal sex, and its unique eroticisms.

Harris, Daniel. 1997. *The Rise and Fall of Gay Culture.* New York: Hyperion. A critical analysis of how the increasing assimilation of gays into mainstream society robs the gay culture of its distinctive sensibility and other values.

Heatherton, Todd F., et al. (eds.). 2000. *The Social Psychology of Stigma.* New York: Guilford Press.

A collection of articles dealing with the development of stigma, its impact on the victims, and the interaction between the stigmatizers and their victims.

Kotula, Dean. 2002. *The Phallus Palace.* Los Angeles, Calif.: Alyson Publications. A full presentation of how it feels to be a female-to-male transsexual and how he is treated by others.

LeVay, Simon, and Elisabeth Nonas. 1995. *City of Friends: A Portrait of the Gay and Lesbian Community in America.* Cambridge, Mass.: The MIT Press. A highly informative guide into the community and lives of gay and lesbian Americans.

Marcus, Eric. 1992. *Making History: The Struggle for Gay and Lesbian Equal Rights.* New York: Harper-Collins. An interesting and enlightening collection of autobiographical accounts of various stages of the gay rights movement.

Miller, Nancy B., and Catherine C. Sammons. 1999. *Everybody's Different: Understanding and Changing Our Reactions to Disabilities.* Baltimore, Md.: Paul Brookes Publishing. Close-up view of various kinds of disabilities.

Nanda, Serena. 2000. *Gender Diversity: Crosscultural Variations.* Prospect Heights, Ill.: Waveland Press. A wide-ranging examination of transgender practices throughout the world.

Rudacille, Deborah. 2005. *The Riddle of Gender: Science, Activism, and Transgender Rights.* New York: Pantheon Books. A detailed look at the lives of transgender people as the most vulnerable minority group in the United States.

Savin-Williams, Ritch C. 2005. *The New Gay Teenager.* Cambridge, Mass.: Harvard University Press. A study of how the gay young people today reject homosexuality as the defining characteristic of their lives while they freely share with each other their same-sex feelings.

Seidman, Steven. 2002. *Beyond the Closet: The Transformation of Gay and Lesbian Life.* New York: Routledge. Shows how U.S. gays and lesbians have emerged from the closet to join mainstream society but more as tolerated minorities than equal citizens.

Suthrell, Charlotte. 2004. *Unzipping Gender: Sex, Cross-Dressing and Culture.* Oxford, U.K.: Berg. A cross-cultural study of transvestism, revealing the greater social acceptance of cross-dressing in India than in Britain.

Swain, John, et al. (eds.). 2004. *Disabling Barriers—Enabling Environments,* 2d ed. London: Sage Publications. A collection of articles presenting the social perspectives on disability, people's views of their own disability, the problems faced by the disabled, and the support offered to the disabled.

Vaid, Urvashi. 1995. *Virtual Equality: The Mainstreaming of Gay and Lesbian Liberation.* New York: Anchor Books. Shows how mainstreamed gays and lesbians are only virtually—but not really—equal to straights.

Warner, Michael. 1999. *The Trouble with Normal: Sex, Politics, and the Ethics of Queer Life.* New York: Free Press. A provocative analysis of conventional sex and marriage as well as gay life and politics.

CRITICAL THINKING QUESTIONS

1. If some heterosexual people engage in homosexual activities, what would you consider them to be? Straight or gay or what? Explain your answer.

2. Can the victims of stigma that we have discussed get rid of the stigma? If yes, how? If not, why not?

PART FIVE

Substance Use and Abuse

CHAPTER
11 Drug Use

Myths and Realities

Myth: Legal drugs such as alcoholic beverages and tobacco cigarettes are less dangerous than illegal drugs such as heroin and cocaine, as legal drugs cause less harm to our bodies.

Reality: Legal drugs are more dangerous; they kill many more people (p. 271).

Myth: If a certain drug is illegal, it must be dangerous.

Reality: The legal prohibition of a drug does not necessarily mean that the drug is dangerous. The prohibition reflects more the temper of a given time or place. For example, opium is today an illegal drug and is widely condemned as a panopathogen (a cause of all ills), but before the twentieth century it was a legal drug and was popularly praised as a panacea (a cure for all ills) (p. 271).

Myth: People who use illegal drugs typically become addicted, compulsive, or heavy users.

Reality: Most people who use illegal drugs do so only experimentally, occasionally, or moderately, without sliding down the slippery slope to compulsive and uncontrollable use (p. 271).

Myth: Marijuana is widely regarded as so dangerous that it is banned in virtually all states in the United States.

Reality: At least eleven states have already legalized medical use of marijuana because it has proved effective for relieving pain and controlling nausea in seriously ill patients (p. 274).

Myth: If people use marijuana they will *inevitably* end up using a harder drug such as heroin and cocaine.

Reality: Marijuana is not the cause of drug escalation; the cause is more likely the marijuana user's having friends who are already using the harder drug (p. 274).

Myth: There is a lot of truth in the popular saying that "once a junkie, always a junkie." If we get hooked on heroin, we won't be able to kick the addiction.

Reality: The addiction can go away if the cause of heroin use is removed. In the 1970s, for example, most (over 90 percent) of the U.S. soldiers who had been addicted to heroin while in Vietnam eventually overcame their addiction after returning home. The reason was that they no longer had the urge to use heroin, which had risen from the extraordinarily stressful experience of the Vietnam War (p. 275).

Myth: Given its tougher laws against drug use, the United States has a lower rate of drug use than do most other countries.

Reality: The United States has the highest rate of drug use in the world, and U.S. high school seniors also have the highest rate among their peers in the industrial world (p. 280).

Myth: Drug use is so pervasive that it invades every nook and cranny of society, enslaving all classes of Americans to the same extent.

Reality: Most drug problems are largely confined to the lower classes, particularly to socially and economically oppressed minorities. Drug use and overdose among the nonpoor, middle class, or affluent is generally far less common (p. 280).

Myth: Drug use causes crime as indicated by the fact that many poor drug users are forced to rob or steal to get the money for their next fix.

Reality: Drug use does not necessarily cause crime because most drug users with a criminal record have started committing crimes *before* using drugs (p. 282).

Myth: Most people who smoke cigarettes are not aware of the hazards of smoking.

Reality: Most smokers are acutely aware of the hazards of smoking. In fact, they tend to greatly overrate the risk of smoking (p. 296).

In the basement of a suburban home in northern New Jersey, a teenage boy fishes out of the front pocket of his backpack a bottle of Ritalin, a prescription medication for ADHD (attention deficit and hyperactivity disorder). He turns to a friend and asks, "Do you have any painkillers? I'll give you some of my Ritalin." With a rap song playing in the background, his friend asks, "Is it generic, or the good stuff?" Upstairs, in the kitchen, several teens are sitting around talking about what prescription drugs they have. One 15-year-old girl says she got her powerful painkiller OxyContin from the medicine cabinet at home. "It was left over from my sister's wisdom-teeth surgery," she explains. What is going on here is a bunch of young people having a "pharming" (from pharmaceutical) party. With the parents having gone out, the youngsters can take prescription drugs in order to get high (Banta, 2005).

Such abuse of legal, prescription drugs by teenagers has gone up sharply over the last decade. The same abuse among adults has also increased significantly. Why? We will find the answer in this chapter, along with an understanding of the nature of various forms of drug use. We will first investigate the effects of various illegal drugs and the connection between such drugs, on the one hand, and AIDS and crime, on the other. We will also examine the extent of illegal drug use, the characteristics of the drug users, the process of becoming a drug user, theories of drug use, and the war on drugs. Finally, we will zero in on the use of OxyContin and tobacco as examples of legal drugs.

Drug Use in Perspective

Contrary to popular belief, *legal* drugs may in some ways be more dangerous than illegal ones. First, the use of such legal drugs as alcoholic beverages and tobacco cigarettes is considerably more prevalent than the use of such illegal drugs as marijuana, heroin, and cocaine. Some 125 million Americans are drinkers and 62 million are smokers, compared with only 20 million users of illegal drugs. Other legal drugs, such as sedatives, tranquilizers, and stimulants, though less popular than alcohol and tobacco, are still more widely used than such illegal drugs as heroin and cocaine. Not surprisingly, the use of legal drugs, particularly alcohol and tobacco, causes far more death, sickness, economic loss, and other social problems than the use of illegal drugs. For example, every year just two legal drugs—alcohol and tobacco—kill at least 60 times as many Americans as do all the illegal drugs combined (NSDUH, 2006; Caulkins et al., 2005).

Contrary to popular assumption, then, legal prohibition—or, more generally, societal disapproval—of a drug does not necessarily indicate how dangerous the drug really is. Instead, the disapproval reflects more the temper of the time and place. Opium is today an illegal drug and is widely condemned as a panopathogen (a cause of all ills), but in the last two centuries it was a legal drug and was popularly praised as a panacea (a cure for all ills). In contrast, cigarette smoking is legal in all countries today, but in the seventeenth century it was illegal in most countries and the smoker was harshly punished in some. The penalty for smoking, for example, included death in Turkey and China, removal of noses in Russia, and slitting of lips in Hindustan (Goode, 2005a).

In assuming that illegal drugs are more dangerous than legal ones, the general public also believes that people who use illegal drugs typically become addicted, compulsive, or heavy users. But empirical evidence suggests that most people who use illicit drugs do so only experimentally, occasionally, or moderately, without sliding down the slippery slope to compulsive and uncontrollable use. This is because the majority of drug users have the ability to draw the line on what they do. Drugs by themselves do not have the power to pull users down the slippery slope. There are, of course, real horrors in drug use, but they befall only a few, not most, users (Goode, 2005a).

Illegal Drugs: Their Effects and Users

Most drugs can be differentiated into three categories according to their effects on the user's central nervous system—the brain and spinal cord. One category includes *stimulants* ("uppers") such as cocaine, crack, caffeine, and nicotine. These drugs can stimulate the activity of the central nervous system, temporarily producing alertness and excitation as well as suppressing fatigue and sluggishness. Another category consists of *depressants* ("downers") such as heroin, PCP, morphine, and aspirin. In direct contrast to stimulants, depressants reduce the activity of the nervous system, so they can relax muscles, relieve anxiety, alleviate pain, create euphoria, or induce sleep. The third category comprises *hallucinogens* (psychedelics) such as LSD and MDMA (Ecstasy). These drugs can disturb the nervous system, altering the user's perception of reality. Most illicit drugs belong in only one of these three categories of drugs, but marijuana does not. Marijuana is in a class by itself, because it can affect the user in the same way as each of the three types of drugs. Thus some experts have classified marijuana as a stimulant, others have categorized it as a depressant, and still others have regarded it as a hallucinogen.

No matter what kind of drugs they are, they do not by themselves produce the effects mentioned above. Certain factors also influence the effects of drugs. One factor is the *dosage*: The higher the dosage or amount of a drug, the stronger its effect on the user. A second factor is the *purity* (or *potency*) of the drug: The more psychoactive substance (such as the chemical THC in marijuana) there is in the drug—or the more actual heroin or cocaine there is in a batch of heroin or cocaine—the easier it is to get "high." A third factor is *drug mixing*: Snorting cocaine while high on marijuana, or taking an injection of "speedball" (a combination of cocaine and heroin) has a synergistic or multiplier effect, which is many times more powerful than either of the two drugs taken separately. A fourth factor is the method of *administration*: Intravenous injection ("mainlining")—putting a drug directly into the bloodstream—produces a stronger effect than intramuscular injection ("skin popping"), which involves injecting the drug into the arm or leg muscles. Smoking cocaine in the form of crack also has a more powerful effect than snorting it. And a fifth factor is the degree of *habituation*: A drug has a greater effect on occasional users than chronic users (Goode, 2005a). Keeping in mind these factors that influence drug effects, let us now take a closer look at the effects and users of today's three most-often-used illegal drugs and three newly popular ones.

Marijuana

Marijuana is the most widely used illegal drug in the United States. It is derived from the Indian hemp plant called *Cannabis sativa*. The top of the plant produces a sticky resin containing a psychoactive substance. A small portion of this psychoactive resin flows downward and coats the lower part of the plant. What is typically sold and bought as marijuana ("grass," "weed," "pot," or "dope") in the United States comes from the entire plant. But when only the top of the plant is harvested, the product is *hashish,* which is far more psychoactively potent than marijuana. Both marijuana and hashish can be eaten or drunk, but are more commonly smoked in the form of cigarettes ("joints" or "reefers"). The cannabis plant can grow all over the world, but the better grades come from the United States, Mexico, Jamaica, and Thailand.

When it was first used in ancient times, marijuana was considered a sacred and useful drug, as suggested by the following passages from ancient Indian literature:

> To the Hindu the hemp plant is holy. A guardian lives in bhang [marijuana]. . . . Bhang is the joy giver, the sky flier, the heavenly guide, the poor man's heaven, the soother of grief . . . No god or man is as good as the religious drinker of bhang. The students of the scriptures of Benares are given bhang before they sit to study. At holy places, yogis take deep draughts of bhang, that they may enter their thoughts on the Eternal. . . . By the help of bhang, ascetics pass days without food or drink. The supporting power of bhang has brought many a Hindu family safe through the miseries of famine. (quoted in Szasz, 1974a)

Yet there has been a great deal of opposition toward using marijuana in our society. This has distorted the judgment of both lay and scientific people about its effects. In the early 1950s, the former head of the Bureau of Narcotics expressed the popular view of the effects of marijuana this way: "In the earliest stages of intoxication the willpower is destroyed and inhibitions and restraints are released; moral barricades are broken down and often debauchery and sexuality result. Where mental instability is inherent, behavior is generally violent" (Anslinger and Thompkins, 1953). But later many researchers found that marijuana tends to inhibit rather than induce aggressive behavior. In an experimental study by two of these researchers, subjects who had taken relatively high doses of marijuana responded less aggressively to provocation than did those who had taken a lower dose (Myerscough and Taylor, 1985).

Today many people, particularly government scientists, argue that there are serious health hazards in smoking marijuana. Smokers can experience short-term effects such as memory loss, anxiety, and increased heart rate. Chronic smokers can eventually develop cancer, respiratory diseases, and heart problems. But critics point out that the majority of marijuana users do not suffer lasting harm while the drug's mild intoxicating effects are no more dangerous than those of alcohol and tobacco (Williams, 2003).

However, if smoked in large doses for an extended period, marijuana can be *physically* addictive. If marijuana use is discontinued, the user will suffer withdrawal symptoms such as mild nausea, restlessness, and loss of appetite, though not as serious as those caused by addiction to heroin and other hard drugs. Marijuana can also be *psychologically* addictive, but only mildly so, because it is not as immensely pleasurable as cocaine or heroin. It is nonetheless easy to get addicted to marijuana in a unique way. Because they see marijuana as harmless, that is, not able to wreck careers, ruin health, destroy marriage, or bring on some other dramatic effects, marijuana users are encouraged to smoke grass repeatedly and thus get addicted to it (Roffman and Stephens, 2006).

If used to the point of intoxication, marijuana can create problems in the same way as alcoholic beverages. It can, for example, impair intellectual judgment, short-term memory, and human psychomotor function. It can thus hamper reading or studying. It can also undermine the performance of car drivers and airline pilots (Murray, 1986; Yesavage et al., 1985). But when used moderately, marijuana can create euphoria, heighten sensitivity, improve perception, and increase appetite (Falco, 1992). Marijuana can also be used for medical purposes, particularly for the benefit of the very ill. In the purified form under the trade name Marinol, or when smoked like a cigarette, marijuana has proved effective for controlling nausea and relieving pain in seriously ill patients with AIDS, cancer, and other diseases. For this reason, eleven states have already legalized medical use of marijuana (Harris, 2006; Conant, 1997; Doblin and Kleiman, 1993).

Many people believe that marijuana is a "gateway" to harder drugs. Indeed, considerable research has shown that almost all heroin and cocaine users started out with weed (Fergusson, 2006; Kandel and Jessor, 2002). But such a finding does not mean that marijuana use inevitably leads to hard drugs in the sense of marijuana itself being the cause of the drug escalation. The cause more likely lies in the marijuana user's involvement with friends who use hard drugs. In other words, pot smokers use heroin or cocaine largely because they have friends already using the harder drug (Goode, 2005a).

Heroin

This drug, also called "P-dope" on the street, was first produced in 1898 from morphine, which was in turn first derived in 1803 from opium. Both morphine and heroin are analgesics (painkillers) and have been used as such. But heroin use is now a major source of our society's concern with the problem of drug abuse. Most of our heroin comes from opium poppies harvested in the Golden Triangle of Southeast Asia (Burma, Thailand, and Laos), the Golden Crescent of South Asia (Pakistan, Afghanistan, and Iran), Mexico, and Colombia.

Heroin can be smoked, sniffed through the nose, taken orally, or injected into the skin, a muscle, or a vein. Injection of the substance into a vein, or mainlining, produces the quickest and most intense high. Traditionally, mainlining has been by far the most common method of ingestion. But fear of AIDS and the greatly increased potency of today's heroin have made smoking or snorting increasingly popular. Taken in moderate doses, heroin not only can dull pain but also diminish anxiety and tension. Most important, heroin can induce euphoria—the feeling of a "flash," "rush," or intense orgasmlike sensation. Actually, heroin itself does not bring about the euphoric feeling; the user has to *learn* to achieve the sense of pleasure from heroin injection. The novice user typically encounters an unpleasant experience from the first shot. Yet the negative experience can easily be rationalized, thus opening the way for taking more heroin trips. Here's how a young woman described her first heroin experience with her boyfriend:

> The rush was so powerful that he almost fell down. He turned white and began to sweat profusely. . . . I, too, began to sweat and tremble. If anyone had seen . . . us walking out of the house, he would have called an ambulance, we could barely walk. For some insane reason, we had decided to drive home immediately after shooting up . . . I had to keep pulling over to throw up on the side of the road . . . I was truly surprised that we both didn't die that very first night. I was more physically miserable than I had ever been before. The whole night was spent vomiting. The thing that surprises me is that we didn't forget about heroin right then and there. It was horrible! But we later decided that our dear friend had given us too much. So I decided to give it another chance. (Goode, 2005a)

Once users try heroin several times, as this woman did, they feel an extreme pleasure from the drug experience. Many heroin users, both male and female, claim that the heroin rush is more satisfying than orgasm and the heroin high far more glorious and pleasurable than anything the nonuser could possibly experience. This, however, can easily lead to psychological dependence on the drug. Furthermore, heroin is physically addictive. If deprived of it for just one day, the addict may suffer withdrawal sickness. The withdrawal symptoms include profuse sweating, running nose, watering eyes, chills, cramps, nausea, and diarrhea (Chase, 1996a).

To relieve or avoid these withdrawal symptoms, the addict obviously has to keep on using heroin. This has led many researchers to believe that once people become addicted, they can no longer experience the pleasurable effects of preaddiction drug use—that addicts use heroin only for *avoiding* the withdrawal distress. As the influential drug researcher Alfred Lindesmith (1968) wrote, "The critical experience in the fixation process is not the positive euphoria produced by the drug but rather the relief of the pain that invariably appears when a physically dependent person stops using the drug." But William McAuliffe and Robert Gordon (1974) presented data to show that, contrary to Lindesmith's belief, addicts do continue to experience *euphoria* following each injection of heroin. McAuliffe and Gordon argued that if it were not for the promise of euphoria, addicts would not persistently take the trouble to steal and hustle to get money for the next fix, and that if they only wanted to avoid withdrawal distress, they would quickly seek help at some drug treatment center. But this is not the case.

Both interpretations may well miss the mark. They above all reflect the researchers' own perceptions of what the experience of the drug effect means to them rather than to the addicts, who were not asked how they themselves actually felt. According to an ethnographic study, which encouraged addicts to express their feelings, most heroin addicts seek *something between* withdrawal avoidance and euphoria—more than the desperate avoidance of withdrawal distress but less than the intense euphoria they initially experienced. What they seek is "a temporary calm and serenity, feelings of normalcy, relaxation, and capability to provide them with a respite from the bleak harshness of their lives. It is the pursuit of normalcy rather than of euphoria that propels these heroin users to continue to use the substance." The pursuit of normalcy, however, does not involve the frantic, pathetic search for relief from the pain of withdrawal symptoms. Instead, heroin addicts see themselves in control rather than as "down-and-out dope fiends." They have a sense of pride in being able to achieve normalcy in a society that has relegated them to a lowly status (Hanson et al., 1985).

Although heroin is addictive, most users do not become addicts. A major reason is that heroin users typically get less and less pleasure from the drug after their early experiences of euphoria. As a former user says, "Luckily, it was no longer feeling good enough to make it worth getting busted for. . . . Heroin had lost its immense power over me. It simply wasn't worth it. The magic ceased to happen long ago. There's only the memory. . . . Right now I'd rather go out for a good dinner than shoot a bag of heroin" (Goode, 1981). There is also no truth to the old saw that "once a junkie, always a junkie." One study shows that, among the returning Vietnam veterans in 1971 who had been addicted to heroin while overseas, over 90 percent were no longer addicted about eight months after their return home. This was largely because they no longer felt the urge to use heroin, the urge that had stemmed from the extraordinarily stressful experience of the Vietnam War (Dodes, 2005; Maddux and Desmond, 1980; Robins, 1973). Even if permanently addicted to heroin, people do not necessarily suffer severe damage to their health. The drug may be harmless when compared with other psychoactive drugs. Unlike cigarette smoking and alcohol drinking, prolonged use of heroin does not necessarily damage the organs, tissues, or cells of the human body. As long as heroin addicts do not neglect other aspects of their lives, they can remain as healthy as the nonuser. As Jerome Jaffe (1965), the physician who later served as President Nixon's adviser on drug problems, observed,

> The addict who is able to obtain an adequate supply of the drug through legitimate channels and has adequate funds, usually dresses properly, maintains his nutrition, and is able to discharge his social and occupational obligations with reasonable efficiency. He usually remains in good health, suffers little inconvenience, and is, in general, difficult to distinguish from other persons.

A good example is the physician addict. Although they use a much greater quantity of narcotics than "street junkies," physician addicts generally manage to maintain their health and practice their profession. They are only less efficient in their work when compared with their addiction-free colleagues (Coombs, 1997).

On the other hand, street junkies are far more likely to suffer the consequences of narcotics laws. Because of these laws, heroin's black market prices are usually so high that the addicts, who are mostly poor, have to spend a great deal of their time frantically searching for money to buy the next fix. The frantic search for money tends to involve the user in committing burglaries, shoplifting, gambling, prostitution, and other acquisitive crimes, which creates a great deal of stress and strain. By the time they get enough money to buy a packet of "junk," they are likely to be both physically drained and emotionally stressed out. In addition, there is no way for them to know how pure or potent the packet is—its heroin content may range from zero to 99 percent. If they are used to no more than 5 percent heroin and happen to buy a packet of 50 percent, they may die of an overdose (Smolowe, 1993).

Cocaine and Crack

Also known as "coke," "snow," and "toot," cocaine is derived from the leaves of coca plants. At least 90 percent of the coca plants in the world are grown on the mountains of Peru and Bolivia, whose governments sometimes treasure the crop as one of their major exports. The coca leaves, however, are processed into cocaine in Colombia, and from there the final product is smuggled into the United States (Wren, 1997).

Before it became illegal at the turn of the twentieth century, cocaine was commonly used as a local anesthetic, for offsetting fatigue and depression, and for curing morphine addiction and stomach disorder. It was even chosen as the official remedy of the Hay Fever Association. Sigmund Freud, the founder of psychoanalysis, not only prescribed cocaine for his patients to treat those ills, but also used the drug himself to stay alert and ward off melancholy. Cocaine was also a major ingredient in numerous patent medicines and in many soft drinks, such as Coca-Cola. In 1885, a well-known pharmaceutical company promoted cocaine as a wonder drug, claiming that it could "supply the place of food, make the coward brave, the silent eloquent, free the victims of alcohol and opium habit from their bondage, and, as an anesthetic, render the sufferer insensitive to pain." One of the best, most popular wines in the late nineteenth century, marketed under the name of Vin Mariani, contained some cocaine. It won endorsement from Pope Leo XIII, Pope Pius X, President

McKinley, the kings of four countries (Spain, Greece, Norway, and Sweden), and many famous writers and artists. The French sculptor who designed the Statue of Liberty swore that if he had only drunk Vin Mariani earlier, he would have been able to build that lady hundreds of meters higher (Goode, 2005a; Musto, 1986).

By the turn of the twentieth century, when laws were passed to make cocaine illegal, it had become widely used as a pleasure drug. At that time most of the users were the powerless, such as African Americans, lower-class whites, and criminals. But since the 1960s cocaine has become a symbol of wealth or status, mostly used by affluent whites. It is the most expensive drug, sometimes called "the champagne of drugs" or "caviar among drugs." Usually snorted, the drug is in the form of white powder—hence also called "powder cocaine." One can seek a greater high by resorting to "freebasing," which involves purifying the drug with ether and then smoking it. Since 1986, however, an increasing number of youths, especially those from poor and working-class families, have used crack cocaine—or simply, "crack." It is a less pure form of cocaine but can still produce an intense high because users typically smoke it rather than snort it. Crack is much cheaper than pure cocaine, which may explain its popular use among the poor and the young.

As a stimulant, cocaine increases the heartbeat and raises blood pressure and body temperature. A snort in each nostril can produce a euphoric lift that lasts for half an hour or so. The cocaine high may be described objectively as an intensely vivid, sensation-sharpening experience. In the view of users themselves, the drug (1) provides exhilaration—a sense of elation, well-being, or a voluptuous, joyous feeling; (2) enhances self-confidence, supplying a sense of mastery and competence in what the user does; and (3) increases energy and suppresses fatigue, enabling the user to continue physical and mental activity more intensely and longer—such as by working for two or three days and nights straight without any sleep. Some users claim that cocaine is an aphrodisiac, but most deny it. There is increasing evidence that sustained use of cocaine can cause sexual dysfunction and impotence (Goode, 2005a).

Cocaine is physically addictive; it produces such withdrawal symptoms as exhaustion and stomach cramps after its use is discontinued. Cocaine is particularly noteworthy for being extremely psychologically addictive, due largely to the high quality of pleasure the user can derive from it. Coming down from a high usually causes such a deep gloom that the only remedy is more cocaine. Bigger doses follow, and soon the urge becomes a total obsession, with all its devastating consequences. As one cocaine user said, "I even hocked my wife's wedding ring. That's not me. Whoever said cocaine isn't addicting should be shot" (Rosenfeld, 1985). The powerful psychological addiction to cocaine has been demonstrated in laboratory experiments with animals. Once hooked on cocaine, rats and monkeys will prefer the drug to food, even though they have not eaten all day. They will keep on pressing the bar (which they have been trained to do) for a cocaine reward until they drop from exhaustion. Crack, the cheapest form of cocaine, is even more addictive than plain cocaine. The rush comes and goes so much more quickly and intensely that the crack user can get hooked much faster. According to the National Institute on Drug Abuse, crack addiction develops after only six to ten weeks, while it takes three to four years for users to get hooked on regular cocaine. When snorted, the coke reaches the brain in about eight minutes to produce a much milder high than that from crack. But crack hits the brain within only seconds in an intensified, concentrated form (Lamar, 1986).

Most people who use cocaine find their experience positive. But the drug can also be extremely dangerous if taken in large doses or used frequently for an extended time. It can cause insomnia, impotence, extreme irritability, paranoia and other symptoms of psychosis, and the sensation of bugs crawling under the skin. A single overdose can also produce an effect like "lighting a fire in the brain," triggering severe headaches, nausea, and convulsions with the possibility of total respiratory and cardiovascular collapse. Crack puts its users even at higher risks. Since it swiftly and dramatically increases blood pressure and heart rate, crack can more easily lead to heart attacks and deaths. Most users of cocaine, however, do not experience these effects, primarily because they use cocaine moderately and infrequently.

Meth and Roofies

Meth (methamphetamine), an injectable stimulant known on the street as "speed," "crank," or "crystal," has, since 1995, risen dramatically in popularity among drug users throughout initially the western United States and now the whole country. The drug itself is not new. During the Second World War, soldiers on both sides used it to reduce fatigue and enhance performance. Hitler was widely believed to be a meth addict. Later, in the 1960s, President John Kennedy also used the drug, and soon it caught on among so-called speed freaks. But because it was extremely expensive as well as difficult to obtain, meth was never close to being as widely used as cocaine.

Today, however, because meth is relatively cheap and easily available, it has supplanted cocaine as the drug of choice for all classes of people. It was initially known as "poor man's cocaine" for being mainly popular among white 18- to 34-year-old working-class or rural men, but today it has made its way into the mainstream, engulfing men and women from different social classes. Since the drug can be easily made from cold medicines like Sudafed, the U.S. Congress has passed the Combat Methamphetamine Act to make it harder to purchase those medications, such as by requiring pharmacies to keep them behind the counter. A major impetus to the popularity of meth stems from the fact that the high from the drug lasts four or five times longer than that from cocaine. When first used, meth is known to suppress appetite, create euphoria, boost self-confidence, and provide a burst of energy. But after users develop a tolerance for the drug, depression is likely to set in, followed by intense paranoia (Mitka, 2006; Jefferson, 2005; Johnson, 2004; Witkin, 1995).

Unlike meth, which is a stimulant, another recently popular drug is a depressant. In tablet form, the drug is known on the street as "roofies," "rope," "the forget pill," and "roach." It is related to the sedative Valium but is 10 times stronger. Roofies are actually Rohypnol, a prescription drug for severe insomnia. Rohypnol is sold over the counter in some 60 countries, and much of the drug used on the street in the United States is smuggled from Mexico and Colombia. The drug is particularly popular with teenagers in the South and Southwest, who like to combine the drug with alcohol for a quick high. This practice is apparently dangerous—it is what sent the grunge-rock star Kurt Cobain into a coma a month before he committed suicide. Like strong liquor, roofies make some users aggressive and fearless, but they often cause blackouts, with a total loss of memory. Consequently, some men use roofies to knock women out and then rape them, and it is from this use that the drug is also known as "the date-rape drug." The drug has also caused a great deal of concern about its potential for addiction and lethal overdosing (Cannon, 1999; Seligmann and King, 1996).

Ecstasy

Ecstasy, which chemists call MDMA (methylenedioxymethamphetamine), is popular with high school and college students and relatively affluent young adults, who typically swallow the drug as a pill at a dance club or party. Ecstasy is a psychedelic, a mood-altering drug. Most of its users report that they feel happier, their mind gets clearer, and their memory improves. They also feel a stronger desire for human connection so that they become compassionate and forgiving toward others. They are thus more inclined to, for example, embrace people, which is why Ecstasy is nicknamed the "hug drug." In short, according to its users, the drug provides a new, better perspective on life. Here is how an Ecstasy user describes how the drug has changed his life:

> Since I've started rolling I'm healthier. I don't smoke, I don't drink, I exercise, I take vitamins. I've gotten interested in meditation. This whole scene for me has been the best thing personally. I've become a better human being. I've become much more calm, much more considerate. I don't freak out about stupid things anymore. (Klam, 2001)

But to the U.S. government and some scientists, the drug is dangerous. In 1985, when the law making Ecstasy illegal was passed, there were false rumors that the drug caused Parkinson's disease and that it could turn your spine into jelly or liquid. In recent years a series of studies have shown that rats and monkeys given large doses of Ecstasy suffered brain damage. As a result, some scientists conclude that even one dose of Ecstasy can damage your brain. Such a conclusion is unwarranted. High doses of Ecstasy, like those given to the rats and monkeys, are indeed dangerous, but so is swallowing a whole bottle of Tylenol, which can wreck your liver and cause you to die. But human users of Ecstasy typically take only a small dose of the drug.

Using Ecstasy does have at least two big problems. One is that the specific doses of Ecstasy may be impure, containing foreign substances that can kill. The other problem is that Ecstasy can cause a body to overheat. If people do not drink enough water to quench the enormous thirst, they may experience dehydration, organ failure, or brain damage. On the other hand, drinking too much water may cause death from thinned-out blood (de Seve, 2006; Klam, 2001).

Social Dimensions of Drug Use

Drug use is not an individual behavior, engaged in simply by one person and affecting one person alone. It is social behavior, involving many drug users and affecting not only the drug user but also many other people—in fact, the entire society. Here we focus on four social dimensions of drug use: the extent of drug use in the United States, how U.S. society reacts to drug use, the impact of drug use on the spread of AIDS, and the influence of drug use on crime.

The Extent of Drug Use

The use of illegal drugs is quite common in the United States. About 12 percent of the U.S. population age 12 or older use illicit drugs every year, half of them at least once a month. Of various age groups, young adults (ages 18 to 25) have the highest rate of drug use and teenagers (ages 12 to 17) the second highest. The United States as a whole has the highest rate of drug use in the world, and U.S. high school seniors also have the highest rate among their peers in the industrial world (Lynch, 2008; NHSDA, 2001; Sallett, Goode, and Pooler, 1999).

All this, however, should not be blown out of proportion. It is true that the United States leads the world in drug use. It is not true that drug use is so pervasive that it invades every nook and cranny of society, enslaving all classes of Americans to the same extent. Most drug problems, especially the most serious ones, such as drug addiction, death from drug overdose, or drug-related homicide, are for the most part confined to the lower classes, particularly to socially and economically oppressed minorities. Drug use and overdose among the nonpoor, middle class, or affluent is generally far less common (Massing, 1998; Currie, 1993).

In fact, for Americans as a whole, the rate of drug use steadily declined from 1980 to 1992, and since 1992 the rate has remained about the same. But for teenagers, the rate has been rising, driven mostly by white youngsters smoking pot, so that today users of marijuana far outnumber users of any other drug (see Table 11.1). The sharpest increase in drug use has occurred among young teens, around age 13 (Caulkins et al., 2005; Sallett, Goode, and Pooler, 1999). Another noteworthy finding: African American students in secondary school are now less likely than their white peers to use drugs because they are more likely to have observed at close hand how drugs wreck lives in black communities (Wren, 1996; Bogert, 1994).

Drugs and AIDS

Intravenous (IV) injection of an illegal drug can spread HIV, the virus that causes AIDS, from one user to another. Most drug users with AIDS are addicted to heroin, and they have

TABLE 11.1   Users of Drugs in 2006

Drug	Number of People Using the Drug in the Past Month
Marijuana	14.8 million
Cocaine	2.4 million
Meth	0.7 million
Ecstasy	0.5 million
Heroin	0.3 million

Source: National Survey of Drug Use and Health, 2006.

caught the deadly disease from sharing needles with other addicts. The connection between drugs and AIDS is remarkably strong in the United States. IV drug users with AIDS make up less than 10 percent of all AIDS cases in Holland, Sweden, and Canada. By sharp contrast, this figure is over 30 percent in the United States. The proportion is considerably higher in some U.S. cities: 40 percent in New York City and 65 percent in Newark. In fact, the spread of the AIDS virus has virtually stopped among gays, but continues among IV drug users (CDC, 2003; Currie, 1993). Why?

A major factor behind the sharp drop in the new incidence of AIDS among gays is the practice of safe sex. But many IV drug users refuse to practice safe needle use, continuing to share needles and rejecting clean needles even if easily available (Decker and Rosenfeld, 1992; Sibthorpe et al., 1991). Why do they take the terrible risk of HIV infection? One reason is that they are drug addicts rather than occasional drug users. Their craving for drugs is so overwhelming that they must shoot up right away and cannot be bothered with taking precautions (Sibthorpe et al., 1991). Another reason is that the essence of the addict's lifestyle is risk taking: "Their habit alone is daily dalliance with mortality. Given a life filled with risks—overdoses, hepatitis, jail—the threat of dying from AIDS seems, to many, merely redundant" (Goode, 2005a). A third reason has to do with the difference in social background between the gays who practice safe sex and the IV drug addicts who spurn safe needle use. Most of the gays are relatively well-off white men, but the majority of the addicts are poor African Americans and Hispanics. Deprived of the opportunities for material success in a society that discriminates against them, the addicts are compelled to seek social status through bravado and derring-do. This includes taking a dangerous drug, especially one that is widely known to be capable of killing the user. In other words, it is overwhelming poverty that makes life so bleak and empty that the risk-taking involved in unsafe drug use appears challenging and thrilling (Currie, 1993).

Drugs and Crime

Research in the United States and other countries has clearly shown a strong link between drug use and crime: People who use illegal drugs generally commit more crime than those who do not. It has been found that close to half of the crime suspects arrested in the United States had used illegal drugs in the prior three days while 55 percent of their counterparts in England had done the same. A review of 30 studies in various countries has further shown that drug users are three to four times more likely than nonusers to commit a crime (Bennett et al., 2008; Wren, 1999; Walchak, 1996). Does all this mean that drug use causes crime? The answer is yes, according to *drug enslavement theory*. The answer is no, according to *general deviance syndrome theory*.

According to drug enslavement theory, drug users are forced into a life of crime because they cannot afford to pay for their prohibitively expensive drug habits unless they rob or steal to get the money for their next fix. This may be true of "deficit users," who live in poverty, have inadequate education, lack job skills, face racial discrimination, and suffer other social disadvantages because they are relatively poor, uneducated, and economically unskilled. But the theory cannot be applied to "leisure users," who are well-off enough to find it unnecessary to commit crime for the purpose of raising funds for drug purchases (Harrison, 1992).

According to general deviance syndrome theory, the high correlation between drug use and crime does not mean that drug use causes crime because most drug users with a criminal record have committed crime *before* using drugs. Becoming a drug user and continuing to commit crime as a drug user are cut from the same cloth—that is, from a general tendency toward deviance. Those with a general deviance syndrome are likely to get involved not only in one form of deviant activities (such as crime) but also in other forms of deviance (such as drug use and drug-related criminality). This syndrome was found in about 77 percent of the drug users in a study conducted at a Denver drug abuse center, while the syndrome was absent in the remaining 23 percent—who committed offenses only after becoming drug users (Dalrymple, 2006; Swan, 1993). It seems clear that drug use does not by itself cause crime for most users, but drug use does *intensify* criminal tendency or *increase* the frequency of criminal activity. This may explain the "astronomical" number of offenses committed by drug users.

Drugs and Socioeconomic Status

Socioeconomic status—measured in terms of education, occupation, and income—is significantly related to the type of illicit drug being used. People of higher status tend to use certain drugs, whereas people of lower status tend to use other drugs (Goode, 2005a).

There is a strong connection between higher status and marijuana: The higher the status, the more likely the use of marijuana. The drug is particularly popular among college and high school students; marijuana is by far their number one drug of choice. This is true not only in the United States. Marijuana is equally popular with the youth in many other wealthy countries such as Canada, Britain, Switzerland, and Spain. The main reason is that young people in wealthy countries enjoy more leisure opportunities than their peers in poor countries. Pot smoking could thus be regarded as the affluent youth's way of pursuing leisure (ter Bogt et al., 2006).

Heroin is far and away the most popular among lower-status people, particularly those who live in poor, inner-city neighborhoods. The affluent, including their children of high school or college age, typically stay away from heroin. This has long been so, and even in the 1960s, when massive numbers of college and high school students experimented with all kinds of drugs, heroin remained at the very bottom of their drug choice. But since the mid-1990s more affluent whites have turned on to heroin, primarily because the drug is now pure enough to snort or smoke, with no risk of getting AIDS from sharing contaminated needles (Wren, 1999; Leland, 1996).

Cocaine has long been associated with affluent people because of its high cost. Today, the drug is still more popular among the affluent than among the poor. But since the drug is much less expensive today, less affluent people have increasingly used it. The cheapest form of cocaine, crack, is particularly popular with the poor. In fact, crack has been called "the poor person's drug." Being socially marginalized, such as being deprived of social support, financial resources, and good health, the poor are likely to use and continue to use crack (Van Der Poel and Van De Mheen, 2006).

As for meth and roofies, they seem to have a special allure among working-class and young people. As has been suggested, some working-class persons use meth to seek euphoria, an enhanced self-confidence, and a burst of energy, and some working-class women use the drug to lose weight because it can suppress appetite. Roofies are also popular with young people, particularly those who like to drink, because as a depressant the drug has the same effect as alcohol, except of course, that it is far more potent. It also seems popular with the working class. As for Ecstasy, it is often associated with high school and college students and young professionals.

While we have discussed users of different drugs separately, we should nonetheless note that the use of a particular drug does not necessarily mean that the individual uses or will continue to use only that drug. Most people who use drugs tend to use more than one type. In addition, under peer influence, they tend to graduate from using relatively soft drugs, such as cigarettes, liquor, or marijuana, to using "harder" drugs, such as heroin and cocaine. Still, most drug users favor a certain drug over others (Fergusson, 2006).

Becoming a Drug User

In their classic study of heroin use, Isidor Chein and his associates (1964) distinguished four stages in the process of becoming involved with the drug. These stages are *experimentation, occasional use* (once a week or less), *regular use* (once a day or more), and *futile efforts to break the habit.* Chein and his associates further note that a user may go through all these stages or may stop at any stage. One person may experiment but not repeat the experiment. Another may use heroin occasionally but never regularly. A third person may become a regular user but manage to break the habit. And a fourth person may go through all the stages to become hooked on heroin, despite strenuous efforts to kick the habit.

Among the users of various drugs, heroin users seem most likely to escalate into the last, fourth stage (addiction), while users of marijuana, cocaine, and other illicit drugs remain in the earlier stages (experimental, occasional, and regular use).

Heroin is most addictive not only because of its chemical properties but, perhaps more important, because the majority of its users are relatively poor and use the drug to cope with the stresses of their life problems, such as low-paying jobs, unemployment, and racism. Since the relief brought by the drug is transitory but the stresses always recur, extended use of heroin is likely to occur; and since the drug is extremely addictive, its users have the greatest chance of getting hooked. On the other hand, users of marijuana, cocaine, and other drugs may be less likely to get addicted to the drugs because, unlike heroin users, they are mostly young people who use drugs for about the same reason they go to the movies, to a party, or out on a date—that is, drugs are a part of their social lives or recreational activities. As a nationwide study of high school seniors found, the reasons most often cited by users of marijuana and cocaine are "to have a good time with friends," "to feel good or get high," and "to see what it's like." Very few of the students mentioned "to get away from my problems," "to deal with anger and frustration," or "to get through the day" (Johnston et al., 1986). Therefore, without the compulsion to use drugs for dealing with difficult, intractable problems, they are more likely to remain occasional users.

Whatever stage drug users may end up in, how do they get involved in drugs in the first place? They usually have been offered the drug by their friends in a simple, casual way.

This can be illustrated by the following accounts of how two young men had their first experiences with heroin (Chein et al., 1964):

> It was raining, and I was tired. I was standing in a doorway when this friend of mine came by. He said, "Want a pick-up [injection]?" I said "Sure," so we popped [took a shot].

> I was at a party. Everybody was having a good time. I wanted to be one of the crowd. I thought, if it didn't hurt them it wouldn't hurt me. That started the ball rolling. They were sniffing it that time. Two or three pulled out a few caps [heroin capsules] and said, "Here, if you want to, try." I accepted. They weren't trying to addict me; they just gave it to me.

Contrary to popular belief, it is not the strange drug peddler, the "merchant of death," who pushes drugs on the innocent young. Instead, it is their friends who introduce them to drug use. This is particularly true of those who use marijuana, the most widely used illicit drug. According to one national survey, an overwhelming majority (nearly 90 percent) of pot smokers obtain their marijuana from a friend or relative (Caulkins and Liccardo, 2006; Osgood et al., 1996).

Once having tried the drug, would-be users may go through a learning process—with explicit or implicit instruction from their drug-introducing friends. Howard Becker (1963) has identified three steps in the process of learning to become a marijuana user.

The first step is learning the *technique* to get high. Since beginners tend to smoke marijuana like an ordinary cigarette, they may fail to induce the desired drug effects. Thus they may watch their experienced friends smoke or they may receive direct coaching from them on the proper way of smoking grass, such as inhaling deeply and then holding the smoke in the lungs long enough for the bloodstream to absorb the psychoactive substance of marijuana.

Becker's second step is learning to *recognize* the drug effects. After learning the proper technique of smoking marijuana, new users may still not get high. So they have to learn from friends that having cold feet, rubbery legs, intense hunger, and unawareness of the passage of time are some of the signs of a marijuana high.

The third step is learning to *enjoy* the drug effects. While being high, novices may have such feelings as dizziness, thirst, and tingling of the scalp; they may misjudge time and distance or feel themselves to be simultaneously at two places; they may hear or otherwise sense things in strange ways. These feelings may be unpleasant or even frightening to beginning drug users. They must learn to redefine these sensations as pleasurable; otherwise they will not use the drug again. New marijuana users usually learn to enjoy these experiences because of the encouragement and reassurances of experienced friends. These friends may tell them such things as, "You sure are lucky; I'd give anything to get that high myself. I haven't been that high in years."

With the use of cocaine, heroin, or other illegal drugs, the beginner may also have to learn the first step—the technique of using the drug. But the second and third steps—learning to recognize and enjoy the drug effects—may not be necessary, because the effects are usually more clear-cut and predictable than the effects of marijuana. In virtually all cases of initial cocaine use, for example, the user feels its effect as extremely pleasurable. Hence, there is no need for users of cocaine and other drugs to learn to recognize and enjoy the drug effects.

A Social Profile of Illegal Drug Users

Illegal drug users are generally distinguishable from nonusers for having certain social and social psychological characteristics. First, users are more likely to be male than female. This reflects the greater general tendency for men to engage in deviant activities. While men are only *slightly* more likely than women to use drugs at all, they are *considerably* more likely to use drugs regularly and *extremely* more likely to use drugs so heavily as to become addicts (Osgood et al., 1996).

Second, drug users are relatively young. The age group with the highest rate of drug use is 18 to 25 years old. Within this group, more drug users are older teenagers (aged 18 or 19) than are young adults (aged 24 or 25). The higher rate of drug use among younger people can be attributed to freedom from parental control and, more important, freedom from adult responsibilities such as employment, marriage, and child rearing. Research has long established that the unemployed, unmarried, and childless are more likely than those with jobs, spouses, and children to use drugs (Goode, 2005a).

Third, drug users learn to use drugs from parents and peers. Users usually have parents who use legal drugs such as tobacco cigarettes, alcoholic beverages, and prescription drugs for relieving tension and combating insomnia. From parents, then, drug users first learn to use legal drugs—before turning to illegal ones. When used for the first time, the drugs are usually given by friends. Unsurprisingly, drug users have at least a few friends who also use the same drugs. Whether they will continue to use the drugs for an extended period also depends significantly on their friends' drug use (Martins et al., 2008; Molotsky, 1999).

Fourth, drug users in high school, when compared with nonusing peers, are more likely to cut classes, skip whole days of school, drop out of school, avoid religious activities, and frequently go out in the evening for fun and recreation. In other words, young drug users are not as strongly tied to three major social institutions—the school, the church, and the home—as the nonusers (Goode, 2005a).

What Causes Illegal Drug Use?

There are over 40 positivist theories about some aspect of drug use. Some of these theories are designed to explain why some individuals are more likely than others to use or abuse drugs. These explanatory theories can be divided into three major types: biological, psychological, and sociological. According to biological theories, the causes of drug addiction inhere in biological factors, such as an inborn high tolerance for drugs or a metabolic disorder that creates a craving for an illicit drug in about the same way that diabetes creates a craving for insulin. According to psychological theories, the causes of drug use are specific personality traits, such as low self-esteem or unconventionality. And according to sociological theories, drug use stems from social forces, such as the drug subculture or peer influence (Goode, 2005a). The first type of theory is the least credible, because scientific research has largely failed to support it. Also, the so-called biological causes could well be the effects of drug abuse. There are ample data to support the other two types of theory, and here we will discuss three specific examples.

Economic Deprivation Theory

After reviewing various studies conducted on drug use since the early 1950s, Elliott Currie (1993) concludes that "the link between drug abuse and deprivation is one of the strongest in 40 years of careful research." More specifically, he writes:

> Forty years of accumulated research, then, confirms that endemic drug abuse is intimately related to conditions of mass social deprivation, economic marginality, and cultural and community breakdown—in Europe as in the United States, in the eighties and nineties as in the sixties, among poor whites and Hispanics as well as inner-city blacks.

Currie further explains why poor people turn to drugs in response to poverty-related social conditions. An important first reason is that drugs can fulfill the need for *status*. In the larger, conventional society, the poor are denied legitimate avenues of attaining esteem, a sense of respect, or even a sense of community. As a consequence, there has developed in the poor neighborhood a drug culture that serves as an alternative source of esteem and respect. As one researcher found, "being in the drug culture is just like being a movie star. So many people depend on you, want to stop you in the street. The police is always on you. . . . You are a very important person." A second reason is that drugs can help the user *cope* with the harsh, oppressive realities of poverty. As Currie writes, "Drugs become a way of getting away from daily problems, medicating emotional anguish, relieving stress, escaping pain." A third reason is that drugs can provide a sense of *structure* or *purpose* to shattered lives. In the absence of steady work or stable family life, the poor cannot find the sense of structure that the nonpoor have. As a substitute, drug use helps relieve monotony and purposelessness among the poor. A fourth, unavoidable reason is that the poor communities are saturated with illicit drugs. Given the pervasiveness and easy availability of drugs along with the ubiquity of drug users, it is easy to drift passively into drug use without considering its consequences (Currie, 1993).

In short, grinding poverty can force people to use drugs as a way of meeting normal human needs that have been systematically thwarted by society. It is obvious that this kind of theory is useful for explaining drug use among the poor, but it is equally obvious that it cannot explain drug use among the affluent.

Cognitive Association Theory

While economic deprivation theory is intended to explain both drug use and abuse, cognitive association theory is designed to explain drug addiction alone. As Alfred Lindesmith (1968) explains,

> The power of the [drug] habit is derived basically from effects which follow when the drug is removed rather than from any positive effects which its presence in the body produces. Addiction occurs only when [drugs] are used to alleviate withdrawal distress, after this distress had been properly understood. . . . If the individual fails to conceive of his distress as withdrawal distress brought about by the absence of [the drugs], he does not become addicted, but, if he does, addiction is quickly and permanently established through further use of the drug.

Lindesmith has collected convincing data to support the theory. He found that, among patients who had been given morphine to kill their postsurgery pain, some later became addicted to the drug but others did not. The difference had to do with whether the patients knew that their nausea and other symptoms of withdrawal sickness were caused by their suddenly discontinuing the use of morphine. Those who did—in other words, who "cognitively associated" the withdrawal distress with their prior use of morphine—ended up addicted to the drug because they demanded that they be given more morphine. By contrast, patients who experienced the same withdrawal sickness *without* knowing the cause of it did not become addicted. Why not? Because they were assured by their doctor that the discomfort was normal for a patient recovering from surgery and that it would eventually stop by itself. These patients then "toughed it out"—rather than demanding more morphine.

In sum, the cause of addiction is the drug user's *cognitive association* between withdrawal distress and prior drug use. To bolster the theory, Lindesmith further observes that the mentally ill, the mentally challenged, young children, and animals usually are immune to addiction because they cannot understand the meaning of withdrawal symptoms even if it is explained to them. The theory can also explain why people with average intelligence can easily get hooked on drugs once they experience withdrawal distress. However, a deeper reason for addiction, we may argue, is that most people in a modern, hedonistic society want to eliminate distress instantly rather than stoically endure it until it passes.

Social Psychological Theory

From various studies we can derive a number of sociological and psychological factors that lead people from virtually all walks of life into drug use.

Among the sociological factors, some exert their influence from the higher societal or cultural level, while others more directly affect individuals in their immediate milieu consisting of family, friends, schoolmates, neighbors, coworkers, and others they meet often.

A prime example of societal factors is the legal drug culture of our society. Such psychoactive drugs as alcoholic beverages, tobacco cigarettes, and various sedatives and tranquilizers are pushed on the general public either directly or indirectly. Each year, the alcohol and tobacco industries spend millions of dollars on advertising—coaxing and seducing people to use their drugs. The pharmaceutical industry sends its sales representatives into doctors' offices with free samples of legal uppers and downers, and these "reps" talk the physicians into pushing the drugs on their patients. On the other hand, the general public demands these drugs to help ease their physical aches and pains, their psychological stresses and strains, a sense of social incompetence and awkwardness, or existential emptiness and boredom. Given this drug culture, many people become accustomed to using legal drugs, which makes it easy to try illegal ones. This is why many people use illegal drugs only after they have drunk or smoked, and many teenagers use illicit drugs only after they have long seen their parents drink or smoke. If a youngster says, "My parents drink—why can't I smoke grass?" it is difficult for adults to talk down that argument.

The social factors that more immediately sway individuals toward drug use can be drawn from various deviance theories, such as social control, differential association, social learning, structured strain, deviant opportunity, and deviant subculture theories. Their significance has been demonstrated by current research. Since these general theories have been discussed in some detail in Chapters 2 and 3, we will mention here only the variables that have been found most useful for explaining drug use. They are (1) lack of attachment to conventional persons or institutions, such as parents, teachers, clergy, and employers, or family, school, religion, and work, (2) having friends who use drugs, (3) being a member of a drug-using subculture, and (4) easy access to drugs (Kilmer et al., 2006; Caulkins and Liccardo, 2006; Kaplan et al., 1986).

As for the psychological reasons behind drug use, research has found the following factors significant: poor self-concept, low self-esteem, self-rejection; feelings of distress, powerlessness, or hopelessness; being unconventional or rebellious; receptivity to uncertainty, risk taking, or new experience; and expecting drugs to enhance status or mitigate life's problems (Kaplan et al., 1986; Jurich and Polson, 1984). Clinical evidence further suggests that people with a certain type of personal problem tend to prefer one particular drug after experimenting with various substances. They tend to use that preferred drug regularly because it helps relieve their specific problem. For example, those who are restless, aggressive, or given to violent eruptions tend to use heroin regularly because they find that it helps them "feel normal, calm, mellow, soothed, and relaxed." Those who often feel depressed, fatigued, bored, or shy are inclined to choose cocaine because they feel that it helps make them energetic, self-assured, and sociable (Khantzian, 1985). Those who worry about losing in sports or looking weak are likely to use steroids and human growth hormone to improve their athletic performance and physical appearance (McCallum, 2008).

The War on Drugs

The war on drugs consists of two basic strategies. One is *punitive*: using law enforcement to stop the supply of drugs and punish drug sellers and users. The other is *supportive*: using drug prevention (or education) and treatment to reduce the demand for drugs and help drug addicts. The U.S. government devotes most of its antidrug budget to law enforcement. In 2008, for example, $8.3 billion was spent on enforcing drug laws while $4.6 billion went toward drug prevention and treatment (Kalb, 2008). One result is a sharp increase in the incarceration of drug offenders. Can this emphasis on law enforcement over drug prevention and treatment solve the drug problem? Let us first analyze the punitive strategy by looking at how it has been applied in the past and how it is applied today. Then we will see how reaction to the punitive strategy has sparked a debate over legalizing drugs. Finally, we will examine the application of the supportive strategy to solving drug problems.

Historical Pattern

Historically, the war on drugs has turned out to be a war on powerless groups, particularly minorities.

The first attempt to battle drug use appeared in the form of a city ordinance against opium dens in San Francisco in 1875. The custom of opium smoking had earlier been introduced to this country by Chinese coolies, unskilled laborers who were imported to work on railroad construction crews. At first, their opium dens were tolerated. But soon the Chinese labor pool was seen to present a threat to the white labor market because they were hired to work long hours for low wages. The white laborers started a campaign against the Chinese and their opium dens. The campaign, effectively led by the president of the American Federation of Labor, conjured "a terrible picture of how the Chinese entice little white boys and girls into becoming 'opium fiends,' [who were] condemned to spend their days in the back of laundry rooms" (Hill, 1973). Consequently, a number of cities followed San Francisco in passing ordinances against opium dens. The antiopium laws were, in practice, anti-Chinese laws, because they provided "a legal basis for unrestrained and arbitrary police raids and searches of Chinese premises" (Helmer, 1975).

Around 1900, many state laws and municipal ordinances were also enacted against the use of another drug—cocaine. These anticocaine laws were, in reality, antiblack laws. In those days, cocaine was widely used by blacks, but whites fearfully believed that a cocaine high could spur blacks to violence against whites, stimulate sexual assaults by black men on white women, improve blacks' pistol marksmanship, make blacks invulnerable to bullets, give blacks superhuman strength, and make them cunning and efficient. The anticocaine laws, then, were useful for controlling blacks and keeping them in "their place."

In 1937 Congress passed the Marihuana Tax Act. This antimarijuana law was, in effect, an anti-Hispanic law. The Mexican migrant workers in the West and Southwest had been known to smoke marijuana, and Anglo Americans, holding a strong prejudice against them, had spread rumors that "weed" often led the Mexicans to commit murder, rape, and other horrible crimes. In 1936, for example, a Colorado newspaper editor wrote to the Bureau of Narcotics: "I wish I could show you what a small marijuana cigarette can do to one of our degenerate Spanish-speaking residents. That's why our problem is so great: the greatest percentage of our population is composed of Spanish-speaking persons, most of whom are low mentally, because of social and racial conditions" (Himmelstein, 1983; Musto, 1973).

In the 1950s the social problem of heroin use was blamed on the communists. They were believed to push heroin as part of their conspiracy against the United States. The Narcotic Drug Control Act, enacted in 1956, was indeed very tough on heroin peddlers: It provided the death penalty for the sale of heroin to a person under 18 by one over 18 (Szasz, 1974a).

In the 1960s horror stories about the effects of marijuana and other illicit drugs were widely publicized. One such story came in 1968 from Pennsylvania's governor, who subsequently became chairman of President Nixon's Marijuana and Drug Abuse Commission. The governor told the press that six college students stared at the sun while under the influence of LSD and were consequently blinded. Although the story was later exposed as a hoax, the general public had already erupted with fear about LSD and other illicit drugs. Then, many new federal and state laws were enacted to increase the severity of punishment for illicit drug use. All these harsh laws served to punish the youth who dared reject conventional values, scorn the establishment, and protest U.S. involvement in the Vietnam War.

Since the late 1960s, however, large numbers of conventional, middle-class whites have used drugs, particularly marijuana. Professional athletes, movie stars, rock stars, business executives, and other successful, respectable people have turned cocaine into a status drug. Drug use has stopped being associated exclusively with powerless minorities, antiestablishment youths, and social undesirables. Consequently, affluent, respectable drug users, instead of being treated like dangerous criminals, are today more likely to go free or receive light sentences. Nevertheless, racial minorities, particularly African Americans, continue to suffer the brunt of antidrug law enforcement.

Punitive Strategy: Law Enforcement

Compared with their affluent and white counterparts, the poor and minority drug users are more often arrested or imprisoned. African Americans, for example, constitute only 12 percent of the U.S. population, but they usually make up over 50 percent of all arrests for various drug offenses. The majority of people convicted of crack cocaine offenses in federal court are also African Americans, who receive much longer sentences than well-off white offenders convicted of selling powder cocaine. All this suggests how today's law enforcement against drugs continues the historical pattern of drug laws against minorities. Today's law enforcement does more than discriminate against African Americans and Hispanics; it worsens their drug problems by siphoning off government funds that could have been used for drug education and treatment programs. Thus, poor black and Hispanic communities continue to have the highest rates of drug addiction and other severe drug problems in U.S. society (Beckett et al., 2006; Friedman, 1998).

Law enforcement is also aimed at poor foreign countries that produce most of the illicit drugs consumed in the United States. Our government has gone to great lengths in urging these countries to eradicate their narcotic plants. Millions of U.S. dollars have been offered in return for the destruction of the plants, and threats to cut off U.S. aid or oppose international lending have often been made to countries that fail to reduce drug production. Even U.S. soldiers and advisers have been dispatched to Latin American countries to destroy cocaine-producing plants and pursue drug lords. The U.S. Customs Service has also caught many people for trying to smuggle illicit drugs into the United States. In addition, the federal Drug Enforcement Agency (DEA) and other law-enforcement agencies have often made headline news seizing tons of illicit drugs throughout the country.

Nevertheless, drugs are still easily available on the street, for the most part because as long as the demand for them is great, there are always some countries and many smugglers to supply them (Shishkin and Crawford, 2006; Wren, 1996).

Debate over Legalizing Drugs

The apparent failure of the law-enforcement approach has led to calls for legalization of drugs. Advocates of legalization contend that, like Prohibition (of alcohol) in the 1920s, current drug laws do more harm than good. They are said to generate many crimes, including homicides. As Milton Friedman (1989) argues, "Addicts are driven to associate with criminals to get the drugs [and] become criminals themselves to finance the habit." The drug laws are also said to encourage official corruption because huge profits from drug sales enable the criminals to bribe police to look the other way. By legalizing drugs, the proponents argue, the government can take away obscene profits from drug traffickers, end police corruption, and reduce crime drastically. Finally, legalizers believe that with legalization the huge amount of money currently spent on law enforcement can be used for drug treatment and education, which will dramatically reduce drug use and addiction (Friedman, 1998; Carter, 1989).

But most Americans oppose legalization. They fear that, if drugs are legalized, drug use and addiction will skyrocket (Walters, 2002). As William Bennett (1989), a former national drug policy director, says, "After the repeal of Prohibition, consumption of alcohol soared by 350 percent." A soaring rate of drug use and addiction, according to another opponent, will hurt the poor and minorities that already suffer the most even more (Rosenthal, 1995). Sociologist Elliott Currie (1993) also argues that legalization cannot solve the problem of widespread drug abuse and crime because the root cause of the problem is poverty, racism, or inequality. Thus, Currie proposes that the government eradicate the cause of the problem by providing employment to all, increasing the minimum wage, expanding the Job Corps, increasing health care for the poor, offering paid family leave, providing affordable housing, and reducing social inequality.

A third approach to controlling the drug problem has recently emerged. It involves striking a middle ground between all-out criminalization and outright legalization. To these "middle grounders," all-out criminalization can lead to great increases in such problems as crime and corruption, just as the legalization advocates have pointed out. But the middle grounders also argue that outright legalization can cause drug use and addiction to soar, just as the criminalization supporters have pointed out. The solution, then, is to reduce harm from these two different kinds of problems. It may involve, for example, legalizing the sale of a small amount of marijuana to adults while criminalizing the sale of marijuana to minors or the sale of hard drugs to anybody. This is already a reality in the Netherlands. Whether it will catch on in the United States is still hard to tell (Goode, 2004a).

Supportive Strategy: Prevention and Treatment

While the U.S. government pays more attention to the punitive strategy, the supportive strategy of preventing drug use via education and treatment for addicts and their drug addiction nonetheless exists. To prevent drug use, school programs, television commercials, and other educational efforts are focused on increasing public awareness of the harmfulness of drugs. Treatment involves hospitals, public-health agencies, and drug-treatment centers in programs for people with drug problems. Let's take a closer look at each of these two types of supportive strategy in the war on drugs.

Drug Prevention.   The most popular program of drug prevention is the Project D.A.R.E. (Drug Abuse Resistance Education). Adopted by more than 60 percent of the U.S. school districts, DARE involves a police officer teaching a drug education class at a local school. The aim of the program is to prevent drug use by teaching students about the perils of drug use and then showing them how to develop social skills, raise self-esteem, resist peer pressure to use drugs, and seek drug-free alternatives, such as tutoring younger children or developing a hobby. According to its administrators and supporters, DARE has, since its establishment in 1982, proven successful in achieving its goal (DeJong, 1986). But researchers have found otherwise: DARE does not significantly prevent drug use, although it does enhance children's self-esteem, polish their social skills, and improve their attitudes toward police (Elliott, 1995).

Nonetheless, parents of most children who have participated in the DARE curriculum seem to agree with its administrators that the program works. They can see that their own children do not use drugs. But they do not realize that, as researchers have generally discovered, DARE works only for children who, like their own, are unlikely to use drugs in the first place. More precisely, then, DARE does prevent drug use by *reinforcing* the existing antidrug attitude that most children have learned from parents. The fact remains that DARE—and other similar programs—does not work for children who are already at risk of using drugs. Who are these children? They are children with the following experiences:

- Family history of alcoholism
- Family history of criminality
- Poor parental child-rearing practices, such as lax supervision and constant criticism
- Parental drug use or permissive attitudes toward drugs
- Early antisocial behavior in school, especially aggressiveness
- Alienation and low commitment to getting an education
- Academic failure in middle to late elementary school education
- Socializing with friends who take drugs (Levine, 1986)

Apparently, drug education alone cannot work for children with these problems unless the family, school, community, and the larger society also work together to deal with the impact of these problems on the children.

Drug Treatment.   Three kinds of treatment exist for drug addicts. The first, *chemical treatment,* may include detoxification and maintenance therapy. *Detoxification* involves the use of a nonnarcotic chemical or a required rest to bring the patient into a drug-free state. Detoxification by itself cannot cure addiction because the craving for drugs remains, but it makes the patient more amenable to psychotherapy or other treatment programs designed to cure addiction. *Maintenance therapy* involves a treatment center giving the patient a drug that has almost the same chemical makeup as that of the illicit drug. The substitute drug, such as methadone for heroin addicts, is able to prevent withdrawal distress and can be used regularly as a safe alternative to the street drug or as a supplement to a treatment designed to cure addiction (Massing, 1998).

A second type of drug treatment is *psychological therapy,* including aversion therapy, personal therapy, and group therapy. *Aversion therapy* involves making patients associate their drug of choice with some unpleasant experience. Thus, if drug addicts undergo a program in which they are administered an electric shock every time they use their drug of choice, they are likely to stop using the drug. *Personal therapy* involves a psychotherapist helping patients discover and then seek to eliminate the psychological causes of their drug abuse, such as low self-esteem or inability to form sound relationships with others. *Group therapy* involves a group of drug addicts discussing and sharing with each other their lives and personal experiences with drug abuse.

A third type of drug treatment is *therapeutic community*. This involves drug addicts living together like members of a family. Cut off from outside contacts, including family and friends, these addicts support each other, helping each other live a drug-free life. The better-known therapeutic communities are Synanon, Odyssey House, and Phoenix House, but they can even be found in many prisons (Early, 1996).

It is difficult, if not impossible, to determine which of these treatments works better than others because patients in different programs vary in such significant factors as age, ethnicity, employment status, length of drug use, and degree of addiction. Thus, for example, a program that treats with great success patients who are only mildly addicted to drugs cannot be said to be more successful than another program that treats with little success patients who are heavily addicted. But many studies suggest that any treatment method can work better if the patients are employed and can earn a good income, receive adequate support from others such as family and friends, or are free from a drug-abuse subculture (Abadinsky, 1993).

Abusing Prescription Drugs, Particularly OxyContin

Drugs prescribed by doctors for patients can be used either licitly or illicitly. The licit use of prescription drugs is meant to eliminate the patient's complaints, such as pain, stress, and fatigue. On the other hand, the illicit use of prescription drugs occurs when nonpatients get high. The misuse has skyrocketed among both teens and adults over the last decade, with the abuse of painkillers rising much more sharply than the abuse of tranquilizers, stimulants, and sedatives (see Figure 11.1). Women and whites are more likely than men, blacks, and Hispanics to abuse prescription drugs. Also, people with some college education are more likely than those with less education to abuse these drugs. Apparently, then, the abuse of prescription drugs is mostly a middle-class problem (ONDCP, 2006; Kalb, 2001).

There are several reasons for the soaring prevalence of prescription-drug abuse. One reason is simply that the drug is easily available, thanks to the sharp increase in the prescriptions written by doctors as well as in the medications sold online without prescription. Another reason is the mistaken assumption that prescription drugs are relatively safe to take because they are legal and come from the doctor and pharmacy rather than illegal and come from the drug dealer. A third reason is that people who abuse prescription drugs are influenced by the same social factors that encourage the use of illegal drugs. These factors include, as discussed previously, peer pressure, the lack of social control, and the legal drug culture that encourages people to use alcohol, tobacco, and various sedatives and tranquilizers (Schepis and Krishnan-Sarin, 2008; Compton and Volkow, 2006).

The skyrocketing abuse of painkillers, particularly OxyContin, seems to have gotten its fuel from the medical establishment and the pharmaceutical industry. For a long time before 1990s, doctors usually paid little attention to their patients' complaints about pain. As the complaints grew increasingly urgent and prevalent, the doctors in the early 1990s began to be much more aggressive in treating the problem. This caused pharmaceutical companies to produce many different painkilling drugs in large quantities. Then, for the next 10 years, these companies launched aggressive marketing campaigns to sell their drugs. One common strategy involved buttering up doctors with free trips and paid speaking engagements. Thus, a pharmaceutical company would pay the transportation and hotel expenses for hundreds of doctors to attend weekend conferences at popular resorts to discuss pain management. The company would also recruit and pay doctors to speak to other

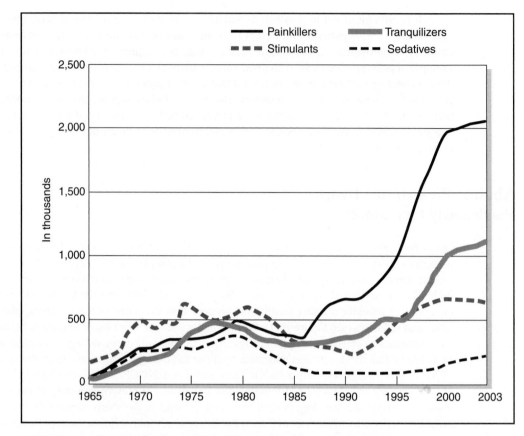

FIGURE 11.1   Soaring Numbers of New Illicit Users of Prescription Drugs

Source: National Household Survey on Drug Abuse (NHSDA), 2004.

doctors at numerous "pain management" seminars all over the country. At those meetings doctors were encouraged to treat their patients with powerful painkillers, particularly Oxy-Contin, the most abused prescription drug (Meier and Petersen, 2001).

Unfortunately, many doctors who were prodded to prescribe OxyContin and other painkillers did not have much experience dealing with such drugs. As a result, they often could not tell if a patient really needed a painkilling drug, and so prescribed it for many patients who lied to get the drug to abuse or sell to others. With pharmaceutical companies flooding the market with painkillers and other prescription drugs and with some doctors too quick to prescribe the drugs, the door to abusing the drugs swung wide open. Many abusers turn into "doctor shoppers," visiting different doctors to get more drugs. This is easy to do. As one abuser said, "I'd walk in and tell them I had a migraine; that's all I had to say." Some abusers obtain drugs by committing fraud, such as using bogus prescriptions or using a doctor's name to phone in prescriptions to pharmacies. Some abusers get drugs by using stolen prescription pads from doctors or breaking into pharmacies or the homes of patients with legitimate prescriptions. Some buy drugs from dealers or patients at prices above those charged by pharmacies. Since 2004, however, the U.S. Drug Enforcement Administration has intensified its regulation of OxyContin and other painkillers (Spencer, 2004; Kalb, 2001).

OxyContin is most popular with abusers of prescription drugs because it is by far the most powerful painkiller, most effective in eliminating severe pain. OxyContin also offers pain relief three times longer than other drugs because of its time-release feature. Licit, legitimate users get these benefits from the drug by swallowing it with water, which releases the drug into the body little by little. But abusers can bypass this time-release system and get an almost immediate and much more powerful rush by chewing the pill or crushing it and then snorting it. It is thus easy to become compulsive about taking the drug, to the point where it threatens the abuser's health or social and professional life (Adler, 2004; Kalb, 2001).

Smoking Cigarettes

As suggested before, compared with illegal drugs, legal drugs are far more prevalent and, over time, much more dangerous. The use of alcohol is the subject of the next chapter. Here we take a look at the smoking of tobacco cigarettes.

Since 1964, when the U.S. Surgeon General first announced the conclusion of a scientific study that smoking is causally related to lung cancer, there have been many reports about the serious health hazards of smoking. Consequently, laws have required warning labels for cigarettes, restriction of tobacco advertising and promotion, and smoke-free workplaces and public areas. In recent years the government has even forced the tobacco industry to pay more than $500 billion over 25 years ($20 billion annually) for health-care costs, an enormous sum in view of the fact that the tobacco business takes in around $30 billion a year. All these efforts have reduced smoking by about 40 percent over the last 40 years, and now the percentage of smokers in the United States is among the lowest in the world (Sullum, 1998; Pollack, 1997).

Still, too many Americans continue to smoke regularly, making up at least 25 percent of the U.S. population. Even among the very young (aged 12 to 17), about 13 percent smoke in any given month. Most of these young smokers are very likely to continue smoking in their adult lives, because most adult smokers started before age 18 (NSDUH, 2006).

As teenagers, whites are much more likely than blacks to smoke. Among adults, however, African Americans are more likely to smoke. Of various racial or ethnic groups, Native Americans have the highest percentage of smokers and Asian Americans the lowest. These racial differences in smoking may have something to do with education. Generally, as many studies have shown, the prevalence of smoking is three times higher among people with less than 12 years of education compared to those with more than 16 years of education. Ethnic groups with less education are thus more likely than other groups to smoke. There is also a gender factor in smoking: Within most ethnic groups, there are many more male smokers than female smokers, the exception being that, among white teenagers, females are just as likely to smoke (Adler, 2008; McMurray, 2004; SAMHSA, 2002; AHA, 1998).

Given the terrible health hazards of smoking, why do smokers continue to smoke rather than quit? Are they irrational, or do they fail to appreciate the hazards of smoking? Many smokers have become addicted, so that they cannot quit. But others continue to smoke even if they could quit because to them the benefits of smoking outweigh the costs. The benefits include releasing tension, feeling relaxed, and enjoying quiet companionship or lively conversation. It is, however, more than these benefits that cause smokers to continue smoking. Smokers are simply much less risk averse than nonsmokers. Contrary to popular belief, most smokers are acutely aware of the hazards of smoking. In fact, they tend to greatly overrate the risks of smoking. In one study, for example, smokers placed the risk of lung cancer at 38 percent, while a more realistic risk is lower than 10 percent (Blizzard, 2004b; Viscusi, 1992).

Whatever benefits smokers claim to enjoy from tobacco use, nonsmokers can still assert their right to be protected from harmful secondhand smoke. But smokers can claim their right to risk their own health by smoking. Faced with this conflict between smokers and nonsmokers, the government has so far tried to bring about a smoke-free society but one in which only smoking in public places is prohibited, not smoking per se.

A Global Perspective on Smoking

Since the 1960s smoking has become less and less prevalent in the United States, Western Europe, and other developed countries. By contrast, the prevalence of smoking has become increasingly higher in the developing countries of Africa, Asia, and Latin America as well as Eastern Europe. As a result, today, there are many more smokers in developing countries than in developed ones. A major reason for the rising prevalence of smoking in developing countries is the lack of laws that require warning smokers of the hazards of smoking, restrict tobacco advertising and promotion, and prohibit smoking at workplaces and public indoor areas. These are the kind of laws that have significantly reduced smoking in developed countries (Mackay and Eriksen, 2002).

During the second half of the last century the prevalence of smoking was higher in developed than in developing countries. Thus the incidence of death from smoking between 1980s and 2000s was higher in developed countries, but it began to decline in the beginning of the current century. Given the currently higher incidence of smoking in developing countries, smoking-related deaths are expected to become more prevalent in 30 years or so in those relatively poor countries (Peto and Lopez, 2001).

In both developed and developing countries, men are more likely than women to smoke. But the ratio of male to female smokers is much greater in developing countries, a reflection of the greater gender inequality in the Third World. But the prevalence of female smokers in these countries has increased rapidly, largely a result of the tobacco industry's efforts to promote smoking among women. Tobacco companies, for example, often advertise their products with the seductive images of female smokers being modern, sophisticated, emancipated, full of vitality, slim, and sexy. The companies also promote female smoking with special brands of cigarettes for women, which are long, slim, low tar, light-colored, or menthol.

All over the world, the overwhelming majority of smokers begin to light up before reaching adulthood. The most common factor in youthful smoking is peer pressure: Young people are likely to smoke if their friends smoke. Another factor is the popular view among youth of tobacco use as normal or "cool." Supporting these two factors are the tobacco industry's advertising and promotion, easy access to cigarettes, and relatively low prices (Mackay and Eriksen, 2002; Peto and Lopez, 2001).

Summary

1. How can illegal drug use be put in proper perspective? We should recognize that illegal drugs are not as widely used and dangerous as some legal drugs. Societal reaction to drugs varies with time and place. Moreover, illegal drugs are for the most part used moderately rather than uncontrollably.

2. What are the effects of various illegal drugs? As a stimulant, marijuana can produce euphoria, heighten sensitivity, improve perception, and increase appetite. It has even proved beneficial to the very ill. But if used to the point of intoxication, marijuana can impair judgment and memory. It is also addictive, and its users are more likely than nonusers to use hard drugs as well. As a depressant, heroin can soothe pain, anxiety, and tension—as well as produce what the user considers to be euphoria. It is highly addictive. Heroin addicts do not necessarily have their health or careers ruined by the drug, but they may suffer both effects if they are not socially privileged and financially successful. As a stimulant, cocaine sharpens the senses, provides exhilaration, enhances self-confidence, and boosts energy. It is also extremely addictive. Crack, the cheaper and smokable form of cocaine, is even more powerful and addictive. Meth and roofies are popular drugs, the former a stimulant and the latter a depressant. The latest popular drug is Ecstasy, which makes most of its users feel good and have a better perspective on life, despite government warnings that it is a dangerous drug.

3. What is the extent of drug use in the United States? The United States has the highest rate of drug use in the world, but most of the drug problems are confined to the lower classes. Drug use in U.S. society steadily declined from 1980s until 1992, when it began to rise among young whites smoking pot.

4. Why are intravenous drug users very likely to get AIDS? IV drug users are reluctant to take precautions by avoiding the sharing of needles. The reasons for such reluctance include an overwhelming need for immediate drug experience, the user's risk-taking lifestyle, and the bleakness and emptiness of life resulting from grinding poverty. **Does drug use cause crime?** The answer is yes according to drug enslavement theory, but no according to general deviance syndrome theory.

5. How is drug use related to socioeconomic status? Users of marijuana and powder cocaine are more likely to be relatively affluent, while users of heroin and crack cocaine are more likely to be poor. Users of meth and roofies seem largely working-class and young. Ecstasy users are mostly students and young professionals. **What is the social profile of illegal drug users?** Illegal drug users tend to be male and young, have drug-using parents and friends, and lack strong ties to social institutions.

6. How does a person become a drug user? There are four stages in the process of becoming an illegal drug user: experimentation, occasional use, regular use, and addiction. A user may go through all these stages until becoming an addict, or may stop at the first, second, or third stage. In Becker's classic study of pot smokers, the smoker characteristically learns three things in a sequential manner: how to get high on the drug, how to recognize the nature of the high, and how to enjoy the high.

7. What causes drug use and addiction? According to Currie's economic deprivation theory, severe poverty causes the victims to use drugs to fulfill their need for status, to cope with the oppressive realities of poverty, and to gain a sense of purpose in their shattered lives with the easy availability of drugs in their community. Lindesmith's cognitive association theory says that we can become addicted to heroin if we associate our withdrawal distress with our previous use of the drug. Finally, according to social psychological theory, both sociological and psychological factors are involved in drug use—the former exemplified by the legal drug culture and lack of social control, and the latter by poor self-concept and low self-esteem.

8. What is the nature of the war on drugs? The war on drugs consists of two basic strategies.

One is punitive, involving the use of law enforcement to stop the supply of drugs and punish drug sellers and users. The other strategy is supportive, involving the use of drug prevention or education to reduce the demand for drugs and the use of treatment to help drug addicts.

9. Why is OxyContin most popular with abusers of prescription drugs? When the drug is crushed and snorted, it can immediately deliver a powerful rush. But its popularity has created such a great demand that abusers commit fraud, burglary, and other crimes to get it. **What is the nature of smoking?** Although smoking can cause serious illnesses, at least 25 percent of Americans smoke regularly, primarily because they believe that the benefits of smoking outweigh the costs.

10. What is the situation of smoking in the world? In the second half of the last century, smoking was more prevalent in affluent countries than in poor countries. But today smoking is more common in poor countries due to the lack of laws that discourage tobacco use. In both affluent and poor countries, men are more likely than women to smoke and most smokers begin to light up at a young age.

FURTHER READING

Boyd, Susan C. 2004. *From Witches to Crack Moms: Women, Drug Law, and Policy.* Durham, N.C.: Carolina Academic Press. A study of how the drug war affects the daily lives of women who use drugs, making them out to be more deviant and immoral than their male peers.

Caulkins, Jonathan P., et al. 2005. *How Goes the "War on Drugs"? An Assessment of U.S. Drug Problems and Policy.* Santa Monica, Calif.: RAND. Analysis of the drug war with the conclusion that it has had a mixed record, with a modest decline in the use of cocaine but a substantial rise in marijuana use.

Cherry, Andrew, Mary E. Dillon, and Douglas Rugh (eds.). 2002. *Substance Abuse: A Global View.* Westport, Conn.: Greenwood. A series of articles discussing the problem of drug abuse in 13 countries.

Coombs, Robert Holman. 1997. *Drug-Impaired Professionals.* Cambridge, Mass.: Harvard University Press. An interview-based analysis of the nature and causes of drug addiction among doctors, lawyers, and other professionals.

Currie, Elliott. 1993. *Reckoning: Drugs, the Cities, and the American Future.* New York: Hill and Wang. An analysis of the drug problems in largely poor minority neighborhoods of large cities across the United States.

Dalrymple, Theodore. 2006. *Romancing Opiates.* New York: Encounter Books. A critical analysis of drug use with such observations that drug addicts usually appear in pain while seeing their therapist but cheerful in the presence of fellow addicts.

Early, Kevin E. (ed.). 1996. *Drug Treatment Behind Bars: Prison-Based Strategies for Change*. Westport, Conn.: Praeger. A collection of articles on the therapeutic communities in U.S. prisons.

Falco, Mathea. 1992. *The Making of a Drug-Free America: Programs That Work*. New York: Times Books. Showcasing effective programs on drug prevention, treatment, and law enforcement.

Gately, Iain. 2002. *Tobacco: The Story of How Tobacco Seduced the World*. New York: Grove. A readable and entertaining history of the weed, showing how it spread throughout the world and, in the process, influenced important global events such as the Atlantic slave trade, the American Revolution, and the opening of international trade.

Goldberg, Ted. 1999. *Demystifying Drugs: A Psychological Perspective*. New York: St. Martin's. Discusses how and why people use drugs as well as how the Swedish and Dutch societies deal with drug abuse.

Goode, Erich. 2005. *Drugs in American Society*, 6th ed. New York: McGraw-Hill. A comprehensive text on the subject, covering drug use in general, many specific drugs such as alcohol, marijuana, and cocaine, and theories of drug use.

Hawdon, James E. 2005. *Drug and Alcohol Consumption as Functions of Social Structures: A Cross-Cultural Sociology*. Lewiston, N.Y.: Edwin Mellen Press. An analysis of how and why drug use is more prevalent in modern, industrialized societies.

Kandel, Denise B. (ed.). 2002. *Stages and Pathways of Drug Involvement: Examining the Gateway Hypothesis*. Cambridge, UK: Cambridge University Press. An anthology of diverse articles presenting various theoretical and empirical analyses of the famous idea that the use of licit or less harmful drugs often leads to the use of harder or more dangerous drugs.

Massing, Michael. 1998. *The Fix*. New York: Simon & Schuster. An analysis of the U.S. drug problem with practical recommendations for treatment as opposed to law enforcement.

Roffman, Roger A., and Robert Stephens (eds.). 2006. *Cannabis Dependence: Its Nature, Consequences and Treatment*. Cambridge, U.K.: Cambridge University Press. A series of articles presenting various aspects of marijuana addiction including the signs and interventions of addiction and the arguments for prohibition or legalization of the drug.

South, Nigel (ed.). 1999. *Drugs: Cultures, Controls and Everyday Life*. Thousand Oaks, Calif.: Sage Publications. A collection of articles dealing with the cultural influences on drug use and various societies' efforts to control it.

Sussman, Steve, and Susan L. Ames. 2001. *The Social Psychology of Drug Abuse*. Philadelphia: Open University Press. A review of studies focusing on social and psychological factors in drug abuse.

Venturelli, Peter J. 1994. *Drug Use in America: Social, Cultural, and Political Perspectives*. Boston: Jones and Bartlett. An anthology of articles on drug use among youth, women, and minorities as well as on drug prevention and decriminalization.

CRITICAL THINKING QUESTIONS

1. If in fighting the war on drugs you had to choose between law enforcement and prevention/treatment, which would you opt for? Why?

2. Some smokers believe that in a free country people should be allowed to smoke even though smoking can kill them. Should smoking be allowed as long as the smoke doesn't get into nonsmokers' lungs? Or should it be banned? Defend your position.

Myths and Realities

Myth: Americans like to drink. They are among the heavy drinkers in the world.

Reality: Globally, Americans appear to be moderate drinkers, ranking neither among the heavy-drinking nations nor among the practically dry ones (p. 302).

Myth: Sex becomes more exciting after several drinks.

Reality: Since alcohol is a depressant rather than a stimulant, a drinker may find it more difficult to perform sexually even if he or she feels less inhibited (p. 303).

Myth: Alcohol usually diminishes the drinker's moral competence, causing the drinker to behave badly.

Reality: Alcohol by itself does not produce moral failings. It is the popular belief that it does, which, in the manner of a self-fulfilling prophecy, causes many people to show moral failings after a few drinks (p. 304).

_____

Myth: Black college students are as likely as their white peers to drink or drink heavily.

Reality: Black college students are much less likely than their white peers to use or abuse alcohol (p. 308).

_____

Myth: Americans of Italian or Chinese descent have one of the lowest rates of alcoholism in the United States because they rarely drink.

Reality: Those two ethnic groups do often drink but tend to avoid becoming alcoholic because drinking is associated with meals and is not meant for getting drunk (p. 309).

_____

Myth: Because their church prohibits the use of alcohol by the faithful, conservative Protestants such as Pentecostals and Southern Baptists have learned to avoid getting drunk.

Reality: There are more nondrinkers and fewer heavy drinkers among conservative Protestants than among liberal Protestants, but if they drink, the conservatives are more likely to end up becoming problem drinkers or alcoholics. One reason is that they have been brought up in a religion that preaches total abstinence from liquor so that they have not learned how to drink in moderation (p. 310).

_____

Myth: There are proportionately more drinkers and therefore more alcoholics in the lower social classes than in the higher classes.

Reality: There are proportionately fewer drinkers but more alcoholics in the lower classes. This may be explained by the fact that, unlike higher-class people who use alcohol positively to smooth social intercourse, lower-class persons tend to drink negatively as a futile attempt to drown personal sorrows or problems (p. 310).

_____

Myth: In the United States, the South has the highest level of alcohol consumption as well as the highest rate of drunkenness.

Reality: The South has the lowest level of alcohol consumption but the highest rate of drunkenness. The reason for the highest rate of drunkenness is having a higher proportion of religiously conservative and lower-class people (p. 311).

_____

Myth: Binge drinking on the U.S. campus has become more common today than in the past.

Reality: Binge drinking is relatively common on U.S. campuses but its incidence has remained the same today as before, while more students abstain from drinking today than before (p. 315).

_____

Myth: The law that raised the minimum drinking age to 21 has helped to reduce risky teen drinking such as binge drinking or alcohol poisoning.

Reality: The drinking-age law has significantly contributed to binge drinking among teenagers by encouraging them to "pregame" or "frontload" in private before attending a public event and also by challenging them to drink to prove their adulthood (p. 324).

_____

On a typical American campus, serious weekend partying begins on Friday. Asked after midnight, "Why do you drink so much?" most students give a succinct answer. "Stress!" says a business major outside a bar. Watched by a bored bouncer, he staggers away. . . . "Stress," whispers a female student as she leans against a wall to avoid falling. Nearby are two bull-necked young men, one wearing a T-shirt with the slogan "Take Me Drunk, I'm Home" and the other's stating, "From Zero to Horny in 2.5 Beers." They lift up the disoriented and giggling young woman by the ankles over a beer keg. Hanging upside down, she seizes its plastic hose and begins to gulp. . . . "Outrageous, awesome, major stress," says a third student outside a club, helping her too-drunk-to-walk friend get into a car. The friend, hair soaked with beer, promptly hangs out the window, hiccuping for a few seconds and then vomiting. All these students engage in what is called binge drinking, which began to appear on many campuses in the late 1980s but still continues in full force today (Seaman, 2005; Matthews, 1993).

Binge drinking is often defined by researchers as the consumption of five or more consecutive drinks for men and four or more for women. According to a national survey, about 44 percent of the students binge at least once within a two-week period (Wechsler et al., 2002). Stress is a contributing factor as most binge-drinking students believe, but other factors are also involved. In this chapter we will discuss those factors along with other facets of drinking and alcoholism.

The Extent of Drinking and Alcoholism

Despite the prevalence of binge drinking on college campuses, most Americans do not become alcoholics, who by definition have lost control over drinking and consequently have problems with health, work, or personal relationships. Only about 6 percent of U.S. adults are alcoholics. About 63 percent drink alcoholic beverages such as liquor, wine, or beer. These are moderate drinkers, among whom the men consume no more than two drinks a day and the women no more than one drink. And a large minority, 37 percent of the adult population, are teetotalers, who completely abstain from drinking (Blizzard, 2004a; SAMHSA, 2002). Globally, Americans also appear to be moderate drinkers, ranking neither among the heavy-drinking nations nor among the practically dry ones. This pattern of moderate drinking has become more popular since the early 1980s. Since that time, moreover, abstinence has increased and heavy drinking has declined, chiefly because of rising health consciousness and caution about the hazards of drinking and driving (Ahlstrom and Osterberg, 2005; Chase, 1996b).

Still, alcohol is far more widely used than all illegal drugs, and its abuse is the most widespread of all drug abuses. Alcoholism is also one of our nation's biggest health problems, surpassed only by heart disease and cancer, and drunk driving is the number one cause of death among young people (ages 16 to 24). The economic cost of alcohol problems is enormous, as much as $90 billion a year in reduced industrial production, illness, and traffic accidents (Rivara et al., 2004; Brake, 1994; Heien and Pittman, 1993).

Myths about Alcohol Abuse

Though prevalent and serious, alcohol problems do not seem to shock the general public. If we, as hosts or hostesses, continually invite our guests to have another drink, we are not considered dope pushers at all. Most important, beer and liquor commercials vie with one another in pushing the drug on a massive audience. It is little wonder that only a small minority of Americans see alcohol use and abuse as a serious problem; most would rather consider the use of other drugs—marijuana, cocaine, and heroin—a serious problem. From this lack of public concern about drinking, there have emerged a number of misconceptions about alcohol and its abuse. Although some of the popular beliefs (e.g., "Drinking on an empty stomach can get you drunk fast") are indeed correct, many are false.

One commonly held notion is the myth that most alcoholics, who have long been disparaged as "skid-row bums," are homeless. The fact is that homeless alcoholics constitute only a very small minority—less than 5 percent—of the entire alcoholic population in the United States. The overwhelming majority of alcoholics are ordinary people who live with their families.

A second, widely believed idea is that mixing different kinds of alcoholic drinks can make a person drunk faster. Actually, it is not the mixture of different drinks, but the total amount of alcohol consumed and the length of time taken to consume it that determine the speed of intoxication.

A third belief held by many people is that drinking black coffee or dousing one's head with cold water can sober one up. In fact, there is no effective method for getting over intoxication other than waiting for the alcohol to leave the body—with the length of the waiting period depending on the percentage of alcohol in the bloodstream.

A fourth popular misconception is that drinking only beer is unlikely to make one an alcoholic. The truth is that beer drinkers are more likely to become alcoholics when compared with drinkers of gin, Scotch, or any other kind of alcoholic beverage. Perhaps because beer is less potent than the other drinks, people tend to drink it for hours on end, and extended, heavy drinking is very likely to lead to alcoholism.

According to a fifth—and seductive—myth, sex becomes more exciting after several drinks. However, since alcohol is a depressant rather than a stimulant of the central nervous system, a drinker may find it more difficult to perform sexually even if he or she feels less inhibited. As Shakespeare writes in *Macbeth,* drinking "provokes the desire, but it takes away the performance." A common problem with heavy drinking for men is loss of erections, particularly among the middle-aged. Also, a drunk man trying to arouse his partner sensitively is like a gorilla trying to play a violin (Hammond and Jorgensen, 1981).

What Alcohol Does to Its Users

Ever since Stone Age people became intoxicated from drinking the liquid oozing from fruit left too long in a warm place, alcohol has been bringing both joy and grief to humankind. Today, for example, most Americans who drink do get a great deal of enjoyment from it, but some end up getting misery from it by becoming alcoholics. Alcohol plays a significant role in holy ceremonies, making people feel religious, but it also has a hand in most cases of murder and aggravated assault. These conflicting effects of alcohol have spawned conflicting ideas in the folk wisdom about alcohol. For example, one Chinese proverb says that "Three glasses of wine can set everything right," yet another states that "Medicine may heal imaginary sickness but wine can never dispel real sorrow." In the Bible we are told that "Wine maketh glad the heart of man," but we are also warned that "Wine is a mocker, strong drink is raging" (Fort, 1973). What exactly does alcohol do to or for its users? Let's take a closer look.

Mental and Physical Impact

Alcohol is a drug since it affects our mental and physical activity. Although it is not a stimulant, alcohol is popularly thought of as one. A stimulant increases the functional activity of the body and mind. But alcohol is a depressant; it belongs to the same class of drugs as anesthetics, sedatives, and narcotics. As a depressant, alcohol reduces our mental and bodily functioning.

> At the sensorimotor level . . . alcohol is an incompetence producer. Its effects on the drinker's equilibrium, for instance, may result in his stumbling, bumping into things, knocking them over, falling down. . . . In addition, things may be dropped or otherwise broken, judgments of time and distance may be thrown askew, tasks may be poorly executed. . . . What is more, we all know that when a person is drunk, these sorts of alcohol-produced failings are both unintentional and beyond the drinker's power to overcome by sheer volition. (MacAndrew and Edgerton, 1969)

Alcohol, then, greatly reduces the drinker's sensorimotor skill—that is, mental and physical functional activity. By itself, however, alcohol does not diminish the drinker's moral competence (Graham et al., 1979; MacAndrew and Edgerton, 1969). It does not, for example, cause people to insult their friends or to make an unwelcome pass at a member of the opposite sex. But the general public believes that alcohol produces moral failings. This popular belief, in the manner of a self-fulfilling prophecy, is so strong that many people in our society do indeed show moral failings after a few drinks. When sober again, they insist that alcohol has made them behave badly, thereby exculpating themselves, with the support of the general public.

Knowing that they will not be condemned for their immoral behavior while drunk, many men in our society often try to get themselves and their women friends drunk. But not all achieve their goal. Some are able to get drunk enough to feel uninhibited; others may get too sick or too drowsy to do or feel anything. This is because one group is more, or less, intoxicated than the other. What is it that determines the different degrees of intoxication? A number of factors:

1. A small-sized person may become intoxicated after drinking only one beer, but a large-sized person may stay sober after three or four. Because alcohol is diluted in the bloodstream, a 100-pound woman cannot tolerate as much liquor as a 200-pound man.
2. The higher the percentage of alcohol in a beverage, the quicker the intoxicating effect. Thus a 90-proof whiskey (containing 45 percent alcohol) is more powerful

than a 6-proof beer (containing 3 percent alcohol). Obviously, the greater the amount of alcohol consumed, the more potent the intoxicating effect.

3. Alcohol is not digested as food; it goes through the walls of the stomach and small intestine and is absorbed directly into the bloodstream. So food in the stomach can retard absorption of alcohol and weaken its intoxicating impact; on the other hand, drinking on an empty stomach will result in quick absorption and quicker intoxication.

4. An individual with a higher level of tolerance for alcohol—through more frequent, heavier drinking—will become less intoxicated than one with lower tolerance if both consume the same amount of alcohol.

Health Effects

A small intake of alcohol can be socially, psychologically, and even physically beneficial. Studies have shown, for example, that occasional or moderate drinking helps rural whites alleviate the tension and pressure of their harsh lives. The aged residents of nursing homes who drink alcoholic beverages moderately also enjoy improved sleep, heightened morale, and general well-being. Moreover, moderate drinkers are generally healthier, live longer, or have lower death rates than abstainers. Moderate drinkers are also much less likely than teetotalers to suffer from heart disease. But the fact that a little bit is good does not mean that a lot would be better. The key, encouraging word here is *moderate,* which, as we have mentioned, means having two drinks a day for men and one drink a day for women. If men and women consume more, they are likely to harm their health in various ways (Underwood, 2005; Burros, 1996).

The most common damage done to the body by immoderate, heavy drinking involves the liver. The constant intake of alcohol, coupled with malnutrition common among problem drinkers, can destroy liver cells and thereby cause fat to accumulate in the liver. The resulting scarred and fatty liver—a condition called *cirrhosis* of the liver—is a major cause of serious illness and premature death in heavy drinkers. Cirrhosis can also lead to sexual impotence. Although at least 60 percent of all cirrhotics who have stopped drinking recover from the disease within five years, their sexual impotence persists (Andreasen and Black, 2001).

Heavy drinking is also likely to cause heart disease and strokes. For one thing, heavy drinkers tend to have clogged blood vessels in the heart and thus suffer from *coronary heart attacks* more often than moderate drinkers. In addition, they are likely to suffer from *cardiomyopathy,* which involves the weakening of the heart muscle, or *hemorrhagic strokes,* which occur when a blood vessel in the brain leaks or ruptures (Mukamal and Rimm, 2001).

When combined with heavy smoking, heavy drinking further increases the risk of developing cancer of the mouth, throat, and other areas of the body that are frequently assaulted by alcohol. The causal impact of alcohol abuse on these cancers seems more indirect than direct: (1) Alcohol acts as an irritant to the tissues of mouth, throat, and other related organs, thereby making them more vulnerable to *carcinogens* (cancer-causing agents) that invade them. (2) Some alcoholic beverages carry their own carcinogens. (3) Poor diet in the heavy drinker facilitates the work of these carcinogens. And

(4) the heavy use of alcohol enhances the cancer-causing impact of smoking (Bagnardi et al., 2001).

Finally, heavy use of alcohol can cause a whole array of other health problems, such as:

- Impaired memory and ability to learn
- Premature aging, with neuropsychological performance more characteristic of much older persons
- Fetal alcohol syndrome, characterized by damage to the fetus's central nervous system, small infant weight and size, and various birth defects (Stark, 1987; Miller, 1986).

Social Consequences

Moderate drinking can bring social benefits, such as sociability and hospitality or relaxation and recreation with others, but excessive use of alcohol helps bring about a number of negative social consequences. One is a relatively high rate of *automobile accidents,* the leading cause of death among young people in the United States. Over half of each year's automobile deaths and injuries can be traced to excessive drinking. As the National Institute on Alcohol Abuse and Alcoholism (NIAAA) has found, "Most people killed in traffic accidents after drinking . . . have very high blood alcohol concentration, averaging twice the level of alcohol considered legally impairing" (NIAAA, 1983). A certain group of young people are especially likely to get involved in auto accidents and deaths. Compared with their peers, they are not just more likely to drink excessively but to use illicit drugs, violate various traffic laws, enjoy taking risks, and exhibit aggressiveness or hostility toward others (Donovan, 1993).

Another consequence is a high rate of *criminal offenses.* Offenses directly related to drinking include public drunkenness, driving while intoxicated, disorderly conduct, vagrancy, and violation of liquor laws. Such offenses result in so many arrests that they put a severe strain on the operation of the criminal justice system. Since 1970, many treatment programs for problem drinkers have helped reduce the number of arrests for alcohol-related offenses, but such offenses still constitute the largest arrest category today (U.S. Census Bureau, 2008). The majority (over 90 percent) of the crimes committed by students on college campuses are also alcohol-related. The perpetrators usually commit multiple crimes, including vandalism, fighting, theft, and alcohol violations. They are more likely than other students to have low grade-point averages, to be athletes, and to drink heavily (Engs and Hanson, 1994; Towson State, 1993).

Heavy drinking further plays a significant part, albeit indirectly, in the commission of more serious, violent crimes, such as homicide, aggravated assault, and forcible rape. As Figure 12.1 indicates, alcohol is implicated in 42 percent of all violent crimes in the United States. Those who commit these crimes seem to use alcohol as an excuse for expressing their aggression. Alcohol can thus become dynamite in the hands of an aggressive person. In one experimental study, subjects with a history of arguments and other aggressive acts were more likely to get involved in interpersonal aggression after they had done some heavy drinking (Boyatzis, 1975).

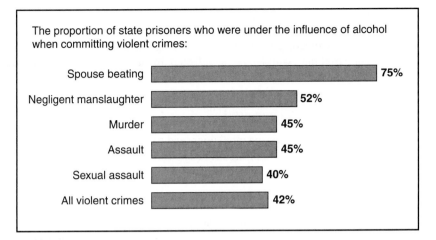

The proportion of state prisoners who were under the influence of alcohol when committing violent crimes:

Spouse beating	75%
Negligent manslaughter	52%
Murder	45%
Assault	45%
Sexual assault	40%
All violent crimes	42%

FIGURE 12.1   Alcohol and Violent Crimes

Source: U.S. Department of Justice, Bureau of Justice Statistics, 1999, 2004.

Social Factors in Drinking

Some Americans are more likely than others to use or abuse alcohol. The difference lies in a number of social factors, such as gender and age, racial and ethnic background, religious affiliation, socioeconomic status, and regional location.

Gender and Age

Drinking is a characteristically male activity. Compared with women, men are not only more likely to drink but also more likely to consume more when they drink and far more likely to get into trouble with drinking. It has been estimated that men are at least four times more likely than women to become alcoholic. But this gender difference has been narrowing over the years, as women have been achieving more equality in various aspects of life. According to many studies, over the last 30 years a significant increase in drinking as well as drinking problems has occurred among college women. The researchers attribute this finding to the women's greater career pressures, their stronger desire for achieving gender equality by behaving like "one of the boys,"and declining social stigma about women getting drunk. Nevertheless, men still drink more and have more alcohol problems than women (Blizzard, 2004a; Rowe, 1995; Gross, 1993; Hanson and Engs, 1992).

One reason for the gender difference is that drinking and drunkenness are more socially acceptable for males than for females. Another reason is that, as a result of gender-role socialization men are more concerned with their masculinity, such as their need for dominance and emotional control, which is further reinforced by the peer pressure to "drink like a man" (Carey, 1993). Research has indeed shown a strong link between masculine concerns and alcohol use or abuse (Huselid and Cooper, 1992).

Apparently more concerned with their masculinity than older men, young men are more likely to drink and to do so heavily. But the age difference in alcohol consumption among women is not as great as that among men, because women are generally uninterested in being masculine. Younger women, though, are still significantly prone to drink more than older women. This suggests that the age factor can have its own, independent influence on drinking, without being affected by the gender factor (Blizzard, 2004a; Breslow and Smothers, 2004; Hanson, 1995).

Racial and Ethnic Background

Americans of different races and ethnicities tend to have different rates of alcohol use and abuse. Apparently, the culture of the countries from which their ancestors came continues to influence the drinking pattern of today's Americans.

African Americans.   Compared with whites as a broad group, African Americans are less likely to drink but significantly more likely to become alcoholics. Moreover, as they get older, African American heavy drinkers are more likely than their white peers to continue drinking heavily (Nielsen, 1999). Thus, as a group, African Americans suffer from a higher rate of alcohol-related diseases, such as alcohol fatty liver, hepatitis, liver cirrhosis, and esophageal cancer (Herd, 1991). This is largely because African Americans have a much higher rate of poverty—and many studies have indeed indicated a strong link between poverty and drinking problems. The alcoholism among poor African Americans can be said to reflect a futile attempt to use alcohol "as a mechanism to escape the stresses of poverty, discrimination, and deprivation" (Neff and Husaini, 1985). Poor blacks, some research suggests, are more likely to abuse alcohol because poverty has caused them to have low self-esteem and little racial pride (Harper and Saifnoorian, 1991). By contrast, middle- and upper-class blacks have higher self-esteem and greater racial pride, which enables them to benefit from traditional Afrocentric values of kinship and spirituality that discourage alcohol abuse. Not surprisingly, many studies have found black college students, who come mostly from the higher social classes, to be much less likely to use and abuse alcohol than even their white peers, let alone poor blacks (Peralta, 2005; Hanson, 1995; Herd, 1991).

Hispanic Americans.   Like African Americans, Hispanic Americans are also more likely than Anglos to drink heavily. This has long been attributed to the Hispanic value of machismo, which emphasizes the importance of masculinity in the form of male dominance, toughness, and honor. But, according to more recent research, machismo does not affect heavy drinking among Hispanics: Hispanics who drink heavily show no greater interest in machismo when compared with those who drink in moderation. Ironically, though, machismo affects heavy drinking among Anglos (Neff et al., 1991). Apparently, in Hispanic culture, men are not expected to prove their machismo through heavy drinking but rather through some other means, such as exhibiting physical courage or sexual prowess. The social expectation for men to prove their manhood through heavy drinking appears instead to be a part of the Anglo culture. A more credible explanation for the higher rate of drinking problems among Hispanics is their higher rate of poverty. Generally, more successful Hispanic groups, such as Cubans and Dominicans, are less likely than others, such as Puerto Ricans and Guatemalans, to abuse alcohol (Hanson, 1995).

Native Americans. Compared with African and Hispanic Americans, Native Americans have more serious problems with alcohol. They suffer from higher rates of such problems as alcoholic cirrhosis, arrests for public drunkenness, and alcohol-related accidental deaths. These problems have been attributed to sociocultural factors, particularly the fact that the life of Native Americans as a poor minority is filled with stress, while the traditional culture that provides them with a sense of pride and dignity has been diminished or destroyed through long years of colonization by Europeans and other immigrants (Schaefer, 1981). However, it is doubtful that the same alcohol problems plague all of the Native American tribes, who, after all, number over 300. While Native Americans as a group have more drinking problems than other Americans, some tribes do have few problems and others have many. Generally, tribes with "an individualistic hunting-gathering tradition" have a higher incidence of alcohol abuse than tribes with "an agricultural tradition stressing communal values and ceremonies" (Hanson, 1995).

Irish Americans. Irish Americans have one of the highest rates of alcoholism in U.S. society. A major reason can be traced to the traditional Irish culture, which accepts heavy drinking as normal and treats the drunk as a lovable person:

> [In Ireland] drunkenness . . . is laughable, pleasurable, somewhat exciting, a punctuation of dull routine to be watched and applauded, and drunken men are handled with care and affection. The drunkard is handled with maternal affection, often referred to as "the poor boy," with a special connotation of sympathy, love, pity, and sorrow. If married, the drunkard is compassionately classed by his wife with "the min, God help us!" The man who is drunk is sometimes regarded with envy by the man who is sober. (Bales, 1962)

Italian and Chinese Americans. Americans of Italian or Chinese ancestry have one of the lowest rates of alcoholism, although they often drink. This is largely because Italian Americans usually drink with meals, do not encourage solitary drinking as a means of drowning sorrows, and have strong sanctions against drunkenness. Similarly, Chinese Americans drink a lot but are relatively free from alcoholism. Like the Italians, the Chinese usually drink with meals, particularly on such special occasions as family ceremonies (births, weddings, rites for the dead) and national and religious celebrations. The Chinese do not think of drunken behavior as funny or comical. They look at it with contempt because they believe that drunkenness can seriously disrupt interpersonal relationships and that only moderate, controlled drinking is a social lubricant (Hanson, 1995).

Religious Affiliation

American Jews start drinking at a very young age, but they have one of the lowest rates of alcohol problems. This has been the case for many years and is still true today. The reason has long been assumed to be the culture of Orthodox Judaism—more specifically, the fact that Jews use wine only for religious rituals and consider it sacrilegious to use the alcohol to get drunk. But sociologist Barry Glassner (1991) finds that Orthodox Judaism cannot fully explain the persistent low rate of drinking problems among Jews. Many Jews today are no longer very religious; instead, they are nominal, nonpracticing, or inactive Jews, who do not go to the synagogue or keep kosher. Instead, there are four factors that reinforce each other in protecting Jews against alcoholism.

One is the widespread belief among Jews that excessive drinking is a non-Jewish characteristic, while *moderate drinking is a Jewish trait*. Jews often use the Yiddish expression *shikker vie a goy* (drunk as a Gentile) and feel that it is not Jewish to get drunk. A second factor that protects Jews against alcoholism is the practice of *moderate drinking since childhood*. They have as children had many opportunities to learn to associate drinking with special positive events, such as religious services, weddings, or dinners. On such occasions, controlled drinking is expected, and excessive drinking is condemned. A third factor is the support for moderate drinking and disapproval of excessive drinking that Jews receive from *their peers*. This kind of peer support and pressure is effective in insulating Jews from alcohol abuse because most of their friends are Jewish. A fourth factor is the Jews' *conscious attempts to avoid excessive drinking* even under social pressures—from non-Jews—to do otherwise. If they are encouraged by non-Jews to drink more than they wish, Jews will often simply say no or will take a few sips rather than gulp down the whole drink (Glassner, 1991).

Conservative Protestants such as Pentecostals and Southern Baptists prohibit the use of alcohol by the faithful. Thus, they have the largest proportion of nondrinkers and the smallest proportion of heavy drinkers when compared with Catholics and liberal Protestants. But if they drink, conservative Protestants are more likely to end up being problem drinkers. One explanation is that conservative Protestants, having been brought up in a religion that preaches total abstinence from liquor, have not learned how to drink in moderation. Another explanation is that the drinking problem of conservative Protestants who drink is merely a part of their overall pattern of deviation from their religious training. Thus, whatever causes their larger pattern of deviance, such as broken homes or joblessness, also causes their alcohol abuse (Galen and Rogers, 2004; Orcutt, 1991).

Socioeconomic Status

Proportionately more people of the higher socioeconomic levels drink when compared with those of the lower levels. Yet there are more problem drinkers and alcoholics from the lower classes. There may be two explanations for this paradoxical finding. One is that drinkers of different classes use alcohol for different purposes. Drinkers of higher social classes seem more likely to use alcohol *positively* as a means to smooth social intercourse, but lower-class drinkers tend more to drink *negatively* as a futile attempt to drown personal sorrows or problems. This may explain why, when drinking, lower-class persons drink significantly more and faster than higher-class persons (Hunter, Hannon, and Marchi, 1982). It is apparent that a large consumption of alcohol can make the lower-class drinkers lose self-control, which in turn makes it harder to solve problems. They may in consequence keep drinking to attempt to achieve a goal that gets progressively harder to achieve the more they drink. Another explanation is that there may in fact be no real difference in alcoholism between the higher and lower classes. Lower-class people may only *appear* more prone to alcoholism because they are not as successful as the higher classes in hiding problem drinking.

The first explanation appears more convincing because the lower classes do have a greater number of distressful life experiences that are associated with drinking problems.

Such experiences include family breakdown (marital violence, separation, or divorce) and job loss. Research has consistently found that people with these kinds of experiences suffer from higher rates of alcoholism than those without (Mulia et al., 2008; Catalano et al., 1993).

Regional Location

Alcohol consumption is highest in the Northeast, lowest in the South, and intermediate in the Midwest and West (see Figure 12.2). The states that have higher rates of alcohol use are generally more urbanized, which suggests that cities and suburbs have proportionately more drinkers than rural areas and small towns. One explanation for the greater consumption of alcohol in more urbanized regions attributes it to the greater stresses and strains of urban life. Another explanation is that regions with higher rates of alcohol use probably have more favorable attitudes toward alcohol, fewer legal restrictions, and weaker traditions of temperance or prohibition against alcohol.

While the South has the lowest level of alcohol consumption, it has the highest rate of drunkenness. In fact, compared with other regions, the South has higher rates of alcoholism and alcohol-related fights, accidents, and problems with work, the police, spouses, and friends (Hilton, 1991). In other words, Southerners are less likely than others to drink, but if they do drink, they are more likely to become problem drinkers. This apparent contradiction between less alcohol consumption and more problem drinking in the South should not be surprising. It is analogous to what we have observed in regard to the religiously conservative and the lower-class, who are less likely than others to drink but, if drinking, are more likely to abuse alcohol. The reasons given earlier are (1) the failure to learn moderate drinking in the case of the religiously conservative and (2) the use of alcohol as a futile attempt to solve personal problems in the case of the lower-class. What about the reason for the higher rate of drinking problems in the South? The reason is having a higher proportion of religiously conservative and lower-class people than other regions.

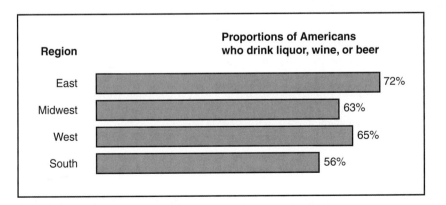

FIGURE 12.2   Prevalence of Drinking by Regions

Source: The Gallup Poll Tuesday Briefing, August 24, 2004.

A Global Perspective on Drinking

Throughout the world, liquor and beer have, over the last quarter century, become much more popular while wine has gotten less so. The consumption of alcoholic beverages as a whole, however, varies from one society to another. Generally, more affluent societies consume greater quantities of alcohol than do poorer societies. The prosperous Western European and North American societies, for example, consume more alcohol than the less economically developed countries in Southeast Asia and in the Middle East. Among prosperous countries, though, France, Germany, and Britain consume more alcohol than do the United States and Canada. Drinking even more than the Europeans are the Russians, who consume the most alcohol in the world (Ahlstrom and Osterberg, 2005; Rehm et al., 2003).

The Russians have been beset with the habit of heavy drinking since they invented vodka, their favorite liquor, 500 years ago. The key reason is apparently the benefits the Russian drinker can obtain from vodka. As a Russian writer explains, "Vodka has provided access to a private life that is closed to the state, a place where it is possible to relax, to forget your troubles, to engage in sex with the illusion of free choice." Heavy drinking has gotten worse since the dissolution of the Soviet Union in the early 1990s, which has brought along severe social and economic problems. Unemployment or poverty has hit more people, the income of the employed has fallen, the prices of goods and services have gone up, and thieves and killers have proliferated. These problems in turn make social life less active. In the past, people often visited friends, patronized cafés and restaurants, went to the movies, attended sports events, or participated in some other social activities. But nowadays people tend to stay home and get drunk (Jukkala et al., 2008; Erofeyev, 2002; Levin, Jones, and Braithwaite, 1998).

In Russia as well as in other countries where the prevalence of drinking is high, the gender difference in drinking is relatively small, with the percentage of male drinkers only slightly exceeding that of female drinkers. But in Islamic countries, which prohibit alcohol use, or in Southeast Asian countries, which are relatively traditional, drinking is almost entirely confined to men, so that drinking by women appears extremely rare (Bloomfield et al., 2006; Rehm et al., 2003).

As the traditional Asian countries become increasingly prosperous, their prevalence of drinking is expected to rise. India and China, the world's most populous countries, are already showing an increase in drinking. Another significant trend is the rising incidence of young people in Europe switching from light or moderate drinking with meals to heavy drinking without meals. This problem can be attributed to the alcohol industry's aggressive marketing to the European youth. After all, liquor and beer companies often promote youthful drinking by sponsoring fun events and putting their banners on Web pages. Young people are thus led to believe that alcohol use is indispensable to recreation, fun, and partying (Hagmann, 2001).

What Is Alcoholism?

There is no universally accepted definition of alcoholism. The most popular definition was offered by the World Health Organization in 1952: "Alcoholics are those excessive drinkers whose dependence upon alcohol has attained such a degree that it shows . . . an interference with their bodily and mental health, their interpersonal relations, and their smooth social and economic functioning" (Cahalan, 1970). This elaborate definition can be boiled down to a shorter sentence like the one offered more recently by psychiatrist Donald Goodwin (1991): "Alcoholism involves a compulsion to drink, causing damage to self and others." Thus alcoholics can be identified on the basis of certain problems that they have as a result of drinking. But those just given in the two definitions are too broad, not specific enough. In a 1991 report from the National Institute on Alcohol Abuse and Alcoholism (NIAAA), specific problems are presented in the form of 33 statements, of which 10 are presented here:

1. I have often taken a drink the first thing when I get up in the morning.
2. I deliberately tried to cut down or quit drinking but was unable to do so.
3. Once I started drinking it was difficult for me to stop before I became completely intoxicated.
4. I have had a quick drink when no one was looking.
5. I have skipped a number of regular meals while drinking.
6. I have awakened the next day not being able to remember some of the things I had done while drinking.
7. I have lost a job, or nearly lost one, because of my drinking.
8. My drinking contributed to getting hurt in an accident (in a car or elsewhere).
9. A physician suggested I cut down on drinking.
10. I have stayed away from work or gone to work late because of a hangover.

According to NIAAA, if a person says yes to at least one of those statements, that person may be identified as an alcoholic. But there is no certainty that a person having any one of these problems is necessarily an alcoholic. Consider the implication of statement 10. Many college students have occasionally stayed away from class because of a hangover from having drunk too much at a party the night before, but they are not necessarily alcoholics, because such experience has occurred only once or twice rather than repeatedly. It is safe to say, however, that the more of the listed problems people have, the more likely they are alcoholics. The problems can be classified into four types (Schuckit, 1984):

1. *Excessive drinking* over an extended period.
2. *Psychological addiction,* an irresistible craving for alcohol.
3. *Physical addiction,* experiencing physical discomfort when drinking stops.
4. *Alcohol-related problems,* such as divorce, car accident, or inability to work because of uncontrolled drinking.

Once a person is identified as an alcoholic, social scientists may still disagree on how to label the alcoholic's problem. Some label it *alcoholism* because they consider it a disease, but others call it *problem drinking* because they see it as a behavior. Still others simply regard alcoholism as chronic drinking, more serious than problem drinking. For our purposes, we use interchangeably various labels, including not only alcoholism and problem drinking but also abusive drinking, uncontrolled drinking, and alcohol abuse. But no matter what label we use, it is intended to mean having those four problems.

Becoming an Alcoholic

When people take a drink for the first time in their lives, they do not immediately, nor inevitably, become alcoholics (Hasin, Grant, and Endicott, 1990). They usually go through a sequence of events that may culminate in being totally dependent on alcohol. That sequence, according to E. M. Jellinek (1952), the influential pioneer in the study of alcoholism, consists of four stages.

Social Drinker

In the first, prealcoholic stage, prospective alcoholics *begin as social drinkers*. Through drinking, they discover their ability to experience some relief from tensions (Orcutt, 1993). But the more they drink, the less their tolerance for tensions; the less their tolerance for tensions, the more they want to drink to seek relief. This results in a vicious circle of more and more episodes of drunkenness and hangover. At the same time, the more individuals drink, the greater their tolerance for alcohol, so that they have to consume more and more alcohol to get drunk. These experiences increase the psychological and physiological impact of alcohol on the drinker. But people in this stage can still control their drinking so that they can continue to function normally in their occupational and social world.

Psychologically Addicted

In this second stage, social drinkers begin to show signs of abusing alcohol if they start to experience blackouts. A *blackout* is an attack of amnesia or memory loss, but it is quite different from passing out. When people drink beyond their alcohol-tolerance level, they may pass out on the spot, totally incapable of interacting with others. On the other hand, individuals experiencing blackouts may be the life of the party, or at least talk with others and move about freely; but the next day they cannot remember what they did.

By now they have become *psychologically addicted* to alcohol, having a strong craving for the drug. The craving is so great that they will drink a lot, drink alone, and drink in the morning. Such excessive drinking begins to hurt their relations with relatives, friends, and fellow workers, and they may feel guilty about drinking too much. Still, they feel they could not help having the strong attraction to alcohol. But they still can stop abusing alcohol if they are determined to do so.

Physically Addicted

In this third stage, the drinkers become *physically addicted* in the sense of having chills, shakes, and other withdrawal distresses when not drinking. By now they could not stop drinking even if they wanted to, because they have lost control over drinking. Therefore, once they start drinking, they tend to keep doing so until the supply is gone or they are too drunk to continue. Although they cannot control their drinking, they typically insist that they can stop if they really want to. To prove that they can, they will go on the wagon for a while or change their drinking patterns—switching types of liquor, trying different ways of mixing it, and altering speeds of consuming it.

But the more these drinkers think they can control their drinking—and the more they try to control it—the more they lose control. Consequently, they begin to invent excuses and rationalizations for drinking. They may, for example, blame their spouses or bosses for causing so much tension that they need to drink for relief. The drinking can break up their relations to bosses, friends, and family. This makes them become even more attached to liquor, and, as a result, they often skip meals in favor of liquor. They are nonetheless still capable of being gregarious and sociable (Morey, Skinner, and Blashfield, 1984).

Hitting Bottom

In this last stage, the alcoholic becomes isolated and withdrawn from others. They now *hit bottom* with total dependence on alcohol, exhibiting spectacular, bizarre behavior. A typical example is drinking and being intoxicated continuously for several days without doing anything else. They are haunted by the tremendous fear that alcohol may be taken away from them. They must have a drink just to be able to get up in the morning. They may be so far gone that to get liquor into their mouths becomes an almost impossible task to perform. But they usually work very hard at it—spending hours stumbling, crawling, vomiting, trembling, and failing to achieve the goal three or four times before finally succeeding in keeping a drink down. Since they rarely eat, they often suffer from malnutrition. They also suffer from delirium tremens, which can produce terrifying hallucinations—such as seeing millions of little flies chasing, suffocating, or eating them.

College Students and Alcohol

Since the late 1980s, many college students have hit the bottle with reckless abandon while an increasing number have abstained from alcohol. As we have suggested at the beginning of this chapter, those alcohol abusers are binge drinkers, men who gulp down five or more drinks in a row and women who put away four or more. What kind of students are these bingers? What has made them go on a binge in the first place?

Binge Drinking in College

Most college students (nearly 56 percent) drink in moderation or abstain from alcohol. In fact, more students today abstain than did in the early 1990s. But over the same period, the relatively high incidence of binge drinking has remained constant. Some 44.4 percent of students engaged in binge drinking in 2001; 44 percent did in 1993. Compared with moderate drinkers and abstainers, binge drinkers are more likely to run into trouble with the police, injure themselves or others, have academic and interpersonal problems, and ride in cars with drivers who are drunk or high. Binge drinkers also cause "secondhand effects" on others, with the latter having their study or sleep interrupted, being forced to take care of drunken students, and getting insulted or humiliated (Seaman, 2005; Wechsler et al., 2002).

Binge drinking started to become a serious problem on many campuses in the late 1980s, about the same time the legal drinking age was raised to 21 throughout the country. Before the enactment of this drinking age law, drinking took place in the open, where it could be supervised by police, security guards, and even health-care workers. After the drinking age went up, drinking did not stop. It simply moved underground to homes, cars, and frat-house basements where, hidden from adults and authorities, it could get out of hand and lead to binge drinking.

More important, most students today have not learned and practiced moderate drinking as their peers did before students under 21 were legally denied access to liquor. When all students were allowed to drink, they learned to do so responsibly at college-sponsored events, where alcoholic beverages were served. They also learned to drink in moderation at the homes of professors who invited them to dinners and receptions. But this kind of drinking experience is no longer available to students. So, Jack Hitt (1999) was able to quip: "Why do college students drink so stupidly? Because drinking intelligently is against the law." Since it is unlawful for most students to drink even moderately, over the last decade college administrators have tried to combat binge drinking with alcohol-free festivals and rock concerts, no-drinking dorms, abstinent fraternities, and the like. The emphasis is on abstinence. But binge drinking remains as prevalent as before (Wechsler et al., 2002).

At a few schools, though, significant headway has been made against binge drinking. In 1996 sociologist Wesley Perkins of Hobart and William Smith Colleges in New York discovered from a survey at his school that students *believed* their peers to be drinking five times a week while in *reality* they were drinking only twice a week. Students at other schools were also found to overestimate their peers' drinking. As a result, Perkins theorized that students would drink in accordance with the real drinking norm at their school if they know it. To test his theory, he used posters and newspaper ads to publicize the fact that most students drank only a little. Over the next two years, Perkins observed a significant drop in excessive drinking. When the same tactic was tried out at several other colleges, the reduction in heavy drinking was also significant (Kluger, 2001).

A Social Profile of College Binge Drinkers

College binge drinkers tend to have the following characteristics:

- Being male
- Being white
- Aged 18 to 23
- Traditional, full-time students, never married, and living independently of their parents
- Having parents with a college degree
- Engaging in risky behaviors, such as smoking pot or cigarettes
- Being involved in athletics
- Being fraternity or sorority members
- Having indulged in binge drinking as high school seniors

Unlike moderate drinkers, who drink to have fun, bingers drink to get drunk. At least four factors lie behind the binging. One is the stress from having to work hard for good grades. Another is the social pressure to get drunk so as to fit in and not be seen by others as uptight or antisocial. A third factor is the adoption of a party-centered lifestyle as an important part of college life. A fourth factor is the *belief* that binge drinking is very common on the campus even if it is really not so (DeSimone, 2007; Jackson et al., 2005; Hoover, 2004; Wechsler et al., 2002).

Women and Alcohol

Compared with men, women are generally more vulnerable to alcohol and less able to hold their liquor. Still, women are increasingly likely to drink and turn into alcoholics—as if they are trying to catch up with men. Here we will discuss why women are more likely to drink today and how women alcoholics differ from their male peers.

Why More Women Drink Today

Scientists have discovered in recent years that moderate drinking is good for health, especially the heart. Moderate drinkers have a better chance of avoiding heart disease and can expect to live longer than teetotalers. But for a woman moderate drinking also increases the risk of getting breast cancer, colon cancer, hip fracture, and infertility. In addition to this vulnerability to alcohol, women's bodies are less able than men's to tolerate drinking, for a number of reasons. First, women generally have smaller bodies and thus less blood volume to dilute alcohol. Second, women have more body fat and less body water, resulting in less alcohol dilution. And third, women have a smaller amount of the stomach enzyme that neutralizes and removes alcohol from the bloodstream. As a result of these differences, a woman drinking the same amount as a man will accumulate more alcohol in her bloodstream, which will affect her more powerfully (HWHW, 2000).

Despite those physiological disadvantages, more women drink today than ever before. Women generally still lag behind men in alcohol use, but this is no longer the case for female youth. In the latest national survey, among current drinkers 42 percent of females are aged 12 or older, compared with 55 percent of males. But for young people aged 12 to 17, females already have about the same rate of alcohol use as males—17.3 percent for females versus 17.2 percent for males (SAMHSA, 2002).

Why, then, do more women drink today? The main reason is apparently the increased power and freedom women enjoy, thanks to greater gender equality in U.S. society. Support for this observation is available from some historical and cross-cultural evidence. In colonial America, upper-class women, who by definition had a great deal of power in society, were free to drink in public. Nowadays, the rates of drinking among women are higher in Western societies, where there is a great deal of gender equality, than in non-Western societies, where there is less gender equality. In the United States, young women enjoy so much gender equality that they are considerably more likely to drink than older women and as likely in the 12 to 17 age group to drink as their male peers. Perhaps most significantly, at all-women colleges, bastions of feminism, the prevalence of binge drinking in the years 1993 to 2001 soared 125 percent (SAMHSA, 2002; Jersild, 2001). All this has prompted an older-generation feminist to say, "Going toe to toe with men is a feminist act [but] going drink for drink with them isn't" (Ehrenreich, 2002).

Nonetheless, the impact of increased gender equality on drinking among women seems irresistible. The many women now working full-time outside the home are more likely than stay-at-home moms to drink. Similarly, those women who have most benefited from greater gender equality, women who are white, business executives, unmarried, or young, are more likely than nonwhite, lower-paid, married, and older women to use alcohol. It is also noteworthy, as Devon Jersild (2002) observed, that "many girls and young women today associate drinking with independence, glamour, and the kind of power once reserved for men." As a college woman said, "To be able to drink like a guy is kind of a badge of honor. For me, it's a feminism thing" (Jersild, 2002).

Alcoholism among Women

Perhaps because they are generally expected not to drink as heavily as men, women tend not to be diagnosed as alcoholics, even when they are known to drink like fish. "I used to carry a big purse full of beer into my psychiatrist's office and drink right through the sessions," recalled a woman about her past alcoholism. "He never said a word to me about it. As I look back, I think I was probably challenging him to say something, to help me. But he never dealt with it." Unable or unwilling to see alcoholism as the source of their female patients' distraught states, doctors often diagnose the problem as merely "nerves," anxiety, depression, or some other emotional ailment and proceed to prescribe tranquilizers, antidepressants, and other psychoactive drugs, which they are far less likely to do for male patients. It is little wonder that women alcoholics are twice as likely as their male counterparts to be addicted to other drugs besides alcohol (Sandmeier, 1992).

The medical profession probably should not be faulted for their lack of knowledge about female alcoholics because most researchers in the field have long studied only male alcoholics, even though at least 25 percent of alcoholics are women. Consequently, doctors tend to rely on popular stereotypes of women alcoholics as loud and rude like male alcoholics or sexually promiscuous like prostitutes. But since most women alcoholics do not behave that way, it is hard for doctors to diagnose them with alcoholism (Jersild, 2001).

The few studies that have been done on women alcoholics show them to be different in some ways from their male peers. First, women are more likely to have a family history of alcoholism. Second, women are more likely to have experienced a stressful event, such as physical or sexual abuse, traumatic loss of loved ones, or loneliness, that precipitates alcoholic drinking. Third, women have their first drink and first intoxication at an older age. Fourth, women often drink abusively after their husbands or boyfriends have become heavy drinkers, but men rarely join their wives or girlfriends in becoming abusive drinkers. Fifth, women drink more at home, while men drink more in bars or other public places. And sixth, women have greater problems with both physical and social functioning, more bodily pain, and poorer physical and mental health (Jersild, 2001; H&MW, 2001).

What Causes Alcoholism?

Researchers from various academic disciplines have offered different positivist theories about the development of alcoholism. Medical scientists and psychiatrists believe that some people are genetically vulnerable to alcoholism. Psychologists attribute alcoholism to certain personality traits collectively called the alcoholic personality. And sociologists ascribe alcoholism to a unique set of environmental factors. Let's take a close look at each theory.

A Biological Predisposition

Some medical scientists have long assumed that alcoholism originates from various physical problems such as nutritional deficiencies, glandular disorders, and malfunctions of the central nervous system. Each of these physical factors is thought to cause a strong craving for alcohol, which then leads to alcoholism. But the medical scientists have been criticized for confusing effect with cause. The physical problems that the medical scientists assume are the causes of alcoholism may well be the effects of alcoholism. In other words, the prolonged, frequent, and heavy consumption of alcoholic beverages is very likely to damage the alcoholic's health, bringing on those physical problems.

Medical and psychiatric researchers have also argued that alcoholism is genetically determined. To support this argument, they point to studies showing, for example, that identical twins have higher concordance rates for alcoholism than fraternal twins. (That is, if an identical twin is alcoholic, the chances of the other identical twin becoming alcoholic are relatively high, but if a fraternal twin is alcoholic, the chances of the other fraternal twin becoming alcoholic are significantly lower.) Since identical twins are more genetically alike than fraternal twins, it is assumed that the cause of alcoholism is genetic.

In the early 1990s, some medical researchers purportedly discovered the so-called A1 gene, which is supposed to make people vulnerable to alcoholism. The A1 gene was found to deprive its carrier of the feeling of pleasure. Therefore, according to the researchers, people born with this defective gene are driven to constantly use alcohol—or some other drug—as a means of seeking the pleasure that genetically normal people can enjoy without excessive drinking. In analyzing the blood of 159 people, the researchers found the A1 gene in 50 percent of the alcoholics they studied, compared with only 21 percent of nonalcoholics (Noble et al., 1991; Parsian et al., 1991).

Another kind of evidence is also used to support the genetic theory of alcoholism. According to many studies, a majority (two-thirds to three-fourths) of Chinese and Japanese have a "flushing response" to alcohol. After they drink a small amount of alcohol (fewer than one or two beers), their faces and upper body parts will blush, to be accompanied by a sensation of warmth, nausea, and general discomfort. Because of this physiological reaction, apparently genetic in origin, many Asians cannot tolerate heavy drinking and, therefore, are unlikely to become alcoholics. By contrast, Caucasians, particularly white males, do not have this response. As a consequence, they are more able to literally hold their liquor—capable of guzzling a large quantity of alcohol without getting drunk. Given their greater tolerance for alcohol, they are more likely to become alcoholics (Hampton, 2006; Nakawatase et al., 1993; Goodwin, 1991).

All this suggests that the biological factor may contribute to the development of alcoholism. But there is no direct evidence that the biological factor causes alcoholism. The biological factor can, at best, only serve as a predisposition to drink excessively, but whether people with that predisposition will actually become alcoholics depends on social and psychological factors (Bower, 1992).

The Alcoholic Personality

Many psychologists attribute alcoholism to one or more negative personality traits. These traits include being antisocial, rebellious, egocentric, gregarious, hyperactive, passive-dependent, depressed, anxious, and hostile. Alcoholics are also assumed to have weak ego, poor self-concept, low frustration tolerance, and neurotic guilt. Such personality deficits have supposedly been found in alcoholics (Donovan, 1986). There is no consensus among the personality researchers as to how many of those traits make up what they call the *alcoholic personality*. To some, only one trait—especially being *antisocial*—reflects the alcoholic personality; to others, many more constitute the alcoholic personality. Another problem with the personality theories is that the traits are often contradictory, such as being hyperactive versus depressed or being hostile versus gregarious. A third problem is that most of the personality researchers focus on adults who have become alcoholics rather than using the prospective, longitudinal method of examining children and then reexamining them when they become adults. As a result, the effects of alcoholism are often confused with the causes. There is evidence that chronic drinking causes rather than results from impulsivity, low self-esteem, anxiety, or depression (Vaillant, 1995; Vaillant and Milofsky, 1982).

Other psychologists consider the need for *dependency* to be the key factor in the development of alcoholism. According to William McCord and Joan McCord (1960), for example, the alcoholic's need for dependency stems largely from a stressful and erratic home environment where the mother often comforts the child with loving indulgence but also often terrifies the child with outright rejection. These conflicting childhood experiences are said to intensify the individual's need for love—the need for dependence on others. But this heightened need is not easy to satisfy, so that the individual becomes overwhelmed with *anxiety,* which in turn leads the person to use alcohol in order to get rid of the anxiety. But David McClelland and his colleagues (1972) contend that the need for *power,* rather than the need for dependency, is the driving force behind alcoholism. As McClelland says, "Societies and individuals with accentuated needs for personalized power are more likely to drink more heavily in order to get the feeling of strength they need so much more than others."

While McClelland regards the concern for power as the cause of alcoholism, the McCords do not necessarily disagree. This is because the McCords acknowledge the power desire as the other, *conscious* aspect of the same alcoholic personality that is characterized by the *unconscious* need for dependency. In these psychoanalytic terms, heavy drinking can be said to provide an appearance of toughness to make the alcoholic feel consciously like a powerful person, which in turn suppresses (i.e., keeps unconscious) the alcoholic's anxiety as a dependent person. In effect, heavy drinking simultaneously fulfills both the conscious need for power and the unconscious need for dependency. It is difficult, however, to demonstrate empirically the concept of the unconscious.

Social and Cultural Forces

In sociology there are two major explanations for alcoholism. One is a strictly sociological theory, useful for explaining why some *groups* have higher alcoholism rates than others. The other theory is social-psychological, explaining why some *individuals* become alcoholics but others do not.

Explaining Individual Differences.   According to a classic social-psychological theory in sociology, the unique factor that turns individuals into alcoholics is the fit between vulnerable personality traits on the one hand, and certain drinking-group values and activities on the other (Trice, 1966). This fit will come about under the following four conditions:

1. People must have the qualifications to be a candidate for alcoholism, namely, the vulnerable personality features. These personality features are the same as some of those identified by psychologists as the traits of the alcoholic personality. As Harrison Trice (1966) says, "A potential alcoholic has intense dependency needs and sharp feelings of worthlessness, self-hate, and inadequacy, which produce an unusual need to be looked upon by others and by himself as a 'man.'" Such dependent individuals have deep anxiety about their own adequacy, which makes them highly susceptible to the influence of drinking groups.

2. Once they join drinking groups, they find that they fit right in. Members of drinking groups characteristically believe that drinking is a sign of masculine prowess. They are fond of encouraging a new member to "drink like a man," and praising him for being able to "hold his liquor." This is what the prospective male alcoholic badly needs because of his "unusual need to be looked upon by others and by himself as a 'man.'"

3. After drinking and enjoying his status as "a man" for some time, the individual finds it necessary to consume more and more liquor to prove his manhood. He reaches the point where he becomes an excessive drinker who has lost self-control. It is at this point that his drinking groups stop rewarding him for his alcohol consumption and start rejecting him as a loser. This is because the same social value that encourages a person to drink like a man also emphasizes the importance of self-control—presumably another aspect of the same masculine character.

4. After being ostracized by the drinking groups that initially encouraged the use of alcohol, the abusive, uncontrolled drinkers seek out more tolerant drinking companions, namely, other abusive, uncontrolled drinkers. In such company, the abusive drinkers encourage each other to drink more and more, until finally they are securely locked into alcoholism.

In short, psychologically vulnerable individuals and their drinking peers come together to generate a force that gradually causes the individuals to become alcoholics.

Explaining Group Differences.   According to another classic sociological theory, three factors work together to create a high rate of alcoholism: (1) the production of acute inner tensions in people by their culture, (2) a culturally induced attitude toward drinking as a means of relieving those inner tensions, and (3) the failure of the culture to provide suitable substitute means for resolving the inner tensions (Bales, 1946).

To take the first factor, *culturally produced inner tensions* include feelings of anxiety, guilt, conflict, suppressed hostility, and sexual frustration. To show the way in which a culture can bring about these inner tensions in its members, Bales presented the case of Irish peasants, noted for their drunkenness during the past several centuries. Irish parents instilled fear, insecurity, and anxiety in their children by disciplining them with the threat of "boogey men," "spooks," and "fairies," and by smothering them with affection at one moment and beating them in a fit of anger at the next. The boys often had to stay on the farm, continuing to work for their father until he retired or died. "So long as they stayed on the farm," Bales observed, "they had to work for him as 'boys' and were treated as boys, even though they might be 45 or 50 years old." This created a huge reservoir of suppressed hostility against the father. Kept under the father's thumb as "boys," these physically mature men could neither marry nor dally in premarital sexual escapades. Such a situation generated powerful sexual tensions.

Acute inner tensions can become a powerful motivating force for compulsive drinking if the *culture has induced in people the attitude that liquor is excellent for relieving the tensions and many other problems,* the second factor. The Irish farmers are said to have such a culture. When going to fairs to buy or sell livestock, they treat each other with a few drinks in order to "soften the other guy up," so that they typically come home in a heavy state of intoxication. But their wives usually treat them with care and affection; their mothers lovingly call them "my poor boy"; and their friends, acquaintances, and others regard their intoxication with envy instead of pity. The Irish also consider alcohol an effective folk remedy for "keeping the cold out of the stomach," curing stomachache, combating insomnia, increasing the feeling of physical and sexual strength, and even getting rid of hangovers. With this attitude, the Irish find it natural to resort to drinking as a means of drowning their personal problems as well. The result is their relatively high rate of alcoholism.

In coping with a culturally induced stress, people will turn to alcohol if they *cannot find another method of resolving the stress,* the third factor. For Jews and Italians, eating seems to be the method of dealing with tension. Many Muslims are said to turn to hashish as well as strong tea and coffee. The Brahmins in India and the Japanese are believed to rely on opium. As a result of their having culturally approved alternatives to the use of alcohol for resolving tension, these groups have low rates of alcoholism. But the Irish, being without an alternative to drinking, have a higher rate of alcoholism.

Of the three types of theories, the sociological theories appear the most satisfactory. As psychologists McCord and McCord (1960) wrote, "Sociologists have produced impressive evidence demonstrating that rates of alcoholism are significantly related to the social factors." But we should not overgeneralize. People who are psychologically vulnerable and exposed by peers to heavy drinking do not necessarily become alcoholics, nor do the majority of the Irish indulge in excessive drinking. What the sociological theories suggest is that people with those social and cultural experiences are more likely than others to become alcoholics.

Controlling Alcohol Use and Abuse

Like illegal drug use, alcohol use or abuse has been subjected to various attempts to control it, but has proved to be a persistent aspect of American life.

Legal Measures

One way to control alcohol use involves the coercive power of the law. Let us see how this has been carried out in the past and present.

The Past. In colonial days, the Puritans enjoyed drinking beer and rum in moderation. They condemned only excessive drinking. Then, in the early nineteenth century, there arose a crusade for total abstinence. This crusade, often called the temperance movement, eventually culminated in the enactment of the Eighteenth Amendment (popularly known as "Prohibition") in 1919. During the next 14 years, drunkenness did not disappear from the face of America. On the contrary, Prohibition turned out to be such a disastrous failure that it was repealed by the Twenty-first Amendment in 1933 (Gusfield, 1991; Wilkinson, 1970).

In some ways similar to the efforts past and present at outlawing psychoactive drugs discussed in the preceding chapter, Prohibition originated chiefly from an attempt to control the powerless segments of society. In postcolonial America, the temperance movement first emerged as an attempt on the part of the wealthy aristocracy to control the new upsurge of democracy among the masses, who happened to engage in some drinking. Later the emergent, dominant middle classes (independent farmers, small-business owners, and self-employed professionals) used the temperance movement to stir up prejudice and discrimination against Irish and German immigrants, Catholics and Jews, and the urban lower classes. The middle classes felt that their puritanical values of hard work were threatened by the "ne'er-do-well, unambitious, and irreligious" immigrants and poor Americans who traditionally drank. But by the time Prohibition came into effect, a new, more powerful group (salaried professionals, white-collar workers, and managerial employees) had begun to emerge from within the middle class. Unlike the old middle class, who advocated total abstinence from drinking, the new one supported moderate use of alcohol, which contributed to the demise of Prohibition. Since then, moderate drinking, as opposed to total abstinence, has continued to be the norm of not just the middle class but of most Americans as well (Gusfield, 1991).

The Present. In the 1990s the Clinton administration wanted to discourage alcohol abuse by imposing a "sin tax" on hard liquor, though not on beer or wine. The increased tax on liquor was designed to help pay some of the enormous, multibillion-dollar expenses for treating diseases caused by heavy drinking. This seemed to be a sensible measure against alcohol abuse, a far cry from the total prohibition of alcohol in the past. But the liquor lobby was so powerful that Clinton changed his mind. In fact, for the last four decades, the excise taxes on various alcoholic beverages have remained relatively low. This has contributed to the low price of alcohol, which has, along with aggressive marketing, encouraged widespread drinking, especially among teenagers (Serdula et al., 2004; Cohn and Hager, 1993).

However, a crusade against teenage drinking and drunk driving has been quite successful. Since 1982 many organizations such as MADD (Mothers Against Drunk Driving) and SADD (Students Against Drunk Driving) have effectively aroused public outrage at drunk driving for causing many traffic deaths. Their biggest achievement has come from lobbying the federal and state governments to raise the minimum drinking age to 21, and by the late 1980s virtually all the states had. As a result, the number of alcohol-related car crashes has declined significantly (Serdula et al., 2004; Hughes and Dodder, 1992).

There is a limit to what the drinking age law can accomplish, though. Although the law has reduced drunk driving and fatal car crashes among teenagers, it has hardly made a dent in risky teen drinking. Binge drinking, along with alcohol poisoning, continues to be relatively common among teenagers. Ironically, this problem can be largely attributed to the drinking age law itself. For one thing, the law unintendedly encourages binge drinking by helping to create a phenomenon called *prepartying, pregaming,* or *frontloading,* in which underage young people consume large quantities of alcoholic beverages in private before attending a party or other event in public where proof of legal age may be required for drinking. Also, the drinking age law effectively challenges teenagers to drink to prove their adulthood. The law seems to say to young people under 21 that they are still children, not yet adults. But young people, particularly those who are 18, 19, or 20, see themselves as adults. With this self-perception, they seek to prove their adulthood by drinking, with some going overboard, getting wasted like there was no tomorrow. After all, alcohol has long been a symbol of adulthood in the U.S. culture, further reinforced by the drinking age law itself. The symbol of adulthood has become particularly powerful for young people anxious to leave behind homeroom, curfew, and hall monitors of the high school days (Pedersen and LaBrie, 2007; Seaman, 2005).

Given the continuing problem of underage binge drinking, at least 24 states have in recent years tried to discourage the practice by passing a "social host" law, which punishes adults, typically parents, for letting teenagers drink in their homes. Some research has shown the law to be effective: The youth whose parents give them alcohol for parties are more likely to binge drink. But other studies have suggested a different result: Kids who drink *with* their parents are less likely to binge drink, presumably because they have learned to drink responsibly from the adults (Cloud, 2008; Schwartz, 2007).

Therapeutic Approaches

While the law against drunk driving or underage drinking treats alcohol users and abusers as offenders, the therapeutic way of dealing with drinking problems is based on the assumption that abusive drinkers are patients who need help.

Detox and Treatment Centers.   In the early 1970s the popular belief in alcoholism as a disease led to the enactment of laws in over 20 states that treat alcohol abusers as patients rather than criminals. In those states today, violators of the public drunkenness law are no longer thrown into jail. They are instead taken to public detoxification centers for treatment and then, if necessary, sent to halfway houses or aftercare facilities where they are helped to stay "on the wagon." Unfortunately, many who have come out of detox centers or halfway houses will go back in again. In fact, research has shown that "detox doors revolve much faster than jail doors." The major reason is that many patients refuse to see themselves as alcoholics and to follow the center's rules for making a recovery (such as attending meetings or talking about drinking problems), two major conditions that have been proven essential for recovering from alcoholism (Rubington, 1991).

For other alcoholics, who do not violate the public drunkenness law, there are numerous community-based alcohol treatment centers throughout the country. These centers provide mostly outpatient services, offering hospitalization only as a last resort. Services primarily include psychological counseling and therapy because the centers are most often operated under the guidance of psychiatrists and psychologists. Much of the psychological treatment involves the use of aversion therapy or a combination of this with group therapy. Group therapy brings together a number of alcoholics (and, in many cases, their spouses and children) and tries to guide them back to sobriety through a series of sessions that include lectures, educational films, and discussions about drinking problems. Aversion therapy calls for the use of electric shock or nausea-inducing drugs designed to condition the alcoholic to feel sick at the very odor of liquor. Generally, this aversion therapy is effective only for a short time—the urge to drink returns within 6 to 12 months. The combination of this therapy with group treatment is more effective. However, most centers are underutilized, so that the enormity of alcohol abuse in the society as a whole remains largely untouched (Roman and Blum, 1991). A more popular—and effective—method does not involve any professional therapist, but simply alcoholics and ex-alcoholics themselves. It is the AA (Alcoholics Anonymous) method.

Alcoholics Anonymous. Founded in 1935, AA is today the largest and most successful organization for helping alcoholics (Weisner et al., 1995). The only requirement for joining AA is the desire to stop drinking. Once having joined the organization, new members may choose another AA member as a sponsor. Sponsors are recovering alcoholics ready to come to a new member's aid whenever needed. The treatment involves attending a series of meetings where any number of alcoholics share their drinking histories. These meetings may be held in offices, schools, churches, lodges, or private homes, and they are open to alcoholics and nonalcoholics alike. At a typical meeting, a volunteer "leader" will begin by saying something like "Hello, I'm John, and I'm an alcoholic." He or she may then introduce some AA members who will discuss their experiences with alcohol as well as their recovery from the drinking problem. Afterward, others may follow suit, relating their own experiences. A crucial part of these sessions is that one admit to oneself and other AA members that one is an alcoholic and is powerless over alcohol.

This program is widely considered the most successful method ever devised for coping with alcoholism. Not surprisingly, it has spawned similar organizations such as Al-Anon (for spouses and other close relatives and friends of alcoholics) and Alateen (for alcoholics' teenage children). Their aim is to help members understand alcoholism and themselves, as well as learn how to live with and help their alcoholic relatives. AA meetings, along with recovery dorms, are also available to students in a growing number of colleges. Apparently, the effectiveness of the AA method is due in great measure to the *group support* provided to alcoholics by people who have deep, personal understanding of drinking problems. Group support is particularly important for alcoholics because they are typically "escape drinkers" (who drink alone in a futile attempt to solve personal problems) rather than social drinkers (who participate in drinking with other people for dietary, religious, or social reasons as the Italians, Jews, Chinese, or higher-status people characteristically do). Research has suggested that AA offers what those alcoholics have always sought before they started to drink heavily, namely, social acceptance, a more positive identity, and feelings of normalcy and confidence, the benefits of group support (Helliker, 2006; Karlin-Resnick, 2004; Hurlburt, Gade, and Fuqua, 1984). AA can provide those benefits because it has effectively become its members' family. As a member said at an AA meeting,

> I lost everything. Family, home, wives, kids, job, everything. Even my parents turned against me. . . . I finally found you people. Now you're my family. Wherever I go, you're there. . . . You give me everything I ever wanted and ever looked for. I feel like I'm needed again. (Denzin, 1991)

Can Alcoholics Learn to Drink Moderately?   AA assumes that alcoholism is an incurable disease. This is why AA often pronounces "once an alcoholic, always an alcoholic." Since they are not expected to fully recover, even members who have remained sober for years are always considered to be, and are called, recovering—not recovered—alcoholics. To continue staying sober, AA insists, recovering alcoholics must completely stay on the wagon. Even taking a small sip of wine, AA believes, will cause recovering alcoholics to relapse into uncontrolled drinking because they still have the disease. Therefore, to AA, alcoholics can never learn to drink moderately, and to talk about moderate drinking can only give alcoholics an excuse to keep on drinking.

But an increasing number of researchers argue that alcoholism is not a disease over which the problem drinker has no control. It is, instead, an unhealthy behavior pattern that can be changed by learning to engage in controlled, moderate drinking. According to moderation theorists, studies in the United States have shown that many alcoholics can learn to drink moderately without suffering a relapse, and studies in many European countries have also demonstrated the ability of alcoholics to learn to drink in moderation without relapsing into uncontrolled drinking (Rotgers et al., 1996; Sobell and Sobell, 1993). We should note, however, that most of these alcoholics may well be merely "problem drinkers" who have not developed a severe addiction to alcohol. But for "hard-core alcoholics," who have long been severely addicted to the drug, AA's insistence on abstinence may still be the safer way of dealing with the addiction (Rivera, 2000; Marriott, 1995).

Summary

1. What is the extent of drinking and alcoholism in the United States? Most Americans drink, but only moderately, while a large minority (one-third) abstain from drinking and a small minority (6 percent) suffer from alcoholism.

2. What are some popular myths about alcohol use? They are as follows: alcoholics are mostly homeless; mixing different kinds of drinks accelerates intoxication; drinking black coffee or pouring cold water on the head can get rid of drunkenness; drinking only beer cannot make one an alcoholic; and sex becomes more exciting after several drinks.

3. What are the effects of alcohol? Alcohol is a depressant drug, and as such, it reduces the drinker's mental and physical ability but not moral competence. How much the mental and physical ability declines depends on the level of intoxication—the percentage of alcohol in the bloodstream. The latter, in turn, depends on such factors as the body size and weight of the drinker, the type and amount of alcoholic beverages consumed, the quantity of food in the stomach, and the drinker's level of tolerance for alcohol. Taken in moderate amounts, alcohol can provide some health and social benefits. But heavy drinking is likely to damage the liver, bring about sexual impotence, and cause heart disease, strokes, cancer, and other health problems. Alcohol abuse further contributes to a number of social problems such as automobile injuries and deaths and criminal offenses.

4. Who is more likely than others to use or abuse alcohol? Those who are more likely to drink are whites, males, young adults, liberal Protestants and Catholics, higher-status persons, and residents of the Northeast and West. But those who are more likely to end up as alcoholics are lower-status persons, and African, Hispanic, Irish, and Native Americans.

5. What is the global pattern of drinking? Alcohol consumption is greater in affluent societies than in poor countries. Among people in affluent societies, Europeans drink more than North Americans, with Russians consuming the largest amount of alcohol. Young people in Europe are now more inclined to engage in heavy drinking than before. In these affluent countries women are only somewhat less likely than men to drink, but in Islamic and Southeast Asian countries it is extremely rare for women to consume alcohol.

6. What is alcoholism? It involves drinking excessively, being psychologically and physically addicted, and experiencing alcohol-related problems. **How does a person become an alcoholic?** The person first begins as a social drinker, then becomes psychologically and physically addicted, and finally hits bottom with total dependence on alcohol.

7. What causes binge drinking in college? The lack of opportunities to learn responsible, moderate drinking because of the drinking-age law. **Who's likely to go on a binge?** Binge drinkers are likely to be, among other things, white males, relatively young traditional full-time students, athletes and fraternity members, and engaged in risky activities. **What could explain the rise in drinking among women, especially female youths?** The increase in gender equality, which encourages women to drink like men. **How do women alcoholics differ from their male peers?** Women alcoholics are more likely to have a family history of alcoholism, experience stressful events, have the first drink older, abuse alcohol to be like their spouse, drink at home, and suffer more physically, mentally, and socially.

8. What causes alcoholism? According to the biological theory, alcoholism is brought on by some problem inside the body such as a nutritional deficiency, a defective gene, or a lack of flushing response. Psychologists attribute alcoholism to the alcoholic personality, which includes being antisocial, the need for being dependent on others, and the need for power. According to one classic sociological theory, alcoholism develops from a social situation in which psychologically vulnerable individuals are pressured by drinking companions to drink heavily. According to another sociological theory, a culture causes alcoholism by producing acute inner tensions in people, encouraging people to view drinking as useful for relieving tensions, and failing to provide suitable substitutes for alcohol in reducing stress.

9. How has U.S. society tried to control alcohol abuse? By legal and therapeutic methods. The law prohibiting the sale of alcohol in the 1920s and early 1930s failed to eradicate drunkenness, and the prohibition reflected an attempt to control the powerless segments of society. The Clinton administration planned to discourage alcohol abuse but to no avail. Still, the crusade against teenage drunk driving since the early 1980s has reduced fatal car crashes but not binge drinking. Therapeutic approaches have also been used to control alcohol abuse. They include treating public drunkenness as a disease rather than a crime, providing treatment at community centers, and offering social support through groups organized by alcoholics themselves, of which the largest and most successful is Alcoholics Anonymous. AA insists that alcoholics must completely abstain from drinking, but a growing number of researchers find that alcoholics (more precisely, problem drinkers) can learn to drink in moderation.

FURTHER READING

Catalano, Ralph, et al. 1993. "Job loss and alcohol abuse: A test using data from the epidemiologic catchment area project." *Journal of Health and Social Behavior,* 34 (September), 215–225. Alcohol abuse is found to be more common among those who have been laid off than among those who have not.

Clark, Walter B., and Michael E. Hilton (eds.). 1991. *Alcohol: Drinking Practices and Problems.* Albany: State University of New York Press. A collection of articles presenting the results of several survey studies on alcohol use and abuse in the United States.

Denzin, Norman K. 1993. *The Alcoholic Society: Addiction and Recovery of the Self.* New Brunswick, N.J.: Transaction. Analyzing the various scholarly views on alcoholism and the experiences of drinking as well as recovering from alcoholism.

Edwards, Griffith. 2002. *Alcohol: The World's Favorite Drug.* New York: St. Martin's. A wide-ranging analysis of scientific facts about alcohol and its impact on people, illustrated with case studies.

Grant, Marcus, and Jorge Litvak (eds.). 1998. *Drinking Patterns and Their Consequences.* Washington, D.C.: Taylor & Francis. A collection of articles about social, cultural, and personal factors in drinking; policies and programs on alcohol use and abuse; and new approaches to controlling alcohol problems.

Heath, Dwight B. (ed.) 1995. *International Handbook on Alcohol and Culture.* Westport, Conn.: Greenwood. A collection of articles on the drinking norms and practices of 27 countries.

Jersild, Devon. 2001. *Happy Hours: Alcohol in a Woman's Life.* New York: HarperCollins. Presenting a mix of scientific data and personal stories about various aspects of drinking and alcoholism among women.

Martin, Jack K., Paul M. Roman, and Terry C. Blum. 1996. "Job stress, drinking networks, and social support at work: A comprehensive model of employees' problem drinking behaviors." *Sociological Quarterly,* 37, 579–599. A study of how stressful working conditions, drinking networks, and social support at work influence problem drinking among employees.

Obot, Isidore S., and Robin Room (eds.). 2005. *Alcohol, Gender and Drinking Problems: Perspectives from Low and Middle Income Countries.* Geneva, Switzerland: World Health Organization. A collection of articles dealing with the gender difference in drinking and alcoholism in eight developing countries.

Orcutt, James D. 1993. "Happy hour and social lubrication: Evidence on mood-setting rituals of drinking time." *Journal of Drug Issues,* 23, 389–407. This study indicates a reduction in stress among college students when they engage in social drinking during weekday evenings.

Perkins, H. Wesley. 1992. "Gender patterns in consequences of collegiate alcohol abuse: A 10-year study of trends in an undergraduate population." *Journal of Studies on Alcohol,* 53, 458–462. The data show that college men continue to have many more alcohol abuse and alcohol-related problems than college women.

Pittman, David J., and Helene Raskin White (eds.). 1991. *Society, Culture, and Drinking Patterns Reexamined.* New Brunswick, N.J.: Rutgers Center of Alcohol Studies. A large collection of articles presenting the social scientific views on various aspects of alcohol use and abuse.

Roman, Paul M. (ed.). 1991. *Alcohol: The Development of Sociological Perspectives on Use and Abuse.* New Brunswick, N.J.: Rutgers Center of Alcohol Studies. A set of essays on the contributions made by sociologists to the understanding of drinking and alcoholism.

Sayette, Michael A., et al. 1993. "Alcohol and aggression: A social information processing analysis." *Journal of Studies on Alcohol*, 54, 399–407. Alcohol use is found to be associated with aggressive responses to provocation.

Seaman, Barrett. 2005. *Binge: What Your College Student Won't Tell You*. Hoboken, N.J.: Wiley & Sons. An ethnographic analysis of today's college life including drinking and alcohol problems.

CRITICAL THINKING QUESTIONS

1. Of the various social factors in drinking, which one would affect you the most and which one the least? Why?

2. How and why has the women's movement for gender equality unintendedly led many young women to the bottle?

PART SIX

Inequality in Deviance

13 Privileged Deviance

Myths and Realities

Myth: The food industry uses chemical additives solely to protect its consumers' health by keeping its products from spoiling.

Reality: The purpose behind the use of chemical additives is not merely to protect the consumers' health but also to reap a huge profit by making the

foods look fresh and appealing to the shoppers (p. 338).

_____

Myth: Since it is illegal to falsely advertise medicine and other products that can seriously harm the consumer, the guilty company is subject to punishment just like a common criminal.

Reality: For the illegal act of false advertising, the company is not subject to punishment as a common criminal. The offender is only required to sign a document stating an agreement to stop the illegal activity (p. 340).

Myth: U.S. corporations are more likely than their counterparts in other countries to bribe foreign government officials to do business abroad.

Reality: Although U.S. companies do occasionally give bribes worth millions of dollars to foreign officials, they are much less likely to do so when compared to their European and Asian counterparts (p. 341).

Myth: If their salaries are relatively low, U.S. corporate executives are likely to boost their income by engaging in illegal or criminal business activities.

Reality: The corporate executives who have recently been charged with or convicted of business crimes received much higher salaries when compared with other, law-abiding executives. Apparently, the sky-high compensation encourages corporate crime by making the executives feel that they are above the law (pp. 342–343).

Myth: Paid less, working-class employees are more likely than their middle-class counterparts to steal from their companies.

Reality: Most employee thieves are middle class. Their reasons for stealing include their companies are too large and impersonal, their society has a tradition of employee–management conflict, and they find their jobs too boring (pp. 343–344).

Myth: Embezzlers are forced to steal after they have repeatedly and unabashedly asked their friends and others for help with a financial problem but to no avail.

Reality: Embezzlers are typically too embarrassed to share their financial problem with friends, spouses, or others who are ordinarily available for help. The embarrassing financial

problem may include being heavily in debt from gambling or from supporting a mistress (p. 345).

Myth: Nowadays white-collar criminals are just as likely as street criminals to receive harsh punishment in the courts.

Reality: White-collar criminals have received harsher punishment in recent years, but the courts still treat them more leniently than street criminals. From 1995 through 2002, for example, only 57 percent of white-collar offenders were sentenced to prison compared to 93 percent of street criminals (p. 350).

Myth: Given their accumulation of sophisticated weapons, the governments of rich countries are more likely than those of poor nations to commit democide—the killing of people by their government.

Reality: Apparently viewing human life as cheap, the governments of poor nations commit democide on a larger scale than do rich countries (p. 355).

Myth: Official corruption is less common in poor countries than in rich ones, simply because poor people are less financially able to bribe their government officials.

Reality: Generally, the poorer a country is, the more corrupt its public officials are. In most of the world's poor countries, corruption is so common that it is considered normal (p. 355).

Myth: When high government officials in the United States promise to the general public that they will get rid of some official deviance, they surely will keep the promise.

Reality: The officials will more likely promise to take action to deal with an issue but fail to carry out any plan of action. In 2006, for example, the U.S. Congress promised to pass tough reform bills to crack down on corrupt lawmakers, but it was widely seen as mere window dressing and expected to result in business as usual, just like many other similar promises (pp. 357–358).

As the boss of the worldwide conglomerate Tyco, Dennis Kozlowski made tons of money for his corporation and for himself. In one decade, he went on a frenzied shopping spree, spending more than $60 billion to buy 200 major corporations and hundreds of smaller ones. As a result, Tyco, once a relatively small industrial-parts manufacturer with $3 billion in yearly sales, turned into a global colossus that annually pulled in $36 billion, selling everything from diapers to fire alarms. For that feat, Kozlowski rewarded himself with more than $300 million in total compensation in his last three years with the company. For his own personal use he acquired, among other things, three Harley-Davidson motorcycles, a 130-foot sailing yacht, a private plane, and lavish homes in four states. Unfortunately, in the summer of 2002, he was first charged with failing to pay $1 million in sales tax on art purchases and then with stealing $150 million from Tyco. In 2005 he was convicted for systematically looting the company and sentenced to serve 8 to 25 years in prison (*Wall Street Journal,* 2007; Eisenberg, 2002; Hill, 2002).

Kozlowski's crime may be called *privileged deviance,* highly profitable deviance that typically occurs among privileged people, the relatively rich and powerful. Privileged deviance can be divided into *white-collar deviance* and *governmental deviance*. In this chapter we will take a closer look at the sociological definition of white-collar deviance, the characteristics of corporate and occupational deviance (the subtypes of white-collar deviance), and the uniqueness and explanations of white-collar deviance. We will then analyze various facets of governmental deviance, including its causes.

What Is White-Collar Deviance?

When sociologist Edwin Sutherland first introduced the concept of white-collar crime in 1939, he defined it as an offense committed by "the upper, white-collar class, which is composed of respectable, or at least respected, business and professional men." Ten years later Sutherland (1949) tried to flesh out the concept:

> White-collar crime may be defined approximately as a crime committed by a person of respectability and high social status in the course of his occupation. Consequently, it excludes many crimes of the upper class, such as most of their cases of murder, adultery, and intoxication, since these are not customarily a part of their occupational procedures.

In this classic definition, two things characterize white-collar crime: (1) It is *occupationally* related, carried out during the course of the offender's occupation, and the occupation involved is *white-collar* as opposed to blue-collar. (2) The economic deviant is a relatively *respectable, high-status* person. By "high-status persons," Sutherland referred to people ranging from business managers and executives to "wage-earning class, which wears good clothes at work, such as clerks in stores" (Sutherland, 1956).

What distinguishes the commission of white-collar crime from the commission of blue-collar or street crime is more than the act itself. It also involves *how* the act is executed. Thus, white collars are more likely to commit an offense with skill, with sophistication, or, most important, with the resources of power, influence, or respectability for avoiding detection, prosecution, or conviction. If blue collars try to commit the same act, they usually do not—and, perhaps, cannot—do it in the same way as white collars. This is why blue collars are far more likely to be arrested, prosecuted, or convicted if they commit the same crimes as white collars (Shapiro, 1990).

While talking about high-status people engaging in economic deviance, Sutherland also had in mind *corporations* participating in similar deviant activities. The concept of corporate deviance was crucial for understanding the sociological nature of white-collar deviance in general. See how Sutherland used the examples of corporate deviance to show what he thought was the absurdity of explaining deviance in psychological terms:

> We have no reason to think that General Motors has an inferiority complex or that the Aluminum Company of America has a frustration-aggression complex or that U.S. Steel has an Oedipus complex, or that the Armour Company has a death wish or that the DuPonts desire to return to the womb. (Sutherland, 1956)

Therefore, for our purposes, white-collar deviance includes both occupational and corporate deviance. It may be noteworthy that we broaden the concept of white-collar *crime* by replacing it with "white-collar *deviance*." This is because what sociologists have traditionally called white-collar crime includes not just criminal offenses but civil and other noncriminal offenses. (A civil offense is legally not a crime because it involves violating a civil rather than a criminal law.) We use the term *white-collar deviance* to refer to both criminal and noncriminal forms of economic deviance carried out by high-status people as part of their occupation for personal gain (hence *occupational deviance*) or on behalf of their corporation (hence *corporate deviance*).

Corporate Deviance

Corporate deviance typically takes place in corporations, carried out by executives for their companies' benefits and their own. It can be divided into four major types: deviance against employees, deviance against customers, deviance against the government, and deviance against the environment.

Deviance against Employees

For many years corporations have been expected to ensure that their employees remain free from known hazards in the work environment. This expectation was finally turned into law in the 1970s, and a federal agency, the Occupational Safety and Health Administration (OSHA), was established to enforce workplace safety. But many workers today are still exposed to various kinds of pollutants in the work environment, for example, coal dust, cotton dust, and radiation. Although these substances have been found to cause cancer, leukemia, and other serious illnesses, corporations tend to ignore or deny the problem rather than take corrective action, such as eliminating the exposures to make their plants safer (Frank, 1993).

Sociologists David Ermann and Richard Lundman (2002) have suggested three reasons for corporations' tendencies to be negligent about their employees' health and safety. The most obvious and important reason is corporate concern with *profit maximization*.

Corporate executives are inclined to ignore health hazards in their plants because elimination of these hazards will eat into their companies' profits.

A second reason for the negligence about workers' safety is the nature of *corporate structure*. One of the major characteristics of corporations is that executives are rewarded for seeking short-term success only. Thus, in determining whether to ignore or eliminate health hazards, corporate executives tend to focus on how great a profit they will derive from a certain decision in a few months or years rather than in 10 or 20 years. It is no wonder that they usually decide against spending what appears, at the moment, to be a large amount of money to improve their employees' working conditions. They simply fail to consider the long-term consequences of such a decision, such as facing the high cost of numerous lawsuits filed against them by their many disabled employees. Another important characteristic of corporate structure is that it motivates executives to judge employees' worth impersonally, focusing only on their contribution to production. As a result, employees tend to be treated as if they were machines—and as machines, they are easily replaceable. If some workers become disabled or die, others can be found easily and quickly to take their place. Such a callous attitude toward employees can understandably lead corporate executives to disregard employee health and safety.

A third reason for corporate deviance against employees is *the government's reluctance to take action against offending corporations*. OSHA often avoids using threats or penalties to deter offenses; instead, negotiation and persuasion are routinely employed to obtain compliance. In cases in which citations and fines are used as a last resort, the companies are allowed to have their penalties reduced if they correct their "deficiencies." In addition to this weak enforcement policy, the government has cut back on OSHA enforcement personnel. Moreover, many states prohibit injured employees from suing their employers unless they are able to prove that the injury was intentional. In other words, employers cannot be sued for negligence (Frank, 1993).

Deviance against Customers

There are many different forms of corporate deviance against customers. The most common ones involve dangerous foods, unsafe products, frauds, deceptive advertising, and antitrust violations.

Dangerous Foods.   The food industry has been known to seek greater profits by selling adulterated or contaminated foods. Meat-packing companies often sell their products without being certain that the meat is safe for human consumption. That's why health experts advise consumers to make sure that their hamburgers are cooked fully. Still, in 1993, nearly 400 people were stricken with *E. coli,* a dangerous colon bacterium, after eating hamburgers at Jack in the Box restaurants. Four children later died from the bacterial infection. According to the U.S. Agriculture Department and state health officials, the bacteria could have been killed if Jack in the Box had cooked the hamburgers to a higher temperature (155 degrees instead of 140). But the problem originated in the slaughterhouse where the meat had been contaminated with feces (McDowell, 1996).

Foods can also be adulterated. Hormel Company, for example, once took stale meat returned by its retail-store customers and then "reconditioned," repackaged, and resold it for a higher profit to other stores—without the legally required reinspection by the U.S. Department of Agriculture officer in charge. As a researcher found, "Spareribs returned for sliminess, discoloration, and stickiness were rejuvenated through curing and smoking, renamed Windsor Loins, and sold in ghetto stores for more than fresh pork chops" (Wellford, 1972).

In fact, it is customary for the food industry to use all kinds of chemical additives in its products, many of which have been suspected by government scientists to cause cancer and other diseases. The apparent purpose is not only to keep the foods from spoiling, but to make them look fresh and appealing as well as to give them the right taste and aroma. Sodium nitrites and nitrates, for example, are added to keep meat products looking blood-red. However, the real purpose behind all this is the pursuit of the big buck. As one food marketer says, "The profit margin on food additives is fantastically good, much better than the profit margins on basic, traditional foods" (Simon, 2006).

Unsafe Products.   The profit motive also underlies the manufacturing and selling of unsafe products by car, drug, tobacco, and other industries. Tobacco companies, for example, have long known that smoking causes cancer and is addictive, but they continue to make and sell cigarettes (Noah, 1997). Dealing in unsafe products also appears frequently in the pharmaceutical industry. Drug companies are often found committing such product-safety offenses as the sale of impure, overstrength, out-of-date, or nonsterile products. The far more serious offense of fraudulent safety-testing of drugs has also been uncovered many times. Experimental rats and monkeys that had developed terrible symptoms such as tumors and blindness in drug trials were replaced by healthy animals. Dead animals were "resurrected" in lab reports—rats that had died from using a new drug reappeared later in the data as alive (Braithwaite, 1993). Falsification of clinical data such as these has set drug companies afoul of the law. In 1990, for example, Bolar's high-blood-pressure drug, generic Dyazide, was recalled because it was found defective and the company was fined $10 million for having forged documents in seeking FDA approval (Gorman, 1992). (The FDA is the federal government's Food and Drug Administration.)

More prevalent than presenting grossly phony data to the FDA is the profit-driven tendency to withhold data from the FDA about a drug's negative side effects. Consequently, many potentially dangerous drugs get FDA approval, and the consumers are, in effect, used as guinea pigs. After using the drugs at their own expense, sometimes for a lengthy period of time, consumers will know whether the medical products are dangerous. Of course, by the time they discover the danger, it is too late. They have already suffered and sometimes died. When this happens, the general public is bound to be greatly scandalized. One of the drug scandals of the 1990s involves Dow Corning's silicone-gel breast implants. In 1992 some customers complained that the implants leaked, ruptured, or caused autoimmune disorders. The FDA was forced to investigate, and found from the company's internal documents that the manufacturer of the breast implants knew about the problems way back in the mid-1970s (Pontell and Calavita, 1993).

Frauds.   Fraudulent practices can be found in various industries such as banking, insurance, real estate, and securities. They are all extremely lucrative, largely made possible by inadequate government control. Let's take a closer look at the nature of bank and insurance frauds.

One of the greatest bank frauds in recent U.S. history involves a number of savings and loan (S&L or thrift) institutions in the 1980s, which cost taxpayers an astounding $1.4 trillion. In a span of only five years, from 1987 through 1992, a staggering 95,045 criminal charges were filed against S&L officials. The suspected frauds can be divided into three types: (1) illegal nonbanking activities—violating banking laws by engaging in unsafe practices, such as concentrating investment in one high-risk area, say, construction loans, without having conducted any marketability study; (2) collective embezzlement—using ownership of an S&L to steal depositors' money, which has prompted a California state official to say, "The best way to rob a bank is to own one"; and (3) covering up—falsifying records to make the institutions look normal or financially healthy. A major cause of all these frauds was the dismantling of "most of the regulatory infrastructure that had kept the thrift industry together for decades" (Pontell and Calavita, 1993; also see Truell and Gurwin, 1992).

Fraud is also a big problem in the insurance industry. Insolvencies among insurance companies are common, often the result of insiders' fraudulent activities. Government regulation is even more inadequate in the insurance industry. There are federal agencies policing banks, savings and loans, securities, and commodities, but there is none for the insurance industry. There are state agencies for regulating insurance, but they are mostly inefficient. They are typically underfunded and understaffed; New Mexico, for example, has only five staff regulators to monitor 1,600 insurance companies. The most common insurance frauds include phony assets and small-business scams. In the phony assets scheme, an insurance company lies about its assets to show that it has the sufficient amount required by law. In small-business scams, a firm administers an MEWA ("Multiple Employer Welfare Arrangement," whereby several small employers combine their money to insure health coverage for their workers) and simply steals the money until it cannot pay any claims (Headden and Witkin, 1993).

Deceptive Advertising. Closely similar to fraud is deceptive advertising. Most advertising is mere puffery, an exaggerated claim for a product. Examples follow (Simon, 2006):

> "Nestle makes the very best chocolate"
>
> "GM—always a step ahead"
>
> "Wheaties, Breakfast of Champions"
>
> "Every kid in America loves Jell-O brand gelatin"
>
> "Seagram's, America's Number One Gin"

Although these claims are false, they are legal. It is also legal to use misleading labels to make food products appear much healthier or less fattening than they actually are. Pam and other cooking sprays, for example, can boast they are fat-free and calorie-free although they are made of 100 percent fat (Parker-Pope, 2003).

But another form of false advertising is illegal because it involves products that can seriously harm the consumer, as the following case illustrates (Simon, 2006):

> The Federal Trade Commission ruled that Anacin had falsely advertised its product by claiming that it: (1) relieved nervousness, tension, stress, fatigue, and depression; (2) was

stronger than aspirin; (3) brought relief within twenty-two seconds; (4) was highly recommended over aspirin by doctors; and (5) was more effective for relieving pain than any other analgesic available without prescription.

For such an illegal act, however, the company is not subject to punishment as a common criminal. The offender is merely required to sign a document stating an agreement to stop the illegal activity. Obviously, the intent of the law here is not to punish the offender, but to stop the illegal action and prevent further damage (Coleman, 2006).

Antitrust Violations.   Antitrust laws prohibit companies from conspiring to reduce or eliminate competition. If there is little or no competition, prices will go up and consumers will have no choice but to pay them. To violate the antitrust laws, companies selling the same kind of products usually get together to fix prices that are abnormally high. Sometimes corporations prevent new competition from entering the market, as can be illustrated by the two largest credit-card companies, Visa and MasterCard, barring banks from issuing American Express and Discover cards (Frank and Wilke, 1997). Antitrust violations consequently can produce enormous profits. Although profit is an obvious prod to antitrust violations, at least three subtle forces may be at work also: (1) a history of cooperation among corporations; (2) an oligopolistic market, dominated by only a few companies, which makes cooperation easy; and (3) a lack of public awareness of antitrust violations (Ermann and Lundman, 2002).

These three elements of antitrust violations can be found in the baby-food industry. Virtually every U.S. family with an infant has bought baby formula, a commercial concoction of milk and vitamins. A few parents may complain about the high price of baby formula, but most do not know that the high price stems largely from antitrust violations. These violations involve three formula companies that, with a long-standing cozy relationship, have dominated the formula industry. Their antitrust violations started in 1980 when the largest of the three companies, Abbott Laboratories, conspired with the other two to prevent a new competitor, Nestle, from entering the formula market in the United States. Since they have dominated the market, they have been able to keep the price of their formulas very high (Wilke, 2004; Jamieson, 1994; Burton, 1993b).

Deviance against the Government

Most corporate deviance against the government involves tax evasion. But tax evasion by corporations is not always illegal. Because of their pervasive and powerful political influence, large corporations can legally evade taxes through tax breaks provided by legislation and through tax loopholes made possible by the complexity of tax laws. This is why, according to a congressional study, the top 148 corporations paid less than half of the official tax rate on profits and 10 percent of these corporations paid no taxes at all (Coleman, 2006; Sloan, 1997).

But taking advantage of the loopholes may go too far and become illegal. Consider, for example, the law that exempts from taxation the profit made by U.S. companies located abroad. To take advantage of this loophole, many giant American companies make themselves multinational corporations by setting up subsidiaries in foreign countries that have very low corporate tax rates and then making it appear that most of their profits are earned abroad. Suppose an item is produced in the United States at a cost of $100 and is sold to an Irish subsidiary for $100. Because there is no profit from this transaction, no U.S. tax is paid. But then the subsidiary resells the item for $200, earning a $100 profit. The company pays only a 4 percent tax ($4) in Ireland, thereby evading the 48 percent tax in the United States. With the Irish subsidiary, then, the American company evades a lot of taxes by making it appear that most of its profits come from the foreign subsidiary (Martz, 1991).

In committing deviance against the government, corporations do not evade payment of taxes alone. They also give huge sums of campaign donations to both political parties to influence legislation toward favoring their business interests (Sabato and Simpson, 1996; Hunt, 1995). Moreover, in today's global economy, giant U.S. corporations may even bribe foreign governments or engage in some other activities abroad that are forbidden by U.S. law. An example is Baxter International Inc., the world's largest hospital-supply company, which in 1993 pleaded guilty to a felony charge of violating the U.S. law that prohibits cooperating with the Arab boycott of Israel. Since 1985 Baxter had tried to enter the vast, lucrative market of the Arab world. Arab boycott authorities would not cooperate unless Baxter first ceased its business in Israel, which Baxter finally did (Burton, 1993a). Most of the illegal activities engaged in by U.S. companies involve giving bribes worth millions of dollars to foreign officials. Still, compared with their European and Asian counterparts, U.S. corporations are much less likely to use payoffs to do business abroad, an extremely common practice in the global economy. In 2007, for example, the giant German technology corporation Siemens was found to have paid millions in bribes to government officials in Nigeria, Russia, and Libya in order to win lucrative contracts for its telecommunication equipment (Crawford et al., 2007; Milbank and Brauchli, 1995).

Deviance against the Environment

Most corporations in one way or another dump their wastes onto the land and into the air and water, primarily because they find it too costly to develop ecologically safer alternatives or antipollution devices. They are also unwilling to clean up the mess or to assume liability for the health of citizens affected by it, because to do so would cut into their profits. According to the U.S. Congress, corporations in the petrochemical, metals, electrical, and transportation industries are the more severe polluters of the environment (Barnett, 1993).

Environmental pollution affects practically all of us in some way. As Ralph Nader (1970) said, "The efflux from motor vehicles, plants, and incineration of sulfur oxides, hydrocarbons, carbon monoxide, oxides of nitrogen, particulates, and many more contaminants amounts to compulsory consumption of violence by most Americans. There is no full escape from such violent ingestions, for breathing is required." According to one Environmental Protection Agency (EPA) study, residents in poor or minority neighborhoods suffer significantly more than others. This is because landfills, garbage incinerators, toxic dump sites, and environmentally hazardous plants tend to be located near the homes of the poor and minorities (Suro, 1993).

The federal government has, since the early 1970s, tried to combat environmental pollution but with little success throughout the decade. Then, in 1980, Congress passed a law called the Comprehensive Environmental Response Compensation and Liability Act, popularly referred to as the Superfund program, intended to clean up some of the worst uncontrolled hazardous waste sites in the nation. In the early 1980s the Superfund program got off to a shaky start because the EPA was "soft" on environmental offenses. Many corporations that polluted the environment were left alone, and the few guilty ones were given every opportunity to negotiate cleanup settlements with the EPA. However, toward the late 1980s, the EPA aggressively began to enforce the Superfund law against guilty corporations. Today, these corporations are under a great deal of EPA pressure to pay for the cleanup. The industry and its insurance companies, though, have been advocating that all the cleanup costs be paid for through taxation. They argue that the general public should help pay for the cleanup because it has enjoyed many products of the industry, having in effect benefited from the production that created hazardous wastes (Barnett, 1993). Given today's widespread opposition to higher taxes, it is doubtful that the general public likes the idea of shelling out more money. Besides, many hold the corporations rather than themselves responsible for industrial waste.

A Social Profile of Corporate Crooks

Recently, many corporate executives were reported to have engaged in illegal business activities (Emshwiller et al., 2006). The most notorious ones included:

- Kenneth Lay and his fellow executives at Enron, a huge energy trading company. They plunged Enron into bankruptcy—the biggest ever in U.S. history—by pocketing millions of dollars from defrauding investors, employees, and pensioners. Lay and his fellow top executive Jeffrey Skilling were later found guilty of many counts of conspiracy and fraud.
- The top executives of the accounting firm Arthur Andersen. They were widely reported to have cooked the books of their client Enron and then shredded the incriminating documents. The shredding caused some executives to be convicted of obstructing justice.
- Scott Sullivan, chief financial officer at WorldCom, a global communications corporation, and his fellow executive Buford Yates. They were charged with masterminding a $7.2 billion securities fraud, which included pumping up the company's earnings to keep its stock price high. Both men pleaded guilty. Their boss, Bernard Ebbers, was later convicted of stock fraud, conspiracy, and false filings with securities regulators. He was sentenced to 25 years in prison.
- The founder of Adelphia, a cable television company, and his two sons. As the company's top executives, they were convicted of defrauding investors out of more than $250 million and giving themselves $2.3 billion in hidden loans from the company.
- The founder and chief executive of ImClone, a biopharmaceutical company. He was found guilty of securities fraud, obstruction of justice, and bank fraud. Domestic style queen Martha Stewart was also convicted of obstructing the federal investigation into her insider trading of ImClone stocks.

Those corporate crooks, along with the chief executive officers (CEOs) of 23 companies under investigation for illegal accounting abuses, earned 70 percent more than the

CEOs at 300 other large corporations. Specifically, the pay for the crooked CEOs averaged $62 million from 1999 to 2001, compared with $36 million for the CEOs at the other companies. As a whole, the shady CEOs at the 23 companies took home a total of $1.4 billion in those three years when the value of their companies plummeted by $530 billion and 162,000 of their employees lost their jobs. Apparently, excessive, sky-high compensation tends to encourage illegal business practices. It makes the executives feel that they, unlike their lowly and dispensable workers, are above the law (Lavelle and Prasso, 2002).

But, more important, those corrupt executives were the product of the business deregulation that has run amok for more than two decades. Their criminal activities are, therefore, not much different from the legal business practices at many U.S. corporations liberated by the same deregulation. Consider, for example, the following legal practices: (1) moving the corporate headquarters, without people, to Bermuda and other such places to evade U.S. taxes, (2) overpaying executives and granting them huge stock options and interest-free loans even when they do their jobs poorly, causing their company to lose money, (3) increasing executive pay for cutting costs by firing masses of workers, which distracts attention from executive mismanagement, (4) stacking the board of directors with insiders and friends who will shower lavish compensation on executives and turn a blind eye to their wrongdoing, and (5) giving campaign contributions to candidates from both major parties to ensure government subsidies, tax breaks, and other favors (Frank et al., 2004).

Occupational Deviance

Compared with the offenses committed by corporations, those perpetrated by individual white-collar employees for their own gain are usually less costly to the victims. But they still cost considerably more than the common crimes committed by the lower classes. There are many different forms of deviant activities in white-collar occupations, but we will analyze only the most common and costly ones.

Employee Theft

Theft by employees from the companies where they work is extremely common and costly. In the 1990s, it accounted for at least 2 percent of sales, costing an estimated $120 billion a year (Buss, 1993). Both businesses and consumers suffer. Because of employee theft, more than a thousand businesses go under every year, and the remaining, nonetheless successful businesses pass the cost of employee theft to consumers by raising prices. According to various expert estimates, about 30 percent of U.S. employees plan to steal from their employer, another 30 percent are basically good employees but may occasionally succumb to the temptation, and 40 percent are basically honest (Buss, 1993). Employee theft is probably the most pervasive and costly form of property deviance of any kind in the United States.

Most employee thieves are middle class. They are "predominantly solid, respectable citizens who pay taxes, root for major league stars, believe in the 'American way of life' and the virtues of hard work and honesty, and are quickly angered by the thought of welfare chiselers, street hoodlums, and the permissiveness and immorality, which they believe is upsetting an established social order" (Altheide et al., 1978). Why, then, do these straight arrows steal? Various researchers have provided at least three explanations (Hollinger and Clark, 1983; Altheide et al., 1978; Conklin, 1977):

1. Employee theft has much to do with *large and impersonal* corporations. Employees tend to feel little or no loyalty to such corporations, regarding them as abstract entities rather than real people. To the employee thief, stealing from a large and impersonal company is like stealing from nobody. The general public may feel the same way. As Jack Douglas and Frances Waksler (1982) say, "If someone steals your $20 calculator, you may well expect sympathy from others; if an employee of IBM steals one, people are less likely to say 'Poor IBM.'"

2. A society with a tradition of *union–management conflict,* such as the United States, tends to have a high incidence of employee theft, because workers feel exploited by and resentful toward the company. Employee theft is thus an expression of the workers' desire to get back at the company. That's why employee theft is more common in cases in which workers feel underpaid or abused by their employers, or frustrated by lack of promotions or salary raises. Such workers regard their stealing not as real theft but as an informal compensation, which they feel they fully deserve (Greenberg, 1996).

3. Workers may steal if they find *their jobs too boring.* Stealing on the job, then, becomes interesting and challenging. One study of employee thieves in a midwestern clothing store found that those who stole for the satisfaction of getting away with it outnumbered those who stole for money alone or on impulse. When not stealing, employees unhappy with their jobs tend to engage in various counterproductive activities, such as doing sloppy work, coming to work late or leaving early, taking extra-long lunch hours or coffee breaks, using a sick leave without being sick, and drinking or using drugs on the job.

Embezzlement

Embezzlement is a form of employee theft, but "embezzlement" is often used to refer to the stealing of money, while "employee theft" usually denotes stealing merchandise. Though less costly than employee theft, embezzlement in the 1990s cost $27.2 billion in one year, and commercial banks lost about five times as much money to embezzlers as they did to armed robbers (Thompson et al., 1992; Conklin, 1977).

Embezzlers range from relatively low-level employees to top executives. Many low-level employees who embezzle are middle-class bank tellers who occasionally steal several hundred dollars to solve some financial problems such as overdue bills or medical expenses. Top-level employees, of course, would make away with much more. In 1991, for example, Donald Houde, a trusted nine-year employee who was the systems director of Denver's Mile Hi Cablevision, was discovered to have embezzled $30,000 every month from the cable television company until he got caught. By then his loot had accumulated to nearly $2 million (Thompson et al., 1992).

Like Houde, most embezzlers are in management positions. Typically, they are white males in their thirties, well-paid, married with one or two children, and living in a respectable neighborhood. Embezzlers are basically hardworking, honest people; some are even pillars of their communities. Why do they steal? According to a classic explanation by sociologist Donald Cressey (1971), prospective embezzlers usually go through a social-psychological process that consists of three phases.

In the first phase, they encounter what they perceive to be an *unshareable* financial problem. They are too embarrassed to share this problem with their spouses, friends, or other people who are ordinarily available for help in financial matters. The reasons include being heavily in debt from gambling, or having a mistress, or simply feeling too much pride to ask others for help.

In the second phase, the individuals become aware of an *opportunity* for secretly solving the financial problem. The opportunity is typically embedded in the very position of trust that they hold by virtue of their respectable occupation.

And in the final, third phase, which is the most crucial, they *rationalize* away the criminal nature of embezzlement, defining the act as merely getting a temporary loan rather than as committing a theft. They expect to return the money later. As one embezzler put it, "I figured that if you could use something and help yourself and replace it and not hurt anybody, it was all right" (Coleman, 2006). This rationalization clinches the decision to carry out the embezzlement. However, compared with those in higher positions in a company, people in lower positions are less likely to rationalize—they tend more to admit that their embezzlement is a crime (Benson, 1985; Zeits, 1981).

Financial Frauds

The most common form of financial frauds involves the failure to pay income taxes. Over half of all taxpayers have been found to evade taxes to some extent. Middle- and upper-income people, especially businesspeople and lawyers, are the most common culprits. Why is tax evasion so prevalent? One reason is the popular perception of tax evasion as a very common activity, which tends to encourage many people to feel that "if everybody does it I'd be a fool if I didn't do it" (Welch et al., 2005). Another reason is the complexity of income tax laws. There are numerous ambiguous legal definitions of what constitutes income, deductions, depreciation, exemptions, and credits. These items can, therefore, be computed and manipulated in different ways, with the result that people with the same income end up paying different amounts of taxes. In effect, how much people pay depends on how well they play the "tax game." Generally, because of being able to hire smart tax accountants or lawyers, higher-income persons can play the game better than others (Coleman, 2006). The richest ones can thus boast that they pay little or no taxes; as Leona Helmsley, one of the wealthiest real estate entrepreneurs in the United States, once said, "Only little people pay taxes."

Less common than tax evasion is violation of securities law. But since most violators are professional stockbrokers and stock traders, the cost per violation is much higher. A popular form of violation by stockbrokers is defrauding customers through sales of worthless securities. Suppose a male stockbroker personally owns a lot of stock in a company that is on the verge of bankruptcy. He gets his friends on Wall Street to put out phony news releases and market analyses that make the stock look like a sure winner. After providing this fraudulent information to his clients, the stockbroker sells them all his stock.

The clients, of course, lose a bundle when the company goes under and the stock hits bottom. Increasingly more prevalent than this securities fraud are sweepstakes schemes, phony Internet stocks, and identity theft, such as using someone else's Social Security number or other personal data to get credit cards or loans (Eaton, 1999).

Another form of securities violation is insider trading. It involves an insider of a company, such as its owner or one of its executives, buying or selling its stock on confidential information not available to the general public, such as advance knowledge about a new product or unanticipated company profits or losses. Insiders can make a killing if they buy a lot of stock in their company before the public knows about the new product or unanticipated profit because the price of the stock will rise significantly after the release of the information. Such insider trading puts the general public at a distinct disadvantage, undermining the fair and honest operation of our securities markets (Szockyj, 1993).

Deviance in the Professions

There are as many forms of professional deviance as there are professions. Here we focus on just three: medical misconduct, lawyerly lawlessness, and accounting abuse.

Medical Misconduct.   Many forms of criminal conduct take place in the medical profession. We will discuss just a few.

One is *fee splitting,* which involves a doctor receiving kickbacks from another for referring patients. The doctor who receives the kickbacks is usually a general practitioner referring his patients to a surgeon or specialist. Fee splitting not only hits the patients in their pocketbooks; it can also literally maim or kill them. The reason is that doctors who seek kickbacks typically send their patients to the surgeon who splits the largest fee rather than the surgeon who does the best surgery. Unfortunately, the surgeon who splits the largest fee tends to be the worst, most dangerous surgeon, who, because of incompetence, must offer maximum kickbacks to get business (Green, 1990).

A second form of medical misconduct is *unnecessary surgery*. In one study in which 1,356 patients recommended for surgery were examined, researchers at Cornell Medical School found that 25 percent of the operations were not needed. The figures were even higher for certain parts of the body: 50 percent of pacemaker implants, 36 percent of eye surgeries, 31 percent of gall-bladder removals, 29 percent of prostate surgeries, 43 percent of hemorrhoid operations, and 32 percent of knee surgeries (Green, 1990). The basic cause of these unnecessary operations is apparently the desire for maximum profits rather than honest misdiagnosis. As research has shown, surgeons who are highly paid by insurance companies on a fee-for-service basis perform considerably more operations than surgeons who are paid much less by health maintenance organizations (HMOs) on a flat salary (Coleman, 2006).

A third form of medical misconduct is *fraudulently claiming payment* for services. This usually involves billing insurance companies and the state and federal Medicaid and Medicare programs for services never rendered, double-billing them for services rendered, or billing them for expensive physician services when, in fact, the services have been performed by nurses or other nonphysicians. Such fraudulent practices seem particularly common among doctors who lack competency and success in their profession and work in poor neighborhoods (Coleman, 2006).

Lawyerly Lawlessness.   Legal lawlessness is widespread, marked mostly by the practice of overcharging clients. According to an auditor who works full-time investigating lawyers' bills, overcharging appears in about 90 percent of the cases he is hired to examine. In one survey, more than 60 percent of lawyers themselves said that they had personal knowledge of bill padding (Budiansky et al., 1995).

The opportunities for profiteering have much to do with the intangible nature of legal work. Unlike plumbers, who render a tangible, visible service by unclogging a stuffed drain or fixing a leaky faucet, lawyers often provide such intangible services as giving a few words of advice, making a telephone call, filling out and filing a form, writing a letter, preparing a document, talking to another attorney or a government agent, negotiating with somebody, or some other similar action that the client is rarely able to observe. Therefore, although any of these actions may take only a few minutes, an attorney can charge an hour's or even several hours' fee for them. It is difficult for the clients to dispute the high fee, because they cannot see what the lawyer does behind closed doors (Stevens, 1995; Green, 1990).

Even when the clients can see the lawyer in action, especially at court appearances, there are still ample opportunities for fraudulent charging of fees. For one thing, a lawyer can intentionally delay the resolution of a case so as to have more court appearances and charge the client accordingly. Lawyers are tempted to engage in this confidence game if the client is rich. But a confidence game can also be played on poor clients, though by the reverse of delay. This tactic involves shortening the duration of a case in order to maximize the number of clients and hence the profit the lawyer can have. The lawyer can pretend to work hard on the client's behalf while persuading the client to plead guilty so that the case can be brought to a quick conclusion (Coleman, 2006).

Regardless of how they inflate their hours of service, this tendency in lawyers has inspired jokes such as this one: "A lawyer appeared at the gates of heaven and began loudly protesting that he was only 42—much too young to die. 'That's funny,' St. Peter replied. 'According to the hours you've billed, we thought you were 93'" (Budiansky et al., 1995).

Accounting Abuse.   In preparing tax returns for companies and individuals, accountants may assist their clients in falsifying their income or deductions in order to pay less taxes. But this is not a profitable area for accounting abuses, because tax preparation provides only a small portion of the accounting profession's revenues. Most of the profession's $46 billion annual revenues comes from examining corporations' financial statements. Thus, most of the abuse involves fraud or negligence in the course of doing audits (Wells, 1993).

The job of auditing a corporation's books to make certain that their accounting is accurate is extremely important in ensuring the stability and health of the nation's economy. If a company is truly as well run as the accountant says it is, then the bank that lends it money and the public that invests in it by buying its stock and becoming its shareholders have a good chance of earning a profit later. But if the accountant says the company is financially sound and strong while, in fact, it is about to go bankrupt, as Enron was, the bank and investors will likely lose their money. But the bank itself can also collude with crooked companies in defrauding their shareholders and investors, with assistance from the lender's own accountants in covering up the seedy deals. In 1993, accountants faced more than 4,000 liability suits—double the total of seven years earlier—and as much as $15 billion in damages. Most of these suits charged the accountants with failure to uncover fraud (Wells, 1993).

The major cause of this accounting abuse is obviously the conflict of interest that is built into the accountant's position as an auditor paid by the company to audit itself. Accountants find it hard to resist the proverbial temptation of not biting the hand that feeds them. They may insist that they can be totally independent of the company so as to be able to examine its books objectively, but the fact remains that they are financially dependent on that company. If they overzealously investigate the company, they will lose the job the next time around. In short, the conflict of interest prevents accountants from doing what they are supposed to do—detect fraud in the company they audit (Wells, 1993).

What Makes White-Collar Deviance Unique?

White-collar deviance is distinguishable from common crime in a number of ways. The most distinctive aspect of white-collar deviance is the rational execution of the offense to maximize profit, along with the use of power, influence, or respectability to minimize detection. Equally distinctive but less obvious are: (1) the deviant's respectable self-image, (2) the victim's unwitting cooperation, and (3) society's relative indifference toward the offense.

The Deviant's Respectable Self-Image

White-collar deviants typically see themselves as respectable individuals rather than as common criminals. This self-image plays an important part in the perpetration of various white-collar deviances.

White-collar deviants usually express their respectable self-image through certain rationalizations. Corporate executives convicted of price fixing have been found to argue that their unlawful price-fixing schemes are far from being criminal. Instead, they view themselves as having really served a worthwhile purpose for the nation's economy by "stabilizing prices," and they congratulate themselves for having effectively helped their companies by "recovering costs." There is no such thing as price fixing in their book. Embezzlers, as we have observed, tend to define their stealing as only "borrowing," insisting that they will pay the money back soon. Perpetrators of the more common employee theft feel that they actually do not steal anything from their companies because the companies are believed to make up the losses by using them as tax deductions and charging customers higher prices. Tax offenders tend to see themselves as victims rather than offenders. They would argue that they are just unlucky enough to get caught for doing something that practically everyone else does. As a convicted tax offender said, "Everybody cheats on their income tax, 95 percent of the people. Even if it's for $10 it's the same principle. I didn't cheat. I just didn't know how to report it" (Benson, 1985).

What all these different types of white-collar offenders have in common is their denial of criminal intent. They admit that they have committed the act that landed them in prison, but regard their actions as mistakes only, not acts motivated by a guilty, criminal mind. In short, they find it hard to see themselves as real criminals. As one businessman, who is in prison for price fixing, said about himself: "Having been in business for 33 years, you don't just automatically become a criminal overnight" (Benson, 1985). Even Charles Keating, who was in prison for conviction on numerous counts of bank fraud and racketeering in 1989, never admitted guilt for his actions (Zagorin, 1997). Similarly, Enron's chairman Ken Lay, after he was convicted of fraud and other corporate crimes, declared, "I firmly believe I'm innocent of the charges against me" (Clark and Lavelle, 2006).

The Victim's Unwitting Cooperation

In contrast to such common crimes as murder, robbery, rape, and assault, white-collar deviance requires an unwitting cooperation from its victims. This cooperation is unwitting because it is based on the victim's carelessness or ignorance. In a home improvement scheme, for example, the victims do not bother to check the work history of the fraudulent company that solicits them, and they sign a contract without examining its contents for such matters as the true price and the credit terms. Some victims purchase goods through the mail without checking the reputation of the firm. Doctors may prescribe untested drugs after having relied on only the drug company's salespeople and advertising. Lest we blame the victims, we should realize the difficulty for them to know they are being victimized, even if they want to find out the true nature of their victimization. Grocery shoppers, for example, are hard put to detect such dangerous substances as residues of hormones, antibiotics, pesticides, and nitrites in the meat they buy.

Society's Relative Indifference

While ignorance or carelessness leads the victim to cooperate unknowingly with white-collar deviants, society's indifference to their offense is a blessing knowingly bestowed on them. Generally, little effort is made to catch white-collar deviants, and if, on rare occasions, they are caught, they seldom go to jail. Even if they are sent to prison, they are not likely to be placed in a harsh institution or to stay there for long.

Since the early 1980s, however, there have been some signs that our society has become more concerned about white-collar deviance. Many large corporations have been prosecuted for illegal activities. In 1985 a Chicago judge gave the most severe sentence ever (25 years) to three corporate executives for an employee's death resulting from their failure to correct unsafe plant conditions. The day after the sentencing, the *Detroit Free Press* asked its readers if murder is "too harsh a charge for negligent employers." An overwhelming 80 percent of those calling in said no (Cahan et al., 1985). Sociologists have also found that most respondents in their studies rated white-collar offenses as serious as—if not more so than—street crimes (Piquero, Carmichael, and Piquero, 2008; Geis, 1984).

Does all this mean that justice can now be expected to be *collar*-blind? Hardly. Most obviously, not a single white-collar offender has been sentenced to death, let alone actually executed, for causing the deaths of many workers or customers, although many lower-class criminals have been executed for killing just one person. Moreover, most white-collar criminals, especially the big-time ones who steal hundreds of millions, continue to be punished less severely than street criminals. From 1987 through 1992, federal agents charged a staggering 95,045 white-collar individuals and corporate executives with various bank and S&L frauds, but more than 75 percent of these charges were dropped from prosecution. The few that were convicted of bank fraud received an average of only 2.4 years in prison, compared with 7.8 years for traditional bank robbery (Pizzo and Muolo, 1993). More recently, from 1995 through 2002, only 57 percent of white-collar offenders were sentenced to prison, compared to 93 percent of street criminals, and among those sent to prison the white-collar convicts served only 11 months compared to 79 months for the street criminals (Shover and Hochstetler, 2006).

It is doubtful that the government can wage an all-out war on white-collar crime because many such criminals are just too powerful, influential, or respectable. Moreover, judges are typically lenient with white-collar offenders. One reason is that most white-collar offenders have never had serious run-ins with the law. Another reason is that it is difficult to prove criminal intent: The criminal intent in robbing a liquor store may be obvious but not so in committing a business fraud that has been approved by the company's lawyers and accountants. Besides, it is difficult for the jury to find the white-collar criminal guilty in the first place. As one prosecutor says, "Look, I can wave a pair of bloody underwear in front of a jury and have their undivided attention. But I can wave a $100 million phony loan statement in front of the same jury and just watch their eyes glaze over" (Pizzo and Muolo, 1993). Their eyes glaze over not only because they find the loan statement boring, but also because they find it too complicated to understand (Jenkins, 2004; Glater, 2002; Eichenwald, 2002).

Causes of White-Collar Deviance

From analyzing the literature on white-collar crime, we can find three basic reasons why corporate executives and other white-collar personnel are likely to engage in deviant activities: deviant motivation, deviant opportunity, and weak social control. They are similar to the reasons provided by Neal Shover and Andy Hochstetler (2006) to explain the commission of white-collar crime: (1) the characteristics of the individuals predisposed to commit the crime, (2) the lure of criminal opportunity, and (3) noncredible oversight. But the data employed by Shover and Hochstetler to illustrate these reasons differ from the data presented here, which have more to do with being in a relatively high social position as suggested by the power theory in Chapter 3.

Deviant Motivation: Fear of Loss and Greed for Gain

Some evidence suggests that fear and greed have much to do with deviant activities in the white-collar world. It is well-known to Wall Street observers that fear and greed are the two most powerful human emotions driving the stock market. The fear of loss causes investors to sell stocks, which brings down their prices. If the fear is great and widely shared, it will cause a market crash. On the other hand, the greed for gain causes investors to buy more stocks, which raises their prices. If the greed is great and widely shared, it will cause a market boom. All this means in economic terms that when the supply of a stock rises—as a result of many investors wanting to sell their shares of the stock—its price falls, and when the demand for a stock rises—as a result of many investors wanting to buy more shares of the stock—its price rises.

Just as fear and greed drive the stock market, these motives seem to propel white-collar deviance. The fear of loss, such as the fear of losing one's house from mortgage foreclosure or the fear of a company going bankrupt, has been found to be associated with white-collar deviance. The deviance is characteristically the type that produces a relatively low profit or high risk of arrest, such as bank embezzlement and credit fraud. This usually involves low-level white-collar workers and small, new, or unsuccessful companies (Wheeler, 1991; Weisburd et al., 1991). The greed for gain—in order to prove to oneself how successful one can be or to turn an already large and successful corporation into an empire—is also likely to cause white-collar deviance. But the deviance is characteristically one that produces huge profit, such as buying political influence with huge donations or violating an antitrust law. It usually involves big-time executives and large, well-established, successful corporations. The greed is a by-product of success. As one researcher on white-collar crime says, "Greed is distinguished as a want that can never be satisfied: Success is ever-receding; having more leads to wanting more again" (Braithwaite, 1992).

The greed is not a psychological abnormality, though. It derives from the culture of competition, which celebrates greed as the engine of capitalism that drives people to get rich (Simpson and Piquero, 2002). This cultural encouragement of greed came through loud and clear when Ivan Boesky, before he was prosecuted and convicted of insider trading in the 1980s, was the honored commencement speaker at the School of Business Administration of the University of California at Berkeley. He told the graduates: "Greed is all right. . . . I want you to know that. I think greed is healthy. You can be greedy and still feel good about yourself." The audience roared with appreciative laughter and applause (Martz, 1986). The business graduates could identify with Boesky probably because greed is basically the same as excessive, boundless ambition, a product of the U.S. culture of success, which greatly emphasizes the importance of achieving material success in our lives.

In short, the greater the fear of loss or the greed for gain, the stronger the motivation for engaging in white-collar deviance.

Deviant Opportunity: The Benefit of High Position and Power

By itself the deviant motivation in the form of fear or greed is not enough to compel a person or corporation to engage in economic deviance. The deviance is more likely to occur if opportunities exist for carrying it out. Generally, the higher the individual's position is in a company, the more likely the "deviantly" motivated individual is to carry out a profitable deviant act, basically because of easier access to the company's resources. Thus managers, officers, or owners can be expected to be more likely than lower-level personnel to steal from the company. Relatively high status and prestige in society also make it easier to defraud unsuspecting victims because status and prestige lend the appearance of legitimacy and trustworthiness and reduce the target's guard against being victimized (Weisburd et al., 1991). A combination of high position, status, and prestige can thus provide the greatest opportunity for deviant activities, which in turn is likely to turn a deviant motivation into a deviant action.

For the same reason, the more power corporations have, the more likely they are to commit corporate crime. There is evidence to support this statement. In one study, for example, large corporations constituted only 42 percent of all companies investigated, but accounted for 70 percent of all violations—compared with 20 percent for medium-sized companies and 10 percent for small firms (Clinard and Yeager, 1980).

Weak Social Control: Lax Law Enforcement

It is widely known that law enforcers do not exercise as much control over white-collar deviance as over street crime. As we have indicated, for example, the penalty for bank fraud committed by a bank's executive or owner averages only 2.4 years in prison, compared with 7.8 years for bank robbery perpetrated by a lower-income person. As a result, white-collar crime by the rich and powerful can be expected to be more prevalent than street crime by the poor and powerless. Sometimes the government even directly encourages the rich to engage in deviance with its deregulation policies, as we can see from the proliferation of banking frauds in the 1980s after the government deregulated the banking industry (Glasberg and Skidmore, 1998). Deregulation may also involve implicitly suggesting to the doctors that the government would not rigorously question their professional judgments on how much to charge for providing Medicare and Medicaid services. This may explain the prevalence of physicians overcharging the government or charging it for services never rendered to the patients (Shover and Hochstetler, 2006).

Some studies, however, claim to have found that the overwhelming majority of white-collar criminals are far from rich and powerful but instead are pitiful middle-class people such as the bank teller who, saddled with overdue bills, embezzles only a few hundred dollars (Weisburd et al., 1991). The sample of such studies is usually a biased one, representing mostly the losers among white-collar criminals, namely, those who are prosecuted or convicted for their crimes. But the plain fact is that most white-collar criminals, particularly those who are rich and powerful, are not caught, which is, in fact, a powerful testimony to the relative lack of law enforcement against them.

Law enforcers are not entirely to blame for the weaker control experienced by more powerful deviants. The huge power commanded by such deviants plays a role too. In the pharmaceutical industry, for example, the government's regulatory agencies may try to confiscate drugs that have not been properly tested. But powerful drug companies can use their considerable resources to stop the confiscation. They may bribe the regulatory agents or pay unethical medical researchers to produce fraudulent evidence that the drugs are safe. To ensure against prosecution for bribery, some pharmaceutical companies even have employees who are, as part of their job description, responsible for going to jail. If a head has to "go on the chopping block," it would be the heads of these employees (Braithwaite, 1993, 1992).

In brief, more powerful corporations and individuals are more likely than others to engage in deviant activities because of weaker social control.

Governmental Deviance

Most of us seem to be ambivalent about our government officials. On the one hand, we expect them to break the law every now and then and we may, when seeing one of them get caught, remark, "There goes another crook." Mark Twain expressed this popular sentiment well when he said way back in 1894: "It could probably be shown with facts and figures that there is no distinctly American criminal class except Congress." On the other hand, we respect and admire them for being our leaders, often so much so that we would scramble in a crowd to get their autographs or shake their hands with a sense of pride and honor. Given these conflicting feelings of revulsion and respect, we nonetheless try to be objective in analyzing governmental deviance. This type of deviance essentially involves the abuse of power by government officials or politicians running for elected office. Here we focus on three types of governmental deviance: political corruption, election improprieties, and official violence.

Political Corruption

Political corruption is usually associated with graft or bribery—the abuse of power for personal gain. It may take the form of an outright bribe, in which case the public official accepts the money offered by a briber who expects a favor in return. Outright bribery routinely takes place in poor countries because it has become a part of their culture (Omestad, 1997). Outright bribery is far less common in the United States. The types of political corruption that occur more often in this country include kickbacks, management of public funds for personal gain, and illegal use of mail privileges.

Receiving Kickbacks from Businesses.   The federal government spends an enormous sum of taxpayer money on goods and services supplied by various businesses. The officials in charge of purchasing these goods and services may find it hard to resist kickbacks from the companies they are dealing with. To receive kickbacks, though, the officials will allow businesses to send the government outrageous bills. Thus, repair contractors and suppliers have been known to bill the government for work that was never done and for materials that were never delivered. Officials in the U.S. Defense Department are also known to have paid hundreds of dollars for a hammer and hundreds more for a toilet seat. Moreover, there are always some U.S. Congress members who receive bribes from companies for helping them get lucrative contracts and other favors from the government (Brush, 2005).

Abusive Management of Public Funds.   The management of public funds is a potential source of political corruption. City or state treasurers can be tempted to misuse the millions of dollars for personal gain, especially because there are many subtle, unprosecutable ways to do it. In deciding which bank to deposit an enormous sum of public money into, government officials may base their decision on whether it will profit themselves financially and politically. Thus, they may choose a bank of which they are shareholders; or a bank that will give their family members or business associates loans at low interest rates; or a bank that has promised to contribute substantially to their political campaigns.

Abusing the Frank.   The most common form of official corruption is probably the abuse of the frank—the privilege of sending mail free of charge. Our Founding Fathers intended the frank to be for official use only, namely, for answering letters from constituents. However, members of Congress routinely abuse the frank for personal purposes by sending out campaign information to ensure reelection. They, in effect, turn the franking system into a "taxpayer-funded propaganda machine" (Sabato and Simpson, 1996). As a congressman explained to his new press aide, "We are going to mail, mail, mail and then mail some more. You're going to mail until you run out of ideas. Then you're going to talk to the rest of the staff and mail until they run out of ideas. After that you're going to come to me and mail until I run out of ideas. And when that happens, we're going to staple my picture to pages of the goddamn Yellow Book and mail them out, too, and lemme tell you, you can't ever run out of them sons of bitches" (Jackley, 1992).

Election Improprieties

Our representative democracy requires that we, the masses, have the right to choose our leaders. This right, however, often has little meaning to those who want to be our leaders. Therefore, various devious means are often used to win elections.

Denial of Voting Right.   The masses of citizenry are encouraged to participate in the presidential election. But in reality it is the electoral college—consisting of political leaders, not the populace—that selects the president. This should largely be blamed on the writers of the Constitution rather than on current political leaders, but it is important to realize that the "voters" are in a way bypassed to let political leaders decide who should be president (Simon, 2006).

Political Dirty Tricks.   Dirty tricks are often employed to ensure victory in an election. They include spreading rumors about the opponent's strange character, kinky sex life, or association with drug kingpins; having individuals in the audience at the opponent's rally heckle or ask embarrassing questions; defacing the opponent's billboards; and stealing the opponent's campaign mail. A more sophisticated form of dirty trick is the "telephone sleaze" in which campaign workers call voters, say they are conducting a nonpartisan survey, then ask loaded questions such as, "Did you know Senator Jones wants to vote against the banning of child pornography?" (Sabato and Simpson, 1996).

Campaign Finance Abuses.   Candidates for elected office often solicit and receive huge campaign contributions from monied interests (large corporations and wealthy individuals) and the donors expect the politicians to return the favor if elected. Incumbent legislators running *unopposed* also receive large contributions from the rich with the same expectation. As a result, the rich can gain access to the White House and Congress that ordinary citizens cannot. All this, in effect, involves the buying and selling of political influence or access to elected officials. When Bill Clinton was president, for example, prominent bankers who had contributed heavily to his reelection campaign were invited to the White House to discuss banking regulations with him and the nation's senior banking regulator, while executives of the giant tobacco company Philip Morris, a huge contributor to the Republicans, were able to discuss their concerns with Republican congressional leaders (van Natta and Fritsch, 1997; Wertheimer, 1996).

Official Violence

There is a long history of governmental violence against various groups of citizens in the United States. The government, for example, drove Native Americans out of their lands and killed many of them in the early period of U.S. history. Today, most official violence involves police brutality against citizens, especially African and Hispanic Americans in large cities. When complaints of police brutality are brought against some officers, they are often dismissed as being without merit. If some complaints are admitted as legitimate, they are blamed on "only a few bad apples" in the police department. But these bad apples are usually kept on the force to rot rather than thrown out. Consequently, in nearly every large city's police department, there's a small group of officers committing most of the police brutality. Some police forces have used a civilian review board to prevent police brutality, but most refuse to subject themselves to outside control, believing that they can police themselves (Kappeler, Sluder, and Alpert, 1998; Gleick, 1995; Herbert, 1995).

As a democracy, however, the United States commits *democide* (the killing of people by their government) to a much smaller extent than many other nations. For the twentieth century, democratic states account for only about 1 percent of all government-sponsored murders throughout the world. The vast majority of such killings have been carried out by Communist and authoritarian governments. The most notorious have been the Soviet Union, China, and the Khmer Rouge, the last of which liquidated about one-third of the Cambodian population. Moreover, the governments of poorer nations commit democide on a larger scale than do richer nations. Apparently, the authorities in poor countries view life as cheap. But as the economy of these nations improves, the incidence of democide tends to decline, because "even ruthless dictators need tax revenue, and you can't collect taxes from dead people" (Scully, 1997).

A Global Perspective on Official Corruption

Official corruption is a common practice around the world. Generally, the poorer a country is, the more corrupt its public officials are. In fact, in most of the world's poor countries, corruption is so prevalent that it is considered normal. There, people have to grease the public official's palm to obtain or retain business, to secure government contracts, or to pay for public service that is supposed to be free such as enrolling children in public school. Corruption hurts the poor more than others, because they spend more on bribes as a share of their small income while their access to badly needed public services is curtailed. Corruption hurts the poor in another way: Every year the World Bank, which gets most of its money from 40 rich countries, loans more than 20 billion dollars to developing countries for the purpose of helping their desperately poor citizens. But an enormous sum of that money ends up in their government officials' pockets (Pound and Knight, 2006; Transparency International, 2004).

Official corruption discourages foreign investment in the corrupt country, which helps to retard its economic growth. This is a major reason why it is extremely difficult for many developing countries to climb out of their poverty. But corruption has helped a few East Asian countries, such as South Korea, Taiwan, Thailand, and Japan, become prosperous. This is because in exchange for bribes and kickbacks from large business companies, government officials offer cheap loans, tax benefits, protection against foreign imports, and other subsidies and support. Unfortunately, though, many developing countries are too poor to have the same large businesses and resource-rich governments that those newly industrialized East Asian countries have (Rock and Bonnett, 2004).

Research in various countries has indicated at least three major causes of official corruption. One is poverty, as suggested by the fact that corruption is much more common in developing countries than in developed ones. This is because the governments in poor countries do not have enough tax revenues to pay their public officials adequately on a regular basis. A second cause of corruption is a large population, which makes surveillance on a massive number of public officials difficult. This may explain why the world's largest country, China, and the fourth largest country, Indonesia, are among the most corrupt on earth while the tiny city state of Singapore is one of the least corrupt. And a third cause of corruption is the lack of democracy. This may explain the higher frequency of corruption in authoritarian countries, which generally do not have what democracies have: the anti-corruption surveillance by citizen groups, the press, and reform-minded politicians (Cheung and Chan, 2008; Xin and Rudel, 2004).

Official Ways of Neutralizing Deviance

Government officials take great care to cover up their deviant acts. Even after such acts have been uncovered, the officials rarely admit their guilt. Instead, they automatically attempt to neutralize their deviance—to make it appear as if they had done nothing wrong. Such an attempt has been called "the ritual of wiggle." There are different ways for government officials to wiggle out of their deviant activities. Let's take a look at their most common techniques of neutralization (Lieberman, 1973).

Denying the Obvious

Public officials tend to deny that any wrongdoing has occurred, no matter how strong the suspicion or how clear the reality. The denial is as frequently and honestly repeated as possible. Even a popular president like Ronald Reagan found it hard to tell the truth. In late 1986, when the arms deal with Iran shocked the nation, he insisted that he did not know of the diversion of funds to the Nicaraguan rebels, although it was clear to many Americans that he did. In a nationwide poll, 47 percent of the respondents said that he was "lying" (the exact word used in the question) while only 37 percent said that he was telling the truth (Church, 1986). More recently, former President Clinton denied that there was anything wrong with him having coffees or lunches in the White House with his wealthy contributors. He said, for example, "I think it is an appropriate thing and can be a good thing for the President and for the Secretary of the Treasury to meet with a group of bankers and listen to them and listen to their concerns" (Mitchell, 1997). Most recently President Bush, along with his vice president and other members of his administration, was reluctant to admit making some mistakes in starting or executing the war in Iraq. The prevalence of this official denial of wrongdoing has led a political observer to conclude: "No one in politics can ever admit to a mistake these days. In real life, none of us is perfect. But in politics, strangely enough, mistakes almost never happen" (Borger, 2006).

Ignoring the Deviance

If an illegal act is a private one committed by individual officials, they ignore it by disconnecting their phones, going into hiding or on a trip away from the press, or simply saying "no comment." If the government is supposed to take action against its officials for some lawbreaking, it resorts to evasive responses by insisting that the facts do not conclusively and absolutely warrant governmental intervention. The government, for example, has failed to address itself adequately to the issue of the legality of the United States' involvement in the Vietnam War. Even if they have been found guilty, officials still tend to act as if their deviance is not really deviant. In 1997, for example, after House Speaker Newt Gingrich was reprimanded and fined $300,000 for years of unethical conduct, he dismissed his misdeeds as only comparable to jaywalking (Weisman, 1997).

Accusing the Accuser

In the case of private offenses, the individual official may threaten or actually file a libel suit against the journalist who publicized the offense. Although it is almost impossible to prove libel, the official hopes that the suit will divert public attention from the official's own wrongdoing. The government hopes for the same thing when it accuses its accuser. This is why the Nixon administration often attacked the news media for distorting facts when its illegal activities were publicized. Also, when CBS-TV News broadcast its critical documentary *The Selling of the Pentagon,* a House committee launched an investigation into CBS-TV News rather than into the Defense Department. In 1992, when Senator Brock Adams of Washington State was accused by a woman of sexually molesting her, he claimed she was mentally ill, though eight other women had independently alleged similar sexual harassment by him (Trost and Thomas, 1993). Most recently, in 2006, the FBI videotaped Congressman William Jefferson of Louisiana receiving a $100,000 bribe and then executed a search warrant of his home and found $90,000 of that money in his freezer. Later the FBI searched his office, also with a warrant from a federal judge. But his lawyer called the search "outrageous," and his congressional leaders accused the federal agents of violating the separation of powers between the legislative and executive branches of government (Isikoff et al., 2006).

Promising to Take Action

When high government officials are under intense pressure to do something about a certain incident, they will publicly promise to take action to deal with it. Yet, behind the scenes, the promised action is not seriously carried out. In the 1970s, when the Watergate scandal broke, the Attorney General promised to make the Justice Department's investigation of the scandal "the most extensive, thorough and comprehensive investigation since the assassination of President Kennedy." But it was only a promise; nothing came of it. In the 1980s, when confronted with the scandal of selling arms to Iran and diverting funds to the Nicaraguan rebels, President Reagan kept repeating that he wanted all the facts to come out. Yet he did not try very hard to get the facts out. He did not even demand from his aides, who were the key figures in the scandal, an accounting of what they did (Church, 1986). More recently, President Clinton repeatedly announced his intent to help clean up the system that effectively encourages politicians to sell access or influence for large campaign contributions. But he continued to raise funds for his political party by soliciting huge donations from big corporations and wealthy individuals (Mitchell, 1997). Similarly, in 2006, the U.S. Congress promised to pass reform bills to crack down on corrupt lawmakers, but it was widely seen as mere window dressing and thus expected to result in business as usual, just like many other broken promises by the government to eliminate official deviance (Knight, 2006; Continetti, 2006).

Justifying the Deviance

This method of neutralization is rationalization par excellence. Although they have implicitly admitted their wrongdoing with their promise to deal with it, the guilty officials rationalize that it was necessary for them to commit the deviant act. This should not be surprising, because it has the support of the popular belief that the end sometimes justifies the means. Thus, many officials justify unlawful wiretapping on the grounds that the danger of not using it against suspected criminals or terrorists is too great. In the early 1970s, President Nixon, the CIA, and the FBI even justified domestic surveillance of U.S. citizens as in the interest of national security. In the 1950s and 1960s, top U.S. military and intelligence officials insisted that it was necessary to use unsuspecting Americans as guinea pigs for mind-control experiments by sneaking powerful mind-altering drugs into their drinks because there had been reports of Soviet success at mind control (Budiansky et al., 1994). In 1997 President Clinton defended his solicitation of big political donations, saying, "I do not believe you will ever get the politics out of politics. And that's not bad" (Mitchell, 1997). In 2004 the Secretary of Defense effectively approved torturing prisoners when he declared that detainees should not get all the rights and privileges accorded prisoners of war under the Geneva Convention because they are unlawful combatants (Barry et al., 2004).

Causes of Governmental Deviance

A review of various studies on governmental deviance suggests at least three important causes of the problem: the superabundance of ambiguous laws, governmental complexity, and power.

Superabundance of Ambiguous Laws

Government officials operate under a *superabundance of ambiguous laws*—lack of clear-cut laws for controlling official action. This enormous collection of ambiguous laws has been described by a legal scholar "as a wall of lattice-work: the thin strips of wood represent all of our legal rules, but the pervasive holes are very prominent; indeed, but for the holes there would be no design at all" (Lieberman, 1973). The "holes" referred to in the quote are popularly known as *loopholes,* meaning the ambiguity of laws through which the intent of the laws can be evaded. Therefore, the superabundance of ambiguous laws inevitably creates a "discretionary wilderness" where government officials are relatively free to rely on their own judgment and self-interest to interpret the law. This kind of interpretation opens up a great deal of opportunity for officials to engage in deviant activities, whenever they so desire, with impunity.

In fact, as is well known among historians studying the U.S. presidency, many laws are purposely ambiguous, designed to give presidents a lot of room to do their job. "The Reagan Administration," for example, "has followed the lead of its predecessors in emphasizing semantic interpretations to exempt its actions from various laws. As the Truman Administration called the Korean war a 'police action' to circumvent the necessity for a declaration of war, so the Reagan Administration said that its assistance to the Nicaraguan rebels was part of a strategy of 'interdicting' supply lines to El Salvador's communist insurgents rather than of undermining the Sandinista Government of Nicaragua" (Tolchin, 1986). Earlier, Presidents Lyndon Johnson and Richard Nixon had also skirted the law when they sent troops into combat in Vietnam without the benefit of a congressional declaration of war. More recently, President Bill Clinton went around the law to raise money for his reelection campaign. Once, for example, after President Clinton received word that a rich man wanted to donate $5 million to his campaign fund, he instructed his White House deputy chief of staff to handle the matter, although it is against the law for a government official to raise campaign funds (Isikoff, 1997).

Governmental Complexity and Power

Given the intricate, complex nature of the government as a huge organization, it is inevitable that its members cannot have complete information and responsibility regarding what and how they should do their jobs in the organization. Due to this lack of information and responsibility, then, officials tend to get involved in deviant activities (Ermann and Lundman, 2002).

This explanation, however, implies that officials are not to blame for committing deviance because, given the lack of information and responsibility, they do not knowingly or intentionally get involved in deviance. Thus, the concept of governmental complexity can best be used to explain *unintentional* deviance among government officials. As for their *intentional* deviance, which essentially involves an abuse of power, it may be better explained by the power theory that we have developed in Chapter 3 and applied to white-collar deviance earlier in this chapter. According to the power theory, there are three reasons why government officials tend to purposely abuse their power: stronger deviant motivation, greater deviant opportunity, and weaker social control. Due to their relatively high position in society, governmental officials tend to be too ambitious, thereby more likely to experience relative deprivation, which would motivate them to employ deviant means to achieve their high goals. They are further encouraged to abuse their power because they enjoy abundant opportunities for doing so and are not subject to stringent social control, thanks again to their lofty position in society.

Summary

1. What is white-collar deviance? Traditionally called white-collar crime, white-collar deviance includes both criminal and noncriminal forms of economic deviance carried out by relatively high-status people as part of an occupation for their personal gain (hence occupational deviance) or on behalf of their corporation (hence corporate deviance).

2. What is the nature of corporate deviance? It can be divided into four types on the basis of who or what their victims are. Deviance against employees involves a corporation ignoring its employees' health and safety; deviance against customers involves a corporation dealing in dangerous foods or unsafe products, engaging in commercial frauds or deceptive advertising, and violating antitrust laws; deviance against the government includes evading payment of taxes, using campaign donations to buy influence, and bribing foreign governments or committing other illegal acts abroad; and deviance against the environment involves polluting the environment.

3. What is the social profile of corporate crooks? They are top corporate executives charged with fraud and other illegal business activities. They are much more highly paid than their already highly paid noncriminal peers. Their sky-high pay may cause them to feel that they are above the law, but their illegal business practices are not much different from the legal practices that result from too much deregulation.

4. What is the nature of occupational deviance? Carried out for the employees' own gain rather than on behalf of their company, occupational deviance includes employee theft, embezzlement, tax and securities violations, and deviance in such professions as medicine, law, and accounting.

5. How does white-collar deviance differ from common, street crime? White-collar deviance is distinguishable for its rational execution of the offense as well as the offender's respectable self-image, the victim's unwitting cooperation, and society's relative indifference toward the offense.

6. What causes white-collar deviance? Generally, the causes of white-collar deviance are stronger deviant motivation, greater deviant opportunity, and weaker social control. The motivation involves the fear of loss and greed for gain. The opportunity inheres in a higher position in a company or in the more powerful corporation. And weaker control comes from less stringent law enforcement against white-collar deviance.

7. What is the nature of governmental deviance? Government deviance involves the abuse of power by government officials or candidates for elected office. Such deviance appears in different forms, including political corruption, election improprieties, and official violence. Political corruption includes receiving kickbacks from businesses, abusing the management of public funds, and abusing the frank. Election improprieties include denial of the right to really elect the president, playing dirty tricks on the election opponent, and the buying and selling of political influence that favors the rich over ordinary citizens. Official violence involves mostly police brutality against crime suspects and innocent citizens, especially African and Hispanic Americans.

8. What are the nature and causes of official corruption around the world? Corruption is a common practice all over the world but more prevalent in poor countries, where it is considered normal. Corruption hurts the poor citizens more than the rich and usually retards the nation's economic growth. Causes of corruption include poverty, large population, and the lack of democracy.

9. What would government officials do if their illegal activities were revealed to the public? They would try to neutralize their deviance. This neutralization takes the form of denying the obvious, ignoring the deviance, accusing the accuser, promising to take action, and justifying the deviance.

10. What causes governmental deviance? The causes of governmental deviance include the superabundance of ambiguous laws, governmental complexity, and power that creates deviant motivation, deviant opportunity, and weak control.

FURTHER READING

Coleman, James William. 2006. *The Criminal Elite: Understanding White-Collar Crime*, 6th ed. New York: St. Martin's. A comprehensive review of the literature on white-collar crime, dealing with the types, characteristics, origins, and legal control of the crime.

Continetti, Matthew. 2006. *The K Street Gang: The Rise and Fall of the Republican Machine*. New York: Doubleday. An analysis of how the lobbyists in the nation's capital corrupt the Republican politicians while enriching themselves.

Croall, Hazel. 2001. *Understanding White-Collar Crime*. Philadelphia: Open University Press. A concise text on white-collar crime, covering the nature, regulation, and explanation of the subject.

Ermann, M. David, and Richard J. Lundman (eds.). 2002. *Corporate and Governmental Deviance*, 6th ed. New York: Oxford University Press. A collection of articles dealing with the characteristics of elite deviance, its impact on people, and societal reactions to it.

Friedrichs, David O. 1996. *Trusted Criminals: White-Collar Crime in Contemporary Society*. Belmont, Calif.: Wadsworth. A comprehensive text covering various types and characteristics of white-collar deviance.

Green, Gary S. 1990. *Occupational Crime*. Chicago: Nelson-Hall. Deals with various kinds of crime committed in the course of one's occupation, as well as the concept, measurements, explanations, and control of occupational crime.

Poveda, Tony G. 1994. *Rethinking White-Collar Crime*. Westport, Conn.: Praeger. An analysis of the theoretical issues about the definition, explanation, and social control of white-collar crime.

Rosoff, Stephen M., Henry N. Pontell, and Robert H. Tillman. 2002. *Profit Without Honor: White-Collar Crime and the Looting of America*, 2d ed. Upper Saddle River, N.J.: Prentice Hall. Describing in great detail the nature of various forms of white-collar crime, including consumer fraud, governmental abuse of power, medical crime, and computer crime.

Sabato, Larry J., and Glenn R. Simpson. 1996. *Dirty Little Secrets: The Persistence of Corruption in American Politics*. New York: Times Book. Discusses how corruption flourishes in the current political system that serves big-money interests more than the ordinary citizenry.

Schlegel, Kip, and David Weisburd (eds.). 1992. *White-Collar Crime Reconsidered*. Boston: Northeastern University Press. A collection of articles by various sociological researchers on the definitions, theories, victimization, and control of white-collar crime.

Simon, David R. 2006. *Elite Deviance*, 8th ed. Boston: Allyn and Bacon. A survey of various forms of elite deviance, including corporate deviance, international deviance, and political deviance.

Simon, David R., and Frank E. Hagan. 1999. *White-Collar Deviance*. Boston: Allyn and Bacon. Presents various aspects of white-collar deviance.

Shichor, David, Larry Gaines, and Richard Ball, eds. 2002. *Readings in White-Collar Crime*. Prospect Heights, Ill.: Waveland Press. An anthology of articles dealing with the sociological definition of the subject, various forms of white-collar crime, and the treatment of white-collar criminals by the criminal justice system.

Shover, Neal, and Andy Hochstetler. 2006. *Choosing White-Collar Crime*. New York: Cambridge University Press. Using rational-choice theory to explain why and how people commit white-collar crime and why it has proliferated over the last several decades.

Shover, Neal, and John Paul Wright, eds. 2001. *Crimes of Privilege: Readings in White-Collar Crime*. New York: Oxford University Press. A collection of articles covering the costs, opportunities, decision-making processes, characteristics, and controlling of white-collar crime.

Sutherland, Edwin H. 1983. *White-Collar Crime: The Uncut Version*. New Haven, Conn.: Yale University Press. A classic on white-collar crime, with introductory remarks by contemporary sociologists Gilbert Geis and Colin Goff.

Weisburd, David, Elin Waring, and Ellen F. Chayet. 2001. *White-Collar Crime and Criminal Careers*. New York: Cambridge University Press. An analysis of the criminal careers of white-collar offenders who repeatedly run afoul of the law.

Weisburd, David, Stanton Wheeler, Elin Waring, and Nancy Bode. 1991. *Crimes of the Middle Classes: White-Collar Offenders in the Federal Courts*. New Haven, Conn.: Yale University Press. An empirical study of middle-class white-collar offenders who get caught for their crimes.

CRITICAL THINKING QUESTIONS

1. Free enterprise, the heart of capitalism, enables business to operate for profit without interference by government and is often credited with the affluence we enjoy as a society. Is corporate deviance, then, a necessary evil of capitalism, a price we have to pay for the affluence? Or is it an insufferable problem that can be eliminated without destroying capitalism? Whatever your answer, provide an explanation.

2. When they are known to have committed a deviant act, why don't politicians and government officials readily confess it to the public? If they do confess, under what circumstances would the public forgive them and under what circumstances would the public not forgive them?

14 Underprivileged Deviance

Myths and Realities

Myth: Robbery is a violent crime because it involves the use of violence or threat of violence against the victim.

Reality: Robbery is simultaneously both a property crime and a violent crime. It is a property crime for illegally taking the victim's possession. It is also a violent crime for using violence or the threat of violence against the victim (p. 365).

Myth: The majority of robbers commit robbery with a gun mostly because they want to enjoy the thrill of power over their cowering victims.

Reality: Most robbers, whether armed or unarmed, are *primarily* interested in money, just like the notorious Willie Sutton. When asked why he robbed banks, he said, "Because that's where the money is" (p. 365).

Myth: Unarmed robberies are less dangerous than armed robberies.

Reality: Unarmed robberies are far more likely to result in injury to the victims because the robbers assume that the victims are more likely to resist when there is no weapon involved than when there is a weapon (p. 366).

Myth: Of all the robberies that take place indoors, a significant number occur in banks.

Reality: Bank robbery is relatively rare, accounting for only about 5 percent of indoor robberies (p. 367).

Myth: Most auto thefts involve teenagers stealing a car for purposes of "joy riding"—driving the car for a while and then abandoning it.

Reality: Joy riding used to be popular in the 1960s and 1970s. Today most auto thieves steal cars in order to sell them for a quick and handsome profit (p. 371).

Myth: Most burglaries occur at night when the victims are sound asleep.

Reality: Most burglaries occur during the day when the homes are empty because the occupants are at work, at school, out shopping, or away on vacation (pp. 372–373).

Myth: Large dogs may deter burglary but small dogs do not.

Reality: Most burglars stay away from a house if they know there is a dog in it. Even small dogs are effective in deterring burglary; as one burglar explains, "Little dogs yap too much. The neighbors look to see what they are so excited about" (p. 373).

Myth: Shoplifting is mostly a female crime, because women shop more often than men.

Reality: Most of the shoplifters are men (p. 374).

Myth: The Mafia is as influential and powerful today as it was some thirty years ago.

Reality: The Mafia has lost some of its dominance over the underworld. Virtually all of the Mafia bosses have been sent to prison (p. 379).

Myth: If the United States is relatively successful in diminishing the power of organized crime, other nations such as Italy, Japan, Hong Kong, and Russia can achieve the same result.

Reality: It is much more difficult for those foreign countries to combat their organized crime because its power and influence have penetrated more deeply into their conventional world of business, politics, and culture (p. 381).

The street gangs of Central America have spun a web of robberies and killings through Guatemala, El Salvador, Honduras, and even the United States. They are estimated to have as many as 100,000 members, of which about 40 percent are young women. Benky used to be one of these women. Having lived on the streets since she was six years old, she decided to join one of these gangs at the age of 14. To do so, she had to have sex with a dozen or so of her homeboys. She recalls sobbing when the last young man climbed off her. After thus becoming a full-fledged member of the gang, she always did what its leader told her to do, such as robbing buses and killing rival gangs' members (Lacey, 2008).

Benky, along with other gang members, can be said to engage in *underprivileged deviance,* deviance that typically occurs among underprivileged people who come from relatively poor and powerless backgrounds. Underprivileged deviance is generally distinguishable from privileged deviance in being less profitable. In this chapter we will discuss various examples of underprivileged deviance, including robbery, auto theft and carjacking, burglary, shoplifting, and organized crime.

Robbery

Robbery is simultaneously both a property and a violent crime. It is a property crime because it involves illegally taking the victim's property; it is a violent crime for the use of violence or threat of violence against the victim in its commission. We will first examine these two connected facets of robbery, and then look at the patterns of robbery, such as where or when robbery usually occurs, what robbers are like, and why they commit robbery.

Robbery as a Property Crime

As a property crime, robbery is a relatively rational, calculated act, and as such, it involves making rational decisions. The decision making consists of a sequence of three elements: (1) deciding to rob mostly for financial gain, (2) deciding what target to rob, and (3) deciding how to carry out the robbery (Conklin, 1972).

Deciding to Rob for Money. For most robbers the decision to rob is based on their desire for money. But psychiatrists tend to assume that armed robbers are basically abnormal, suffering from a sense of inadequacy and weakness and, therefore, committing robbery with a firearm as a way of seeking self-adequacy and power. One armed robber is quoted as saying, "When I have a gun in my hands nothing can stop me. It makes me feel important and strong. With a revolver you're somebody" (Gabor et al., 1987). This may be true of some robbers, but *most* robbers, whether armed or unarmed, are *primarily* interested in money, just like the notorious Willie Sutton. When asked why he robbed banks, Sutton replied, "Because that's where the money is." The pursuit of power in robbery, if it exists, is only a *secondary* motive (Haran and Martin, 1984).

Deciding Which Target to Rob. Once they have decided to rob, would-be robbers have to select a certain target. Target selection is generally based on two factors: (1) Robbers usually consider *lucrative* establishments—such as banks, grocery stores, and other places where large sums of cash are available—as potential targets. (2) They usually select from among these targets one with a *lower risk of arrest*. Thus, most robbers choose, for example, to hold up a branch bank in an outlying commercial area with few people that is close to a highway, rather than the main bank in the busy central business district.

Deciding How to Rob. This last decision involves varying degrees of planning. At one extreme, some robbers, particularly professional ones who are after a big score, plan their crimes with great care and minute detail. At the other extreme, some robbers, especially amateur ones who suddenly feel the need for a small sum of cash, commit robbery on the spur of the moment, with hardly any planning. The majority of robberies are more carefully planned than not, as evidenced by the relatively low rate of arrest for such a crime; only about one out of four robberies ends in arrest (FBI, 2008).

Robbery as a Violent Crime

There are two facets to robbery as a violent crime: One involves actual violence, the other potential violence. Because they do not carry a weapon, *unarmed robbers* usually have to resort to *actual violence* to subdue the victim; hence the crime is also called *strong-arm robbery*. But *armed robbers* tend more to rely only on *potential violence*—the threat of force—made to appear real and frightening to the victim by the sight of a weapon. Nowadays, in many communities there is a lack of faith in the police's ability to control crime. As a result, robbers are more likely to use a gun than not, assuming that they can get away with the crime and that their victims will carry a gun to protect themselves (Warner, 2007).

Unarmed Robbery and Actual Violence.   Unarmed or strong-arm robberies are often viewed by the public as less dangerous than armed robberies. But, in reality, the opposite is true: Unarmed robberies are far more likely to result in injury to the victims. According to one study, 66 percent of unarmed-robbery victims, compared to only 17 percent of armed-robbery victims, were injured (Feeney and Weir, 1975). Of course, armed robberies are more likely to result in the victim's death. But the likelihood of fatality is extremely small: Victims die in fewer than one percent of all robberies carried out with a gun (Wright, Rossi, and Daly, 1983; Feeney and Weir, 1975).

Unarmed robberies are more dangerous because offenders believe that victims are more likely to resist when there is no weapon involved than when there is a weapon. As one unarmed robber says, "In strongarms, you have to put [the victim] out of commission for a few minutes. When you haven't got a gun or knife, he won't do anything. He'll tell you to go to hell or turn on you. So all you can do is knock him out" (Luckenbill, 1981).

Armed Robbery and Potential Violence.   As a threat of force, potential violence in armed robbery rarely turns into real violence because the use of a weapon, particularly a firearm, often ensures the successful execution of the crime. There are four ways in which a weapon can help robbers accomplish their goal efficiently (Conklin, 1972).

First, the weapon creates a *buffer zone* between offender and victim. Many robbers believe that the firearm is the most effective weapon because it frightens the victim the most. With the firearm holding the victim at a distance, the robber can cover a large area and can also control many victims at the same time. Second, the weapon *intimidates* the victim, making it unnecessary for the robber to resort to violence. If the show of a weapon fails to intimidate the victims enough to give up their money, the offender often tries to increase the level of intimidation by cocking the pistol or holding it to the victim's head. If this attempt also fails, the robber may be compelled to use the weapon for the third purpose—to *make good the threat*. A few robbers stab or shoot the victim, but most simply strike—without seriously hurting—the victim on the side of the head or in the stomach to show that they "mean business." If this still does not work and the victim resists strongly, most robbers would not hesitate to kill the victim (Wright and Decker, 1997). According to an analysis of over 815 robberies reported to Chicago police, only a few (7 percent) of the victims did resist actively and most of these victims were killed (Meer, 1985). Fourth, the weapon *ensures escape* after the completion of the crime, as robbers use the weapon to prevent the victims, witnesses, and even police officers from interfering with their escape.

Patterns of Robbery

Robbery is basically a *big-city* crime. The robbery rate in large cities is many times higher than in rural areas. Relatedly, the more urbanized a region, the higher its rate of robbery. This is because, unlike homicide, which typically occurs between acquaintances as offender and victim, robbery involves mostly strangers—and opportunities abound for encountering strangers in large cities. Thus, as the northeastern states are more urbanized than the southern states, so the northeastern states have a higher robbery rate (U.S. Census Bureau, 2008).

Robbery occurs most frequently in the *cold winter* months, reaching its peak in volume during the holiday season in December, when stores are making more money and people are carrying more cash with them on the streets. There are additional reasons for the higher frequency of robbery in the winter than in other seasons. The cold weather keeps most people off the streets, thereby making it easier for robbers to victimize isolated individuals without having any discouraging witnesses around. The cold weather also makes it look natural for robbers to wear a heavy coat, which is ideal for hiding a shotgun or other weapon. The increase in hours of darkness in the winter further enhances the opportunity for robbing without getting caught. All these factors involve the opportunity for committing robbery. Other factors have to do with the increased motivation for committing the crime. One such factor is a higher rate of unemployment in the winter, which largely comes from the loss of seasonal jobs such as construction, tourism, and other outdoor work. Another motivational factor is the economic pressure from the rising cost of living in the winter, because there is greater need for money to be spent on such goods as clothing, shelter, and heating (Landau and Fridman, 1993).

Most robberies (about six out of ten) take place *outdoors,* on the streets and highways. Of those that occur indoors, the general public assumes that a significant number take place in banks. But *bank robbery is relatively rare,* accounting for only about 5 percent of indoor robberies (see Figure 14.1). Since the early 1990s, though, bank robberies have increased significantly. This is largely because it is much more convenient to rob banks today. Unlike the fortresslike banks built in the past, many banks today make themselves vulnerable to robbery by having potted plants, subdued lighting, long hours, and open teller stations in order to please customers. To avoid violence from angry robbers, bank tellers are instructed

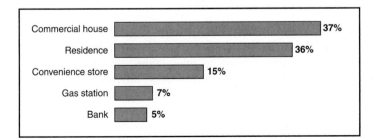

FIGURE 14.1 Locations of Indoor Robberies

Source: U.S. Census Bureau, *Statistical Abstract of the United States, 2008.*

to quickly hand over the money without a fight, which makes it convenient even for a 12-year-old or an 80-year-old to rob the bank. The road system further makes it easy to pull off a robbery at selected banks—it can take less than a minute after the heist to zoom away on the freeway. This may explain why California, which has the nation's most extensive network of freeways, has more bank robberies than any other state (St. John, 2004; Hechinger, 2002; Johnston, 1997).

Most of the robberies today are *armed*. Over the years, armed robberies have increased faster than unarmed ones. Most of these robberies involve the use of firearms rather than knives and other cutting instruments, and are more likely to be committed by adults than youngsters. In contrast, unarmed robberies, which include purse snatching, mugging, and other violent confrontations, involve youngsters more often than adults. Compared with armed robberies, unarmed robberies also take place closer to the offender's home. This is largely due to the spontaneity and predominance of foot travel in unarmed robbery—as opposed to the planned nature of armed robbery and the common use of a vehicle in its commission (FBI, 2008; Capone and Nichols, 1976).

In contrast with violent crimes such as homicide and rape, which are predominantly intraracial in nature, robbery is more likely to be *interracial*—involving blacks robbing whites (Wilbanks, 1985). This is probably because robbery is more premeditated and impersonal than homicide and rape. "More premeditated" suggests that the robber, being more rational and calculative, would rather victimize people with more money than those with less, and "impersonal" implies that the robber would rather rob strangers than relatives, friends, or acquaintances. This victim profile—having more money and being strangers—is more likely to fit whites than blacks. Therefore, black offenders tend more to rob whites than other blacks.

Amateur and Professional Robbers

There are two kinds of robbers: amateurs and professionals. Compared with professionals, amateurs generally commit robbery for smaller sums of money with less planning and skill and higher risks of arrest. Adults are more likely than youngsters to be professionals; youngsters tend more to be amateurs. Nowadays robbers are more desperate and unpredictable, more prone to violence, and more likely to drink and use drugs. Most of these robbers are amateurs and their number has increased over the last several decades while the number of their professional peers has shrunk (Matthews, 2002).

Amateur Robbers.   Amateur robbers can further be divided into three types: (1) opportunist robbers, (2) addict robbers, and (3) alcoholic robbers (Haran and Martin, 1984; Conklin, 1972).

The majority of amateur robbers are *opportunist robbers*. Usually committing such forms of theft as larceny and shoplifting, opportunists infrequently rob. When they do rob, they tend to target individual persons rather than commercial establishments. Typical targets are older women with purses, drunks, cab drivers, and people who walk alone on dark or empty streets. The criteria for choosing such targets are the victim's easy accessibility and vulnerability rather than large sums of cash. Perhaps because such targets are easy to rob, opportunists rarely carry firearms and often have no weapon of any kind. Yet they are likely to form a gang, three or four young opportunists working together to overpower the victim in a strong-arm robbery. So the group itself operates as a weapon of sorts, comparable in threatening power to a knife.

Since the early 1980s, however, opportunist robbers have caused a surge in bank robberies, which are traditionally associated with professional robbers. This new breed of bank robber is mostly young and unsophisticated. There is little planning to their heists. Confederates are casually chosen and form loose groups thrown together "for the job." The robberies are so amateurishly conceived that the amount of loot is often the result of pure chance. The average take is about $3,000, but it does not seem much because it has to be split two, three, or four ways (Kaplan, 1991; Haran and Martin, 1984).

Addict robbers commit robbery to buy their next "fix." Like opportunists, addicts rarely go after lucrative targets and thus often commit robberies that yield small sums of money. But the high cost of their drug habit drives the addict robbers, out of desperation, to carry out more acts of property crime than the opportunist. Moreover, addicts are more reluctant to resort to physical force and thus more likely to use a firearm. Their robberies are often committed on the street against vulnerable targets for ready cash. Such targets often include drug dealers, who carry a lot of cash and as wanted criminals themselves can't call the police, and white folks, who are much less likely than blacks to offer resistance (Jacobs, 2000; Wright and Decker, 1997).

Among amateurs, *alcoholic robbers* are least likely to engage in robbery, and most likely to be caught when they rob. They usually do not plan their crime; neither do they try to make their crime easier by seeking a vulnerable victim. Instead, they often get involved in a situation that unexpectedly leads to a robbery. They may get into fistfights or drunkenly assault people, and then take away their victims' money as an afterthought. The random nature of the alcoholic's crime may be illustrated by one alcoholic who walked into a liquor store to buy a bottle of whiskey. After he had given the clerk the money to pay for it, the clerk asked whether he wanted anything else. At that instant, the alcoholic decided that he did, telling the clerk to hand over all the money in the register. Surprised and angered, the clerk refused. During the ensuing fight, the alcoholic managed to take some money and then fled.

Professional Robbers. Professionals carefully plan their robberies, execute them with one or more accomplices and with skill, and make away with large sums of money. There are two types of professional robbers, one more specialized in robbery than the other. The more specialized ones commit robbery almost exclusively; the less specialized, being also committed to other forms of crimes, commit robbery only occasionally but nonetheless with professional skill. The first type of professional robber was more common in the past, while the second type is more common today.

Professional robbers as a whole have a strong commitment to robbery as a way of earning a living, and seek a series of big scores to support an expensive, hedonistic lifestyle. After executing a robbery, professionals often leave the city for a few weeks, perhaps taking a trip to a resort area. Once there, they spend the money like millionaires, to satisfy luxurious whims and pleasures. When the supply of money is depleted, they will start developing specific plans for more robberies. At other times they just keep their eyes open, watching for possible scores. Since they are mostly interested in big scores, they will typically rob commercial establishments that contain large sums of money. Because these targets generally take greater precaution against theft than individuals do, professional robbers usually have developed considerably more skill and do more careful planning than amateur offenders, who usually rob individuals of smaller sums of money.

Professional robbers tend to see their crime as an honest enterprise. Unlike burglary and other thefts, which involve furtiveness or deception, robbery calls for an open, direct, face-to-face confrontation with the victim. It is this quality of candor that, in the eye of the professional robber, transforms the crime into an honest activity. Professional robbers even consider their crime more honest than the business activity of the companies they victimize. As one of them explains, "To me this is perfectly honest, because these companies are cheating people anyway. When you go and just take it from them, you are actually more honest than they are. Most of the time, anyway, they are insured and make more money from the caper than you do" (Irwin, 1970).

Causes of Robbery

Two positivist theories seem useful for explaining robbery. One focuses on the motivation to commit robbery and the other on the *opportunity* for committing robbery as the causes of the crime. According to the first theory, the motivation is socially created *relative deprivation,* the feeling of frustration from failing to realize a heightened expectation in the lower classes, and to the second theory, the opportunity is provided by the *economic abundance* in the larger society.

Relative Deprivation.   John Conklin (1972) has used the concept of relative deprivation to explain the surge in robbery rates in major U.S. cities during the 1960s. Conklin noticed that from 1960 to 1969 the social and economic condition of poor African Americans improved significantly as a result of the federal government's many antipoverty and civil rights programs. But at the same time the rates of robbery among poor African Americans also went up significantly. Conklin attributed this ironical increase in robbery rates to relative deprivation among the poor blacks: The absolute improvement in their life induced them to hold higher expectations of enjoying as many opportunities as whites, but when they failed to realize these expectations, they felt frustrated and, as a consequence, tended to commit robbery.

Economic Abundance.   Leroy Gould (1969) has used not only the concept of relative deprivation but also economic abundance to explain why the rate of property crime that had remained relatively low during the 1930–1943 period of economic scarcity rose sharply during the period of abundance from 1944–1965. As Gould says, "Increases in the amount of property would serve to increase the relative deprivation of those who were still not sharing in the ownership of the property, while at the same time *making it easier for these people to steal the property for their own use*."

According to Gould, people with money problems feel particularly frustrated when they know that many others are doing very well because of the general affluence around them. At the same time, the society's economic abundance creates a lot of opportunities for committing robbery. Many banks, especially branch banks, are located close to highways and shopping centers—a convenience obviously designed for customers but tempting to robbers as well (Johnston, 1997; Duffala, 1976; Gould, 1969). The opportunities for robbery are also available in many other business establishments and private residences, where the robber can find a great deal of money, jewelry, and other precious objects. Since people have more money, they are also likely to carry more cash with them on the streets. In brief, economic abundance enhances what some sociologists have called "target suitability" for robbery (Cohen, Cantor, and Kluegel, 1981).

Auto Theft and Carjacking

Over the last 20 years or so various property crimes have declined significantly. But the decline in auto theft was much less when compared to robbery and burglary (see Table 14.1).

Characteristics and Trends

Many people seem to associate auto theft with teenagers stealing a car for purposes of "joy riding"—driving the car for a while and then abandoning it. Indeed, joy riding was once quite common, especially in the 1960s and 1970s. But today most auto thieves steal cars in order to sell them for a quick and handsome profit. In fact, auto theft has become big business. Every year, about 1.2 million cars are stolen, costing at least $8 billion, which accounts for nearly half of all the property lost to crime (FBI, 2008).

The overwhelming majority of auto thefts do not involve any violence against the victim because the offender typically steals the car when the owner is not around. However, since 1990s, there has been a trend toward the use of violence to force drivers to give up their cars. Cars have been hijacked at highway rest stops, gas stations, fast-food outlets, car washes, red lights, and shopping-mall parking lots. In a typical carjacking, a single robber puts a pistol to the head of a startled driver. Some carjackers would do a "bump and run" by staging a minor rear-end accident. When the unsuspecting motorist gets out to investigate the damage, one robber holds up the victim while the other drives off with the victim's car. A few of these carjackings are extremely violent, resulting in the victim being severely beaten or brutally killed (Hyatt, 1993; Witkin, 1992).

According to the U.S. Justice Department, every year in the 1990s there were about 49,000 attempted carjackings and in half of these cases the offender got away with the car.

TABLE 14.1 Property Crimes, 1986–2003

Crime	Rate per 100,000 population		Change from 1986 to 2003
	1986	**2003**	
Auto theft	507.8	433	−15%
Robbery	225.1	142	−35%
Burglary	1344.6	741	−45%

Source: U.S. Census Bureau, *Statistical Abstract of the United States, 2006.*

Most of the carjackers are African Americans, but so are most of their victims. The most vulnerable to carjacking are people who are most likely to become victims of violent crime in general. They include men more than women, blacks more than whites, Hispanics more than non-Hispanics, the divorced more than the married, and urban residents more than rural or suburban dwellers (Klaus, 1999).

Causes

The *motivation* for committing auto theft appears to be about the same as for other property crimes. Like other property criminals, car thieves have a strong motivation for monetary gain. Their criminal motivation derives largely from the poor, lower-class environment where they have suffered deprivation resulting from income inequality, racial discrimination, or society's failure to fulfill aspirations for decent jobs. But auto thieves are unique in being offered abundant *opportunities* for stealing cars (Rice and Smith, 2002).

First, *inadequate law-enforcement* makes it easy to steal cars without getting caught. Overwhelmed by violent crime, the police have too little time left for dealing with auto theft. Of the nation's 500,000 police officers, fewer than 3,000 (less than one percent) investigate auto theft. Moreover, prisons are so overcrowded with violent offenders that most car thieves do not serve any time—they are simply set free on probation. A second reason for auto theft is the *profitability* of stolen cars and car parts, the demand for which is relatively high. Some of this demand comes from foreign countries, to which some 200,000 "hot" cars are shipped a year, because a stolen American car can double or triple in value there. Auto-repair shops also like to buy the parts removed from stolen cars because the illegal items are sold cheaper and delivered faster than legal ones from the manufacturer. A third reason for auto theft is *insurance fraud*. To collect insurance money, a car owner can contract with a thief to steal the car, abandon the automobile on a city street for any thief to steal, or simply run the vehicle into a river (Christian, 1995; Witkin, 1992).

What about the upsurge in carjacking? The reason for this increase in carjacking is ironical: the *increased sophistication of the car's security devices,* such as the alarm systems, steering-wheel locks, and ignition-control systems. These antitheft devices are likely to encourage car thieves, particularly young amateurs, to hijack a car, because it is considerably easier to rob a motorist at gunpoint than to steal a car parked somewhere with its engine turned off (Bradsher, 1999; Witkin, 1992).

Burglary

Compared with other property crimes, burglary has declined the most (see Table 14.1). Nevertheless, burglars still steal more than $4 billion worth of property in a year, about half the cost of auto thefts (Armes, 2004).

Modus Operandi

Burglars are characteristically rational and calculating in executing their crime. Thus, most burglaries are committed during the day when the homes are empty because the occupants are at work, at school, out shopping, or away on vacation. The most popular time for burglars to do their thing is between 9 and 11 A.M. and from 1 to 3 P.M. These are the hours when people are most likely to go out. Contrary to popular belief, burglaries are not crimes of the night, because breaking into a house at night may cause a confrontation with its occupants. There are exceptions, though. A few cat burglars may break into a home without waking up its occupants. This is especially easy to do in houses with loud window air conditioners. As a burglar says, "If you can't hear the air conditioner when you're asleep, you can't hear me when I break into your home." A few other burglars would work at night only if the family is away on vacation (Sussman, 1992; Cromwell, Olson, and Avary, 1991).

To ensure that the house they want to break into is empty, most burglars have a bag of tricks at their disposal. One common trick is to pass themselves off as a door-to-door salesperson. They knock on a door or ring a doorbell, ready to deliver a sales pitch. A similar stratagem is to knock on the door, ready to ask for a nonexistent person ("Is Mr. Smith home?") or directions to a nearby address. If nobody answers the door, they may quickly break into the house. But the more cautious burglars would leave a card in the door. If the card is still there the next day, it is a sure sign that the family is away. Another common trick is to get the prospective victim's name from the mailbox, look up the telephone number, and repeatedly make the call. If nobody answers, the house is assumed to be unoccupied (Cromwell, Olson, and Avary, 1991).

After making sure that nobody is in the house, most burglars still want to find out whether there is a burglar alarm. If there is, the burglars will go away. They will even pass over a house with a mere sign or window sticker that says the house is protected by an alarm system. They do not want to take chances with anyone who takes some precaution against burglary. As one burglar says, "Why take a chance? There's lots of places without alarms. Maybe they're bluffing, maybe they ain't." Dogs are another effective deterrent. Most burglars will stay away from a house if they know there is a dog in it. Even small dogs deter burglary, because, as one burglar explains, "Little dogs yap too much. The neighbors look to see what they are so excited about. I don't like little yapping dogs" (Helm, 2006; Cromwell, Olson, and Avary, 1991).

Causes of Burglary

Like other property crimes, burglary can be explained by deviant motivation and opportunity. But the specific nature of motivation and opportunity for burglary is not the same as that for other economic deviances.

In the case of burglaries, the primary motivation is the desire to obtain money to *meet expressive needs,* specifically the needs to maintain a "fast life," to party, and to use drugs and alcohol. Burglars have developed these needs from their street culture that emphasizes partying as the most important purpose of life (Wright and Decker, 1994).

The opportunity for committing burglary largely comes from the frequent *absence of capable guardians.* Capable guardians are people whose presence deters others from committing crime. Members of a family can become capable guardians against burglary simply by being present in their home. But there is no guardianship against burglary in many homes when husbands and wives go to work and children go to school. Moreover, the lack of community integration, as indicated by the absence of many neighbors watching each other's homes, reduces the neighbors' capability as antiburglary guardians (Lynch and Cantor, 1992).

Shoplifting

Shoplifting has become a scary word, conjuring up an image of thieves mingling with customers. Who wants to shop at a store known to be crawling with thieves? Understandably, store owners, to avoid frightening away customers, euphemistically refer to shoplifting as "shrinkage." Whatever it is called, shoplifting has become a serious problem in the United States. It costs U.S. shops about $31 billion a year. This is roughly equivalent to 2 percent of their total merchandise, compared with 1.5 percent for shops in Canada and less than 1 percent in Japan. Ultimately, however, it is the honest customers who are forced to pay for the cost of shoplifting because prices of goods are routinely raised to reduce the loss from shrinkage (Jacobs, 2005; Clarke, 2002; Adler, 2002; *The Economist,* 1991).

A Social Profile of Shoplifters

Only a few shoplifters are *boosters,* professional criminals who shoplift for profit. Most shoplifters are *snitches,* amateurs who steal articles of small value for personal use.

Shoplifting is predominantly a juvenile offense. Individuals under age 21 are most likely to shoplift and, among these young people, those between ages 11 and 15 shoplift the most. This explains the increased incidence of shoplifting on nonschool days, afternoons and evenings, and late in the week, from Wednesday through Saturday. The youth of the common shoplifters further explains why the items most often stolen include beauty products, music CDs and movie videos, and apparel from athletic shoes to designer clothing. The prevalence of youthful shoplifters has also led some malls to prohibit teenagers from entering them during evening hours without adult companions (Lee, 2006; Adler, 2002).

The incidence of shoplifting is lowest for people above age 50. Still, older shoplifters are more often featured in newspapers and magazines than their numbers warrant, because they can offer heartrending stories like, "I'm tired of eating dog food, and I felt like eating a decent piece of meat." It is also extremely rare for movie stars and other celebrities to shoplift, but the few that are charged with the offense make headlines. They, unlike ordinary folks, are said to lack the intent to steal because they "unfortunately" suffer from kleptomania, a neurotic impulse to steal (Clarke, 2002).

The general public seems to believe that shoplifting is mostly a female crime. Some criminologists have also assumed the same thing. But this assumption was based on old studies that dealt with *apprehended* shoplifters only. Apprehended shoplifters do not represent the population of shoplifters, most of whom are not caught by the police. In more recent studies, when random samples of ordinary people were asked whether they had shoplifted, men turned out to be more likely than women to commit the crime (Klemke, 1992).

The lower-class, the unemployed, the homeless, and drug addicts also have clearly higher rates of shoplifting. As for race, African Americans are more likely than whites to shoplift in cases in which the items taken are relatively expensive, while whites are more inclined to take things of little value (Clarke, 2002; Klemke, 1992).

Causes of Shoplifting

Like other property crimes, shoplifting can be explained by criminal motivation and opportunity. But a unique configuration of motivations and opportunities differentiates shoplifting from other crimes.

There are both economic and social psychological motivations for shoplifting. As for economic motivations, poverty is a factor, as suggested by the evidence that poor people are more likely than others to shoplift and that shoplifting becomes more common when unemployment is high or when the economy is sluggish. But severe economic hardship alone cannot explain most cases of shoplifting. In fact, many shoplifters are merely frugal customers, who can afford to buy the things they need, but are driven to steal by a desire to stretch their budget through bargain hunting, as encouraged by the consumption-driven society. Also, many young shoplifters commit the offense because they do not have the money to buy designer jeans, fancy shoes, and other fashionable items that enhance peer acceptance (Dugas, 2008; Klemke, 1992).

Of the social psychological motivations for shoplifters, the most common is the *sense of thrill, excitement,* or *fun* that shoplifters expect to experience when committing the crime. Another important motivation is the *desire for social acceptance,* which makes youngsters, in particular, highly vulnerable to peer pressure. When asked why they shoplift, many would say "because my friends are doing it." A third motivation is a cluster of *rationalizations* that the shoplifter can use to justify the crime before committing it. Thus, many shoplifters deny responsibility (saying, for example, "My friends make me do it" or "I'm high or drunk"); deny injury to the victim ("It's only a cheap bottle of perfume" or "It's such a big store they won't miss it"); or argue that the victim deserves it ("It serves them right because they rip us off every time we buy something from them"). Armed with these rationalizations, shoplifters are able to decriminalize their offense, thereby continuing to see themselves as respectable, law-abiding citizens rather than as criminals (Klemke, 1992).

Those economic and social psychological motivations seem by themselves powerful enough to cause people to shoplift because the opportunities for shoplifting are available to everybody. Anyone can, without any difficulty, walk into a store as a prospective shoplifter in the guise of a customer. And the risk of being apprehended for shoplifting is minimal, thanks to the laxness of law-enforcement against such offense. Even when a shoplifter is caught, most stores are reluctant to press charges for fear of publicity and possible liability over false arrest (Adler, 2002).

Organized Crime

The entertainment media, through vehicles like the movie *The Godfather,* first shown more than 30 years ago, often romanticizes mobsters as men of honor, courage, and toughness, but it also sensationalizes them as ruthless killers. Actually, the participants in organized crime, like the average Americans, try to achieve the American Dream, except by using more socially disreputable, deviant means. Let's take a closer look at organized crime.

Organizational Structure

There are many different organized crime groups in the United States, each consisting of members of the same race or ethnicity. The best known and most powerful is *the Mafia,* also called *la Cosa Nostra, the mob,* or *the syndicate*. Composed mostly of Italian Americans, the Mafia is a relatively loose, informal confederation of diverse groups of professional criminals operating independently in large cities around the country. Each group is known to law enforcers as a crime family identified by the name of its founder, such as Genovese, Gambino, or Bonanno. Each family consists of a *hierarchical structure* of positions, ranging from the highest to the lowest as follows: "don" or boss, underboss, lieutenants, counselor, and "soldiers" or button men (so-called because they do the bidding of the higher-ranking members when the latter "push the button"). The boss of each family directs the criminal activities of the members of his family.

Members are governed by *a code of conduct*. The most important rules in the code concern *loyalty* ("Be loyal to the family") and secrecy ("Don't squeal on fellow members"). If these rules are violated, the individual will be killed. That's why the U.S. government has to spend an enormous sum of money on the witness-protection program, providing informers with new identities, houses in different locations, and new jobs.

Those two basic characteristics of organization—a well-defined hierarchy of positions and a code of conduct—also exist, with some variation, in many other ethnic crime groups, such as those dominated by African Americans, Hispanic Americans, and Asian Americans. But these ethnic gangs not only differ among themselves but also from the Italian American Mafia in regard to the nature of their deviant activities.

Organized Crime Activities

The largest criminal organization is the 6,000-strong Herrera family founded by immigrants from Mexico, operating mostly in Southern California. They are notorious for smuggling heroin into the United States. Then there are some 200 Colombian crime families in Florida who engage in cocaine smuggling. Chinese, Vietnamese, Korean, and Japanese gangs have been found on the East and West Coasts, active in smuggling drugs and extorting money from businesses in their communities. Scores of other groups can be found in various cities: Israelis dominating insurance fraud in Los Angeles, Cubans running illegal gambling operations in Miami, Canadians engaging in gun-smuggling and money-laundering in Miami, Russians carrying out extortion and contract murders in New York, and so on (Kleinknecht, 1996; President's Commission, 1986). Despite their differences, all these groups have one thing in common: They specialize in one or two forms of economic deviance while confining their operation to a limited area, usually an ethnic community. In contrast, Italian American crime groups operate *all over the country,* engaging in a *variety* of deviant activities, such as those disclosed below.

Selling Illegal Goods and Services. The illegal goods and services sold by the Mafia include illicit gambling, loan sharking, and narcotics. *Illicit gambling* includes betting on horse races, lotteries, and sporting events. But it has become less profitable today because of the increasing legalization of lotteries and off-track betting. In the early 1990s illicit gambling brought in only about $2 billion a year, which was small potatoes in view of the Mafia's annual income of at least $60 billion (Angelo, 1992; President's Commission, 1986).

Far more profitable is *loan sharking,* the lending of money at exorbitantly high rates, typically more than 100 percent a year. In fact, when the economy is in a depression or recession, hordes of businesspeople and bill-payers are forced to borrow money from loan sharks at up to between 200 and 300 percent annual interest. Since customers can put up only their bodies as security for the loan (if they had valuable property, they would have gone to a legitimate loan company), it seems logical that the loan sharks may resort to violence or the threat of violence to ensure repayment. But the loan sharks hardly need to threaten violence, let alone actually use it, because they already have a bad reputation for being violent, which is enough to scare the borrowers (Block, 1991).

In the field of *illicit drugs,* the Italian American Mafia operates for maximum profit at minimum risk of interference from law enforcers. They restrict their activities to importing and wholesale distribution, letting independent drug pushers take over the risky business of selling narcotics on the street. The narcotics trade is the most lucrative source of revenues for organized crime. Not surprisingly, the "new Mafias"—consisting of African Americans, Asians, or Hispanics—rely on drug trafficking as their *primary* source of income.

Engaging in Large-Scale Thefts and Racketeering. The Mafia steals in a big way. Small-scale thefts such as holdups and burglaries are left to independent criminals. The mob turns to wholesale operations instead: They steal huge quantities of negotiable stocks and bonds as well as credit cards and airline tickets, whole carloads of merchandise (sometimes with the car itself) from docks, railway stations, and international airports, and millions of dollars' worth of automobiles, which they furnish with proper engine identification numbers and registration papers necessary for selling them. To sell these "hot" items, they have fences who work like big-time merchandising operators.

Another form of organized crime activity is known as racketeering. It may take the simple form of a "protection racket," which involves the extortion of money from legitimate businesspeople. They are given the proverbial offer they cannot refuse: The sale of the mob's "insurance policy" against such "accidents" as the burning of their stores and the breaking of their store windows or their heads—to be carried out by the mobsters if the businesspeople refuse to buy the "insurance." The more elaborate and more common form is *labor racketeering*. This involves the manipulation of workers' employers and unions. Racketeers may forcibly offer businesspeople a "sweetheart contract," whereby the employers pay them a fee for having their employees join the racketeers' nonexistent union; extort money from employers by threatening them with labor strife; or demand that the employing company put their relatives on the company's payroll.

Corrupting Public Officials. To help ensure success in all the above patterns of activities, it may be necessary to corrupt the appropriate public officials. The mob usually targets three kinds of officials: law enforcers, politicians, and officials in licensing, supervisory, or regulatory agencies (Block, 1991). The manner of corruption is outright bribery or, in the case of politicians, contribution to a political campaign. The goal is to have their "political front person" pass laws favoring their interests and prevent the passage of laws damaging to their illegal activities, to have the police and other law enforcers ignore their criminal activities, or to get regulatory agencies to turn a blind eye to their illegal way of operating legitimate businesses—such as threatening competitors with violence.

Infiltrating Legitimate Businesses.   This activity is the most profitable and yet the safest for the mobsters to engage in. The types of businesses that they have infiltrated include Las Vegas casinos, nightclubs and restaurants, hotels and motels, trucking companies, wholesale food distributors, as well as the industries of banking and investment, insurance, real estate, electronics, health services, stock brokerage, and prepaid telephone cards. The Mafia's penetration into these legitimate businesses is so deep that many law-abiding citizens routinely deal with it. Even the FBI, always busy fighting organized crime, once unknowingly hired a mob's moving company (Raab, 1997; President's Commission, 1986). By acquiring any one of those legitimate businesses, the mobsters aim to achieve certain objectives: to gain respectability, to establish a legitimate source of income for paying taxes and thus avoid income tax prosecution, to invest "bad" money (from racketeering and other illegal activities) in a legitimate business for legitimate profit, and to use the legitimate business as a front for carrying out illegitimate schemes.

The most common objective of entering a legitimate business is the last one because it produces the most profit. An illegitimate scheme may involve insurance fraud: Taking over businesses and then hiring professional arsonists to burn buildings and their contents in order to then collect on the fire insurance. Increasingly, to avoid detection by law enforcers, the Mafia has resorted to the more sophisticated methods of fraud typically used by white-collar and corporate criminals like those we discussed in the preceding chapter.

Ethnicity and Organized Crime

The roots of organized crime reach deep into the American past. During the eighteenth century, there were pirates at many U.S. ports and rivers, as well as robbers, gamblers, and slave-snatchers operating mostly in the rural, frontier settings. The frontier lawlessness continued to reign throughout the nineteenth century. It spawned such legendary train- and bank-robbery gangs as the Reno brothers and the Jesse James gang.

Toward the end of the nineteenth century, many criminal gangs began to emerge in the cities. The major ones were Irish, Jewish, and Italian, but these three groups were not equally powerful at the same time. The Irish dominated the organized crime scene in the first two decades of the last century, controlling large cities' political machinery and such industries as construction, trucking, public utilities, and the waterfront. Then, in the 1920s, the Jews took over the dominant position in organized crime, controlling gambling and labor racketeering. In the same decade Prohibition (the law against the manufacture and sale of liquor) began to prepare the Italians to succeed the Jews. By the end of Prohibition in the early 1930s, the Italians were firmly in control of organized crime. In fact, Italian dominance has continued to this day, largely because of Prohibition.

Prohibition ushered in a new era of organized crime. Before Prohibition, criminal groups were mostly local in the scope and extent of their activities, confined to single ethnic neighborhoods. During and after Prohibition, however, the Italian gangs went beyond the local setting to control criminal activities of more extensive territories—covering the entire country. Prohibition brought this about by making bootlegging a complex, large-scale operation. The illicit alcohol had to be manufactured, transported, and distributed to thousands of retail outlets across the country. Successful bootlegging required complex operations involving huge breweries and distillers, giant warehouses, fleets of tank cars and trucks, and protection from hijackers. It also required the bribery and cooperation of the Coast Guard, customs officials, politicians, and police. Since the liquor came from Europe or Canada, it further required international as well as interstate connections (Hills, 1980; Homer, 1974).

All this explains why the Mafia is the only crime group that exists in all the major U.S. cities today. But, since the early 1980s, the Mafia has lost some of its dominance over the underworld. The country's most celebrated Mafia boss in recent years, John Gotti, was finally convicted and sentenced to prison. Virtually all of the other Mafia bosses have also been put away. Every single one of the nation's 24 Mafia families has some members now doing time. The Mafia has also suffered severe internal problems. Threatened with long imprisonment unless they talk, many mafiosi are willing to violate the organization's sacred code of "omerta" (silence or secrecy) by testifying in court against fellow members. The Mafia membership is also shrinking because the crime families' children and grandchildren prefer to pursue conventional careers as lawyers, doctors, or businesspeople. Given all these problems plaguing the Mafia, criminal gangs of other ethnicities that have emerged over the last three decades are tempted to move in on the lucrative crime markets that the Italians have monopolized for the last 60 years (Corliss and Crittle, 2004; Griffin, 2003; Kleinknecht, 1996; Reuter, 1995).

But it will take some time for some of the new ethnic gangs to wrest the underworld leadership from the Italians. The history of ethnic succession in organized crime—the leadership first held by the Irish, then by the Jews, and finally by the Italians—suggests that an ethnic gang has to go through at least four stages before it can attain supremacy in the U.S. underworld. In the first stage, common street criminals get together to *form gangs in their own ethnic neighborhood* where they extort or otherwise victimize its residents. In the second stage, confined to the same area, different gangs are compelled to *compete with one another* in dominating the local crime scene. Frequent violent conflict occurs, including murders. In the third stage, the gangs *resolve their conflict* by forming a larger crime organization that allocates turfs to gangs and settles intergang disputes by peaceful means. The organization, stronger than each individual gang, is powerful enough to move its crime operations beyond the ethnic neighborhood and into the larger society. In the fourth stage, various ethnic crime organizations compete with one another, resulting in the emergence of *one ethnic organization as the victor,* which then dominates the underworld across the country. This is what the Italians have been doing since they became victorious over the Jews and Irish in the 1930s (O'Kane, 1992).

Today, African, Hispanic, Asian American, and other gangs are stuck in the second stage, as shown by the constant conflicts among ethnic gangs in their own ethnic neighborhoods. Most of the conflicts are drug-related, because the new ethnic gangs typically rely on drug trafficking as the primary source of their income. This is reminiscent of the 1930s when the Italians were also in the second stage, finding themselves locked in a liquor war comparable to the drug war of today. In fact, the new ethnic gangs seem to have taken over drug trafficking and other traditional street crime activities but only in their own ethnic communities, as the Italians did in the 1930s. But none of these new ethnic gangs—or the nonethnic motorcycle gangs—has managed to have the Mafia's success in developing a diversified portfolio that includes not just drug trafficking but many other crime activities throughout the country (Kleinknecht, 1996; Nordland, 1992). In short, the Mafia has been losing its power, but no other ethnic crime organization has emerged to replace it as the dominant force in organized crime.

The War on Organized Crime in the United States

In the 1980s the federal government began in earnest to crack down on organized crime. Special strike forces were set up in 26 cities to arrest and prosecute numerous mobsters and seize their assets. This was done by pulling together the resources of the Justice Department's lawyers; the FBI; the Drug Enforcement Administration; the Department of Labor; the Internal Revenue Service; the Customs and Postal Services; and the Bureau of Alcohol, Tobacco, and Firearms in order to ensure that the mobsters did not slip through the law-enforcement cracks. These federal agents also had the cooperation of local police, a far cry from the situation in the past when they distrusted each other and often collided in their organized-crime investigations. President Ronald Reagan also helped out by removing the limits on court-ordered wiretaps. With these electronic weapons, federal agents were able to listen in on countless conversations among mobsters in their cars, social clubs, and other places where they met. The federal agents were even successful in using the threat of heavy sentences to pressure many mafiosi to violate their crime family's centuries-old tradition of silence by testifying against their former partners. These turncoats were mostly the new generation, who found a long prison sentence too stiff a price to pay for family loyalty.

Because of the combination of all these factors, the war on organized crime showed impressive results. In only four years, from 1981 to 1985, 2,554 mafiosi were prosecuted and 809 convicted (Magnuson, 1986). The campaign against organized crime has been even more successful in the 1990s, as none of the nation's 24 Mafia families escaped successful prosecution (Nordland, 1992). By 2004 the bosses of four of New York's Mafia families have been convicted or imprisoned, with the last, fifth boss awaiting trial (Corliss and Crittle, 2004).

All this has undoubtedly dealt a serious blow to the Mafia. But it does not signal the death of organized crime. Those members of the crime families who have escaped the dragnet are now much more careful in concealing their activities and identities. They have begun to shift increasingly to more sophisticated, less detectable white-collar crimes (Raab, 1997, 1994). They have also stopped attracting public attention by shedding their former flamboyant lifestyles. It is doubtful that they would again behave like the mobster who turned himself into "a one-man parade" everywhere he went and impressed others by tipping a bartender $100 just for keeping the ice cubes cold (Pileggi, 1986).

Perhaps most important to the future, it seems impossible to stamp out organized crime because the two basic social causes of such deviance remain: (1) a strong demand for illicit drugs and other vices or a great opportunity for illicit gain in the white-collar and corporate world, and (2) a contingent of the ambitious poor or immigrants who cannot achieve the American Dream the conventional way.

A Global Perspective on Organized Crime

A tour of the underworld in Italy, Japan, Hong Kong, and Russia reveals that organized crime in these countries resembles that in the United States in some ways but differs in other ways.

Like in the United States, organized crime is a crooked way for the ambitious poor youth to get rich. For example, recruits for the *Yakuza,* the crime family in Japan, are mostly lower-class youths who have been rejected by the business world. They include school dropouts, drug users, and members of motorcycle gangs. Before being initiated into the Yakuza, these social rejects must undergo an apprenticeship that usually lasts five years. They learn the values and customs of the syndicate, such as taking responsibility for one's failure by cutting off the little pinkie or, more important, being absolutely loyal to the boss, who is considered more important than one's wife and children, or life itself. At the end of the apprenticeship, the recruits join the Yakuza and earn four times as much as the average salaried person (Kaplan, 1998).

Organized crime is basically the same in most countries in that it is a hierarchical organization in which lower-level members are relatively obedient and loyal to their leaders. Members of the crime syndicate called Triad in Hong Kong, for example, have sworn absolute loyalty to the organization 36 times during the initiation ceremony so that they will always remember they have only two choices in their lives—loyalty to the Triad or death. Thus they are likely to become absolutely loyal, knowing that disloyalty is punishable by death. The exception is the organized crime in Russia. It is rife with distrust and betrayal, with members who are willing to sell out to the police to save their own skins. The crime syndicate is unpredictable and volatile enough to project an image of *disorganized* rather than organized crime (Booth, 2000; Friedman, 1999; Bohlen, 1994).

Organized crime in Russia is nonetheless more pervasive, influential, or powerful than in the United States. A large majority of commercial banks and private enterprises in Russia's major cities, for example, are forced to pay a tribute of 10 to 20 percent of their profit to organized crime. The reason is apparently economic: The capitalism in Russia is less mature than that in the United States so that organized crime in Russia is less controllable and more pervasive. Organized crime in Italy, Japan, and Hong Kong is also more pervasive than that in the United States, but the reason is mostly cultural: Organized crime in those foreign countries is more socially acceptable and integrated into the legitimate world of business and politics. In Italy, victims of robbery have a much greater chance of getting their possessions back if they seek help from the Mafia than if they go to the police. In Japan, the Yakuza is heavily involved not only in banking and other legitimate businesses but also in politics, as businesspeople and politicians actively seek out Yakuza as clients and providers of unique and essential services. In Hong Kong, the Triad has similarly penetrated into legitimate businesses (Ward and Mabrey, 2005; Kaplan, 1998; Nicastro, 1992).

Due to the underworld's deeper penetration into the conventional upperworld in those countries, it is extremely difficult, if not impossible, to get rid of organized crime. Given its limited influence in U.S. society, though, American authorities are more successful in keeping it under their thumb.

Summary

1. What are the characteristics of robbery? Robbery has the characteristics of both a property and a violent crime. As a property crime, robbery is a rational act, which involves making rational decisions about the execution of a robbery. As a violent crime, robbery is carried out with actual or potential violence against the victim; unarmed or strong-arm robbery involves actual violence, while armed robbery involves potential violence.

2. What are the patterns of robbery? Most robberies are committed in large cities, during the cold winter months, and most occur outdoors. While bank robbery is relatively rare, it has increased significantly. Most robberies are armed, and robberies are more interracial than such violent crimes as homicide and rape.

3. How do amateur robbers differ from professional robbers? The amateurs are generally younger, and tend to commit robbery for smaller sums of money with less planning and skill and a higher risk of arrest. In addition, professional robbers have a stronger commitment to robbery as a way of earning a living and see their crime as an honest enterprise. **What causes robbery?** According to sociological theories, the causes of robbery are relative deprivation in the lower classes and economic abundance in the larger society.

4. What are the characteristics of auto theft and carjacking? Most auto thieves steal cars for the purpose of selling them for a quick and handsome profit. While a great majority of auto thieves quietly steal cars left alone by their owners, a few thieves resort to violence by hijacking cars. **What causes auto theft and increase in carjacking?** The causes of auto theft include inadequate law enforcement against car theft, profitability of stolen cars and auto parts, and insurance fraud. The increased sophistication of the car's security devices is an additional factor behind the upsurge in carjacking.

5. How do burglars go about breaking and entering? They try to avoid confrontations with victims by breaking into empty houses, which explains why most burglaries occur during the day when people go out to work rather than during the night. **What causes burglary?** The causes include the offender's expressive needs for maintaining a fast life, partying, and using drugs and alcohol, and the deviant opportunity provided by the frequent absence of capable guardians against burglary.

6. What is the social profile of shoplifters? Shoplifters are mostly young people under age 21. They are more likely to be men and to be lower-class, unemployed, homeless, or addicted to drugs. **What causes shoplifting?** Causes of shoplifting include economic motivations such as being poor and trying to be frugal and social psychological motivations such as the desires for thrill, social acceptance, and rationalizations.

7. What is the nature of organized crime as an organization? It has a well-defined hierarchy of positions and a code of conduct governing the behavior of members. **What crime activities do organized criminals participate in?** While most ethnic crime groups specialize in drug trafficking or only a few crimes, the Italian-American Mafia gets involved in many diverse deviances that include selling illegal goods and services, engaging in large-scale thefts and racketeering, corrupting public officials, and infiltrating legitimate businesses.

8. How is ethnicity associated with organized crime? Toward the end of the nineteenth century, the most powerful crime groups were Irish, Jewish, and Italian. Organized crime was first dominated by the Irish, then by the Jews, and finally, beginning in the 1930s, by the Italians. Prohibition—the period in which alcohol was made illegal—helped the Italians develop a nationwide dominance of organized crime, which continues to this day. Since the early 1980s, pressure from law enforcement has chipped away the Italian dominance, and other ethnic groups, particularly African, Hispanic, and Asian Americans, have emerged. But the Italian Mafia still retains its nationwide leadership in the underworld.

9. How has the U.S. government dealt with organized crime? Since the early 1980s, the federal government has consolidated its various law-enforcement efforts—with impressive results—toward putting organized crime out of business. Numerous mobsters, and their bosses, have been successfully prosecuted and put away. But the demise of organized crime is doubtful because

the criminals tend to become more careful in concealing their activities and identities—and, perhaps most important, the basic social causes of organized crime continue to exist.

10. Is organized crime the same or different in various countries? It is basically the same in some ways, such as serving as a means for the ambitious poor to achieve success and operating as a hierarchical organization in which the rank and file swear their loyalty to their leaders. But organized crime is more pervasive and powerful in other countries than in the United States. Government attempts to crack down on organized crime are, therefore, less successful in other countries.

FURTHER READING

Albanese, Jay S., Dilip K. Das, and Arvind Verma (eds.). 2003. *Organized Crime: World Perspectives.* Upper Saddle River, N.J.: Prentice Hall. A collection of articles on the concept of organized crime, its nature and extent, and the methods of dealing with it in 20 different countries on all continents.

Block, Alan A. (ed.). 1991. *The Business of Crime: A Documentary Study of Organized Crime in the American Economy.* Boulder, Colo.: Westview. A collection of government reports on organized crime's infiltration and control of garment, air freight, waste disposal, and other industries.

Booth, Martin. 2000. *The Dragon Syndicates: The Global Phenomenon of the Triads.* New York: Carroll & Graf Publishers. A comprehensive study of the past and present conditions of Chinese organized crime.

Cromwell, Paul F., and James N. Olson. 2004. *Breaking and Entering: Burglars or Burglary,* 2d ed. Belmont, Calif.: Thomson/Wadsworth. A thorough-going look into the world of burglary.

Handelman, Stephen. 1995. *Comrade Criminal: Russia's New Mafiya.* New Haven, Conn.: Yale University Press. Offers a guide to the frontierlike, ruthless, and chaotic world of organized crime in Russia.

Jacobs, Bruce A. 2000. *Robbing Drug Dealers: Violence beyond the Law.* New York: Aldine de Gruyter. An ethnographic analysis of what motivates robbers to stick up drug dealers and how they choose their targets, carry out the robbery, and deal with the retaliation from the victim.

Kenney, Dennis J., and James O. Finckenauer. 1995. *Organized Crime in America.* Belmont, Calif.: Wadsworth. A textbook on organized crime, covering its history, crime activities, and association with various groups of Americans, as well as the attempts to deal with organized crime.

Kleinknecht, William. 1996. *The New Ethnic Mobs: The Changing Face of Organized Crime in America.* New York: Free Press. A detailed presentation of organized crime among various ethnic minorities in the United States.

Klemke, Lloyd W. 1992. *The Sociology of Shoplifting: Boosters and Snitches Today.* Westport, Conn.: Praeger. A comprehensive theoretical and empirical analysis of various aspects of shoplifting.

Liddick, Donald R., Jr. 2004. *The Global Underworld: Transnational Crime and the United States.* Westport, Conn.: Praeger. Describing the nature of transnational crime and its impact on the United States.

O'Kane, James M. 1992. *The Crooked Ladder: Gangsters, Ethnicity, and the American Dream.* New Brunswick, N.J.: Transaction. An analysis of how a succession of ethnic minorities has been using organized crime to climb the ladder of success in the United States.

Rengert, George F., and John Wasilchick. 2000. *Suburban Burglary: A Tale of Two Suburbs,* 2d ed. Springfield, Ill.: Charles C. Thomas. An empirical analysis of how burglars choose which communities and houses to break into.

Reppetto, Thomas. 2004. *American Mafia: A History of Its Rise to Power*. New York: Henry Holt. A detailed description of the development of organized crime during the first half of the twentieth century.

Schulte-Bockholt, Alfredo. 2006. *The Politics of Organized Crime and the Organized Crime of Politics: A Study in Criminal Power*. Lanham, Md.: Lexington Books. A neo-Marxist analysis of organized crime as an ally of the political elites in the country where it operates.

Shover, Neal. 1996. *Great Pretenders: Pursuits and Careers of Persistent Thieves*. Boulder, Colo.: Westview. An ethnographic analysis of the experiences of criminals who persist in pursuing an unsuccessful career of committing robbery, burglary, and other property crimes.

Tunnell, Kenneth D. 1992. *Choosing Crime: The Criminal Calculus of Property Offenders*. Chicago: Nelson-Hall. An empirical study of robbers, burglars, auto thieves, and other property offenders with a focus on how they have come up with their motivation and decision to commit the crime.

Wright, Richard T., and Scott H. Decker. 1994. *Burglars on the Job: Streetlife and Residential Break-ins*. Boston: Northeastern University Press. A close-up analysis of how burglars do their crime and live their lives.

Wright, Richard T., and Scott H. Decker. 1997. *Armed Robbers in Action: Stickups and Street Culture*. Boston: Northeastern University Press. A detailed ethnographic analysis of how street robbers go about deciding to rob, choosing targets, and carrying out the offense.

CRITICAL THINKING QUESTIONS

1. Given what you have learned about robbery, how would you go about preventing robbery in your community?

2. Do you agree or disagree that it is impossible to get rid of organized crime? Why?

PART SEVEN

Cyberspace: Wild Frontier

15 Internet Deviance

Myths and Realities

Myth: Just as high technology has brought us the Internet, it has enabled law-enforcement agencies to catch and convict at least 10 percent of the online identity thieves in the United States.

Reality: It is extremely easy for online identity thieves to get away with their crime; far less than one, or nearly zero, percent of online identity thefts results in a conviction (p. 389).

Myth: Keylogging programs, also known as spywares or Trojans, which thieves use to steal the computer user's name, password, and ultimately cash, are highly sophisticated so that only a few criminals know how to use them.

Reality: The keyloggers are not particularly sophisticated and are easily available to anybody, including parents who want to keep an eye on what their children are doing online. The easy availability of the keyloggers greatly contributes to the prevalence of identity thefts (p. 390).

———————

Myth: Since strangers in foreign countries can steal our personal data, it is not surprising that most identity thefts are committed by people far away from the companies and consumers they victimize.

Reality: The majority of identity thefts are perpetrated by corporate insiders, including the victimized companies' skilled employees, authorized computer users, and other trusted personnel (p. 390).

———————

Myth: Because it is illegal to engage in Internet gambling that involves more luck than skill, such as sports betting, poker, and blackjack, fewer Americans play these games than the legal online games such as chess, backgammon, and eight-ball pool.

Reality: Far more Americans play the illegal games, and the number of gambling sites that cater to these players has soared over the last few years, from a mere 700 in 1999 to 2,400 in 2006 (p. 391).

———————

Myth: Since everybody likes sex, all kinds of people from various social and ethnic backgrounds are equally likely to participate in cybersex.

Reality: Most of the cybersex participants are white, male, and college-educated, with many, or about half, being married (p. 392).

———————

Myth: It is difficult for cyberporn to become popular in the United States, a predominantly Christian nation that frowns on pornography whether it is online or offline.

Reality: Soon after pornography went online about 10 years ago, it spread like wildfire. In only one year in the late 1990s, the number of pornographic Web sites soared from a mere 900 to somewhere between 20,000 and 30,000 (p. 393).

———————

Myth: Most of the cyberporn enthusiasts are teenagers.

Reality: The typical regular consumers of cyberporn are not teenagers, but adults. The majority of the cyberporn viewers are more than 30 years old, married, white, and middle class (p. 394).

———————

Myth: Since online affairs do not involve face-to-face contacts including sexual intercourse and other physical intimacies, as traditional, offline affairs do, most people in the general public do not consider online affairs a real case of marital infidelity.

Reality: Most people in the general public do consider online affairs just as real as offline affairs (p. 395).

———————

Myth: The Internet makes it easy for people to *both* express their prejudice and practice discrimination against minorities.

Reality: The Internet makes it easy to express prejudice but difficult to practice discrimination (p. 397).

———————

Myth: Because it doesn't involve physical contact with the victim, cyberstalking is more benign and less harmful than offline, traditional stalking.

Reality: Cyberstalking is often more disturbing and dangerous than traditional stalking. Cyberstalkers have, among other things, greater access to the victim's personal data—hence are more capable of disrupting the victim's personal and professional life—than a prowler lurking in the dark (p. 398).

———————

Deborah Majoras recently bought a pair of shoes from a footwear company and paid for it with a credit card. Later she found that somebody had stolen her credit card number stored in that company's database, and they had used her card to buy all kinds of stuff in her name. At least 1.4 million other Americans have been victimized that way. Yet the identity thief who robs a databank with a computer runs a much lower risk of getting caught than a traditional robber who holds up a bank with a gun, thanks to the tendency of many banks, credit card companies, and credit bureaus to look the other way (Acohido and Swartz, 2008; Levy and Stone, 2005).

Identity theft is part of the new, wild frontier of deviance today. Like the wild, wild West of the old frontier days, the Internet world is full of various kinds of deviant activities that can be carried out with relative impunity. Just consider how easy it is for online identity thieves to get away with their crimes. Far less than one—or nearly zero—percent of identity thefts leads to a conviction. No wonder identity theft is the fastest-growing crime of this century (Levy and Stone, 2005).

In this chapter we will explore the nature of not only identity theft but also other forms of Internet deviance. Internet deviance, or cyberdeviance, involves the commission of a deviant act through the use of a computer. Researchers have divided cyberdeviances into two broad types: (1) disrupting a computer network as a *target,* such as hacking (or breaking into a computer network) and cyberterrorism, and (2) using the computer as a *tool* to commit such deviant acts as identity theft, pornography, and stalking. The second type of cyberdeviance is by far more common than the first, and it can be subdivided into three categories according to what the computer is used as a tool for: seeking easy money, searching for sex, and expressing hate. We will first take a look at these three subtypes of cyberdeviance and then at hacking and cyberterrorism.

Seeking Easy Money Online

Many people would like to make money without having to work hard for it if there is an opportunity to do so. Such an opportunity is now available with the proliferation of computers throughout the world. Thanks to the new technology, one can seek easy money by committing identity theft online or by gambling online. To turn the computer into a cash cow, the online identity thief needs only some computer skill, but the online gambler doesn't need the skill—just luck.

Online Identity Theft

Online identity theft involves stealing (with the aid of a computer) credit card numbers, Social Security numbers, or other personal information. The thief can then buy anything online and offline for free because the purchases are charged to the owners of those card numbers. This online theft, compared to traditional forms of theft such as burglarizing a store or bank, is much more easily carried out and extremely profitable if it is pulled off. Consider, for example, computer technician Carlos Salgado, who managed to steal more than 100,000 credit card numbers by using a ready-made computer-intrusion program he found on the Web to hack into several e-commerce databases on the Internet. Those cards had a combined credit line of more than one billion dollars. Unfortunately for Salgado, though, the FBI caught him, and after pleading guilty he was sentenced to two and a half years in prison (Hansen, 2004).

Hacking into the databases of commercial establishments as Salgado did is one common practice among identity thieves. Another popular method of identity theft called "phishing" is targeted at individual consumers. The consumers are sent bogus e-mails that appear to come from legitimate banks or e-commerce sites. The recipients are asked to confirm or update their accounts by providing their personal data such as their bank account, Social Security, or credit card numbers. Even longtime Internet users can fall for the phishing trick. Store owner Mark Nichols, for example, once received an e-mail from what he thought was eBay, telling him that his account with that company had been suspended and asking him to supply his credit card number. Since he had replaced his old credit card number with a new one, he went to a site as instructed and entered his user name and password, ready to supply his new credit card number. Fortunately, though, he did not go through with it because he discovered that the site was not an official eBay site (Mann, 2006).

But a relatively new way of stealing consumers' personal information is through the use of keylogging programs that copy the computer users' keystrokes and send that information to the crooks. These monitoring programs are secretly planted in certain Web sites, e-mail messages, e-mail attachments, and ordinary software downloads. They are thus known as spyware or Trojan horses (or simply Trojans). These hidden programs are not particularly sophisticated. They are even available for sale to parents who want to keep an eye on what their children are doing online, and to people who want to find out what their significant others are doing in online chat rooms. But keyloggers are usually used by thieves to steal their victims' user names and passwords and ultimately cash. Such crimes often cross international borders, putting Internet users everywhere at risk. Joe Lopez, a small company owner in Florida, recently became a victim when cyber-crooks used a keylogging Trojan planted in his business computers to obtain his bank account information and transfer $90,000 to the Eastern European country of Latvia (Zeller, 2006).

While some strangers in faraway foreign countries may steal our personal information, it is noteworthy that *most* of the identity thefts are inside jobs. According to a study by a criminal justice researcher at Michigan State University, more than 50 percent of identity thefts involve corporate insiders. They are the victimized companies' skilled employees, authorized computer users, and trusted personnel. As the researcher said, "the biggest problem is the workplace, and the biggest problem in the workplace is there's a lack of personnel security." In one example cited by the researcher, an employee at General Motors took home the personal information on thousands of company executives during her last day of work. She was caught and convicted, but while still on probation, she was hired by another company and did the same thing again (Mann, 2006).

This failure to monitor what insiders may do with customers' personal information is not the only problem that is the fault of companies. There are other problems that contribute to identity theft. Some companies, for example, fail to use a firewall to prevent wireless intrusions. Some futilely try to protect information with easy-to-guess default passwords. Sometimes personal data under the care of a company are inadvertently sold to crooks. This is what happened with Choice-Point, the information broker that keeps 19 billion records on American consumers. It once sold the personal data of at least 145,000 customers to a fake company. There are many cases like these that show how insecure the computer networks of the corporate world are that hold our sensitive personal information (Levy and Stone, 2005).

Internet Gambling

Internet gambling is illegal in the United States. Online games that require more skill than chance, such as chess, backgammon, and eight-ball pool, are legal; only games that involve more luck than skill are illegal. Examples are sports betting, poker, and casino-type games such as blackjack and slot machines (Walsh, 2005). Although such games are illegal, there are far more Americans playing them, and the number of these gamblers has soared over the last few years. To cater to this horde of online gamblers, the number of Internet gaming sites has mushroomed from a mere 700 in 1999 to 2,400 in 2006. As a result, the revenue that is pulled in by the Internet gambling industry has skyrocketed—from less than $1 billion in the late 1990s to over $12 billion in 2006. The explosive growth of Internet gambling is expected to continue (Miller, 2006).

Why can't the U.S. law against Internet gambling stop it? One major reason is the *global and borderless* nature of Internet gambling. While it is illegal to gamble online in the United States, it is legal in foreign countries, and most of the Americans who engage in Internet gambling do so by visiting foreign gaming Web sites. These foreign sites are beyond the reach of U.S. law even though many of them are owned and operated by American citizens. Another reason for the failure to stop Internet gambling is the *lack of law enforcement* against the gambling Web sites operated from within the United States. Although the U.S. government can legally go after these domestic sites, it usually refrains from taking any enforcement action, primarily because combating other social problems such as terrorism and drugs is considered more important (Stone, 2005).

Still, the U.S. government continues to treat Internet gambling as an illegal activity. Many in the U.S. Congress further want to ban online gambling completely. Some have introduced bills to prevent banks and credit card companies from making payments for online bets but failed to get them passed into laws. There are a number of reasons for the continuing effort to keep Internet gambling at least technically illegal. (1) If Internet gambling were legal, it would have thrown the door wide open for *minors* to gamble. It is already extremely difficult to prevent minors from gambling online. After all, gambling Web sites cannot look at their customers to assess their age and request photo identification as is possible with offline, land-based casinos. By keeping Internet gambling illegal, it could at least discourage minors from gambling. (2) Online gambling can easily bankrupt *compulsive gamblers* because the gamblers can gamble at any time continuously until they are broke. (3) The potential for *fraud* associated with casinos and bookmaking operations in cyberspace is much greater than in the physical space. This is particularly true of online casinos and bookmakers that operate in foreign countries where effective regulation and law enforcement is minimal or absent. (4) The potential for the involvement of *organized crime* in online gambling is there, since organized crime has traditionally gotten involved in land-based gambling. And (5) it is much easier for criminals to *launder their ill-gotten money* through online casinos than through banks, because online casinos are subjected to less scrutiny and regulation than are banks (Malcolm, 2005).

There is a price for the continuing illegality of Internet gambling: the loss of taxes the government could have obtained from the legalization of online gambling. According to one estimate, Internet gambling, if legalized, could produce $900 million in taxes in one year (Miller, 2006). The legalization could also help regulate the online gambling industry, reducing many of the existing problems mentioned above, such as youthful and compulsive gambling, fraud, and money laundering. The continuing prohibition of Internet gambling, however, keeps driving the online operators away from the United States and further beyond the reach of U.S. law. Moreover, without the regulation that comes with legalization, the Internet bookmakers and other online operators do not have the incentive to voluntarily keep out underage or compulsive gamblers (Strumpf, 2005).

Whether legalized or not, Internet gambling seems to attract certain types of people. According to one study, people who have gambled at land-based casinos are much more likely than the general population to participate in online gambling. Those who have tried Internet gambling are likely to continue gambling online and stay away from a land-based casino. Compared to those who have not gambled online, Internet gamblers are younger, more likely to try new things, more educated, and more willing to bank online (Woodruff and Gregory, 2005). Another study shows how online gamblers differ from offline, traditional gamblers. One significant difference is that online gamblers are more financially stable. They are more likely to stop gambling when they run out of the money they have initially set aside for gambling. But traditional gamblers tend more to keep on gambling with money they cannot afford. This lack of financial control among traditional gamblers apparently reflects their lower level of education as previously suggested. It does not suggest that traditional gambling is highly addictive. In fact, gamblers are more likely to gamble excessively online rather than when they gamble offline. This suggests that Internet gambling can be very addictive because it is highly convenient, enjoyable, solitary, and anonymous—no one knows who is gambling (Griffiths and Parke, 2002).

Searching Cyberspace for Sex

While the computer is increasingly used as a tool to seek easy money by stealing others' identities and gambling online, a fast-growing number of people are using the computer to find easy sex. Thus they end up having solitary sex while online, making love with someone offline, viewing pornography online, and conducting an extramarital affair online or offline.

Cybersex

To experience cybersex, most people first find their partners by placing or answering personals on the Internet or by entering an online chat room. Then they exchange erotic e-mails, trade pornographic pictures of themselves, or engage in steamy conversations in a chat room, and in the process get sexually stimulated and, most often, masturbate. Some of these cybersex enthusiasts go offline to meet their partners in person. If the meeting is mutually satisfactory, they will have sex (Cooper, 2004; Wysocki, 1998; Lamb, 1998).

Most of the cybersex participants are white, male, and college-educated. Many, or about half, are married. Whether married or not, why do these people take part in cybersex? At least five reasons have emerged from an empirical study by sociologist Diane Wysocki (1998).

One reason is the need for *anonymity*. Unlike the real world in which sexual partners can see each other, the virtual, cybernetic world enables them to keep their true identities under wraps. They can thus take on whatever persona they want within the comfort of their home. If a man is shy and becomes tongue-tied when meeting partners face-to-face, online he can shed his shyness, feel bold, and turn chatty, projecting himself as the life of the party. Some women feel fat, old, and undesirable in person, but online they feel slim, young, wanted, and sexy—and this is the image they try to get across to the men on the other side of the electronic connection.

A second reason for participating in cybersex is the relative *ease and convenience* of finding sex partners. Trying to find a person with similar sexual attitudes and desires is difficult and time-consuming in the real world, where most of the people you meet do not share your interests. But it is much easier to find sex partners in the virtual world because it attracts only people with the same interests. This ease and convenience of finding a partner is especially important for people who are too busy to pursue friendships and sexual contacts on the face-to-face basis.

A third reason for engaging in cybersex is *sharing sexual fantasies*. Most people entertain sexual fantasies, such as engaging in sexual activities outdoors, having sex with more than one partner, or being a transvestite by wearing the clothing of the opposite sex. Since conventional society frowns on these fantasies, most people find them too embarrassing to share with others or even with their wives or husbands in the real world. But in the virtual world, where people with similar fantasies get together, the fantasies can be freely talked about and can even be turned easily into reality with willing partners.

A fourth reason for seeking online sex is the easy availability of partners as an *outlet for masturbation*. As a woman who is a regular participant in cybersex says, "I love it when the guy gets off . . . it starts with teasing and flirting . . . I usually rub my clit and we eventually get off. I most often am wearing a miniskirt or nude and it goes from there . . . usually the men are online for a hot chat and wanting to come" (Wysocki, 1998).

A fifth reason is the expectation that online sex can lead to *real sex* with a willing partner face-to-face. Most of the online partners find their sexual experience in the real world very satisfactory. But some find the experience disappointing because either one or both partners have lied online about their physical appearance. One man, for example, complains that some people he has met have not been completely honest: "[They] tell you how good of shape they're in . . . you know like 38-22-36 and 128 lbs . . . when you get there they are more like 180 or so . . . or they will tell you things like yes, I want to do this or that and when you meet it is different" (Wysocki, 1998).

Internet Pornography

Internet pornography, or cyberporn, is not new. Soon after the Internet came on the technological scene, people started to trade dirty pictures on the Net. But amateur swapping has now given way to commercial ventures. By mid-1997, according to an online guide to cyberporn, there were already about 900 sex sites on the Web. Only one year later, this number had soared to somewhere between 20,000 and 30,000. These commercial sites vary in size from small outfits with just a few hundred paying members to major networks with thousands of subscribers. By 2001 the top five porn sites received nearly twice as many visitors as the top five news sites (Webb, 2001; Barnako, 1998; Weber, 1997).

Cyberporn has become big business, raking in some $700 million a year. Sex sites are comparable in popularity to sports or weather sites and have only slightly fewer visitors than business and travel sites. A onetime stripper's site brings in so much revenue that she has given up stripping for good. In her former profession, she made only $1,500 a month, but right after going on the Web, her monthly earnings jumped to somewhere between $10,000 and $15,000. A 23-year-old man makes even much more, reaping $20 million annually after forming a company called Internet Entertainment. It offers a wide range of online pornographic shows. One type, called "live video," features exotic nude dancers in full color on the customers' computer screens, while allowing the viewers to chat on the phone with the gyrating performers. Customers can also click their way to different virtual rooms: In the "bedroom" the visitor can see a naked dancer rolling around on a giant mattress, and in the "health club" the performer works out on a step exerciser with no clothes on. Not surprisingly, cyberporn has become so profitable as to turn some porn companies into respectable corporate giants on Wall Street (Whitehead, 2005; Barnako, 1998; Weber, 1997).

Cyberporn has become popular primarily because customers can view racy material in the privacy of their homes. They no longer have to sneak into a sleazy adult bookstore or the back room of a video shop. But the popularity of cyberporn has caused many parents to fear that children can easily look up pornographic material when going online. Curious about sex, youngsters may want to do so, and they can find the Web sites that provide what they are looking for. Theoretically, masses of youngsters will habitually consume cyberporn for several reasons: (1) they can obtain the material in the privacy of their home, without having to walk into an adult bookstore or cinema; (2) they can download only the portions of the material that turn them on, rather than buy an entire magazine or video; and (3) they can explore sex without risking public ridicule or communicable diseases (Jerome et al., 2004; Elmer-Dewitt, 1995). But, as we will see in the next section, the reality is that the typical viewers of cyberporn are men over age 30, not teenagers (Webb, 2001).

Nevertheless, the U.S. Senate tried to pass a bill in 1995 prohibiting anyone from making "indecent" material available to children under 18. But the bill failed to become law, not only because many believed it violated the First Amendment guarantee of free speech but also because many feared it could transform the vast library of the Internet into a children's reading room where only subjects suitable for kids could be discussed (Elmer-Dewitt, 1995). However, the computer industry has come up with programs such as SurfWatch and Net Nanny that can block children's access to questionable material. In addition, most pornographic sites on the Web require an adult ID and a credit card. Parents, too, can help solve the problem by raising their children to shun pornography (Biskupic, 2004; Onstad, 1996).

A Social Profile of Cyberporn Surfers

Contrary to popular belief, the typical, regular consumers of cyberporn are not sex-crazed teenagers. They are, instead, older and married men. According to demographic data from the porn site Sex Tracker, two-thirds of the cyberporn viewers are more than 30 years old and they are mostly married, white, and middle class. These cyberporn surfers, as a sociological study suggests, have a relatively weak tie to religion and suffer from a relative lack of marital happiness. According to another study, 70 percent of the cyberporn traffic occurs during work hours, not at home after teens are let out of school. Teenagers are much less inclined to view cyberporn because it doesn't seem like a big deal to them; they have been growing up in an environment saturated with pornographic stimuli. But the same cyberporn may be more intriguing to older men because it is more striking than the porn they grew up with (Albright, 2008; Stack, Wasserman, and Kern, 2004; Tuesday, 2002).

Research specifically on child porn in cyberspace has shown about the same demographics: Most viewers of child porn are white men in their thirties and forties. Their occupations, however, are highly diverse, ranging from the unemployed to taxi drivers to scientists and engineers. They can be considered pedophiles because of their attraction to young children and their discomfort with adult women. They often use child porn as masturbation aids. But they also like to trade their pornographic pictures with others in order to satisfy their "collective fetish," which is the same as normal people's desire to collect cards, militaria, and Star Trek memorabilia. A broad spectrum of attitudes and opinions exists among child-porn consumers. Some say that what they do is wrong, but others insist it is not. Some maintain that they are only interested in "innocent" fantasies, while others admit that they have molested young children (Jenkins, 2001; Webb, 2001).

Online Affairs

In online affairs, married people cheat on their spouses by engaging in extramarital activities with somebody else in cyberspace, specifically through the use of e-mails or chat rooms. These online extramarital activities differ from the offline, traditional ones. While offline affairs involve *face-to-face* contacts including sexual intercourse and other physical intimacies, online affairs do not. Instead, they call for two individuals sitting in front of their computers in different locations and engaging in erotic conversations, sharing sexual fantasies, or sexual self-stimulation such as masturbation.

It may appear that online affairs are not really marital infidelity, so they are basically harmless. In fact, to some people, an online affair is not a case of infidelity for the following reasons:

- It is "just a friendship."
- It is merely flirtation or fun.
- It involves a relationship with an object (the computer), not a real human being.
- It involves two people who have never met in person and do not ever intend to meet.
- It can't be infidelity because no physical sex takes place. (Whitty, 2004)

This seems to be the way the participants in online affairs are likely to rationalize their betrayal of their spouses. However, only a few people see online affairs that way. As research has indicated, *most* people in the general public consider online affairs just as real as offline affairs. They further see online affairs as seriously harmful to marriages as offline affairs are. To most people, then, online infidelity is highly likely to lead to marital discord, separation, or divorce just as offline infidelity is (Whitty, 2005). Perhaps because they see cybercheating as the same as traditional offline cheating, most people to whom their spouse has been unfaithful would feel hurt and react in the same negative way as the victims of traditional infidelity. This may explain why online infidelity does have the same serious impact on marital relations as offline infidelity (Young et al., 2000).

Nonetheless, the Internet encourages online infidelity by making it more appealing than offline infidelity to potential cheaters. One reason is the *anonymity* of cybercommunication, which enables people to commit infidelity without the fear of getting caught by their betrayed spouses. Another reason is the convenience of finding partners all over the world without having to leave one's familiar and comfortable home or office. A third reason is the escapism provided by the Internet, which enables the users to escape from the stress and strain of real life and into the fantasy world where "a lonely wife in an empty marriage . . . is desired by her many cyberpartners, and a sexually insecure husband can transform into a hot cyberlover whom all the women in a chat room fight over" (Young et al., 2000).

Those three reasons for the Internet to facilitate online infidelity may cause the cheaters to progress toward offline, real-life liaisons. Indeed, research has shown that some 30 percent of married people who have online affairs eventually meet their partners in person and have sex with them (Drapkin, 2005). Most of these people already plan on going offline to have the sexual encounter when they initiate the online search for partners. These offline sexual affairs are mostly transitory. After having sex with a partner, the cheater moves on to another. Here is how Ted, a 40-year-old married salesman from Dallas got involved in a series of offline affairs with the help of the Internet: Just wanting to have casual sex with other women, he posted an ad at a small online dating service, saying that he was seeking "a special friend who doesn't mind the fact that I'm married." Almost immediately, several women responded, and two weeks later, for the first time in his 10 years of marriage, he had sex with one of them. He was nervous in the lead-up to that encounter, but afterward he was giddy with excitement and eagerly looking forward to another affair (Orr, 2004).

Ted's experience further illustrates how easy and fast it is for the Internet to facilitate infidelity because of the anonymity, convenience, and escapism mentioned earlier. It took only about two months for him to transform from a husband with a "cheating mind to first-time cheater and then to habitual cheater" (Orr, 2004). After he became a habitual cheater, his extramarital liaison turned into a weekly event and sometimes he squeezed in two on a single Saturday. He had no desire to leave his wife because he just was no longer happy with their sex life. He was what the Internet dating services call an NSHM ("not so happily married"). He was thus not interested in looking for a steady girlfriend; he just wanted to have sex with many different women. Many of the women he met were just like him, married and only wanting to have sex with other men (Orr, 2004).

Expressing Hate Online

People may use the Internet as a tool for expressing their hate of others. The victim is often someone whom the deviant knows, such as a former girlfriend or boyfriend. In a few cases, the victim is a stranger. Such an online expression of hate often takes the form of cyberstalking, the repeated harassment of others through the Internet. People may also use the Internet to express their hate of some minority group. This expression of hate often involves showing prejudice and practicing discrimination against the minority in cyberspace.

Prejudice and Discrimination in Cyberspace

In the current era of civil rights, people who are prejudiced against minorities tend to refrain from expressing their antiminority beliefs and feelings. But with the availability of the Internet, it is easier for people to express their prejudice and get away with it without being subjected to ridicule, attack, or some other retaliation. They no longer have to stand on street corners to spew out their hatred toward minorities; they can instead achieve the same objective from the relative safety of their homes. This is because the Internet is anonymous in nature, allowing the users to conceal their true identity if they so wish. Thus antiminority extremists and hate groups have proliferated in cyberspace. Through e-mails, chat rooms, and Web sites, they appear everywhere, not only across the United States but also in Canada, South America, and Europe. Due to the Internet's anonymity, then, prejudice is more likely to be expressed in cyberspace than in face-to-face interactions (Glaser and Kahn, 2005).

There are efforts to combat prejudice, though. Organizations such as the Anti-Defamation League, the Southern Poverty Law Center, and the Simon Wiesenthal Center maintain Web sites that track prejudice and promote tolerance. Some software companies offer filtering programs to shelter children from access to hate-group or racist Web sites. In Germany it is a crime to run a Web site advocating hate crimes. And in the United States a 21-year-old man has been convicted of committing a hate crime over the Internet for sending e-mail threats to dozens of Asians. All this may serve to reduce prejudice, especially among young people who are typically targeted online by racist groups. But research is still needed to find out how effective those antiprejudice efforts are (Glaser and Kahn, 2005; *Telephony,* 1998).

While the anonymity of the Internet makes it relatively easy for people to express their prejudice with impunity, the same anonymity makes it difficult for them to discriminate against minorities. But the anonymity serves two different kinds of people. The anonymity that promotes the expression of *prejudice* protects the *bigot* by concealing his or her true identity, but the anonymity that prevents *discrimination* protects the potential *victims* by hiding their identity from the bigot. Prejudice is a covert, psychological state, such as unjust thoughts and feelings against the minorities, whereas discrimination is overt behavior characterized by disadvantageous treatment of the minorities. The identity of the minorities as potential victims of prejudice and discrimination consists of their group-identifying cues such as their ethnicity, gender, sexual orientation, and disability. Since these cues are more likely to be concealed in cyberspace than in physical space, there is consequently less discrimination in cyberspace. In physical space, if people apply and interview for a job or mortgage loan, the employer or loan officer can see their ethnicity and gender. As a result, the decision to reject the applicant or disapprove the loan is likely to be an act of discrimination, based on the applicant's physical appearance. But in cyberspace, prevented from knowing the physical appearance, the employer or loan officer would be hard put to discriminate in the same way (Glaser and Kahn, 2005).

In short, through its anonymity, the Internet influences prejudice and discrimination in paradoxical, conflicting, or opposite ways. Specifically, in cyberspace, people are more likely to express their prejudice, if they have it, but they are less likely to practice discrimination.

Stalking through Cyberspace

Stalking through cyberspace, or cyberstalking, involves the use of the Internet or e-mail to repeatedly harass or threaten another person. Since computer technology has become cheaper, more accessible, and easier to use than ever before—helping the cyberstalker avoid arrest by concealing his identity—cyberstalking has been growing fast. A study at the University of New Hampshire has already found about 10 percent of students there having repeatedly received harassment, threats, or insults through their e-mails (Finn, 2004).

Lack of physical contact may make cyberstalking seem more benign than offline, traditional stalking, but cyberstalking is often more disturbing and dangerous than traditional stalking. Cyberstalkers have greater access to the victim's personal data—hence are more capable of disrupting the victim's personal and professional life—than a prowler lurking in the dark. Cyberstalkers can easily harass the victim anywhere in the world because of the swift global access provided by the Web. While all this can cause the victim serious emotional and mental harm, it may also result in physical or sexual assault, kidnapping, and even murder (Bocij, 2004; Newton, 2004).

However, cyberstalkers are similar to traditional stalkers in some ways. Like traditional stalkers, most cyberstalkers are males while their victims are females, and most cyberstalkers are older persons victimizing younger ones. Most cyberstalkers also know their victims. A typical example is a 50-year-old ex-security guard in Los Angeles seeking revenge on a 28-year-old woman who rejected his romantic interest. Posing as her, the man posted numerous online messages about "her" fantasies of being raped, along with her real phone number and home address. As a result, six men who saw the message came on separate occasions to the woman's home at night, knocking on her door and announcing their desire to rape her. The offender was finally arrested, pleaded guilty to stalking and soliciting sexual assaults, and received a six-year sentence (Sheridan and Grant, 2007; Newton, 2004).

Like traditional stalkers, a few cyberstalkers are strangers to their victims. An example of such an online stalker is a man who had just graduated with honors from a university in San Diego. Convinced that five female students had made fun of him as well as caused others to do the same, he spent 12 months bombarding them with up to four or five threatening e-mails every day, a common cyberstalking tactic called "e-mail bombing." After he was arrested, the police found that he was unbalanced and none of the women had ever met him (Newton, 2004). Mentally normal people, however, may engage in this kind of cyberdeviance against strangers. At a university in New Hampshire, for example, apparently normal students with prejudice against sexual minorities are more likely to send harassing e-mails to strangers who are gays and bisexuals than to strangers who are heterosexuals (Finn, 2004). If the so-called normal students knew the sexual minority students as friends rather than strangers, they would not have harassed them online.

Disrupting Computer Networks

We have so far discussed the cyberdeviances that involve the use of the computer as a tool for committing some deviant act. Here we turn our attention to those cyberdeviances that target the computer network, specifically computer hacking and cyberterrorism.

Computer Hacking

Computer hacking involves "breaking into a computer network and then proceeding to plant viruses, steal data, change user names and passwords, manipulate web pages, or just simply explore the network" (Hale, 2006). The most well-known form of hacking is the planting of viruses in our computers. This is called computer sabotage because the virus is designed to delete important files or otherwise cause the computers to function abnormally. Once a computer is infected, the virus can spread quickly from one machine to another with the aid of the users. As a consequence, virtually everybody who uses a computer has been a victim of computer sabotage. A similar kind of computer sabotage is the creation and dissemination of a worm, a malicious program that makes so many copies of itself, without any assistance from a computer user, that it finally crashes the computer system. A German teenager, for example, created a computer worm in 2004 that caused thousands of computers to crash while also slowing Internet traffic. He was convicted but given only a suspended sentence in 2005 (Alexander, 2006).

This kind of hacking involving the use of a virus or worm is usually malicious in nature. Other kinds of hacking that do not use a virus or worm can also be malicious, such as breaking into a telephone company's computer network and knocking out the phone service for an entire city. But hacking can be relatively innocent and harmless, such as breaking into computer systems only for the challenge and then notifying system administrators how the break-in is done so that they can improve their network security. There are still other forms of hacking that are merely mischievous though still illegal. Such was the case involving a Massachusetts teenager who in 2005 pleaded guilty to hacking into hotel heiress Paris Hilton's cellular phone and then posting her photographs and contact information online. In the same year a British man was arrested for hacking into U.S. military computer networks by illegally gaining access to 97 U.S. government computers, which, according to prosecutors, had caused $700,000 in damage (Alexander, 2006). This mischievous kind of hacking has also hit American high schools where students can break into their schools' computer systems to change grades, delete teachers' files, or steal data. Most of these hackers are not computer geeks with highly sophisticated skills; they are instead average students who take advantage of the lax security and the "anywhere, anytime" accessibility of school computer systems (Borja, 2006; Stover, 2005).

Whether malicious, innocent, or mischievous, these hackings are not intended to seek monetary gain, and their incidence has declined. Nowadays most of the hackings appear to be aimed at seeking money by stealing personal information or identities (Alexander, 2006). Increasing numbers of these hackings involve corporations in rich Western countries being victimized by organized criminal gangs in relatively poor countries that lack antihacking laws or enforcement of such laws. The foot soldiers of this new cybercrime gang are either smart youngsters or frustrated men in their twenties or thirties. Alexey Ivanov is a typical example. A computer whiz kid in an economically depressed area in Russia, he dropped out of college, then worked as a low-paid furniture mover, and finally joined a team of computer experts hacking corporate Web sites to steal credit card numbers (Piore et al., 2006). But most of the hacking for financial gain still originates from within rich countries such as the United States. And much of this hacking relies on what the hacker community calls "social engineering"—tricking a company's employees into revealing passwords or other secret information by posing, for example, as colleagues or other trusted insiders (Yount, 2006).

The most striking thing about hacking is that it is mostly a juvenile deviance; adolescents are simply much more likely to engage in hacking than adults. This has prompted sociologists to see if hacking is just another case of juvenile delinquency. Indeed, the characteristics and causes of juvenile delinquency in general have been found to resemble those of hacking. First, like juvenile delinquency, hacking is an overwhelmingly male activity, with the male-female ratio being estimated to be as high as 99 to 1. This massive overrepresentation of males among hackers is attributed to males' greater interest in mathematical and logical problem solving as well as in mastery over machines and domination over others. Second, like many juvenile delinquents, hackers are likely to come from dysfunctional families, experiencing parental neglect, parental conflict or divorce, physical abuse, parents' alcoholism, and the like. Despite such family problems, however, hackers can be "normal kids," largely indistinguishable from their peers. Finally, like juvenile delinquents, hackers often associate with a peer group and engage in activities encouraged by the group, such as participating in a fierce competition by "out-hacking" each other (Yar, 2005).

Terrorism in Cyberspace

To plan and carry out their terrorist activities, the members of the terrorist organization al Qaeda nowadays use mostly the Internet to communicate with one another. Some messages are posted in code on various Web sites. Other messages are transmitted electronically. After they are sent and read by the recipient, the whole communication and related files are deleted to maintain secrecy. Moreover, e-mail addresses are generally used only once or twice (Jehl and Rohde, 2004).

The terrorists are further able to launch a direct digital attack on the United States by hacking into its computer networks. The cyberattack could bring the country to its knees by disrupting or disabling its infrastructure. This infrastructure comprises many of the nation's vital facilities and services, such as the power and water supply, gas and oil production and storage facilities, telecommunications and banking networks, air traffic control systems, and transportation and emergency services (Mazzetti, 2004; Hosenball, 2002). For example, a cyberterrorist can break into an air traffic control system, tamper with it, and cause jets to collide, so that hundreds of people die. Such cyberattacks have not taken place yet, but they can happen as suggested by the success in the last several years of nonpolitical, recreational hackers in briefly disabling Yahoo!, Amazon.com, and other online giants.

By using computers as a weapon of mass disruption, cyberterrorists can reach the United States more easily than intercontinental ballistic missiles, disregarding the physical barriers of two broad oceans (the Atlantic and the Pacific) and two large peaceful neighbors (Canada and Mexico) that have long enhanced America's sense of safety. In today's computer-driven world, the terrorists no longer have to physically invade the territory or the airspace of the United States in order to damage its resources and disrupt the lives of its people. Indeed, as Congressperson Jane Harman of California has said, expressing the belief of most government officials, "Cyberterrorism presents a real and growing threat to American security. What I fear is the combination of a cyberattack coordinated with more traditional terrorism, undermining our ability to respond to an attack when lives are in danger" (Newton, 2004; Will, 2001).

The threat of cyberterrorism, however, remains only a threat. In the last 10 years, there has not been a single cyberattack on the United States. This does not mean that the terrorists have lost interest in attacking the United States—and other nations. After all, in those 10 years, there have been 1,813 international terrorist attacks and 217,394 computer hacking incidents, none of which knocked out the United States' infrastructure or created nationwide panic (Lewis, 2005). The key reason that cyberterrorism has not occurred—or, to some critics, is unlikely to happen—is that hacking into the computer network of the nation's infrastructure requires specialized knowledge, which the terrorists still do not possess—or, according to critics, are not likely to (Green, 2006; Lewis, 2005).

A Global Perspective on Cyberdeviance

Cyberdeviance is truly global and borderless. It takes place anywhere in the world, and it can easily cross national borders with the culprit in one country defrauding or otherwise preying on the victim in another country. A classic case is the Nigerian scam that cheated Americans out of five billion dollars from the early 1980s to 1996. It still continues to this day, though to a lesser extent now than before. The scam may involve sending an e-mail to countless Americans, enticing them to send in a few thousand dollars with the tempting but false promise that they will make millions of dollars from a newly discovered gold mine in an African nation (Marshall, Robinson, and Kwak, 2005). In another case, a group of meth addicts in Canada regularly stole credit card numbers, Social Security numbers, and other personal information and then got on the Internet Relay Chat room to sell the loot to crime rings in countries as far away as Romania, Austria, and Egypt (Acohido and Swartz, 2005).

Online fraud, which includes identity theft, as illustrated by these cases, is by far the most common cyberdeviance in the world. As Table 15.1 indicates, fraud makes up as much as 26 percent of all cyberdeviances reported to the International Web Police. Another significant fact about international cyberdeviance is its enormous increase in occurrence. According to the same Web Police, there were only 640 reports of cybercrime in 1993 but the number soared to 1,351,897 in 2002 (Marshall, Robinson, and Kwak, 2005).

TABLE 15.1 Distribution of Cyberdeviances Worldwide

Fraud	26%
Child pornography	17%
Stalking	11%
E-mail abuse	9%
Harassment	9%
Hacking with virus	9%
Copyright violations	4%
Terrorism	3%
Chat room abuse	2%
Other	10%
Total	**100%**

Source: Data from InterGOV International's Office of Public Information, cited by Marshall, Robinson, and Kwak, 2005.

The meteoric rise in cyberdeviance can be attributed to two major factors. One is the phenomenal increase in the use of computers and the Internet over the last decade. The other factor is the relative lack of law enforcement against cybercrime all over the world. This problem is particularly severe in Russia, Eastern Europe, and other countries with widespread unemployment, where Internet access is high and its policing is low. Many computer-savvy youngsters are recruited by criminal groups through Internet chat rooms. In South Korea, for example, an organized crime syndicate once used a chat room to hold a bogus hacker contest and recruited the most promising young contestants. Not surprisingly, hacker crimes in that country skyrocketed from 449 in 2000 to 14,065 in 2003 (Anderson, 2008; Piore et al., 2006). In addition to the lax law enforcement in those countries, the lack of international cooperation in catching cybercriminals further makes it easy for them to get away with their crimes. In 2000, for example, a man in the Philippines created the "I Love You" virus that caused millions of dollars in damage in various countries but he got away with it. He could not be prosecuted in his home country due to the lack of applicable laws there, and he could not be extradited to the United States for trial, either, due to the lack of cooperation between the two countries' law enforcement agencies (Archick, 2003).

Summary

1. What is the nature of Internet deviance? Internet deviance, or cyberdeviance, involves the commission of a deviant act through the use of a computer. It can be divided into two broad types: disrupting a computer network as a target and using the computer as a tool to commit deviant acts. The second type can further be divided into three subtypes. One involves seeking easy money online; another, searching cyberspace for sex; and a third, expressing hate online.

2. What are the characteristics of online identity theft? It involves the use of a computer to steal credit card numbers, Social Security numbers, or other personal data. It can be carried out by hacking into the databases of business companies, by sending customers bogus e-mails that appear to come from legitimate companies, or by secretly planting keylogging programs into the victim's computer. Most of these identity thefts are inside jobs, carried out by people associated with the victimized companies such as their employees.

3. Why can't the U.S. law against Internet gambling stop it? One reason is the global and borderless nature of Internet gambling. Since it is legal to gamble online in foreign countries, Americans who want to gamble can easily visit foreign gaming Web sites. Another reason for the ineffectiveness of the U.S. law against Internet gambling is the lack of law enforcement against the gambling Web sites run from within the United States. **What kind of people are likely to gamble online?** They are likely to have gambled at land-based casinos, be relatively young, inclined to try new things, well educated, willing to bank online, and financially stable. But they are more likely to gamble excessively when online than when offline in land-based casinos.

4. Why do some people engage in cybersex with strangers they meet on the Internet? The reasons include being anonymous, the ease and convenience of finding online sex partners, being able to share sexual fantasies, the easy availability of online partners for masturbation, and having real sex with partners that one has met online. **What is cyberporn?** It is sexually explicit material accessible via the Internet. It has become very popular today, and many parents fear that their children will be exposed to cyberporn. But there are ways to block children's access to it. **What is the profile of cyberporn surfers?** Cyberporn surfers are mostly over 30, married, white, and middle-class men. They have weak ties to religion and suffer from a lack of marital happiness; and they tend to access cyberporn during work hours. Consumers of Internet child porn have about the same demographic backgrounds as porn surfers in general, but they are mostly pedophiles who like to use the porn for masturbation and collection.

5. Are online affairs as real and harmful as traditional offline cheating? Yes, according to most people in the general public. Research further indicates that online infidelity has the same serious impact on marriage as does a traditional affair. **Why do some married people have online affairs?** The reasons are the anonymity of cybercommunication, the convenience of finding partners, and the escapism provided from a stressful life into the fantasy world of being desired by many sex partners.

6. Does the Internet encourage the expression of prejudice against minorities? Yes, because the anonymity provided by the Internet makes it safer for bigots to express their prejudice, without the fear of being ridiculed, attacked, or retaliated against in some other way. **Does the same anonymity encourage the practice of discrimination?** No, because the anonymity hides from the bigot the potential victim's group-identifying cues such as his or her ethnicity, gender, sexual orientation, and disability. Unable to know these cues, the bigot cannot know, for example, that a job applicant is black and therefore cannot discriminate against him or her.

7. Is online stalking less dangerous than offline, face-to-face stalking? On the contrary. Because they have greater access to the victim's personal data, online stalkers can disrupt the victim's personal and professional life more than a prowler lurking in the dark can. But online stalkers are similar to offline, traditional stalkers in some ways. Like traditional stalkers, most online stalkers are males while their victims are females, and most online stalkers are older persons victimizing younger ones.

8. What is the nature of computer hacking? It involves breaking into a computer system and then planting viruses and worms in the system to delete its files or otherwise make it function abnormally. It is usually malicious in that it sabotages the computer system, but it can be merely mischievous although illegal. However, most of the hackings today seem aimed at seeking financial gain from stealing personal information or identity. **What is the most striking thing about hacking?** Hacking is mostly a juvenile deviance, as adolescents are much more likely to engage in hacking than adults. Like juvenile delinquency, hacking is an overwhelmingly male activity, a product of dysfunctional families, and an activity of a peer group.

9. Is cyberterrorism a serious threat to the United States? Yes, especially to government officials. But critics disagree, arguing that not a single incident of cyberterrorism has ever occurred because terrorists do not have the specialized knowledge required for hacking into the government's computer network in the first place.

10. What can a global perspective tell us about cyberdeviance? Cyberdeviance is truly global and borderless, taking place in all countries and able to cross national borders with deviants in one country preying on their victims in another. Online fraud, including identity theft, is by far the most prevalent cyberdeviance in the world. The incidence of cyberdeviance in general has skyrocketed since the 1990s, fueled by the tremendous increase in the use of the Internet and by the lack of law enforcement against cybercrime all over the world.

FURTHER READING

Amichai-Hamburger, Yair (ed.). 2005. *The Social Net: Human Behavior in Cyberspace*. New York: Oxford University Press. A collection of 10 essays on the social and social-psychological influences of the Internet.

Blane, John V. 2003. *Cybercrime and Cyberterrorism*. New York: Novinka Books. A brief statement of how the governments in seven countries fight cybercrime and cyberterrorism and prevent these attacks from happening.

Calder, Martin C. (ed.). 2004. *Child Sexual Abuse and the Internet: Tackling the New Frontier*. Dorset, England: Russell House Publishing. A series of articles about the use of the Internet to distribute child pornography and have sexual contacts with children in Great Britain.

Colarik, Andrew M. 2006. *Cyber Terrorism: Political and Economic Implications*. Hershey, Penn.: Idea Group. Discussing the power of terrorism, the development of cyberterrorism, the cyberattack methods, and the cyberattack scenarios.

Furnell, Steven. 2002. *Cybercrime: Vandalizing the Information Society*. London: Addison-Wesley. Presenting the nature and impact of computer crime, especially hacking, on society as a whole.

Henderson, Harry. 2005. *Library in a Book: Internet Predators*. New York: Facts on File, Inc. An informative guide to the nature of cyberdeviances including a chronology of important events relating to Internet crimes and a list of biographical sketches of cybercriminals.

Jenkins, Philip. 2001. *Beyond Tolerance: Child Pornography on the Internet*. New York: New York University Press. Discussing the nature of Internet child porn and society's reactions to it.

Joyce, Bryan H. 2002. *Internet Scams: What to Be Afraid of in Cyberspace*. Pembroke Pines, Fla.: Net Works. Reviewing a variety of attacks with computer viruses, social engineering, cons, and scams facing Internet users.

Mitnick, Kevin D., and William L. Simon. 2005. *The Art of Intrusion: The Real Stories Behind the Exploits of Hackers, Intruders & Deceivers*. Indianapolis, Ind.: Wiley. A series of stories about computer hacking followed by insights gained from them.

Orr, Andrea. 2004. *Meeting, Mating, and Cheating: Sex, Love, and the New World of Online Dating*. Upper Saddle River, N.J.: Reuters. An ethnographic, close-up view and analysis of the world of online dating.

Taylor, Max, and Ethel Quayle. 2003. *Child Pornography: An Internet Crime*. New York: Brunner-Routledge. An analysis of how child porn is used online and how social factors influence such use.

Waskul, Dennis D. (ed.). 2004. *net.seXXX: Readings on Sex, Pornography, and the Internet*. New York: Peter Lang. A collection of essays on various aspects of cybersex and cyberporn.

Worley, Becky. 2004. *Security Alert: Stories of Real People Protecting Themselves from Identity Theft, Scams, and Viruses*. Indianapolis, Ind.: New Riders Publishing. Showing with supporting anecdotes the nature of such cyberdeviances as identity theft, scams, viruses, stalking, and sexual exploitation of children, and providing advice on how to avoid becoming a victim.

Yount, Lisa. 2006. *Does the Internet Increase the Risk of Crime?* Detroit, Mich.: Greenhaven Press. A presentation of conflicting views on various aspects of Internet deviance including hacking, cyberterrorism, identity theft, and cyberstalking.

CRITICAL THINKING QUESTIONS

1. A major characteristic of the Internet is the anonymity that people can use to hide their identity when going online. Is it good for the user and the society? Why or why not?

2. Cyberdeviance has proliferated at a tremendously fast rate all over the world. What is the cause of this problem? Can various countries come together to thrash out an international plan to minimize the problem? Support your answer with logic and facts.

REFERENCES

Abadinsky, Howard. 1993. *Drug Abuse,* 2d ed. Chicago: Nelson-Hall.

Ackman, Dan. 2004. "A star is porn." *Wall Street Journal,* August 27, p. W13.

Acohido, Byron, and Jon Swartz. 2005. "Meth addicts' other habit: Online theft." *USA Today,* December 15, p. 1A.

Acohido, Byron, and Jon Swartz. 2008. *Zero Day Threat: The Shocking Truth of How Banks and Credit Bureaus Help Cyber Crooks Steal Your Money and Identity.* New York: Union Square Press.

Adams, Mike S., et al. 2003. "Labeling and delinquency." *Adolescence, 38,* 171–186.

Adams-Curtis, Leah E., and Gordon B. Forbes. 2004. "College women's experiences of sexual coercion: A review of cultural, perpetrator, victim, and situational variables." *Trauma, Violence, & Abuse, 5,* 91–122.

Adler, Jerry. 1996. "Adultery: A new furor over an old sin." *Newsweek,* September 30, 54–60.

Adler, Jerry. 2002. "The 'thrill' of theft." *Newsweek,* February 25, pp. 52–53.

Adler, Jerry. 2004. "In the grip of a deeper pain." *Newsweek,* October 20, pp. 48–49.

Adler, Jerry. 2008. "The working-class smoker." *Newsweek,* March 31, p. 16.

Agnew, Robert. 1992. "Foundation for a general strain theory of crime and delinquency." *Criminology, 30,* 47–87.

AHA (American Heart Association). 1998. "Tobacco smoke biostatistical fact sheet." http://www.amhrt.org.

Ahlstrom, Salme K., and Esa L. Osterberg. 2005. "International perspectives on adolescent and young adult drinking." *Alcohol Research & Health, 28,* 258–268.

Ahmadu, Fuambai. 2000. "Rites and wrongs: An insider/outsider reflects on power and excision." In Bettina Shell-Duncan and Ylva Hernlund (eds.), *Female "Circumcision" in Africa.* Boulder, Colo.: Lynne Rienner.

Akers, Ronald L. 1985. *Deviant Behavior: A Social Learning Approach,* 3d ed. Belmont, Calif.: Wadsworth.

Akers, Ronald L., and Gang Lee. 1999. "Age, social learning, and social bonding in adolescent substance use." *Deviant Behavior, 20,* 1–25.

Al-Arian, Laila. 2004. "Perceptions of U.S. in the Arab World." Washington Report on Middle East Affairs, September, pp. 69–70.

Albrecht, Steven F. 2001. "Stalking, stalkers, and domestic violence: Relentless fear and obsessive intimacy." In Joseph A. Davis (ed.), *Stalking Crimes and Victim Protection.* Boca Raton, Fla.: CRC Press.

Albright, Julie M. 2008. "Sex in America online: An exploration of sex, marital status, and sexual identity in internet sex seeking and its impacts." *Journal of Sex Research, 45,* 175–186.

Alder, Christine. 1984. "The convicted rapist: A sexual or a violent offender?" *Criminal Justice and Behavior, 11,* 157–177.

Alder, Christine. 1985. "An exploration of self-reported sexually aggressive behavior." *Crime & Delinquency, 31,* 306–331.

Alessio, Vittoria. 1996. "Born to be gay?" *New Scientist, 151,* September 28, 32–35.

Alexander, Steve. 2006. "Computer and information systems." pp. 160–166 in *Encyclopaedia Britannica: 2006 Book of the Year.*

Allam, Abeer. 2004. "Egypt: Torture charged." *New York Times,* March 2, p. A6.

Allan, Graham. 2004. "Being unfaithful: His and her affairs." pp. 121–140 in Jean Duncombe et al. *The State of Affairs: Explorations in Infidelity and Commitment.* Mahwah, N.J.: Lawrence Erlbaum Associates.

Altheide, David L., et al. 1978. "The social meanings of employee theft." In John M. Johnson and Jack D. Douglas (eds.), *Crime at the Top.* Philadelphia: Lippincott.

Altman, Lawrence K. 1999. "New York study finds gay men using safer sex." *New York Times,* June 28, pp. A1, A17.

Alvarez, Alex. 2001. *Governments, Citizens, and Genocide.* Bloomington: Indiana University Press.

Amir, Menachem. 1971. *Patterns in Forcible Rape.* Chicago: University of Chicago Press.

Anderson, C. A. 1989. "Temperature and aggression: Ubiquitous effects of heat on occurrence of human violence." *Psychological Bulletin, 106,* 74–96.

Anderson, K. E., Hugh Lytton, and David M. Romney. 1986. "Mothers' interactions with normal and conduct-disordered boys: Who affects whom?" *Developmental Psychology, 22,* 604–609.

Anderson, Mark. 2008. "Crimeware pays." *IEEE Spectrum,* July, p. 13.

Andreasen, Nancy C., and Donald W. Black. 2001. *Introductory Textbook of Psychiatry,* 3rd ed. Washington, D,C,: American Psychiatric Press.

Angelo, Bonnie. 1992. "Wanted: A new godfather." *Time,* April 13, p. 30.

Anslinger, Harry J., and W. S. Thompkins. 1953. *The Traffic in Narcotics.* New York: Funk and Wagnalls.

APA (American Psychiatric Association). 1994. *Diagnostic and Statistical Manual of Mental Disorders,* 4th ed. Washington, D.C.: APA.

Archer, Dane, and Rosemary Gartner. 1984. *Violence and Crime in Cross-National Perspective.* New Haven, Conn.: Yale University Press.

Archick, Kristin. 2003. "Cybercrime: The Council of Europe Convention." pp. 1–6 in John V. Blane (ed.), *Cybercrime and Cyberterrorism.* New York: Novinka Books.

Arenson, Karen W. 2004. "Worried colleges step up efforts over suicide." *New York Times,* December 3, pp. A1, A15.

Armes, Audrie. 2004. "Keep your castle secure." *Family Safety & Health,* Fall, pp. 24–29.

Armstrong, Louise. 1993. *And They Call It Help: The Psychiatric Policing of America's Children.* Reading, Mass.: Addison-Wesley.

Arrigo, Bruce A., and Thomas J. Bernard. 1997. "Postmodern criminology in relation to radical and conflict criminology." *Critical Criminology, 8,* 39–60.

Athens, Lonnie. 1985. "Character contests and violent criminal conduct: A critique." *Sociological Quarterly, 26,* 419–431.

Atkinson, Michael. 2003. *Tattooed: The Sociogenesis of a Body Art.* Toronto: University of Toronto Press.

Avio, Kenneth L. 1979. "Capital punishment in Canada: A time-series analysis of the deterrence hypothesis." *Canadian Economic Review, 12,* 647–676.

Bachman, R., and Karl A. Pillemer. 1991. "Retirement: Does it affect marital conflict and violence?" *Journal of Elder Abuse and Neglect, 3,* 75–88.

Bagnardi, Vincenzo, et al. 2001. "Alcohol consumption and the risk of cancer: A meta-analysis." *Alcohol Research & Health, 25,* 263–270.

Bailey, William C. 1998. "Deterrence, brutalization, and the death penalty: Another examination of Oklahoma's return to capital punishment." *Criminology, 36,* 711–733.

Baker, Al. 2007. "City homicides still dropping, to under 500." *New York Time,* November 23, p. 1.

Bales, Robert F. 1962. "Attitudes toward drinking in the Irish culture." In David J. Pittman and Charles R. Snyder (eds.), *Society, Culture, and Drinking Patterns.* New York: Wiley.

Bales, Robert Freed. 1946. "Cultural differences in rates of alcoholism." *Quarterly Journal of Studies on Alcohol, 6,* 480–499.

Balkan, Sheila, Ronald J. Berger, and Janet Schmidt. 1980. *Crime and Deviance in America: A Critical Approach.* Belmont, Calif.: Wadsworth.

Ball-Rokeach, Sandra J. 1973. "Values and violence: A test of the subculture of violence thesis." *American Sociological Review, 38,* 739–743.

Banta, Carolyn. 2005. "Trading for a high." *Time,* August 1, p. 35.

Barnako, Frank. 1998. "Sex sites: $1 billion and growing fast." *CBS MarketWatch,* October 8.

Barnett, Harold C. 1993. "Crimes against the environment: Superfund enforcement at last." *The Annals of the American Academy of Political and Social Science, 525* (January), 119–133.

Barnett, Ola W., Cindy L. Miller-Perrin, and Robin D. Perrin. 2005. *Family Violence Across the Lifespan: An Introduction,* 2d ed. Thousand Oaks, Calif.: Sage Publications.

Baron, Beth. 2006. "Women, honour, and the state: Evidence from Egypt." *Middle Eastern Studies, 42,* 1–20.

Baron, James N., and Peter C. Reiss. 1985. "Same time, next year: Aggregate analyses of the mass media and violent behavior." *American Sociological Review, 50,* 347–363.

Baron, Stephen W. 2007. "Street youth, gender, financial strain, and crime: Exploring Broidy and Agnew's extension to general strain theory." *Deviant Behavior, 28,* 273–302.

Barry, John, et al. 2004. "Abu Ghraib and beyond." *Newsweek,* May 17, pp. 32–37.

Barry, Kathleen. 1995. *The Prostitution of Sexuality.* New York: New York University Press.

Barstad, Anders. 2008. "Explaining changing suicide rates in Norway 1948–2004: The role of social integration." *Social Indicators Research, 87,* 47–64.

Barstow, Anne Llewellyn (ed.). 2000. *War's Dirty Secret.* Cleveland, Ohio: Pilgrim Press.

Barstow, Donald G. 2004. "Female genital mutilation." In Alex Thio and Thomas C. Calhoun (eds.), *Readings in Deviant Behavior,* 3d ed. Boston: Allyn and Bacon.

Bart, Pauline B., and Patricia H. O'Brien. 1984. "Stopping rape: Effective avoidance strategies." *Signs, 10,* 83–101.

Bart, Pauline B., and Patricia H. O'Brien. 1985. *Stopping Rape: Successful Survival Strategies.* New York: Pergamon.

Bartell, Gilbert D. 1971. *Group Sex.* New York: Signet.

Bawer, Bruce. 1993. *A Place at the Table: The Gay Individual in American Society.* New York: Poseidon Press.

Bayer, Ronald. 1985. "AIDS and the gay community: Between the specter and the promise of medicine." *Social Research, 52,* 588–589.

Bearman, Peter S., James Moody, and Katherine Stovel. 2004. "Chains of affection: The structure of adolescent romantic and sexual networks." *American Journal of Sociology, 110,* 44–91.

Beasley, James O. II. 2004. "Serial murder in America: Case studies of seven offenders." *Behavioral Sciences and the Law, 22,* 395–414.

Bechhofer, Laurie, and Andrea Parrot. 1991. "What is acquaintance rape?" In Andrea Parrot and Laurie Bechhofer (eds.), *Acquaintance Rape: The Hidden Crime.* New York: John Wiley & Sons.

Beck, Melinda. 1990. "Trading places." *Newsweek,* July 16, pp. 48–54.

Becker, Howard S. 1963. *Outsiders: Studies in the Sociology of Deviance.* New York: Free Press.

Becker, Howard S. 1974. "Labeling theory reconsidered." In Paul Rock and Mary McIntosh (eds.), *Deviance and Social Control.* London: Tavistock.

Beckerman, Nancy L. 1995. "Suicide in relation to AIDS." *Death Studies, 19,* 223–234.

Beckett, Katherine, et al. 2006. "Race, drugs, and policing: Understanding disparities in drug delivery arrests." *Criminology, 44,* 105–137.

Begley, Sharon. 1996. "Born happy?" *Newsweek,* October 14, pp. 78–80.

Begley, Sharon. 2004. "Alternative peer groups may offer way to deter some suicide bombers." *Wall Street Journal,* October 8, p. B1.

Bem, Daryl. 2008. "Is there a causal link between childhood gender nonconformity and adult homosexuality?" *Journal of Gay & Lesbian Mental Health, 12,* 61–79.

Benedict, Jeffrey R. 1998. *Athletes and Acquaintance Rape.* Thousand Oaks, Calif.: Sage Publications.

Benjamin, Harry, and R. E. L. Masters. 1964. *Prostitution and Morality.* New York: Julian.

Bennett, Trevor, et al. 2008. "The statistical association between drug misuse and crime: A meta-analysis." *Aggression & Violent Behavior, 13,* 107–118.

Bennett, William J. 1989. "A response to Milton Friedman." *Wall Street Journal,* September 19, p. A32.

Benson, Michael L. 1985. "Denying the guilty mind: Accounting for involvement in white-collar crime." *Criminology, 23,* 585–607.

Berendzen, Richard, and Laura Palmer. 1993. *Come Here: A Man Overcomes the Tragic Aftermath of Childhood Sexual Abuse.* New York: Villard Books.

Bergen, Raquel Kennedy. 1996. *Wife Rape: Understanding the Response of Survivors and Service Providers.* Thousand Oaks, Calif.: Sage Publications.

Berger, Joseph. 1994. "The psychotherapeutic treatment of male homosexuality." *American Journal of Psychotherapy, 48,* 251–261.

Berger, Lawrence M. 2004. "Income, family structure, and child maltreatment risk." *Children and Youth Services Review, 26,* 725–748.

Berk, Richard A., and Phyllis J. Newton. 1985. "Does arrest really deter wife battery? An effort to replicate the findings of the Minneapolis spouse abuse experiment." *American Sociological Review, 50,* 253–262.

Berke, Richard L. 1998. "Chasing the polls on gay rights." *New York Times,* August 2, Section 4, p. 3.

Berrill, Kevin T. 1992. "Anti-gay violence and victimization in the United States: An overview." In Gregory M. Herek and Kevin T. Berrill (eds.), *Hate Crime.* Newbury Park, Calif.: Sage Publications.

Berry, Jason. 2000. *Lead Us Not Into Temptation.* Urbana: University of Illinois Press.

Bettridge, Brenda J., and Olga Eizner Favreau. 1995. "Suicidal behavior among adolescent females: The cry for connection." In Silvia Sara Canetto and David Lester (eds.), *Women and Suicidal Behavior.* New York: Springer.

Bilefsky, Dan. 2005. "Belgian experiment: Make prostitution legal to fight its ills." *Wall Street Journal,* May 26, pp. A1, A8.

Biskupic, Joan. 2004. "It may be up to parents to block Web porn." *USA Today,* June 30, p. 6A.

Bjorksten, Karin Sparring. 2005. "Suicides in the midnight sun—a study of seasonality in suicides in West Greenland." *Psychiatry Research, 133,* 205–213.

Black, Jane A. 2008. "The not-so-golden years: Power of attorney, elder abuse, and why our laws are failing a vulnerable population." *St. John's Law Review, 82,* 289–314.

Blakely, Mary Kay. 1983. "The New Bedford gang rape." *Ms.,* July, p. 53.

Blank, Jonah, Jason Vest, and Suzie Parker. 1998. "The children of Jonesboro." *U.S. News & World Report,* April 6, pp. 16–22.

Blizzard, Rick. 2004a. "Americans and alcohol: Drink, drank, drunk?" The Gallup Poll Tuesday Briefing, August 24. www.gallup.com.

Blizzard, Rick. 2004b. "Smoking: Will education overpower addiction?" The Gallup Poll Tuesday Brief, August 31. www.gallup.com.

Block, Alan A. 1991. *The Business of Crime.* Boulder, Colo.: Westview.

Bloomfield, Kim, et al. 2006. "Introduction to special issue 'gender, culture and alcohol problems: A multi-national study.'" *Alcohol and Alcoholism,* October/November, pp. 13–17.

Blumenfeld, Warren J. (ed.). 1992. *Homophobia: How We All Pay the Price.* Boston: Beacon.

Blumenfeld, Warren J., and Diane Raymond. 1993. *Looking at Gay and Lesbian Life.* Boston: Beacon.

Blumstein, Alfred. 1995. "Violence by young people: Why the deadly nexus?" *National Institute of Justice Journal,* August, pp. 2–9.

Blumstein, Philip, and Pepper Schwartz. 1990. "Intimate relationships and the creation of sexuality." In David P. McWhirter, et al. (eds.), *Homosexuality/ Heterosexuality.* New York: Oxford University Press.

Bocij, Paul. 2004. *Cyberstalking: Harassment in the Internet Age and How to Protect Your Family.* Westport, Conn.: Praeger.

Boffey, Philip M. 1986. "Schizophrenia: Insights fail to halt rising toll." *New York Times,* March 16, p. 1.

Bogert, Carroll. 1994. "Good news on drugs from the inner city." *Newsweek,* February 14, pp. 28–29.

Bohlen, Celestine. 1994. "Graft and gansterism in Russia blight the entrepreneurial spirit." *New York Times,* January 30, p. 1.

Bolen, Rebecca M. 2001. *Child Sexual Abuse: Its Scope and Our Failure.* New York: Kluwer Academic/ Plenum Publishers.

Booth, Martin. 2000. *The Dragon Syndicates: The Global Phenomenon of the Triads.* New York: Carroll & Graf Publishers.

Borger, Gloria. 2006. "A real shot . . . in the foot." *U.S. News & World Report,* February 27, p. 32.

Borja, Rhea R. 2006. "Cyber-security concerns mount as student hacking hits schools." *Education Week,* January 18, pp. 1–13.

Botchkovar, Ekaterina V., and Charles R. Tittle. 2005. "Crime, shame and reintegration in Russia." *Theoretical Criminology, 9,* 401–442.

Bower, Bruce. 1992. "Alcoholism: Nurture may often outdo nature." *Science News, 141,* February 1, p. 69.

Bower, Bruce. 1994. "Mental disorders strike about half of U.S." *Science News,* January 22, p. 55.

Bowers, William J., and Glenn L. Pierce. 1980. "Deterrence or brutalization: What is the effect of execution?" *Crime and Delinquency, 26,* 453–484.

Boy, Angie, and Andrzej Kulczycki. 2008. "What we know about intimate partner violence in the Middle East and North Africa." *Violence Against Women, 14,* 53–70.

Boyatzis, Richard E. 1975. "The predisposition toward alcohol-related interpersonal aggression in men." *Journal of Studies on Alcohol, 36,* 1196–1207.

Bradsher, Keith. 1999. "For car thieves, a technological arms race." *New York Times,* March 28, Section 4, p. 3.

Braithwaite, John. 1989. *Crime, Shame and Reintegration.* New York: Cambridge University Press.

Braithwaite, John. 1992. "Poverty, power, and white-collar crime." In Kip Schlegel and David Weisburd (eds.), *White-Collar Crime Reconsidered.* Boston: Northeastern University Press.

Braithwaite, John. 1993. "Transnational regulation of the pharmaceutical industry." *The Annals of the American Academy of Political and Social Science, 525,* January, 13–14.

Braithwaite, John. 2000. "Shame and criminal justice." *Canadian Journal of Criminology,* July, 42, 281–299.

Brake, Mike. 1994. "Needed: A license to drink." *Newsweek,* March 14, p. 11.

Breault, K. D. 1986. "Suicide in America: A test of Durkheim's theory of religious and family integration, 1933–1980." *American Journal of Sociology, 92,* 628–656.

Breggin, Peter. 1997. *Empathy and the Creation of a Healing Presence.* New York: Springer.

Brener, N., et al. 2004. "Violence-related behaviors among high school students—United States, 1991–2003." *JAMA (Journal of American Medical Association), 292,* 1168–1169.

Breslow, Rosalind A., and Barbara Smothers. 2004. "Drinking patterns of older Americans: National health interview surveys, 1997–2001." *Journal of Studies on Alcohol, 65,* 232–240.

Brewer, John D. 2000. *Ethnography.* Buckingham, U.K.: Open University Press.

Brinson, Susan L. 1992. "The use and opposition of rape myths in prime-time television dramas." *Sex Roles, 27,* 359–375.

Broder, John M. 2005. "Los Angeles files recount decades of priests' abuse." *New York Times,* October 12, pp. A1, A16.

Brody, Jane E. 1997. "Quirks, oddities may be illnesses." *New York Times,* February 4, pp. B9, B11.

Brown, Judith K. 1992. "Introduction." In D. A. Counts, J. K. Brown, and J. C. Campbell (eds.), *Sanctions and Sanctuary: Cultural Perspectives on the Beating of Wives.* Boulder, Colo.: Westview.

Brown, Marjorie E. 1979. "Teenage prostitution." *Adolescence, 14,* 665–680.

Browne, Angela. 1987. *Why Battered Women Kill.* New York: Free Press.

Brownell, Kelly D., and Katherine Battle Horgen. 2004. *Food Fight: The Inside Story of the Food Industry, America's Obesity Crisis, and What We Can Do About It.* Chicago: Contemporary Books.

Brownmiller, Susan. 1975. *Against Our Will: Men, Women and Rape.* New York: Simon & Schuster.

Bruni, Frank. 1997. "In an age of consent, defining abuse by adults." *New York Times,* Section 4, p. 3.

Brush, Lisa D. 2003. "Effects of work on hitting and hurting." *Violence Against Women, 9,* 1213–1230.

Brush, Silla. 2005. "Who's sorry now?" *U.S. News & World Report,* December 12, pp. 35–43.

Bryan, James H. 1966. "Occupational ideologies and individual attitudes of call girls." *Social Problems, 13,* 441–450.

Bryant, Marshall A. 1977. "Prostitution and the criminal justice system." *Journal of Police Science and Administration, 5,* 384.

Budiansky, Stephen, et al. 1995. "How lawyers abuse the law." *U.S. News & World Report,* January 30, pp. 50–56.

Bullough, Bonnie. 1993. "The causes of homosexuality: A scientific update." *Free Inquiry, 13* (Fall), 40–47.

Burgess, Ann Wolbert. 1995. "Rape trauma syndrome." In Patricia Searles and Ronald J. Berger (eds.), *Rape and Society.* Boulder, Colo.: Westview.

Burgess, Robert L., and Ronald L. Akers. 1966. "A differential association-reinforcement theory of criminal behavior." *Social Problems, 14,* 128–147.

Burr, Chandler. 1996. *A Separate Creation: The Search for the Biological Origins of Sexual Orientation.* New York: Hyperion.

Burros, Marian. 1996. "In an about-face, U.S. says alcohol has health benefits." *New York Times,* January 3, pp. A1, B6.

Burt, Martha R. 1991. "Rape myths and acquaintance rape." In Andrea Parrot and Laurie Bechhofer (eds.), *Acquaintance Rape.* New York: Wiley.

Burton, Thomas M. 1993a. "Caught in the act." *Wall Street Journal,* March 26, pp. A1, A5.

Burton, Thomas M. 1993b. "Spilled milk." *Wall Street Journal,* May 25, pp. A1, A6.

Burton, Velmer S., et al. 1998. "Gender, self-control, and crime." *Journal of Research in Crime and Delinquency, 35,* 123–147.

Busch, Amy L., and Mindy S. Rosenberg. 2004. "Comparing women and men arrested for domestic violence: A preliminary report." *Journal of Family Violence, 19,* 49–57.

Buss, Dale. 1993. "Ways to curtail employee theft." *Nation's Business,* April, p. 36.

Butterfield, Fox. 1999. "Prisons brim with mentally ill, study finds." *New York Times,* July 12, p. A10.

Byrne, C. A., et al. 1999. "The socioeconomic impact of interpersonal violence on women." *Journal of Consulting and Clinical Psychology, 67,* 362–366.

Cahalan, Don. 1970. *Problem Drinkers.* San Francisco: Jossey-Bass.

Cahan, Vicky, et al. 1985. "A murder verdict jolts business." *Business Week,* July 1, p. 24.

Cahill, Tom. 1985. "Rape behind bars." *The Progressive,* November, p. 32.

Calhoun, Lawrence G., James W. Selby, and Michael E. Faulstich. 1980. "Reactions to the parents of the child suicide: A study of social impressions." *Journal of Consulting and Clinical Psychology, 48,* 535–536.

Campbell, Rebecca, and Sharon M. Wasco. 2005. "Understanding rape and sexual assault: 20 years of progress and future directions." *Journal of Interpersonal Violence, 20,* 127–131.

Campo-Flores, Arian. 2002. "A crackdown on call girls." *Newsweek,* September 2, p. 59.

Canetto, Silvia Sara, and David Lester (eds.). 1995. *Women and Suicidal Behavior.* New York: Springer.

Cannon, Angie, and Jeffrey L. Sheler. 2002. "Catholics in crisis." *U.S. News & World Report,* April 1, pp. 51–57.

Cannon, Angie. 1999. "Sex, drugs, and sudden death." *U.S. News & World Report,* May 24, p. 73.

Caplan, Gerald M. 1984. "The facts of life about teenage prostitution." *Crime & Delinquency, 30,* 69–74.

Capone, Donald L., and Woodrow W. Nichols, Jr. 1976. "Urban structure and criminal mobility." *American Behavioral Scientist, 20,* 199–213.

Carey, Benedict. 2008. "Drawn lines: Making sense of the great suicide debate." *New York Times,* February 10, p. 1.

Carey, Kate B. 1993. "Situational determinants of heavy drinking among college students." *Journal of Counseling Psychology, 40,* 217–220.

Carlson, Eric Stener. 2006. "The hidden prevalence of male sexual assault during war: Observations on blunt trauma to the male genitals." *British Journal of Criminology, 46,* 16–25.

Carlson, Margaret. 1995. "The sex-crime capital." *Time,* November 13, pp. 89–90.

Carrithers, David W. 1985. "The insanity defense and presidential peril." *Society, 22* (July/August), 22–27.

Carter, Bonnie Frank, and Allan Brooks. 1991. "Child and adolescent survivors of suicide." In Antoon A. Leenaars (ed.), *Life Span Perspectives of Suicide: Time-lines in the Suicide Process.* New York: Plenum.

Carter, David, and Andra J. Bannister. 2002. "Computer-related crime." In David Shichor, Larry Gaines, and Richard Ball (eds.), *Readings in White-Collar Crime.* Prospect Heights, Ill.: Waveland.

Carter, Hodding. 1989. "We're losing the drug war because prohibition never works." *Wall Street Journal,* July 13, p. A15.

Cashdan, Sheldon. 1972. *Abnormal Psychology.* Englewood Cliffs, N.J.: Prentice Hall.

Castle, Tammy, and Jenifer Lee. 2008. "Ordering sex in cyberspace: A content analysis of escort websites." *International Journal of Cultural Studies, 11,* 107–121.

Catalano, Ralph, et al. 1993. "Job loss and alcohol abuse: A test using data from the epidemiologic catchment area project." *Journal of Health and Social Behavior, 34,* 215–225.

Caulkins, Jonathan P., and Rosalie Liccardo. 2006. "Marijuana markets: Inferences from reports by the household population." *Journal of Drug Issues, 36,* 173–200.

Caulkins, Jonathan P., et al. 2005. *How Goes the "War on Drugs"?* Santa Monica, Calif.: RAND.

Cazenave, N. A., and Murray A. Straus. 1990. "Race, class, network embeddedness, and family violence: A search for potent support systems." In M. A. Straus and R. J. Gelles (eds.), *Physical Violence in American Families.* New Brunswick, N.J.: Transaction.

Centers for Disease Control and Prevention (CDC). 2008. "CDC: School-based homicides on the decline in recent years." *Canadian Electronics, 23,* 6.

CDC, 2003. "Drug-associated HIV transmission continues in the United States." www.cdc.gov/hiv/pubs/facts/idu.htm.

Chambliss, William J. 1969. *Crime and the Legal Process.* New York: McGraw-Hill.

Chambliss, William J., and Robert Seidman. 1971. *Law, Order, and Power.* Reading, Mass.: Addison-Wesley.

Chamlin, Mitchell B., and John K. Cochran. 2005. "Ascribed economic inequality and homicide among modern societies." *Homicide Studies, 9,* 3–29.

Chappell, Allison T., and Alex R. Piquero. 2004. "Applying social learning theory to police misconduct." *Deviant Behavior, 25,* 89–109.

Chappell, Duncan, Gilbert Geis, Stephen Schafer, and Larry Siegel. 1971. "Forcible rape: A comparative study of offenses known to the police in Boston and Los Angeles." In James M. Henslin (ed.), *Studies in the Sociology of Sex.* New York: Appleton-Century-Crofts.

Chase, Marilyn. 1996a. "Health journal." *Wall Street Journal,* August 26, p. B1.

Chase, Marilyn. 1996b. "Americans seem to drink a lot or hardly at all." *Wall Street Journal,* December 30, p. B1.

Chein, Isidor, Donald L. Gerard, Robert S. Lee, and Eva Rosenfeld. 1964. *The Road to H.* New York: Basic Books.

Cherry, Rona, and Laurence Cherry. 1973. "Depression: The common cold of mental ailments." *New York Times Magazine,* November 25, p. 38.

Chervyakov, Valerity V., et al. 2002. "The changing nature of murder in Russia." *Social Science and Medicine, 55,* 1713–1724.

Chesney-Lind, Meda. 1997. *The Female Offender: Girls, Women, and Crime.* Thousand Oaks, Calif.: Sage Publications.

Cheung, Hoi Yan, and Alex W. H. Chan. 2008. "Corruption across countries: Impacts from education and cultural dimensions." *Social Science Journal, 45,* 223–239.

Chiroro, Patrick, et al. 2004. "Rape myth acceptance and rape proclivity: Expected dominance versus expected arousal as mediators in acquaintance-rape situations." *Journal of Interpersonal Violence, 19,* 427–442.

Christensen, Russ, and Peter W. Dowrick. 1983. "Myths of mid-winter depression." *Community Mental Health Journal, 19,* 177–186.

Christian, Nichole. 1995. "New generation of car thieves restructures the business." *Wall Street Journal,* July 19, p. B1.

Church, George J. 1986. "What he needs to know." *Time,* December 22, pp. 17–18.

Clark, Kim, and Marianne Lavelle. 2006. "Guilty as charged!" *U.S. News & World Report,* June 5, pp. 44–45.

Clarke, Ronald V. 2002. *Shoplifting.* Washington, D.C.: U.S. Department of Justice.

Clausen, John A., and Carol L. Huffine. 1975. "Sociocultural and social-psychological factors affecting social responses to mental disorder." *Journal of Health and Social Behavior, 16,* 405–420.

Clifton, A. Kay, and Dorothy E. Lee. 1995. "Gender socialization and women's suicidal behaviors." In Silvia Sara Canetto and David Lester (eds.), *Women and Suicidal Behavior.* New York: Springer.

Clinard, Marshall B., and Peter C. Yeager. 1980. *Corporate Crime.* New York: Free Press.

Cloud, John. 1998. "For better or worse." *Time,* October 26, pp. 43–44.

Cloud, John. 2001. "A license to kill?" *Time,* April 23, p. 66.

Cloud, John. 2008. "Should you drink with your kids?" *Time,* July 30, pp. 44–47.

Cloward, Richard, and Lloyd E. Ohlin. 1960. *Delinquency and Opportunity: A Theory of Juvenile Gangs.* New York: Free Press.

Cochrane, Raymond. 1983. *The Social Creation of Mental Illness.* London: Longman.

Cohen, Albert K. 1955. *Delinquent Boys: The Culture of the Gang.* New York: Free Press.

Cohen, Lawrence E., David Cantor, and James R. Kluegel. 1981. "Robbery victimization in the U.S.: An analysis of a nonrandom event." *Social Science Quarterly, 62,* 645–657.

Cohen, Murray, Ralph Garofalo, Richard Boucher, and Theoharis Seghorn. 1971. "The psychology of rapists." *Seminar in Psychiatry, 3,* 310.

Cohn, Bob, and Mary Hager. 1993. "The power of sin." *Newsweek,* October 4, p. 51.

Coleman, James William. 2006. *The Criminal Elite: The Sociology of White Collar Crime,* 5th ed. New York: St. Martin's.

Collier, Theresa J. 1993. "The stigma of mental illness." *Newsweek,* April 26, p. 16.

Colvin, Mark, and John Pauly. 1983. "A critique of criminology: Toward an integrated structural-Marxist theory of delinquency production." *American Journal of Sociology, 89,* 513–551.

Compton, Wilson M., and Nora D. Volkow. 2006. "Abuse of prescription drugs and the risk of addiction." *Drug and Alcohol Dependence, 83S,* S4–S7.

Conant, Marcus. 1997. "This is smart medicine." *Newsweek,* February 3, p. 26.

Conklin, John E. 1972. *Robbery and the Criminal Justice System.* Philadelphia: Lippincott.

Conklin, John E. 1977. *"Illegal but Not Criminal": Business Crime in America.* Englewood Cliffs, N.J.: Prentice Hall.

Contexts. 2004. "From the polls: Assisted suicide." *Summer,* p. 58.

Continetti, Matthew. 2006. *The K Street Gang: The Rise and Fall of the Republican Machine.* New York: Doubleday.

Cook, Philip J., and Mark H. Moore. 1999. "Guns, gun control, and homicide: A review of research and public policy." In M. Dwayne Smith and Margaret A. Zahn (eds.), *Homicide: A Sourcebook of Social Research.* Thousand Oaks, Calif.: Sage Publications.

Cookson, Peter W. Jr., and Caroline Hodges Persell. 1985. *Preparing for Power: America's Elite Boarding Schools.* New York: Basic Books.

Coombs, Robert Holman. 1997. *Drug-Impaired Professionals.* Cambridge, Mass.: Harvard University Press.

Cooper, Al. 2004. "Online sexual activity in the New Millennium." *Contemporary Sexuality,* March, pp. 1–8.

Cooperman, Nina A., and Jane M. Simoni. 2005. "Suicidal ideation and attempted suicide among women living with HIV/AIDS." *Journal of Behavioral Medicine, 28,* 149–156.

Corliss, Richard, and Simon Crittle. 2004. "The last don." *Time,* March 29, pp. 44–52.

Corliss, Richard. 2006. "How the west was won over." *Time,* January 30, pp. 60–63.

Corzine, Jay, Lin Huff-Dorzine, and Hugh P. Whitt. 1999. "Cultural and subcultural theories of homicide." In M. Dwayne Smith and Margaret A. Zahn (eds.), *Homicide: A Sourcebook of Social Research.* Thousand Oaks, Calif.: Sage Publications.

Cose, Ellis. 2008. "The lessons of Rwanda." *Newsweek,* April 21, p. 33.

Cottle, Thomas J. 2004. "A teen suicide in the family." In Alex Thio and Thomas C. Calhoun (eds.), *Readings in Deviant Behavior,* 3d ed. Boston: Allyn and Bacon.

Cowley, Geoffrey. 1997. "Can marijuana be medicine?" *Newsweek,* February 3, pp. 22–27.

Coyne, James C., and Geraldine Downey. 1991. "Social factors and psychopathology: Stress, social support, and coping processes." *Annual Review of Psychology, 42,* 401–425.

Crabb, Peter B. 2005. "The material culture of suicidal fantasies." *The Journal of Psychology, 139,* 211–220.

Crawford, David, et al. 2007. "Siemens ruling details bribery across the globe." *Wall Street Journal,* November 16, pp. A1, A17.

Cressey, Donald R. 1971. *Other People's Money: A Study in the Social Psychology of Embezzlement.* Belmont, Calif.: Wadsworth.

Critelli, Joseph W., and Jenny M. Bivona. 2008. "Women's erotic rape fantasies: An evaluation of theory and research." *Journal of Sex Research, 45,* 57–70.

Cromwell, Paul F., James N. Olson, and D'Aunn Wester Avary. 1991. *Breaking and Entering: An Ethnographic Analysis of Burglary.* Newbury Park, Calif.: Sage Publications.

Crossen, Cynthia. 1996. "Losing it." *Wall Street Journal,* December 3, pp. A1, A10.

Crosset, Todd W., J. Ptacek, M. A. Mcdonald, and J. R. Benedict. 1996. "Male student-athletes and violence against women: A survey of campus judicial affairs offices." *Violence Against Women, 2,* 163–179.

Cross-National Collaborative Group. 1992. "The changing rate of major depression: Cross-national comparisons." *JAMA (Journal of American Medical Association), 268,* 3098–3105.

Crouch, Margaret A. 2001. *Thinking about Sexual Harassment.* New York: Oxford University Press.

Current Science. 2008. "Autism epidemic a myth." March 28, p. 14.

Currie, Elliott. 1993. *Reckoning: Drugs, the Cities, and the American Future.* New York: Hill and Wang.

Cuvelier, Monique. 2002. "Victim, not villain." *Psychology Today,* May/June, p. 23.

Dalmas, Paul C. 2007. "Looking for answers to my nephew's death." *Newsweek,* April 23, p. 18.

Dalrymple, Theodore. 2002. "Marks of shame." *National Review,* March 11, pp. 28–30.

Dalrymple, Theodore. 2006. *Romancing Opiates.* New York: Encounter Books.

Danigelis, Nick, and Whitney Pope. 1979. "Durkheim's theory of suicide as applied to the family: An empirical test." *Social Forces, 57,* 1081–1106.

Davies, Scott, and Julian Tanner. 2003. "The long arm of the law: Effects of labeling on employment." *Sociological Quarterly, 44,* 385–404.

Davis, Alan J. 1982. "Sexual assaults in the Philadelphia prison system and sheriff's vans." In Anthony M. Scacco, Jr. (ed.), *Male Rape.* New York: AMS Press.

Davis, Bernard D. 1990. "Right to die: Living wills are inadequate." *Wall Street Journal,* July 31, p. A12.

Davis, Kingsley. 1971. "Sexual behavior." In Robert Merton and Robert Nisbet (eds.), *Contemporary Social Problems,* 3d ed. New York: Harcourt Brace Jovanovich.

Davis, Nanette J. (ed.). 1993. *Prostitution: An International Handbook on Trends, Problems, and Policies.* Westport, Conn.: Greenwood.

Davis, Nanette J., and Clarice Stasz. 1990. *Social Control: The Production of Deviance in the Modern State.* New York: McGraw-Hill.

Davison, Gerald C., and John M. Neale. 1996. *Abnormal Psychology,* 6th ed. New York: Wiley.

De Seve, Karen. 2006. "The perils of ecstasy." *Current Health 2,* February, pp. 26–29.

De Visser, Richard, and Dee McDonald. 2007. "Swings and roundabouts: Management of jealousy in heterosexual 'swinging' couples." *British Journal of Social Psychology, 46,* 459–476.

Decker, Scott, and Richard Rosenfeld. 1992. "Intravenous drug use and the AIDS epidemic: Findings from a 20-city sample of arrestees." *Crime & Delinquency, 38,* 492–509.

Deitz, Sheila R., et al. 1984. "Attributions of responsibility for rape: The influence of observer empathy, victim resistance, and victim attractiveness." *Sex Roles, 10,* 261–280.

DeJong, William. 1986. "Project DARE: Teaching kids to say no to drugs and alcohol." *NIJ Reports,* no. 196, pp. 2–5.

DeKeseredy, Walter S., and Martin D. Schwartz. 1996. *Contemporary Criminology.* Belmont, Calif.: Wadsworth.

Demyttenaere, K., et al. 2004. "Prevalence of mental disorders in Europe: Results from the European Study of the Epidemiology of Mental Disorders project." *Acta Psychiatrica Scandinavica, 109,* 21–27.

Denfeld, Duane. 1974. "Dropouts from swinging." *The Family Coordinator,* January, pp. 45–49.

Denham, Susanne A., Susan M. Renwick, and Robert W. Holt. 1991. "Working and playing together: Prediction of preschool social-emotional competence from mother-child interaction." *Child Development, 62,* 242–249.

Denzin, Norman K. 1991. "The AA group." In David J. Pittman and Helene Raskin White (eds.), *Society, Culture, and*

Drinking Patterns Reexamined. New Brunswick, N.J.: Rutgers Center of Alcohol Studies.

DeSimone, Jeff. 2007. "Fraternity membership and binge drinking." *Journal of Health Economics, 26,* 950–967.

Desmarais, Sarah L., and Kim A. Reeves. 2007. "Gray, black, and blue: The state of research and intervention for intimate partner abuse among elders." *Behavioral Sciences and the Law, 25,* 377–391.

Dickermann, Mildred. 1995. "Wilson's panchreston: The inclusive fitness hypothesis of sociobiology re-examined." *Journal of Homosexuality, 28,* 147–183.

Dickey, Christopher. 2002. "Inside Suicide, Inc." *Newsweek,* April 15, pp. 26–32.

Diken, Bulent, and Carsten Bagge Laustsen. 2005. "Becoming abject: Rape as a weapon of war." *Body & Society, 11,* 111–128.

Diller, Lawrence H. 1998. *Running on Ritalin.* New York: Bantam Books.

Dobash, Russell P., R. Emerson Dobash, Margo Wilson, and Martin Daly. 1992. "The myth of sexual symmetry in marital violence." *Social Problems, 39,* 71–91.

Doblin, Rich, and Mark A. R. Kleiman. 1993. "Marijuana as medicine." *Wall Street Journal,* February 19, p. A13.

Dobrzynski, Judith H. 1996. "For more and more job seekers, an aging parent is a big factor." *New York Times,* January 1, pp. 1, 24.

Dodes, Lance M. 2005. "Psychological factors, not the chemical properties of drugs, cause addiction." pp. 26–33 in Mercedes Munoz (ed.), *What Causes Addiction?* Detroit, Mich.: Thomson/Gale.

Dodge, David L. 1985. "The over-negativized conceptualization of deviance: A programmatic exploration." *Deviant Behavior, 6,* 17–37.

Dohrenwend, Bruce P. 1975. "Sociocultural and social-psychological factors Iin the genesis of mental disorders." *Journal of Health and Social Behavior, 16,* 365–392.

Dohrenwend, Bruce P., and Barbara Snell Dohrenwend. 1974. "Psychiatric disorders in urban settings." In S. Arietti and G. Caplan (eds.), *American Handbook of Psychiatry.* New York: Basic Books.

Dohrenwend, Bruce P., and Barbara Snell Dohrenwend. 1976. "Sex differences and psychiatric disorders." *American Journal of Sociology, 81,* 1447–1454.

Dokoupil, Tony. 2007. "Trouble in a 'black box'." *Newsweek,* July 16, p. 48.

Donnerstein, Edward, et al. 1987. *The Question of Pornography: Research Findings and Policy Implications.* New York: Free Press.

Donovan, James M. 1986. "An etiologic model of alcoholism." *American Journal of Psychiatry, 143,* 5–6.

Donovan, John E. 1993. "Young adult drinking-driving: Behavioral and psychosocial correlates." *Journal of Studies on Alcohol, 54,* 600–613.

Douglas, Jack D. 1967. *The Social Meanings of Suicide.* Princeton, N.J.: Princeton University Press.

Douglas, Jack D., and Frances C. Waksler. 1982. *The Sociology of Deviance.* Boston: Little, Brown.

Drapela, Laurie A. 2005. "Does dropping out of high school cause deviant behavior? An analysis of the national education longitudinal study." *Deviant Behavior, 26,* 47–62.

Drapkin, Jennifer. 2005. "PT data mine." *Psychology Today,* July/August, p. 30.

Dubin, Louis I., and Bessie Bunzel. 1933. *To Be or Not to Be.* New York: Harrison Smith and Robert Haas.

Duffala, Dennis C. 1976. "Convenience stores, armed robbery, and physical environmental features." *American Behavioral Scientist, 20,* 227–246.

Dugas, Christine. 2008. "More consumers, workers shoplift as economy slows." *USA Today,* June 19, p. 1B.

Dugger, Celia W. 1999. "Calcutta's prostitutes preach about condoms." *New York Times,* January 4, pp. A1, A8.

Duncombe, Jean, et al. (eds.). 2004. *The State of Affairs: Explorations in Infidelity and Commitment.* Mahwah, N.J.: Lawrence Erlbaum Associates.

Dunkle, John H., and Patricia L. Francis. 1990. "The role of facial masculinity/femininity in the attribution of homosexuality." *Sex Roles, 23,* 157–167.

Dunlap, David W. 1995. "Two steps forward for homosexuals." *New York Times,* October 18, p. A12.

Dunn, Jennifer. 2004. "'Everyone knows who the sluts are': How young women get around the stigma." In Alex Thio and Thomas C. Calhoun (eds.), *Readings in Deviant Behavior,* 3d ed. Boston: Allyn and Bacon.

Durkheim, Émile. 1897/1966. *Suicide.* New York: Free Press.

Durose, Matthew R., et al. 2005. *Family Violence Statistics.* Washington, D.C.: U.S. Department of Justice, Bureau of Justice Statistics.

Dutton, Donald G. 1986. "Wife assaulters' explanations for assault: The neutralization of self-punishment." *Canadian Journal of Behavioral Sciences, 18,* 381–390.

Dutton, Donald G. 1994. "Patriarchy and wife assault: An ecological fallacy." *Violence and Victims, 9,* 167–182.

Early, Kevin E. 1992. *Religion and Suicide in the African-American Community.* Westport, Conn.: Greenwood.

Early, Kevin E. 1996. *Drug Treatment Behind Bars: Prison-Based Strategies for Change.* Westport, Conn.: Praeger.

Early, Kevin E., and Ronald L. Akers. 1995. "'It's a white thing': An exploration of beliefs about suicide in the African-American community." In Alex Thio and Thomas Calhoun (eds.), *Readings in Deviant Behavior.* New York: HarperCollins.

Eaton, Leslie. 1999. "Assault with a fiscal weapon." *New York Times,* May 25, pp. C1, C25.

Edmundson, Mark. 1999. "Save Sigmund Freud." *New York Times Magazine,* July 13, pp. 34–35.

Edwards, Hodee. 1993. "Rape defines sex." *Off Our Backs, 23* (August), 16–17.

Egan, Timothy. 2000. "Technology sent Wall Street into market for pornography." *New York Times,* October 23, pp. A1, A20.

Ehrenreich, Barbara. 2002. "Libation as liberation." *Time,* April 1, p. 62.

Ehrlich, Isaac. 1975. "The deterrent effect of capital punishment: A question of life and death." *American Economic Review, 65,* 397–417.

Eichenwald, Kurt. 2002. "White-collar defense stance: The criminal-less crime." *New York Times,* March 3, Section 4, p. 3.

Eigen, Joel Peter. 1981. "Punishing youth homicide offenders in Philadelphia," *Journal of Criminal Law and Criminology, 72,* 1075.

Einstadter, Werner, and Stuart Henry. 1995. *Criminological Theory: An Analysis of Its Underlying Assumptions.* Fort Worth, Texas: Harcourt Brace.

Eisenberg, Daniel. 2002. "Dennis the menace." *Time,* June 17, pp. 46–49.

Elias, Marilyn. 2005. "Mental illness: Surprising, disturbing findings." *USA Today,* June 2005, p. 8d.

Elliott, Diana M., et al. 2004. "Adult sexual assault: Prevalence, symptomatology, and sex differences in the general population." *Journal of Traumatic Stress, 17,* 203–211.

Elliott, Jeff. 1995. "Drug prevention placebo." *Reason, 26* (March), 14–21.

Elliott, Robert E., et al. 1985. *Explaining Delinquency and Drug Use.* Beverly Hills, Calif.: Sage Publications.

Elmer-Dewitt, Philip. 1995. "On a screen near you: Cyberporn." *Time,* July 3, pp. 38–45.

Empfield, Maureen, and Nicholas Bakalar. 2001. *Understanding Teenage Depression.* New York: Henry Holt.

Emshwiller, John R., et al. 2006. "Symbol of an Era: Lay, Skilling Convicted of Conspiracy." *Wall Street Journal,* May 26, pp. A1, A9.

Engs, Ruth C., and David J. Hanson. 1994. "Boozing and brawling on campus: A national study of violent problems associated with drinking over the past decade." *Journal of Criminal Justice, 22,* 171–180.

Erikson, Kai T. 1962. "Notes on the sociology of deviance." *Social Problems, 9,* 307–314.

Erlanger, Howard S. 1974. "The empirical status of the subculture of violence thesis." *Social Problems, 22,* 280–292.

Ermann, M. David, and Richard J. Lundman (eds.). 2002. *Corporate and Governmental Deviance: Problems of Organizational Behavior in Contemporary Society,* 6th ed. New York: Oxford University Press.

Erofeyev, Victor. 2002. "The Russian god." *New Yorker,* December 16, pp. 56–63.

Essex, Marilyn, et al. 1981. "On Weinstein's 'Patient attitudes toward mental hospitalization: A review of quantitative research.'" *Journal of Health and Social Behavior, 21,* 393–396.

Fahim, Kareem, and Nate Schweber. 2008. "Three youths in Montclair are charged in sex attack." *New York Times,* March 12, p. A3.

Falk, Gerhard. 2001. *Stigma: How We Treat Outsiders.* Amherst, N.Y.: Prometheus Books.

Falkenrath, Richard A. 2006. "Grading the war on terrorism." *Foreign Affairs, 85,* 122–128.

Fang, Bay. 2005. "Young lives for sale." *U.S. News & World Report,* October 24, pp. 30–34.

Farberow, Norman L. 1991. "Adult survivors after suicide: Research problems and needs." In Antoon A. Leenaars (ed.), *Life Span Perspectives of Suicide: Time-lines in the Suicide Process.* New York: Plenum.

Farley, Melissa. 1994. "Prostitution: The oldest use and abuse of women." *Off Our Backs, 24,* 14–15.

Farrington, David P. 1977. "The effects of public labelling." *British Journal of Criminology, 17,* 112–125.

Farwell, Nancy. 2004. "War rape: New conceptualizations and responses." *Affilia, 19,* 389–403.

Fazel, Seena, et al. 2005. "Suicides in male prisoners in England and Wales, 1978–2003." *Lancet, 366,* 1301–1302.

FBI (Federal Bureau of Investigation). 2008. *Uniform Crime Reports.* Washington, D.C.: Government Printing Office.

Feeney, Floyd, and Adrianne Weir. 1975. "The prevention and control of robbery." *Criminology, 13,* 104.

Feldman, Douglas A. 1985. "AIDS and social change." *Human Organization, 44,* 343–348.

Felson, Richard B., and Henry J. Steadman. 1983. "Situational factors in disputes leading to criminal violence." *Criminology, 21,* 39–74.

Fergusson, David M. 2006. "Cannabis use and other illicit drug use: Testing the cannabis gateway hypothesis." *Addiction, 101,* 556–569.

Ferrell, Jeff, and Mark S. Hamm (eds.). 1998. *Ethnography at the Edge: Crime, Deviance, and Field Research.* Boston: Northeastern University Press.

Ferro, Christine, et al. 2008. "Current perceptions of marital rape: Some good and not-so-good news." *Journal of Interpersonal Violence, 23,* 764–779.

Fields, Gary. 2006. "No way out: Trapped by rules, the mentally ill languish in prison." *Wall Street Journal,* May 5, pp. A1, A16.

Fields, Suzanne. 1993. "Rape as sport: The culture is at the root." *Insight on the News, 9* (May 3), 19–20.

Fillion, Kate. 1991. "Rape on campus." *Chatelaine, 64* (August), 33–35.

Fine, M., and A. Asch. 1988. "Disability beyond stigma: Social interaction, discrimination, and activism." *Journal of Social Issues, 44,* 3–22.

Finkelhor, David, et al. 1989. "Sexual abuse and its relationship to later sexual satisfaction, marital status, religion, and attitudes." *Journal of Interpersonal Violence, 4,* 379–399.

Finkelhor, David. 1984. *Child Sexual Abuse: New Theory and Research.* New York: Free Press.

Finn, Jerry. 2004. "A survey of online harassment at a university campus." *Journal of Interpersonal Violence, 19,* 468–483.

Firth, Raymond. 1961. "Suicide and risk-taking in Tikopia society." *Psychiatry, 24,* 4.

Fisher, Bonnie S., Francis T. Cullen, and Leah E. Daigle. 2005. "The discovery of acquaintance rape: The salience of methodological innovation and rigor." *Journal of Interpersonal Violence, 20,* 493–500.

Fisher, Helen E. 1992. *Anatomy of Love: The Natural History of Monogamy, Adultery, and Divorce.* New York: Norton.

Fishman, Scott M., and David V. Sheehan. 1985. "Anxiety and panic: Their cause and treatment." *Psychology Today,* April, p. 26.

Fleishman, Ellen Gerschitz. 1983. "Sex-role acquisition, parental behavior, and sexual orientation: Some tentative hypotheses." *Sex Roles, 9,* 1051–1059.

Flowers, Amy. 1998. *The Fantasy Factory: An Insider's View of the Phone Sex Industry.* Philadelphia: University of Pennsylvania Press.

Foderaro, Lisa W. 1995. "Mentally ill gaining new rights, with the ill as their own lobby." *New York Times,* October 14, pp. 1, 8.

Folse, Kimberly A., and Dennis L. Peck. 1995. "A phenomenological analysis of suicide." In Alex Thio and Thomas Calhoun (eds.), *Readings in Deviant Behavior.* New York: HarperCollins.

Fort, Joel. 1973. *Alcohol: Our Biggest Drug Problem.* New York: McGraw-Hill.

Fox, James Alan, Jack Levin, and Kenna Quinet. 2005. *The Will to Kill.* Boston: Allyn and Bacon.

Fox, James Alan. 1996. "Trends in juvenile offending." *National Institute of Justice Journal,* August, pp. 15–23.

Francis, Andrew M. 2008. "The economics of sexuality: The effect of HIV/AIDS on homosexual behavior in the United States." *Journal of Health Economics, 27,* 675–689.

Frank, Nancy. 1993. "Maiming and killing: Occupational health crimes." *The Annals of the American Academy of Political and Social Science, 525,* 107–118.

Frank, Robert, et al. 2004. "Scandal scorecard." *Wall Street Journal,* October 3, pp. B1, B4.

Frank, Stephen E., and John R. Wilke. 1997. "Visa, Master-Card may face antitrust suit." *Wall Street Journal,* February 7, p. A3.

Frederick, Sharon. 2001. *Rape: Weapon of Terror.* River Edge, N.J.: Global Publishing.

Fredriksen, K. I. 1989. "Adult protective services: A caseload analysis." *Journal of Interpersonal Violence, 4,* 245–250.

Freund, Matthew, et al. 1991. "Sexual behavior of clients with street prostitutes in Camden, N.J." *Journal of Sex Research, 28,* 579–591.

Friedman, Milton. 1989. "An open letter to Bill Bennett." *Wall Street Journal,* September 7, p. A18.

Friedman, Milton. 1998. "There's no justice in the war on drugs." *New York Times,* January 11, p. 19.

Friedman, Robert I. 1999. "White collar and dangerous." *New York Times,* August 27, p. A25.

Fritz, Mark. 2006. "Strong medicine." *Wall Street Journal,* February 1, pp. A1, A12.

Fritz, Robert, et al. 2007. "Antidepressants can lead to teen suicide." pp. 133–137 in David Becker and Cynthia Becker (eds.), *Problems with Death.* Detroit, Mich.: Greenhaven Press.

Furr, Susan R. 2001. "Suicide and depression among college students: A decade later." *Professional Psychology: Research and Practice, 32,* 97–100.

Gabor, Thomas, et al. 1987. *Armed Robbery: Cops, Robbers, and Victims.* Springfield, Ill.: Charles C. Thomas.

Gagnon, John H., Martin Levine, and Peter Nardi (eds.). 1997. *Encounters with AIDS: The Impact of the HIV/AIDS Epidemic and the Gay and Lesbian Communities.* Chicago: University of Chicago Press.

Galea, S., et al. 2002. "Psychological sequelae of the September 11 terrorist attacks in New York City." *New England Journal of Medicine, 346,* 982–987.

Galen, Luke W., and William M. Rogers. 2004. "Religiosity, alcohol expectancies, drinking motives and their interaction in the prediction of drinking among college students." *Journal of Studies on Alcohol, 65,* 469–476.

Gallagher, Bernard. 2002. *The Sociology of Mental Illness,* 4th ed. Upper Saddle River, N.J.: Prentice Hall.

Gallup-Black, Adria. 2005. "Twenty years of rural and urban trends in family and intimate partner homicide: Does place matter?" *Homicide Studies, 9,* 149–173.

Gambetta, Diego (ed.). 2005. *Making Sense of Suicide Missions.* New York: Oxford University Press.

Gamerman, Ellen. 2006. "Legalized 'cheating.'" *Wall Street Journal,* January 21, pp. 1, 8.

Gamper, Catharine M. 2004. "Perceived social competence and rape myth endorsement." *Deviant Behavior, 25,* 133–150.

Gamwell, Lynn, and Nancy Tomes. 1995. *Madness in America: Cultural and Medical Perceptions of Mental Illness before 1914.* Ithaca, N.Y.: Cornell University Press.

Ganzini, Linda, et al. 2008. "Why Oregon patients request assisted death: Family members' views." *JGIM: Journal of General Internal Medicine, 23,* 154–157.

Garber, Kent. 2008. "Who's behind the bible of mental illness." *U.S. News & World Report,* January, pp. 25–26.

Garfinkel, Harold. 1967. *Studies in Ethnomethodology.* Englewood Cliffs, N.J.: Prentice Hall.

Garland, David. 1993. *Punishment and Modern Society: A Study in Social Theory.* Chicago: University of Chicago Press.

Gauthier, DeAnn K., and William B. Bankston. 2004. "'Who kills whom' revisited: A sociological study of variation in the sex ratio of spouse killings." *Homicide Studies, 8,* 96–122.

Gavey, Nicola. 2005. *Just Sex? The Cultural Scaffolding of Rape.* London: Routledge.

Gearan, Ann. 2006. "U.S. cites countries for human trafficking." www.yahoo.com, June 5, 2006.

Geis, Gilbert, and Robley Geis. 1979. "Rape in Stockholm: Is permissiveness relevant?" *Criminology, 17,* 315.

Geis, Gilbert. 1984. "White-collar and corporate crime." In Robert F. Meier (ed.), *Major Forms of Crime.* Beverly Hills, Calif.: Sage Publications.

Gelles, Richard J. 1985. "Family violence." *Annual Review of Sociology, 11,* 347–367.

Gelles, Richard J. 1995. *Contemporary Families: A Sociological View.* Thousand Oaks, Calif.: Sage Publications.

Gelles, Richard J. 1998. "Family violence." In Michael Tonry (ed.), *The Handbook of Crime and Punishment.* New York: Oxford University Press.

Gelles, Richard J., and Murray A. Straus. 1987. "The cost of family violence." *Public Health Reports, 102,* 638–641.

Gelles, Richard J., and Murray Straus. 1988. *Family Violence.* Beverly Hills, Calif.: Sage Publications.

Gelman, David, et al. 1994. "The rapist: An overview." In Karin L. Swisher, Carol Wekesser, and William Barbour (eds.), *Violence Against Women.* San Diego, Calif.: Greenhaven.

George, Robert, Fred Wulczyn, and David Funshel. 1994. "A foster care research agenda for the 90s." *Child Welfare, 73,* 525–549.

Gianelli, Diane M. 1999. "Oregon suicide report contains some surprises." *American Medical News, 42,* March 8, pp. 9, 11.

Gibbs, Nancy. 1993a. "R for Death." *Time,* May 31, p. 37.

Gibbs, Nancy. 1993b. "'Til death do us part." *Time,* January 18, p. 41.

Gibbs, Nancy. 1995. "Love and let die." In Robert Emmet Long (ed.), *Suicide.* New York: Wilson.

Gibbs, Nancy. 2007. "Darkness falls: One troubled student rains down death on a quiet campus." *Time,* April 30, pp. 37–53.

Gidycz, Christine A., and Mary P. Koss. 1991. "The effects of acquaintance rape on the female victim." In Andrea Parrot and Laurie Bechhofer (eds.), *Acquaintance Rape.* New York: Wiley.

Gilbert, Neil. 1995. "Realities and mythologies of rape." In Alex Thio and Thomas C. Calhoun (eds.), *Readings in Deviant Behavior.* New York: HarperCollins.

Gilgoff, Dan, and Jay Tolson. 2003. "Losing friends?" *U.S. News & World Report,* March 17, p. 40.

Gill, Carol J. 2001. "Divided understanding: The social experience of disability." In Gary L. Albrecht et al. (eds.), *Handbook of Disability Studies.* Thousand Oaks, Calif.: Sage Publications.

Gillespie, Michael, Valerie Hearn, and Robert A. Silverman. 1998. "Suicide following homicide in Canada." *Homicide Studies, 2,* 46–63.

Gillespie, Terry. 1996. "Rape crisis centers and 'male rape': A face of the backlash." In Marianne Hester et al. (eds.), *Women, Violence and Male Power.* Philadelphia: Open University Press.

Gilmartin, Brian G. 1975. "That swinging couple down the block." *Psychology Today,* February, pp. 54–58.

Girard, Chris. 1993. "Age, gender, and suicide: A cross-national analysis." *American Sociological Review, 58,* 553–574.

Glasberg, D. S., and D. Skidmore. 1998. "The dialectics of white-collar crime: The anatomy of the savings and loan crisis and the case of Silverado Banking, Savings and Loan Association." *American Journal of Economics and Sociology, 57,* 423–449.

Glaser, Daniel. 1956. "Criminality theories and behavioral images." *American Journal of Sociology, 61,* 433–444.

Glaser, Jack, and Kimberly Kahn. 2005. "Prejudice, discrimination, and the Internet." pp. 247–274 in Yair Amichai-Hamburger (ed.), *The Social Net: Understanding Human Behavior in Cyberspace.* New York: Oxford University Press.

Glass, Shirley P., and Thomas L. Wright. 1992. "Justifications for extramarital relationships: The association between attitudes, behaviors, and gender." *Journal of Sex Research, 29,* 361–387.

Glassner, Barry. 1991. "Jewish sobriety." In David J. Pittman and Helene Raskin White (eds.), *Society, Culture, and Drinking Patterns Reexamined.* New Brunswick, N.J.: Rutgers Center of Alcohol Studies.

Glater, Jonathan D. 2002. "Mad as hell: Hard time for white-collar crime." *New York Times,* July 28, Section 4, p. 5.

Gleick, Elizabeth. 1995. "The crooked blue line." *Time,* September 11, pp. 39–42.

Gleick, Elizabeth. 1996. "Putting the jail in jailbait." *Time,* January 29, pp. 33–34.

Goetting, Ann. 1989. "Patterns of marital homicide: A comparison of husbands and wives." *Journal of Comparative Family Studies, 22,* 341–354.

Goetting, Ann. 1995. *Homicide in Families and Other Social Populations.* New York: Springer.

Goffman, Erving. 1961. *Asylums.* Garden City, N.Y.: Anchor.

Gold, Martin. 1958. "Suicide, homicide, and the socialization of aggression." *American Journal of Sociology, 43,* 651–661.

Goldberg, Carey. 1998. "Little drop in college binge drinking." *New York Times,* September 11, p. A12.

Goldner, Norman S. 1972. "Rape as a heinous but understudied offense." *Journal of Criminal Law, Criminology and Police Science, 63,* 402–407.

Goldsmith, S. K., et al. 2002. *Reducing Suicide: A National Imperative.* Washington, D.C.: National Academies Press.

Goleman, Daniel. 1986. "Aid in day-to-day life seen as hope for schizophrenics." *New York Times,* March 19, pp. 1, 12.

Goleman, Daniel. 1992. "A rising cost of modernity: Depression." *New York Times,* December 8, p. B6.

Goode, Erica. 2002. "Antidepressants lift clouds, but lose 'miracle drug' label." *New York Times,* June 30, pp. 1, 18.

Goode, Erich. 1981. "Drugs and crime." In Abraham S. Blumberg (ed.), Current Perspective on Criminal Behavior. New York: Knopf.

Goode, Erich. 1991. "Positive deviance: A viable concept?" *Deviant Behavior, 12,* 289–309.

Goode, Erich. 2004a. "Legalize it? A bulletin from the war on drugs." *Contexts,* Summer, pp. 19–25.

Goode, Erich. 2004b. "The stigma of obesity." In Alex Thio and Thomas C. Calhoun (eds.), *Readings in Deviant Behavior,* 3d ed. Boston: Allyn and Bacon.

Goode, Erich. 2005a. *Drugs in American Society,* 6th ed. New York: McGraw-Hill.

Goode, Erich. 2005b. *Deviant Behavior,* 7th ed. Upper Saddle River, N.J.: Prentice Hall.

Goodwin, Donald W. 1991. "The etiology of alcoholism." In David J. Pittman and Helene Raskin White (eds.), *Society, Culture, and Drinking Patterns Reexamined.* New Brunswick, N.J.: Rutgers Center of Alcohol Studies.

Gordon, Margaret T., and Stephanie Riger. 1989. *The Female Fear.* New York: Free Press.

Gorman, Christine, and Wendy Cole. 2004. "Between the sexes." *Time,* March 1, pp. 54–56.

Gorman, Christine. 1992. "Can drug firms be trusted?" *Time,* February 10, p. 43.

Gosselin, Denise Kindschi. 2000. *Heavy Hands: An Introduction to the Crimes of Domestic Violence.* Upper Saddle River, N.J.: Prentice Hall.

Gosselin, Denise Kindschi. 2005. *Heavy Hands: An Introduction to the Crimes of Family Violence,* 3d ed. Upper Saddle River, N.J.: Prentice Hall.

Gottesman, Irving I. 1995. "Genetic factors contribute to schizophrenia." In David Bender and Bruno Leone (eds.), *Mental Illness: Opposing Viewpoints.* San Diego, Calif.: Greenhaven.

Gottfredson, Michael R., and Travis Hirschi. 1990. *A General Theory of Crime.* Newbury Park, Calif.: Sage Publications.

Gould, Leroy C. 1969. "The changing structure of property crime in an affluent society." *Social Forces, 48,* 50–59.

Gould, Terry. 2000. *The Lifestyle: A Look at the Erotic Rites of Swingers.* Buffalo, N.Y.: Firefly Books.

Gove, Walter R. 1970. "Societal reaction as an explanation of mental illness: An evaluation." *American Sociological Review, 35,* 882.

Gove, Walter R. 1982. "Labeling theory's explanation of mental illness: An update of recent evidence." *Deviant Behavior, 3,* 307–327.

Gove, Walter R. 1984. "Gender differences in mental and physical illness: The effects of fixed roles and nurturant roles." *Social Science and Medicine, 19,* 77–84.

Gove, Walter R. 2004. "The career of the mentally ill: an integration of psychiatric, labeling/social construction, and lay perspectives." *Journal of Health and Social Behavior, 45,* 357–375.

Gove, Walter R., and Michael Hughes. 1980. "Reexamining the ecological fallacy: A study in which aggregate data are critical in investigating the pathological effects of living alone." *Social Forces, 58,* 1157–1177.

Graham, Kathryn, William Turnbull, and Linda LaRocque. 1979. "Effects of alcohol on moral judgment." *Journal of Abnormal Psychology, 88,* 442–445.

Gray, Susan H. 1982. "Exposure to pornography and aggression toward women: The case of the angry male." *Social Problems, 29,* 387–398.

Greeley, Andrew M. 2004. *Priests: A Calling in Crisis.* Chicago: University of Chicago Press.

Green, Edward, and Russell P. Wakefield. 1979. "Patterns of middle and upper class homicide." *Journal of Criminal Law and Criminology, 70,* 172–181.

Green, Gary S. 1990. *Occupational Crime.* Chicago: Nelson-Hall.

Green, Joshua. 2006. "Cyberterrorism is not a major threat." pp. 56–65 in Lisa Yount (ed.), *Does the Internet Increase the Risk of Crime?* Detroit, Mich.: Greenhaven Press.

Green, Sara, et al. 2005. "Living stigma: The impact of labeling, stereotyping, separation, status loss, and discrimination in the lives of individuals with disabilities and their families." *Sociological Inquiry, 75,* 197–215.

Greenberg, David F. (ed.). 1981. *Crime and Capitalism: Readings in Marxist Criminology.* Palo Alto, Calif.: Mayfield.

Greenberg, Michael, and Dona Schneider. 1994. "Violence in American cities: Young black males is the answer, but what was the question?" *Social Science and Medicine, 39,* 179–187.

Greenberg, Scott. 1996. "Why do workers bite the hands that feed them? Employee theft as a social exchange process." *Research in Organizational Behavior, 18,* 111–156.

Greenhouse, Linda. 1999. "Sex harassment in class is ruled schools' liability." *New York Times,* May 15, pp. A1, A24.

Greenwald, Harold. 1970. *The Elegant Prostitute.* New York: Walker.

Greer, Frank I., and Rhona Strasberg Weinstein. 1979. "Suicide prevention outreach: Callers and noncallers compared." *Psychological Reports, 44,* 387–393.

Gregory, Raymond F. 2004. *Unwelcome and Unlawful: Sexual Harassment in the American Workplace.* Ithaca, N.Y.: Cornell University Press.

Griffin, Sean Patrick. 2003. "'Emerging' organized crime hypotheses in criminology textbooks: The case of African-American organized crime." *Journal of Criminal Justice Education, 14,* 287–300.

Griffin, Susan. 1971. "Rape: The all-American crime." *Ramparts,* September, pp. 4–5.

Griffiths, Mark D., and Jonathan Parke. 2002. "The social impact of Internet gambling." *Social Science Computer Review, 20,* 312–320.

Gross, William C. 1993. "Gender and age differences in college students' alcohol consumption." *Psychological Reports, 72,* 211–216.

Grossman, Dave. 1995. *On Killing: The Psychological Cost of Learning to Kill in War and Society.* Boston: Little, Brown.

Groth, A. Nicholas, and H. Jean Birnbaum. 1979. *Men Who Rape.* New York: Plenum.

Groth, A. Nicholas. 1983. "Rape: Behavioral aspects." In S. H. Kadish (ed.), *Encyclopedia of Crime and Justice.* New York: Free Press.

Gruenbaum, Ellen. 2001. *The Female Circumcision Controversy: An Anthropological Perspective.* Philadelphia: University of Pennsylvania Press.

Gunnell, David, Helen Wehner, and Stephen Frankel. 1999. "Sex differences in suicide trends in England and Wales." *Lancet, 353,* 556–557.

Gusfield, Joseph R. 1991. "Status conflicts and the changing ideologies of the American temperance movement." In David J. Pittman and Charles R. Snyder (eds.), *Society, Culture, and Drinking Patterns.* New York: Wiley.

Guthrie, Patricia. 2006. "Assisted suicide debated in the United States." *CMAJ: Canadian Medical Association Journal, 174,* 755–756.

H&MW (Health & Medicine Week). 2001. "Study finds women at greater risk of harm by alcoholism." *H&MW,* April 2, pp. 13–14.

Hagmann, Michael. 2001. "Alcohol takes its toll on Europe's youth." *Bulletin of the World Health Organization, 79,* 380.

Hale, Chris. 2006. "Internet crime is increasing." pp. 10–18 in Lisa Yount (ed.), *Does the Internet Increase the Risk of Crime?* Detroit, Mich.: Greenhaven Press.

Hammond, D. Corydon, and Gary Q. Jorgensen. 1981. "Alcohol and sex: A volatile cocktail." *USA Today: The Magazine of the American Scene,* July, pp. 44–46.

Hampton, Tracy. 2006. "Interplay of genes and environment found in adolescents' alcohol abuse." *JAMA: Journal of the American Medical Association, 295,* 1760–1762.

Handel, Warren. 1982. *Ethnomethodology: How People Make Sense.* Englewood Cliffs, N.J.: Prentice Hall.

Hannon, Lance E. 2005. "Extremely poor neighborhoods and homicide." *Social Science Quarterly, 86,* 1418–1434.

Hansen, Brian. 2004. "The proliferation of cybercrimes." In Alex Thio and Thomas C. Calhoun (eds.), *Readings in Deviant Behavior,* 3d ed. Boston: Allyn and Bacon.

Hanson, Bill, et al. 1985. *Life with Heroin: Voices from the Inner City.* Lexington, Mass.: Health.

Hanson, David J. 1995. "The United States of America." In Dwight B. Heath (ed.), *International Handbook on Alcohol and Culture.* Westport, Conn.: Greenwood.

Hanson, David J., and Ruth C. Engs. 1992. "College students' drinking problems: A national study, 1982–1991." *Psychological Reports, 71,* 39–42.

Haqqani, Husain, and Daniel Kimmage. 2005. "Suicidology." *New Republic,* October 3, pp. 14–15.

Haran, James F., and John M. Martin. 1984. "The armed urban bank robber: A profile." *Federal Probation, 48* (December), 51.

Harman, Lesley D. 1985. "Acceptable deviance as social control: The case of fashion and slang." *Deviant Behavior, 6,* 1–15.

Harned, Melanie S. 2005. "Understanding women's labeling of unwanted sexual experiences with dating partners: A qualitative analysis." *Violence Against Women, 11,* 374–413.

Harper, Dee Wood, and Lydia Voigt. 2007. "Homicide followed by suicide: An integrated theoretical perspective." *Homicide Studies, 11,* 295–318.

Harper, Frederick D., and Elaheh Saifnoorian. 1991. "Drinking patterns among black Americans." In David J. Pittman and Helene Raskin White (eds.), *Society, Culture, and Drinking Patterns Reexamined.* New Brunswick, N.J.: Rutgers Center of Alcohol Studies.

Harries, Keith D. 1990. *Serious Violence: Patterns of Homicide and Assault in America.* Springfield, Ill.: Charles C. Thomas.

Harris Interactive. 2004. *Therapy in America 2004.* http://cms.psychologytoday.com/pto/topline_report_042904.pdf.

Harris, Andrew, and Arthur J. Lurigio. 2007. "Mental illness and violence: A brief review of research and assessment strategies." *Aggression and Violent Behavior, 12,* 542–551.

Harris, Gardiner. 2006. "F.D.A. dismisses medical benefit from marijuana." *New York Times,* April 21, pp. A1, A23.

Harrison, Lana D. 1992. "The drug-crime nexus in the USA." *Contemporary Drug Problems, 19,* 257–258.

Harry, Joseph, and Mary C. Sengstock. 1978. "Attribution, goals, and deviance." *American Sociological Review, 43,* 278–280.

Harry, Joseph. 1983. "Parasuicide, gender, and gender deviance." *Journal of Health and Social Behavior, 24,* 350–361.

Hasin, Deborah S., Bridget Grant, and Jean Endicott. 1990. "The natural history of alcohol abuse: Implications for definitions of alcohol use disorders." *American Journal of Psychiatry, 147,* 1537–1541.

Hassanin, Ibrahim, et al. 2008. "Prevalence of female genital cutting in Upper Egypt: 6 years after enforcement of prohibition law." *Reproductive BioMedicine Online, 16,* 27–31.

Hawkins, Joseph R. 2000. "Japan's journey into homophobia." *Gay & Lesbian Review Worldwide,* 7 (Winter), pp. 36–38.

Hawton, Keith, and Louise Harriss. 2008. "Deliberate self-harm by under-15-year-olds: Characteristics, trends, and outcome." *Journal of Child Psychology and Psychiatry, 49,* 441–448.

Hayes, Lindsay M. 1995. *Prison Suicide: An Overview and Guide to Prevention.* Washington, D.C.: U.S. Department of Justice.

Headden, Susan, and Gordon Witkin. 1993. "Preying on the helpless." *U.S. News & World Report,* May 24, pp. 48–52.

Hebl, Michelle R., and Julie M. Turchin. 2005. "The stigma of obesity: What about men?" *Basic and Applied Social Psychology, 27,* 267–275.

Hebl, Michelle R., and Robert E. Kleck. 2000. "The social consequences of physical disability." In Todd F. Heatherton et al. (eds.), *The Social Psychology of Stigma.* New York: Guilford Press.

Hechinger, John. 2002. "Easy money." *Wall Street Journal,* October 8, pp. A1, A18.

Heckert, Alex, and Druann Maria Heckert. 2002. "A new typology of deviance: Integrating normative and reactivist definitions of deviance." *Deviant Behavior, 23,* 449–479.

Heckert, D. Alex, and Edward W. Gondolf. 2000. "The effect of perceptions of sanctions on batterer program outcomes." *Journal of Research in Crime and Delinquency, 37,* 369–346.

Heidensohn, Frances. 1995. *Women and Crime,* 2d ed. New York: New York University Press.

Heidensohn, Frances. 2002. "15. Gender and crime." pp. 491–530 in Mike Maguire and Rodney Morgan (eds.), *Oxford Handbook of Criminology.* New York: Oxford University Press.

Heien, Dale M., and David J. Pittman. 1993. "The external costs of alcohol abuse." *Journal of Studies on Alcohol, 54,* 302–307.

Helliker, Kevin. 2006. "The case for Alcoholics Anonymous: It works even if the science is lacking." *Wall Street Journal,* October 17, p. D1.

Helm, Burt. 2006. "Common-sense home safety." *Business Week Online,* May 9, p. 5.

Helmer, John. 1975. *Drugs and Minority Oppression.* New York: Seabury.

Hendin, Herbert. 1979. "A saner policy on suicide." *Psychology Today,* May, p. 115.

Hendin, Herbert. 1995. *Suicide in America.* New York: Norton.

Hendin, Herbert. 1997. *Seduced by Death: Doctors, Patients, and the Dutch Cure.* New York: Norton.

Hendrie, Caroline. 2004. "Report examining sexual misconduct taps some nerves." *Education Week,* July 14, pp. 1–2.

Hendrix, Melissa. 1993. "Is it a boy or a girl?" *Johns Hopkins Magazine,* November, pp. 10–16.

Henry, Andrew, and James Short. 1954. *Suicide and Homicide.* New York: Free Press.

Henry, William A. III. 1993. "Gay parents: Under fire and on the rise." *Time,* September 20, pp. 68–71.

Henshel, Anne-Marie. 1973. "Swinging: A study of decision making in marriage." *American Journal of Sociology, 78,* 885–891.

Hensley, Christopher, and Richard Tewksbury. 2005. "Wardens' perceptions of prison sex." *The Prison Journal, 85,* 186–197.

Henslin, James M. 1970. "Guilt and guilt neutralization: Response and adjustment to suicide." In Jack D. Douglas (ed.), *Deviance and Respectability.* New York: Basic Books.

Hepburn, John R. 1977. "Social control and the legal order: Legitimated repression in a capitalist state." *Contemporary Crises, 1,* 84.

Herbert, Bob. 1995. "Killer cops." *New York Times,* September 15, p. A15.

Herd, Denise. 1991. "Drinking patterns in the black population." In Walter B. Clark and Michael E. Hilton (eds.), *Alcohol in America.* Albany: State University of New York Press.

Herdt, Gilbert. 1990. "Developmental discontinuities and sexual orientation across cultures." In David P. McWhirter et al. *Homosexuality/Heterosexuality.* New York: Oxford University Press.

Herman, Ellen, and Martin B. Duberman. 1995. *Psychiatry, Psychology, and Homosexuality.* New York: Chelsea House.

Herman, Judith Lewis. 1995. "Considering sex offenders: A model of addiction." In Patricia Searles and Ronald J. Berger (eds.), *Rape and Society.* Boulder, Colo.: Westview.

Hess, John H., and Herbert E. Thomas. 1963. "Incompetency to stand trial: Procedures, results, and problems." *American Journal of Psychiatry, 119,* 713–720.

Hill, Andrew. 2002. "Ex-Tyco chairman free on $10m bail." FT.com, September 27.

Hill, Herbert. 1973. "Anti-oriental agitation and the rise of working-class racism." *Society, 10,* January/February, p. 52.

Hill, Simon A., et al. 2005. "Changing patterns of suicide in a poor, rural county over the 20th century." *Social Psychiatry & Psychiatric Epidemiology, 40,* 601–604.

Hills, Stuart L. 1980. *Demystifying Social Deviance.* New York: McGraw-Hill.

Hilton, Michael E. 1991. "Regional diversity in U.S. drinking practices." In Walter B. Clark and Michael E. Hilton (eds.), *Alcohol in America: Drinking Practices and Problems.* Albany: State University of New York Press.

Hilts, Philip J. 1987. "AIDS infection found in 11% of U.S. prostitutes." *Washington Post,* March 27, pp. A1, A10.

Himmelstein, Jerome L. 1983. *The Strange Career of Marijuana: Politics and Ideology of Drug Control in America.* Westport, Conn.: Greenwood.

Hinrichsen, Gregory A., Nancy A. Hernandez, and Simcha Pollack. 1992. "Difficulties and rewards in family care of depressed older adults." *Gerontologist, 32,* 486–492.

Hirschi, Travis. 1962. "The professional prostitute." *Berkeley Journal of Sociology, 7,* 44–45.

Hirschi, Travis. 1969. *Causes of Delinquency.* Berkeley and Los Angeles: University of California Press.

Hirschi, Travis. 1973. "Procedural rules and the study of deviant behavior." *Social Problems, 21,* 166–171.

Hirschi, Travis, and Michael R. Gottfredson (eds.). 1994. *The Generality of Deviance.* New Brunswick, N.J.: Transaction.

Hirschi, Travis, and Michael Gottfredson. 2000. "In defense of self-control." *Theoretical Criminology, 4,* 55–69.

Hitt, Jack. 1999. "The battle of the binge." *New York Times Magazine,* October 24, pp. 31–32.

Hochstetler, Andy. 2004. "Interactional dynamics in robbery." pp. 303–307 in Alex Thio and Thomas C. Calhoun (eds.), *Readings in Deviant Behavior,* 3d ed. Boston: Allyn and Bacon.

Hochstetler, Andy, Heith Copes, and Matt DeLisi. 2002. "Differential association in group and solo offending." *Journal of Criminal Justice, 30,* 559–566.

Hodgson, James F. 1997. *Games Pimps Play: Pimps, Players and Wives-in-Law.* Toronto: Canadian Scholars' Press.

Hollinger, Richard C., and John P. Clark. 1983. *Theft by Employees.* Lexington, Mass.: Lexington Books.

Holmes, Ronald M., and Stephen T. Holmes. 1992. "Understanding mass murder: A starting point." *Federal Probation, 56,* 53–61.

Holtzworth-Munroe, Amy. 2005. "Male versus female intimate partner violence: Putting controversial findings into context." *Journal of Marriage and Family, 67,* 1120–1125.

Holzman, Harold R., and Sharon Pines. 1982. "Buying sex: The phenomenology of being a john." *Deviant Behavior, 4,* 105.

Homer, Frederic D. 1974. *Guns and Garlic: Myths and Realities of Organized Crime.* West Lafayette, Ind.: Purdue University Press.

Hoover, Eric. 2004. "Studies find 'social norms' strategy reduces drinking at colleges." *Chronicle of Higher Education,* August 13, p. A32.

Hornblower, Margot. 1993. "The skin trade." *Time,* June 21, p. 45.

Horwitz, Allan V., and Jerome C. Wakefield. 2006. "The epidemic in mental illness: Clinical fact or survey artifact?" *Contexts, Vol. 5* (Winter), pp. 19–23.

Horwitz, Allan V., Susan C. Reinhard, and Sandra Howell-White. 1996. "Caregiving as reciprocal exchange in families with seriously mentally ill members." *Journal of Health and Social Behavior, 37,* 149–162.

Hosansky, David. 2004. "Should government fund more prevention programs?" *CQ Researcher,* February, pp. 1–32.

Hosenball, Mark. 2002. "Islamic cyberterror." *Newsweek,* May 20, p. 10.

Hughes, Stella P., and Richard A. Dodder. 1992. "Changing the legal minimum drinking age: Results of a longitudinal study." *Journal of Studies on Alcohol, 53,* 568–575.

Humphreys, Laud. 1970. "Tearoom trade: Impersonal sex in public places." *Transaction, 7,* 17–18.

Humphreys, Laud. 1972. *Out of the Closets.* Englewood Cliffs, N.J.: Prentice Hall.

Hunt, Albert R. 1995. "The best Congress money can buy." *Wall Street Journal,* September 7, p. A15.

Hunter, Patricia A., Roseann Hannon, and David Marchi. 1982. "Alcohol consumption in natural settings as a function of sex, age, and income level." *Journal of Studies on Alcohol, 43,* 387–392.

Hurlburt, Graham, Eldon Gade, and Dale Fuqua. 1984. "Personality differences between Alcoholics Anonymous members and nonmembers." *Journal of Studies on Alcohol, 45,* 170–171.

Huselid, Rebecca Farmer, and M. Lynne Cooper. 1992. "Gender roles as mediators of sex differences in adolescent alcohol use and abuse." *Journal of Health and Social Behavior, 33,* 348–362.

Hutson, Matthew. 2008. "Vice or virtue?" *Psychology Today,* February, p. 18.

HWHW (Harvard Women's Health Watch). 2000. "Women and moderate drinking: Health in the balance." *HWHW,* November, pp. 2–3.

Hyatt, Ralph. 1993. "Carjacking: A sign of the times." *USA Today: The Magazine of the American Scene, 22,* September, pp. 40–41.

Ibrahim, Farah A. 1995. "Suicidal behavior in Asian-American women." In Silvia Sara Canetto and David Lester (eds.), *Women and Suicidal Behavior.* New York: Springer.

Irvine, Janice M. 2002. *Talk about Sex: The Battles over Sex Education in the United States.* Berkeley: University of California Press.

Irwin, John. 1970. *The Felon.* Englewood Cliffs, N.J.: Prentice Hall.

Irwin, Katherine. 2001. "Legitimating the first tattoo: Moral passage through informal interaction." *Symbolic Interaction, 24,* 49–73.

Isikoff, Michael, et al. 2006. "How the Jefferson search put Bush in a bind." *Newsweek,* June 5, p. 6.

Isikoff, Michael. 1995. "Crack, coke and race." *Newsweek,* November 6, p. 77.

Isikoff, Michael. 1997. "The White House shell game." *Newsweek,* February 10, pp. 34–35.

Itzin, Catherine (ed.). 1993. *Pornography: Women, Violence, and Civil Liberties: A Radical View.* New York: Oxford University Press.

Jackley, John L. 1992. *Hill Rat: Blowing the Lid Off Congress.* Washington, D.C.: Regnery Gateway.

Jackson, James O. 1996. "The lost children." *Time,* March 25, pp. 44–45.

Jackson, Kristina M., et al. 2005. "Drinking among college students: Consumption and consequences." pp. 85–117 in Marc Galanter (ed.), *Recent Developments in Alcoholism.* New York: Kluwer Academic/ Plenum Publishers.

Jackson, Lois, et al. 1992. "Varied potential risks of HIV infection among prostitutes." *Social Science and Medicine, 35,* 281–286.

Jacobs, Andrew. 2005. "As shoplifters improve game, police do, too." *New York Times,* December 24, pp. B1, B4.

Jacobs, Bruce A. 2000. *Robbing Drug Dealers: Violence Beyond the Law.* New York: Aldine de Gruyter.

Jacobs, Jerry. 1967. "A phenomenological study of suicide notes." *Social Problems, 15,* 60–72.

Jaffe, Jerome H. 1965. "Drug addiction and drug abuse." In Louis S. Goodman and Alfred Gilman (eds.), *The Pharmacological Basis of Therapeutics.* New York: Macmillan.

Jamieson, Katherine M. 1994. *The Organization of Corporate Crime: Dynamics of Antitrust Violation.* Thousand Oaks, Calif.: Sage Publications.

Janus, Samuel S., and Cynthia L. Janus. 1993. *The Janus Report on Sexual Behavior.* New York: Wiley.

Jasper, Jann. 1992. "Rape: Are you at risk?" *New Woman, 22,* 80–86.

Jefferson, David J. 2005. "America's most dangerous drug." *Newsweek,* August 8, pp. 41–48.

Jehl, Douglas, and David Rohde. 2004. "Captured Queda figure led way to information behind warning." *New York Times,* August 2, p. A1.

Jellinek, E. M. 1952. "Phases of alcohol addiction." *Quarterly Journal of Studies on Alcohol, 13,* 673–684.

Jenkins, Holman W. Jr. 2004. "Is corporate fraud too hard for juries?" *Wall Street Journal,* April 14, p. A15.

Jenkins, Philip. 2001. *Beyond Tolerance: Child Pornography on the Internet.* New York: New York University Press.

Jenks, Richard J. 1985. "Swinging: A test of two theories and a proposed new model." *Archives of Sexual Behavior, 14,* 517–527.

Jenks, Richard J. 1998. "Swinging: A review of the literature." *Archives of Sexual Behavior, 27,* 507–521.

Jenness, Valerie. 1990. "From sex as sin to sex as work: COYOTE and the reorganization of prostitution as a social problem." *Social Problems, 37,* 403–420.

Jerome, Richard, et al. 2004. "The cyberporn generation." *People,* April 26, pp. 72–76.

Jersild, Devon. 2001. *Happy Hours: Alcohol in a Woman's Life.* New York: HarperCollins.

Jersild, Devon. 2002. "Alcohol in the vulnerable lives of college women." *Chronicle of Higher Education,* May 31, pp. B19–11.

Johnson, Charles Felzen. 2004. "Child sexual abuse." *Lancet, 364,* 462–470.

Johnson, Dirk, and Adam Piore. 2004. "At home in two worlds." *Newsweek,* October 18, pp. 52–54.

Johnson, Dirk. 2004. "Policing a rural plague." *Newsweek,* March 8, p. 41.

Johnson, Dirk. 2006. "A terrible connection." *Newsweek,* January 9, p. 31.

Johnson, Matthew C., and Glen A. Kercher. 2007. "ADHD, strain, and criminal behavior: A test of general strain theory." *Deviant Behavior, 28,* 131–152.

Johnston, David. 1997. "The mystery of the violent bank jobs." *New York Times,* March 30, p. E4.

Johnston, Lloyd D., et al. 1986. *Drug Use Among American High School Students, College Students, and Other Young Adults.* Rockville, Md.: National Institute on Drug Abuse.

Joiner, Thomas. 2005. *Why People Die by Suicide.* Cambridge, Mass.: Harvard University Press.

Jones, Peter, et al. 1993. "Premorbid social underachievement in schizophrenia: Results from the Camberwell Collaborative Psychosis Study." *British Journal of Psychiatry, 162,* 65–71.

Jukkala, Tanya, et al. 2008. "Economic strain, social relations, gender, and binge drinking in Moscow." *Social Science & Medicine, 66,* 663–674.

Jurich, Anthony P., and Cheryl J. Polson. 1984. "Reasons for drug use: Comparison of drug users and abusers." *Psychological Reports, 55,* 371–378.

Kahan, Dan M. 1997. "It's a shame we have none." *Wall Street Journal,* January 15, p. A14.

Kalb, Claudia. 2001. "Playing with painkillers." *Newsweek,* April 9, pp. 45–48.

Kalb, Claudia. 2008. "And now, back in the real world . . . " *Newsweek,* March 3, p. 41.

Kandel, Denise B., and Richard Jessor. 2002. "The gateway hypothesis revisited." pp. 365–372 in Denise B. Kandel (ed.), *Stages and Pathways of Drug Involvement.* Cambridge, U.K.: Cambridge University Press.

Kanin, Eugene J. 1984. "Date rape: Unofficial criminals and victims." *Victimology: An International Journal, 9,* 95–108.

Kanin, Eugene J. 1985. "Date rapists: Differential sexual socialization and relative deprivation." *Archives of Sexual Behavior, 14,* 219–231.

Kanin, Eugene J., and Stanley R. Parcell. 1981. "Sexual aggression: A second look at the offended female." In Lee H. Bowker (ed.), *Women and Crime in America.* New York: Macmillan.

Kantor, Glenda, and Murray A. Straus. 1990. "The 'drunken bum' theory of wife beating." In M. A. Straus and R. J. Gelles (eds.), *Physical Violence in American Families.* New Brunswick, N.J.: Transaction.

Kantrowitz, Barbara. 1996. "Gay families come out." *Newsweek,* November 4, pp. 50–57.

Kaplan, David A. 1991. "The bank robbery boom." *Newsweek,* December 9, p. 63.

Kaplan, David E. 1998. "Yakuza Inc." *U.S. News & World Report,* April 13, pp. 40–47.

Kaplan, David E. 2003. "Playing offense." *U.S. News & World Report,* June 2, pp. 18–29.

Kaplan, David E., and Kevin Whitelaw. 2004. "Terror's new soldiers." *U.S. News & World Report,* November 1, pp. 34–35.

Kaplan, Howard B. 1972. *The Sociology of Mental Illness.* New Haven, Conn.: College and University Press.

Kaplan, Howard B., et al. 1986. "Escalation of marijuana use: Application of a general theory of deviant behavior." *Journal of Health and Social Behavior, 27,* 44–61.

Kappeler, Victor E., Mark Blumberg, and Gary W. Potter. 1993. *The Mythology of Crime and Criminal Justice.* Prospect Heights, Ill.: Waveland.

Kappeler, Victor E., Richard D. Sluder, and Geoffrey P. Alpert. 1998. *Forces of Deviance: Understanding the Dark Side of Policing,* 2d ed. Prospect Heights, Ill.: Waveland.

Karlin-Resnick, Joshua. 2004. "Helping students stay clean and sober." *Chronicle of Higher Education,* August 31, pp. A31–A33.

Kart, Gary S. 1990. *The Realities of Aging,* 3d ed. Boston: Allyn and Bacon.

Katchadourian, Herant. 1985. *Fundamentals of Human Sexuality,* 4th ed. New York: Holt, Rinehart and Winston.

Katz, Bonnie L. 1991. "The psychological impact of stranger versus nonstranger rape on victims' recovery." In Andrea Parrot and Laurie Bechhofer (eds.), *Acquaintance Rape.* New York: Wiley.

Katz, Jack. 1988. *Seductions of Crime: Moral and Sensual Attractions in Doing Evil.* New York: Basic Books.

Kaufman, Joan, and Edward Zigler. 1987. "Do abused children become abusive parents?" *American Journal of Orthopsychiatry, 57,* 186–192.

Kaufman, Joan, and Edward Zigler. 1993. "The intergenerational transmission of abuse is overstated." In Richard J. Gelles and Donileen R. Loseke (eds.), *Current Controversies on Family Violence.* Newbury Park, Calif.: Sage Publications.

Kay, William K., and Leslie J. Francis. 2006. "Suicidal ideation among young people in the U.K.: Churchgoing as an inhibitory influence?" *Mental Health, Religion & Culture, 9,* 127–140.

Kaysen, Susanna. 1993. *Girl, Interrupted.* New York: Turtle Bay Books/Random House.

Kelley, Jack. 2001. "Wired for death." *USA Today,* June 26, p. 12.

Kelly, Katy. 2005. "Just don't do it!" *U.S. News & World Report,* October 17, pp. 44–51.

Kemp, Alan. 1998. *Abuse in the Family: An Introduction.* Pacific Grove, Calif.: Brooks/Cole.

Kempf, Kimberly L. 1993. "The empirical status of Hirschi's control theory." In Freda Adler and William S. Laufer (eds.), *New Directions in Criminological Theory.* New Brunswick, N.J.: Transaction.

Kendall-Tackett, Kathleen A., Linda Meyer Williams, and David Finkelhor. 1993. "Impact of sexual abuse on children: A review and synthesis of recent empirical studies." *Psychological Bulletin, 113,* 164–180.

Kendler, Kenneth S. 1983. "Overview: A current perspective on twin studies of schizophrenia." *American Journal of Psychiatry, 140,* 1413–1425.

Kessler, Ronald C., and Harold W. Neighbors. 1986. "A new perspective on the relationships among race, social class, and psychological distress." *Journal of Health and Social Behavior, 27,* 107–115.

Kessler, Ronald C., and James A. McRae, Jr. 1983. "Trends in the relationship between sex and attempted suicide." *Journal of Health and Social Behavior, 24,* 98–110.

Kessler, Ronald C., et al. 1985. "Social factors in psychopathology: Stress, social support, and coping processes." *Annual Review of Psychology, 36,* 560–561.

Kessler, Ronald C., et al. 2004. "Prevalence, severity, and unmet need for treatment of mental disorders in the World Health Organization world mental health surveys." *JAMA (Journal of the American Medical Association),* 2581–2590.

Kessler, Ronald C., et al. 2005a. "Lifetime prevalence and age-of-onset distribution of DSM-IV disorders in the national comorbidity survey replication." *Archives of General Psychiatry, 62,* 593–602.

Kessler, Ronald C., et al. 2005b. "Prevalence, severity, and comorbidity of 12-month DSM-IV disorders in the national comorbidity survey replication." *Archives of General Psychiatry, 62,* 617–627.

Kessler, Ronald., et al. 1994. "Lifetime and 12-month prevalence of DSM-III-psychiatric disorders in the United States." *Archives of General Psychiatry, 51,* 8–19.

Kety, Seymour S. 1974. "From rationalization to reason." *American Journal of Psychiatry, 131,* 957–963.

Khantzian, Edward J. 1985. "The self-medication hypothesis of addictive disorders: Focus on heroin and cocaine dependence." *American Journal of Psychiatry, 142,* 1259–1264.

Kilmer, Jason R., et al. 2006. "Misperception of college student marijuana use: Implications for prevention." *Journal of Studies on Alcohol, 67,* 277–281.

Kilpatrick, Dean G., et al. 2007. "Rape-related PTSD: Issues and interventions." *Psychiatric Times, 24,* 50–58.

King, David R. 1978. "The brutalization effect: Execution publicity and the incidence of homicide in South Carolina." *Social Forces, 57,* 683–687.

Kingston, Drew A., et al. 2008. "Pornography use and sexual aggression: The impact of frequency and type of pornography use on recidivism among sexual offenders." *Aggressive Behavior, 34,* 341–351.

Kinsey, Alfred C., et al. 1948. *Sexual Behavior in the Human Male.* Philadelphia: Saunders.

Kinsey, Alfred C., et al. 1953. *Sexual Behavior in the Human Female.* Philadelphia: Saunders.

Kirkpatrick, Clifford, and Eugene Kanin. 1957. "Male sex aggression on a university campus." *American Sociological Review, 22,* 52–58.

Kirn, Walter. 1998. "Crank." *Time,* June 22, pp. 26–32.

Kisch, Jeremy, et al. 2005. "Aspects of suicidal behavior, depression, and treatment in college students: Results from the spring 2000 national college health assessment survey." *Suicide & Life-Threatening Behavior, 35,* 3–13.

Kishor, Sunita, and Kiersten Johnson. 2004. *Profiling Domestic Violence: A Multi-Country Study.* Calverton, Md.: ORC Macro.

Kite, Mary E., and Bernard E. Whitley, Jr. 1996. "Sex differences in attitudes toward homosexual persons, behaviors, and civil rights: A meta-analysis." *Personality and Social Psychology Bulletin, 22,* 336–353.

Kitsuse, John I. 1962. "Societal reaction to deviant behavior: Problems of theory and method." *Social Problems, 9,* 247–256.

Klam, Matthew. 2001. "Experiencing Ecstasy." *New York Times Magazine,* January 21, pp. 38–43, 64–79.

Klaus, Patsy. 1999. "Carjackings in the United States, 1992–96." *Bureau of Justice Statistics Special Report,* March, U.S. Department of Justice.

Kleck, Gary, and M. Hogan. 1999. "National case-control study of homicide offending and gun ownership." *Social Problems, 46,* 275–293.

Kleinknecht, William. 1996. *The New Ethnic Mobs: The Changing Face of Organized Crime in America.* New York: Free Press.

Klemke, Lloyd W. 1992. *The Sociology of Shoplifting: Boosters and Snitches Today.* Westport, Conn.: Praeger.

Klinger, David A. 2001. "Suicidal intent in victim-precipitated homicide." *Homicide Studies, 5,* 206–226.

Kluger, Jeffrey. 2001. "How to manage teen drinking (the smart way)." *Time,* June 18, pp. 42–44.

Kluger, Jeffrey. 2003. "Medicating young minds." *Time,* November 3, pp. 48–57.

Knight, Danielle. 2006. "Ethically challenged." *U.S. News & World Report,* May 22, pp. 24–25.

Knight, Zelda G. 2006. "Some thoughts on the psychological roots of the behavior of serial killers as narcissists: An object relations perspective." *Social Behavior and Personality, 34,* 1189–1206.

Knowles, Gordon James. 1999. "Male prison rape: A search for causation and prevention." *Howard Journal of Criminal Justice, 38,* 267–282.

Koch, Wendy. 2008. "Ban on child porn web forums affects few." *USA Today,* June 13, p. 3A.

Kolata, Gina. 1992. "The burdens of being overweight: Mistreatment and misconceptions." *New York Times,* November 22, pp. 1, 18.

Kolb, Lawrence C., and H. Keith H. Brodie. 1982. *Modern Clinical Psychiatry,* 10th ed. Philadelphia: Saunders.

Konty, Mark. 2005. "Microanomie: The cognitive foundations of the relationship between anomie and deviance." *Criminology, 43,* 107–131.

Kopelowicz, Alex, and T. George Bidder. 1992. "Outcomes of schizophrenia." *American Journal of Psychiatry, 149,* 426.

Koss, Mary P. 1995. "Hidden rape: Sexual aggression and victimization in a national sample of students in higher education." In Patricia Searles and Ronald J. Berger (eds.), *Rape and Society.* Boulder, Colo.: Westview.

Koss, Mary P., et al. 1987. "The scope of rape: Incidence and prevalence of sexual aggression and victimization in a national sample of higher education students." *Journal of Consulting and Clinical Psychology, 55,* 162–170.

Kotula, Dean. 2002. *The Phallus Palace.* Los Angeles: Alyson Publications.

Krislov, Marvin. 2007. "Mental illness on campus: A quiet danger no longer." *USA Today,* December 20, p. 13A.

Kristof, Nicholas D. 1996a. "Asian childhoods sacrificed to prosperity's lust." *Time,* April 14, pp. 1, 6.

Kristof, Nicholas D. 1996b. "Guns: one nation bars, the other requires." *New York Times,* March 10, p. E3.

Kristof, Nicholas D. 2008. "The pimps' slaves." nytimes.com, March 16.

Krueger, Alan, and Jitka Maleckova. 2002. "Does poverty cause terrorism?" *New Republic,* June 24, pp. 27–33.

Krummel, Sabine. 2001. "The elderly are vulnerable to abuse." In J. D. Lloyd, *Family Violence.* San Diego, Calif.: Greenhaven.

Kuo, Michelle. 2001. "Asia's dirty secret." *Harvard International Review, 22* (summer), 42–45.

Kuo, Wen H. 1984. "Prevalence of depression among Asian-Americans." *Journal of Nervous and Mental Disease, 172,* 449–457.

Kuo, Wen H., and Yung-Mei Tsai. 1986. "Social networking, hardiness and immigrant's mental health." *Journal of Health and Social Behavior, 27,* 133–149.

Kurst-Swanger, Karel, and Jacqueline L. Petcosky. 2003. *Violence in the Home: Multidisciplinary Perspectives.* New York: Oxford University Press.

Kushner, Howard I. 1985. "Women and suicide in historical perspective." *Signs, 10,* 543.

Kushner, Howard I. 1995. "Women and suicidal behavior: Epidemiology, gender and lethality in historical perspective." In Silvia Sara Canetto and David Lester (eds.), *Women and Suicidal Behavior.* New York: Springer.

Kutchins, Herb, and Stuart A. Kirk. 1997. *Making Us Crazy.* New York: Free Press.

Labaton, Stephen. 1995. "As pornography arrests grow, so do plans for computer stings." *New York Times,* September 16, pp. 1, 8.

Labovitz, Sanford. 1968. "Variation in suicide rates." In Jack P. Gibbs (ed.), *Suicide.* New York: Harper & Row.

Lacayo, Richard. 2004. "For better or for worse?" *Time,* March 8, pp. 26–33.

Lacey, Marc. 2004. "Amnesty says Sudan militias use rape as weapon." *New York Times,* July 19, p. 9.

Lacey, Marc. 2008. "Abuse trails Central American girls into gangs." *New York Times,* April 11, p. A1.

LaFree, Gary D. 1982. "Male power and female victimization." *American Journal of Sociology, 88,* 312–313.

LaFree, Gary D., Barbara F. Reskin, and Christy A. Visher. 1985. "Jurors' responses to victims' behavior and legal issues in sexual assault trials." *Social Problems, 32,* 389–406.

LaFree, Gary. 1999. "Homicide: Cross-national perspectives." pp. 115–139 in M. Dwayne Smith and Margaret A. Zahn (eds.), *Studying and Preventing Homicide.* Thousand Oaks, Calif.: Sage Publications.

Laing, R. D. 1965. *The Divided Self.* Baltimore, Md.: Penguin Books.

Laing, R. D. 1967. *The Politics of Experience.* New York: Ballantine.

Laing, R. D. 1985. *Wisdom, Madness and Folly.* New York: McGraw-Hill.

Lalumiere, Martin L., et al. 2005. *The Causes of Rape: Understanding Individual Differences in Male Propensity for Sexual Aggression.* Washington, D.C.: American Psychological Association.

Lamar, Jacob V. 1986. "Crack." *Time,* June 2, p. 17.

Lamb, Michael. 1998. "Cybersex: Research notes on the characteristics of the visitors to online chat rooms." *Deviant Behavior, 19,* 121–135.

Landau, Simha F., and Daniel Fridman. 1993. "The seasonality of violent crime: The case of robbery and homicide in Israel." *Journal of Research in Crime and Delinquency, 30,* 163–191.

Langton, Lynn, Nicole Leeper Piquero, and Richard C. Hollinger. 2006. "An empirical test of the relationship between employee theft and low self-control." *Deviant Behavior, 27,* 537–565.

Lanning, Kenneth V. 1992. *Child Molesters: A Behavioral Analysis.* Arlington, Va.: National Center for Missing and Exploited Children.

Laubscher, Leswin R. 2003. "Suicide in a South African town: A cultural psychological investigation." *South African Journal of Psychology, 33,* 133–143.

Lauderdale, Pat, Jerry Parker, Phil Smith-Cunnien, and James Inverarity. 1984. "External threat and the definition of deviance." *Journal of Personality and Social Psychology, 46,* 1058–1068.

Laumann, Edward O., et al. 1994. *The Social Organization of Sexuality: Sexual Practices in the United States.* Chicago: University of Chicago Press.

Lavelle, Louis, and Sheridan Prasso. 2002. "The fat wages of scandal." *Business Week,* September 9, p. 8.

Lavelle, Marianne. 1998. "The new rules of sexual harassment." *U.S. News & World Report,* July 6, pp. 30–31.

LaViolette, Allyce D., and Ola W. Barnett. 2000. *It Could Happen to Anyone: Why Battered Women Stay,* 2d ed. Thousand Oaks, Calif.: Sage Publications.

Lawson, Andrea, and Gregory Fouts. 2004. "Mental illness in Disney animated films." *Canadian Journal of Psychiatry, 49,* 310–314.

Lawson, Annette. 1988. *Adultery: An Analysis of Love and Betrayal.* New York: Basic Books.

Leaning, Jennifer. 2004. "Diagnosing genocide—The case of Darfur." *New England Journal of Medicine, 351,* 735–738.

Lear, Martha Weinman. 1972. "Q. If you rape a woman and steal her TV, what can they get you for in New York? A. Stealing her TV." *New York Times Magazine,* January 30, pp. 62–63.

Lee, Louise. 2006. "Kick out the kids, bring in the sales." *Business Week,* April 17, p. 42.

Lee, Matthew R., Timothy C. Hayes, and Shaun A. Thomas. 2008. "Regional variation in the effect of structural factors on homicide in rural areas." *Social Science Journal, 45,* 76–94.

LeGrand, Camille E. 1973. "Rape and rape laws: Sexism in society and law." *California Law Review, 61,* 929–930.

Lehrer, Eli. 2001. "Hell behind bars." *National Review,* February 5, pp. 24–25.

Leland, John. 1995. "Bisexuality." *Newsweek,* July 17, pp. 44–50.

Leland, John. 1996. "The fear of heroin is shooting up." *Newsweek,* August 26, pp. 55–56.

Leland, John. 2000. "Shades of gay." *Newsweek,* March 20, pp. 46–49.

Lemelson, Robert. 2001. "Strange maladies." *Psychology Today,* December, pp. 60–64.

Lemert, Edwin M. 1951. *Social Pathology.* New York: McGraw-Hill.

Lemonick, Michael D. 2004. "How we grew so big." *Time,* June 7, pp. 66–74.

Leonard, Eileen B. 1982. *Women, Crime, and Society: A Critique of Criminology Theory.* New York: Longman.

Lester, David, and Bruce L. Danto. 1993. *Suicide Behind Bars: Prediction and Prevention.* Philadelphia: Charles Press.

Lester, David. 1985. "Accidental deaths as disguised suicides." *Psychological Reports, 56,* 626.

Lester, David. 1988. "Toward a theory of parasuicide." *Corrective and Social Psychiatry, 34,* 24–26.

Lester, David. 1990. "Suicide, homicide and the quality of life in various countries." *Acta Psychiatrica Scandinavica, 81,* 332–334.

Lester, David. 1991. "Childlessness, suicide and homicide." *Psychological Reports, 69,* 990.

Lester, David. 2000. *Why People Kill Themselves,* 4th ed. Springfield, Ill.: Charles C. Thomas.

LeVay, Simon, and Elisabeth Nonas. 1995. *City of Friends: A Portrait of the Gay and Lesbian Community in America.* Cambridge, Mass.: MIT Press.

LeVay, Simon. 1996. *Queer Science: The Use and Abuse of Research into Homosexuality.* Cambridge, Mass.: MIT Press.

Levin, B. M., Anthony Jones, and Kim Braithwaite. 1998. "Principal factors of the spread of alcoholism in society in a time of social changes." *Russian Social Science Review, 39* (November/December), 38–50.

Levin, Jack, and James Alan Fox. 1985. *Mass Murder: America's Growing Menace.* New York: Plenum.

Levin, Kate A., and Alastair H. Leyland. 2005. "Urban/ rural inequalities in suicide in Scotland, 1981–1999." *Social Science & Medicine, 60,* 2877–2890.

Levine, Art. 1986. "Drug education gets an F." *U.S. News & World Report,* October 13, pp. 63–64.

Levinson, David. 1988. "Family violence in a cross-cultural perspective." In V. B. Van Hasselt et al. (eds.), *Handbook of Family Violence.* New York: Plenum.

Levy, Ariel. 1999. "Sex clubs." *New York,* May 3, p. 72.

Levy, Steven, and Brad Stone. 2005. "Grand theft identity." *Newsweek,* July 4, pp. 38–47.

Lewin, Tamar. 1993. "Rape and the accuser: A debate still rages on citing sexual past." *New York Times,* February 12, p. B12.

Lewin, Tamar. 1995. "Parents poll finds child abuse to be more common." *New York Times,* December 7, p. A17.

Lewis, Helen Block. 1985. "Depression vs. paranoia: Why are there sex differences in mental illness?" *Journal of Personality, 53,* 150–178.

Lewis, James. 2005. "The threat of cyberterrorism is exaggerated." pp. 101–109 in James D. Torr (ed.), *The Internet: Opposing Viewpoints.* Detroit, Mich.: Greenhaven Press.

Lewis, Mindy. 2003. "Those who hold the keys are listening." *Newsweek,* October 6, p. 24.

Li, Spencer De. 2004. "The impacts of self-control and social bonds on juvenile delinquency in a national sample of midadolescents." *Deviant Behavior, 25,* 351–373.

Liddick, Don. 2004. "Political deviance: Two case studies." pp. 280–283 in Alex Thio and Thomas C. Calhoun (eds.), *Readings in Deviant Behavior,* 3d ed. Boston: Allyn and Bacon.

Lieberman, Jethro K. 1973. *How the Government Breaks the Law.* Baltimore, Md.: Penguin.

Liebling, Alison. 1992. *Suicides in Prison.* London: Routledge.

Lilienfeld, Scott O., and Hal Arkowitz. 2007. "Is there really an autism epidemic?" *Scientific American Special Edition, Vol. 17,* Issue 4, pp. 58–61.

Lindesmith, Alfred R. 1968. *Addiction and Opiates.* Chicago: Aldine.

Link, Bruce G., and Jo C. Phelan. 1999. "Public conceptions of mental illness: Labels, cause, dangerousness, and social distance." *American Journal of Public Health, 89,* 1328–1333.

Link, Bruce G., Bruce P. Dohrenwend, and Andrew E. Skodol. 1986. "Socio-economic status and schizophrenia: Noisome occupational characteristics as a risk factor." *American Sociological Review, 51,* 242–258.

Link, Bruce G., Jerrold Mirotznik, and Francis T. Cullen. 1991. "The effectiveness of stigma coping orientations: Can negative consequences of mental illness labeling be avoided?" *Journal of Health and Social Behavior, 32,* 302–320.

Link, Bruce G., Mary Clare Lennon, and Bruce P. Dohrenwend. 1993. "Socioeconomic status and depression: The role of occupations involving direction, control, and planning." *American Journal of Sociology, 98,* 1351–1387.

Linz, Daniel, and Neil Malamuth. 1993. *Pornography.* Newbury Park, Calif.: Sage Publications.

Linz, Daniel, Edward Donnerstein, and Steven Penrod. 1984. "The effects of multiple exposures to filmed violence against women." *Journal of Communication, 34,* 130–147.

Liptak, Adam. 2002. "Judge blocks U.S. bid to ban suicide law." *New York Times,* April 18, p. A16.

Liptak, Adam. 2007. "Does death penalty save lives? A new debate." *New York Times,* November 18, pp. 1, 32.

Littlejohn, Christopher. 2004. "Rediscovering the 'social' in the biopsychosocial perspective." *Mental Health Practice, 8,* 14–17.

Livingston, Michael. 2008. "Alcohol outlet density and assault: A spatial analysis." *Addiction, 103,* 619–628.

Lockwood, Daniel. 1985. "Issues in prison sexual violence." In Michael Braswell et al., *Prison Violence in America.* Cincinnati, Ohio: Anderson.

Loftus, Jeni. 2001. "America's liberalization in attitudes toward homosexuality, 1973–1998." *American Sociological Review, 66,* 762–782.

Lonsway, Kimberly A., and Louise F. Fitzgerald. 1994. "Rape myths are attitudes and generally false beliefs about rape." *Psychology of Women Quarterly, 18,* 133–164.

Loseke, Donileen R., and Demie Kurz. 2005. "Men's violence toward women is the serious social problem." pp. 79–95 in Donileen R. Loseke, Richard J. Gelles, and Mary M. Cavanaugh (eds.), *Current Controversies on Family Violence,* 2d ed. Thousand Oaks, Calif.: Sage.

Love, Sharon RedHawk. 2006. "Illicit sexual behavior: A test of self-control theory." *Deviant Behavior, 27*, 505–536.

Lucas, Ann M. 2005. "The work of sex work: Elite prostitutes' vocational orientations and experiences." *Deviant Behavior, 26*, 513–546.

Luckenbill, David F. 1981. "Generating compliance: The case of robbery." *Urban Life, 10*, 25–46.

Luckenbill, David F. 1985. "Entering male prostitution." *Urban Life, 14*, 131–153.

Luckenbill, David F. 1986. "Deviant career mobility: The case of male prostitutes." *Social Problems, 33*, 283–296.

Lussier, Patrick, Jean Proulx, and Marc LeBlanc. 2005. "Criminal propensity, deviant sexual interests, and criminal activity of sexual aggressors against women: A comparison of explanatory models." *Criminology, 43*, 249–281.

Lyman, Stanford M. 1995. "Without morals or mores: Deviance in postmodern social theory." *International Journal of Politics, Culture and Society, 9*, 197–235.

Lynch, James P., and David Cantor. 1992. "Ecological and behavioral influences on property victimization at home: Implications for opportunity theory." *Journal of Research in Crime and Delinquency, 29*, 335–362.

Lynch, Sarah N. 2008. "An American pastime: Smoking pot." *Time*, July 11, http://www.time.com/time/health/article/0,8599,1821697,00.html

MacAndrew, Craig, and Robert B. Edgerton. 1969. *Drunken Comportment*. London: Nelson.

Macdonald, John M. 1971. *Rape*. Springfield, Ill.: Charles C. Thomas.

Macdonald, John M. 1995. *Rape: Controversial Issues*. Springfield, Ill.: Charles C Thomas.

MacFarquhar, Neil. 2001. "Bin Laden and his followers adhere to an austere, stringent form of Islam." *New York Times*, October 7, p. B7.

Mackay, Judith, and Michael Eriksen. 2002. *The Tobacco Atlas*. Geneva, Switzerland: World Health Organization.

Maddux, J. F., and D. P. Desmond. 1980. "New light on the maturing out hypothesis in opioid dependence." *Bulletin on Narcotics, 32*, 15–25.

Madge, Nicola, and John G. Harvey. 1999. "Suicide among the young—The size of the problem." *Journal of Adolescence, 22*, 145–155.

Madigan, Lee, and Nancy C. Gamble. 1991. *The Second Rape: Society's Continued Betrayal of the Victim*. New York: Lexington Books.

Magnuson, ed. 1986. "Headhunters," *Time*, December 1, p. 32.

Maguire, Kathleen, and Ann L. Pastore (eds.). 1996. *Sourcebook of Criminal Justice Statistics—1995*. Washington, D.C.: Government Printing Office.

Malcolm, John G. 2005. "Internet gambling is a serious problem." pp. 61–66 in James D. Torr (ed.), *The Internet: Opposing Viewpoints*. Detroit, Mich.: Greenhaven Press.

Mancoske, Ronald J., et al. 1995. "Suicide risk among people living with AIDS." *Social Work, 40*, 783–787.

Mandoki, Catalina A., and Barry R. Burkhart. 1991. "Women as victims: Antecedents and consequences of acquaintance rape." In Andrea Parrot and Laurie Bechhofer (eds.), *Acquaintance Rape*. New York: Wiley.

Mann, Coramae Richey. 1996. *When Women Kill*. Albany: State University of New York Press.

Mann, Joseph. 2006. "Internet use increases the risk of identity theft." pp. 66–72 in Lisa Yount (ed.), *Does the Internet Increase the Risk of Crime?* Detroit, Mich.: Greenhaven Press.

Mao, Tse-tung. 1967. *Selected Works of Mao Tse-tung, Vol. 1*. Peking: Foreign Languages Press.

Marcos, Anastasios C., Stephen J. Bahr, and Richard E. Johnson. 1986. "Test of a bonding/association theory of adolescent drug use." *Social Forces, 65*, 135–169.

Marcus, Eric. 1992. *Making History: The Struggle for Gay and Lesbian Equal Rights*. New York: HarperCollins.

Marcus, Eric. 1993. *Is It a Choice?* San Francisco: HarperSanFrancisco.

Margolin, Leslie. 1992. "Deviance on record: Techniques for labeling child abusers in official documents." *Social Problems, 39*, 58–70.

Markowitz, Fred E. 2005. "Sociological models of mental illness stigma: Progress and prospects." pp. 129–144 in Patrick W. Corrigan (ed.), *On the Stigma of Mental Illness*. Washington, D.C.: American Psychological Association.

Marks, Alan. 1980. "Socioeconomic status and suicide in the state of Washington: 1950–1971." *Psychological Reports, 46*, 924–926.

Marriott, Michel. 1995. "Half steps vs. 12 steps." *Newsweek*, March 27, p. 62.

Marshall, Chris E., T. Hank Robinson, and Dae-Hoon Kwak. 2005. "Computer crime in a brave new world." pp. 114–138 in Philip Reichel (ed.), *Handbook of Transnational Crime & Justice*. Thousand Oaks, Calif.: Sage.

Martin, Elaine K., et al. 2007. "A review of marital rape." *Aggression & Violent Behavior, 12*, 329–347.

Martin, Patricia Yancey, and Robert A. Hummer. 1995. "Fraternities and rape on campus." In Alex Thio and Thomas C. Calhoun (eds.), *Readings in Deviant Behavior*. New York: HarperCollins.

Martin, Patti. 2001. *Teenage Blues Might Be More*. Asbury Park, N.J.: Asbury Park Press.

Martin, William T. 1984. "Religiosity and United States suicide rates, 1972–1978." *Journal of Clinical Psychology, 40*, 1166–1169.

Martins, Silvia A., et al. 2008. "Adolescent ecstasy and other drug use in the national survey of parents and youth: The role of sensation-seeking, parental monitoring, and peer's drug use." *Addictive Behavior, 33*, 919–933.

Martz, Larry. 1986. "True greed." *Newsweek*, December 1, p. 48.

Martz, Larry. 1991. "The corporate shell game." *Newsweek,* April 15, pp. 48–49.

Marx, Gary T. 1981. "Ironies of social control: Authorities as contributors to deviance through escalation, nonenforcement, and covert facilitation." *Social Problems, 28,* 221–246.

Maso, Ilja. 2001. "Phenomenology and ethnography." In Paul Atkinson et al. (eds.), *Handbook of Ethnography.* London: Sage Publications.

Massing, Michael. 1998. *The Fix.* New York: Simon & Schuster.

Masters, William H., and Virginia E. Johnson. 1979. *Homosexuality in Perspective.* Boston: Little, Brown.

Mathis, James L. 1972. *Clear Thinking About Sexual Deviations.* Chicago: Nelson-Hall.

Mattern, Jody L., and Clayton Neighbors. 2004. "Social norms campaigns: Examining the relationship between change in perceived norms and changes in drinking levels." *Journal of Studies on Alcohol, 65,* 489–494.

Matthews, Anne. 1993. "The campus crime wave." *New York Times Magazine,* March 7, p. 41.

Matthews, Dawn D. (ed.). 2004. *Domestic Violence Sourcebook,* 2d ed. Detroit, Mich.: Omnigraphics, Inc.

Matthews, Roger. 2002. *Armed Robbery.* Portland, OR: Willan.

Mauro, Robert. 1996. "Suicide—not the answer." *Accent on Living, 41* (Winter), 68–69.

May, William F. 1991. "The molested." *Hastings Center Report, 21,* 9–17.

Mazzetti, Mark. 2004. "Rethinking the next wars." *U.S. News & World Report,* January 5, p. 70.

McAuliffe, William E., and Robert A. Gordon. 1974. "A test of Lindesmith's theory of addiction: The frequency of euphoria among long-term addicts." *American Journal of Sociology, 79,* 795–840.

McCaghy, Charles H. 1968. "Drinking and deviance disavowal: The case of child molesters." *Social Problems, 16,* 43–49.

McCaghy, Charles H., and James K. Skipper, Jr. 1969. "Lesbian behavior as an adaptation to the occupation of stripping." *Social Problems, 17,* 262–270.

McCallum, Jack. 2008. "The real dope." *Sports Illustrated,* March 17, pp. 28–36.

McClelland, David C., et al. 1972. *The Drinking Man.* New York: Free Press.

McCord, William, and Joan McCord. 1960. *Origins of Alcoholism.* Stanford, Calif.: Stanford University Press.

McDowell, Bill. 1996. "Jack in the Box battles back with some help from a clown." *Advertising Age, 67,* November 25, p. 11.

McGeary, Johanna. 2002. "Can the church be saved?" *Time,* April 1, pp. 29–39.

McGinn, Daniel, and Ron Depasquale. 2004. "Taking depression on." *Newsweek,* August 23, pp. 59–60.

McGirk, Tim. 2002. "Lifting the veil on sex slavery." *Time,* February 18, p. 8.

McGirk, Tim. 2008. "Israel's secret war." *Time,* March 24, pp. 30–31.

McIntosh, John L. 1991. "Epidemiology of suicide in the United States." In Antoon A. Leenaars (ed.), *Life Span Perspectives of Suicide: Time-lines in the Suicide Process.* New York: Plenum.

McKegney, F. Patrick, and Mary Alice O'Dowd. 1992. "Suicidality and HIV status." *American Journal of Psychiatry, 149,* 396–398.

McLanahan, Sara S., and Jennifer L. Glass. 1985. "A note on the trend in sex differences in psychological distress." *Journal of Health and Social Behavior, 26,* 328–336.

McMullen, Richie J. 1990. *Male Rape: Breaking the Silence on the Last Taboo.* London: GMP Publishers.

McMurray, Coleen. 2004. "Number of teen smokers holding steady." The Gallup Poll Tuesday Briefing. www.gallup.com.

McNeil, Donald G., Jr. 1995. "For gay Zimbabweans, a difficult political climate." *New York Times,* September 10, p. 3.

McNeil, Donald G., Jr. 1998. "Mugabe attacks, and gay Zimbabweans fight back." *New York Times,* July 14, p. A4.

McNeil, Donald G., Jr. 1999. "Condoms for women gain approval among Africans." *New York Times,* July 24, pp. A1, A6.

Medea, Andra, and Kathleen Thompson. 1974. *Against Rape.* New York: Farrar, Straus and Giroux.

Meer, Jeff. 1985. "Living through robbery." *Psychology Today,* May, p. 20.

Meier, Barry, and Melody Petersen. 2001. "Sales of painkiller grew rapidly, but success brought a high cost." *New York Times,* March 5, pp. A1, A15.

Meier, Robert F., Steven R. Burkett, and Carol A. Hickman. 1984. "Sanctions, peers, and deviance: Preliminary models of a social control process." *The Sociological Quarterly, 25,* 67–82.

Meiselman, Karin C. 1990. *Resolving the Trauma of Incest: Reintegration Therapy with Survivors.* San Francisco: Jossey-Bass.

Meloy, J. Reid, and Alan R. Felthous. 2004. "Introduction to this issue: Serial and mass homicide." *Behavioral Sciences and the Law, 22,* 289–290.

Meloy, J. Reid, et al. 2004. "A comparative analysis of North American adolescent and adult mass murderers." *Behavioral Sciences and the Law, 22,* 291–309.

Menard, Scott. 1995. "A developmental test of Mertonian anomie theory." *Journal of Research in Crime and Delinquency, 31,* 136–174.

Merkin, Rebecca S. 2008. "Cross-cultural differences in perceiving sexual harassment." *North American Journal of Psychology, 10,* 277–289.

Merry, Engle. 1980. "Manipulating: Streetwalkers' strategies for safety in the city." *Ethnos, 45,* 157–175.

Merton, Robert K. 1938. "Social structure and anomie." *American Sociological Review, 3,* 672–682.

Merton, Robert K. 1957. *Social Theory and Social Structure,* rev. ed. New York: Free Press.

Messerschmidt, James W. 1986. *Capitalism, Patriarchy, and Crime: Toward a Socialist Feminist Criminology.* Totowa, N.J.: Rowman & Littlefield.

Messner, Steven F. 1982. "Poverty, inequality, and the urban homicide rate." *Criminology, 20,* 102–114.

Messner, Steven F. 1983. "Regional and racial effects on the urban homicide rate: The subculture of violence revisited." *American Journal of Sociology, 88,* 997–1007.

Messner, Steven F., and Kenneth Tardiff. 1985. "The social ecology of urban homicide: An application of the routine activities' approach." *Criminology, 23,* 241–267.

Messner, Steven F., and Reid M. Golden. 1992. "Racial inequality and racially disaggregated homicide rates: An assessment of alternative theoretical explanations." *Criminology, 30,* 421–445.

Messner, Steven F., and Richard Rosenfeld. 2001. *Crime and the American Dream,* 3d ed. Belmont, Calif.: Wadsworth.

Messner, Steven F., Robert D. Baller, and Matthew P. Zevenberger. 2005. "The legacy of lynching and southern homicide." *American Sociological Review, 70,* 633–655.

Michael, Richard P., and Doris Zumpe. 1983. "Sexual violence in the United States and the role of season." *American Journal of Psychiatry, 140,* 883–886.

Michael, Robert T., et al. 1994. *Sex in America: A Definitive Survey.* Boston: Little, Brown.

Michels, Scott. 2006. "For gays, new math." *U.S. News & World Report,* August 14, pp. 34–36.

Miethe, Terance D., and Wendy C. Regoeczi, with Kriss A. Drass. 2004. *Rethinking Homicide: Exploring the Structure and Process Underlying Deadly Situations.* Cambridge, U.K.: Cambridge University Press.

Milbank, Dana, and Marcus W. Brauchli. 1995. "Greasing wheels." *Wall Street Journal,* September 29, pp. A1, A14.

Miller, Howard L., et al. 1984. "An analysis of the effects of suicide prevention facilities on suicide rates in the United States." *American Journal of Public Health, 74,* 340–343.

Miller, JoAnn L. 1991. "Prostitution in contemporary American society." In Elizabeth Grauerholz and Mary A. Koralewski (eds.), *Sexual Coercion.* Lexington, Mass.: Lexington Books.

Miller, Laurence. 1986. "Pickled brains age faster." *Psychology Today,* January, p. 16.

Miller, M., and D. Hemenway. 1999. "The relationship between firearms and suicide: A review of the literature." *Aggression and Violent Behavior, 4,* 59–75.

Miller, Matthew. 2006. "Catch me if you can." *Forbes,* March 27, pp. 112–116.

Miller, Matthew, et al. 2007. "State-level homicide victimization rates in the US in relation to survey measures of household firearm ownership, 2001–2003." *Social Science & Medicine, 64,* 656–664.

Millett, Kate. 1973. *The Prostitution Papers.* New York: Avon.

Mills, Linda G. 2003. *Insult to Injury: Rethinking Our Response to Intimate Abuse.* Princeton, N.J.: Princeton University Press.

Milner, Christina, and Richard Milner. 1972. *Black Players.* Boston: Little, Brown.

Mishara, Eric. 1983. "R. D. Laing's new home." *Omni,* August, p. 35.

Mitchell, Alison. 1997. "President regrets top U.S. regulator met with bankers." *New York Times,* January 29, pp. A1, A12.

Mitchell, Roger E., and Rudolf H. Moos. 1984. "Deficiencies in social support among depressed patients: Antecedents or consequences of stress?" *Journal of Health and Social Behavior, 25,* 438–452.

Mithers, Carol Lynn. 1980. "Date rape: When 'nice guys' won't take NO for an answer." *Mademoiselle,* November 8, pp. 210–211.

Mitka, Mike. 2006. "Methamphetamine bill." *JAMA: Journal of the American Medical Association, 295,* 2130.

Mixson, Paula M. 1995. "An adult protective services perspective." *Journal of Elder Abuse and Neglect, 7,* no. 2–3, 69–87.

Modan, Baruch, et al. 1992. "Prevalence of HIV antibodies in transsexual and female prostitutes." *American Journal of Public Health, 82,* 590–591.

Moen, Phyllis, Julie Robison, and Donna Dempster-McClain. 1995. "Caregiving and women's well-being: A life course approach." *Journal of Health and Social Behavior, 36,* 259–273.

Moffatt, Gregory K. 2000. *Blind-Sided: Homicide Where It Is Least Expected.* Westport, Conn.: Praeger.

Mohler-Kuo, Meichun, et al. 2004. "Correlates of rape while intoxicated in a national sample of college women." *Journal of Studies on Alcohol, 65,* 37–45.

Molotsky, Irvin. 1999. "Study links teen-age substance abuse and paternal ties." *New York Times,* August 31, p. A14.

Monahan, John. 1992. "Mental disorder and violent behavior." *American Psychologist,* April, pp. 511–521.

Monastersky, Richard. 2007. "Is there an autism epidemic?" *Chronicle of Higher Education,* May 11, p. 19.

Moniruzzaman, Syed, and Ragnar Andersson. 2005. "Age- and sex-specific analysis of homicide mortality as a function of economic development: A cross-national comparison." *Scandinavian Journal of Public Health, 33,* 464–471.

Monroe, Scott M., and Katholiki Hadjiyannakis. 2002. "The social environment and depression: Focusing on severe life stress." In Ian Gotlib and Constance Hammen (eds.), *Handbook of Depression.* New York: Guilford Press.

Moreau, Ron. 1992. "Sex and death in Thailand." *Newsweek,* July 20, p. 50.

Morey, Leslie C., Harvey A. Skinner, and Roger K. Blashfield. 1984. "A typology of alcohol abusers: Correlates and implications." *Journal of Abnormal Psychology, 93,* 408–417.

Morin, Stephen F., et al. 1984. "The psychological impact of AIDS on gay men." *American Psychologist, 39,* 1288–1293.

Morris, Allison. 1987. *Women, Crime, and Criminal Justice.* New York: Basil Blackwell.

Morris, Jeanette, and Lisa A. Cubbins. 1992. "Dating, drinking, and rape." *Psychology of Women, 16,* 179–191.

Morris, Monica B. 1977. *An Excursion into Creative Sociology.* New York: Columbia University Press.

Morrison, Dan. 2006. "Remember Darfur?" *U.S. News & World Report,* February 13, p. 25.

Mosher, William D. 2005. "With males in the mix, federal sex survey takes on greater importance." *Contemporary Sexuality, Vol. 39,* November, pp. 1–6.

Mukamal, Kenneth J., and Eric B. Rimm. 2001. "Alcohol's effects on the risk for coronary heart disease." *Alcohol Research & Health, 25,* 255–262.

Mulia, Nina, et al. 2008. "Stress, social support, and problem drinking among women in poverty." *Addiction, 103,* 1283–1293.

Mullen, Paul E., et al. 2000. *Stalkers and Their Victims.* Cambridge, U.K.: Cambridge University Press.

Mullins, Christopher W. 2006. *Holding Your Square: Masculinities, Streetlife, and Violence.* Portland, OR: Willan.

Mulrine, Anna. 2001. "Where do hopes go?" *U.S. News & World Report,* May 7, pp. 41–44.

Mulvihill, Donald J., and Melvin M. Tumin with Lynn A. Curtis. 1969. *Crimes of Violence, Vol. 11.* Washington, D.C.: Government Printing Office.

Murray, John B. 1986. "Marijuana's effects on human cognitive functions, psychomotor functions, and personality." *Journal of General Psychology, 113,* 25–40.

Musto, David F. 1973. *The American Disease: Origins of Narcotic Control.* New Haven, Conn.: Yale University Press.

Musto, David F. 1986. "Lessons of the first cocaine epidemic." *Wall Street Journal,* June 11, p. 30.

Myers, Mary Beth, Donald Templer, and Ric Brown. 1984. "Coping ability of women who become victims of rape." *Journal of Consulting and Clinical Psychology, 52,* 73–78.

Myerscough, Rodney, and Stuart Taylor. 1985. "The effects of marijuana on human physical aggression." *Journal of Personality and Social Psychology, 49,* 1541–1546.

Nader, Ralph. 1970. "Foreword" to John C. Esposito, *Vanishing Air.* New York: Grossman, p. viii.

Nagel, Barbara, et al. 2005. "Attitudes toward victims of rape: Effects of gender, race, religion, and social class." *Journal of Interpersonal Violence, 20,* 725–737.

Nakawatase, Tomoko V., et al. 1993. "The association between fast-flushing response and alcohol use among Japanese Americans." *Journal of Studies on Alcohol, 54,* 48–53.

Namaste, Viviane K. 2000. *Invisible Lives: The Erasure of Transsexual and Transgendered People.* Chicago: University of Chicago Press.

Nanda, Serena. 2000. *Gender Diversity: Crosscultural Variations.* Prospect Heights, Ill.: Waveland.

Nathan, Debbie. 1995. "Justice in Wenatchee." *New York Times,* December 19, p. A19.

Nation's Health. 2008. "UN agencies unite against female genital mutilation." April, p. 10.

Neff, James Alan, and Baqar A. Husaini. 1985. "Stress-buffer properties of alcohol consumption: The role of urbanicity and religious identification." *Journal of Health and Social Behavior, 26,* 207–222.

Neff, James Alan, et al. 1991. "Machismo, self-esteem, education and high maximum drinking among Anglo, black and Mexican-American male drinkers." *Journal of Studies on Alcohol, 52,* 458–463.

Nelson, Roxanne. 2004. "Oregon court upholds assisted-suicide law." *The Lancet, 363,* 1877.

Nettler, Gwynn. 1974. "On telling who's crazy." *American Sociological Review, 39,* 893–894.

Neugeboren, Jay. 2006. "Meds alone couldn't bring Robert back." *Newsweek,* February 6, p. 17.

Newman, Katherine S. 2004. *Rampage: The Social Roots of School Shootings.* New York: Basic Books.

NewsRx.com. 2004. "Asian suicide rate higher in women." April 22.

Newton, Michael. 2004. *The Encyclopedia of High-Tech Crime and Crime-Fighting.* New York: Facts on File.

NHSDA (National Household Survey on Drug Abuse). 2001. *National Survey on Drug Abuse.* Washington, D.C.: Government Printing Office.

NIAAA (National Institute on Alcohol Abuse and Alcoholism). 1983. *Alcohol and Health.* Rockville, Md.: NIAAA.

Nicastro, Franco. 1992. "All is quiet in Corleone." *World Press Review,* December, p. 13.

Nichols, Margaret. 1990. "Lesbian relationships: Implications for the study of sexuality and gender." In David P. McWhirter, et al. (eds.), *Homosexuality/Heterosexuality.* New York: Oxford University Press.

Niebuhr, Gustav. 1998. "Laws aside, some in clergy quietly bless gay 'marriage'". *New York Times,* April 17, pp. A1, A20.

Nielsen, Amie L. 1999. "Testing Sampson and Laub's life course theory: age, race/ethnicity, and drunkenness." *Deviant Behavior, 20,* 129–151.

Noah, Timothy. 1997. "OK, OK, cigarettes do kill." *U.S. News & World Report,* March 31, pp. 29–30.

Noble, Ernest P., et al. 1991. "Allelic association of the D$_2$ dopamine receptor gene with receptor-binding characteristics in alcoholism." *Archives of General Psychiatry, 48,* 648–654.

Noonan, David. 2008. "Doctors who kill themselves." *Newsweek,* April 28, p. 16.

Nordland, Rod. 1992. "The 'Velcro Don': Wiseguys finish last." *Newsweek,* April 13, p. 35.

Nordland, Rod, and Jeffrey Bartholet. 2001. "The web's dark secret." *Newsweek,* March 19, pp. 44–51.

Nordland, Rod, et al. 2007. "Surge of suicide bombers." *Newsweek,* August 13, pp. 30–32.

Norman, Michael. 1998. "Getting serious about adultery." *New York Times,* July 4, pp. A13, A15.

Norris, Frank H., et al. 2002. "The epidemiology of sex differences in PTSD across developmental, societal, and research contexts." In Rachel Kimerling, Paige Ouimette, and Jessica Wolfe (eds.), *Gender and PTSD.* New York: Guilford.

Norris, Joel. 1989. *Serial Killers.* New York: Anchor Books.

NSDUH (National Survey on Drug Use & Health). 2006. http://oas.samhsa.gov/NSDUHLatest.htm

O'Boyle, Michael, and Elisif A. A. Brandon. 1998. "Suicide attempts, substance abuse, and personality." *Journal of Substance Abuse Treatment, 15,* 353–356.

O'Hanlan, Katherine A. 1996. "Homophobia is a health hazard." *USA Today: The Magazine of the American Scene, 125,* November, pp. 26–29.

O'Kane, James M. 1992. *The Crooked Ladder: Gangsters, Ethnicity, and the American Dream.* New Brunswick, N.J.: Transaction.

O'Sullivan, Chris S. 1991. "Acquaintance gang rape on campus." In Andrea Parrot and Laurie Bechhofer (eds.), *Acquaintance Rape.* New York: Wiley.

Omestad, Thomas. 1997. "Bye-bye to bribes." *U.S. News & World Report,* December 22, pp. 39–44.

ONDCP (Office of National Drug Control Policy). 2006. "Prescription drug abuse." http://www.whitehouse drugpolicy.gov/

Onstad, Katrina. 1996. "The cyberporn flap: An update." *Canadian Business, 69,* Fall, p. 58.

Orcutt, James D. 1991. "Beyond the 'exotic and the pathologic': Alcohol problems, norm qualities, and sociological theories of deviance." In Paul M. Roman (ed.), *Alcohol: The Development of Sociological Perspectives on Use and Abuse.* New Brunswick, N.J.: Rutgers Center of Alcohol Studies.

Orcutt, James D. 1993. "Happy hour and social lubrication: Evidence on mood-setting rituals of drinking time." *Journal of Drug Issues, 23,* 389–407.

Orr, Andrea. 2004. *Meeting, Mating, and Cheating: Sex, Love, and the New World of Online Dating.* Upper Saddle River, N.J.: Reuters.

Osborne, Lawrence. 2001. "Regional disturbances." *New York Times Magazine,* May 6, pp. 100–102.

Osgood, D. Wayne, et al. 1996. "Routine activities and individual deviant behavior." *American Sociological Review, 61,* 635–655.

Overall, Christine. 1992. "What's wrong with prostitution? Evaluating sex work." *Signs, 17,* 705–724.

Painter, Kim. 2008. "Spring's dark side: Upswing in suicides." *USA Today,* May 5, p. 4D.

Pakhomou, Serge-Moses. 2004. "Serial killers: Offenders' relationship to the victim and selected demographics." *International Journal of Police Science & Management, 6,* 219–233.

Palson, Charles, and Rebecca Palson. 1972. "Swinging in wedlock." *Society,* February, pp. 28–37.

Pape, Robert. 2005. *Dying to Win: The Strategic Logic of Suicide Terrorism.* New York: Random House.

Park, Alice. 2008a. "The obese feel more discrimination." *Time,* April 11, http://www.time.com/time/health/article/0,8599,1730150,00.html

Park, Alice. 2008b. "What the gay brain looks like." *Time,* June 17, http://www.time.com/time/health/article/0,8599,1815538,00.html

Parker, Robert Nash, with Linda-Anne Rebhun. 1995. *Alcohol and Homicide: A Deadly Combination of Two American Traditions.* Albany: State University of New York Press.

Parker, Robert Nash. 1989. "Poverty, subculture of violence, and type of homicide." *Social Forces, 67,* 983–1007.

Parker-Pope, Tara. 2002. "A new reason for teens to avoid sex: It could be harmful to their health." *Wall Street Journal,* August 27, p. D1.

Parker-Pope, Tara. 2003. "A 'fat-free' product that's 100% fat: How food labels legally mislead." *Wall Street Journal,* July 15, p. D1.

Parnaby, Patrick F., and Vincent F. Sacco. 2004. "Fame and strain: The contributions of Mertonian deviance theory to an understanding of the relationship between celebrity and deviant behavior." *Deviant Behavior, 25,* 1–26.

Parsian, Abbas, et al. 1991. "Alcoholism and alleles of the human D$_2$ dopamine receptor locus: Studies of association and linkage." *Archives of General Psychiatry, 48,* 655–663.

Passas, Nikos, and Robert Agnew (eds.). 1997. *The Future of Anomie Theory.* Boston: Northeastern University Press.

Paul, Pamela. 2004. "The porn factor." *Time,* January 19, pp. 99–100.

Paveza, Gregory J., et al. 1992. "Severe family violence and Alzheimer's disease: Prevalence and risk factors." *Gerontologist, 32,* 493–497.

Pearson, Veronica, and Meng Liu. 2002. "Ling's death: An ethnography of a Chinese woman's suicide." *Suicide and Life-Threatening Behavior, 32,* 347–358.

Peck, Dennis L. 1984. "Lethality of method of suicide among a youthful sample of committers: An examination of the intent hypothesis." *Psychological Reports, 55,* 861–862.

Peck, Dennis L. 1985–1986. "Completed suicides: Correlates of choice of method." *Omega, 16,* 309–323.

Peck, M., and A. Schrut. 1971. "Suicidal behavior among college students." *HSMHA Health Report, 86,* 149–156.

Pedahzur, Ami, Arie Perliger, and Leonard Weinberg. 2003. "Altruism and fatalism: The characteristics of Palestinian suicide terrorists." *Deviant Behavior, 24,* 405–423.

Pedersen, Eric R., and Joseph LaBrie. 2007. "Partying before the party: Examining prepartying behavior among college students." *Journal of American College Health, 56,* 237–245.

Peen, Jaap, et al. 2007. "Is the prevalence of psychiatric disorders associated with urbanization?" *Social Psychiatry & Psychiatric Epidemiology, 42,* 984–989.

Pelka, Fred. 1995. "Raped: A male survivor breaks his silence." In Patricia Searles and Ronald J. Berger (eds.), *Rape and Society.* Boulder, Colo.: Westview.

Pennebaker, James W., and Robin C. O'Heeron. 1984. "Confiding in others and illness rates among spouses of suicide and accidental-death victims." *Journal of Abnormal Psychology, 93,* 473–476.

Peplau, Letitia Anne, and Susan D. Cochran. 1990. "A relationship perspective on homosexuality." In David P. McWhirter et al. (eds.), *Homosexuality/ Heterosexuality.* New York: Oxford University Press.

Peplau, Letitia Anne. 1981. "What homosexuals want." *Psychology Today,* March, pp. 28–38.

Peralta, Robert L. 2005. "Race and the culture of college drinking." pp. 127–141 in Wilson R. Palacios (ed.), *Cocktails & Dreams: Perspectives on Drug and Alcohol Use.* Upper Saddle River, N.J.: Prentice Hall.

Perkins, Roberta. 1991. *Working Girls: Prostitutes, Their Life and Social Control.* Canberra: Australian Institute of Criminology.

Perry, Alex, and Mae Sai. 2002. "How I bought two slaves, to free them." *Time,* March 11, p. 7.

Pescosolido, Bernice A., and Robert Mendelsohn. 1986. "Social causation or social construction of suicide? An investigation into the social organization of official rates." *American Sociological Review, 51,* 80–101.

Peterson, Elicka S. 1999. "Murder as self-help: Women and intimate partner homicide." *Homicide Studies, 3,* 30–46.

Peterson, Ruth D. 1992. "Rape and dimensions of gender socioeconomic inequality in U.S. metropolitan areas." *Journal of Research in Crime & Delinquency, 29,* 162–177.

Peterson, Virginia. 2000. *Child Abuse: Fear in the Home.* Wylie, Tex.: Gale Group.

Peto, Richard, and Alan D. Lopez. 2001. "Future worldwide health effects of current smoking patterns." p. 154 in C. Everett Koop, Clarence E. Pearson, and M. Roy Schwartz (eds.), *Critical Issues in Global Health.* San Francisco: Jossey-Bass.

Petrovich, Michael, and Donald I. Templer. 1984. "Heterosexual molestation of children who later became rapists." *Psychological Records, 54,* 810.

Phillips, David P. 1979. "Suicide, motor vehicle fatalities, and the mass media: Evidence toward a theory of suggestion." *American Journal of Sociology, 84,* 1150–1174.

Phillips, David P. 1980a. "Airplane accidents, murder, and the mass media: Towards a theory of imitation and suggestion." *Social Forces, 58,* 1001–1024.

Phillips, David P. 1980b. "The deterrent effect of capital punishment: New evidence on an old controversy." *American Journal of Sociology, 86,* 139–148.

Phillips, David P. 1981. "The complementary virtues of qualitative and quantitative research: Reply to Altheide." *Social Forces, 60,* 597–599.

Phillips, David P. 1983. "The impact of mass media violence on U.S. homicides." *American Sociological Review, 48,* 560–568.

Phillips, David P. 1993. "Adequacy of official suicide statistics for scientific research." *Suicide & Life-Threatening Behavior, 23,* 307–319.

Phillips, David P., and Kenneth A. Bollen. 1985. "Same time, last year: Selective data dredging for negative findings." *American Sociological Review, 50,* 364–371.

Pileggi, Nicholas. 1986. *Wiseguy: Life in a Mafia Family.* New York: Simon & Schuster.

Pillemer, Karl A., and David Finkelhor. 1988. "The prevalence of elder abuse: A random sample survey." *The Gerontologist, 28,* 51–57.

Piore, Adam, et al. 2006. "Hacking for dollars." pp. 27–33 in Lisa Yount (ed.), *Does the Internet Increase the Risk of Crime?* Detroit, Mich.: Greenhaven Press.

Piquero, Nicole Leeper, Stephanie Carmichael, and Alex R. Piquero. 2008. "Assessing the perceived seriousness of white-collar and street crimes." *Crime & Delinquency, 54,* 291–312.

Pittman, Frank III. 1993. "Beyond betrayal: Life after infidelity." *Psychology Today,* May/June, p. 36.

Pitts, Marian K., et al. 2004. "Who pays for sex and why?" *Archives of Sexual Behavior, 33,* 353–358.

Pizzo, Stephen P., and Paul Muolo. 1993. "Take the money and run." *New York Times Magazine,* May 9, p. 26.

Platt, Steven. 1984. "Unemployment and suicidal behavior." *Social Science and Medicine, 19,* 93–115.

Pollack, Andrew. 1997. "Overseas, smoking is one of life's small pleasures." *New York Times,* August 17, p. E5.

Ponse, Barbara. 1984. "The problematic meanings of 'lesbian.'" In Jack D. Douglas (ed.), *The Sociology of Deviance.* Boston: Allyn and Bacon.

Pontell, Henry N., and Kitty Calavita. 1993. "White-collar crime in the savings and loan scandal." *The Annals of the American Academy of Political and Social Science, 525* (January), 31–45.

Porter, Roy. 1996. "Born that way?" *New York Times Book Review,* August 11, p. 8.

Potterat, John J., et al. 1990. "Estimating the prevalence and career longevity of prostitute women." *Journal of Sex Research, 27,* 233–243.

Pound, Edward T., and Danielle Knight. 2006. "Cleaning up the World Bank." *U.S. News & World Report,* April 3, pp. 40–51.

Pratt, Timothy. 2001. "Sex slavery packet: A growing concern in Latin America." *Christian Science Monitor,* January 11, p. 7.

Pratt, Travis C., and Francis T. Cullen. 2000. "The empirical status of Gottfredson and Hirschi's general theory of crime: A meta-analysis." *Criminology, 38,* 931–964.

President's Commission on Organized Crime. 1986. *The Impact: Organized Crime Today.* Washington, D.C.: Government Printing Office.

Previti, Denise, and Paul R. Amato. 2004. "Is infidelity a cause or a consequence of poor marital quality?" *Journal of Social and Personal Relationships, 21,* 217–230.

Pridemore, William Alex, and Andrew L. Spivak. 2003. "Patterns of suicide mortality in Russia." *Suicide and Life-Threatening Behavior, 33,* 132–150.

Pridemore, William Alex. 2002. "Using newly available homicide data to debunk two myths about violence in an international context." *Homicide Studies, 5,* 267–275.

Pridemore, William Alex. 2008. "A methodological addition to the cross-national empirical literature on social structure and homicide: A first test of the poverty-homicide thesis." *Criminology, 46,* 133–154.

Prior, Jo. 2007. "Psychosis in the group." *Therapy Today,* December, pp. 40–42.

Pristina, Andrew Purvis, and Jan Stojaspal Chisinau. 2001. "Human slavery." *Time Europe,* February 19, pp. 18–21.

Pritchard, C., and D. S. Baldwin. 2002. "Elderly suicide rates in Asian and English-speaking countries." *Acta Psychiatrica Scandinavica, 105,* 271–275.

Procida, Richard, and Rita J. Simon. 2003. *Global Perspectives on Social Issues: Pornography.* Lanham, Md.: Lexington.

Prus, Robert, and Scott Grills. 2003. *The Deviant Mystique: Involvements, Realities, and Regulation.* Westport, Conn.: Praeger.

Psychology Today. 1976. "Wrist-cutting—a road to life, not death." April, p. 20.

Quindlen, Anna. 1994. "Sex for sale." *New York Times,* November 26, p. 15.

Quinney, Richard. 1974. *Critique of Legal Order: Crime Control in Capitalist Society.* Boston: Little, Brown.

Quinney, Richard. 1975. *Criminology.* Boston: Little, Brown.

Raab, Selwyn. 1994. "Mob tightens secretive style in retreat from prosecutors." *New York Times,* May 29, pp. 1, 13.

Raab, Selwyn. 1997. "Officials say mob is shifting crimes to new industries." *New York Times,* February 10, pp. A1, A10.

Rapaport, Karen R., and C. Dale Posey. 1991. "Sexually coercive college males." In Andrea Parrot and Laurie Bechhofer (eds.), *Acquaintance Rape.* New York: Wiley.

Rapaport, Karen, and Barry R. Burkhart. 1984. "Personality and attitudinal characteristics of sexually coercive college males." *Journal of Abnormal Psychology, 93,* 216–221.

Ratey, John J., and Catherine Johnson. 1997. *Shadow Syndromes.* New York: Pantheon Books.

Rawe, Julie. 2004. "The case against Ken Lay." *Time,* July 19, pp. 62–63.

Reed, Susan E. 2000. "New economy, same harassment problems." *New York Times,* August 12, Section 3, pp. 1, 11.

Rehm, Jurgen, et al. 2003. "The global distribution of average volume of alcohol consumption and patterns of drinking." *European Addiction Research, 9,* 147–156.

Reid, Scott A., Jonathan Epstein, and D. E. Benson. 1995. "Does exotic dancing pay well but cost dearly?" In Alex Thio and Thomas C. Calhoun (eds.), *Readings in Deviant Behavior.* New York: HarperCollins.

Rein, Mei Ling. 2001. *Child Abuse: Betraying a Trust.* Detroit, Mich.: Gale Group.

Rescorla, L., et al. 2007. "Epidemiological comparisons of problems and positive qualities reported by adolescents in 24 countries." *Journal of Consulting and Clinical Psychology, 75,* 351–358.

Reuter, Peter. 1995. "The decline of the American Mafia." *Public Interest,* Summer, 89–99.

Riccio, R. 1992. "Street crime strategies: The changing schemata of streetwalkers." *Environment and Behavior, 24,* 555–570.

Rice, Kennon J., and William R. Smith. 2002. "Socioecological models of automotive theft: Integrating routine activity and social disorganization approaches." *Journal of Research in Crime and Delinquency, 39,* 304–336.

Richards, Bill. 1992. "Burden of proof." *Wall Street Journal,* December 8, pp. A1, A8.

Richtel, Matt. 2008. "Sex trade monitors a key figure's woes." nytimes.com, June 17.

Rickgarn, Ralph L. V. 1994. *Perspectives on College Student Suicide.* Amityville, N.Y.: Baywood.

Ridley, Mark. 1996. "The gay brain." *Natural History, 105* (August), 10–11.

Rieger, Gerulf, et al. 2008. "Sexual orientation and childhood gender nonconformity: Evidence from home videos." *Developmental Psychology, 44,* 46–58.

Rimer, Sara. 1993. "Campus lesbians step into unfamiliar light." *New York Times,* June 5, p. 6.

Ripley, Amanda. 2002. "Why suicide bombing . . . is now all the rage." *Time,* April 15, pp. 32–39.

Risman, Barbara, and Pepper Schwartz. 2002. "After the sexual revolution: Gender politics in teen dating." *Contexts,* Spring, pp. 16–24.

Rivara, Frederick, et al. 2004. "Mortality attributable to harmful drinking in the United States, 2000." *Journal of Studies on Alcohol, 65,* 530–536.

Rivera, Elaine. 2000. "License to drink." *Time,* July 31, p. 47.

Robins, Lee N. 1973. *The Vietnam Drug User Returns.* Washington, D.C.: Government Printing Office.

Robins, Lee N., et al. 1984. "Lifetime prevalence of specific psychiatric disorders in three sites." *Archives of General Psychiatry, 41,* 949–958.

Rock, Michael T., and Heidi Bonnett. 2004. "The comparative politics of corruption: Accounting for the East Asian paradox in empirical studies of corruption, growth and investment." *World Development, 32,* 999–1017.

Rodgers, Bryan, and Susan L. Mann. 1993. "Rethinking the analysis of intergenerational social mobility: A comment on John W. Fox's 'Social class, mental illness, and social mobility.'" *Journal of Health and Social Behavior, 34,* 165–172.

Roffman, Roger A., and Robert Stephens. 2006. *Cannabis Dependence: Its Nature, Consequences and Treatment.* Cambridge, U.K.: Cambridge University Press.

Roman, Paul M., and Terry C. Blum. 1991. "The medicalized conception of alcohol-related problems: Some social sources and some social consequences of murkiness and confusion." In David J. Pittman and Helene Raskin White (eds.), *Society, Culture, and Drinking Patterns Reexamined.* New Brunswick, N.J.: Rutgers Center of Alcohol Studies.

Rosack, Jim. 2007. "Antidepressants do not increase teen suicide." pp. 138–145 in David Becker and Cynthia Becker (eds.), *Problems with Death.* Detroit, Mich.: Greenhaven Press.

Rose, Harold M., and Paula D. McClain. 1990. *Race, Place, and Risk: Black Homicide in Urban America.* Albany: State University of New York Press.

Rosenau, Pauline. 1992. *Postmodernism and the Social Sciences.* Princeton, N.J.: Princeton University Press.

Rosenberg, Debra. 2004. "The Will & Grace effect." *Newsweek,* May 24, pp. 38–39.

Rosenberg, Debra. 2007. "(Rethinking) gender." *Newsweek,* May 21, pp. 50–57.

Rosenblum, Karen E. 1975. "Female deviance and the female sex role: A preliminary investigation." *British Journal of Sociology, 26,* 169–185.

Rosenfeld, Barry. 2004. *Assisted Suicide and the Right to Die.* Washington, D.C.: American Psychological Association.

Rosenfeld, Sam A. 1985. "The lady is addictive." *Psychology Today,* January, p. 20.

Rosenhan, D. L. 1973. "On being sane in insane places." *Science,* January 19, p. 256.

Rosenthal, A. M. 1995. "The cruelest hoax." *New York Times,* January 3, p. A11.

Rosenthal, Elisabeth. 1999. "Suicide gains ground on women in rural China." *New York Times,* January 24, pp. 1, 8.

Rosoff, Stephen M., Henry N. Pontell, and Robert H. Tillman. 2002. *Profit without Honor: White-Collar Crime and the Looting of America,* 2d ed. Upper Saddle River, N.J.: Prentice Hall.

Ross, Michael W., and Willem A. Arrindell. 1988. "Perceived parental rearing patterns of homosexual and heterosexual men." *Journal of Sex Research, 24,* 275–281.

Rotgers, Frederick, et al. 1996. *Treating Substance Abuse: Theory and Practice.* New York: Guilford.

Roubach, Michael. 2004. "Meaning, phenomenology, and being." *Inquiry, 47,* 189–199.

Rowe, Paul M. 1995. "Alcoholism in USA." *Lancet, 345,* April 1, 860.

Rubin, Arline M., and James R. Adams. 1986. "Outcomes of sexually open marriages." *Journal of Sex Research, 22,* 311–319.

Rubington, Earl. 1991. "The chronic drunkenness offender: Before and after decriminalization." In David J. Pittman and Helene Raskin White (eds.), *Society, Culture, and Drinking Patterns Reexamined.* New Brunswick, N.J.: Rutgers Center of Alcohol Studies.

Ruch, Libby O., Susan Meyers Chandler, and Richard A. Harter. 1980. "Life change and rape impact." *Journal of Health and Social Behavior, 21,* 248–260.

Rudacille, Deborah. 2005. *The Riddle of Gender: Science, Activism, and Transgender Rights.* New York: Pantheon Books.

Ruiz, Dorothy S. 1982. "Epidemiology of schizophrenia: Some diagnostic and sociocultural considerations." *Phylon, 43,* 315–326.

Rumney, Philip N. S. 2008. "Policing male rape and sexual assault." *Journal of Criminal Law, 72,* 67–86.

Russell, Diana E. H. 1984. *Sexual Exploitation.* Beverly Hills, Calif.: Sage Publications.

Russell, Diana E. H. 1990. *Rape in Marriage.* Bloomington: Indiana University Press.

Russell, Diana E. H., and Rebecca M. Bolen. 2000. *The Epidemic of Rape and Child Sexual Abuse in the United States.* Thousand Oaks, Calif.: Sage Publications.

Rust, Paula C. 1995. *Bisexuality and the Challenge to Lesbian Politics: Sex, Loyalty, and Revolution.* New York: New York University Press.

Sabato, Larry J., and Glenn R. Simpson. 1996. *Dirty Little Secrets.* New York: Times Books.

Sachs, Andrea. 1993. "9-Zip! I love it!" *Time,* November 22, pp. 44–45.

Saghir, Marcel T., and Eli Robins. 1980. "Clinical aspects of female homosexuality." In Judd Marmor (ed.), *Homosexual Behavior: A Modern Reappraisal.* New York: Basic Books.

Sallett, Alphonse, Erich Goode, and William Pooler. 1999. "The death of a paradigm? The onset and dynamics of an adolescent drug epidemic, 1991–1998." Unpublished paper.

SAMHSA (Substance Abuse and Mental Health Services Administration). 2002. *Annual Household Survey.* www.hhs.gov/news.

Sanday, Peggy Reeves. 1981. "The socio-cultural context of rape: A cross-cultural study." *Journal of Social Issues, 37,* 5–27.

Sanday, Peggy Reeves. 1990. *Fraternity Gang Rape: Sex, Brotherhood, and Privilege on Campus.* New York: New York University Press.

Sanday, Peggy Reeves. 1996a. *A Woman Scorned: Acquaintance Rape on Trial.* New York: Doubleday.

Sanday, Peggy Reeves. 1996b. "Rape-prone versus rape-free campus cultures." *Violence Against Women, 2,* 191–208.

Sandmaier, Marian. 1992. *The Invisible Alcoholics: Women and Alcohol,* 2d ed. Bradenton, Fla.: Blue Ridge Summit.

Santtila, Pekka, et al. 2008. "Potential for homosexual response is prevalent and genetic." *Biological Psychology, 77,* 102–105.

Santtila, Pekka, et al. 2001. "The structure of crime-scene actions in Finnish homicides." *Homicide Studies, 5,* 363–387.

Sapp, M., et al. 1999. "Attitudes toward rape among African American male and female college students." *Journal of Counseling and Development, 77,* 204–208.

Sarrel, Philip M., and William H. Masters. 1982. "Sexual molestation of men by women." *Archives of Sexual Behavior, 11,* 117–131.

Sarrel, Philip, and Lorna Sarrel. 1981. "Can a man be raped by a woman?" *Redbook,* May, p. 94.

Satel, Sally. 1996. "The madness of deinstitutionalization." *Wall Street Journal,* February 20, p. A22.

Saunders, Daniel G. 2002. "Are physical assaults by wives and girlfriends a major social problem? A review of the literature." *Violence Against Women, 8,* 1424–1448.

Savin-Williams, Ritch C. 2005a. "The new gay teen: Shunning labels." *The Gay & Lesbian Review,* November/December, pp. 16–19.

Savin-Williams, Ritch C. 2005b. *The New Gay Teenager.* Cambridge, Mass.: Harvard University Press.

Savin-Williams, Ritch C. 2005c. "Who's gay? Does it matter?" *Current Directions in Psychological Science, 15,* 40–44.

Scarce, Michael. 1997. *Male on Male Rape: The Hidden Toll of Stigma and Shame.* New York: Insight Books.

Scelfo, Julie. 2007. "Men & depression: facing darkness." *Newsweek,* February 26, pp. 43–49.

Schaefer, James M. 1981. "Firewater myths revisited: Review of findings and some new directions." *Journal of Studies on Alcohol,* Supplement No. 9 (January), 108–109.

Scheff, Thomas J. 1964. "Social condition for rationality: How urban and rural courts deal with the mentally ill." *American Behavioral Scientist, 7,* 21–27.

Scheff, Thomas J. 1966. *Being Mentally Ill.* Chicago: Aldine.

Scheff, Thomas J. 1974. "The labeling theory of mental illness." *American Sociological Review, 39,* 448–449.

Schepis, Ty S., and Suchitra Krishnan-Sarin. 2008. "Characterizing adolescent prescription misusers: A population-based study." *Journal of the American Academy of Child & Adolescent Psychiatry, 47,* 745–754.

Schiff, Frederick. 1999. "Nude dancing: Scenes of sexual celebration in a contested culture." *Journal of American Culture,* Winter, pp. 9–16.

Schiffren, Lisa. 1996. "Gay marriage, an oxymoron." *New York Times,* March 23, p. 37.

Schildkrout, Enid. 2004. "Inscribing the body." *Annual Review of Anthropology, 33,* 319–344.

Schlenger, William, et al. 2002. "Psychological reactions to terrorist attacks: Findings from the National Study of Americans' Reactions to September 11." *JAMA, 288,* 581–588.

Schlosser, Eric. 1997. "The business of pornography." *U.S. News & World Report,* February 10, pp. 42–50.

Schmitt, Richard B. 1996. "Defenses down." *Wall Street Journal,* February 29, pp. A1, A6.

Schuckit, Marc A. 1984. "Overview: Epidemiology of alcoholism." In Marc A. Schuckit (ed.), *Alcohol Patterns and Problems.* New Brunswick, N.J.: Rutgers University Press.

Schur, Edwin M. 1984. *Labeling Women Deviant.* New York: Random House.

Schuster, Mark, et al. 2001. "National survey of stress reactions after the September 11, 2001 terrorist attacks." *New England Journal of Medicine, 345,* 1507–1512.

Schutz, Alfred. 1962. *Collected Papers I: The Problem of Social Reality.* Ed. Maurice Natanson. The Hague: Martinus Nijhoff.

Schwartz, Emma. 2007. "A host of trouble." *U.S. News & World Report,* October 8, pp. 47–50.

Schwartz, Martin D. 1987. "Gender and injury in spousal assault." *Sociological Focus, 20,* 61–75.

Schwartz, Martin D., and Walter S. DeKeseredy. 1997. *Sexual Assault on the College Campus: The Role of Male Peer Support.* Thousand Oaks, Calif.: Sage Publications.

Schwartz, Sharon. 1991. "Women and depression: A Durkheimian perspective." *Social Science and Medicine, 32,* 127.

Schwendinger, Julia R., and Herman Schwendinger. 1983. *Rape and Inequality.* Beverly Hills, Calif.: Sage Publications.

Scull, Andrew. 1988. "Deviance and social control." In Neil J. Smelser (ed.), *Handbook of Sociology.* Newbury Park, Calif.: Sage Publications.

Scully, Diana, and Joseph Marolla. 1984. "Convicted rapists' vocabulary of motive: Excuses and justifications." *Social Problems, 31,* 530–544.

Scully, Diana, and Joseph Marolla. 1985. "Riding the bull at Gilley's: Convicted rapists describe the rewards of rape." *Social Problems, 32,* 251–263.

Scully, Diana. 1990. *Understanding Sexual Violence: A Study of Convicted Rapists.* Boston: Unwin Hyman.

Scully, Gerald W. 1997. *Murder by the state.* Paper published by the National Center for Policy Analysis at the University of Texas, Dallas.

Seaman, Barrett. 2005. *Binge: What Your College Student Won't Tell You.* Hoboken, N.J.: Wiley & Sons.

Segal, Lynne. 1993. "Does pornography cause violence?: The search for evidence." In Pamela Church Gibson and Roma Gibson (eds.), *Dirty Looks: Women, Pornography, Power.* London: BFI Publishing.

Seidman, Steven. 2002. *Beyond the Closet: The Transformation of Gay and Lesbian Life.* New York: Routledge.

Seligman, Dan. 2003. "Transsexuals and the law." *Forbes,* October 13, pp. 68–69.

Seligmann, Jean, and Patricia King. 1996. "'Roofies': The date-rape drug." *Newsweek,* February 26, p. 54.

Selkin, James. 1975. "Rape." *Psychology Today,* January, p. 74.

Sellers, Christine, John Cochran, and Kathryn Branch. 2005. "Social learning theory and partner violence: A research note." *Deviant Behavior, 26,* 379–395.

Sellin, Thorsten. 1938. *Culture Conflict and Crime.* New York: Social Science Research Council.

Serdula, Mary, et al. 2004. "Trends in alcohol use and binge drinking, 1985–1999: Results of a multi-state survey." *American Journal of Preventive Medicine, 26,* 294–98.

Sergo, Peter. 2008. "Mental illness in America." *Scientific American Mind, Vol. 19,* Issue 1, p. 15.

Serrill, Michael S. 1993. "Defiling the children." *Time,* June 21, pp. 53–55.

Shapiro, Joseph P. 1996. "The elderly's vulnerability to abuse is exaggerated." In A. E. Sadler (ed.), *Family Violence.* San Diego, Calif.: Greenhaven.

Shapiro, Susan P. 1990. "Collaring the crime, not the criminal: Reconsidering the concept of white-collar crime." *American Sociological Review, 55,* 346–365.

Sharon, Jayson. 2008. "Study challenges myths of teen sex." *USA Today,* May 20, p. 7D.

Sharpe, Anita. 1997. "Psyched up." *Wall Street Journal,* January 24, pp. A1, A11.

Sheehy, Gail. 1971. *Hustling.* New York: Delacorte.

Shellenbarger, Sue. 2001. "A colleague's suicide has a lasting impact on fellow employees." *Wall Street Journal,* June 13, p. B1.

Shenon, Philip. 1996. "AIDS epidemic, late to arrive, now explodes in populous Asia." *New York Times,* January 21, pp. 1, 8.

Sheridan, L. P., and T. Grant. 2007. "Is cyberstalking different?" *Psychology, Crime & Law, 13,* 627–640.

Shihadeh, Edward S., and James Flynn. 1996. "Segregation and crime: The effect of black social isolation on the rates of black urban violence." *Social Forces, 74,* 1325–1352.

Shishkin, Philip, and David Crawford. 2006. "Heavy traffic: In Afghanistan, heroin trade soars despite U.S. aid." *Wall Street Journal,* January 18, pp. A1, A8.

Shneidman, Edwin S. 1975. "Classification of suicidal phenomena." In Simon Dinitz, Russell R. Dynes, and Alfred C. Clarke (eds.), *Deviance.* New York: Oxford University Press.

Short, James F. Jr. 1960. "Differential association as a hypothesis: problems of empirical testing." *Social Problems, 8,* 14–25.

Shotland, R. Lance, and Lynne Goodstein. 1983. "Just because she doesn't want to doesn't mean it's rape: An experimentally based causal model of the perception of rape in a dating situation." *Social Psychology Quarterly, 46,* 220–232.

Shover, Neal, and Andy Hochstetler. 2006. *Choosing White-Collar Crime.* New York: Cambridge University Press.

Shrout, Patrick E., et al. 1992. "Mental health status among Puerto Ricans, Mexican Americans, and Non-Hispanic whites." *American Journal of Community Psychology, 20,* 729–749.

Sibthorpe, Beverly, et al. 1991. "Needle use and sexual practices: Differences in perception of personal risk of HIV among intravenous drug users." *Journal of Drug Issues, 21,* 699–712.

Siegal, Lewis J., and Jacob H. Friedman. 1955. "The threat of suicide." *Diseases of the Nervous System, 16,* 45.

Silbert, Mimi H., and Ayala M. Pines. 1981. "Occupational hazards of street prostitutes." *Criminal Justice and Behavior, 8,* 397–398.

Silverman, Morton M. 2008. "Campus security begins with caring." *Chronicle of Higher Education,* April 18, pp. A51-A52.

Simmons, J. L. 1965. "Public stereotypes of deviants." *Social Problems, 13,* 223–224.

Simon, David R. 2006. *Elite Deviance,* 8th ed. Boston: Allyn and Bacon.

Simon, Rita J., and Dagny A. Blaskovich. 2002. *A Comparative Analysis of Capital Punishment: Statutes, Policies, Frequencies, and Public Attitudes the World Over.* Lanham, Md.: Lexington Books.

Simon, William, and John H. Gagnon. 1974. "The lesbians: A preliminary overview." In John H. Gagnon and William Simon (eds.), *Sexual Deviance.* New York: Harper & Row.

Simons, Marlise. 1993. "The sex market: Scourge on the world's children." *New York Times,* April 9, p. A3.

Simpson, Sally S., and Nicole Leeper Piquero. 2002. "Low self-control, organizational theory, and corporate crime." *Law & Society Review, 36,* 509–548.

Skapinakis, Petros. 2007. "Commentary: Socioeconomic position and common mental disorders: What do we need to know?" *International Journal of Epidemiology, 36,* 786–788.

Skipp, Catharine, and Arian Campo-Flores. 2006. "Street-walker stalker." *Newsweek,* March 27, p. 39.

Skrapec, Candice A. 2001. "Phenomenology and serial murder: Asking different questions." *Homicide Studies, 5,* 46–63.

Sky and Telescope. 1985. "The moon and murder." Vol. 70, p. 28.

Sloan, Allan. 1997. "A sexy new loophole." *Newsweek,* February 3, pp. 37–38.

Smith, Michael D. 1990. "Patriarchal ideology and wife beating: A test of a feminist hypothesis." *Violence and Victims, 5,* 257–273.

Smith, Wesley J. 1993. "The whispers of strangers." *Newsweek,* June 28, p. 8.

Smolowe, Jill. 1993. "Choose your poison." *Time,* July 26, p. 57.

Smyth, Angela, and Chris Thompson. 1990. *SAD: Seasonal Affective Disorder.* New York: Unwin.

Snyder, David. 2008. "See no evil." *U.S. Catholic,* January, pp. 30–35.

Sobell, Mark B., and Linda C. Sobell. 1993. *Problem Drinkers: Guided Self-Change Treatment.* New York: Guilford.

Socall, Daniel W., and Thomas Holtgraves. 1992. "Attitudes toward the mentally ill." *The Sociological Quarterly, 33,* 435–445.

Socarides, Charles, et al. 1997. "Don't forsake homosexuals who want help." *Wall Street Journal,* January 9, p. A10.

Sontag, Deborah. 2002. "Who was responsible for Elizabeth Shin?" *New York Times Magazine,* April 28, pp. 57–61, 94, 139.

Sorboro, John. 2007. "The trouble with psychiatry." *Skeptic, 13,* 37–43.

Spake, Amanda. 2002. "A fat nation." *U.S. News & World Report,* August 19, pp. 40–47.

Specter, Michael. 1995. "Gay Russians are 'free' now but still stay in fearful closet." *New York Times,* July 8, pp. 1, 4.

Spencer, Jane. 2004. "Crackdown on drugs hits chronic-pain patients." *Wall Street Journal,* March 16, pp. D1, D10.

Spencer, Jennifer, et al. 2002. "Self-esteem as a predictor of initiation of coitus in early adolescents." *Pediatrics, 109,* 581–584.

Spivey, Sue E. 2005. "Distancing and solidarity as resistance to sexual objectification in a nude dancing bar." *Deviant Behavior, 26,* 417–437.

St. John, Warren. 2004. "Today's bank robber might look like a neighbor." *New York Times,* July 3, pp. A1, A16.

Stacey, Judith, and Timothy J. Biblarz. 2001. "(How) does the sexual orientation of parents matter?" *American Sociological Review, 66,* 159–183.

Stack, Steven, and Jim Gundlach. 1992. "The effect of country music on suicide." *Social Forces, 71,* 211–218.

Stack, Steven, Ira Wasserman, and Roger Kern. 2004. "Adult social bonds and use of Internet pornography." *Social Science Quarterly, 85,* 75–88.

Stack, Steven. 1979. "Durkheim's theory of fatalistic suicide: A cross-national approach." *Journal of Social Psychology, 107,* 161–168.

Stack, Steven. 1982. "Suicide: A decade review of the sociological literature." *Deviant Behavior, 4,* 49–51.

Stack, Steven. 1983. "The effect of religious commitment on suicide: A cross-national analysis." *Journal of Health and Social Behavior, 24,* 362–374.

Stack, Steven. 1986. "A leveling off in young suicide." *Wall Street Journal,* May 28, p. 30.

Stack, Steven. 1987. "Celebrities and suicide: A taxonomy and analysis, 1948–1983." *American Sociological Review, 52,* 401–412.

Stack, Steven. 1991. "Social correlates of suicide by age: Media impacts." In Antoon A. Leenaars (ed.), *Life Span Perspectives of Suicide: Time-lines in the Suicide Process.* New York: Plenum.

Stark, Elizabeth. 1987. "Forgotten victims: Children of alcoholics." *Psychology Today,* January, pp. 58–62.

Steel, Emily. 2008. "My legal cameo: Why we convicted Thurman stalker." *Wall Street Journal,* May 7, pp. A1, A16.

Steffensmeier, Darrell. 1996. "Gender and crime: Toward a gendered theory of female offending." *Annual Review of Sociology, 22,* 459–487.

Steffensmeier, Renee Hoffman. 1984. "Suicide and the contemporary woman: Are male and female suicide rates converging?" *Sex Roles, 10,* 613–631.

Steinberg, Jacques. 1999. "The coming crime wave is washed up." *New York Times,* January 3, Section 4, p. 4.

Stephens, Joyce. 1995. "The pseudocidal female: A cautionary tale." In Silvia Sara Canetto and David Lester (eds.), *Women and Suicidal Behavior.* New York: Springer.

Stevens, Amy. 1995. "Ten ways (some) lawyers (sometimes) fudge bills." *Wall Street Journal,* January 13, pp. B1, B10.

Stickley, Andrew, et al. 2008. "Attitudes toward intimate partner violence against women in Moscow, Russia." *Journal of Family Violence, 23,* 447–456.

Stockard, Jean, and Robert M. O'Brien. 2002. "Cohort effects on suicide rates: International variations." *American Sociological Review, 67,* 854–872.

Stolberg, Sheryl Gay. 1999. "Science looks at Littleton, and shrugs." *New York Times,* May 9, pp. 1, 4.

Stone, Brad. 2005. "Going all in for online poker." *Newsweek,* August 15, pp. 40–41.

Stover, Del. 2005. "Students 'hacking' school computer systems." *Education Digest,* December, pp. 54–56.

Straus, Murray A. 1991. "Discipline and deviance: Physical punishment of children and violence and other crime in adulthood." *Social Problems, 38,* 133–154.

Straus, Murray A. 2005. "Women's violence toward men is a serious social problem." pp. 55–77 in Donileen R. Loseke, Richard J. Gelles, and Mary M. Cavanaugh (eds.), *Current Controversies on Family Violence,* 2d ed. Thousand Oaks, Calif.: Sage.

Straus, Murray A., Richard J. Gelles, and Suzanne K. Steinmetz. 1980. *Behind Closed Doors.* Garden City, N.Y.: Anchor Books.

Strom, Kevin J., and John M. MacDonald. 2007. "The influence of social and economic disadvantage on racial patterns in youth homicide over time." *Homicide Studies, 11,* 50–69.

Struckman-Johnson, Cindy. 1991. "Male Victims of Acquaintance Rape." In Andrea Parrot and Laurie Bechhofer (eds.), *Acquaintance Rape.* New York: Wiley.

Strumpf, Koleman. 2005. "Internet gambling should be legalized." pp. 67–71 in James D. Torr (ed.), *The Internet: Opposing Viewpoints.* Detroit, Mich.: Greenhaven Press.

Stylianou, Stelios. 2002. "The relationship between elements and manifestations of low self-control in a general theory of crime: Two comments and a test." *Deviant Behavior, 23,* 531–557.

Suitor, Jill J., Karl Pillemer, and Murray A. Straus. 1990. "Marital violence in a life course perspective." In Murray A. Straus and Richard J. Gelles (eds.), *Physical Violence in American Families: Risk Factors and Adaptations to Violence in 8,145 Families.* New Brunswick, N.J.: Transaction.

Sullum, Jacob. 1998. *For Your Own Good: The Anti-Smoking Crusade and the Tyranny of Public Health.* New York: Free Press.

Summers, Randal W., and Allan M. Hoffman. 2002. *Domestic Violence: A Global View.* Westport, Conn.: Greenwood Press.

Suro, Roberto. 1993. "Pollution-weary minorities try civil rights tack." *New York Times,* January 11, pp. A1, A12.

Sussman, Vic. 1992. "To stop a thief." *U.S. News & World Report,* March 30, pp. 55–58.

Sutherland, Edwin H. 1939. *Principles of Criminology,* 3d ed. Philadelphia: Lippincott.

Sutherland, Edwin H. 1949. *White-Collar Crime.* New York: Holt, Rinehart and Winston.

Sutherland, Edwin H. 1956. "Crimes of corporations." In Albert K. Cohen, Alfred Lindesmith, and Karl Schuessler (eds.), *The Sutherland Papers.* Bloomington, Ind.: Indiana University Press.

Sutherland, Edwin H., and Donald R. Cressey. 1978. *Criminology,* 10th ed. Philadelphia: Lippincott.

Suthrell, Charlotte. 2004. *Unzipping Gender: Sex, Cross-Dressing and Culture.* Oxford, U.K.: Berg.

Swan, Neil. 1993. "Researcher's problem, which comes first: Drug abuse or antisocial behavior?" *NIDA (National Institute on Drug Abuse) Notes, 8* (May/June), 6–7.

Sweet, Ellen. 1985. "Date rape: The story of an epidemic and those who deny it." *Ms.,* October, p. 58.

Szasz, Thomas. 1974a. *Ceremonial Chemistry.* Garden City, N.Y.: Anchor.

Szasz, Thomas. 1974b. *The Myth of Mental Illness,* rev. ed. New York: Harper & Row.

Szasz, Thomas. 1994. "Mental illness is still a myth." *Society,* May/June, pp. 34–39.

Szockyj, Elizabeth. 1993. "Insider trading: The SEC meets Carl Karcher." *The Annals of the American Academy of Political and Social Science, 525* (January), 46–58.

Tannenbaum, Frank. 1938. *Crime and the Community.* New York: Columbia University Press.

Taylor, Steven J. 2004. "'You're not a retard, you're just wise.'" In Alex Thio and Thomas C. Calhoun (eds.), *Readings in Deviant Behavior,* 3d ed. Boston: Allyn and Bacon.

Telephony. 1998. "Crosstalk." February 16, *Vol. 234,* Issue 7, p. 8.

ter Bogt, Tom, et al. 2006. "Economic and cultural correlates of cannabis use among mid-adolescents in 31 countries." *Addiction, 101,* 241–251.

Tewksbury, Richard. 2007. "Effects of sexual assaults on men: Physical, mental and sexual consequences." *International Journal of Men's Health, 6,* 22–35.

The Economist. 2004. "It's their business." *Vol. 372,* September 4, p. 12.

The Economist. 1979. "Sexual therapists." December 2, p. 26.

The Economist. 1991. "Shoplifting in America." January 19, p. 65.

Thio, Alex. 1973. "Class bias in the sociology of deviance." *The American Sociologist, 8,* 1–12.

Thompson, Terri, et al. 1992. "Crime and the bottom line." *U.S. News & World Report,* April 13, p. 57.

Thornton, Bill, and Richard M. Ryckman. 1983. "The influence of a rape victim's physical attractiveness on observers' attributions of responsibility." *Human Relations, 36,* 549–562.

Time. 1980. "Deadwood's defunct houses." July 28, p. 77.

Tittle, Charles R. 1995. *Control Balance: Toward a General Theory of Deviance.* Boulder, Colo.: Westview.

Tittle, Charles R. 2004. "Refining control balance theory." *Theoretical Criminology, 8,* 395–428.

Tolchin, Martin. 1986. "On breaking, or bending, or ignoring the law." *New York Times,* November 28, p. 12.

Torrey, E. Fuller. 1974. *The Death of Psychiatry.* Radnor, Pa.: Chilton.

Torrey, E. Fuller. 1997. *Out of the Shadows: Confronting America's Mental Illness Crisis.* New York: Wiley.

Totman, Jane. 1978. *The Murderers: A Psychosocial Study of Criminal Homicide.* San Francisco: R and E Research Associates.

Toubia, Nahid, and Susan Izett. 1998. *Female Genital Mutilation.* Geneva: World Health Organization.

Toufexis, Anastasia. 1992a. "Bisexuality: What is it?" *Time,* August 17, p. 49.

Toufexis, Anastasia. 1992b. "Do mad acts a madman make?" *Time,* February 3, p. 17.

Toufexis, Anastasia. 2002. "A psychiatrist's-eye view of murder and insanity." *New York Times,* April 23, p. D5.

Towson State. 1993. "A study on campus crime by Towson State University's Center for the Study and Prevention of Campus Violence." *New York Times Magazine,* March 7, p. 40.

Trad, Paul V. 1991. "The ultimate stigma of mental illness." *American Journal of Psychotherapy, 45,* 463–466.

Transparency International. 2004. *Global Corruption Report 2004.* London: Pluto Press.

Trice, Harrison M. 1966. *Alcoholism in America.* New York: McGraw-Hill.

Troiden, Richard R. 1979. "Becoming homosexual: A model of gay identity acquisition." *Psychiatry, 42,* 362–373.

Trost, Cathy, and Paulette Thomas. 1993. "Sexual politics." *Wall Street Journal,* March 10, p. A6.

Truell, Peter, and Larry Gurwin. 1992. *False Profits: The Inside Story of BCCI, the World's Most Corrupt Financial Empire.* Boston: Houghton Mifflin.

Tuesday, Vince. 2002. "The naked truth about porn surfers." *Computerworld,* June 24, p. 40.

Tumulty, Karen. 2006. "Abortion: Where the real action is . . ." *Time,* January 30, pp. 50–53.

Tumulty, Karen. 2006. "The politics of fat." *Time,* March 27, pp. 40–43.

U.S. Census Bureau. 2008. *Statistical Abstract of the United States.* Washington, D.C.: Government Printing Office.

U.S. Congress, Office of Technology Assessment. 1990. *Indian Adolescent Mental Health (OTA-H-446).* Washington, D.C.: Government Printing Office.

Underwood, Anne. 2005. "A healthy toast." *Newsweek,* October 3, p. 70.

Unnithan, N. Prabha, Lin Huff-Corzine, Jay Corzine, and Hugh P. Whitt. 1994. *The Currents of Lethal Violence: An Integrated Model of Suicide and Homicide.* Albany: State University of New York Press.

USA Today. 2005. "One priest is punished, but church's progress still lags." February 16, p. 10a.

Vachss, Alice S. 1994. *Sex Crimes: Ten Years on the Front Lines Prosecuting Rapists and Confronting Their Collaborators.* New York: Holt.

Vail, D. Angus. 2004. "Tattoos are like potato chips . . . You can't have just one." In Alex Thio and Thomas C. Calhoun (eds.), *Readings in Deviant Behavior,* 3d ed. Boston: Allyn and Bacon.

Vaillant, George E. 1995. *The Natural History of Alcoholism Revisited.* Cambridge, Mass.: Harvard University Press.

Vaillant, George E., and Eva S. Milofsky. 1982. "The etiology of alcoholism: A prospective viewpoint." *American Psychologist, 37,* 494–503.

Valentino, Benjamin A. 2004. *Final Solutions: Mass Killing and Genocide in the 20th Century.* Ithaca, N.Y.: Cornell University Press.

Van Der Poel, Agnes, and Dike Van De Mheen. 2006. "Young people using crack and the process of marginalization." *Drugs: Education, Prevention & Policy, 13,* 45–59.

van Gelder, Paul J., and Charles D. Kaplan. 1992. "The finishing moment: Temporal and spatial features of sexual interactions between streetwalkers and car clients." *Human Organization, 51,* 253–263.

Van Mourik, Orli. 2007. "The origin of schizophrenia." *Discover,* December, p. 19.

van Natta, Don Jr., and Jane Fritsch. 1997. "$250,000 buys donors' best access to Congress." *New York Times,* January 27, A1, A10.

van Poppel, Frans, and Lincoln H. Day. 1996. "A test of Durkheim's theory of suicide—Without committing the 'ecological fallacy'." *American Sociological Review, 61,* 500–507.

Van Tubergen, Frank, et al. 2005. "Denomination, religious context, and suicide: Neo-Durkheimian multilevel explanations tested with individual and contextual data." *American Journal of Sociology, 111,* 797–823.

Vaughan, Diane. 1983. *Controlling Unlawful Organizational Behavior: Social Structure and Corporate Misconduct.* Chicago: University of Chicago Press.

Victor, Jeffrey S. 2004. "Sluts and wiggers: A study of the effects of derogatory labeling." *Deviant Behavior, 25,* 67–84.

Viscusi, W. Kip. 1992. *Smoking: Making the Risky Decision.* New York: Oxford University Press.

Voeller, Bruce. 1990. "Some uses and abuses of the Kinsey scale." In David P. McWhirter, Stephanie A. Sanders, and June Machover Reinisch (eds.), *Homosexuality/Heterosexuality.* New York: Oxford University Press.

Walchak, David G. 1996. "Drugs and violent crime." *Police Chief, 63,* March, p. 6.

Walker, Jayne, John Archer, and Michelle Davies. 2005. "Effects of rape on men: A descriptive analysis." *Archives of Sexual Behavior, 34,* 69–80.

Walker, Lenore F. 1990. *Terrifying Love: Why Battered Women Kill and How Society Responds.* New York: Harper Perennial.

Wall Street Journal. 2007. "Tyco convictions upheld." November 16, p. C2.

Wallace, Harvey. 1996. *Family Violence: Legal, Medical, and Social Perspectives.* Boston: Allyn and Bacon.

Waller, Willard. 1936. "Social problems and the mores." *American Sociological Review, 1,* 922–933.

Walsh, Mark. 2005. "You can bet—but don't call it gambling." *Business Week,* September 19, p. 14.

Walters, Anne K. 2005. "'Hostile environment' is found at academies." *Chronicle of Higher Education,* September 9, p. 36.

Walters, John P. 2002. "Don't legalize drugs." *Wall Street Journal,* July 19, p. A10.

Wang, Philip S., et al. 2005. "Twelve-month use of mental health services in the United States." *Archives of General Psychiatry, 62,* 629–640.

Wang, S. S., et al. 2004. "The influence of the stigma of obesity on overweight individuals." *International Journal of Obesity, 28,* 1333–1337.

Ward, Richard H., and Daniel J. Mabrey. 2005. "Organized crime in Asia." pp. 387–401 in Philip Reichel (ed.), *Handbook of Transnational Crime & Justice.* Thousand Oaks, Calif.: Sage.

Warner, Barbara D. 2007. "Robberies with guns: Neighborhood factors and the nature of crime." *Journal of Criminal Justice, 35,* 39–50

Wartik, Nancy. 1995. "Jerry's choice: Why are our children killing themselves?" In Robert Emmet Long (ed.), *Suicide.* New York: Wilson.

Wasserman, Ira. 1984. "Imitation and suicide: A reexamination of the Werther effect." *American Sociological Review, 49,* 427–436.

Webb, Gary. 2001. "Sex and the internet." *Yahoo! Internet Life, 7,* 88–98.

Weber, Thomas E. 1997. "The X files." *Wall Street Journal,* May 20, pp. A1, A8.

Wechsler, Henry, et al. 2002. "Trends in college binge drinking during a period of increased prevention efforts." *Journal of American College Health, 50,* 203–217.

Weicker, Lowell P., Jr. 1985. "Dangerous routine." *Psychology Today,* November, pp. 60–62.

Weinstein, Raymond M. 1981. "Mental patients' attitudes toward hospital staff." *Archives of General Psychiatry, 38,* 487.

Weinstein, Raymond M. 1983. "Labeling theory and the attitudes of mental patients: A review." *Journal of Health and Social Behavior, 24,* 70–84.

Weis, Kurt, and Sandra S. Borges. 1973. "Victimology and rape: The case of the legitimate victim." *Issues in Criminology, 8,* 81–85.

Weisberg, Kelly. 1985. *Children of the Night: A Study of Adolescent Prostitution.* Lexington, mass.: Lexington Books.

Weisburd, David, et al. 1991. *Crimes in the Middle Classes.* New Haven, Conn.: Yale University Press.

Weisheit, Ralph. 1992. "Patterns of female crime." In Robert G. Culbertson and Ralph Weisheit (eds.), *Order Under Law.* Prospect Heights, Ill.: Waveland.

Weisman, Steven R. 1997. "Spin nation." *New York Times,* January 26, p. 12.

Weisner, Constance, et al. 1995. "Trends in the treatment of alcohol problems in the U.S. general population, 1979 through 1990." *American Journal of Public Health, 85,* 55–60.

Weitz, Eric D. 2003. *A Century of Genocide: Utopias of Race and Nation.* Princeton, N.J.: Princeton University Press.

Weitzer, Ronald. 1991. "Prostitutes' rights in the United States: The failure of a movement." *Sociological Quarterly, 32,* 23–41.

Weitzer, Ronald. 2000. "Deficiencies in the sociology of sex work." *Sociology of Crime, Law and Deviance, 2,* 259–279.

Weitzer, Ronald. 2005a. "Flawed theory and method in studies of prostitution." *Violence Against Women, 11,* 934–949.

Weitzer, Ronald. 2005b. "New directions in research on prostitution." *Crime, Law & Social Change, 43,* 211–235.

Weitzer, Ronald. 2006. "Moral crusade against prostitution." *Society,* March/April, pp. 33–38.

Welch, Michael R., et al. 2005. "'But everybody does it . . . ': The effects of perceptions, moral pressures, and informal sanctions on tax cheating." *Sociological Spectrum, 25,* 21–52.

Wellford, Harrison. 1972. *Sowing the Wind: A Report from Ralph Nader's Center for Study of Responsive Law on Food Safety and the Chemical Harvest.* New York: Grossman.

Wells, Joseph T. 1993. "Accountancy and white-collar crime." *The Annals of the American Academy of Political and Social Science, 525* (January), 86–87.

Wertheimer, Fred. 1996. "Stop soft money now." *New York Times Magazine,* December 22, pp. 38–39.

Wheeler, John, and Peter R. Kilmann. 1983. "Comarital sexual behavior: Individual and relationship variables." *Archives of Sexual Behavior, 12,* 304–310.

Wheeler, Stanton. 1991. "The problem of white-collar crime motivation." In Kip Schlegel and David Weisburd (eds.), *White-Collar Crime Reconsidered.* Boston: Northeastern University Press.

White, Jacquelyn W., and John A. Humphrey. 1991. "Young people's attitudes toward acquaintance rape." In Andrea Parrot and Laurie Bechhofer (eds.), *Acquaintance Rape.* New York: Wiley.

Whitehead, Barbara Dafoe. 2005. "Online porn." *Commonweal,* October 21, p. 6.

Whitty, Monica T. 2004. "Cybercheating." *CPJ: Counseling & Psychotherapy Journal, 15,* 38–39.

Whitty, Monica T. 2005. "The realness of cybercheating: Men's and women's representations of unfaithful Internet relationships." *Social Science Computer Review, 23,* 57–67.

Wickelgren, Ingrid. 1999. "Discovery of 'gay gene' questioned." *Science,* April 23, p. 571.

Widom, Cathy Spatz. 1989. "The intergenerational transmission of violence." In Neil Alan Weiner and Marvin E. Wolfgang (eds.), *Pathways to Criminal Violence.* Newbury Park, Calif.: Sage Publications.

Wilbanks, William. 1984. *Murder in Miami: An Analysis of Homicide Patterns and Trends in Dade County (Miami) Florida, 1917–1983.* Lanham, Md.: University Press of America.

Wilbanks, William. 1985. "Is violent crime intraracial?" *Crime & Delinquency, 31,* 117–128.

Wilentz, Amy. 1985. "When brother kills brother." *Time,* September 16, p. 33.

Wilke, John R. 2004. "Price-fixing investigations sweep chemical industry." *Wall Street Journal,* June 22, pp. A1, A6.

Wilkins, James. 1967. "Suicidal behavior." *American Sociological Review, 32,* 286–287.

Wilkinson, Kenneth P. 1984. "A research note on homicide and rurality." *Social Forces, 63,* 445–452.

Wilkinson, Rupert. 1970. *The Prevention of Drinking Problems.* New York: Oxford University Press.

Wilkinson, Wayne W. 2004. "Religiosity, authoritarianism, and homophobia: A multidimensional approach." *The International Journal for the Psychology of Religion, 14,* 55–67.

Will, George F. 2001. "Now, weapons of mass disruption?" *Newsweek,* October 29, p. 76.

Williams, Armstrong. 2006. "Teen suicide." *New York Amsterdam News,* January 5, p. 13.

Williams, Kirk R. 1984. "Economic source of homicide: Reestimating the effects of poverty and inequality." *American Sociological Review, 49,* 283–289.

Williams, Kirk R., and Susan Drake. 1980. "Social structure, crime and criminalization: An empirical examination of the conflict perspective." *The Sociological Quarterly, 21,* 563–575.

Williams, Mary E. 2003. *Marijuana.* San Diego, Calif.: Greenhaven Press.

Wilson, Margo I., and Martin Daly. 1992. "Who kills whom in spouse killings? On the exceptional sex ratio of spousal homicides in the United States." *Criminology, 30,* 189–215.

Wilson, Mitchell. 1993. "DSM-III and the transformation of American psychiatry: A history." *American Journal of Psychiatry, 150,* 399–410.

Winerip, Michael. 2002. "The never-promised rose garden and the snake pit." *New York Times,* May 5, Section 4, p. 3.

Wingfield, Nick. 2004. "Problem for cops on eBay beat: Crooks keep getting smarter." *Wall Street Journal,* August 3, pp. A1, A8.

Winick, Charles, and Paul M. Kinsie. 1971. *The Lively Commerce.* Chicago: Quadrangle.

Winslow, Ron, and Peter Landers. 2002. "Obesity: A worldwide woe." *Wall Street Journal,* July 1, pp. B1, B4.

Witkin, Gordon. 1992. "Willing to kill for a car." *U.S. News & World Report,* September 21, pp. 40–43.

Witkin, Gordon. 1995. "A new drug gallops through the West." *U.S. News & World Report,* November 13, pp. 50–51.

Wittig, Monique. 1990. "The straight mind." In Russell Ferguson et al. (eds.), *Out There: Marginalization and Contemporary Culture.* Cambridge, Mass.: MIT Press.

Wolfe, Alan. 1998. "The homosexual exception." *New York Times Magazine,* February 8, pp. 46–47.

Wolfgang, Marvin E. 1958. *Patterns in Criminal Homicide.* Philadelphia: University of Pennsylvania Press.

Wolfgang, Marvin E. 1967. "A sociological analysis of criminal homicide." In Marvin E. Wolfgang (ed.), *Studies in Homicide.* New York: Harper & Row.

Wolfgang, Marvin E., and Franco Ferracuti. 1967. *The Subculture of Violence: Towards an Integrated Theory in Criminology.* London: Tavistock.

Wolpert, Lewis. 2000. *Malignant Sadness: The Anatomy of Depression.* New York: Free Press.

Wonders, Nancy A., and Raymond Michalowski. 2004. "The globalization of sex tourism." In Alex Thio and Thomas C. Calhoun (eds.), *Readings in Deviant Behavior,* 3d ed. Boston: Allyn and Bacon.

Wondrak, Isabel, and Jens Hoffmann. 2007. "A personal obsession." *Scientific American Mind, 18,* 76–81.

Wood, Elizabeth Anne. 2001. "Strip club dancers: Working in the fantasy factory." In Alex Thio and Thomas C. Calhoun (eds.), *Readings in Deviant Behavior,* 2d ed. Boston: Allyn and Bacon.

Woodruff, Christopher, and Susan Gregory. 2005. "Profile of Internet gamblers: Betting on the future." *UNLV Gaming Research & Review Journal, 9,* 1–14.

Wren, Christopher S. 1996. "Adolescent drug use rose in latest survey from 1995." *New York Times,* December 20, p. A8.

Wren, Christopher S. 1997. "Keeping cocaine resilient: Low cost and high profit." *New York Times,* March 4, pp. A1, A10.

Wren, Christopher S. 1999. "Study compares U.S. and English drug crimes." *New York Times,* May 14, p. A10.

Wright, Bradley R. E., et al. 2004. "Does the perceived risk of punishment deter criminally prone individuals? Rational choice, self-control, and crime." *Journal of Research in Crime and Delinquency, 41,* 180–213.

Wright, James D. 1995. "Ten essential observations on guns in America." *Society,* March/April, pp. 62–68.

Wright, James D., Joseph F. Sheley, and M. Dwayne Smith. 1992. "Kids, guns, and killing fields." *Society,* November/December, pp. 84–89.

Wright, James D., Peter H. Rossi, and Kathleen Daly. 1983. *Under the Gun: Weapons, Crime, and Violence in America.* New York: Aldine.

Wright, Richard T., and Scott H. Decker. 1994. *Burglars on the Job: Streetlife and Residential Break-ins.* Boston: Northeastern University Press.

Wright, Richard T., and Scott H. Decker. 1997. *Armed Robbers in Action: Stickups and Street Culture.* Boston: Northeastern University Press.

Wysocki, Diane Kholos. 1998. "Let your fingers do the talking: Sex on an adult chat-line." *Sexualities, Vol. 1,* pp. 425–452.

Xin, Xiaohui, and Thomas K. Rudel. 2004. "The context for political corruption: A cross-national analysis." *Social Science Quarterly, 85,* 294–309.

Yamamoto, J., et al. 1983. "Symptom checklist of normal subjects from Asian-Pacific islander population." *Pacific/Asian American Mental Health Research Center Research Review, 2,* 6–8.

Yar, Majid. 2005. "Computer hacking: Just another case of juvenile delinquency?" *The Howard Journal, 44,* 387–399.

Yen, Hope. 2005. "High court to review assisted suicide law." Yahoo! News, February 22, http://story.news.yahoo.com.

Yesavage, Jerome A., et al. 1985. "Carry-over effects of marijuana intoxication on aircraft pilot performance: A preliminary report." *American Journal of Psychiatry, 142,* 1325–1329.

Yonkers, Kimberly A., and George Gurguis. 1995. "Gender differences in the prevalence and expression of anxiety disorders." In Mary V. Seeman (ed.), *Gender and Psychopathology.* Washington, D.C.: American Psychiatric Press.

Young, Kimberly S., et al. 2000. "Online infidelity: A new dimension in couple relationships with implications for evaluation and treatment." *Sexual Addiction & Compulsivity, 7,* 59–74.

Young, T. J. 1991. "Suicide and homicide among Native Americans: Anomie or social learning?" *Psychological Reports, 68,* 1137–1138.

Yount, Lisa (ed.). 2006. *Does the Internet Increase the Risk of Crime?* Detroit, Mich.: Greenhaven Press.

Zagorin, Adam. 1997. "Charlie's an angel?" *Time,* February 3, pp. 36–38.

Zeisel, Hans. 1982. "A comment on 'The deterrent effect of capital punishment' by Phillips." *American Journal of Sociology, 88,* 167–169.

Zeits, Dorothy. 1981. *Women Who Embezzle or Defraud.* New York: Praeger.

Zeller, Tom., Jr. 2006. "Cyberthieves silently copy as you type." *New York Times,* February 27, pp. A1, A16.

Zezima, Katie. 2004. "Girl, 17, was raped by a group of teenagers, Boston police say." *New York Times,* December 10, p. 27A.

Zillmann, Dolf, and Jennings Bryant. 1982. "Pornography, sexual callousness, and the trivialization of rape." *Journal of Communication, 32,* 10–21.

Zimmerman, Jacqueline Noll. 2003. *People Like Ourselves: Portrayals of Mental Illness in the Movies.* Lanham, Md.: Scarecrow Press.

Zorza, Joan, and Laurie Woods. 1994. *Mandatory Arrest: Problems and Possibilities.* New York: National Center for Women and Family Law.

NAME INDEX

SUBJECT INDEX